MONUMENTAL INSCRIPTIONS

OF

THE BRITISH WEST INDIES.

INDUS·UTERQUE·SERVIET·UNI

Monumental Inscriptions
of the
British West Indies

From the Earliest Date,

with Genealogical and Historical Annotations, from Origina
Local, and Other Sources, Illustrative of the Histories
and Genealogies of the Seventeenth Century,
the Calendars of State Papers, Peerages
and Baronetages; with Engravings
of the Arms of the Principal
Families

Chiefly Collected on the Spot

by

Captain J. H. Lawrence-Archer

HERITAGE BOOKS
2014

HERITAGE BOOKS

AN IMPRINT OF HERITAGE BOOKS, INC.

Books, CDs, and more—Worldwide

For our listing of thousands of titles see our website
at
www.HeritageBooks.com

A Facsimile Reprint
Published 2014 by
HERITAGE BOOKS, INC.
Publishing Division
5810 Ruatan Street
Berwyn Heights, Md. 20740

Originally published
London:
Chatto and Windus
Piccadilly
1875

International Standard Book Numbers
Paperbound: 978-0-7884-5543-8
Clothbound: 978-0-7884-9009-5

TEMPLA·QUAM·DILECTA

𝔇𝔢𝔡𝔦𝔠𝔞𝔱𝔢𝔡, 𝔟𝔶 𝔓𝔢𝔯𝔪𝔦𝔰𝔰𝔦𝔬𝔫,

TO

HIS GRACE

THE DUKE OF BUCKINGHAM AND CHANDOS,

FORMERLY SECRETARY OF STATE FOR THE COLONIES.

CONTENTS.

PREFATORY REMARKS.

THE Author formed the design of visiting the older English colonies of the West Indies, and of examining, so far as he might be permitted, their local records, with a view to the production of a work which should contribute, through the genealogical medium, to a better knowledge of the social origin of those colonies, in the seventeenth and eighteenth centuries.

It may not be unworthy of note, that those early settlers were, as a rule, men of great energy, with moderate political opinions. They belonged to the same class from which the titled aristocracy is for the most part derived, and many of their numerous descendants are to be found in the present peerage and baronetage, holding posts of honour under the Crown.

The higher class of planters or proprietors almost invariably educated their children in England ; and, although in those days, the voyage was so much longer and more difficult than at present, it is surprising how frequently those colonial gentry made it ; and many of their adventures might, even now, afford subject of interest for the novelist.

There was, towards the close of the seventeenth century, another element in the social condition of these colonies—namely, *white* slaves,—an institution perhaps suggested by Cromwell's Government, but only carried out to its full extent, by James the Second, while disposing of the unfortunate adherents of Monmouth.

Another principal object of the present collection is, to preserve records which, in the course of a few generations, would otherwise be destroyed through neglect, spoliation, the effects of climate, and other causes.

In Jamaica, most of the handsome old mausoleums—at Port Royal, for instance—being secluded from the town, and partially concealed by gigantic cacti, cashaw, and mangrove trees, have been, from time to time, broken into and plundered—the leaden coffins stolen, the marble tablets carried off, and sold again for the like purposes, and the empty vault left for the lugubrious pic-nics of the " dangerous," or at any rate, idle classes, whose broken bottles, mingled with the relics of humanity, bear witness to the revelries by which they have been desecrated.

b

In many other places, the older slabs have been broken up, to supply the ordinary necessities of repairing walls, &c., while, in some of the disused cemeteries, the monuments themselves have been gradually and surely entombed, by the encroachments of the matted crab-weed. In numerous instances, the larger sepulchres have been insidiously destroyed by the seeds of overhanging trees, which, vegetating in their fissures, and striking their roots downwards, in search of nourishment, have so disintegrated the masonry, as, in some places, to carry it up in their growth, and in others, to reduce it to mouldering heaps. Such a struggle between robust nature and frail art, in the less frequented private cemeteries, has generally resulted in the entire destruction of tombs scarcely half a century old.

The present collection was made in 1858 and 1864-5,* and almost entirely annotated by the author, under circumstances of considerable personal difficulty, in the churches and cemeteries of Jamaica, and Barbados. Later, he discovered that some pamphlets, entitled "Church Notes," and "A History of the Parish of St. James', Jamaica,"† had been printed by the late Mr. Roby, of the latter island, and from portions of these, which fell into his hands, and also from a small MS. collection of pedigrees given to him by the late Mr. H. L. Long, of Hampton Lodge, he has made several useful extracts, which will be found duly acknowledged, along with other desultory contributions.

After many researches amongst the local public records of the West Indies, the author, on his return to England, continued his annotations in the various registries of the three Kingdoms; but, ultimately finding these too extensive for the limits of his work, he made a careful selection, and then abridged the latter.‡

One of the objects of the present work being to link, however slightly, the Home and Colonial records of the seventeenth century, the author made an application to His Grace the Secretary of State for the Colonies (1867), who very liberally endeavoured to facilitate his farther inquiries in the islands which he had just left; but owing to unforeseen obstacles this attempt was frustrated, and, consequently, many valuable sources of information yet remain available for some future labourer in the same field.

In Barbados, the task of transcribing epitaphs, owing to the highly cultivated and open character of the country, was comparatively easy; but in Jamaica, where the wild vegetation of nature is so remarkable, the explorer of its older and private

---

* The author's term of service in command of the depot of his regiment—2nd Batt. 60th Rifles—having then expired.

† Unfortunately, the author was unable to discover the 1st and 2nd Parts of the latter, until the greater part of Jamaica had passed through the press.

‡ The present object being to present the materials in as condensed a form as possible, it has seemed unnecessary to repeat in every instance local official titles, names of the estates of their owners, and much interesting collateral matter, which may be reserved for another occasion.

cemeteries, must resort to manual labour; and the author has, not unfrequently passed days, from breakfast-time until sunset, with the common woodman's cutlas, clearing away the dense and matted undergrowth, while approaching the objects of his search.

In these dark and humid spots, shut up in woods which have undone the labours, in some instances, of generations, the loneliness is equal to, if not greater, than that of the great forests of India, for here animal life—with the exception of birds and insects —is almost unknown, and the perfect solitude is quite undisturbed. But although there may be grander trees in the Indian forests, they cannot compare with those of the West Indies in the wealth of gorgeous blossoms, and in variety of aspect, from the wild tamarind, whose graceful boughs hang out their scarlet clusters, and the spicy pimento, with its chaste myrtle bloom—to the cedars, and the giant cotton tree, overgrown with delicate or brilliant flowering orchids, and festooned with climbing plants of exquisite beauty.

Without a record of *every* consecrated ground in the West Indies, and more especially, in a densely wooded island like Jamaica, it would be impossible to make a complete collection of these mortuary memorials; and moreover, without very unusual advantages, a private explorer would meet with incessant and vexatious obstacles. The author made this collection as exhaustive as possible, where he had the opportunity, but much has been left undone.

He did not confine himself, as will be observed, to the transcription of merely old, curious, or dignified epitaphs, but included many of no particular interest, and which can only be expected to acquire a slight value in the lapse of time. Nor did he desire to make, by a studied selection, any invidious distinction between social classes, and different races and nationalities. There are doubtless inconveniences in thus treating the subject—especially since the period of the negro emancipation—but there is a classical excuse, which may be accepted as sufficient apology—

> " Nil nimiùm studeo, Cæsar, tibi velle placere ;
> Nec scire utrùm *sis albus an ater homo.*"

The intention of the author was originally restricted to a collection of epitaphs, from the earliest period to the year 1750, but, for reasons which will be apparent, this limit has been frequently exceeded, except as regards the island of Barbados, in which his stay was so short that it would have been impossible to do otherwise, while on the other hand, where inscriptions, mostly of modern date, were received from a few minor islands, it seemed undesirable to reject them, in conformity to an arbitrary arrangement.

The endeavour has been made to avoid, in annotation, the error of over-estimating the importance of families whose influence was only local, but, at the same time, not to overlook anything curious in their histories, and also to give space to their genealogies, in preference to those already before the public, and which are readily accessible.*

J. H. L.-A.

---

* Archbishop Whately was, doubtless, just in the following remarks, but, as much of this spirit of which he complained will always prevail, it is scarcely safe to be generous :—" I have always desired to repress that narrow, provincial spirit, that would separate island from island, county from county, one portion of the British empire from the other. Two eminent prelates, raised to the bench of bishops in England, are natives, not of Great Britain, but of Barbados. Suppose the narrow feeling had been nourished of Barbados for the Barbadians, could these prelates ever have attained their high dignity ?"

ΓΙΚUS   M I   ETSI

T

RECINCTUS

JAMAICA.

JAMAICA.

THE idea of making Jamaica an English colony seems to have been started about that period when, from our increasing settlements on the American Continent, the want of convenient harbours among the West India Islands began to be felt. (Cal. S. P., Col. S. 1613.)

The project was revived at intervals, but as is well known, the immediate cause of our obtaining possession of the Island of Springs, was the failure of the expedition against Hispaniola.

On the capture of the former island (May 10th, 1655), by Penn and Venables, about fourteen hundred of the inhabitants took refuge in the almost inaccessible fastnesses of its mountains, while a few of the Negro and Portuguese population submitted to the conquerors.

Although the commanders were subjected to censure for their conduct in other particulars, the capture of Jamaica was a source of pride to the Lord Protector, who addressed himself with energy to its colonization, for which purpose immigrants were invited from all the other English settlements, while the officers and soldiers of the force which had taken possession of the island received, shortly afterwards, allotments of land on a species of military tenure, a practice observable in many patents even so late as the year 1743.*

While Barbados had from the first been so exclusively *British* that at one time the Island legislature even passed a law adverse to Irishmen, the English in Jamaica seem at once to have fraternized with the races already there, and to have sedulously invited the influx of strangers from all parts. The mother country provided *administrative* talent, and the *energy*, aroused amongst their cadets by the decay of good houses during those troubled times at home. The Jewish settlers brought their proverbial talents into its commercial interests ; and to the Spaniard was perhaps due much of the social style of the people. There was another element of prosperity in the frequent visits of Buccaneers, who called to dispose of their plunder on the wharfs of Port Royal, and whose personal gallantry and quasi-crusade against Spain were no mean recommendations. Moreover, many of them were gentlemen by birth, and in every way fitted to mingle with the higher class of residents.

---

* A useful and economical system of defence might be organized in this and the other islands, by granting temporarily small allotments of waste land (strategically distributed) to pensioned soldiers and their white offspring, renewable periodically, and under conditions which would develop the resources of these colonies, check continental propagandism, and relieve the mother country of a serious burden in time of war.

Hither came likewise many of the unfortunate victims of the *Darien* intrigue, and introduced a strong and useful Scotch element.

Still the island felt the want of skilful agriculturists, and although it had received at the outset every encouragement, it required the steady diligence of the acclimatized Barbadian to bring its great estates into that working order which resulted in such colossal fortunes in the following century.

Sir Charles Lyttleton convened the first Legislative Assembly of thirty representatives ; who formed, so to speak, the nucleus of the local aristocracy (1664—75).

Of the French invasions of 1691 and 1702 there is little to be said ; while the history of the Maroon war, which lasted thirty-seven years, can only be brought within the scope of these introductory remarks as the field where the warlike reputation of the militia leaders was tried, and, notwithstanding their frequent reverses, well sustained.

Earthquakes, servile revolts, and terrible epidemics followed each other at comparatively short intervals, and are sometimes briefly noticed on the tombstones of the early settlers. Many of these inscriptions are quaint, but the majority are in objectionable taste—a fault rather of the period than of the place, and introduced from England, where, during the eighteenth century, a bombastic style of epitaph was usual. There are, however, many magnificent marble sepulchral monuments in Jamaica, from the chisels of the first sculptors of Europe, and which, in discussing the whole collectively, are sufficient to redeem the faults of some others. A few remarks on the parishes of Jamaica may here be necessary.

In the time of Sir Thomas Modyford (1664) there were seven parishes, namely, St. Catherine, St. John, Port Royal, Clarendon, St. David, St. Andrew, and St. Thomas, but there was only one church—the present Cathedral of Spanish Town. It is true that about the time when Colonel Edward D'Oyley received his commission as Governor, from Charles II. in 1661, or soon afterwards, the island was divided into twelve *districts*, which, according to Long, included the subsequent parishes, in addition to those already mentioned, of St. George, St. Mary, St. Anne, St. James, and St. Elizabeth ; and this number has been further increased by the addition of Vere, Portland, St. Thomas ye Vale, Metcalf, Kingston, Manchester, Westmoreland, Hanover, St. Dorothy, and Trelawney.

St. Thomas in the Vale and St. Dorothy were constituted parishes in 1675 ; the former was originally a part of St. Catherine. St. Dorothy separated from Clarendon, in 1675.

Westmoreland was separated from St. Elizabeth, in 1703, and Hanover, from the former, in 1723.

Trelawney separated from St. James in 1770 ; Portland was taken from St. George, and St. Thomas in the East, in 1723.

Manchester was formed out of portions of St. Elizabeth, Clarendon, and Vere, in 1814.

Metcalfe was severed from St. George and St. Mary, in 1841.

Vere was separated from Clarendon, in 1673.

The Parishes were thus constituted :—

Between 1661-4—St. Catherine, St. John, Port Royal, Clarendon, St. David, St. Andrew, St. Thomas in the East.

1665—St. George, St. Mary, St. Ann, St. James, St. Elizabeth.

1673—Vere.

1675—St. Thomas ye Vale, St. Dorothy.

When the division of St. James's was first contemplated, in 1733, it was proposed to name the new subdivision Brunswick, but on the third reading, the bill was lost, and it was called Trelawney, after Sir W. Trelawney, the governor from 1767 to 1772.

The Duke of Portland was appointed Governor of Jamaica, 9th September, 1721 ; arrived 22nd December, 1722 ; and died in Spanish Town, 4th July, 1726—hence the name of the parish.

Metcalfe was so named after the eminent and liberal-minded governor of that name.

Manchester received the name of the ducal governor.

In allusion to the patron saint of its discoverer Columbus, in 1494, the emblem* of St. James, from whom Jamaica takes its name (although by a curious phonetic coincidence it was previously known by its Indian name Xaymaca, Isle of Springs) has, along with the arms of Jamaica,† been adopted in the Parochial Seals of the island.

By an act passed in 1789, burying in Churches was prohibited, and a penalty of £500 imposed on any Rector permitting it ; but two local bills dispensing with that act, were specially passed in the case of the Earl and Countess of Effingham, who were the last so interred, in Jamaica ; hence, at the present day, the few additions to the monuments within the Church, and, as it were, an abstract of inscription on the grave-stone without.

Besides the cemeteries of the Church of England, there are, of course, many others, which go on increasing with the progress of dissent and sectarianism, but these are comparatively modern, and therefore scarcely come within the scope of the present undertaking ; at the same time, a few such collections have been preserved, and will, at any rate, afford a curious contrast in nomenclature, inasmuch as they contain chiefly the epitaphs of the blacks, who, since the era of Emancipation, have not been backward in seeking to flatter "the dull cold ear of death!"

---

* The Emblem of St. James are a pilgrim's staff and a gourd bottle—hence the seal of the Churchwardens of Jamaica bears according to the Local Act, 7 Vic. cap. 39—"Argent—a palmer's staff erect, depending from its rest, by a leathern thong, a gourd bottle, ppr. On a border gules five Pine Apples *Or.* Sigill : Ædelium Sancti Jacobi in Jamaica. (Roby.)

The double gourd bottles of the Chinese and Japanese, so frequently represented in their works of art, are called by them, also, pilgrim bottles, and may be observed attached to the girdles of the Fusiyama excursionists.

† The inscription on the Great Seal of Jamaica bearing these Arms is—

"ECCE ALIUM RAMOS PORREXIT IN ORBEM
NEC STERILIS EST CRUX."

Bridges says, "This Seal was designed by the Archbishop of Canterbury." At that time (1662) the Metropolitan See was filled by William Juxon, who, when Bishop of London, attended Charles I. on the scaffold.

In giving a short account of the various religious denominations, I cannot do better than quote the words of a gentleman, whose acquaintance with the subject entitles him to be considered an authority.

" It is now (1865) two hundred and ten years ago, since the island of Jamaica passed into the hands of the English nation. One hundred and sixty-four years before this, it was possessed by the Spaniards. At three hundred and seventy-two years from this present year, it was the home of the aboriginal Indians. The latter are exterminated,* and we do not recognize any of their descendants occupying the homes of their fathers."

" The Spaniards were the first Europeans who possessed these islands. They failed to Christianize them ; and destroyed the people. Scarce more than two hundred years back, the English took Jamaica, and drove out the Spaniards. Now, in addition to the Spaniards, there were Portuguese settlers here, but they were Jews, and not Christians. When the Spanish Inquisition drove the Jews, as well as the Moors out of Spain, the Jews found an asylum in Portugal. The family of Columbus, the discoverer of America, had received this island as a sovereign possession."

" His son, Diego, was created Marquis of St. Jago de la Vega. On the grand-daughter of Columbus marrying into the house of Braganza (the family that now occupies the throne of Portugal), the Jews from Portugal came to Jamaica in numbers. Though the English drove out the Spaniards from the colony on its capture, they suffered the *Portugals*, as they were called, to remain. These were the Jewish settlers, whose families are perpetuated to this day, in their descendants—the Dasilvas and Soarezes, the Cordozos, the Belisarios, and Belinfantes, the Nunezes, the Fonsecas, the Guttereces, the Da Cordovas, and a hundred such names. They became the first traders and merchants of the English Colony, and owe to their precedence, as a people holding to a *revealed faith*, the preponderance of social and political influence they possess at this day, as Magistrates, as Members of the Legislature, and as members of learned professions."

" The first introduction of the Jews into Jamaica, is thus recorded by Sir Wm. Beeston. ' On the 31st March, 1663, H. M. Ship the " Great Guest," Captain Bernard, Commander, arrived from London, and brought six Jews (with a rich cargo), who

---

* A cursory glance over public documents supplies us with a number of Swiss and French Huguenots : James Zellar, Rector of St. Andrew's ; Hausyer, Rector of St. Catherine's ; Calvin Galpine, Rector of St. John's ; Mignot, Rector of a midland Parish. Joseph Delaunay, Peter Valette, and Leopold de Stapelton, Justices and Vestrymen of Port Royal in 1725. The Honourable Gabriel Marquis Duquesne, Commander of the Fort of Port-Royal,—Woolmer, Merchant of Kingston, who endowed the Grammar School of that City. There was a Huguenot Merchant, who bequeathed an annuity for a School in St. Andrew's ; and the Bernards, of St. James' ; the Le Contes and the Grignons, allied families of Lord Abinger, were all French Protestant settlers.

In a MS. in the *House of Assembly Library*, entitled " The State of the Church in his Majesty's Island of Jamaica," dated May, 1675, twenty years after the capture, it is there stated, after enumerating the then Stipended Ministers of Religion, " All the other Parishes on the North side, and St. Elizabeth's on the South, are great and ill-settled, *without Churches*, they being most planted in Sir Thomas Lynch's time, who ordered Glebe Lands to be reserved in two or three places in every Parish, that in time may prove convenient. He likewise, observing how *prejudicial and dishonourable* it was for the Ministers to be at the *will of the vestrys*, prevailed with the Assembly to make a Law that every Parish should pay their Parson £100 per annum *at least.*"

pretended they came to discover a gold mine, known to them in the Spaniard's Government, but concealed for fear it might bring grievances on a place so weakly manned, as Jamaica was, in the Spaniard's time; but this was basely a pretence, for their design was only to insinuate themselves into the country, for the sake of trade, and was managed by Sir John Davidson, who sent them with Mr. Watson, a German, who managed all.'"

The Jews, for a long time, were not taxed like other residents, but were obliged to pay an annual tribute, which the government of Sir T. Lynch assessed at £750 per annum, besides five per cent on their rents.

The oldest inscribed Jewish monument is that of Leah Gedaleah :—

"The earliest missionary teachers here, under the English, were the *Independents* that came with the army of Venables, in 1655. They were the first *stipended* ministers, and when they were *unstipended*, by the operation of the Act of Uniformity, they became the first Christian teachers, supported by *voluntary* contributions. Their numbers were augmented by the imported Nonconformists, who were not emigrants to Jamaica, but shipped off to be sold for slaves to the planters."

After these came hither the Huguenots—French Protestants, who were driven out of France, on account of their Protestant faith, at the Revocation of the Edict of Nantes. Many of them were accepted as stipended ministers, and became the early rectors of parishes.*

The Moravians, under the auspices of the families of Barham and Foster, followed, about the year 1765.

These were followed by the Baptists, and other sects.

Besides the public cemeteries, there were other places of sepulture; but, "when we consider that many monuments have doubtless been destroyed by earthquake and hurricane, particularly at the times when Port Royal and Savanna-la-Mar were submerged—that some tombs have been thrown down by wanton violence, and others mutilated, or lost in the fires, alterations, or desecrations of the buildings that contained them—we ought not to be surprised at the comparative rarity of monuments of the seventeenth century. No doubt, many of these exist, in the depths of impenetrable 'bush,' or jungle, never again to meet the eye; but there are also others on private estates, which are, I am told, well known, although I have not been able to obtain any accurate description of them."

On the estate called "Greenwich," for instance, and likewise at Spitzbergen, and Dublin Castle (the latter in the Port Royal mountains), are some old tombs. Such names are often apt to put the genealogist on a wrong scent, but they are at times correct guides; and by even so faint a light, we are sometimes enabled to trace a family back to the registers of some remote parish church at home.

"Parnassus," "Bellevue," "Golden Grove," "Running Gut" (probably a corruption, by some seafaring man, of *Harangutta*, a branch of the Ganges), "Romsey," "Arcadia," Lacovia, and Luana are amongst the names of old estates; while it is not

---

* A lecture by R. Hill, Esq.

altogether unworthy of note, in connection with one of the old stories of the island, that the celebrated buccaneer Governor of Jamaica, Sir Henry Morgan, lived on an estate near Spanish Town, which was called Laurencefield.*

Most of the handsome old mausoleums at Port Royal, secluded as they are from the town, and partially concealed by cashaws, gigantic cacti, and mangrove-trees, have been broken into and plundered, the lead of the coffins stolen, and the empty

---

* In a letter from Sir S. Watson to the Committee of Plantations, 27 Oct., 1689, speaking of the depredations of freebooters on the coasts of Jamaica, the writer says :—"Major Lawrence, with a ship and pirago, and about 200 men, the last month, touched at Mantega (Montego) Bay, on the north side of this island, did no harm then, but gave out that he would sail up to Petit Goave, a French settlement upon Hispaniola, and procure a commission from the governor, wherewith he will return with greater force, and plunder all the north side, killing man, woman, and child, which has so affrighted the inhabitants of these parts, they have sent away their wives and children to Port Royal."

Lawrence and Towneley were two buccaneer captains, commanding in the fleet of Sir H. Morgan.

The Earl of Inchiquin, in a letter to the same committee, 6 July, 1690, says of the Calapatch, and some small vessels, which had been sent to the Camanas for turtle, "They were there found by Lawrence, the great pirate of Petit Goave, who bore down upon the Calapatch, and engaged him. * *" That Lawrence has taken her, is the conclusion.

For further notices of the name Lawrence in these parts, *vide* Appendix.

When, and where, the piratical brotherhood first settled as planters in Jamaica, cannot with accuracy be determined, prior to the proclamation of George I., dated 5th September, 1717, when he promised and declared, that each and all of the pirates who should submit before the 5th September, 1718, should have the royal pardon for piracies committed.

The adventurers who entered the fraternity of freebooters in the time of Lawrence,* were influenced by reasons for their lawlessness different from those which existed amongst the earlier buccaniers.†

Their act was hostility to the Spaniard, because the government of Spain, having made all trading within their declared lines of empire, unlawful, *put it down as piracy;* but, after the restoration of Charles II., and the disputed succession to the British throne on the abdication of James, enabled Louis XIV. to resort to his avowed and decided warfare, as a partizan of James against William and Mary, it gave an abiding salvo to the consciences of English desperadoes (similar to those under the belligerent Federals and Confederates, in the *quasi* piratical Alabamas, Georgias, and Floridas which swept the high seas), and gentlemen like Lawrence did not hesitate to become adventurers. Such men yielded in acquiescence, when the king's proclamation, on the succession of the Hanoverian line, assured a settlement of all differences, by the suppression of the Scotch rebellion of 1715. Those that held out, on the chances of continued disorder in England, were such runagates as Blackbeard (Teach of Spanish Town), Rackham, and the petty rascals distinguished as *Piccaroons.*

The later history of the freebooters assumes a different aspect from that of the legitimate (so to speak) Buccaniers, and belongs rather to the HOME, than the FOREIGN department.

At the present day, an islet and reef on the coast of Jamaica bear the name of Rackham; and on the former may be noticed the site of the gibbet where perished the last of the Piccaroons.

There was in the possession of a late President of the Executive Committee, a deed of his maternal ancestor, Claver Tayler, a member of "the fraternity," dated in 1655, at Cabo Bonito, in Westmoreland (parish), the year of the capture of the island by Penn and Venables. Claver Tayler was a grandson of Tayler, one of the pilgrim fathers of the "Mayflower," and perhaps a settler from among the crew. His location was Rhode Island. The Taylers (probably through their previous common adventures) formed family alliances with the Lawrences.

There exists a MS. account of European families in Jamaica, compiled by a member of the Hinds' family. My informant had not seen it himself, but had no doubt of its existence.

The Honourable Alexander Bravo (Auditor-General's office), of a Portuguese family, is said to possess much valuable information as to the rise of the older Jewish families in Jamaica, which, it may be observed, have developed no small amount of ability amongst their members.‡ Amongst the earliest of the converts from Judaism were the Vidals, of Spanish Town, and the Israels, of St. Dorothy.

---

* He was twice married, first in 1729.
† Properly so spelt.
Amongst desultory works on the buccaneers of the West Indies, is one more immediately connected with the present subject, "An Account of the Rise and Growth of the West India Colonies, by Dalby Thomas, London, 1690."—Harleian Misy., vol. ix., p. 422.
"Memoranda of West Indian History," divided into "One Hundred and Fifty Years Ago" and "Supplement" to the same, ending with the disastrous war with Spain, in 1702.
‡ Mr. Bernal Osborne, for example, is the son of Bernal, an extensive proprietor of the Vega. (St. Cath. Par.)

vault left for the lugubrious picnics of the "dangerous classes," whose broken bottles, mixed up with human bones, bear witness to the revelries by which these solemn scenes have been desecrated.

No doubt the social vagabond of these parts sees little to reverence in such monuments. His own remains may be hastily consigned to the deep, or disposed of by the local authorities.

"And in the next generation let his name be clean put out." "Root out the *memorial* of them from off the earth."

These, and many similar expressions in Scripture, show the estimation in which records of the dead were held ; and that it was no derogation from spiritual hopes, or any evidence of pride and vanity in the living, to be solicitous of such mementos.

I have endeavoured to curtail as much as possible the conventional eulogies of these epitaphs, most of which contrast unfavourably with the pathetic simplicity of one, which recalls those of the early Christians at Rome.

"LYTTLETON, D.D., SUÆ IN VICINIA SEPULTÆ FILIOLUS OB. 1662."

A suspicion also rests, in many instances, on the heraldry of some of the more recent monuments ; but this is a question apart from the collection.

There are two inscriptions which perhaps require special notice in these remarks, the one published by Sir Hans Sloane* is thus described as then still existing, at Sevilla D'Oro, a few miles from St. Ann's Bay (Jamaica), and where, it is said, many Spanish mortuary memorials still remain concealed by the encroaching turf :—

---

* Sir Hans Sloane mentions in his work on Jamaica (published in 1725, but written from notes made in 1688, while he was physician to the Governor, the Duke of Albemarle), a number of little incidents and names of persons residing in that island, which are, in connection with the present work, not altogether uninteresting.

He alludes to his own account of the destruction of Port Royal, published in "Philosophical Transactions," No. 209, p. 77.

His description of the asthmatic Sir Francis Watson and his plethoric "lady" is graphic. "The Lady Watson, aged 50, and very fat." Sir Francis Watson, aged 55, "wheezing and asthma." Sir Henry Morgan is depicted in 1688, when he was about 45 years of age, as "lean, sallow coloured," his eyes a little yellowish, and belly a little setting out or prominent—Mrs. Banett, aged 45, as of a spare body—Dr. Cooper, aged 45, of a yellowish swarthy complexion."

"Major Thomas Ballard is aged 35," is said to be "much given to extravant drinking," that he is "plethoric and of sanguine complexion. Mrs. Aylmer, a lean woman of 35."

Amongst other names of residents, he mentions D——, an English physician who lived at Guatemala, and who had been taken prisoner by the Spaniards ; Captain Hemmings, living near Seville ; Captain Harrison, a planter in Liguanea ; Colonel Ballard ; Mr. Barnes, a carpenter living at Guanaboa ; Mr. Rowe, in Spanish Town ; one Captain Gough ; Colonel Crew, Captain Groves, Captain Powell, Mr. Rhadish, Mr. Lane, a child of Colonel Fuller, Mr. Anthony Gamble, a cook ; Colonel Walker, Mr. Rayney, Colonel Needham, Mrs. Pain, Colonel Ryves, Mr. Halstead, Mrs. Cope, Mr. Molines, John Parker, a lusty fellow ; Roger Flower, a baker ; Rev. Mr. Lenning, Mr. Wm. Kay, Dr. Rose, Stephen Legs, a wheelwright ; Rob. Nichols, Mrs. Barrett, Mrs. Duke, Geo. Thrieve, a bricklayer ; Harris, a joiner, &c.

On his way from St. Ann's to Orange River, Sir Hans Sloane returned from the North side of the island, by a road on the ridge of hills called *Archer's Ridge*, near the Orange River, probably alluding to a place so called after a certain John Archer, who received various grants of land in the time of Charles II., and who, one is strongly disposed to believe, is the person mentioned by Sir John Archer, judge of the Common Pleas, in his unpublished Diary, as his son by his first wife.

"There were two coats of arms lay by not set up ; a ducal one, and that of a Count, I suppose belonging to Columbus, his family proprietors of the Island." (D. of Varaguas.)

"Over the door" (of the old Spanish church at Sevilla) . . . "was our Saviour's head with a crown of thorns, between two angels ; on the right side a small round figure of some saint with a knife stuck into his head ; on the left a Virgin Mary or Madonna, her arm tied in three places, Spanish fashion. Over the gate, under a coat of arms, this inscription" (in Roman capitals)—

"'PETRUS. MARTIR. AB. ANGLERIA. ITALUS. CIVIS. MEDIOLANEN. PROTHON. APOS. HUIVS. INSULE. ABBAS. SENATUS. INDICI CONSILIARIUS. LIGNEAM. PRIUS. ÆDEM. HANC. BIS. IGNE. CONSUMPTAM. LATERICIO. ET. QUADRATO. LAPIDE. PRIMUS. A. FUNDAMENTIS EXTRUXIT.'

"The words are entire except Mediolanensis, which I supplied because this Peter Martir, a famous man, wrote himself of Milan."

The other is the spurious epitaph, written by the historian, Edwards, and inscribed on a piece of ordnance set up as a monument near Martha Brae.* As it has been the source of much _local_ error, it is here given—

"STRANGER !—ERE THOU PASS, CONTEMPLATE THIS CANON!—NOR REGARDLESS BE TOLD—THAT NEAR ITS BASE LIES DEPOSITED THE DUST OF—JOHN BRADSHAW— WHO, NOBLY SUPERIOR TO ALL SELFISH REGARDS—DESPISING ALIKE THE PAGEANTRY OF COURTLY SPLENDOUR— THE BLAST OF CALUMNY—OR THE TERROR OF ROYAL VENGEANCE—PRESIDED IN THAT ILLUSTRIOUS BAND OF HEROIC PATRIOTS—WHO FAIRLY AND OPENLY ADJUDGED—CHARLES STUART—TYRANT OF ENGLAND—TO A PUBLIC AND EXEMPLARY DEATH—THEREBY REPRESENTING TO THE AMAZED WORLD—THE MOST GLORIOUS EXAMPLE—OF UNSHAKEN VIRTUE AND LOVE OF FREEDOM—AND IMPARTIAL JUSTICE—EVER EXHIBITED ON THE BLOOD-STAINED THEATRE—OF HUMAN ACTIONS—O, READER !—PASS NOT, TILL THOU HAST BLESSED HIS MEMORY—AND NEVER NEVER FORGET—THAT REBELLION TO TYRANTS—IS OBEDIENCE TO GOD."

Many of the monumental inscriptions recorded in the following pages have ceased to exist, even since the compiler noted them nine years ago. Others, such as slabs, which once occupied an honourable place, within the walls of the church, have from time to time been cast forth into the churchyard, and could no longer be recognized. In my task of restoration, I have been assisted by the "Spanish Town Church Notes, &c.," of the late Mr. Roby, whose work, however, I was not aware of when first I made my collection. To it, also, many of the purely local annotations are due.

In the parish of St. Andrew's are some of the oldest cemeteries in Jamaica ; but it so happens, that not always the oldest consecrated ground, contains the oldest existing

---

* Trelawney, Jamaica.

mortuary remains. So rapidly does nature in that warm climate, and rich soil, mask the evidence of mortality, that even now tombs not dating a hundred years back, are comparatively rare, concealed as they are in many instances under the turf, as at Half-Way-Tree,* or enveloped in an impenetrable net-work of interlacing and often prickly plants.

Again, although Kingston only rose on the fall of Port Royal, yet so effectually have the sands of the Palisades swept over the tombs on that long and mournful, though beautiful, spit of land which enclosed the harbour, that while the former is comparatively rich in these remains, few are to be met with at the latter, and these few have for the most part been despoiled of their tablets for the sake of the value of the marble.

The compiler trusts that his labours as a pioneer in a comparatively new field may be taken up by some one with better opportunities, who, from this starting-point, might undertake to show the connection between these remote abodes, and the parent homes in England—and, entering into the domestic life of those early emigrants, unfold their schemes, trace their steps to local power and affluence, and, gradually commencing with individuals, proceed to communities, and then, overtaking those writers who have already ably written the political history of the West Indies, move onwards with them, in showing the course of declining and reviving prosperity in the present century.†

Retracing his steps homewards, such an author would find in the records of the State Paper Office, Diocesan Registries, and archives of the great Guilds of London, &c., many of those lost links which are still wanting in several instances to connect the colonial families, with those of the political exiles of the most troublous period of our modern national history.

---

* It is said that the foundations of an old Spanish chapel still exist in Half-Way-Tree Churchyard, and that underneath the present turf there are many Spanish monumental slabs.

† See "Private Diary of Richard, Duke of Buckingham and Chandos, K.G." (London, 1862), under Feb. 28, 1828.

CHRONOLOGICAL TABLE.

Date.	Events.	Governors.
1494	Jamaica discovered by Columbus. Columbus on his discovery of Jamaica in 1494, May 3, landed at the present Ora Cabessa.	
to	In June, 1503, during his fourth voyage, was shipwrecked on the spot now known as St. Ann's Bay.	
1504.	Governed by Indian Chiefs.	
1509.	Spanish Colony commenced.	D'Ojeda and Nicuessa.
1526.	Towns of Sevilla d'Ora, Melilla, and Oristan built.	Don Juan de Esquimel, and others.
	Indians nearly exterminated—700,000, in 13 years, perished.	
1538.	St. Jago de la Vega (or Spanish Town) built, —gave the title of Marquis to the heir of Diego Columbus.	
1605.	Island plundered by Sir A. Shirley.	
1645.	,, ,, by Col. Jackson.	Don Pedro de Esquimel, and others.
1655.	The *Flibustiers* and Bucaneers. Oristan destroyed, and Sevilla d'Ora and Melilla abandoned.	
,,	Penn and Venables conquer it; when it became a British colony.	} Don Sasi. } Serle and Winslow, } and Butler.
1656.	Council of State in England ordered 1000 young men and 1000 girls to be sent from Ireland to people the island.	} Sedgwicke and D'Oyley.
25 June, 1656.	Commander-in-Chief Sedgwicke died, and the command devolved on Colonel D'Oyley, who executed Major Throgmorton for mutiny.	
Dec., 1656.	Spaniards flee to Cuba, leaving their slaves, who regained freedom, and became the Maroons.	

Date.	Events.	Governors.
Dec., 1656.	General Stokes with 1600 men from Nevis, arrived and settled near Port Morant.	
Sept., 1657.	Settlers arrive from Nevis and Barbados.	Lt.-General Brayne.
Aug., 1660.	Conspiracy of the Parliament men defeated—D'Oyley at the head of the Royalists.	
1661.	Island divided into 12 parishes—St. David, St. Andrew, St. Catherine, St. John, St. Thomas, St. George, St. Mary, St. Anne, St. James, St. Elizabeth, Port Royal, and Clarendon.	
1662.	200 Settlers arrived from the Windward Islands and elsewhere.	D'Oyley.
Aug., 1662.	Spaniards return under Don Sasi, are defeated by D'Oyley—Rise of Port Royal, Rendezvous of Bucaneers — Revolt of the planters, and execution of 2 officers, Raymond and Tyson.	
Aug. 11, 1662.	Thos. Windsor Hickman, Lord Windsor, afterwards Earl of Plymouth, arrived as Governor.	Lord Windsor.
,,	Several extensive grants of land. The whole of *Liguanea* (Kingston) divided between Col. Archbould, Major Hope, and Sir W. Beeston.	
Oct., 1662.	Expedition to Cuba.	
1663.	First General Assembly—viz., Robt. Freeman, Edw. Waldron, Richd. Lloyd, Edw. Mullens, Jno. Colbeck, Humph. Freeman, Lewis Ashton, W. Beeston, Saml. Long, Rob. Byndloss, Anth. Collier, Wm. Clee, Thos. Freeman, Richd. Bryan, Wm. Ivy, Southwell Adkins, and Abraham Rutter.	Sir Chas. Lyttleton.
1664.	Speaker of Assembly—Rob. Freeman.	
1671.	First Members of Council—Maj.-Gen. Jas. Bannister, Col. Sir Jas. Modyford, John Cope, Thos. Freeman, Thos. Ballard, Wm. Ivy, Robt. Byndloss, Chas. Whitfield, Thos. Fuller, Anth. Collier, and Capt. Helder Molesworth.	

Date.	Events.	Governors.
1675.	Privateering suppressed. Census taken—7768 Whites. 　　　　　　9504 Negroes.	} Col. Lynch. } Sir Hen. Morgan.
July, 1678.	Forts Carlisle and Charles burnt.	Lord Vaughan.
,,	Rupture in Assembly.	Lord Carlisle.
1684.	Privateering recommenced. Sir H. Morgan died in a Spanish prison.	Sir Th. Lynch.
Apl., 1688.	First great Insurrection among the slaves.	Sir H. Molesworth.
Oct., 1688.	Attempt to revive Roman Catholicism.	Duke of Albemarle.
Jan., 1691.	Another Insurrection —Attack of French on North Coast.	Sir F. Watson.
June 7, 1692.	Port Royal destroyed by Earthquake; 3000 perished—President White died of injuries thereat, and was succeeded by John Bourden.	} Earl of Inchiquin. } President of Council, } John White.
March, 1693	Island in distress from late Earthquake.	John Bourden.
July, 1694.	French Invasion—Commencement of Maroon war under Cudjoe, which lasted 37 years.	Sir Wm. Beeston.
1700.	Usher Tyrrell, who had been expelled the Assembly by Governor Beeston, re-elected for St. James.	
1702.	Brig.-Gen. Selwyn, Colonel of 22nd Foot, and Governor, died. Adm. Benbow encountered and defeated M. Du Casse—mortally wounded—buried in Kingston church.	
Jan. 9, 1703.	Rise of Kingston.	
	Col. Thos. Handasyd, 22nd Foot, appointed Lt.-Governor.	} Major-Gen. Selwyn. } Col. Beckford. } Earl of Peterborough.
Feb., 1703.	Port Royal again destroyed by Fire.	
1711.	Great dissensions.	Genl. Handasyd.
,,	Admiral Lord Archbd. Hamilton, son of Wm. Douglas, 3d Duke of H., and Anne, Duchess in her own right, arrived as Governor.	Lord Hamilton.
1716.	Great dissensions.	
Aug. 1718.	Insurrections—Hordes of Pirates.	Peter Heywood.

Date.	Events.	Governors.
1721.	The parish of St. Anne suffered severely from fire.	
Aug. 22, 1722.	Hurricane.	Sir Nich. Lawes.
1724.	Attorney-General Monk expelled the Assembly for "infringing the liberties of the people."	
1734.	Coffee introduced from St. Domingo, by Sir N. Lawes.	Gen. Hunter.
1738.	White soldiers defeated by Rebel Negroes, 150 killed.	} John Ayscough. John Gregory. H. Cunningham.
,,	Governor Edwd. Trelawney—was afterwards Colonel of 40th Foot.	
	Col. Grant, of Jamaica, killed at the storming of Fort de St. Lazan, Carthagina.	Edw. Trelawney.
1739.	Maroon war terminated by negotiations.	
1744.	Hurricane and Earthquake, Oct. 20.	
	Guinea grass introduced by Ellis.	
1756.	Henry Moore, Governor, and afterwards a Baronet.	
1758.	108 families of Immigrants arrive, most of whom soon die.	} Admiral Knowles. Lt.-Governor Moore.
1759 to 1762.	Rebellion; loss of 90 whites and 400 negroes —King's House, S. T., completed.	} Haldane. Moore.
	Thos. Raffles introduced that pest—the *formica omnivora.*	
1764.	Thos. Wilson, a Marshal's deputy, levied on the carriage of John Oliphant, Esq., a Member of Assembly ; it was resisted.	
1766.	Vast treasures brought from Havana, which had been plundered by the British.	
	Magazine of Fort Augusta struck by lightning ; 300 persons killed.	
1767.	Sir Wm. Trelawney, Captain in Royal Navy, Governor.	
	Col. John Dalling, afterwards Baronet, Lt.-Governor.	Wm. Lyttleton.
	Sir Basil Keith, Capt. R.N.	
1768.	Census—Whites, 17,000.	Lt.-Governor Elletson.
	Blacks, 167,000.	
1772.	Negro Conspiracy discovered.	Sir Wm. Trelawney.

Date.	Events.	Governors.
1775 to 1777.	Peaceful and prosperous — Hutchinson's terrible murders.	Lt.-Gov. Dalling.
	Conspiracy of negroes in Hanover and Westmoreland discovered, and 30 executed.	Sir Basil Keith.
1780-1.	Savanna La Mar destroyed by fire—Earthquakes and hurricanes nearly ruin the island.	Lt.-Gov. Dalling.
1784.	The notorious Three-Fingered Jack lived— Lord Rodney's victory over the French.	Maj.-Gen. Campbell.
,,	Dreadful earthquake and hurricane, July 10	
1790.		Genl. Clarke.
1791.		Earl of Effingham.
1795.	Bread-fruit, Mango, China orange, Cocoanuts, Plums, &c., brought from East Indies.	Maj.-Gen. Williamson.
1798.	Montego Bay burnt.	
1801.	Second Maroon war terminated by bloodhounds—Slave insurrection.	Earl of Balcarres.
1806.	Slave trade abolished by Great Britain— Kingston made a city.	Lt.-Gov. Nugent.
Mar., 1808.	Conspiracy amongst Coromantee negroes ; their chief executed.	Sir Eyre Coote.
	Mutiny in West India Regiments, March 27, at Fort Augusta,—15 killed.	
	Conspiracy amongst negroes.	Duke of Manchester.
1812.	Hurricane, Oct. 12, followed in a few hours by Earthquake.	Gen. Morison. Maj.-Gen. Conran, acting for Duke of Manchester.
1815.	Port Royal destroyed by fire, July 13.	
,,	Hurricane, Oct. 18–19.	
	Conspiracy in Portland, St. George's, and St. Mary's.	
1829.	Colony declines.	Sir John Keane.
1831.	Rebellion in Cornwall—Slaves executed— Caused by Missionaries.	Earl of Belmore.
,,	Sir W. Anglin Scarlett, Kt., Ch. Just., died Oct. 6, at Cedar Grove, Manchester.	

Date.	Events.	Governors.
1833–4.	Abolition of Slavery—Apprenticeship.	Hon. G. Cuthbert, provisional. Earl of Mulgrave.
Aug., 1836.	Compensation for slaves, £20,000,000.	Lord Sligo.
Sept., 1839.	Complete Emancipation.	Sir Lionel Smith.
to		
May, 1842		Sir C. Metcalfe.
Nov., 1845.	Coolies introduced.	Earl of Elgin.
1846.	Coolie Immigration.	Gen. Berkeley.
1850.	Ravages of the Cholera.	Sir C. Grey.
1852.	Epidemic of the Yellow Fever.	
	The Hon. R. Hill,—a patron of local literature, and himself an author.	Sir H. Barkly. C. H. Darling.
1859.	Soulouque, ex-Emperor of Hayti, seeks an asylum in Jamaica—Riots.	E. J. Eyre.
1864.	A 5th W. I. Regiment raised—Its disorganisation and ultimate disbandment.*	
Oct. 11, 1865.	Insurrection at Morant Bay—Gallantry of the Volunteers—Captain Hitchins, and the brothers William, Norman, and Richard Harrison, &c.	
,,	Murder of the Baron von Kettleholdt, &c. Maj.-Genl. O'Connor, Commanding the Forces. Captain De Horsey, R.N.	
Oct. 17, 1865.	Bogle's rebellious proclamation.	
Oct. 23, 1865.	G. W. Gordon, an instigator of the Insurrection, executed under unsatisfactory circumstances.	
Nov. 1, 1865.	The Insurrection "stamped out."†	

* The particulars of these transactions, alike discreditable to the Government and its agents, have not yet been published, although references to them will be found in the "Examiner," Aug. 2, 1873; the "Broad Arrow," 28 Dec., 1871, Jan. 7 and 27, 1872, April 19, 1873, &c.; the "New Monthly Magazine," Oct., 1873, &c. It is a singular fact that the public has never required the production of the balance-sheet of this corps, on its final extinction, as such a document would throw a valuable light on a system by which the public funds are not the less squandered, because the accounts are *formally* balanced.

† See an article on the subject, by the author, in "Fraser's Magazine," Feb., 1866, &c.

Date.	Events.	Governors.
Nov. 1, 1865.	A Commission appointed to inquire into its causes and results.	Sir H. Storks (*ad interim.*)
Jan., 1866.	The Legislative Assembly abolished by its own act.	
1866.		Sir J. P. Grant.
1869–70.	Disendowment of the Established Church —A new system of judicature introduced.	
	Supreme authority practically vested in the Governor, assisted by a Privy Council of six, and a Legislative Council of twelve.	
1870.	[Revenue, £434,564. Expenditure, 430,154. Public Debt, 619,353.]	

GOVERNORS AND LIEUT.-GOVERNORS OF JAMAICA.

WITH THE YEARS WHEN THEY COMMENCED THEIR ADMINISTRATION.

| 1655 to 1658......Searle .... ⎫ | |
| Winslow .... ⎪ |
| Butler .... ⎬ Administered the Government. |
| Sedgwick and D'Oyley ⎪ |
| Brayne.................... ⎭ |

Governors.		Lieut.-Governors and Presidents.	
Colonel D'Oyley	1660	Sir C. Lyttleton, Kt....................	1662
Lord Windsor	1662	(P) Colonel T. Lynch	1664
Sir T. Modyford	1664	Sir T. Lynch, Kt.	1671
Lord Vaughan	1675	Sir H. Morgan, Kt.	1675
Earl of Carlisle	1678	„ „ „	1678
Sir Thos. Lynch	1682	„ „ „	1680
Duke of Albemarle	1687	Colonel H. Molesworth	1684
Earl of Inchiquin	1690	(P) Sir F. Watson	1688
William Selwyn, Esq.	1702	(P) John White, Esq..................	1690
Lord A. Hamilton....................	1711	(P) John Bourden	1692
Peter Heywood, Esq.	1716	Sir W. Beeston, Kt.	1693
Sir N. Lawes, Knt.	1718	P. Beckford, Esq.	1702
Duke of Portland	1722	T. Handaysd, Esq.	1702
Major-Genl. Hunter*	1728	(P) John Ayscough, Esq.	1722
Edwd. Trelawney, Esq...............	1738	(P) John Gregory, Esq..............	1735
Charles Knowles, Esq.	1752	Henry Moore, Esq.	1756
Geo. Haldane, Esq.	1758	„ „ „	1759
W. H. Littleton, Esq.	1762	R. H. Elletson, Esq.	1766
Sir W. Trelawney......................	1767	Lt.-Col. Dalling........................	1771
Sir Basil Keith	1773	Br.-Genl. Alured Clarke	1784
Major-Genl. Dalling	1777	Maj.-Genl. A. Williamson	1791
„ A. Campbell.....................	1782	Earl of Belcarres	1795
Earl of Effingham	1790	Lt.-Genl. Nugent	1801
Duke of Manchester	1808	Sir Eyre Coote	1806
„ „	1813	Lt.-Genl. Morrison	1811
„ „	1822	Maj.-Genl. Couran...................	1821
Earl of Belmore.......................	1829	Sir John Keane	1827
Earl of Mulgrave	1832		

* Henry Cunningham appointed governor in 1735, but not regularly inducted.

Governors.		Lieut-Governors and Presidents.	
Marquis of Sligo	1834	(P) George Cuthbert	1830
Lt.-Gen. Sir Lionel Smith	1836	,, ,,	1834
Sir C. T. Metcalfe, Bart.	1839	Sir A. Norcott	1834
Earl of Elgin and Kincardine	1842	Sir W. M. Gomm	1839
Sir C. E. Grey, Kt.	1846	Maj.-Genl. Berkeley	1846
Sir H. Barkly, Kt.	1853	,, ,, Bell	1856
C. H. Darling	1857	Edwd. J. Eyre	1862
E. J. Eyre	1864		
Sir H. Storks	1866		
Sir J. P. Grant	1868 to 1873		

SPEAKERS OF "THE ASSEMBLY."

DATES OF ELECTION.

Robert Freeman	1664	Hugh Totterdell	1714
Sir Thos. Whitestones	1664	John Blair	1715
Samuel Long	1671	Peter Beckford	1716
Thos. Colbeck	1671	Wm. Nedham	1718
Wm. Beeston	1677	Edmd. Kelly	1719
Samuel Bernard	1680	Geo. Modd	1721
George Nedham	1686	Fr. Melling	1727
R. Elletson	1688	Thos. Beckford	1727
T. Sutton	1691	John Stewart	1731
A. Langley	1693	Wm. Nedham	1733
James Bradshaw	1694	Chas. Price	1746
Thos. Sutton	1698	Edwd. Manning	1755
Andrew Langley	1701	Charles Price	1756
Francis Rose	1702	C. Price, Junr.	1765
A. Langley	1703	W. Nedham	1766
Edwd. Stanton	1704	Edward Long	1768
M. Gregory	1705	Nicholas Bourke	1770
Hugh Totterdell	1706	Chas. Price	1770
Peter Beckford	1709	Ph. Pinnock	1775
Wm. Brodrick	1711	S. M. Houghton	1781
Peter Beckford	1713	William Blake	1793

D. Campbell	1797
Keane Osborne	1799
Ph. Kedwood	1802
James Lewis	1809
D. Finlayson	1821
Richd. Barrett	1830
R. Allwood	1832
Edwd. Panton	1839
S. J. Dallas	1842
C. M. Morales	1849

THE FIRST GENERAL ASSEMBLY OF JAMAICA,

IN 1663, WAS COMPOSED AS FOLLOWS :—

Robert Freeman, Edward Waldron, Richard Lloyd, Edward Mullins, John Colbeck, Humphrey Freeman, Lewis Ashton, Wm. Beeston, Samuel Long, Robert Byndloss, Anthony Collyer, Wm. Clee, Thomas Freeman, Richard Bryan, Willm. Ivy, Southwell Adkins, Abraham Rutter.* Speaker—Robt. Freeman.

1671. FIRST PRIVY COUNCIL :—

Major-General James Bannister, Colonel Sir James Modyford, John Cope, Thomas Freeman, Thomas Ballard, William Ivy, Robert Byndloss, Charles Whitfield, Thomas Fuller, Anthony Collier, Captain Sir Helder Molesworth.

CLERGY IN THE DIOCESE OF JAMAICA.

PARISHES, 22.

2 Bishops—of Jamaica, and Kingston (1 Coadjutor); 2 Archdeacons; 2 Commissaries; 6 Chaplains to the Bishop; 1 Secretary; 1 Registrar and 1 Assistant; 1 Clerk; 1 Apparitor; 22 Rectors of Parishes; 70 "Island" and other Curates and Chaplains.

SECTARIANS HAVING PLACES OF WORSHIP.

Presbyterians, Wesleyans, Moravians, Baptists, Roman Catholics, American Mission, Independents, Wesleyan Association, United Methodist Free Church, English and German Synagogue, Spanish and Portuguese Synagogue, Spanish Town Synagogue, Montego Bay Synagogue.†

---

* There was but one representative for the whole of the north side of the island, viz., Abraham Rutter, Gent. In the next Assembly Mr. Samuel Jenks was added.

† The island is 150 miles long by 50 at the broadest part, and had a population, according to the census of 1861, of Whites, 13,816; Blacks, 346,374; Coloured, 81,074—Total, 441,264, showing an average of 31,519 to each denomination.

CIVIL LIST.*

1 Captain-General and Governor-in-Chief.

1 Lieut.-Governor.

1 Secretary, 1 Private Secretary, and A. D. C.

Privy Council—1 President and 15 Members (styled "Honorable").

Executive Committee—3 Members (styled Honbles.), and 1 Secretary and Clerks.

Legislative Council—1 President and 16 Members (styled Honbles.), Secretary, &c.

Honble. House of Assembly—1 Speaker and 42 Members; Clerk, Sergt.-at-Arms, Chaplain, Clerks, &c.

Public Offices — 1. Governor's; 2. Island Secretary's; 3. Receiver-General's, Board of Audit, &c., &c.

LAW DEPARTMENT.

Court of Chancery—Court of Ordinary—Court of Vice Admiralty—Vice Admiralty Session—Court of Judicature—the Circuit Courts and Courts of Petty Sessions.

CROWN OFFICE.

ARMY.

Commander of the Forces.

1 Military Secretary; 1 A. D. C.; 1 Assist. Adjutant-General; 1 Assist. Quartermaster General; Fort Adjutant; Engineers; Artillery; 1 Regiment of the Line; 1 West India Regiment; Militia; Volunteers; Clerks.

---

* As constituted *prior* to 1866 (see Chronological Table). This note refers also to the Church Establishment.

PARISH OF ST. CATHERINE.

THE CATHEDRAL.

THE cathedral church of St. Catherine stands in the south-east part of St. Jago de la Vega,* more commonly called Spanish Town, and occupies the site of the Spanish church of the Red Cross, which, together with an abbey, and another church, called the White Cross, was destroyed, at the capture of the town by Venables, in May, 1655.

On the outside of the west end of the cathedral tower, over the door, and under a pointed window, is this inscription, on a white marble tablet:

"D. O. M.

"This Church Dedicated to ye Service of Almighty God was thrown downe by ye dreadfull Hurricane of August ye 28th Anno Domini MDCCXII and was by ye Divine Assistance, through ye Piety and at ye expense of ye Parishioners, more beautifully and substantially rebuilt upon its old foundation in ye thirteenth year of ye Reigne of our most gracious Sovereigne Queen ANN and in ye Government of his Excellency the Lord Archibald Hamilton, in the year of our Lord MDCCXIV

Matthew Gregory, Esqr
&   } Church Wardens "
Mr. Beaumont Pestell

Below this, on another marble slab,

"THIS TOWER WAS ERECTED,
And the above Tablet removed from the inner wall,
In the year MDCCCXVII.
His Grace the DUKE of MANCHESTER Governor.
JOHN LUNAN, FRANCIS SMITH, Churchwardens."

---

* *St. James of the Plains*, so called from the patron saint of Spain, and its champaign situation. Long and Edwards agree in the probable correctness of the tradition, which ascribes its foundation to Diego, son of Christopher Columbus, about 1523, on the decay of New Seville, the former capital of the island, near the present village of St. Ann's Bay. Lewis, eldest son of Diego, was created Duke de Veragua, with the second title of Marquess *de la Vega*, derived from this town.—Edwards' *West Indies*.

4

On the east wall is the following tablet of—

"Benefactors to the Poor.

"Matthew Gregory Esq M. D. in the y^r 1765, granted (under the direction of the Honble the Chief Justice, the Honble the Custos of this Precinct, and the Rev^d. the Rector of S. Catherine as Trustees) a yearly income to the amount of £230 for the following benevolent purposes, viz To relieve any distressed Object of this island coming to S^t. Jago de la Vega, To bind out poor children to trades, and to portion orphan girls at Marriage.

Erected 1779 { Honble R. Welch Esq Ch Jus :
Honble W. P. Browne Esq C^s R^m
Revd J. Lindsay D. D. R^r Treas^r."*

I.

TO THE MEMORY OF—ANDREW ARCHDECKNE, ESQ., A NATIVE OF THE KINGDOM OF IRELAND, MANY YEARS BARRISTER AT LAW AND REPRESENTATIVE OF THIS TOWN IN THE GENERAL ASSEMBLY OF THE ISLAND. HE DEPARTED THIS LIFE ON THE 17th DAY OF AUGUST, 1763, AGED 72 YEARS, LAMENTED BY HIS FRIENDS, AND REGRETTED BY HIS RELATIONS. HIS CHILDREN, IN TESTIMONY OF THE GREAT LOVE AND AFFECTION THEY BORE HIM WHEN ALIVE, AND IN GRATITUDE FOR HIS PATERNAL TENDERNESS, HAVE ERECTED THIS MONUMENT TO THEIR FATHER, FRIEND AND BENEFACTOR.

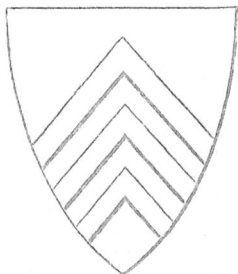

Arms, Arg^t., three chevronels Gu.

HE was of Gleveny Hall, Suffolk, and married a daughter of Francis Love Beckford, Esq., of Basing Park. For an account of the ancient family of Archdeckne, *vide* Banks' *Baronia Anglica Concentrata,* and *Journals of the Kilkenny Archæological Society.* Mr. Archdeckne was returned M.A. for this parish so early as 1718.

The city of Kilkenny appears, as well as Galway, to have had its own "ten tribes," thus recapitulated—

---

* By indenture, dated 22nd March, 1765, Dr. Gregory conveyed a house and land in Spanish Town to Mr. Edward Aldred, surgeon, upon trust for the Hon. Thomas Fearon, Chief-Justice, the Hon. William Wynter, and the Rev. Samuel Griffith, rector of the parish, and their successors, "for and towards the maintenance and support of poor persons in or from any part of the said island, and in and for putting poor boys and poor girls apprentices in the said island, and for giving portions in marriage with any poor girls in or from any part of the said island." But in the year 1792, the House having fallen into decay, an Act was passed (33 Geo. III. c. 14) vesting the messuage and land in the Hon. William Jackson, Chief-Justice, the Hon. William Mitchell, Custos, and the Rev. Robert Stanton Woodham, rector, for the purpose of sale, and for investment of the remaining proceeds and the interest therefrom to the charitable purposes before mentioned.

Of the subscribers to this tablet were Richard Welch, Chief-Justice, and William Patrick Browne, Custos. It is somewhat remarkable that of the numerous rectors of this parish there is not to be found a single memorial in the church or churchyard.

"Archdekin, Archer, Cowley, Langton, Ley,
Knaresborough, Lawless, Ragget, Rothe and Shee."

Of these, "Archdekin" was of more note in the county than in the city.

According to Banks (*Baronia Anglica Concentrata*), the male line of Thomas le Archdekne (summoned to parliament, 14 Edw. II.) expired in the person of his grandson, Warine, who married Elizabeth, daughter of John Talbot, of Richard's Castle.

2.

JOHN ATKINSON, OBIIT. 10th OF NOVEMBER IN YE 28th YEAR OF HIS AGE ANO DO 16(83).

HERE LYETH INTERR'D THE BODY OF ITHAMAR THE WIFE OF THE HONBLE ROSE FULLER ESQ WHO DEPARTED THIS LIFE THE 22d DAY OF APRll 1738 AGED 17 YEARS.

HERE LYETH INTERRED, THE BODY OF THE HONBLE RICHARD MILL, ESQ MEMBER OF THE COUNCIL, RECEIVER GENERAL AND LATE CHIEF JUSTICE OF THIS ISLAND, WHO DEPARTED THIS LIFE THE 16th DAY OF JUNE 1739 AGED 60 YEARS.

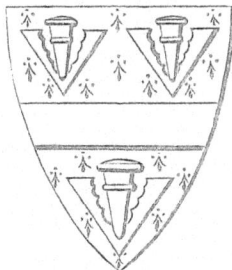

M. Slab, with a brass plate on which are engraven armorial ensigns ; *Arms*, Ermine a fess (or) between 3 pheons (argt.) ; *Crest*, A pheon. These are a narration of the arms assigned to Atkinson or Atchinson of Newark and Yourkshire. (Burke's *Genl. Arm.*)

3 A.

C.Y. * * MR. FRANCIS ARCHER * DEPARTED THIS LIFE THE 8th OF FEBRUARY 1824 AGED 35. (Ten verses follow) * *

FRANCIS ARCHER appears to have been of an Irish family, connected with the Commissariat department of the army. There were other families of this name in Jamaica during the 17th and 18th centuries, *viz.*—1. Archer from Swindon, co· Wilts ; 2. Archer of Wexford ; 3. Archer of Wicklow ; 4. Archer of Essex ; 5. Archer from Barbados, but previously from Suffolk (Q. Bury St. Edmund's and Sudbury ?).

3 B.

TO THE MEMORY OF ANNA MARIA ALDRED—DAUGHTER OF DANIEL BROADBELT ESQR. AND ANNA MARIA HIS SPOUSE— AND WIFE OF MR. EDWARD ALDRED SURGEON—WHO DIED IN CHILDBED ON THE 21st DAY OF DECEMBER 1761—AGED 19 YEARS AND SIX DAYS. THIS STONE IS ERECTED AND IN- SCRIBED—BY HER AFFECTIONATE HUSBAND—(Verses).

IT appears * that a Mr. Rigby Pennoyre Broadbelt was a trustee to a deed executed in Jamaica in favour of a Mrs. Elizabeth Crowder Nixon, &c.

M. Monument, sculptured ; On a bat's wing a skull.

---

* See advertisement in the *Times*—"To Genealogists, &c. * * Address care of Mr. F. May, 9, King Street, St. James', London. (1867.)

Captain Rigby, of whom a beautiful mezzotint portrait still exists, was an officer of the Navy on the Jamaica station, but for some reason a veil has been drawn over his memory. (See proceedings of his trial.)

4.

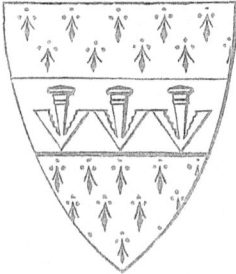

B. M. ; *Arms*, Ermine on a fess, 3 pheons. *Crest*, A pheon. (These are the arms assigned to Atkinson of Newark.)

HERE LYETH THE BODY OF CHARLES ATDKINSON ESQ: A GENTLEMAN THAT BY A GENEROUS AND PUBLIC SPIRIT, PUR-CHASED NO INCONSIDERABLE ADDITIONS OF HONOUR, TO HIS GOOD EXTRACTION, BEING SECRETARY SUCCESSIVELY TO THE HONOURABLE SR. THOMAS LYNCH, AND THE RIGHT HONOUR-ABLE THE LORD VAUGHAN. THRICE IMPLOYED IN FORRAIN NEGOTIATIONS HE ACQUIT HIM SELFE WITH HONOUR AND PUBLICK SATISFACTION. AFTER ALL, BEING READY TO EM-BARK ON AN EMBASSY FOR ENGLAND WAS SEIZED BY AN IN-VIDIOUS AND MALIGNANT FEAVER UNDER A PAROXISME WHEREOF HE DEPARTED THIS LIFE NOVEMBER YE 20th,

ANNO $\begin{cases} \text{AETATIS SUAE, } 31 \\ \text{SALUTIS } 1678. \end{cases}$

5.

B. M. Slab ; *Arms*, ... A fess between three asses passant. . . . .

WILLIAM ASSAM DIED IN 1730 IN HIS 45th YEAR. HIS WIFE MARY " LATE THE WIFE OF LAWRENCE PEAT " DIED 1734, IN HER 76th YEAR.

6.

RICHARD BATTY, ESQRE—DIED APRIL 10th 1796 AGED 53 YEARS—THROUGHOUT THY SHRINE BENEVOLENCE ENDEAR'D !—AFFECTION'S TRIBUTARY LAMP IS REARED ; —YET VAIN THE RECORD WHICH THE SCULPTUR'D STONE—WOULD RAISE TO THOSE PRE-EMINENTLY KNOWN—HIS STERLING WORTH AND VIRTUES STAND CON-FEST—GRAVED ON THE WORTHY AND THE VIRTUOUS BREAST.

W. and gray M.   Sculp. J. Bacon, London, 1798.

ON this monument is represented a female figure leaning over an altar tomb, on which appears in relief, a pelican feeding her young, &c. The deceased was Cust. Rot., and Member of Assembly for " Vere " parish.

7.

HERE LYETH BURRYED ELIZABETH BEESTON DAUGHTER OF SR. WILLIAM BEES-TON KNT. (PRESENT GOVERNOUR OF THIS ISLAND) BY ANN HIS WIFE, WHO DYED YE 18 OF AUGUST ANNO DI. 1693 AND IN YE 18 YEAR OF HER AGE.

B. M. Slab.

WILLIAM BEESTON, "Gent.," who had obtained large grants of land in Liguanea from Lord Windsor in 1662, was returned a member for "Cagua" (the present Port-Royal), in the first Assembly of the island, 20th Jan., 1663-4. He was four times elected Speaker of the House, *viz.*, 9th April, 1677 ; 4th September, 1677 ; 3rd September, 1678, and 19th August, 1679, having been each time returned for Port-Royal. —*Journals.* He was distinguished in that office, by his resistance to the attempt of the Governor, the Earl of Carlisle, to enforce "Poynings law" (of Ireland) on the island ; and his successful vindication of the privileges of the Assembly is fully detailed in the histories of Long, Edwards, and Bridges. On the 9th of March, 1692-3, having been knighted by William III., he arrived at Port-Royal with the commission of Lieut.-Governor of the island. In this situation he repelled a formidable invasion from St. Domingo, under Du Casse, who, after some predatory attacks about Port-Morant, landed 1500 men in Carlisle-Bay, but was compelled to retreat to his ships, with a loss of 700 men, after several encounters with the militia of the island, in July, 1694. In 1701 Sir William was appointed Governor, which office he held about one year, when he was superseded by Major-General Selwyn.

8.

HERE LYETH THE BODY OF COLL—JOHN BOURDEN—BORNE IN THE CITY OF COLRAIN—IN THE KINGDOM OF IRELAND, IN YE — YEAR 1633 — ONE OF HIS MAJESTIES COUNSELL OF—JAMAICA, AND SOMETIME PRESIDENT — A LOVER OF JUSTICE—A LOVING HUSBAND—A FAITHFUL FRIEND AND A GOOD MASTER — DYED THE 18th DAY OF AUGUST—1697.

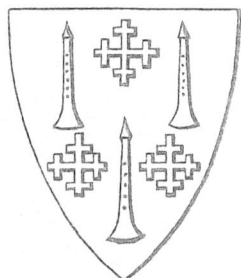

B. M. Slab ; *Arms*, 3 hautboys, 2 and 1, between as many crosses crosslet.

BOURDEN* was first returned to the Assembly as Member for Vere, 26 April, 1675. He afterwards represented St. Catherine in five Assemblies. He was then called up to the Council, where, resisting the Arbitrary measures of Christopher (Monk) 2d Duke of Albemarle, he was displaced by that Governor, but restored, on the accession of William and Mary, Feb. 22, 1688-9. On the death of the Governor, William (O'Brien) 2d Earl of Inchiquin, Jan. 16, 1691, the Government devolved upon the President of the Council, John White, who was killed at Port-Royal, in the earthquake which destroyed that place, June 7, 1692 ; when Bourden succeeded to the presidency of the Council, and, as President, to the chief command of the Island. In the latter he was superseded by Sir William Beeston, who arrived at Port Royal as Lieut.-Governor, on March 9, 1692-3.

---

* There was a Governor of the Bermudas between 1612 and 1622, of this surname, but whether of the same family as the above, is uncertain.

9.

HERE LYES THE BODY OF—SAMUEL BERNARD, ESQRE., CHIEF JUSTICE OF THIS COUNTREY FOR THE SPACE OF TEN YEARS, IN WHICH TRUST HE ACQUITTED HIM SELF AS BECAME A JUST AND PRUDENT MAGISTRATE, TO HIS OWN HONOUR THE GOOD OF YE COMMUNITY AND YE SATISFAC- TION OF ALL HONEST MEN—HE DYED MARCH YE 29th 1695, IN YE 59th YEAR OF HIS AGE.

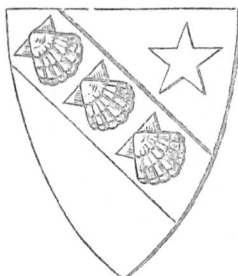

B. M. Slab; *Arms*, On a bend, 3 escallops. In the Sinr. Ch. a mullet.

10.

HERE ALSO LIES THE BODY OF JOHN THE SON OF THOMAS BERNARD WHO DIED JULY 24th 1720.—HERE ALSO LIES THE BODY OF SAMUEL ELDEST SON OF THE SAID THOMAS BER- NARD ESQR. WHO DIED NOVBR. YE 17. 1720 AGED 2 YEARS AND 11 MONTHS.

11.

MARY WIFE OF THOMAS BERNARD ESQR. WHO DIED AUGUST 13. 1724, IN THE 25th YEAR OF HER AGE.

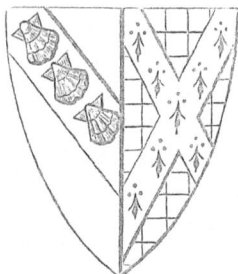

M—; *Arms*, Argt. on a bend az., 3 escallops of the field; impaling checquy, arg and gu. a saltire ermine. *Crest*, a demi-lion arg. holding in his jamb a serpent sable.

12.

(All on the same.)

HERE LYES INTERR'D THE BODY OF THE HONBLE COLL[LL] PETER BECKFORD LATE PRESIDT. OF YE COUNCILL, SOMETIME LIEUT.-GOVR. AND COMMANDER IN CHIEF OF THIS ISLAND, WHO DEPARTED THIS LIFE YE 3[d] APRLL 1710, IN THE 67th YEAR OF HIS AGE.

ALSO THE BODYS OF WILLM THE SON OF GEORGE BECKFORD, LATE OF EALING, IN YE COUNTY OF MIDDX, ESQ WHO DYED YE 11th DECR 1708 IN THE 18th YEAR OF HIS AGE. AND PHILLIS THE DAUGHTER OF PETER BECKFORD YE YOUNGER ESQ WHO WAS BORN YE 21st OF MAY 1708 AND DYED THE 28th DAY OF JULY FOLLOWING.

W. M.; *Arms*, On a chev. betw. 3 martlets, an eagle displayed. *Crest*, A heron's head erased, holding a fish in its bill.

ALSO THE BODY OF PETER BECKFORD ESQR SON OF THE HONBLE COLL[LL] PETER BECKFORD ESQR WHO DIED THE 23[d] OF SEPTEMBER 1735 IN THE 62[d] YEAR OF HIS AGE.

LIKEWISE THE BODY OF PETER BECKFORD ESQ. JUNIOR HIS SON, WHO DYED THE 16th OF AUGUST 1737 IN THE 32[d] YEAR OF HIS AGE.

ON the death of Governor Major-General Selwyn, on April 5th, 1702, when the Legislature was sitting, Colonel Beckford, who had a dormant commission of old date, caused himself to be proclaimed Lieutenant-Governor. In his speech to the Assembly he said, "I have gone through most of the offices of this island, though with no great applause, yet without complaint," and Bridges adds, " He carried on the business in a manner which redeemed the pledge he had given." He was succeeded in the office of Lieutenant-Governor by Lieutenant-General Thomas Handasyde, the same year. The cause of his death is thus graphically described by Bridges. " During a warm debate in the Assembly, on June 8, 1711, on the right of adjournment for a longer period than *de die in diem*, Peter Beckford, the Speaker (son of the President), repeatedly called to order, and was at length compelled to enforce it by adjournment. But irritation had gone so far that, when he rose to quit the chair, the Members drew their swords and held him there while the obnoxious questions in debate were put and carried. The doors were barred; the uproar was alarming; and the Speaker's father heard the disturbance in the Council-Chamber. He recognized the voice of his son crying aloud for help, and rushed into the Governor's apartment. Thomas Handasyde seized his sword, ordered the sentinels to follow him, forced the door of the Court-House, and dissolved the Assembly in the Queen's name. But the fray was fatal to the elder Beckford; in his agitation his foot slipped, and he was precipitated down the staircase, and the effects were deadly on his aged frame. His personal property amounted to £478,000, and his real estate to as much more !"

The second Peter Beckford, son and heir of the first, was elected Member of Assembly for Port Royal in 1704, and in the next Assembly, 1705, was chosen for three parishes, St. John, Westmoreland, and St. Elizabeth, but made his election for the last. He continued to serve as a Member in every Assembly of the island until his death—in the earlier Assemblies generally for St. Elizabeth, in the latter for St. Catherine. As Member for the former parish he was five times chosen Speaker, *viz.*, 29th December, 1707, when he was also returned for three parishes; January 4, 1708-9; 11th April, 1711; 26th November, 1713; and 17th September, 1716. He was also Comptroller of his Majesty's Customs in this island. On the 3rd of February, 1730, he gave "for a school and poor house-keepers" in this parish £2000. He married Bathshua, daughter of Julines Herring, Esq., of this island, and in the " Gentleman's Magazine" for December, 1735, he is said to have died worth £300,000.

Besides the " Peter Beckford, Esq., junior," who was M.A. for Westmoreland in 1728, the Speaker left a daughter, Elizabeth, wife of the second Earl of Effingham, and mother of the Governor of this island, and also a son, William, the celebrated Lord Mayor and M.P. for the City of London, who, in his second mayoralty made the memorable reply to George III., on May 23, 1770, which the citizens thought so worthy of commemoration as to inscribe it on a most magnificent monument in their Guildhall. Medals were struck on the occasion, having on their obverse the head of " WILLIAM BECKFORD, ESQ., LORD MAYOR OF London," in a large wig, with the civic robe and chain. On the reverse a female figure, seated on a pile of books, one of which is opened, and inscribed " MAGNA CHARTA," her right hand holding " the balance," and her left a staff, with the cap of liberty thereon; motto, " TRUE TO HIS TRUST." On the exergue, "1770." He married Maria, daughter and co-heir of the Honourable George Hamilton, second surviving son of James, sixth Earl of Abercorn, by whom he had issue William Beckford, Esq., author of "Vathek" (which he wrote and published originally in French, and afterwards translated into English), and proprietor of Fonthill. In right of his mother, who was descended in a direct line from James, second Lord Hamilton, by Mary Stuart, his wife, eldest daughter of James II. of Scotland, Mr. Beckford bore, under grant of the Earl Marshal, in addition to his paternal coat (Per pale gules and azure, on a chevron argent, between three martlets or, an eagle displayed sable), on a bordure or, a double tressure flory counter flory, gules, as in the arms of Scotland. William Beckford, of Fonthill, had by his wife (daughter of the Earl of Aboyne) a daughter, Susanna Euphemia, who married the 10th Duke of Hamilton, and was grandmother of the present Duke.

His cousin, William Beckford, Esq., formerly of Somerly, in Suffolk, was the gentleman to whom Brydone addressed his very amusing "Tour in Sicily and Malta," and was himself the author of "Remarks on the Negroes in Jamaica," 1 vol., 8vo., 1788, and "A Descriptive Account of Jamaica," 2 vols., 8vo., 1790. Another of this family was author of "Thoughts upon Hare and Fox Hunting."

[For other notices of this family see the "Peerages" of *Ancaster, Rivers*, &c.]

13.

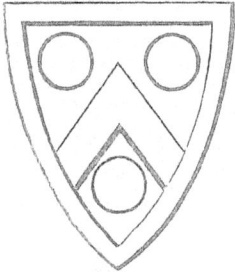

Arms, A chevron between three roundles, all within a border. *Crest*, A dove rising. *Motto*, "Virtute tutus."

NEAR THIS PLACE LIES THE BODY OF—JOHN BLAIR ESQR. —ONLY SON OF THE LATE—COLL JOHN BLAIR ESQR. DECEASED —WHO DIED THE 22D DECR. 1742—AGED 26.

(On the same.)

HERE LIES NIDEME, THE WIFE OF JOHN BLAIRE, ESQR AGED 29 YEARS, DIED YE 5th MARCH, 1707.

(On the same.)

HERE LIES THE BODY OF JAMES HAY, ESQ., ONE OF THE JUDGES OF THE GRAND COURT, AGED 39 YEARS, WHO DEPARTED THIS LIFE THE 7th DAY OF OCTOBER, 1735.

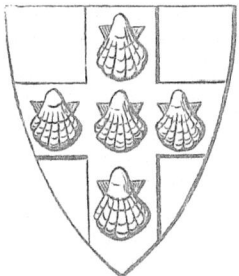

Arms, On a cross five escallops. *Crest*, A lion rampant.

THE Blairs of Jamaica are supposed to have been descended from the family of Balthyock, Perthshire ; this, however, is a mere conjecture, the first of the family in the island having been John Blair, a Darien refugee, who, in 1701, was elected Member for St. Thomas in the East, and filled many other offices of trust.

14.

HERE LYES INTERR'D THE BODY OF ELIZABETH THE LATE WIFE OF JOHN BLAIR ESQR. WHO DEPARTED THIS LIFE THE 7th OF 7BER 1721 AGED TWENTY SEVEN YEARS—LIKEWISE THEIR FOUR CHILDRN, JOHN, THOMAS, CHRISTIAN AND MARY—HERE ALSO LIETH INTERR'D YE BODY OF THE HONBLE JOHN BLAIR ESQR. WHO DEPARTED THIS LIFE YE 27th DAY OF JUNE 1728 AGED 60 YEARS.

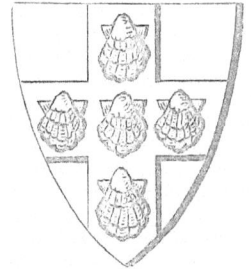

W. M. Monument ; *Arms* On a cross five escallops *Crest*, A lion rampant.

THE Honourable Colonel John Blair (*see* epitaphs of his first wife and son, already transcribed), was a surgeon, and one of the Scotch colonists of Darien.

There is a large collection of interesting wills and administrations of many of these Darien refugees, preserved in the Register House, Edinburgh, some of which would repay the trouble of publishing.

15.

HERE LYETH THE BODY OF HEARCEY BARRITT, WHO DE-PARTED THIS LIFE THE 5th DAY OF MARCH 1726 IN THE 76th YEAR OF HER AGE.

B. M. slab ; *Arms*, ... A chevren between three eagles' talors [Q. lion's jambs] erased and reversed. *Crest*, A talbot's head erased, collared.

16.

HENRY BARHAM, SEN : ESQR. DIED 1726 IN HIS 56th YEAR.

B. M. Slab ; *Arms*, ... On a fess betw. three boars statant ; a fleur de lis betw. two ducks, close...... *Crest*, A heron among reeds, close.

17

SACRED TO THE MEMORY OF THE HONBLE WILLIAM BLAKE ESQR. SPEAKER OF THE HONBLE HOUSE OF ASSEMBLY. HE DIED 24th JANUARY 1797 AGED 56 YEARS.

Stone Slab.

5

DURING the illness of Samuel Williams Haughton, Member for Hanover, the Speaker of the House, Mr. Blake, was twice elected *pro tempore.* He was re-elected for Westmoreland in the Assembly of 23rd March, 1790, and on the death of Mr. Haughton, (by a fall from his horse in August, 1793,) Mr. Blake was unanimously chosen Speaker, 22nd October, 1793. He was again elected for Westmoreland, and again unanimously chosen Speaker on Oct. 28th, 1796. He was succeeded in that high office by Donald Campbell, Esq., Member for St. George, who was elected 25th July, 1797.—*Journals of House of Assembly.*

In 1755 we find the will of Nicholas Blake, of Jamaica, and in it mention made of his brother Benjamin, and his son Nicholas Allen Blake, &c.

In 1766 is recorded the will of Samuel Blake, in which occur the names of his sons and daughters—Joseph, William, Samuel, Bonella, and Margaret.

The will of Nicholas Allen Blake, the nephew of Nicholas as above, is dated July 16, 1789, and contains bequests to his son Matthew Gregory Blake, his brother William, and his cousins the Burkes of Loughrea, in Ireland.

A few years earlier, in the will of Benjamin William Blake (1785), his nieces are named Jane Gregory and Helen Haughton, his brother-in-law Samuel Williams Haughton, and his brothers William and Nicholas Allen Blake, &c.

The first entry of this name in the parish registers of Jamaica is in 1671, and in 1717 is recorded the birth of Benjamin, the son of Benjamin and .... Blake. In 1743 is recorded the marriage of Alexander Blake* and Hagar Williams (probably a daughter of Williams of Carowena) ; and still later, in the Hodges family the baptism of an Alexander Blake Hodges, the nephew of Robert Francklyn Hodges, who married a daughter of the Hon. Hugh Lewis (Ch. Justice).

Robert Francklyn Hodges, younger, of Maxfield, was so named after a Mr. Francklyn, who married his aunt, Margaret Blake.†

In so extensive a family as that of Blake, it is natural to suppose that even uncommon surnames will be frequently adopted instead of ordinary Christian names, to distinguish individuals ; but when we find a double combination of this description, we attach more importance to the *coincidence* (?).

A reference to the pedigree of the Allens of Blackwell Grange, and a comparison of the names of Blake and Burke therein, suggests some connection with the family of Blake in Jamaica ; and if so, of necessity it appears with that of Barbados, in the

---

* It may not be unworthy of attention, that in no other but the Taunton Blake pedigree, is the name Alexander Blake to be found. Colonel Williams, of Carowena, married Elizabeth, daughter of Colonel John Guthrie. On his decease, she married (1735) Colonel Richard Haughton. The above (Hagar) was, however, not the daughter of *this* Colonel Williams.

† This gentleman's seal, now in the possession of Ana Archer, wife of Rev. John Campbell, Rectory, St. Thomas in the Vale, bears on one side the initials J. F. ; on the other a ship in full sail ; and on the third, Arg. on a bend engrailed gu., between two dolphins naiant embowed, three lions' heads erased, of the first.

seventeenth century, and of another family of the name in Ireland, one of whose members, Nicholas Blake, is described as of Barbados at the period to which we allude.

On referring, however, to the registers of Andover, we find that Nicholas Blake of that town was also of Barbados; while in the will of the wife of Nicholas Blake of Barbados (1663), we discover that her husband was also of " Bishop's Mead, near Craford, Kent."

Leaving, however, such branches of this family out of the question, and turning to the pedigree of *Benjamin*, Nicholas, and *Alexander*, three of the younger brothers of the celebrated Admiral Blake,* we find very strong presumptive evidence of its being represented in Jamaica; and this is probable, moreover, from the interest which Cromwell took in his valuable insular acquisition; and the date on the tomb of Alexander Blake, at Eaton Socon, 1690, brings the record of the Taunton family close upon modern times.

It is probable that there were two families of Blake in Jamaica, which became united in one, about the commencement of the eighteenth century.

The will of Elizabeth Blake, wife of Nicholas Blake, merchant, of London, entered (Barbados) Oct. 26, 1663, states:—" I bequeath unto my son Nicholas my land called Bishop's Mead, in the parish of Craford, county of Kent, and bought of Wm. Borman, and to his half-brother my son John Wilson, my cousins John Blake and Nicholas Prideaux, &c. Witnesses: Nicholas Prideaux, H. Turvile, Thomas Mortimer, and Hercules Tervile" (*sic*).

(Vide also the Baronetage; and Pedigrees of Blake at the Heralds' College and Brit. Mus., " Notes and Queries," &c. Very extensive *private* collections of Blake records exist.)

The name is probably identical with that of Black, and therefore has had various " centres of origin;" although, so far as we know, its earliest appearance was in Hampshire and Wilts, whence all the other *recorded* branches are assumed to have been derived.

In Hardiman's " History of Galway," (Dublin, 1820,) we find the following remarks:—" This family is of British extraction, and although the name seems derived from the Saxon *Blac*, a colour; yet Debrett, in his ' Baronetage,' says, ' they are traditionally descended from *Ap Lake*, one of the *Knights of King Arthur's Round Table* ' (!). Nothing ought to surprise us after such an announcement.

" In 1651 Government caused a map of this county to be made, and on the third sheet are, amongst others, the Arms of Blake, and also, with other inscriptions, the words (' Marilandiæ, Carolinæ, Verginiæ, et *Jamaicæ*,' being on the second sheet with the name Marline) on the third sheet: ' Bermude, Barbude, Montserrat, et Sancti Christophore.'"

---

* It may be incidentally noticed that the late representative of this family, the Rev. H. J. C. Blake (descended from Humphrey Blake), possessed the sword, and an interesting original portrait of the great Admiral. The Admiral died in August, 1657, and his epitaph is given by Pettigrew.

The peculiar baptismal name (probably in compliment to some Spanish family) of *Bonella*, seems to have been peculiar to certain families intermarried in Jamaica. Bonella Hodges, mother to (Pennant) first Lord Penrhyn, (see " Peerage,") gave her name to the Blakes, Haughtons, Vassalls, and Archers. Through other ramifications it passed into the families of Scarlett, &c.

From Pedigree of the Rev. J. H. C. Blake.

Humphrey Blake [s. of Robt. & Margt., of Bridgewater] had, by his w. Sarah Williams, 14 sons, & 1 dau.

The sons were in the following order [see Ped. Her. Coll. & Harl. MSS., 1141] :—

1. Robert ; 2. Humphrey ; 3. William ; 4. George ; 5. George ; 6. Nicholas ; 7. Samuel ; 8. Edward ; 9. John ; 10. Thomas ; 11. .... *ob. inf.* ; 12. Benjamin. 13. ....; 14. Alexander.

Robert, the celebrated Admiral, 1st son, died *s.p.*

Humphrey, 2nd son, left issue, and was represented by the late Rev. J. H. C. Blake.

George, 4th son, *ob. inf.*

George, 5th son, had issue male: Benjamin.

Nicholas, 6th son, had issue male : Nicholas (*viv.* 1695), and the latter had— 1. Alexander ; 2. John ; 3. William.

Samuel, 7th son, had issue male : 1. Samuel ; 2. Robert.

John, 9th son, died *s.p.*

Alexander, 14th son.

Admiral Blake's uncle, Benjn. B., m. 1614, Elizth, d. of Sidrach Blake, Stepney, Middx.

18.

HERE LYES INTERR'D — MR. GERALD BERMINGHAM — OF THE NOBLE AND ANTIENT FAMILY—OF ATHENRY—OF THE KINGDOM OF IRELAND—HE WAS A MAN OF STRICT VIRTUE —AND PRUDENCE ;—FAITHFULL TO HIS TRUSTS—AND SINCERE IN HIS FRIENDSHIPS,—TO WHOSE MEMORY HIS RELICT—MRS. ANNE BERMINGHAM—ERECTED THIS MONUMENT.—HE DIED DECEMBER THE 11th 1742—AGED 48 YEARS.

B. M. Slab ; *Arms,* Per pale indented two spears' heads paleways, points up. *Crest,* A goat's head erased. *Motto,* " Tout au Rien."

THERE was a great feudal family of this name, a branch of which settled in Ireland.

The Barony of Athenry de Bermingham was the premier Barony of Ireland, and fell into abeyance on the death of Thomas, Earl of Louth, the 22nd Baron, in 1799, when the Earldom of Louth became extinct.

The Berminghams and Barnewalls were two powerful families, at an early period, in the South East of Ireland. The Barony of Kingsland in the latter, was restored in the person of a Dublin hotel waiter, but is again dormant.

There was a branch of this family, as may be seen by reference to the Inquis. P. M. of Leinster, which was twice intermarried with that of Archer of Kilkenny, at an early period ; hence their coat being now quartered with others of note in the armorial achievement of The-O'Shee-of-Garden-Morris family. (Vide " Notes and Queries," 1867, voce *O'Shee*.)

19.

SACRED TO THE MEMORY OF—FRANCIS RIGBY BROADBELT ESQRE. M D—WHO IN HIS PASSAGE THRO' THIS PROBATIONARY STATE—WAS EMINENTLY DISTINGUISHED—FOR PURITY OF SENTIMENT, INTEGRITY OF LIFE—AND THE EXEMPLARY DISCHARGE OF EVERY RELATIVE AND SOCIAL DUTY — AND WAS EQUALLY RESPECTED AND BELOVED—AS A PHYSICIAN AND AS A MAN.   HE WAS BORN OCTOBER 9th 1746 ; AND DIED DECEMBER 9th 1795—THIS MONUMENT WAS ERECTED BY HIS SON—FRANCIS RIGBY BROADBELT—1799—

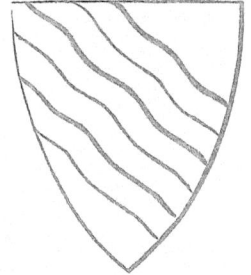

J. Bacon Sculpt.

W. M. ; *Arms*, Gu. three bendlets wavy or. *Crest*, A double headed eagle displayed sa. *Motto*, " Altius ibunt, qui ad summa nitantur."

O N this monument, the Genius of Medicine is represented supporting a figure of Hope, beside an altar, on which is sculptured the parable of the Good Samaritan, and beneath is the following couplet :

" When the physician shares the patient's pain,
Medicine may well our fainting hope sustain."

Dr. Broadbelt, junior M. of C., gained the silver medal of the Med. Soc. London, Feb. 23, 1795.

20.

THOMAS YE SONN OF THOMAS BRAY DIED 1699 AGED 7.   ELIZABETH BRAY BORN FEBRUARY 1698/9 DIED DECEMBER 1699.

Stone Slab.

21.

SUSANNA WIFE OF THOMAS BARRITT ESQ. DIED JANUARY 14, 1727/8 IN HER 36th YEAR, AND FOUR OF THEIR CHILDREN THOMAS, THOMAS, SUSANNA, AND HEARCEY—ELIZABETH HIS SECOND WIFE DIED 1740 AGED 47.

T HE families of Barrett, Hodges, Haughton, and Molton were connected with each other by various intermarriages.

The poetess Elizabeth Barrett Browning was of this family, having been a sister of the late Mr. Barrett, of Cinnamon Hill, Par. Trelawny.

B. M. Slab ; *Arms*,...... A chevron between three lions' jambs erased. *Crest*, A talbot's head erased, collared and langued...... [see p. 29.]

The name John Baret, 1463, St. Mary's, Bury St. Edmunds, occurs in Pettigrew's work.

22.

G. M. Slab; *Arms*, ...
Per cross, fesswise indented
.......on a bend, a rose between two martlets......Im-
paling a chevron between
three bucks' heads cabossed.
Crest, A sagittarius.

HERE LYETH THE BODY OF COLONEL ROBERT BYNDLOS
HE DYED THE 16th DAY OF JUNE 1687 IN YE 50 YEAR OF HIS
AGE.

HE was one of the original members of the first General
Assembly, and subsequently of the first "Council."

By his wife, Anne-Petronella, daughter of General Edward
Morgan and his wife, daughter of Baron Pollnitz, he had a
daughter, who married Thomas Beckford, grandson of Colonel
Peter Beckford.

There was a baronetcy in the family of Bindlosse of Bor-
wick, which became extinct, on the death of Sir Robert Bindlosse, in 1688.

23.

WILLIAM BALDWIN ESQR. DIED 17 JULY 1755 AGED 54,
ALSO MARY HIS WIDOW WHO DIED 12th APRIL 1760 AGED 68.

M. Tablet; *Arms*, Arg. three oak branches, slipped, leafed, and fructed ppr.

24.

HERE LYETH BURIED YE BODY OF CAPT WALTER BREAREY SON TO THE
RIGHT WORSHIPLL MR. BREARY LATE LORD MAYOR OF THE CITTY OF YORKE,
WHO DEPARTED THIS LIFE YE 29th DAY OF NOVEMBR ANO DOM 1681.

B. M. Slab.

25.

MR THOMAS BREWSTER SENR. DIED 1701 IN HIS 33d YEAR. SAMUEL HIS
SON DIED 1721 IN HIS 29th YEAR. JOHN BREWSTER SON OF JOHN & GRANDSON
OF THOMAS BREWSTER DIED 1733 AGED $\frac{8}{12}$. MRS JOYCE RAISBECK FORMERLY
WIFE OF THOMAS BREWSTER DIED 1734 IN HER 71st YEAR. SAMUEL SON OF

JOHN BREWSTER DIED 1737 AGED 10 YEARS MRS JOYCE BREWSTER, DAUGHTER
OF JOHN BREWSTER DIED 1737 AGED 14 YEARS.

W. M. Slab.

THE Brewsters are frequently mentioned in connection with the affairs of New
England in the seventeenth century. (S. P. O.) They were also numerous in
Barbados, where they intermarried with the family of Archer.*

There was a family of Raisbeck at Stockton, of which was Thomas, (*temp.* Carl.
II.,) who married Sarah, daughter of the Rev. T. Stapylton, son of Miles Stapylton,
Auditor to Cosins, Bishop of Durham (*temp.* Carl. II.).

See also Notes in Misc. Gen. et Herald., July, 1870, (No. 4), on the family of the
celebrated Maj.-Gen. Skippon.

26.

HERE LYETH INTERR'D YE BODY OF—FRANCIS BLACK-
MORE ESQ—ONE OF HIS MATIES COUNCIL OF JAMAICA—
AND SON OF SIR JOHN BLACKMORE OF QUANTRIX HOUSE—
IN THE COUNTY OF SOMERSET KT—WHO DEPARTED THIS
LIFE THE 24th —DAY OF OCTOBER 1697—AND IN YE 39th
YEAR OF HIS AGE

B. M. Slab ; *Arms*, ... On
a fess between three Moors' heads, as many crescents ...... *Crest*, An arm embowed, grasping a lance with a
swallow-tailed pennon.

27.

HERE LYETH INTERR'D THE BODY OF MAJOR GENERALL
JAMES BANNISTER LATE GOVERNOR OF SARRENHAIM WHO
DEPARTED THIS LIFE THE 10th OF NOVEMBER ANO DOMI
1674 IN THE 50th YEARE OF HIS AGE.

THE colony of Surinam was granted by Charles II. in 1662,
to Francis Lord Willoughby of Parham, and Lawrence B. M. Mont. *Arms*,......A
Hyde (afterwards Earl of Rochester), second son of the great cross flory, impaling ......
three battle-axes. *Crest*, A
Lord Chancellor Clarendon. In 1664 the English captured the griffin's head erased, ducally
gorged.
New Netherlands, the present New York, from the Dutch. In
1667 Surinam was taken by surprise by the Hollanders, under Captain Abraham

* Parish Register, Barbados. Richard Brewster and Sarah Archer married in 1681. Brewster is also
named in the will of Edward Archer, of St. Philip and St. Lucy, 1693.

Criuvon, but retaken the same year by Commodore Sir John Harman. By treaty, in 1673–4, it was finally agreed that Surinam should be the property of the Dutch, in exchange for the province of New York.

Major-General Bannister appears to have been President of the Council of Jamaica in 1671, his name being first on the list of that body, as given by Sir Thomas Lynch, on August 20 ; and he is the first named of the Council to John Lord Vaughan, appointed by Charles II., April 3, 1674. The 51st Article of the Instructions to that Nobleman, dated 3rd December, 1674, says, " Whereas we are now providing for the removal of such of our subjects from Surinam, as shall desire to transport themselves from thence under our obedience, in pursuance of the articles made at the surrender of that colony, our pleasure is, that for the encouragement of such of our said subjects, as shall be willing to remove from Surinam, you receive and use with kindness as many of these as come to Jamaica, and take care that they be furnished with provisions and other necessaries at a moderate rate, until they shall be able to get or procure them themselves, and that you proportion out to them twice as much land as used to be granted to other planters coming thither." Accordingly, in 1675, about 1200 persons from Surinam arrived in Jamaica, and were located in that district in the parish of St. Elizabeth, which still retains the name of " The Surinam Quarters." General Bannister was murdered by a " Mr. Burford, who was tried and hanged for it."— *Stedman's Narrative, Appendix to Journals, and Bridges' Annals.*

Major-General J. Bannister was murdered by a Mr. Charles Burford, who was tried and convicted on the 2nd December, 1674, and hanged three days afterwards. The *executioner*, Edward Hackett, died the same day. (Vide Reg. of St. Cath. Parish, Jamaica.)

28.

HERE LYETH INTERRED THE BODY OF MRS. MARY LEWIS WIFE OF MR SAMUEL LEWIS AND DAUGHTER OF MAJOR GENERALL JAMES BANNISTER WHO DEPARTED THIS LIFE THE 2d OF JANUARY ANO DOMI 1676-7 IN THE 18th YEARE OF HER AGE.

THAT DEATH MIGHT HAPPY BEE TO LIVE LEARN'D I
THAT LIFE MIGHT HAPPY BEE I HAVE LEARN'D TO DYE.

B. M. ; *Arms*, Chequy on a fess, three leopards' faces ; impaling a cross flory. *Crest*, A griffin's head erased, ducally gorged.

29.

ALEXR MACGREGOR MURRAY BURGE—THE INFANT SON OF—WM AND HELEN GRACE MURRAY BURGE—DEPARTED THIS LIFE THE 16th OF JUNE 1822—AGED 7 MONTHS AND 3 WEEKS.

(Also)

BENJAMIN MILWARD BURGE—DEPARTED THIS LIFE—ON THE 16th JUNE 1819, AGED 23 YEARS.

(Also)

WILLIAM LEE BATSON BURGE—THE INFANT SON OF—WILLIAM AND HELEN GRACE—MURRAY BURGE—DEPARTED THIS LIFE ON THE 19th NOVR—1819 AGED ELEVEN MONTHS AND—THREE WEEKS.

C. Y.

THE first two were sons of the Attorney General; the third and fourth, brother and daughter of the same.

30.

(*Ab.*) ALEX. BAYLEY ESQ. OF WOODHALL—ST DOROTHY—D. 14 JULY 1832, IN HIS 60th YEAR.

31.

HERE LYETH THE BODY OF COLONELL THEODORE CARY, ONE OF THE SONNES OF COCKINGTON HOUSE IN DEVON-SHIRE, BROTHER TO SR HENRY CARY CAPTAINE OF HIS MATIES FORT AT PORT ROYALL, ONE OF HIS MATIES COUNCIL, AND ONE OF THE JUDGES OF THE GRAND COURT IN JAMAICA. HE DIED JUNE 26th 1683 IN YE YEARE OF HIS AGE 63.

HE was also brother to Robert Cary, author of *Paleologia Chronica*, born at Cockington.

B. M. Slab; Arms, On a bend three roses, a mullet in sinister chief for differ-ence.

For an elaborate and interesting genealogy of this family, see the *Herald and Genealogist*, from which periodical the following is ex-tracted :—

"William Cary of this family had a daughter, who was married to Dr. William Helyar, and was buried in Exeter Cathedral, July, 1607. Dr. Helyar was a divine of some eminence, and claimed (I presume through his wife) kinship with Queen Eliza-beth. At any rate he was her Majesty's chaplain, and probably through her, if not directly from her, received his other important preferments. He seems to have been a great pluralist in an age of pluralism, and enjoyed a prebendal stall both at Exeter and Chester, the archdeaconry of Barnstaple, the treasurership of Chelsea College, and various livings in Devon and Somerset. He died in 1645, and was, I think, buried in Exeter Cathedral ; but at East Coker, in Somersetshire, he founded an almshouse and built a handsome residence, Coker Court, which his descendants have occupied in succession to the present day. The archdeacon's eldest son, Henry Helyar, formed a *second* connection with the Cary family. According to the Visitation of Somerset, 1672 (confirmed by Cole's Escheats), he married in 1621, Christian, daughter of William Cary of Clovelly, co. Devon, and by her had several children, amongst whom

6

was Cary Helyar, who migrated as a merchant to Jamaica, and there died, in 1672, aged 39. His monument is in the church of Spanish Town in that island, and in the same church is another to Colonel Theodore Cary, 'one of the sons of Cockington House, co. Devon, brother to Sir Henry Cary, a judge of the Grand Court.' He died in 1683, aged 63, and was therefore contemporary with Cary Helyar ; and, it is not unreasonable to conjecture, was related to him. There can be little doubt that Colonel Theodore Cary was one of the younger sons of George Cary of Cockington, of whom Prince says, that his 'youngest sons became soldiers of fortune, and died, I think, beyond the seas, without issue.' This last statement is perhaps open to queston, as the MS. I have quoted records the marriage, in 1676, of Colonel Theodore Cary with Dorothy Wale ; and, in 1679, of Penelope Cary with Thomas Edward.

"The immediate cause of the rapid rise of the Cary family is to be found in its close connection with Queen Elizabeth. William Cary (second son of Thomas Cary of Chilton Foliot) married Mary Boleyne, sister of Queen Anne, and aunt of Queen Elizabeth. From this marriage descended the Earls of Dover and Monmouth and the Barons Hunsdon ; while from Sir John Cary, William's elder brother, came the Viscounts Falkland, whose fame is well preserved in the annals of our country."

B. M. Slab ; sculptured dove and olive branch.

32.

MR. JOHN CHILDERMAS DIED 1699 AGED 33 : RACHAEL OB : 1720 ÆT 15 ; & SEBRAN LARSON HER FATHER OB. 1725 ÆT 50.

IN the Journal of the House of Lords, 17th August, 1660, mention is made of the "Bill for Naturalizing Renée de *Sebran*, an infant of 8 years."

Sebran Larson was governor of the Spanish Town gaol, &c.

33.

HERE LYETH THE BODY OF—JANE COOPER—WHO DEPARTED THIS LIFE—IN THE YEAR OF OUR LORD 1749, IN THE 86th YEAR OF HER AGE—

G. M. Slab.

PERHAPS related to the family of Major Christopher Cooper, who lost his life in Jamaica, as appears by the petition of his widow in 1656. (Cal. S. P.)

34.

CHRISTIAN DAUGHTER OF RICHARD AND MARY CASTELL DIED 1720 IN HER 13th YEAR.

W. M. Slab.

35.

ON THE 17th DAY OF JUNE—IN THE YEAR OF OUR LORD—1780—DEPARTED THIS LIFE—UNIVERSALLY LAMENTED—GEORGE CUTHBERT ESQ—ONE OF THE REPRESENTATIVES—IN ASSEMBLY—FOR THE PARISH OF—PORT ROYAL—AND LATE—PROVOST MARSHAL GENERAL—OF THIS ISLAND—AGED 42 YEARS—UNDER-NEATH THIS STONE—HIS REMAINS ARE DEPOSITED.

Stone Slab.

TWO brothers, Lewis (father of the Hon. George Cuthbert, sometime President of the Council), and George (Provost-Marshal-General, whose epitaph is above tran-scribed), descended from a family in the county of Inverness, came out to this island and married two sisters of the Hon. George Pinnock, late President of the Council. A third brother, a Roman Catholic, was consecrated Bishop of Rhodes (in partibus infidelium).

36.

SACRED TO THE MEMORY—OF—ANNE THE DUTIFUL AND AFFECTIONATE DAUGHTER OF JOHN CLEMENT OF PETERS-FIELD IN THE COUNTY OF SOUTHAMPTON ESQUIRE AND THE TRULY VIRTUOUS, MUCH BELOVED AND LAMENTED WIFE OF GEORGE RAMSAY ESQ REGISTRAR IN CHANCERY AND CLERK OF THE PATENTS IN THIS ISLAND. SHE DIED OF THE SMALL POX ON THE 14th DAY OF AUGUST 1764 AGED 32 YEARS AND WAS BURIED WITHIN THE COMMUNION RAILS OF THIS CHURCH —AND ALSO OF—PETER RAMSAY ESQUIRE REGISTRAR IN CHANCERY AND CLERK OF THE PATENTS ON THE RESIGNA-TION OF HIS BROTHER IN THE YEAR 1770. THE EASE AND UNAFFECTED DEPORTMENT OF THIS GENTLEMAN IN PRIVATE LIFE DID NOT MORE TRULY ENDEAR HIM TO HIS NUMEROUS AC-QUAINTANCE THAN THE UNIFORMLY UPRIGHT AND ATTENTIVE DISCHARGE OF THE PUBLIC TRUSTS REPOSED IN HIM JUSTLY SECURED HIM THE RESPECT AND ESTEEM OF THE WHOLE COMMUNITY—HE DIED THE 27th DAY OF OCTOBER 1781, AGED 48 YEARS, AND WAS BURIED ON THE WEST SIDE OF THE NORTH DOOR OF THIS CHURCH, UNDER A MARBLE SLAB IN THE CHURCHYARD.—A SMALL TRIBUTE OF CON-JUGAL AFFECTION—AND BROTHERLY REGARD.*

Arms, Suspended from the crest, an unicorn's head sable, two shields : on dexter, argent, an eagle displayed within a bordure sable. Im-paling, gules, three garbs or, for Clement. On sinis-ter, Ramsay, as in pedigree.

* For Pedigree see following page.

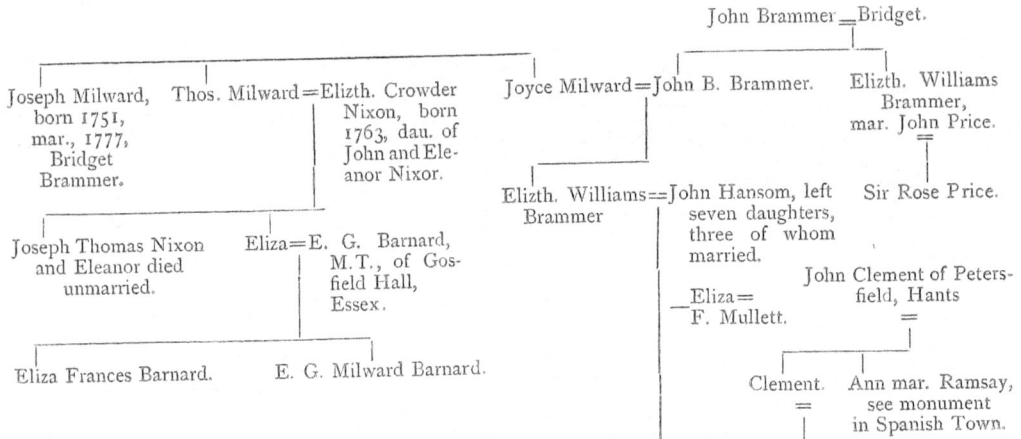

John Brammer＝Bridget.

Joseph Milward, born 1751, mar., 1777, Bridget Brammer.

Thos. Milward＝Elizth. Crowder Nixon, born 1763, dau. of John and Eleanor Nixor.

Joyce Milward＝John B. Brammer.

Elizth. Williams Brammer, mar. John Price.

Joseph Thomas Nixon and Eleanor died unmarried.

Eliza＝E. G. Barnard, M.T., of Gosfield Hall, Essex.

Elizth. Williams Brammer ＝＝John Hansom, left seven daughters, three of whom married.

Sir Rose Price.

Eliza Frances Barnard.

E. G. Milward Barnard.

Eliza＝F. Mullett.

John Clement of Petersfield, Hants ＝

Clement. ＝

Ann mar. Ramsay, see monument in Spanish Town.

ARMS.

MILWARD.—Ermine on a fess gules three plates. *Crest,* A lion's jamb sa., grasping a sceptre or.

HANSON.—Three mascles sable ; on a chief of the Second, as many lions rampant of the First. *Crest,* A lion rampant, holding a mascle.

CLEMENT.—Three garbs within a bordure.

ST. JOHN.—The same as the Bolingbroke family. Capt. St. John was the son of Lieut. St. John, of Devonshire.

[Contrd. by E. G. M. B.]

Anna Wilhemina, mar. Capt. James Humphrey St. John. ＝

Frances＝Clement.

—sons died unmarried.

Henry, a son now living.

Frances＝Revd. Thos. Robinson, son of the Master of the Temple.

Charles Grey.   Celeste.   Thomas.   &c., &c.

37.

HERE LYETH YE BODY OF COLLNEL JOHN COLBECK OF COLBECK IN ST DOROTHYES WHO WAS BORN YE 30 OF MAY 1630 AND CAME WITH YE ARMY THAT CONQUERED THIS ISLAND YE 10th DAY OF MAY 1655 WHERE HAVEING DISCHARGED SEVERAL HONBLE OFFICES BOTH CIVILL AND MILITARY WITH GREAT APPLAUSE HE DEPARTED THIS LIFE YE 22d DAY OF FEBRUARY 1682.

B. M. Slab.

IT is remarkable that the names of *Colbeck,* who "came with ye army that conquered this island,"—of *Freeman,* "who was at ye takeing of this island,"—and of *Fuller* (buried in the Church of St. Dorothy), "one of the first takers of this island," are altogether omitted in the list of "some of the principal persons who held official situations in the expedition" under Penn and Venables, as given by Bridges, in his Appendix, Note XLIX., although the circumstance of their being among the original captors of Jamaica, is particularly recorded on their respective gravestones.—Roby.

In 1664, Captain Colbeck was distinguished during the negro rebellion of that year.

38.

JOSEPH CRASSWELL ESQ LATE OF THIS PARISH, DIED 1768 AGED 39.

Stone Slab.   (Vide HANSON).

39.

MR. FRANCIS COLEPEPPER BORN AT HOLLINGBOURN IN KENT DIED 1761
AGED 44.

W. M. Slab; *Arms*, A chev. engrailed in sinister chief, a crescent. *Crest*, A hawk rising (with a branch in its talons).

THE Colepeper, or Culpeper family, of great antiquity in Kent, was, before the time of Edward III., divided into two branches, the claim to precedence between which has never been decided.

The above was a descendant of Walter, son of Sir John Culpeper, from whom came "the Barons Colepeper, the Colepepers of Wiggshall and Folkington, and the Colepepers of Hollingborn, &c." (Ext. Baronetage.)

This family was eminent in the seventeenth century.

40.

HERE RESTETH YE BODY OF ANTHONY COLLYER ESQ BORN IN THE CITY OF
GLOCESTER ONE OF HIS MATIES COUNCIL FOR THIS ISLAND AND COLL OF A
FOOT REGMT IN YE SAME: WHO DEPARTED THIS LIFE ON YE TENTH DAY OF
AUGUST IN YE YEARE OF OUR LORD GOD ONE THOUSAND SIX HUNDRED SEAVENTY
AND SEAVEN, AND IN THE FORTIETH YEARE OF HIS AGE.

B. M. Slab; *Arms*, A chev. between three bats volant proper. *Crest*, A wyvern passant.

ANTHONY COLLYER was one of the first Representatives of Jamaica, being returned to the Assembly of 20th January, 1663-4, as Member for "Seven Plantations." He was probably called up to the Council soon afterwards, as we do not find his name in the Returns of any future Assembly, and in 1671 Sir Thomas Lynch mentions him as one whom he found a Member of the Council on his arrival in this island. He was also "constituted and appointed" one of the Council by Charles II., in his Commission to the Governor John Lord Vaughan, dated April 3, 1674.

Anthony Collyer bequeathed one thousand acres to Samuel Long. Collyer's widow, Elizabeth, married secondly, Sir Francis Watson, Knt. (Major-General, Member of Congress, and President of Council), who administered the Government from the death of the Duke of Albemarle in 1688, until the arrival of the Earl of Inchiquin in 1690.

Sir Francis was buried in the chancel of Spanish Town Church, 19th August, 1691, and Lady W. on 18th April, 1698.

Probably of the same family was "Giles Collier, of Bristol, clothier," who presented Joseph Collier to the living of Steple, Longford, Wilts, 1607.

1635. Henry Collier, p.m., J.C.	1703. Ann Collier, presented.
1670. Arthur Collier, p.m., H.C.	1704. „ „
1698. Ann Collier, presented.	1732. Arthur Collier, died.

41.

HIC JACET ROSANNA UXOR DILECTA—ROGERI DAVIES MD—NATU MAXIMA
ET COHERES—THOMAE BROOKS DE BROOKSHALL—PAROCH STAE MARIAE IN HAC
INSULA ARMIG.—OBIIT 17º DIE XBRIS A.D. 1753—AETATIS SUAE 30—
QUICQUID AMAS CUPIAS NON PLACUISSE NIMIS.
B. M. Slab.

42.

M. Mont. (Westmacott,
Sculpt.); *Arms*, 2ndly, 1
& 4. Per pale or and azure ;
A sun in splendour, counter-
changed. 2 & 3. Gules, on
a bend or, three mullets
sable within a border ar-
gent. *Crest*, A ram pas-
sant gules.

TO THE MEMORY OF—CAPTAIN GEORGE DYSON OF THE
ROYAL ENGINEERS, BORN AT WINCHESTER 12th OF MARCH
1783 DIED AT SPANISH TOWN 26th OF JUNE 1806.

YE WHOM THE RECORDS OF THE TOMB MISTRUST,
AND DEEM SEPULCHRAL PRAISE MORE FOND THAN JUST,
MAY IN THIS STONE'S SINCERITY CONFIDE
AND READ A SOLDIER'S PRAISE WITH UNCHECK'D PRIDE ;
HERE IN THE WORDS OF WARM BUT SOBER TRUTH
AN HONOUR'D CHIEF EMBALMS A GALLANT YOUTH
HERE—SHALL NO FATHER'S FONDNESS INTERFERE
TO CLAIM THE HOMAGE OF A GENERAL TEAR
CONTENT TO HOPE HIS SON'S DISTINGUISH'D PRAISE
SHALL KINDRED FLAMES IN OTHER BOSOMS RAISE
IN VIRTUE'S SERVICE, AS IN HONOUR'S BRAVE
AND BLEST WITH LAURELS WHICH SURVIVE THE GRAVE.

On the base of the monument :—

" SORRY, VERY SORRY AM I INDEED, THAT IT HAS FALLEN
TO MY LOT TO COMMUNICATE THIS LAMENTABLE LOSS TO
YOU OF A SON, WHOSE UNEXCEPTIONABLE PIOUS AND DO-
CILE DISPOSITION, SUPERIOR TALENTS, AND PROFOUND
KNOWLEDGE OF HIS PROFESSION, IN SHORT EVERY NOBLE
AND GOOD QUALITY, HAD ENDEARED HIM TO ME AS A
BROTHER.—EYRE COOTE, LIEUT GOVr. 28th JUNE 1806."

43.

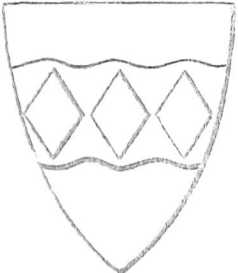

B. M. Slab ; *Arms*, On a
fess wavy three lozenges.
Crest, An anchor erect with

UNDER THIS STONE LYETH BODYS OF EDMON DUCKE
ESQ ... [MARTHA] HIS WIFE SHE BEING MOST ...BAROUSLY
MURTHERED BY SOME OF THEIR ... SLAVES DEPARTED THIS
LIFE THE ... OF APRIL 1678 AND HEE FOLLOW ... 14th DAY
OF OCTOBER 168[3] ...

HERE LYES THE BODY OF ... EXCELLENCY HENRY CUN-
NINGHAM ESQR GOVERNOR OF JAMAICA WHO DEPARTED
THIS ...... 12th DAY OF FEBRUARY 1735-6 IN THE 59th YEAR
OF HIS AGE.

E DMUND DUCKE was Attorney-General of Jamaica in 1671. He was probably a near relative of Dr. Duck, Chancellor of London, whom the Privy Council desired, in 1637, to settle some disputes among the inhabitants of, and others connected with, the Island of St. Christopher.

There was a Sir John Duck created a Baronet in 1687, whose rise to fortune deserves a place in the romance of the Baronetage. He had a brother named Robert, and several nieces, but no issue.

Henry Cunningham, Esq., of Balquhan, Stirlingshire, was M.P. for that county several times. He was appointed Governor of Jamaica in 1734, but did not assume office before Dec. 22, 1735.

Henry Cunningham held the government only three months, and fell by "an act of his own intemperance at a public entertainment." He was a Scotchman, and favourite of Sir Robert Walpole, whom he had rescued from the mob, during the Excise Riots. ("Roby." *Gentleman's Magazine.* "Bridge's Annals.")

44.

TO THE MEMORY OF—THOMAS EARL OF EFFINGHAM BARON HOWARD—CAPTAIN GENERAL, AND CHIEF GOVERNOR OF THIS ISLAND 1790 AND 1791—AND OF CATHERINE HIS WIFE—THE LATTER DEPARTED THIS LIFE ON THE THIRTEENTH DAY OF OCTOBER 1791—IN A VOYAGE UNDERTAKEN FOR THE BENEFIT OF HER HEALTH IN HIS MAJESTY'S SHIP DIANA:—THE FORMER ON THE 19th OF THE FOLLOWING MONTH—THE THIRD WEEK AFTER THE MELANCHOLY RETURN OF THE DIANA WITH THE REMAINS OF HIS BELOVED CONSORT—WHOM HE SEEMED UNWILLING TO SURVIVE—AND WITH WHOM HE WAS DEPOSITED IN THE SAME GRAVE—THUS UNITED IN THEIR LIVES BY THE MOST TENDER AND EXALTED TIES——

HE—THE FOND AND INDULGENT HUSBAND
SHE—THE CHEERFUL AND OBEDIENT WIFE—
IN THEIR DEATHS THEY WERE NOT DIVIDED!

TO PERPETUATE THE REMEMBRANCE OF SO ILLUSTRIOUS A PATTERN OF CONJUGAL AFFECTION—TO MANIFEST THE PUBLIC SENSE—OF THE MANY PUBLIC AND PRIVATE VIRTUES OF THEIR RESPECTED GOVERNOR, AND TO RECORD FOR THE BENEFIT OF POSTERITY—THE CLEARNESS OF THAT SAGACITY, THE EXTENT OF THAT KNOWLEDGE—AND THE PURITY AND FIRMNESS OF THAT INTEGRITY—WHICH RENDERED HIS ADMINISTRATION THE BOAST AND SECURITY OF A GRATEFUL PEOPLE:—THE ASSEMBLY OF JAMAICA—HAVE CAUSED THE

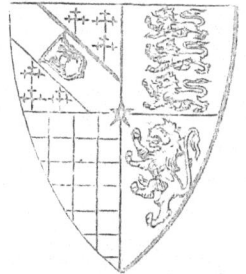

This handsome monument has been thus described : Marble, and of a pyramidal form festooned with flowers. An earl's coronet over the following coat armorial. Quarterly—I. *Gules* on a bend betw. six crosses crosslet fitchée *arg̑t.*, an escun. of the fd. chd., with a demi lion ramp. pierced through mouth with an arrow; within a d. tressure fly. c. fly. II. *Gu.* 3 lions pass. guard. in pale *or.;* a label of 3 points. III. Checquy *or* and *azure.* IV. *Gules:* a lion rampant *arg̑t.* A mullet for difference in fess point. Supporters 2 lions rampant. Motto, "Virtus mille scuta."
A female figure emblematic of Jamaica, and a cherub or genius, the latter's right hand resting on a shield, which bears the arms of Jamaica, viz., Argenton a cross gules five pineapples or. To this shield are supporters — dexter

a female Blackamoor, hold- REMAINS OF THIS NOBLE AND LAMENTED PAIR—TO BE
ing in her dexter hand a
basket of fruit. Sinister, INTERR'D WITH FUNERAL HONOURS AT THE PUBLIC EX-
an Indian warrior holding
a bow, plumed proper. PENCE—THE WHOLE HOUSE ATTENDING EACH PROCESSION
Crest, An alligator. Motto, AS MOURNERS—AS A FURTHER TESTIMONY OF MERITED
"Indus uterque serviet
uni." ESTEEM INSCRIBE THIS MONUMENT.

J. Bacon Sculptor, London,
1796.

THOMAS HOWARD, third Earl of Effingham, was born January 13, 1746-7. Married
October, 1765, Catharine (born Sept. 17, 1746), daughter of Metcalfe Proctor, of
Thorpe, near Leeds, co. York, Esq. Appointed Master of the Mint, January, 1784,
which office he resigned on his obtaining the Government of Jamaica. Dying without
issue, he was succeeded in title and estates by his only brother Richard. The Earl's
mother was Elizabeth, daughter of Peter Beckford, Esq.

45.

IN MEMORY OF

ELIZABETH MARY, COUNTESS OF ELGIN AND KINCARDINE, ONLY CHILD OF
CHARLES LENNOX CUMMING BRUCE ESQR, OF ROSEISLE AND KINNAIRD IN
SCOTLAND, MEMBER OF PARLIAMENT FOR THE COUNTIES OF ELGIN AND NAIRN,
AND OF MARY ELIZABETH BRUCE, GRAND-DAUGHTER AND REPRESENTATIVE OF
THE DISTINGUISHED TRAVELLER IN ABYSSINIA. BORN ON THE 13th APRIL 1821,
SHE WAS MARRIED ON THE 22nd APRIL 1841, AND HAVING ACCOMPANIED HER
HUSBAND, HIS EXCELLENCY JAMES EARL OF ELGIN AND KINCARDINE, TO JAMAICA
IN APRIL 1842, SHE DIED AT CRAIGTON, IN THE PARISH OF ST. ANDREWS, ON
THE 7th JUNE 1843: RESTING WITH ASSURED FAITH ON THE LOVE OF HER RE-
DEEMER, AMIDST THE UNSPEAKABLE SORROW OF DEAR RELATIONS AND FRIENDS,
AND THE DEEP LAMENT OF THE COMMUNITY THAT HAD WITNESSED THE RICH
PROMISE OF HER EARLY VIRTUES. THIS MONUMENT WAS ERECTED BY THE
LEGISLATURE OF THE COLONY, NOT AS A COLD TRIBUTE OF RESPECT DUE TO
EXALTED RANK, BUT TO MARK THE PUBLIC REGRET, FOR DISTINGUISHED WORTH
AND TALENT, SO EARLY LOST TO HER COUNTRY AND HER FAMILY.

"BLESSED ARE THE PURE IN HEART FOR THEY SHALL SEE GOD."

46.

HERE LYETH INTERR'D THE BODY OF ITHAMAR THE WIFE OF THE HONBLE
ROSE FULLER ESQ, WHO DEPARTED THIS LIFE THE 22nd DAY OF APRLL 1738,
AGED 17 YEARS.

JOHN FULLER, Esq., of Brightling, co. Sussex (*vide* Fuller of Rose Hill, *Burke's
L. G.*), M.P., married Elizabeth, daughter and co-heir of Fulk Rose, Esq., of Jamaica, by Elizabeth, daughter and co-heir of John Langley, Alderman of London (she

married, secondly, Sir Hans Sloane), and had issue six sons, of whom the fifth, Stephen Fuller, merchant, of London, and many years agent for Jamaica, married Miss Noakes, and by her had, with two daughters, who died unmarried, three others, viz., 1. Philippa, married W. Dickenson, Esq., M.P. for Somerset ; 2. Elizabeth, married to her cousin, Hans Sloane, son of William Sloane, of Stoneham.

47.

HERE LYETH THE BODY OF MERIDETH THE WIFE OF COLLNEL MODYFORD FREEMAN—THE DAUGHTER OF COLLNEL EDWARD STANTON AND PRISCILLA HIS WIFE—WHO DEPARTED THIS LIFE YE 19th DAY OF SEPTEMBR 1697 IN YE 20th YEARE OF HER AGE.

48.

HERE LYETH INTERRED — THE BODY OF HUMPHREY FREEMAN ESQR—WHO WAS AT YE TAKEING OF THIS ISLAND —HE DEPARTED THIS LIFE THE 6th—OF AUGUST 1692 IN THE 64th YEAR—OF HIS AGE.

IN the first Assembly of this island, meeting January 20, 1692, we find " Humphrey Freeman, *Gent.*," a Member for " Old Harbour." In the third Assembly, 8th Jan., 1671-2, "Humphrey Freeman, *Esq.*" was returned " for the the town of St. Jago.' —Roby.*

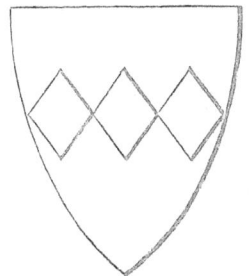

B. M. Slab ; *Arms*, Three lozenges. *Crest*, A demi-lion holding in his jambs a lozenge.

49.

SACRED TO THE MEMORY—OF ALEXANDER FORBES ESQR PROVOST MARSHAL GENERAL—AND ONE OF HIS MAJESTY'S COUNCIL OF JAMAICA—BELOVED AND RESPECTED—FOR HIS GREAT ABILITY—UNSPOTTED INTEGRITY—AND UNIVERSAL BENEVOLENCE—HE WAS YE SECOND SON—OF SR DAVID FORBES—OF NEWHALL IN YE COUNTY—OF EDINBURGH— IN SCOTLAND—BORN AT EDINBURGH—THE 27th JULY 1689— DIED AT JAMAICA—THE 13th NOVEMBER 1729.

Arms (As Forbes of Newhall), Azure on a chev. between three boars' heads erased argent, as many unicorns' heads erased, gules. *Crest*, A cubit arm grasping a snake, gules.

50.

(*Ab.*) BREVET MAJOR FITZGERALD 8th FOOT DIED 5th JULY 1835 AGED 57.

---

* There was a Sir Robert Freeman connected with the affairs of Virginia, about the middle of the seventeenth century. In 1671, William Freeman was Member of Council in Jamaica. Thomas, Robert, and Humphrey Freeman were members of the first General Assembly of Jamaica in 1663. Robert was Speaker of the House of Assembly in 1664. The arms on this monument appear to be the same as those of Freeman of Castle Cor.

51.

BARTHOLOMEW FAUTT DIED 1703 AGED 35.

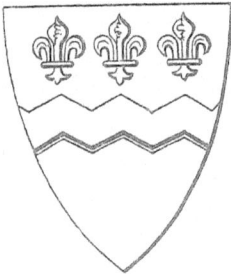

52.

(*Ab.*) MR. JOSHUA FEAKE DIED 1684 AGED 33.

FEAKE or Feeke (Stafford; London; and Gadston, co. Surrey), sa, a fesse dancette, in chief three fleurs-de-lys or.— Burke's " General Armoury."

B. M. Slab; *Arms*, a fesse
dancette, in chief three fleur-de-lys.

53.

TO THE MEMORY—OF MATTHEW GREGORY ESQR MD— AND LUCRETIA HIS WIFE—SHE DIED THE 29th OF JANUARY MDCCL—IN THE FORTY THIRD YEAR OF HER AGE—HE ON THE 31st DECEMBER MDCCLXXIX—AGED EIGHTY SIX YEARS— THIS MONUMENT WAS ERECTED BY THEIR DAUGHTERS— MARY DEHANY AND ELIZABETH TROWER.*

B. & W. M. Mont., richly
sculptured as follows : A female figure resting on an anchor, and gazing on two urns, on which appear the arms of
Gregory, with an escutcheon of pretence......six fleur-de-lys...... a chief danzette.

54.

NEAR THIS PLACE—LIETH THE BODY OF—MATTHEW GREGORY SENR. ESQ :—WHO DEPARTED THIS LIFE THE 6th DAY—OF SEPTEMBER—IN THE YEAR—OF OUR LORD—1715 AND IN—THE 60th YEAR OF—HIS AGE.

THIS family appears by its arms, to have derived a descent from the ancient family, which is said to be now represented by that of Stivic Hall.

Arms, Or, two bars, a lion
in chief : passant gules.
Crest, A boar's head or,
colld. and langd. gules.

Archer Martin, and Matthew Gregory, the nephews of John Archer, of St. Thomas-in-the-Vale (of a Wiltshire family), received by the will of their uncle, (dated 1663, and recorded 1689), considerable legacies.

---

* "Matthew Gregory, the younger, was elected Member in Assembly for St. James, 1st August, 1718 ; re-elected for the same parish, 14th June, 1722 ; and chosen for St. Ann, 1st March, 1726-7 ; after which he appears to have declined the senatorial honour. By his will dated 24th December, 1778, he bequeathed his estate of Swansey and other properties in St. John's, to his daughters, Mary, widow of George Dehany, Esq., and Elizabeth Trower, the erectors of this monument."—" Journals of House of Assembly (Roby)."

55.

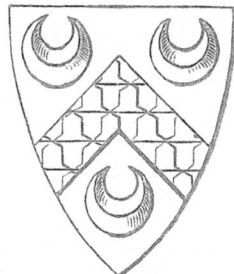

HERE LYETH THE BODY OF JAMES GODDARD,* SECOND SON TO JAMES GODDARD GENT OF SOUTH MARSTON IN THE COUNTY OF WILTSHEARE IN THE KINGDOM OF INGLAND HE WAS SECRETARY TO ONE SR THO LYNCH GOVERNOR OF THIS PLACE WHO DEPARTED THIS LIFE THE TWENTY FIRST DAY OF JULY 1691 IN THE THIRTY THIRD YEAR OF HIS AGE.

B. M. Slab; *Arms,* ...... A chev. vair, between three crescents. *Crest,* A stag's head.

56.

(*Ab.*) * * ROBERT GIBBINS * * (OB) 1752.

C. Y.

57.

(*Ab.*) * * WILLIAM GRAY * * (OB) 1755.

C. Y.

58.

IN THIS CHURCH LYES INTERRED—THE BODY OF—THE HONBLE JOHN HUDSON GUY ESQR.—WHO DEPARTED THIS LIFE—THE 7th OF FEBRY 1749—IN THE 52d YEAR OF HIS AGE —HIS MERIT PROMOTED HIM TO SEVERAL PUBLIC OFFICES —IN THIS ISLAND ;—WHICH HE EXECUTED WITH HONOUR— AND INTEGRITY—AND SUPPORTED THEM WITH DIGNITY—HE SERVED HIS COUNTRY AS A MEMBER OF—THE ASSEMBLY— WAS MADE AN ASSISTANT JUDGE OF THE COURTS OF LAW— AND ACTED IN THAT STATION FOR NINE YEARS—WITH SO STRICT AN ADHERENCE TO—THE RULES OF JUSTICE—THAT HE WAS RAISED TO THE CHIEF JUDGE'S SEAT—AS A REWARD FOR HIS UNIFORM AND STEADY REGARD—TO THE LAWS OF HIS COUNTRY.

A richly sculptured Monument (Marble); *Arms,* Azure, on a chev. argent, three fleurs-de-lys gules: between three leopards' heads or.

AND ALSO OF MRS ELIZ: VOSSAL—WHO DYED SEPTBER 27 1725—IN THE 43d YEAR OF HER AGE—SHE WAS A GOOD WIFE, AN AFFECTIONATE MOTHER—AND A SINCERE FRIEND.

---

* Survey of Manors of the Prince of Wales. Temp. Jac. I. Albourne, &c.
Richard Goddard, Esq., 1 Messuage, 867 acres at £28 18s. 8d. 19 years, £130.
Henry Martyn, Esq., ,, 276 ,, 8 3 4 58 ,, 70.
Henry Martyn, Esq., holds 2 yard lands mentioned in his lease, lying in Upham, called Pratt and Pomates,* late in the tenure of William Goddard, by Copy, and after in the tenure of Richard Yate (Gate?), which 2 yard lands about 60 acres, &c. The land is expressed in a grant made by William Longspee to Lord Turbarde without date.

² Mention is made of the same grant to Edward Walrond.

59.

(*Ab.*) TO THE MEMORY OF CHARLES GRAHAM ESQ LATE OF THIS PARISH—DIED 9 MAY 1801 AGED 50—BY HIS MUCH AFFLICTED WIDOW (A CENOTAPH).

B. and W. M. ; An urn, &c., inscribed in gold, on a black ground.

60.

SACRED TO THE MEMORY—OF—FRANCIS GRAHAM* ESQRE OF TULLOCH CASTLE—IN ST THOMAS IN THE VALE—AND FOR SOME TIME MEMBER OF—THE HONOURABLE HOUSE OF ASSEMBLY—SON OF THE LATE—ALEXANDER GRAHAM ESQRE OF DRYNIE—BRITISH CONSUL AT FAYAL—BORN ON THE 17th OF OCTOBER 1773—DIED THE 1st OF FEBRUARY 1820—AND OF HIS INFANT SON—COLIN— BORN ON THE 23d OF OCTOBER 1814—AND DIED ON THE SAME DAY—ALSO OF HIS DAUGHTER - AGNES—BORN ON THE 5th OF OCTOBER 1816—DIED THE 30th OF DECEMBER 1817—ALSO—COLIN GRAHAM—ELDEST SON OF—COLONEL COLIN DUNDAS GRAHAM K W &C—BORN ON THE 31st OF AUGUST 1801—DIED THE 21st OF OCTOBER 1814.

C. Y.

61.

IN MEMORY OF—JOHN HEYLIGER—MAJOR—IN HIS BRITANNIC MAJESTY'S— 55th REGIMENT—WHO WAS BORN—IN THE ISLAND OF ST. CROIX—AUGUST 23d 1782—AND DEPARTED THIS LIFE—OCT 8th 1808.

C. Y.

62.

(*Ab.*) JOHN HANSON ESQR. DIED 1745 AGED 27; HIS WIFE MRS FRANCES HANSON 1761 AGED 43—ELIZABETH HANSON OB 1786 AET 40 JOHN HANSON ESQ OB 1812 AET 70—JOSHUA CRASSEWELL ESQ OB 1768 AET 39.
(*Vide* Crasswell.)

W. M. Slab.

---

* Mr. Graham was a large planting attorney, and Member for St. Thomas-in-the-Vale. Tulloch is a considerable sugar-estate in that parish, which Mr. Graham purchased. The name is taken from Tulloch Castle, in the county of Ross. Lieut.-Col. Colin Dundas Graham, K.W. (*i.e.*, of the Order of William of the Netherlands), and Lieut.-Governor of St. Mawes, in Cornwall, died at Cromarty House in Scotland, 7th July, 1828, aged 76. His daughter was the wife of Francis Graham above noticed.

63.

HERE LYES—YE BODY OF YE HONBLE ALEXR HENDER-
SON—ESQR—ONE OF THE HONBLE THE COUNCIL—AND HIS
MAJESTIES ATTORNEY GENERAL—OF THIS ISLAND—OBIIT 13th
APRIL 1732—AETATIS SUAE 36.

M R. HENDERSON first came into the Assembly as Member for
St. John's (on the death of its representative, George Modd,
the Speaker of the House) Oct. 8, 1723. He was twice elected
for St. Andrew and once for Clarendon, and was called to the
Council on June 17, 1730.—*Journals.* He was succeeded in the
office of Attorney-General of this island by Matthew Concanen,
" damn'd to everlasting fame " in the " Dunciad " of Pope.—Roby.

Arms, On a chev. between three martlets as many cres-cents. *Crest,* A griffin's head collared.

64.

HERE LYETH THE BODY OF MR. CARY HELYAR MAR-
CHANT WHO DYED THE 5th DAY OF JULY 1672 AND IN THE
39 YEARE OF HIS AGE—REV 14th " BLESSED ARE THE DEAD
THAT DIE IN THE LORD. THEY REST FROM THEIR LABOURE."

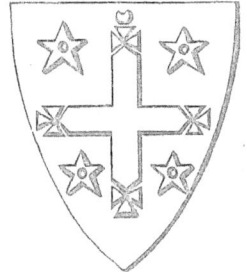

S IR THOMAS LYNCH, in his " Present State of the Government
of Jamaica, August 20, 1671," says of this " Marchant":—" I
have appointed a Chief Treasurer, Mr. Cary Helyar; he is an
honest gentleman, and an excellent accomptant; he has other
employs here, so does it at 8d. per pound."

A Thomas Helyar was Member for St. Ann's in 1675.

For a further account of this family see the " Herald and
Genealogist," *voce* " Cary family."

Cary Helyar married, 13th Oct., 1671, Priscilla Houghton, who re-married, 10th
May, 1675, Colonel Edward Stanton.

B. M. Slab; *Arms,* A cross pointed patee [a curious va-riation of a cross urdee], be-tween four mullets pierced, a crescent for difference. *Crest,* Behind a dunghill cock a cross crosslet patee fitchee.

65.

HERE LYETH THE BODY OF MARY HALL DAUGHTER OF WILLIAM HALL ESQ
IN WESTMORELAND, WHO DEPARTED THIS LIFE THE 25th DAY OF JULY 1735—
AGED 12 YEARS.*

W. M. Slab.

66.

NEAR THIS PLACE—LIES INTERRED THE BODY OF—JOHN HENCKELL ESQR
CHIEF JUDGE—OF THIS ISLAND WHO DEPARTED THIS LIFE ON THE 10th—OF

---

* See " Hall of Arrow'sfoot ;" Burke's " Landed Gentry ;" " Peerage," *voce* Harrington.

DECEMBER 1801 IN THE 50th YEAR OF HIS AGE. AT HIS PARTICULAR REQUEST
HIS REMAINS ARE—-DEPOSITED NEAR THE ASHES—OF HIS MUCH VALUED FRIENDS
T HARRISON ESQR—AND DR F RIGBY BROADBELT.

W. M.

67.

(*Ab.*) * * "ELIZABETH WIFE OF CAPT JAS : HALFHIDE. (Date effaced.)

C. Y.

68.

HERE LIETH THE BODY OF HILL, LATE THE WIFE OF
ROBERT HOTCHKYN ESQ—OB, 1706, AET, 43 ; ALSO ROBERT
HOTCHKYN, OB, 1709. AET 42—

ROBERT HOTCHKYN was Attorney-General of that Island. He
was the eldest son of Robert Hotchkin, Esq., and Mary his
wife, of Bradmore, Nottinghamshire. He was born in 1667. He
married Hill, the widow of Henry Brabant, Esq., Provost-Marshal.
He survived his wife, and died in 1709 without issue, leaving to his
brothers in England—Thomas Hotchkin, a physician, and the Rev.
John Hotchkin, Rector of Abbot's Ripton, Huntingdonshire—a

B. M. ab. ; *Arms*, Per
pale, azure and gules three
lions rampant or. *Crest*,
A lion's head erased du-
cally crowned.

very considerable property, both real and personal. Part of the former is still in the
possession of one of his brother's descendants. He left £60 to the poor of the parish of
St. Katharine, and desired to be buried by the side of his dear wife, Hill Hotchkin, in
that church.

Hill Hotchkin, the wife of the Attorney-General, was probably of an Irish
family. Her maiden name was Bolton. She first married John Childermas, the only
son of a wealthy planter, also from Ireland ; he died in 1699. In 1701 she again
married Henry Brabant, Esq., Provost-Marshal of the Island. On the death of the
Provost-Marshal she married the Attorney-General, and died shortly after, in 1706.
Her third husband was laid beside her in the grave in 1709. Only ten years elapsed
between the death of her first husband and that of the third, who survived her. (See
the *Annual Register*, Aug. 15, 1775.)

69.

EDWARD HALSTEAD ESQR. LIEUT. OF YE TROOP, SON OF LAWRENCE—DIED
25th DEC. 1744 AGED 26.

B. M. Slab.

LAURENCE HALSTEAD was connected with the family of Whitgyft Aylmer of
Jamaica.

70.

(*Ab.*) JOSEPH JORDAN DIED 1715, IN HIS 31st YEAR. HIS SISTER JANE, WIFE OF HENRY BARHAM* DIED, 1717, IN HER 24th YEAR.

B. M.

THE Jordans of Jamaica seem to have been a branch of the Barbadian family of the same name (*vide* " Baronetage," *voce* Gibbes.)

71.

(*Ab.*) SACRED—TO THE MEMORY—OF—MARY ANN JACKSON JAMES—DAUGHTER OF HUGO AND EMILY—WHO DIED THE 11th JUNE 1820—AGED 2 YEARS 2 MONTHS AND 13 DAYS.

C. Y.

THE family of James, in Jamaica, derives from Robert James, who, in 1652, married Margaret Dalton, by whom he had, besides other sons, Hugh, born 1669, ob. 1758, who, by his second wife, Anne, daughter of the Rev. Gawen Noble, of Cockermouth, had a son William, who, by his wife, Jane Senhouse, was mother of Hugh (born 1750), who, by his second wife, —— Cargill, had a son, Hugo James, appointed Attorney-General of Jamaica, who married Æmilia, daughter of Samuel Jackson, Member of Council, &c., and had, with other issue, Hugh Rees James, C.B., Commission in the Punjab, &c.

72.

```
. . . . . . ARCH . . . . . . . . JOH . . . . . . . . . . . . .
. . . . . . 2th . . . . . . . . . . . 16 . . . . . . . . . . . . . . .
. . . . . . . . . . . . . . . . . . . . . . . . . . . . . . . . . 167 . .
```

Fragment—perhaps " Archibald Johnston."

C. Y.

---

* Dr. Henry Barham, author of " Hortus Americanus," preceded Sir Hans Sloane, and was, therefore, a gatherer of information as early as 1680. He had married into the family of " Foster," of St. Elizabeth's Parish, and through it acquired a considerable fortune. It was the Foster family that introduced the Moravian Mission, to which sect Dr. H. Barham belonged. Through the Fosters he was connected with the " Stevenson" family. He retired to England in 1740, and settled at Staines, near Egham, where he died. He bequeathed his property to the youngest son of Mrs. Barham, whom he had married when the widow of Thomas Foster. Joseph Foster was the father of Joseph Foster Barham, M.P., about 1793, and who married Lady Caroline, daughter of the then Earl of Thanet. In 1794 Alexander Aikman published Dr. Barham's " Jamaica Botany," and dedicated the work to the Hon. William Blake, Speaker of the House of Assembly. The present Mr. William Thomas March, Clerk of the Crown, Jamaica, is of a family whose patronymic was Foster, who sought an asylum in the West Indies about 1715, and acquired extensive estates in the Parishes of St. Catherine, and St. Thomas-in-the-Vale; these, however, have long since been alienated. [R. Hill.]

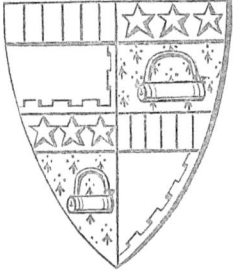

73.

SACRED TO THE MEMORY OF—SIR BASIL KEITH KNT.*— GOVERNOR OF JAMAICA—WHO DEPARTED THIS LIFE ON THE 15th DAY OF JUNE 1777—IN THE DUTIES OF HIS OFFICE HE WAS ASSIDUOUS—WISE AND IMPARTIAL IN THE ADMINISTRA- TION OF JUSTICE—A FRIEND TO MANKIND AND A FATHER TO THE PEOPLE—OVER WHOM HE PRESIDED—THIS MONU- MENT WAS ERECTED BY THE ASSEMBLY—TO TRANSMIT TO POSTERITY THE GRATITUDE OF THE PEOPLE—OF THIS ISLAND FOR THE HAPPINESS THEY ENJOYED—UNDER HIS MILD AND UPRIGHT GOVERNMENT.

G. Marble Mont., richly sculptured (cenotaph) by J. Wilton, R.A. ; *Arms,* 1 & 4, Arg. a chief paly or and gules, base and sinister embattled of the third. 2 & 3, Erm. a fetter lock proper. On a chief azure, three mullets ; a crescent for difference. *Crest,* A fox trippt (?). *Motto,* "Candore decus." (N.B.—The House of Assembly on 11 Nov., 1777, voted three thousand guineas for this monument.)

BRIDGES says, " Keith, after a popular administration of less than two years, fell sick and died." The duration of his government is incorrectly stated. He opened a Session of the Legislature on the 8th Feb., 1774, and died 15th June, 1777, so that he must have presided more than three years and four months.

74.

SARAH KELSALL DIED 1734 AGED 49. ALSO HER NIECE JOHANNA BOWER- MAN 1729 AGED 26.

Stone Slab.

75.

HERE LYETH INTERR'D—THE BODY OF—MR. SAMUEL KNIGHT SON OF DOCTOR—SAMUEL KNIGHT DECEASED—WHO DEPARTED THIS LIFE THE 7th OF MARCH—ANNO DOMINI 1708-9 IN THE 24th YEAR—OF HIS AGE.

HIS father, Dr. Samuel Knight, was member for Kingston in 1691. See Kingston.

B. M. Slab; *Arms,......*On a canton......a spur. *Crest,* An eagle displayed.

---

* Keith of Powburn, Bart., cr. 4 June, 1663 (ext.). The Hon. John Keith, fourth son of William, second Earl Marischal, had parts of the estates of Craig and Garrock from his father. These were sold by his descendant, Colonel Robert Keith, whose son, Robert Keith, of Craig (ambassador to the Courts of Vienna and St. Peters- burg), was father of Sir Robert Murray Keith, K.B., of Murray's Hall (ambassador at Dresden, &c.) and of Sir Basil Keith, Governor of Jamaica ; both of whom died without legitimate issue. See Burke's " Ext. and Dormt. Peerage," in which, however, *Keith* is blazoned, " azure on a chief or, three pellets gules."

76.

SAMUEL LONG

PIETATIS ILLUSTRIS, INGENIO INCLYTUS

JUSTITIA ORNATUS, FAMA CLARISSIMUS

CORPORE RECTO, ANIMO VEGETO

PRAEMATURE....................(*obl.*)

POST [QUADRAGINTA QUATUOR] ANNOS

QUOS VIXERAT PROUT VIRUM GENEROSUM, ET VERE

CLARISSIMUM DECUIT

TANDEM FATO CEDENS

QUOD HABUIT TERRENUM, TERRÆ REDDIDIT

IGNE RECOCTUM—DIEI NOVISSIMO

DENUO RESUMPTURUS

ET CÆLITUS QUOD ERAT

ET PATRI, ET PATRIAE SPIRITUM, ET AMATÆ REDIT ASTREAE

OBIIT ANNO DOMINI MDCLXXXIII

JUNII 28º.

Slab; *Arms*,......A lion passant collared. On a chief three crosses crosslet. *Crest*, Over an esquire's helmet, a lion's head langued, ...issuing from a ducal coronet.

N.B. —The inscription being half concealed by a pew, the present is partly taken from a MS. of the late C. E. Long, Esq.

THE family of Long, of Longville, Jamaica, Hampton Lodge, Surrey, and originally from Wilts, is descended from John Longe, of Netheravon, in the latter county, who died in 1630. Samuel, the grandson of John, having subsequently participated in the conquest of Jamaica by Penn and Venables, became a person of great consideration in that Island, where his great-grandson, Edward Long, Esq., filled the office of Chief Justice of the Admiralty Court.

77.

THE CHILDREN OF SAMUEL LONG AND ELIZ: HIS WIFE WHO DIED IN 1677.

THIS family, so eminent, and distinguished in the earlier history of Jamaica, gave to the Island its chief historian, namely, Edward Long, eldest son of Samuel Long, the eldest son of Charles Long, whose fourth son, Beeston Long, was father of the first Lord Farnborough.—See Peerages of Orford, Rivers, &c., and Burke's "Landed Gentry."

B. M. Slab; *Arms* and *Crest*, Long as above.

78.

SACRED TO THE MEMORY OF—THE REV RICHARD BRISSETT LAWRANCE—WHO DEPARTED THIS LIFE—THE 13th DAY OF OCTOBER 1821—AGED 31 YEARS AND 3 MONTHS.

W. M. Slab. C. Y

HE was the fourth son of James, third son of James Lawrence, of Fairfield. For a fuller account of this family see "History of Parish of St. James," the *Gentleman's Magazine*, "The Herald and Genealogist," &c.

8

79.

HERE LVETH INTERRED THE BODY OF JOHN LAWRENCE WHO DEPARTED THIS LIFE JANUARY YE 7th 17$\frac{17}{18}$ AND IN THE 46th YEAR OF HIS AGE.

B. M. Slab.

THERE were, at any rate, four distinct families of this name at the period referred to, settled in Jamaica. The first settled in the Parish of St. Catherine; the second in St. James', is supposed to have been from St. Ives in Huntingdon. The next came from New England, and originally, perhaps, from Iver. There were other Lawrences in the Parish of St. Thomas-ye-East, who were of Irish extraction. The above was a Buccaneer.

80.

SACRED TO THE MEMORY OF—THE HONOURABLE JAMES LEE ESQR. M D—MEMBER OF HIS MAJESTY'S PRIVY COUNCIL —OF THIS ISLAND WHO DIED IN THE GULPH OF—FLORIDA IN HIS PASSAGE TO ENGLAND, WHERE—HE WAS GOING FOR THE RECOVERY OF HIS HEALTH—ON THE 30th OF MAY 1821 AGED 68—THIS MONUMENT WAS ERECTED—BY HIS AFFECTION- ATE FRIEND—FRANCIS RIGBY BRODBELT 1822.

B. M. Pyramidal, sculptured in relief on a sarcophagus (Reeves & Son, Bath), a ship in full sail, with the legend, "His body was committed to the deep." *Arms* (argent?), A chev. sable, between three leopards' faces. *Crest*, A leopard's face (*vide* Lee of Quarrendon, "Herald and Genealogist").

DR. LEE acquired a large fortune by his practice in Spanish Town. He was the junior partner of Dr. Broadbelt, sen., whose epitaph, in the nave of this church, has been already transcribed; and the senior partner of Sir Michael Benignus Clare, Knt., Member of the Legion of Honour in France, Member of the Honourable the Council, and Provincial Grand Master of Freemasons in this Island.—Roby.

81.

SACRED—TO THE MEMORY OF—MRS. CHRISTIAN LANE—WIFE OF JAMES SETON LANE—OF THE PARISH OF ST THOMAS IN THE VALE—SHE DEPARTED THIS LIFE ON THE 28th DAY OF SEPTEMBER—IN THE YEAR OF OUR LORD 1808—AGED 23 YEARS. THE EXQUISITE TENDERNESS OF HER ATTACHMENT TO HIM—WHO HAS ERECTED THIS MEMORIAL—WAS THE GREATEST SOURCE OF HAPPINESS HE EVER —YET ENJOYED – HER FERVENT PIETY TOWARDS ALMIGHTY GOD LEAVES HIM— THE ONLY CONSOLATION, THAT BY ENDEAVOURING—TO IMITATE HER LIFE, HE MAY IN DEATH BE—UNITED TO HER.

C. Y.

82.

SEBRAN LARSON DIED 1730 AGED 42—MARY HIS WIFE 1725 AGED 50— RACHAEL THEIR ONLY DAUGHTER 1720—AGED 15.

SEBRAN LARSON was keeper (qy. governor?) of the gaol at Spanish Town.

RENEE DE SEBRAN—a bill for naturalizing this infant aged eight years.—Journal of the House of Lords, 17th August, 1660.

83.

IN THE NAME OF GOD AMEN—HERE RESTETH THE BODY OF—ELIZABETH LATE WIFE TO THE HONBLE COLL NICHOLAS LAWES AND ONLY DAUGHTER TO SIR THOMAS MODYFORD BARRONETT, DECEASED WHO WAS FIRST MARRIED UNTO THE HONBLE COLL SAMUEL BARRY AND DEPARTED THIS LIFE THE 11th DAY OF NOVEMBER IN THE YEARE OF OUR LORD GOD 1694 AND YE THIRTIETH OF HER AGE.

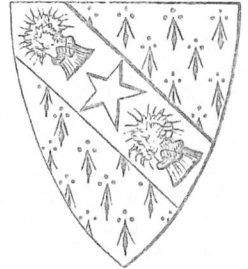

B. M. Slab; *Arms*, Erm. on a bend...a mullet...between two garbs.

SEE the pedigrees of Barry, Modyford, Lawes, and Long. Sir Nicholas Lawes was one of the most eminent of the governors of Jamaica, and to him is due the credit of having introduced the coffee plant, which has since become a staple product. His monument in St. Andrew's Parish Church (see that Parish), affords further particulars.

84.

HERE LYES INTERRED THE BODY—OF THE HONBLE HENRY LOWE—ESQR WHO DEPARTED—THIS LIFE THE 15th DAY OF—FEBRUARY ANNO DOMINI 1714—AGED 51 YEARS.

HENRY LOWE served in the Assembly of 9th June, 1691, for Vere; and in that of 4th May, 1693, for Clarendon. In 1696, he was appointed a Member of the Council, which office, together with a Colonelcy of Militia, he enjoyed until his death. —Roby.

(Lowe of Goadby, Marwood, Leicestershire) Henry Lowe had a daughter, Susanna, married to Theobald Taaffe.

B. M. Slab; *Arms*, A fess ermine between two greyhounds courant. Impaling ...a lion passant. *Crest*, A talbot's head.

85.

HIC SITUS EST HENRICUS LYTTLETON D.D.—CAROLI LITTLETON ET CATHERINAE UXORIS—SUAE IN VICINIA SEPULTAE FILIOLUS SEMESTRIS—OBIIT FEBR. I A.D. 1662.

B. M.

SIR CHARLES LYTTELTON, son of Sir Thomas Lyttelton, first Bart. of Frankley, co. Worcester, and heir to his brother, Sir Henry, the second Bart., was distinguished for his loyal and valiant activity in the cause of Charles I., and was engaged with Sir George Booth in the unsuccessful Cheshire rising in 1659. In 1662 he was knighted, and accompanied the Governor Thomas (Windsor) Lord Windsor, as Lieut.-Governor and Chancellor of this Island. On his lordship's departure, October 28th of the same year, the command devolved on Sir Charles, who, as " Deputy Governor," issued "an Ordinance," dated at "Point Cagua, 23d October, 1663," addressed to Lieutenant-Colonel Thomas Lynch, Provost-Marshal-General, "to have an Assembly fairly and indifferently chosen by the votes of the inhabitants of the several precincts of this Island." This Legislative Assembly, the first in Jamaica, met at the town of St. Jago de la Vega, 20th January, 1663-4.

Sir Charles left Jamaica in May, 1664. On his arrival in England, he was appointed Colonel of the Duke of York's Regiment, and in 1673, Governor of Sheerness and Languard Fort. He represented the borough of Bewdley, co. Worcester, in the reign of James II.—Roby.

Sir Charles died at Hagley, May 2nd, 1716, and was succeeded by his only surviving son, by his second wife, Anne, dau. and coheir of Thomas Temple, of Frankton.

86.

MEMORIÆ SACRUM

HIC JACET CATHERINA LYTTLETON FILIA D D GULIELMI FAIRFAX DE STEETON IN COMITATU EBORACENSI EQUITIS AURATI, UXOR D D CAROLI LYTTLETON EQUITIS AURATI, ET IN JAMAICA VICE GUBERNATORIS—OBIIT JANUAR 26 AD 1662.

B. M. Slab.

Sir William Fairfax, of Steeton, was knighted by Queen Elizabeth in 1562. His grandson, Sir William Fairfax, Knt., of Steeton, married Frances, daughter of Sir Thomas Chaloner, Governor and Chamberlain to Prince Henry, and, being slain in 1644, left, besides sons, two daughters, one of whom, Catherine, married, first, Sir Martin Lister, Knt., and, secondly, Sir Charles Lyttleton, Bart., of Hagley.

87.

LYTTLETON, D. D. SUÆ IN VICINIA SEPULTÆ FILIOLUS, OB. 1662.

Vide "Peerage," "Baronetage," &c.

88.

M. Pyramidal, richly sculptured Monument : a medallion portrait in relief. *Arms*,

NEAR THIS PLACE ARE INTERRED—THE REMAINS OF—HUGH LEWIS ESQR.—BARRISTER AT LAW HIS MAJESTY'S ADVOCATE-GENERAL FOR THIS ISLAND—AND—REPRESENTATIVE IN ASSEMBLY FOR THE PARISH OF PORT ROYAL—HE WAS BORN THE 3d AUGUST 1753—HE DIED THE 23d JANRY 1785—EARLY AND ZEALOUSLY ATTACHED TO THE PROFESSION OF THE LAW—WHICH NATURE HAD PREPARED HIM TO ADORN—HE CULTIVATED HER PARTIAL ENDOWMENTS—WITH UNREMITTING ASSIDUITY—TO A VOICE CLEAR AND STRONG—

TO ACTION GRACEFUL AND AFFECTING—HE ADDED KNOW-
LEDGE THE MOST ACCURATE AND EXTENSIVE—SUPERIOR
BOTH FROM INTEGRITY AND ABILITIES—TO THE MEANNESS
OF SOPHISTRY—HIS ARGUMENTS AT THE BAR WERE NATURAL
AND FORCIBLE—HIS ELOQUENCE IN THE SENATE DIGNIFIED
AND PERSUASIVE—THO' HIS MERIT RAISED HIM WITH UN-
USUAL RAPIDITY—TO THE HIGHEST HONOURS OF HIS PRO-
FESSION—YET SUCH WAS HIS LIBERALITY AND CONDESCEN-
SION—SO TRULY BENEVOLENT WAS HE AND SINCERE—THAT
HE ENJOYED THE UNCOMMON FELICITY—TO BE—UNENVIED
BY ANY—THE DELIGHT AND ADMIRATION OF ALL.

Quarterly azure, 1 & 4, azure, a chev. argent, between three garbs. 2, Per chev. azure and argent, in ch. two falcons rising, or. 3, Argent on a cross gules five escallops or. *Crest,* A lion rampant.

M. T. C. Sculpt.

HUGH LEWIS was the son of John Lewis, Member for Port Royal in 1701. There was a family of this name in Jamaica, last century, on whose seal is borne the arms of Lewis, of Harpton Court.

89.

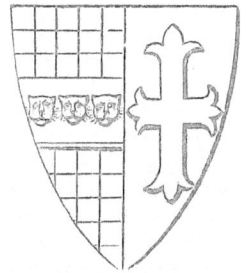

HERE LYETH INTERRED THE BODY OF MRS MARY LEWIS
WIFE OF MR SAMUEL LEWIS AND DAUGHTER TO MAJOR
GENERALL JAMES BANNISTER—WHO DEPARTED THIS LIFE
THE 2d OF JANUARY ANO DOMI 1676-7 IN THE 18th YEARE
OF HER AGE.

THAT DEATH MIGHT HAPPY BEE, TO LIVE LEARN'D I
THAT LIFE MIGHT HAPPY BEE I HAVE LEARN'D TO DYE.

B. M. Slab ; *Arms,* Chec-quy or and sable : on a fess, three leopards' heads affrontée. Impaling…a cross flory. *Crest,* A wyvern's head erased, ducally gorged.

THERE is recorded in Jamaica, in 1686, the will of John Lewis, whose brother, Richard Lewis, was of Shrewsbury, and of the ship " Elizabeth," of Honduras.

Samuel Lewis appears to have been the father of John Lewis, who sat in the first " Assembly " of 1722.

John Lewis, of Clarendon parish, left a will, in 167⅞, in which he mentions only a daughter.

Thomas Lewis, by his will (1701), leaves to his brother Hugh and his sister Gwinn his real estate in the parish of Cwmr Toyddwr (?), Wales, called Nant Lamptir.*

---

* Probably incorrectly copied. Of this family was the celebrated Matthew Gregory Lewis, whose *West Indian Journal* gives so graphic a picture of Jamaica, but which is less identified with his name than his novel " The Monk."

90.

HERE LYES SIR THOMAS LYNCH IN PEACE, AT EASE, AND BLEST

WOULD YOU KNOW MORE—THE WORLD WILL SPEAK YE REST.

CAPTAIN THOMAS LYNCH was very active in settling the public affairs of Jamaica on the restoration of Charles II. It was he who proposed that the Government of this Island should be supreme over all the others of the Caribbean Group. —Cal. S. P., Nov., 1660.

B. M. Slab; *Arms,* Three lynxes rampant. *Crest,* A lynx statant.

There was an extensive family of this name among the original settlers in the province of Connaught, and another of the same name in Kent, to which latter, perhaps, belonged the subject of this note.

Sir Thomas Lynch was Governor of Jamaica in 1684.*

91.

(*Ab.*) * * DANIEL MASTERS ESQ * * (OB) 170$\frac{4}{5}$ (AET) 46.

PROBABLY of the family of Masters, connected in New England with those of Allen, Penn, and Lawrence.

Arms, ... A lion rampant guardant. In dexter chief a mullet of six points pierced. ...... *Crest,* Two serpents.

92.

(*Ab.*) * * THE SON OF THOMAS MASY * * (OB) 1693.

93.

(*Ab.*) * * MR. FRANCIS MATTHE DIED 1766 AGED ...5—FIVE OF HIS CHILDREN BY HIS WIFE ELIZABETH DIED IN THEIR INFANCY.

Stone Slab.

---

* Colonel Thomas Lynch, as well as Sir William Beeston, obtained extensive grants of fertile land in Liguanea from Lord Windsor in free soccage in 1662.—Bridges. He held the patent office of Provost-Marshal-General of this Island, and was President of the Council to Sir Charles Lyttleton, on whose departure from Jamaica, in May, 1664, he assumed the Government, but was quickly superseded by Colonel Henry Morgan, the famous Buccaneer, captor of Panama, Maracaybo, &c., who was appointed Lieut.-Governor. Lynch then proceeded to England, where he received the honour of Knighthood, and came out again to Jamaica in 1671, as Lieutenant-Governor, his Commission being dated 5th January, 1670-1.—Roby.

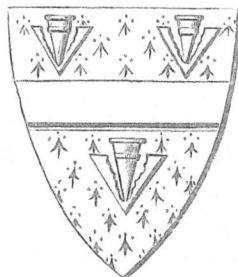

94.

HERE LYETH INTERRED THE BODY OF THE HONBLE. RICHARD MILL, ESQ., MEMBER OF COUNCIL, RECEIVER GENE-RAL, AND LATE CHIEF JUSTICE OF THIS ISLAND, WHO DE-PARTED THIS LIFE THE 16th DAY OF JUNE, 1739, AGED 60 YEARS.

Brass. *Arms*, Ermine, a fesse between three pheons.

95.

(*Ab.*) MR. WILLIAM MERRICK DIED 1714 AGED 49—& HIS 3 SONS & 3 DAURS BY ANN HIS WIFE; AND A GRANDDR ELIZABETH DAUR OF JOHN & MARY, DIED 1728. AGED 2½ YEARS.

W. M. Slab.

96.

(*Ab.*) MRS. ANN MARCH, WIFE OF FOSTER MARCH ESQ &c —OB 1739 AET 47—MRS SARAH SPENCER, WIFE OF MR. JOHN SPENCER DAUGHTER OF AFORESAID FOSTER MARCH OB 1740 AET 21 MISS ANN SPENCER DAUGHTER OF JOHN AND SARAH SPENCER OB 1724 AET 35.

GEORGE MARCH, a merchant, had a pass in 1652, to transport himself and family, to the Island of St. Christopher.—C.S.P. The family of Foster March was of some local distinction. The name was originally Foster, March having been subsequently assumed. This family was related to that of Barham, as already shown.

M. Mont. *Arms*, Argent, a cross moline between four lions' heads erased gules, a mullet for difference.

97.

SACRED TO THE MEMORY OF—DAVID MILLIGAN ESQUIRE —SON OF THE LATE ROBERT MILLIGAN ESQUIRE OF LONDON MERCHANT,—BORN IN THAT CITY THE 27th OF APRIL—1789 DIED IN JAMAICA AFTER A SHORT ILLNESS ON THE 16th OF FEBRUARY 1818.—HE LEFT HIS OWN COUNTRY TO ATTEND UPON A BELOVED BROTHER,—WHO DIED AT SEA ON HIS WAY TO THIS ISLAND FOR THE RECOVERY OF HIS HEALTH—AND WHOM HE SURVIVED ONLY A FEW MONTHS.—HE WAS A MAN OF STRICT INTEGRITY,—HUMANE, GENEROUS, DISINTERESTED AND AFFECTIONATE, ESTEEMED BY HIS FRIENDS, AND BE-LOVED BY HIS FAMILY;—AT WHOSE DESIRE THIS MEMORIAL

W. M. Tablet. *Arms*, 2ndly, 1 & 4, between two spears in pale, a dexter hand in chief, and a heart in base. 2 & 3, A lion rampant, within a border engrailed

charged with four mullets OF HIS WORTH—IS PLACED ON THESE SACRED WALLS, NEAR
and four lozenges alternately. WHICH HE IS BURIED,—IN A LAND WHERE HE EXPERIENCED
UNBOUNDED HOSPITALITY AND KINDNESS.

                                                                  Regnart, Sculpt.

ROBERT MILLIGAN, of London, merchant, was Deputy Chairman of the West India
Dock Company, when the first stone of that......magnificent undertaking was
laid on July 12, 1800, by the concurring hands of the Lord Chancellor (Wedderburn),
Lord Loughborough, the Right Hon. William Pitt, George Hibbert, Chairman of the
Company, and himself. Mr. Milligan was the principal promoter of the work, and a
noble bronze statue erected at the entrance of the dockyard, perpetuates his fame.

Mr. Milligan carried on an extensive and lucrative business in Kingston, Jamaica,
under the firm of "Dick and Milligan."—Roby.

98.

MISTAKE NOT READER, FOR HERE LYES NOT ONELY THE
DECEASED BODY OF THE HONOBLE SR THOMAS MODYFORD
BARRONETT, BUT EVEN THE SOULE AND LIFE OF ALL JA-
MAICA, WHO FIRST MADE IT WHAT IT NOW IS. HERE LYES
THE BEST AND LONGEST GOVERNOUR, THE MOST CONSIDER-
ABLE PLANTER, THE ABLEST AND MOST UPRIGHT JUDGE
THIS ISLAND EVER INJOYED—HE DYED THE SECOND OF
SEPTEMBER 1679.

B. M. Slab. *Arms*, Ermine,
on a bend a mullet between
two garbs; the baronet's
badge in the dexter chief.
Impaling a chev. between
three palmers' scrips. *Crest*,
A garb.

HERE ALSO LYES SR THOMAS MODYFORD JUNR BAR-
RONETT, THAT HOPEFUL AND FLOURISHING BRANCH—WHICH,
THE ROOT BEING DEAD, SOONE AFTER WITHERED, WHO AS
THEY LIVED IN CONTINUALL UNITY WERE NOT EVEN IN
DEATH TO BE SEPERATED. HE DYED THE NINETEENTH OF
OCTOBER 1679.

SIR THOMAS, by his own sole authority, twice proclaimed war against the Spaniards,
but in so doing, and in his encouragement of the Buccaneers, he was countenanced
by Charles II., who empowered him "to commission whatever persons he thought
good to be partners with his majesty in the plunder, 'they finding victuals, wear and
tear.' So that his majesty entered very seriously into the privateering business, and
held this reputable partnership for some years."—Appendix to Long, vol. i.

Sir Thomas Modyford, like his brother, Sir James Modyford, Bart., was also
Governor of Jamaica. He was created a baronet March 1st, 1663-4; married Elizabeth, daughter of Lewin Palmer, Esq., of Devonshire; and died in Jamaica, according
to his epitaph, in 1679.

His successors matched with the families of Sir Thomas Norton, Bart., Guy of
Barbados, Hathenstall of London, and lastly, of Sir William Beeston, Knt., Governor

of Jamaica, whose daughter and heiress, Jane, married Sir Thomas Modyford, fifth and last Baronet, and on the death of the latter she married Charles Long, Esq., of Jamaica.

Sir Thomas, the first Baronet, was one who moved with the times, and, although a subscriber to the loyal defiance sent to the summons of Sir George Ayscue, we find him the following year assuring President John Bradshaw that his master's counsels tend to the good of the English nation (S. P. O. Cal., 1652), and that the "people of Barbadoes would delight to have the same form of government as England;" and declares that the powerful regicide had "sweetly captivated" his mind by his "unexpected civilities."

He seems to have had strong prejudices against the Irish; and was a Member of the Council of Barbados, in 1660, which decided that no Irishman was to be commander, or sharer of any boat belonging to the Island. He was afterwards Governor of Barbados.*

99.

HERE LYETH THE BODY OF DAME ELIZABETH—THE WIFE OF SR. THOMAS MODYFORD BARRONETT—GOVERNOUR OF HIS MAJESTIES ISLAND OF JAMAYCA—WHO DIED THE 12th OF NOVEMBER 1668—BEING THE 29th YEARE OF THEIR—HAPPY WEDLOCKE.

> HER LIFE WAS PURE, AS CLEARE HER FAME
> NONE ERE THOUGHT EVILL OF THIS DAME.

Arms, Ermine, on a bend azure, between two garbs or, a mullet argent.

THIS was Elizabeth Palmer, daughter of Lewin Palmer, Esq., of Devonshire, who died . . . 1668. There was a large family of this name, in the parish of St. James, one of whose monuments, by Flaxman, is in that parish.

John Palmer, Chief Justice of Jamaica, married Mary Ballard, daughter of Colonel Peter Beckford.

100.

HERE LYETH INTERR'D THE BODY—OF JOSEPH MAXWELL ESQR—SECRETARY OF THIS ISLAND, WHO—DIED THE 9th OF JULY 1735—AGED 51 YEARS.

W. M. Slab.

---

* "At Lord Berkeley's I dined with Sir Thomas Modiford, late Governor of Jamaica, and with Colonel Morgan," &c.—Evelyn, 1671, Sept. 21. "I was at the wedding of my nephew, John Evelyn, of Wooton, married by the Bishop of Rochester, in Henry the Seventh's Chapel. * * The solemnity was kept with a few friends only at Lady Beckford's, the lady's mother."—Evelyn, 1681.

101.

(*Ab.*) .... MARY MCLARTY, ONLY DAUGHTER OF THE HON. CHARLES MCLARTY, AND MARY MORALES, BORN ON THE 9th FEB. 1838 & DIED, 16th JUNE 1857.

102.

(*Ab.*) .... BOSWELL MIDDLETON ESQ, LATE ADVOCATE GENERAL OF THIS ISLAND, WHO DIED HERE, DURING THE GREAT CHOLERA EPIDEMIC, ON THE 16th DAY OF MAY 1854 .... AN ABLE & SUCCESSFUL MEMBER OF THE BAR; AND ONE OF THE MOST GENEROUS AND INDEPENDENT MEN OF HIS TIME. .

103.

(*Ab.*) . . THE SON OF THOMAS MASY OB. 1693.

104.

(*Ab.*) . . DANIEL MASTERS, ESQ . . OB. . . 170$\frac{4}{5}$ AET. 46

Arms,...A lion rampant guardant ; in dexter chief, a mullet of six points pierced. *Crest,* Two serpents.

105.

M. Mont. ; *Arms,* Argent, on a bend engrailed, between two deers' heads cabossed sable, attired or.. .....*Crest,* A phœnix gules, in flames proper.*

NON PROCUL AB HOC MARMORE—CONDUNTUR CINERES —GULIELMI NEDHAM ARMIGERI—QUI SPATIO VITÆ FELICI BENE PERACTO—ÆTERNAM EXPECTANS BEATITUDINEM—RE-CESSIT.—BEATUS IN HAC VITA FUIT—QUOD IN DEO SEMPER ESSENT—SPES, AMOR, VENERATIO :—QUOD IN SE FUERIT ANIMUS FELIX ATQUE PLACENS.—CONJUX AMANS, BENEVOLUS PATER—ATQ IN SERVOS JUSTISSIMUS.—QUOD DOMUM SUIS, VICINITATEM OMNIBUS—CONSERVAVERIT PLACIDISSIMAM— MULTIS AMICITIAM, PLURIMIS AMOREM—NULLI INFERENS INIMICITIAS—AUT ODIUM.—QUOD SERVUS PATRIÆ FIDUS— SEMPER PARATUS, MAXIME VOLENS,—ET, QUANTUM POTUIT, UTILIS.—QUOD MULTOS ANNOS JUDICIS OFFICIUM—PLURIMOS SUMMI JUSTICIARII—INTEGER AGERET.—QUOD AB UNA PATRIÆ VOCE TER ELECTUS—PROLOCUTOR COMITIALIS—QUOD UNUS E CONCILIO A REGE SUO HONORATE AVOCATUS—ET PRIVATO DIGNATUS FUERIT SIGILLO :—QUOD VITÆ VIGORE PENITUS EXTINCTO—SERVITIUM PATRIÆ CUM VITA IPSA—TANDEM

---

* See Burke's " Landed Gentry," " Peerage," and " Baronetage."

FINIERIT—PRIMO DIE JULII MENSIS—ANNO DOMINI 1746—ÆTATIS 77.—HOC MARMOR POSUIT FIDELE—IN MEMORIAM PARENTUM CARISSIMORUM—GULIELMI NEDHAM, ET OLIVIÆ MATRIS,—QUÆ EODEM IN LOCO DEPOSITA JACET,—FILIUS HAMPSONIUS NEDHAM.

106.

(*Ab.*) GEORGE NEALE DIED MARCH YE 23^d 1708-9.

Stone Slab.

107.

HERE LYETH H. N.

B. M. Slab.

N.B.—Supposed to be the burial place of Hampson Nedham.—*Vide* pedigree of Long, &c.

108.

HERE LYETH THE BODY OF ...... ORGILL SENR. WHO DEPARTED .... THE 19th OF SEPTEMBER 168 ...

B. M. Slab.

MOST probably this was Andrew Orgill, who was Member of Assembly twice for St. George, and three or four times for St. Mary. Andrew Orgill, probably the junior, was returned for St. Mary, in the Assembly of 13th Jan., 1702-3.—Journal of the House of Assembly. William Anderson Orgill, late Custos of St. George, was probably a descendant.—Roby.

109.

(*Ab.*) MR. GEORGE OSBORNE DIED 1695, IN HIS 56th YEAR.

THERE was a John Osborne killed in the expedition under Penn and Venables, in 1655; but it is more probable that the family in question came at a later period from Barbados.

B. M. Slab; *Arms*, Quarterly ermine and ...... on a cross ... five annulets. *Crest*, A hippopotamus.

110.

NEAR THIS PLACE LYES INTERRD THE BODY OF SAMUEL OSBORNE ESQ, WHO DEPARTED THIS LIFE MARCH THE 26th 1723, AGED 36. AND LIKEWISE YE BODY OF ELIZABETH SPRUCE, WHO DEPARTED THIS LIFE DECR 19 1725 IN YE 55th YEAR OF HER AGE.

IN the Calendars of State Papers, frequent mention is made, early in the seventeenth century, of a family of this name M. Mont.; *Arms*, Quarterly, ermine and azure, a cross or.

9—2

which was raised to the baronetage; and also of a Captain Christopher Osborne, who does not appear to have been *too* adventurous.—Pet. of Capt. Squibb, July 5, 1626, Cal. S. P.

Roger Osborne, Governor of Montserrat, in 1654, (an Irishman, and probably a member of the well-known Wexford family of the same name), was accused of a " barbarous and inhuman murder " in that year.

III.

FRAGMENT of armorial sculpture, probably on the tomb of a person apparently named PALMER, as indicated by the sculptured arms.

Arms, A chevron between three rudely represented escallops or palmer's scrips. *

112.

MARY WIFE OF DAVID PUGH ESQ, DIED 1710 IN HER 29th YEAR—HER MOTHER MARY WATSON DIED 1691 AGED 33—ALSO THE BODY OF MARY MARTIN, BESIDE ARCHER MARTIN ESQR, HER FORMER HUSBAND, WHO DIED 1703.

B. M. Slab. ; *Arms,...*A lion passant between three fleurs-de-lys : impaling, on a cross between four fleurs-de-lys, a crescent. *Crest,* A demi-lion, holding in his jamb, a fleur-de-lys.

113.

(*Ab.*) * * MR. ROBERT PITCAIRN DIED 22d JULY 1799 AGED 62 * *

C. Y.

HERE LYETH INTERRED—THE BODY OF—ELIZABETH PESTELL—WHO DEPARTED THIS LIFE—THE 31st OF DECEMBER—ANNO 1710.

HERE ALSO RESTS INTERR'D YE BODY OF MR. BEAUMONT PESTELL WHO DIED THE 4th DAY OF SEPR 1714 IN YE FIFTY-SIXTH YEAR OF HIS AGE AND YE SECOND YEAR OF HIS CHURCHWARDENSHIP IN WCH OFFICE HE INDUSTRIOUSLY ASSISTED TOWARDS YE REBUILDING OF THIS CHURCH.

ALSO BEAUMONT SON OF ALGR & JANE PESTELL BORN YE 23d DAY OF OCTR 1721 AND DY'D YE 29th OF NOVR 1724.

B. M. Slab.

114.

UNDER THE PAVEMENT OF THE PEW—BENEATH THIS MONUMENT—ERECTED TO HER MEMORY—BY HER AFFECTIONATE HUSBAND—THE HONOURABLE CHARLES PRICE ESQR—SPEAKER OF THE ASSEMBLY—LIE THE REMAINS OF MRS ELIZABETH HANNAH PRICE—DAUGHTER OF JOHN HUDSON GUY ESQR—AND ELIZABETH HIS

---

* See these Arms impaled at No. 98, p. 60.

WIFE.—ENDOWED WITH UNCOMMON SENSIBILITY—AND FORTITUDE OF MIND—
SHE EXHIBITED AN AMIABLE EXEMPLAR—OF CONSTANCY IN LOVE—AND SINCERITY
IN FRIENDSHIP.—SHE DIED JULY 5th 1771—IN THE 34th YEAR OF HER AGE.

THE Hon. Charles Price was second baronet, and married the widow of John Woodcock, Esq. He died s. p. in 1778, when he was succeeded by his brother, Sir
Rose Price, third and last baronet.

Francis Price, a captain in the army under Venables at the capture of Jamaica,
married the widow of Lieutenant-Colonel " Rose, also one of the conquerors of that
Island, and the scion of an ancient family long settled in the counties of Dorset, and
Gloucester." By Sarah, daughter of P. Edmunds, Esq., of Jamaica, he was father of
Charles, the first baronet, whose son, as above, succeeded him.

115.

HERE LYETH INTERR'D THE BODY OF THOMAS PRICE
ESQ, SON OF THE HONOURABLE COLL CHARLES PRICE, WHO
DEPARTED THIS LIFE, THE 20th DAY OF MAY 1731, AGED 20
YEARS.

three spear heads.... *Arms*,.. A chev. between *Crest*, A wyvern's head erased......

116.

HERE LYES THE BODY OF THE HONBLE—FRANCIS ROSE,
ESQ—LATE PRESIDENT OF THE COUNCIL OF—THIS ISLAND,
WHO DEPARTED THIS LIFE—YE 20th OF NOVEMBER 1720 IN
THE 67th YEAR OF HIS AGE.

W. M. Mont.; *Arms*, sable,
on a bend argent, three roses gules.

FRANCIS ROSE represented St. Thomas-in-the-Vale in two Assemblies, 4th May,
1693, and 27th Sept., 1698 ; and St. Catherine in three, 24th June, 1701, 17th
March, 1701-2, and 6th Aug., 1702, on which last date he was elected Speaker of the
House. In the Assembly of Jan. 13, 1702-3, he was chosen Member for St. George,
and on the 27th of May, 1703, was called up to the Council, of which body he died
President. In 1714 he gave a very handsome chandelier to this church.—Roby.

See, also, Burke's " Peerage " (Harrington), " Baronetage " (Buller East), and
" Landed Gentry " (Hall).

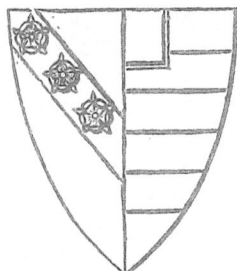

117.

NEAR THIS PLACE—LYES INTERRED YE BODY OF— THOMAS ROSE ESQR—WHO DEPARTED—THIS LIFE—YE 12th OF NOV. 1724—AGED 35 YEARS.

M. Mont. ; *Arms*, Sable,
on a bend argent, three roses gules : impaling, barry of six, argent and gules, a canton of the second.

118.

HERE LYETH THE BODY OF—MRS ELIZABETH ROSE—LATE WIFE OF—THE HONBLE THOMAS ROSE ESQ—WHO DEPARTED THIS LIFE—THE 8th DAY OF OCTOBER —1722, AGED 25 YEARS.

W. M. Slab. *Arms*,......On a bend...three roses .....: impaling, barry gules and argent a canton of the second.

Lieutenant-Colonel Rose, the founder of this family in Jamaica, was one of the officers under Venables at the conquest of the Island.

119.

(*Ab.*) HIC SEPULTUS EST JOHANNES VEZEY RENNALLS, ARTIS MEDICINALIS ET CHIRURGICAE PROFESSOR. NATUS 9 DIES JULII 1743 : OBIIT...DIE OCTOBRIS 1794.

120.

HENRY RENNALLS DIED 1797: JOSEPH RENNALLS 1798: AMELIA VEZEY RENNALLS 1804 THE OLDEST NOT 5 YEARS OF AGE.

Stone Slab.

121.

TO THE MEMORY OF—STEPHEN RICHARD REDWOOD ESQRE—WHO WAS BORN IN SPANISH TOWN—ON THE 1st OF DECEMBER 1726, AND DIED ON THE—8th OF DECEMBER 1781, AND WAS, FOR MANY YEARS, ONE OF THE—REPRESENTATIVES IN ASSEMBLY FOR ST THOMAS IN THE VALE.

ALSO, TO THE MEMORY OF HIS SON—THE HONOURABLE PHILIP REDWOOD, BARRISTER AT LAW,—WHO WAS A REPRESENTATIVE FOR ST CATHERINE—UPWARDS OF TWENTY FIVE YEARS,—WAS CHOSEN SPEAKER OF THE ASSEMBLY IN 1802,—APPOINTED CHIEF JUSTICE OF THIS ISLAND IN 1808, AND DIED—ON THE 9th OF FEBRUARY 1810 IN LONDON IN HIS 60th YEAR.

THIS MONUMENT IS ERECTED BY—SUSANNAH RENNALLS IN TESTIMONY OF —HER AFFECTION AND GRATITUDE—TO A FATHER AND BROTHER.

W. M. Tablet.

122.

HERE LIES INTERRED THE BODY OF—THE HONBLE COLL : JAMES RISBY—WHO DEPARTED THIS LIFE AUGT. THE 22^d—1726 AGED 63 YEARS.—ALSO THE BODY OF JANE HIS WIFE—AGED 19 YEARS.

HERE LIES THE BODY OF—CHARLES KELLY ESQ—WHO DEPARTED THIS LIFE OCT YE 7th 1731—AGED 32 YEARS—ALSO THE BODYS OF JANE, MARY—AND EDMUND KELLY CHILDREN—OF THE SAID CHARLES KELLY ESQ.

Stone Slab.

CHARLES was probably the brother of Edmund Kelly, Attorney-General and Speaker of the House of Assembly.

123.

SACRED—TO THE MEMORY OF—JOHN RODON ESQUIRE A NATIVE OF THIS ISLAND—WHO FILLED FOR MANY YEARS THE PUBLIC SITUATIONS—OF REPRESENTATIVE IN ASSEMBLY FOR THIS PARISH,—OF MEMBER OF HIS MAJESTY'S PRIVY COUNCIL,—AND OF CUSTOS ROTULORUM AND CHIEF MAGISTRATE FOR THIS PARISH AND PRECINCT.—HE WAS EMINENTLY DISTINGUISHED FOR THE FAITHFUL DISCHARGE OF—HIS DUTIES BOTH IN PUBLIC AND PRIVATE LIFE.—IN BENEVOLENCE AND STRICT INTEGRITY HE WAS EQUALLED BY FEW.—HE DIED IN LONDON—ON THE 21st DAY OF JANUARY 1808 AGED 63 YEARS—SINCERELY AND DESERVEDLY REGRETTED BY ALL—WHO KNEW HIM.

W. M. Tablet.

MR. RODON was an Attorney-at-Law, and partner with Mr. Finlayson.

124.

(*Ab.*) FOUR SONS AND TWO DAUGHTERS OF JOHN AND SUSANNA SPENCER WHO DIED FROM 1751 TO 1760 THE OLDEST NOT 13 YEARS OF AGE.

Stone Slab.

125.

(*Ab.*) * * SUSANNA SPENCER * * (OB) 1751 * *

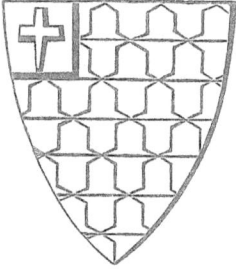

126.

HERE LYETH THE BODY OF COLONEL EDWARD STANTON.
HE DEPARTED THIS LIFE THE 22^d DAY OF JUNE ANO. DOMI.
1705 AND IN THE 65th YEAR OF HIS AGE.

ALSO PRISCILLA WIFE OF YE SAID EDWARD STANTON
WHO DEPARTED THIS LIFE YE 11th DAY OF SEPTEMBR ANO.
DOMI. 1709 AND IN YE 56th YEAR OF HER AGE.

B. M. Slab; *Arms*, Vair, on a canton, a cross patée fitchée. *Crest*, A greyhound sejeant.

EDWARD STANTON was chosen Member for St. David, 8th January, 1671. In twelve succeeding Assemblies he served for St. Thomas-in-the-East, and in three for Kingston. When representative of the last-mentioned parish, he was chosen Speaker of the House, April 11, 1704.—Roby.

It is not improbable that this officer was a near relative of Serjeant Edward Staunton, who agreed to train and exercise the inhabitants of Providence Island, in the use of arms.—Cal. S. P., Col. S., March 9, 1636.

There was an ancient family named Staunton, settled in Notts. in the time of Edward I.—Banks' " Baronia," &c.

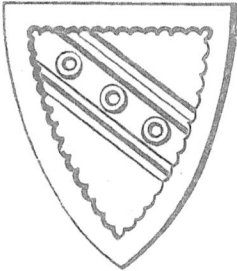

127.

TO THE MEMORY—OF THE RT HONBLE WILLIAM SELWYN, ESQR OF MATSON, IN YE COUNTY OF GLOUCESTER, COLONEL OF A REGIMENT OF FOOT, AND MAJOR GENERAL OF HER MATIES FORCES, GOVERNOR OF GRAVESEND AND TILBURY FORT, CAPTN GENERAL AND COMMANDER IN CHIEF OF HER MATIES ISLAND OF JAMAICA AND YE TERRETORIES THERETO BELONGING, AND VICE ADMIRAL OF THE SAME, WHO DIED YE 5th APRIL 1702.

W. M. Mont., Sculpture, an urn, &c.; *Arms*, On a bend cotised, within a border engrailed, three annulets.

OSTENDENT INSULAE HUNC TANTUM FATA, NEQUE ULTRA ESSE SINENT.

IN 1703 Major-General Selwyn, Colonel Beckford, and the Earl of Peterborough administered the government of Jamaica.

128.

AENEUS STUERT DYED 1734 AGED 24—MARY WIFE OF PETER WARD DIED 1740 AGED 55—MARY THEIR DAUGHTER, DIED 1734 AGED 6.

W. M. Slab.

129.

(*Ab.*) * * MR. GEORGE TAYLOR * * (OB) * 1724 (AET) 52 * *

Also

(*Ab.*) * HIS WIFE MRS SUSANNA TAYLOR * * (OB) 1732 IN HER 53^d YR.

130.

(*Ab.*) * * MARY TRUELOVE * DIED * 1749 * * AGED 29.

B. M. Slab.

TRUELOVE'S Company is mentioned, in the muster of the inhabitants of Virginia, in 1625.

131.

DERBYE TOLDERBYE YE SONNE OF JOHN TOLDERBYE ESQR BY HANNAH HIS SECOND WIFE—DIED—1682 IN HIS 15th MONTH.

B. M. Slab.

132.

HERE LYETH YE BODY OF CAPT JOHN TOLDERBYE, WHO DYED YE SIXTEEN DAY OF DECEMBER 1682, AND IN YE FORTIETH YEAR OF HIS AGE: AFTER HAVING GAYNED A VERY FAIR REPUTATION IN YE WARRS OF YE FRENCH KING AGAINST YE EMPEROUR.

HE DEATH OUTBRAVED ON MANY A BLOODY FEILD
YET DEATH AT LAST HAS MAD THE SOLDIER YIELD.

B. M. Slab; *Arms,...* A fess between three crosses crosslet fitchée.... *Crest,* An arm embowed holding a wreath.

DERBYE TOLDERBY. This peculiar surname seems to be identical with Toldervey. In 1604 (Cal. S. P.) there is a notice of Christopher Toldervey being continued as collector of tithes in London, on the translation of the Bishop of Chester to that see. See the pedigree of Manjoy or Mangye.

133.

MARY TAAFE. (Neither date nor remark.)*

C. Y.

SHE was probably the wife of Michael Taafe. The Taaffes of Jamaica were apparently allied to the noble house of the same name in Ireland. However the local tradition may have originated, there is still enough to be gleaned from the wills of the family, in both islands, to justify a respect for it.

---

* Towards the close of the seventeenth century and earlier part of the eighteenth, Ireland was in so unsettled a state, that there are few parochial registers there, which may be referred to, for the confirmation of pedigrees ; and the remarkable vicissitudes of the family in question, would make such difficulties insurmountable, were it not for the comparative rarity of the name itself forming a useful clue. The earliest will on record in Jamaica of this family, is that of Arthur Taafe, dated in 1750, and entered Jan. 30, 1752. In it, the testator leaves legacies to his father Christopher and his mother Mary, of the kingdom of Ireland, "if still alive." Arthur Taafe also mentions his brother, the rector of St. Thomas-in-the-Vale, Henry Taafe, and his nephew Henry Gordon. The question is, who was this Christopher Taafe? A Christopher Taaffe, of Mansfields Town, co. Louth, was attainted in 1691 at *Ardee.* He was an adherent of James II., in whose own regiment of infantry he was a lieutenant. "I find," says the author of a valuable work on a kindred subject,* "the chattel property of a Christopher Taaffe" (probably the above lieutenant), "sold in 1725, who, dying in Dublin in 1736, made a will, which is recorded there, from which I think that he is identical with the Christopher named in the will of Arthur Taafe of Jamaica. The latter had sons, Arthur and Henry, and I am inclined to think, that he had also a son George, who passed into

---

* "King James II.'s Army List annotated." It is not shown how the author came by the knowledge of Christopher, the attainted officer, having left two sons, for there is no mention in his will either of wife or children.

134.

M. Mont., sculpture—a female figure leaning on a column, surmounted with an urn bearing the initials A. W., &c. ; *Arms*, Quarterly, 1 & 4, or, a chev. gules betw. three trefoils sa. 2nd, sable, three lozenges argent, on a chev. or, three fleurs-de-lys. 3rd, quarterly, 1 & 4, argent, on a fess, three mullets.. in chief a boar's head couped. 2 & 3, azure, three garbs. Impaling, quarterly, 1 & 4, sable, a lion rampant within a border engrailed or. 2 & 3, gules, a cross on three greeces, argent (*i.e.*, in "degrees"). *Crest*, Out of a mural crown gules, a wyvern's head or. *Motto,* "Adsum." Supporters, two lions rampant (*tinctures* imperfect).

SACRED TO THE MEMORY OF—ANNE,[*] THE BELOVED AND LAMENTED CONSORT OF HIS EXCELLENCY — SIR ADAM WILLIAMSON K. B.—CAPTAIN GENERAL, OF HIS MAJESTY'S POSSESSIONS IN ST. DOMINGO—AND FORMERLY LIEUTENANT GOVERNOR OF THIS ISLAND—SHE WAS THE ORNAMENT OF SOCIETY, & A PATTERN OF HER SEX—POSSESSING ALL THOSE VIRTUES, AND EXERCISING THAT BENEVOLENCE—WHICH RENDERED HER LIFE A BLESSING—HER DEATH AN IRREPARABLE LOSS—TO THE COMMUNITY—SHE DIED THE 19th OF SEPTEMBER 1794, IN THE 48th YEAR OF HER AGE—DEPLORED BY ALL ;—BUT BY NONE WITH MORE HEARTFELT ANGUISH—THAN THE DESOLATE, THE INDIGENT, AND THE AFFLICTED :—WHOSE SORROWS HER TENDERNESS ANTICIPATED, AND HER BOUNTY RELIEVED—TO SUCH DISTINGUISHED EXCELLENCE, THE ASSEMBLY OF JAMAICA COULD NOT BE INSENSIBLE—WITH GENERAL ASSENT, AND THE UNIVERSAL APPROBATION OF THEIR CONSTITUENTS—THEY VOTED THIS MEMORIAL—OF PUBLIC GRATITUDE AFFECTION AND ESTEEM.

J. Bacon, Sculpt. London, 1798.

M AJOR-GENERAL WILLIAMSON was sworn into office as Lieut.-Governor, and announced in General Orders as Commander-in-Chief, in November, 1790, during

---

Connaught and settled there."[*] It seems, however, more probable that he was the Christopher, son of George Taaffe (Corballa, co. Meath) mentioned in the will of Stephen Taaffe, 1730. The next will is that of Henry Taafe (entered May 30, 1771). He was rector of St. Thomas-in-the-Vale, Jamaica. His sons are named : 1. Arthur Rodger, 2. John Armistead, 3. Richard Brownrigg, 4. Thomas Wheeler. He appoints John Gordon the guardian of his sons. Anne, the sister of Henry Taaffe, was married to Mr. Gordon,[†] said to have been originally of Enniskillen, and who was father of the Henry Gordon mentioned in the will of Arthur Taafe, his uncle. Henry Taafe names, among other bequests, "his gold watch and tortoise-shell box set in gold." In the record of his matriculation, in 1740, at Trinity College, Dublin, Henry is described as being then seventeen years of age, and the son of Christopher Taaffe.—"Generosus in Com. Derriæ." In the will of William Gordon, of St. Elizabeth, Jamaica (Nov. 27, 1759), there is a bequest to *Susanna*, daughter of *Harry* Gordon, of St. James's ; and in the will of Henry Gordon, of St. James's, Jamaica, dated Jan. 18, 1788, we find references to his (mother's, Anne Taafe) claims to real and personal estate in Ireland. The next Taafe will, is that of Michael Taafe (dated May 19, 1761), of St. James's, Jamaica, in which the testator mentions his mother *Anne* residing at *Dromisken*, co. Louth. N.B.—Theobald Taafe, Earl of Carlingford, had a grant of land, in 1668, in the parish or townland of *Dromisken,* co. Louth. In 1762 is entered the will (dated in 1754) of *Susanna* Taafe, "wife of *Theobald* Taafe, of Hanover Square, in the parish of St. George, Middlesex, England, . . . and youngest daughter of Henry *Lowe.*"[‡]

[*] Her death announced in the *Gentleman's Magazine*, Dec., 1794, vol. lxiv. p. 1150.

---

[*] He bequeaths his sword and pistols to his relative Theobald Taaffe (1736).
[†] He was twice married ; his first wife is said to have been Mary Jones, a lady of the Ranelagh family. But there is another lady of this name, and the widow, about 1720, of Penn, who had inherited his father, William Penn's, Irish estate. There was also a connection by marriage between the Taaffes of Smermor, and the founder of Pennsylvania's family, while again the above-mentioned Henry Gordon married a very near relative of the Penns.—See "History of the Taaffe Family," Vienna, 1856 ; *Notes and Queries,* 1873-4 ; "Ulster Records," &c
[‡] *Not* "Long," as given in the Long pedigree.—*Vide* the "Peerage," &c.

the Government of the Earl of Effingham. On that nobleman's decease, 19th Nov., 1791, he assumed the Government of the Island, in virtue of the dormant commission before mentioned. He had been previously joined by his wife, who arrived in Jamaica, from London, on Oct. 31, 1791. He continued in the government until the arrival of Alexander (Lindsay), 6th Earl of Balcarras, at Port Royal, on April 15, 1795, and on the 21st of the same month, he was invested by the hands of the earl, his successor, as Commissioner, with the ribbon and badge of the Order of the Bath. On May 9, in the same year, he left Jamaica for Port-au-Prince, having been appointed Governor-General and Commander-in-Chief of such parts of St. Domingo as then were, or hereafter might be, under the Government of Great Britain. Sir Adam died at Avesbury House, co. Wilts, Oct. 21, 1798, from the effects of a fall. He was Colonel of the 73rd Regiment.

Mrs. Williamson (for the Knighthood of the Bath was not conferred on her husband till after her death) was buried in this church, and an Act (as in the cases of the Earl and Countess of Effingham) passed the Legislature, to indemnify the Rev. R. S. Woodham, the rector, from the penalties imposed by the Law of 1789, for burying in churches.

135.

HERE LYES THE BODY OF THE HONOURABLE COLLONELL JOHN WALTERS, LATE CHIEF JUSTICE OF THIS ISLAND, AND ONE OF HER MAJESTIES COUNCILL HERE. BORN AT ASH-PRENTON* IN THE COUNTY OF DEVON, THE 6th OF APRIL 1659, AND DYED THE 5th OF NOVEMBER 1706, AGED 47 YEARS

B. M. Slab; *Arms,*...A fess dancette between three eagles displayed. *Crest,* On a cap of maintenance, a lion's head erased....

136.

(*Ab.*) * * ELIZABETH WALTERS * * DIED * * 1690 * *

137.

(*Ab.*) CAPT WILLIAM WALTER, OB. 1701, AET 36—HIS TWO SONS BOTH NAMED WILLIAM OB. 1692 & 1701.

WILLIAM WALTER was Member of Assembly for St. George, 27th Sept., 1698.— Roby.

138.

THREE INNOCENTS, THE DEARLY BELOVED CHILDREN OF JOHN AND ANN WRIGHT ... ROBERT, BORN 1786—MARY FRANCES, BORN 1791—AND EDWARD BORN, 1790— ... WHO ALL DIED IN 1792———

* Ashprington on the Dart (?).

(These uncouth rhymes follow) :

AH ! DEAR BABES YOU HAVE LEFT YOUR PARENTS HERE
FOR HEAVEN'S ABOVE NOT WANTING O' THEIR CARE
BLEST NOW SUPREMELY SO YOU MUST BE
FOR EVERMORE AND ALL ETERNITY.

G. M. Slab.

139.

DOCTR JOHN WIGAN—OBIIT 5 DECR 1739 AETAT. 43.

B. M. Slab.

140.

MR JOHN WELCH DIED 17 APRIL 1798 AGED 40.

141.

HERE LYETH INTERRED THE BODY OF MR HENRY WILLIS, JUNIER, WHO
DEPARTED THIS LIFE THE 4th DAY OF NOVEMBER, 1702, AGED 26 YEARS.

HERE ALSO LYETH INTERRED THE BODY OF MARY ELYES, DAUGHTER OF
GERSHOM ELYES, ESQ, AND MARY HIS WIFE. SHE WAS BORN THE 30th OF
JANUARY, 1715, AND DEPARTED THIS LIFE, THE 14th DAY OF APRIL, 1716.

AND ALSO THE BODY OF MARY ELYES, LATE WIFE OF GERSHOM ELYES, ESQ,
WHO DEPARTED THIS LIFE THE SIXTEENTH DAY OF OCTOBER, ONE THOUSAND
SEVEN HUNDRED AND THIRTY SIX, IN THE THIRTY SEVENTH YEAR OF HER AGE.

B. M. Slab.

COLONEL GERSHOM ELYES was Colonel of the St. Ann's regiment, and Member for
St. Mary, in the first Assembly of 1711.

142.

CAPT. WILLIAM WORLEY DEPARTED THIS LIFE THE
ELEVENTH DAY OF APRILL, ANNQ. DOM. 1690, AND IN THE
TWENTY NINTH YEAR OF HIS AGE—ALSO ELIZABETH HIS
WIFE DEPARTED . . . . THE 22d DAY OF AUGST ANN. DOM.
1696 AETATIS SUAE 33o.

G. M. Slab; *Arms,*...A
chev. between three birds close... *Crest,* A wolf's head erased.

CAPT. WORLEY was chosen Member for this parish 20th July, 1688.

143.

(*Ab.*) TIMOTHY WAKELING OB. 1741, AET. 44

W. M. Slab.

144.

(*Ab.*) RACHAEL WILSON DIED 1736 AGED 16. SAMUEL KING DIED 1742 AGED 41.

Stone Slab.

145.

(*Ab.*) EDWARD YOUNG DIED, 1710—HIS WIFE MARY, 1696,

B. M. Slab; *Arms*, Lozengy,
on a bend, three heraldic antelopes' heads erased....

FORT AUGUSTA.

FORT AUGUSTA, the principal defence of the harbour of Kingston, was built, for the greater part, under the immediate direction and superintendence of the Governor, Rear-Admiral Knowles (afterwards Sir Charles Knowles, of Lovel Hill, co. Berks, Bart.; and Rear-Admiral of England).

1.

DEPARTED THIS LIFE DECEMBER 25th 1807—MAJOR GEORGE CRAWFORD—OF THE 2d W. I. REG—SON OF JAMES CRAWFORD OF AUBURN IRELAND ESQ,—WAS MAJOR OF THE 33d REG.—IN THE EAST INDIES;—SERVED UNDER SIR RALPH ABERCROMBY;—WAS AT THE CAPTURE OF THE DUTCH FLEET—BY LORD KEITH AND SIR JAMES CRAIG;—WAS AT THE SIEGE AND STORM OF SERINGAPATAM;— AND WAS FROM HIS EARLIEST YEARS—ALWAYS ACTIVELY EMPLOYED IN THE— SERVICE OF HIS KING AND COUNTRY (&c).

W. M.

2.

SACRED TO THE MEMORY OF LIEUTENANT JAMES CAMPBELL MACLACHLAN OF THE 82d REGT, SON OF COLONEL MACLACHLAN H.P. 69th REGIMENT, AGED 20 YEARS.

3.

SACRED TO THE MEMORY OF—ANDREW ROBERT CHARLESTON, MAJOR IN THE 92ᵈ HIGHLANDERS WHO DEPARTED THIS LIFE, MONDAY AUGUST 15ᵗʰ, 1825, AGED 30 YEARS.

4.

SACRED TO THE MEMORY OF—JOHN SANKEY DARLEY— MAJOR OF THE 2ⁿᵈ WEST INDIA REGMT—WHO BRAVELY LOST HIS LIFE—IN THE ZEALOUS DISCHARGE OF HIS DUTY— ON THE 27ᵗʰ OF MAY 1808—HIS CONDUCT AS A MAN AND A SOLDIER, ENDEARING HIM TO ALL,—HE DIED BELOVED AND REGRETTED—BY HIS FAMILY—FRIENDS AND BROTHER OFFI- CERS—WITH THE DEEPEST SORROW THIS LAST SAD TRIBUTE IS PAID—BY HIS AFFECTIONATE FATHER—GEORGE DARLEY-- OF THE CITY OF DUBLIN—AGED 80 YEARS NOV 12ᵗʰ 1810.

B. Stone; *Crest*, A unicorn's head couped, bridled, with crescent on breast. *Motto*, Dure.

THE LORD GAVE AND THE LORD HATH TAKEN AWAY, BLESSED BE THE NAME OF THE LORD.

Job, 1st Chapter, 21st verse.

MAJOR DARLEY'S death is thus related in the "Continuation to Edwards' West Indies:" "Fifty-four Chamba and Koromantyn negroes, who had been purchased to serve in the Colonial corps, broke out into mutiny at Fort Augusta, while under drill, and massacred two of their officers, Major Darley and Lieutenant Ellis, who rode up to them to inquire into the cause of the tumult. They were speedily chastised for their disobedience and barbarity. Fifteen of them were killed on the spot, five were wounded, and seven were afterwards executed. The reason which they assigned for their conduct was, that they were too often drilled, and that they were desirous of returning to their native country." The date is incorrectly stated as August instead of May, 1808, and the Report of the Committee of Assembly says "that the mutiny was not by any means confined to the recruits, but that many of the old soldiers, if not openly and directly concerned in it, did persuade and excite the troops to mutiny." The "Chronology" of the "Jamaica Almanack" is more correct in its detail : "1808, May 27. Recruits of the 2nd West India Regiment mutinied on parade : Lieutenant and Adjutant Ellis was killed, and Major Darley died of the wounds he received. Nine of the mutineers were killed ; one died of wounds ; fifteen were tried by a court-martial, and found guilty ; seven of them were shot." The reader, desirous of further particulars, may consult the 12th vol. Journals of House of Assembly, where the examination of many witnesses is given at length. The "Violation of the privileges of the Assembly, in the case of Major-General Carmichael, commanding his Majesty's forces in this island," (who had directed the officers under his command not "to answer any questions that the Legislative Body of this island might put upon the subject of a late mutiny, or upon the government or discipline of his Majesty's forces,") has been inserted by Mr. Aikman, sen., in an Appendix to his re-publication in 1810 of " The Privileges of Jamaica vindicated," in the case of John Olyphant, Esq., a Member of Assembly.

The major was brother to Alderman Darley, of Dublin, of Orange notoriety.—Roby.

5.

SACRED TO THE MEMORY OF CAPT JOSEPH GREENWOOD OF HM'S 22d REGT., WHO DIED AT FORT AUGUSTA, 31st OCTR, 1828, AGED 32 YEARS.

6.

SACRED TO THE MEMORY OF J. HINDS, ADJUTANT 2nd WEST INDIA REGT. OF FOOT WHO DEPARTED THIS LIFE, MONDAY AUGUST 13th, 1825—AGED 30 YEARS.

7.

BENEATH THIS STONE—LIE THE REMAINS OF—COLL. CHARLES HILL—WHO DIED 31st OF AUGUST 1819—AGED 57 YEARS. IN THE COMMAND OF—THE 50th REGIMENT OF FOOT.

HE is honourably mentioned in the " Percy Anecdotes," under "Humanity."

8.

SACRED TO THE MEMORY OF ARTHUR J. JONES, CAPTAIN OF H.M'S R.E, WHO DEPARTED THIS LIFE, ON THE 18th OF MAY, 1816, AGED 50 YEARS.

9.

SACRED TO THE MEMORY OF—CAPTAIN GEORGE ROSS MUNRO—LATE OF THE 85th REGIMENT—WHO DIED NOVEMBER THE 11th 1802—AGED 19 YEARS—THIS MONUMENT WAS ERECTED BY HIS BROTHER—OFFICERS AS A TESTIMONY OF THEIR SINCERE ESTEEM—FOR HIS AMIABLE CHARACTER.

W. M.

CAPT. GEORGE ROSS MUNRO " was the only son of Duncan Munro, Esq., of Culcairn, in the county of Ross, in Scotland, the nephew of Sir Hugh Munro, of Fowlis, Bart., and the presumptive heir to his title and estates."—*Royal Gazette*, 1802.

10.

HENRY STANLEY MONK, CAPTAIN IN THE 13th REGT OF FOOT, WHO DIED 9 JULY 1791, IN HIS 32d YEAR.

Dilapidated Tomb.

II.

SACRED TO THE MEMORY OF J. W. PARKINSON OF THE ROYAL ENGINEERS WHO DEPARTED THIS LIFE, ON THE 17th OF JUNE 1819. AGED 40 YEARS.

GREEN BAY.

I.

HERE LYETH THE BODY OF CAPT EDWARD JAMES, A LATE EMINENT MERCHANT OF THIS ISLAND, WHO WAS ALWAYS LOYAL TO HIS PRINCE, FAITHFUL TO HIS FRIEND, KIND AND CHARITABLE TO HIS RELATIONS, READY UPON ALL OCCASIONS OF DOING GOOD OFFICES TO HIS ACQUAINTANCES. DEPARTED THIS LIFE THE 28th DAY OF APRIL 1720, IN THE 50th YEAR OF HIS AGE, MUCH LAMENTED BY ALL WHO KNEW HIM.

2.

Brick tomb with Marble Slab; *Arms*, A cock between two mullets in chief and a crescent in base. *Crest*, Over an esquire's helmet, a plume. *Motto*, "Dieu sur tout."

HERE LYES THE BODY OF LEWIS GALDY ESQR, WHO DEPARTED THIS LIFE AT PORT ROYAL, THE 22d DECEMBER 1739 AGED 80 YEARS. HE WAS BORN AT MONTPELIER IN FRANCE, BUT LEFT THAT COUNTRY FOR HIS RELIGION, AND CAME TO SETTLE IN THIS ISLAND, WHERE HE WAS SWALLOWED UP IN THE GREAT EARTHQUAKE IN THE YEAR 1692, AND BY THE PROVIDENCE OF GOD, WAS BY ANOTHER SHOCK THROWN INTO THE SEA, AND MIRACULOUSLY SAVED BY SWIMMING UNTIL A BOAT TOOK HIM UP: HE LIVED MANY YEARS AFTER IN GREAT REPUTATION, BELOVED BY ALL THAT KNEW HIM, AND MUCH LAMENTED AT HIS DEATH

THIS remarkable inscription is copied from a note in Edwards' "West Indies," and in the text of Bridges' "Annals." Both writers have incorrectly transcribed the date of Galdy's death, stating it to have occurred in 1736 instead of 1739. Mr. Galdy was an affluent merchant of Port Royal, Member of Assembly for St. Mary, 29th December, 1707; for Port Royal, 4th January, 1708-9; for St. George, 17th April, 1711; for Port Royal, 17th September, 1716, and for St. Anne, August 1, 1718, besides sitting in other Assemblies for which there are no returns.—Journals; Roby.

Mr. Galdy probably exaggerated the circumstances of his escape, especially as there was no one left to contradict his statement.

3.

HERE LYES THE BODY OF CAPTN ROBERT SHORTING, COMMANDER OF HIS MAJESTY'S SHIP DEALE CASTLE, WHO DEPARTED THIS LIFE ON THE ELEVENTH

DAY OF MAY 17... IN THE ... YEAR OF HIS AGE. HE WAS SON OF THOMAS SHORTING ESQ. .... CLOUDSLY SHOVEL, REAR ADMIRAL OF GREAT BRITAIN.

Stone Altar Tomb: Sculpture, A man of war in full sail.

4.

HERE LYETH YE BODY OF CAPT. WILLIAM WAKELIN, LATE COMMANDER OF HER MAJESTY'S SHIP YE SUFFOLK, WHO DEPARTED THIS LIFE, YE I[th] OF OCTOBER 1705. AGED 46 YEARS.

THOSE, WAKELIN, WEEP AND WANT, AND MOURN THEE MOST
WHO, HAPPY, COULD THY HONEST FRIENDSHIP BOAST.
SEAS MAY BE KIND, AND EARTH MAY RICHES LEND
TO SEARCHING MAN, BUT CANNOT GIVE A FRIEND.

PARISH OF KINGSTON.

KINGSTON CATHEDRAL CHURCH.

INTRA MURAL MONUMENTS.

I.

NEAR THIS SPOT, IN THE ADJOINING CEMETERY, ARE DEPOSITED THE REMAINS OF EDWARD BAKER, MIDSHIPMAN IN THE ROYAL NAVY OF GREAT BRITAIN, SECOND SON OF WILLIAM BAKER OF BAYFORDBURY, IN THE COUNTY OF HERTFORD, BY SOPHIA, THIRD DAUGHTER OF JOHN CONYERS, LATE OF COPPED HALL IN THE COUNTY OF ESSEX. A YOUTH WHOSE RARE ENDOWMENTS BY NATURE, IMPROVED BY EDUCATION, AND CONFIRMED BY THE EXAMPLE AND INSTRUCTION OF HIS COMMANDER, COMMODORE JOHN THOMAS DUCKWORTH, GAVE THE FAIREST PROMISE TO HIS COUNTRY (HAD IT PLEASED THE ALMIGHTY TO SPARE HIS LIFE), OF A DISTINGUISHED CHRISTIAN HERO, AND TRUELY VALUABLE MAN, INITIATED IN THE PROFESSION OF HIS CHOICE. WITH THESE ADVANTAGES, HE SERVED ON BOARD THE ORION, IN THE MEMORABLE ACTION OF THE 3^{d} OF JUNE 1794, AND SHARED, WITH SINGULAR MERIT, IN THE GLORIES OF THAT IMPORTANT DAY. WITH EQUAL GALLANTRY, BUT LESS PROPITIOUS FORTUNE, UNDER THE SAME RESPECTABLE OFFICER, ON THE 21st OF MARCH 1796, HE WAS ENGAGED IN THE ATTACK MADE BY THE LEVIATHAN, AND AFRICA, ON THE FORTS OF LEOGANE, IN THE ISLAND OF ST DOMINGO, BUT YIELDING ALAS! TO THE FATIGUES OF THAT DISASTROUS SERVICE, SUCCEEDED BY THE PREVAILING MALADY OF THE CLIMATE, HE CLOSED A BRILLIANT CAREER OF HONOUR AND VIRTUE, IN THE 17th YEAR OF HIS AGE.

IF HARD INDEED HIS LOT, AND PREMATURE HIS FALL, DEPRIVED IN THAT AWEFUL MOMENT OF THE CONSOLING CARE OF HIS DEAREST RELATIVES, YET HAPPY AT LEAST IN THIS, THAT WITH FACULTIES UNIMPAIRED, AND HOPEFUL OF THE BLISS WHICH AWAITED HIM, HE BREATHED HIS LAST IN THE ARMS OF HIS PROTECTOR AND FRIEND, AND WAS ATTENDED TO THE GRAVE, BY THE UNFEIGNED TEARS, AND HEARTFELT SIGHS OF THE COMPANIONS OF HIS NAVAL FORTUNES— THE ZEALOUS ADMIRERS OF HIS EXCELLENCE AND CHARACTER.

NAT. V^{o} DIE SEPTEMBRIS MDCCLXXIX OB. XXI DIE APRILIS MDCCXCVI.

OSTENDENT TERRIS HUNC TANTUM FATA NEQ. ULTRA ESSE SINENT.

SI QUA FATA ASPERA RUMPAS TU MARCELLUS ERIS!

2.

IN MEMORY OF—MRS. FRANCES INGLIS—WHO DIED THE 9th OF JANY 1791—AGED 66 YEARS—ALSO OF JOHN SUTHERLAND ESQRE—WHO DIED THE 12th OF FEBY. 1796:— AGED 62 YEARS—AND OF MRS. ANN SUTHERLAND—WHO DIED THE 1st OF DECR 1797; AGED 51 YEARS.

Mural, Gray Marble—gilding and blazonry; *Arms*, Or, within a tressure flory counter flory gules, three mullets or. Impaling, or, a lion rampant (facing to the sinister side) azure, on a chief of the first, three mullets of the last.

N. B.—It is clear that in transferring these coats to the marble, the sculptor reversed them. A remarkable instance of the same error is to be seen on the tombs of the O'Shee family, in Kilkenny.

3.

(*Ab.*) ELIZABETH CRICHTON, WIFE OF WILLIAM LAMBIE ESQR. OF THIS ISLAND; DAUGHTER OF PATRICK CRICHTON ESQ. OF THE CITY OF EDINBURGH; WHO DIED IN KINGSTON, ON THE 20th DECR 1821, AGED 23 YEARS.

Mural, W. Marble; *Arms*, Per fess, argent and azure; in chief three spears,...and in base a saltire.... Impaling, argent, a lion rampant, within a border engrailed, azure.

SIXTEEN eulogistic lines follow, in which she is described as a daughter, wife, sister, and mother.

4.

(*Ab.*) JOSEPH FITCH ESQR OF THIS TOWN—MERCHANT, WHO DIED ON THE 21st OCTOBER 1778 AET 43 (ERECTED BY HIS BROTHER.)

Mural, W. & G. Marble, &c., gilding and blazonry; *Arms*, Vert, three leopards' heads affronté or. *Crest*, A leopard's head affronté, or.

5.

SACRED—TO THE MEMORY OF—BARTHOLOMEW SAMUEL ROWLEY ESQRE—ADMIRAL OF THE BLUE—AND COMMANDER IN CHIEF OF HIS MAJESTY'S FLEET—AT JAMAICA—WHO DIED ON THE 7th OF OCTOBER A.D. 1811—AGED 47 YEARS. THIS MONUMENT IS ERECTED—AS A TRIBUTE OF AFFECTION BY HIS WIDOW—ARABELLA.

Mural, G. & W. Marble; *Arms*, Argent, on a fess azure, between two Cornish choughs, three escallops. Impaling, argent, two bars gules. *Crest*, A rowel pierced.

11—2

HE was second son of Sir Joshua Rowley, cr. Bart., in 1786.

6.

HENRY ROBARTS HIBBERT, YOUNGEST SON OF GEORGE HIBBERT ESQ., OF LONDON, AGENT FOR THIS ISLAND, DIED ON THE 14th DAY OF JULY 1825.

Mural, W. M., plain.

7.

(*Ab.*) MARK O'SULLIVAN ESQR. OB 3d NOV: 1825, AET 74; & 47 YEARS A RESIDENT.

Mural, W. M., plain.

8.

IN MEMORY OF THOMAS T. GITTINGS, OF BALTIMORE, M.D. U.S.A. WHO DIED HERE, JUNE 6th 1857, AGED 21 YEARS & 5 MONTHS.

Mural, very mean appearance, though W. M.

9.

TO THE MEMORY OF—GEORGE HINDE ESQR—WHOSE FAITHFUL SERVICES—ENDEARED HIM TO HIS COUNTRY— AND HIS SOCIAL VIRTUES TO—HIS FRIENDS—HE DIED A REAL LOSS TO BOTH—JULY 21. 1756—AGED 46—YEARS.

Mural, a sumptuous Monu-
ment of white and coloured marbles, with gilding and blazonry ; *Arms,* Gules, a chev. between three hinds or. Impaling, barry of eight, or and gules.

10.

(*Ab.*) JOHN DANIEL ORRETT ESQ., A NATIVE OF THIS CITY, WHO DIED AT NEW YORK, DEC 6. 1858. AET 59. (Six verses follow.)

11.

(*Ab.*) VIRGINIA FAIRFAX, WIFE OF PETER ALEXR. ESPEUT ESQR, OF THIS CITY, AND DAUGHTER OF COLONEL ROBERT MUNROE HARRISON, CONSUL GENERAL OF THE U.S. OF AMERICA, FOR THIS ISLAND—BORN 28th AUGT 1821 : DIED 5th NOVR 1841, AGED 20 YEARS & 2 MONTHS &C. ALSO.—VIRGINIA MARGARET GROSETT, 2d DAUR. OF THE ABOVE, BORN 28th OCT 1839, DIED 7 JANY. 1841, AGED 14 MTHS & 11 DAYS. ALSO—CHARLES ALLEN BANCROFT, 2d SON OF P.A. ESPEUT ESQ., BY HIS 2 WIFE MARIANNE AUGUSTA, THIRD DAUGHTER OF THE LATE EDWARD NATHANIEL BANCROFT, ESQ. M.D. DEPY. INSP. GENL: OF ARMY HOSPITALS IN THIS ISLAND—DIED OF CHOLERA, 12 NOV 1850, AET. 5 YRS, & 6 MTHS.

Mural, G. M., surmounted by a cross, &c.

THE Espeuts were a French refugee family, from St. Domingo.

12.

(*Ab.*) HENRY RODON, OF FRANKFIELD, & CRAWLE RIVER ESTATES, PAR: CLA-
RENDON. OB. 6 FEB. 1835, AET 33.

Mural, W. & G. Marble.

13.

(*Ab.*) ELIZABETH WIFE OF ANDREW DUNN, M.D. & 2d DAU. OF W. S. TONGE, BAR-
RISTER AT LAW. OB. OCT. 26 1852. AET 44 YRS. 5 MTHS, & 10 DAYS.

Mural, W. & G. Marble.

IN the lines that follow, she is described as wife and mother. It is unnecessary to
give them, as they are poetically discreditable.

14.

(*Ab.*) MRS ANNE SMITH WIFE OF MR. W SMITH OF THIS CITY, MERCHANT, AND
SECOND DAUGHTER OF JOHN LUNAN ESQ. OF SPANISH TOWN—OB. 11 DEC. 1825.
AET 21. ERECTED BY HER AFFLICTED HUSBAND.

Mural, B. & W. Marble ; curious sculpture of Death drawing her bed-curtain, while an angel lifts her up, to receive
the visitation.

SIX highly eulogistic lines in rhyme, follow.

15.

THE HONBLE JOSEPH BARNES, LATE MAYOR AND CUSTOS OF THIS CITY, AND
PARISH : MR. OF ASSLY., &C—OB. 6 MAY 1829, AET 66. ERECTED BY THE CORPOR-
ATE BODY.

Mural, G. & W. Marble.

16.

SACRED TO THE MEMORY OF AUGUSTUS LEVESON GOWER, CAPTAIN IN HIS
MAJESTY'S NAVY, BORN THE 21st OF JUNE 1782. HE GAVE EARLY PROMISE OF
BEING AN ORNAMENT TO HIS PROFESSION, AND AN HONOR TO HIS COUNTRY,
AND DIED MUCH LAMENTED, AT PORT ROYAL IN THIS ISLAND, ON THE 3d OF
AUGUST 1802, BEING THEN CAPTAIN OF HIS MAJESTY'S SHIP SANTA MARGARETTA

Mural, gray-white and reddish-brown Marble and Stone ; a naval trophy, inscription on a boat's square sail of
W. Marble.

CAPT. A. L. G. not found in Burke's " Peerage."

17.

SACRED TO THE MEMORY—OF—SIR ALEXANDER LEITH BART.—LIEUT. COLL
OF THE 88th REGIMENT—WHO DIED OCTOBER THE 3d 1781—AGED 40 YEARS—
THIS MONUMENT WAS ERECTED, BY HIS AFFECTIONATE SON SIR GEORGE LEITH
BART—OF BURUGH ST PETER'S—NORFOLK.

Mural, W. Marble.

SIR ALEXANDER, cr. Bart. in 1775, married Margaret, eldest daughter of Thomas
Hay, Sen. Coll. of Jus., Scotland.

18.

(*Ab.*) THE REVD GEORGE WATSON ASKEW B.A. OF QUEEN'S COLLEGE OXFORD. OB. 27th OCTR 1831. AET. 31. 10. 10.

Handsome mural sarco-phagus, W. & G. M.; *Arms,* A fesse between three horses passant.

19.

(*Ab.*) ERECTED BY HIS WIDOW, TO THE MEMORY OF MR JOHN BURROWS, MERCHANT OF KINGSTON, WHO DIED 12 FEB, 1807, AGED 39.

Mural, W. Marble.

20.

(*Ab.*) WM. JAS. STEVENSON ESQ., BORN 29 OCT 1764; DIED 15 APRIL 1830, AGED 66. ERECTED BY THE MERCHTS OF KINGSTON

Mural, W. Marble.

HE was Receiver-General of Jamaica, and grandfather of the late Sir W. Stevenson, Governor of Mauritius.

21.

SACRED TO THE MEMORY—OF THOMAS STOPFORD ESQR LATE COMMANDER OF H.M.S. CARNATION—WHO DEPARTED THIS LIFE—ON THE 11 DAY OF OCTOBER 1824—AGED 32 YEARS

Mural, W. & G. Marble (chaste design).

22.

(*Ab.*) EBENEZER REID, SENIOR, A NATIVE OF SCOTLAND OB: 25 MAY 1843 AET 66. HE WAS ELECTED HEAD MASTER OF WOLMER'S FREE SCHOOL IN 1815, AND RESIDED ALTOGETHER 43 YEARS, AS A TEACHER IN JAMAICA.

Mural, Black Marble, gold lettered.

HE is described as a husband and father. The tablet was erected by his pupils.

23.

(*Ab.*) BARTH OWEN WILLIAMS ESQRE—A KIND HUSBAND AFFECTIONATE FATHER, TRUE FRIEND, AND SINCERE CHRISTIAN. OB. 10 APRIL 1830, AET 66— ERECTED BY HIS BRETHERN OF THE SUSSEX LODGE OF FREE MASONS, OF WHICH HE WAS THE FOUNDER—

Mural, W. & G. Marble.

24.

(*Ab.*) ROBERT MC CLELLAND OF THE ROYAL LODGE NO. 250. PROVL NO. I. GRAND REGISTRAR OF THE PROVINCIAL LODGE OF EAST JAMAICA—HE DIED 15 SEP, 1860 —ERECTED BY THE BRETHERN OF THE LODGE—

Mural, Black Marble Tablet, Royal Archmasonic devices.

25.

SACRED—TO THE MEMORY OF—MARY CARR—WIFE OF DAWKINS CARR ESQRE. —COMMANDER OF—THE JUPITER—WHO DIED JUNE 4th 1798—AGED 28.

Mural, W. & G. Marble ; a sculptured urn.

26.

(*Ab*). MR NATHANIEL MILWARD, A NATIVE OF THE CITY OF BRISTOL ; AND LATE OF THIS PARISH, MERCHANT—HE WAS A TRULY HONEST MAN, &c &c. OB. JUNE 6th 1775 AET 37. ERECTED BY FRIENDS

Mural, W. & Coloured Marble.

27.

(*Ab.*) ALEXANDER EVANS—ALDERMAN OF KINGSTON, OB. 8 JANY 1858. HE WAS 27 YRS IN THE MAGISTRACY. ERECTED BY THE CORPORATION OF KINGSTON.

Mural, W. Marble.

28.

(*Ab.*) GEORGE MARTIN, ELDEST SON OF WILLIAM MARTIN, ESQR. OF HEMING-STONE HALL, IN CO: SUFFOLK—BORN 15th SEP: 1796 & DIED, OFF ST JAGO DE CUBA, ON BOARD H.M.S. BUSTARD 13th JANY. 1822.

Mural, W. Marble.

29.

(*Ab.*) THE REVD FRANCIS HUMBERSTONE, CHAPLAIN TO THE CORPORATION OF KINGSTON ; OB AUGT. 9th 1819. AET. 28—AFTER ONLY 9 MTHS RESIDENCE IN THE ISLAND.

Mural Monument, W. & G. Marble ; the Bible encircled by a snake.

HE was one of the first stirring men, after the emancipation. He died of tetanus, caused by preaching a sermon, immediately after the extraction of a tooth.

30.

(*Ab.*) THE REVD ISAAC MANN, B.A. ONE OF THE CHAPLAINS TO THE LORD BISHOP OF JAMAICA, AND FOR FIFTEEN YEARS, THE BELOVED & RESPECTED

RECTOR OF THIS PARISH. HE DIED, OCTOBER 31st 1828, AGED 51 YEARS. ERECTED BY THE MAYOR & COMMONALTY.

Mural, Black & White Marble.

31.

THIS MARBLE—INTENDED AS A MONUMENT OF—PUBLIC GRATITUDE—TO A —PUBLIC BENEFACTOR—IS SACRED TO THE MEMORY OF—JOHN WOLMER, GOLD-SMITH—FOUNDER OF A FREE SCHOOL AT KINGSTON. OBT. 29th JUNE 1729

Mural, G. & W. Marble; J. Bacon, R.A., Sculpt., 1789. A life-size female figure, subscribed "Liberalitas."

32.

SACRED TO THE MEMORY OF EMANUEL THOMAS POE, MAJOR OF HIS MAJESTY'S 50th REGT., BORN 12th NOVR 1782; DIED 7th JANY 1822.

Mural, B. & W. Marble.

33.

SACRED TO THE MEMORY OF CAPTAIN EDWARD ROWLEY, THIRD SON OF SIR WILLIAM ROWLEY, BART. OF TENDRING HALL, IN THE COUNTY OF NORFOLK; WHO DIED AT NASSAU, NEW PROVIDENCE, ON THE 8th OF JULY 1817, WHILE COMMANDING H.M. BRIG SHEARWATER, AND WAS BURIED AT THAT PLACE, ON THE 15th OF THE SAME MONTH—BORN, THE 16th OF APRIL 1792.

Mural, B. & W. Marble.

34.

IN MEMORY OF WILLIAM BROWN OF LEESTHORPE, IN THE COUNTY OF LEICESTER, ESQUIRE, A REAR ADMIRAL OF THE RED, & COMMANDER IN CHIEF AT JAMAICA, WHERE TO THE REGRET OF THE WHOLE COLONY, HE DIED ON THE 20th DAY OF SEPTEMBER 1814; IN THE FIFTIETH YEAR OF HIS AGE. HE MARRIED FIRST, CATHERINE, DAUGHTER OF JOHN TRAVERS ESQUIRE, A DIRECTOR OF THE EAST INDIA COMPANY; AND SECONDLY, MARTHA VERE, DAUGHTER OF JOHN FOTHERGILL OF HANDSWORTH, IN THE COUNTY OF STAFFORD, ESQUIRE, WHO HAS ERECTED THIS MOUNUMENT, AS A FAINT RECORD OF HER UNBOUNDED AFFECTION, AND AS A SLENDER TRIBUTE, TO HIS UNSHAKEN AND ACKNOWLEDGED WORTH.

Mural Monument, B. & W. Marble sculptured; Arms, On a fess, between three mallets sable, a crescent argent. Impaling, vert, a deer's head couped at the shoulder, within a border engrailed, argent. Crest, A demi-eagle displayed, its neck entwined by a snake.

35.

NEAR THIS MARBLE LIE INTERRED THE REMAINS—OF MALCOLM LAING ESQUIRE—WHO DEPARTED THIS LIFE THE 1st OF AUGUST 1781—AGED 63 YEARS—ALSO THE REMAINS OF ELEANOR HIS WIFE—THE DAUGHTER OF MRS MARY SHARPE—WHO DEPARTED THIS LIFE THE 29th OF SEPTEMBER 1747—AGED 35 YEARS.

THIS MONUMENT IS ERECTED IN GRATITUDE TO THEIR MEMORY, AND AS A LASTING TESTIMONY OF THEIR WORTH, BY JOHN JAQUES ESQRE

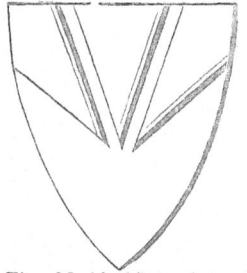

Fine Marble Mont., bearing a sculptured female figure, beautifully designed and executed by J. Bacon, R.A., 1794; *Arms*, Argent, three piles azure.

36.

(*Ab.*) IN MEMORY OF LIEUT. BURTON ROWLEY, SECOND SON OF REAR ADMIRAL SIR CHARLES ROWLEY, COMMANDER IN CHIEF IN THE WEST INDIES, WHO DIED ON THE 15th OF SEPTR. 1822, ON BOARD H.M.S. SIBYLLE, AT CARTHAGENA, IN THE 20th YEAR OF HIS AGE.

Mural, White Marble.

37.

(*Ab.*) SACRED TO THE MEMORY OF ENSIGN JOHN SKINNER, 58th REGT., SECOND SON OF LIEUT. GENL: SKINNER, WHO FELL A SACRIFICE TO THIS CLIMATE, 28th NOVEMBER 1821, AGED 19 YEARS & 3 MONTHS—

Mural, B. & W. Marble, sculptured; *Arms*, Sable, a chev. or, between three eagles' heads erased, a mullet in chief.

TWELVE eulogistic lines follow.—These arms appear as a quartering in the escutcheon of Skinner, of Carisbrooke.—Burke's "Landed Gentry."

38.

(*Ab*). JEAN DAUR. OF SAMUEL GREGORY, MERCHANT, BORN NOV. 30, 1753 : DIED OCT 12. 1776. ERECTED BY HER HUSBAND, HUGH POLSON ESQRE.

Mural, W. Marble.

39.

SACRED TO THE MEMORY OF MRS. ANN NEUFVILLE, DAUGHTER OF MRS. FRANCIS DWARRIS, BY HER FIRST HUSBAND, JOHN DUNSTON ESQRE., SHE DEPARTED THIS LIFE ON THE 15th AUGUST 1782, AGED 24 YEARS.

"MANY DAUGHTERS HAVE DONE VIRTUOUSLY BUT THOU HAST EQUALLED THE BEST."

12

LIKEWISE, THE HONORABLE FORTUNATUS DWARRIS, ESQR. M.D., AND CUSTOS ROTULORUM FOR THE PARISH OF ST. GEORGE, IN THIS ISLAND. HE DEPARTED THIS LIFE, ON THE 5th OF FEBRUARY 1790, AGED 63 YEARS

WITH JUST APPLAUSE EACH STAGE OF LIFE HE RAN, AND DIED LAMENTED AS AN HONEST MAN.

THIS MONUMENT (A JUST TRIBUTE DUE TO DEPARTED MERIT) IS ERECTED BY THE AFFLICTED PARENT, AND DISCONSOLATE WIDOW, MRS. FRANCES DWARRIS IN TENDER REGARD TO THEIR RESPECTIVE MEMORIES, AND MANY VIRTUES

Beautiful W. Marble Mont., by J. Bacon, R.A., Sculptor, London, 1792. Figures in bas relief, and on an urn in the arm of the principal these lines :

" Ascend to Bliss ye gentle spirits
Where yon angel soars above
There, virtue her reward inherits
Crown'd with Heav'ns Eternall Love."

40.

IN THE CEMETERY OF THIS PARISH LIE INTERRED THE MORTAL REMAINS OF COLONEL CHARLES HILL, LIEUT. COLONEL OF THE 50th REGIMENT OF FOOT, AND A COMPANION OF THE MOST HONORABLE MILITARY ORDER OF THE BATH. AS MAJOR, AND AFTERWARDS AS LIEUT COLONEL COMMANDING THIS BRAVE AND DISTINGUISHED REGIMENT, HE WAS HIMSELF EMINENTLY CONSPICUOUS IN THE NUMEROUS ACTIONS OF THE WAR, IN WHICH IT WAS ENGAGED, AND ASSISTED, IN PLACING ON ITS COLOURS THE GLORIOUS DISTINCTIONS OF VIMIERA, VITTORIA, PYRENEES, AND PENINSULA. COVERED WITH WOUNDS, AND WITH HONOR, HE MIGHT, AT THE PEACE, HAVE RETIRED TO THE ENJOYMENT OF HIS COUNTRY'S BLESSINGS AND APPLAUSE ; BUT ANXIOUS TO SEE HIS OLD REGIMENT RESTORED TO ITS WONTED FORCE, AND DISCIPLINE ; AND THEN UNWILLING TO QUIT IT WHEN AGAIN ORDERED ON DISTANT DUTY, AND AN UNFAVOURABLE CHANGE OF CLIMATE, HE ULTIMATELY FELL A VICTIM TO HIS EVER ANXIOUS SOLICITUDE FOR THOSE WITH WHOM HIS BLOOD HAD BEEN SO OFTEN SHED ; AND, TOGETHER WITH A NUMEROUS BAND OF HIS GALLANT OFFICERS AND SOLDIERS, PERISHED BY A DESOLATING FEVER, ON THE 31st OF AUGUST 1819, IN THE 57th YEAR OF HIS AGE, & THE 41st OF HIS MILITARY SERVICE. THIS STONE IS ERECTED TO HIS MEMORY BY HIS AFFECTIONATE WIFE ANNE HILL.

Mural, White Marble ; a military trophy, in relief.

41.

(*Ab.*) COLONEL HENRY CAPADOSE, DIED AT UP PARK CAMP, 29th FEB: 1848, AGED 70—ERECTED TO THEIR LATE COMMANDING OFFICER, BY THE OFFICERS OF THE 1st W. I. REGT.

W. M. Mural Sarcophagus.

42.

MEMORIAE SACRUM—JOANNIS BECHER ARMIGERI APUD
ANGLOS—INDIGENAE PROBI JURISPERITI ; QUI QUUM—IN HAC
INSULA MULTOS ANNOS COMMORATUS — FUISSET, ARTEMQ
SUAM FIDE SUMMA—JUDICIO SUMMO EXERCUISSET, PRAE
PROPERE—NIMIS AMICIS ABREPTUS EST, NUNQUAM—SATIS
DEFLENDUS SATIS DESIDERANDUS—OBIIT 27 SEPTR 1762
AETAT SUAE 35.

White Mural Mont., with
an obelisk of yellow variegated marble ; *Arms*, Vair, or and gules, on a canton of the first, a deer's head caboshed azure. Im paling, azure, a fess nebulé, between three lions' heads erased, argent.

43.

TO THE MEMORY OF—GEORGE ORLEBAR, FRANCIS W HODGES, JOIIN SMITH
HANDCOCK, CECIL F.P. HALE, & HENRY DYSON, MIDSHIPMEN ON BOARD H.M.S.
SANSPAREIL, WHO IN THE BLOOM OF YOUTH—& WITH EVERY PROMISE OF—
ADORNING THEIR PROFESSION—OF BEING USEFUL TO THEIR COUNTRY—AND A
BLESSING TO THEIR FRIENDS—PREMATURELY PERISHED—IN 1800, & 1801—BY
THE FELL FEVER OF—THE WEST INDIES.

Mural, White Marble Tablet ; oval on gray.

G. ORLEBAR, born 1782, was son of Richard Orlebar [O. of Hanwick], by his second
wife, Charlotte Willing. See Hale, of King's Walden, pedigree. Of the Hodges
family a notice will be found farther on.

44.

MEMORIAE SACRUM CAROLI LLOYD ARMIGERI QUI E
FAMILIA GLOCESTRIENSI ORIUNDUS ET LIBERALIBUS HUMA-
NIORIS VITAE STUDIIS IN ANGLIA PROBE EXCULTUS. HIC
MATURUS SEDEM FIXIT UBI MERCATURAM FELICITER EXER-
CENS INTEGERRIMÆ VITAE EXEMPLAR SE PRAESTANS, ET
OMNIUM QUIBUSCUM VEL COMMERCIUM VEL CONSORTIUM
HABUIT, FAVOREM SIBI CONCILIANS, IN HAC PROVINCIA
PRAEFECTUS AERARII COOPTATUS EST : QUO MUNERE SUMMA
CUM PROBITATE. SUMMO OMNIUM PLAUSU PERFUNCTUS
EST ; POST FACULTATES SATIS AMPLAS HONORIFICE ACQUI-
SITAS QUAS (PAENETOTAS) SINGULIS SUIS NEPOTIBUS EX
AEQUO LEGARAT. LANGUORE CORREPTUS OBIIT DIE SEPTEM-
BRIS 28º. A.D. MDCCLI ET AETATIS SUAE LX.

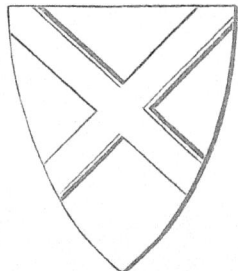

Mural, White Marble ;
Arms, Argent, a saltire
gules.

HOC QUALECUNQUE AFFECTUS ET DESIDERII TESTI-
MONIUM P.P. NATHANIEL LLOYD ARMIGER NON MINUS COM-
MERCII QUAM FRATERNITATIS VINCULO OLIM CONJUNCTISSI-
MUS : JOHANNES LLOYD S.T.P. & THOMAS CRAWLEY BOEVEY
ARMIGER.

E NEPOLITIUS ET TESTAMENTI HAEREDIBUS.

TREVOR, third son of Sir Evan Lloyd [cr. Bart. in 1647], a Captain in the army of Charles I., was the ancestor of this family. Thomas, second son of T. Crawley, merchant of London, assumed the additional surname of Boevey, on inheriting the estate of Flaxley Abbey, and succeeding to the baronetage conferred on Sir C. Barrow, his wife's cousin.—See "Baronetage," *Boevey.*

45.

SACRED—TO THE MEMORY OF—MRS MARGARET TAYLOR—WIFE OF WILLIAM TAYLOR—MERCHANT IN THIS CITY—WHO DIED THE 14th OF JUNE 1806—AGED 28 YEARS—FEW WOMEN HAVE BEEN—MORE BELOVED IN LIFE—OR MORE LAMENTED IN DEATH

Simple design : an urn, &c. ; Mural, G. & W. Marble.

46.

(*Ab.*) TO THE MEMORY OF MESSRS. CHARLES INMAN, & RALPH PRESTON FROM LANCASTER, IN GREAT BRITAIN, BUT LATE OF THIS PARISH, MERCHANTS. THE FORMER DIED 14 AUG 1767, AET 42—THE LATTER—THE 29th OF JANY. 1772, ONLY TWENTY SIX.

Mural, W. G. & B. Marble.   (Ford, Bath, Sculp.)

SIX eulogistic lines follow.—C. Inman, born 1725, son of Christopher Inman, by his wife, Mary Patefield, married "Lady M. Bowlby," and by her had a son, ancestor of the Inmans of Upton Manor, co. Chester.

47.

SACRED TO THE MEMORY OF—HORATIO S. CROSS—OFFICER OF H.M.'S CUSTOMS —OBIIT JANY 29 1854. ETATIS SUAE 28.

REQUIESCAT IN PACE.

White Marble Mural Tablet on a Black Marble ; representation of a curtain drawn aside, and these words, " Thy will be done as it is in Heavn."

48.

TO THE MEMORY OF THE FOLLOWING—

(*Ab.*) CAPT. ROBT. MOSTYN, 3d W.I.R., DIED OF YELLOW FEVER, AT NASSAU, BAHAMAS, 23 JULY 1853, AET 27.

ENSIGN JOHN ALEXR GORDON PRINGLE, 3d W.I.R., DIED OF YELLOW FEVER, AT KINGSTON, JAMAICA, 31 JULY 1853, AET 21.

ASST: SUR: WALTER WM. HARRIS, 1st W.I.R., ATTACHED TO 3d W.I.R., DIED AT UP PARK CAMP, OF YELLOW FEVER, 4 AUGT 1853, AET 24.

LIEUT. JOHN MARYON WILSON, 3d W.I.R., DIED AT U.P.C., OF YELLOW FEVER, 13 AUGT 1853, AET. 22.

ELIZA CHANCELLOR WILSON, WIFE OF THE ABOVE, DIED AT U.P.C., OF YELLOW FEVER, 5th SEPTR 1853, AET. 22.

CATH : ELIZABETH, WIFE OF LIEUT. WM HENY WILSON HAWTAYNE, 3. W.I.R., DIED OF YELLOW FEVER AT NASSAU, BAHAMAS, 9 AUGT. 1853 AET 23.

ASST. SURG. GIDEON JAS WM GRIFFITH 3. W.I.R. DIED OF YELLOW FEVER, AT LUCEA, 26th AUG 1853, AET 23.

ALSO, SELINA MARIA, WIFE OF CAPT C.S.H HINGSTON, 3 W.I.R. DIED AT U.P.C. 11th APL 1854, AET. 23.

ERECTED BY THE OFFICERS OF THE 1st & 3d W.I. REGTS.

Mural, W. Marble Tablet.

LIEUTENANT J. M. WILSON, son of J. M. Wilson, second son of Sir T. M. Wilson, seventh Bart.—Ensign Pringle was probably of the *Whytbank* family.

49.

IN MEMORY OF ISAAC JONES OF THIS CITY, WHO DEPARTED THIS LIFE, 16th JANUARY 1853, AGED 62 YEARS—ERECTED BY THE BRETHERN OF THE SUSSEX LODGE, IN TOKEN OF THEIR ESTEEM.

Mural, White Marble.

50.

(*Ab.*) NEAR THIS PLACE LIES BURIED, THE BODY OF RICHARD CARGILL, OF THE PARISH OF ST THOMAS IN THE EAST, ESQR. LATE COLL. OF THE ST THOMAS'S REGIMENT OF FOOT MILITIA, AND A REPRESENTATIVE IN THE ASSEMBLY OF THIS ISLAND FOR THE SAID PARISH—WHO DIED IN MARCH 1781. AGED 37 YEARS. AT THE EAST PART OF THIS CHURCH, ALSO LIES BURIED, THE BODY OF JOHN CARGILL ESQ; FORMERLY MERCHANT IN THIS TOWN, WHO DIED IN SEPTEMBER 1780, AGED 35 YEARS. ERECTED BY THEIR BROTHER

Handsome Mural Monument of coloured Marble and blazonry; *Arms*, Gules, three martlets, or.

EULOGISTIC lines follow.—The Cargill family was from Scotland, some time during the Stuart rebellions, and were connected in Jamaica with the Marstons, Lascelles, and Dallas families.

51.

(*Ab.*) EDWARD NATHANIEL BANCROFT M.D. CANTAB ; FELLOW OF THE ROYAL COLLEGE OF PHYSICIANS, LONDON ; AND DEPUTY INSPECTOR GENERAL OF ARMY HOSPITALS. (ERECTED BY THE PHYSICIANS & SURGEONS OF JAMAICA) OB. AT KINGSTON, 18 SEP. 1842, AET. 70.

Mural, W. M. Tablet.

52.

NEAR THIS MONUMENT—LIES INTERRED THE BODY OF EDWARD MANNING, ESQ.—ONE OF THE HONOURABLE PRIVY COUNCIL—SPEAKER OF THE ASSEMBLY—AND CUSTOS ROTU-LORUM OF THIS PARISH—IN WHICH STATIONS HE DISTIN-GUISHED HIMSELF. (HIS VIRTUES ARE THEN RECORDED, AND THE INSCRIPTION THUS TERMINATES): HE DIED GREATLY LAMENTED—DECEMBER 6th, 1756—AGED 46 YEARS.

Arms, Gules, a cross moline, between three trefoils slipped...... A marble bust of the deceased.

EDWARD MANNING was married to the sister of Sir Henry Moore, but they were divorced, Ballard Beckford having been what is termed the co-respondent.

INTRA MURAL SLABS.

53.

SACRED TO THE MEMORY OF ROBERT FOSTER ESQR, OF KINGSTON, WHO DEPARTED THIS LIFE, DECEMBER 5th 1768, AGED 55 YEARS.

Black Marble.

54.

FRANCIS MARY, THE WIDOW OF THE HONBLE JOHN SCOTT, ESQR., AND DAUGHTER OF THE HONBLE ALEXANDER HENDERSON ESQ., LATE ONE OF HIS MAJESTY'S PRIVY COUNCIL, AND ATTORNEY GENERAL OF JAMAICA—DIED 20th NOVEM. 1755. AGED 27.

B. M.

EIGHT eulogistic lines follow.

55.

HERE LIES INTERR'D THE BODY OF FLORENTIUS SON OF FLORENTIUS VASSAL ESQR BORN 18th OF APRIL 1732 & DEPARTED THIS LIFE 29th OF MAY FOLLOWING.

B. M. ; *Arms,* In chief, the sun in splendour ; and in base, an uncovered cup. *Crest,* Over an esquire's helmet, a three-masted ship with sails furled (a kind of lymphad).

SEE pedigree of " Vassal of Milford."

56.

(*Ab.*) HERE LYETH INTERRED, THE BODY OF ELIZABETH COLLY, WIFE OF WM. COLLY OF THIS PAR : WHO DEPARTED THIS LIFE JULY 9, 1717—AND ALSO THREE OF THEIR CHILDREN VIZ—

WILLIAM COLLY		29 FEBY. 1711
RICHARD COLLY	OB	5 NOV. 1715
JANE COLLY		3d JANY. 17

WILLM. COLLY, OBIIT THE 10th OF FEBRUARY, 1736, AGED 64.

B. M.

57.

HERE LYETH THE BODY OF—MRS ELIZABETH FREEMAN—WHO DYED JULY 2d 1728—AGED 50 YEARS—ALSO ANN GOAD, HER NIECE, OBIIT 11 SEP 1731, AGED

—31 YEARS—LIKEWISE, YE BODY OF CAPTAIN GAYWOOD GOADE, HER NEPHEW—OBIIT 1st SEPTR. 1758, AGED 45 YRS.

B. M.

58.

(*Ab.*) LUCY, WIFE OF WM LEVER, MERCHANT, OB. AUGT. 10, 1720, AET. 43 YRS. & 3 MONTHS.

B. M.

59.

ANN GOODIN, WIDOW, MOTHER TO ROBT G...... OF GOODIN.......... (obl.)

B. M. ; apparently one of the oldest ; no date.

60.

HERE LYETH THE BODY OF—WATERHOUSE .... RNELEY ESQ—OBIIT THE 6th OF ....LY 1723—AGED 43 YEARS.

B. M. ; *Arms*, On a bend
three deers' heads caboshed.   *Crest*, Over an esquire's helmet a talbot passant.

61

HERE LYES INTERR'D, YE BODY OF—WILLIAM HAY—OF THE PARISH OF WESTMORELAND IN JAMAICA—WHO DEPARTED THIS LIFE—THE 16th DAY OF APRIL A.D 1717—AGED THIRTY SIX YEARS.

B. M.

62.

DR JAMES COCKBURN, AND SARAH HIS WIFE ; ALSO PRUDENCE, LATE WIFE OF DR THOMAS COCKBURN—SHE DIED AGED 31 .... AUGUST 1738 WITH HER ONLY CHILD.

G. M. ; *Arms*, Quarterly,
1 & 4, three cocks ; 2 & 3, six mascles, 3, 2, & 1.

THESE are the arms of Cockburn, Bart., of *Langton* (now represented by the Lord Chief Justice of England). Perhaps, however, they should be those of *Ryslaw*.—See "Baronetage."

63.

HERE LIES INTERR . . . .

EDDE THE WIFE OF . . . .

HIS MAJESTY'S . . . .

THE 6th OF JULY 173 . . . .

. . . . OF HER . . . .

B. M. ; *Arms*, A chev.
between three animals like does.   Impaling, ... *Crest*, Over an esquire's helmet, out of a ducal coronet, a bird
(Phœnix ?) rising.

64.

(*Ab.*) JOHN DAVIS, OB. 30 JUNE, 1728, AET. 32.

B. M.

65.

(*Ab.*) BASILLEA HAWKS, WHO DIED AFTER HER BROTHER RICHARD THE 17
FEB 1739.

G. M.

TWENTY eulogistic lines follow.

66.

HERE LIETH THE BODY OF EDWARD EVANS—SON OF
JOHN AND ELIZABETH EVANS—·WHO DEPARTED THIS LIFE
YE 4th DAY OF FEBY 1745-6—AGED 24 YEARS, JOHN EVANS
SENR DYED YE 7th DAY OF OCTR 1746—AGED 70 YEARS.

White veined M. ; *Arms,*
Quarterly, argent and or, four demi-lions rampant gu.   *Crest*, On an esquire's helmet a demi-lion holding an escallop.

67.

(*Ab.*) JONATHAN HURST, OF KINGSTON, MERCHT. OB : DEC : 22 1744, AET. 42.

W. M.

68.

(*Ab.*) MARY FLETCHER, WIFE OF LEWIS FLETCHER, OB. JULY 20 1712, AET.
53. ALSO, JAMES DICKSON, SON OF DANIEL DICKSON, HER GRANDSON, OB. AUGT
28 1713, AET. 2 MTHS.

B. M.

69.

HERE LYETH THE BODY OF MR SAMLL. SHAWE, LATE OF BRISTOLL, MARCHT., WHO DEPARTED THIS LIFE, DECR. THE 3, 1716, AGED 42 YEARS.

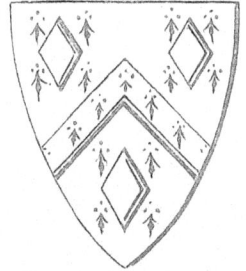

ermine between three lozenges, each with four ermine spots.   *Crest,* Over an esquire's helmet, a bundle of seven arrows, points down, three and three in saltire, and one in pale.

B. M. ; *Arms,* A chev.

70.

HERE LYETH THE BODY OF MR. ⸱⸱⸱⸱⸱⸱⸱⸱⸱⸱ LATE OF KINGSTON, WHO DEPARTED THIS LIFE, JAN. THE 4th 1717, AGED 43 YRS.

voided, or fimbriated, between three fleurs-de-lys.   *Crest,* On an esquire's helmet, a demi-eagle displayed.

B. M. ; *Arms,* A chev.

71.

(*Ab.*) ELIZABETH BATTERSLY WIFE OF BENJAMIN BATTERSLY OF YE PARISH OF KINGSTON MERCHT OB DEC 10 1737 AET 21 11 MTHS & 2 DAYS : ALSO THEIR DAUR HANNAH OB: OCT. 26. 1739 AET 3.

G. M.

THE name is probably " Batters*by*."

72.

IN VERTUOUS AND—GRATEFUL REMEMBRANCE OF—MRS MARY OBURNE—THE WIFE OF WILLIAM OBURNE, OF THIS—PARISH MERCHT.—SHE SURRENDERED HUMAN LIFE, UNDER THE AGONIES AND EXTREME PANGS IN TRAVEL, WITH HER —FIRST CHILD NAMED FRANCES, DECEMBER THE 21st—ANNO DOM: 1724, IN THE TWENTIETH YEAR OF HER—AGE—

AND IN COLD EARTH REPOSED, THE CORPS HERE LYS
UNTIL LAST TRUMPET SOUND A⸱⸱⸱⸱⸱⸱⸱T ARISE.

1 Cor. xv.

WITH HIM, WHO ALL THINGS MADE WITHOUT CONTROL,
IN HEAV'NLY BLISS, IS HER IMMORTAL SOUL.

Gen. i. ; Luke xvi.

ALSO HERE LYETH ⸱⸱⸱⸱⸱⸱⸱⸱⸱⸱⸱⸱⸱⸱ 1725—6

Sculptured.

13

73.

HIC JACET—SAMUEL KNIGHT, M.D.—QUI TRIGINTA QUA-
TUOR—ANNOS IN HOC INSULA—MEDICINAM MAGNA—CUM
LAUDE EXERCUIT.—OBIIT 12° JAN. 1707-8—AETATIS SVAE 65.

B. M.; On a fess, three
cinquefoils pierced; in chief a unicorn's head erased. *Crest,* Over an esquire's helmet a goat's head with a cherry
leafed in its mouth.

HE was Member of Assembly for Kingston in 1691 and 1701.

74.

UNDERNEATH THIS MARBLE—ARE INTER'D THE REMAINS OF—THE HONOUR-
ABLE JAMES LAWRENCE—OF FAIRFIELD IN THE PARISH OF ST. JAMES, ESQ.—WHO
DEPARTED THIS LIFE—IN THE YEAR OF OUR LORD—1756—IN THE 47th YEAR
OF HIS AGE—HE WAS BURIED THERE 16th JUNE.

COLONEL JAMES LAWRENCE was Custos Rotulorum of St. James's parish. By his
wife Mary, daughter of Colonel Richard James, of Hanover (the first child born
of English parents in Jamaica after its conquest), he had a numerous family.

Richard James Lawrence, his eldest son, married Mary, fourth daughter of
Thomas Hall, of Kirkpatrick, a Member for the parish of Westmoreland in 1752. He
died in London, Nov. 8, 1830, aged eighty-five years. Mr. R. J. Lawrence had five
sons, viz., 1. James; 2. George; 3. Charles (who had issue: 1. G. H. Lawrence, 2. Rev.
C. W. Lawrence, 3, Major-General A. Lawrence); 4. Henry; 5. Frederick Augustus,
Captain, and Gentleman of the P. Chamber to King George IV., when regent.

His eldest son was the late (Sir) James Lawrence, Knight of Malta, and author
of several works, one of which, on the "Nobility of the British Gentry," is well known.
George, the second son, was the late proprietor of Cowsfield House, near Salisbury.*

* *Lineage:*—Henry Lawrence, President of the Council of State, under Cromwell, was of St. Ives, in Huntingdonshire, and came of an ancient family, a long account of which is to be found in the *Gentleman's Magazine*
(1815 and 1829), Sir Egerton Brydge's edition of Milton, and other works. He married Amy, only daughter and
heiress of Sir Edward Peyton, of Isleham (*vide* the "Extinct Baronetage"), and died in 1664. One of his daughters married an Earl of Barrymore, while John—one, it is believed, of his seven sons—emigrated to Barbados, with
John Bradshaw, nephew of the regicide, and ultimately removed to Jamaica, about 1675. His (J. L.'s) will is dated
May 10th, 1690. By his wife Jane, daughter of —. Collins, and relict of Richard Dunn, of Cabrete, he had three
sons, of whom the eldest, John, married Susanna Petgrave, and by her, had six sons and three daughters. His
third son, James Lawrence, of Fairfield, was the ancestor, as already stated, of the late (Sir) James Lawrence.
1. The eldest daughter of John Lawrence and Susanna Petgrave was named Susanna. She married Lawrence
Lawrence,* of a New England family (of *his* family there are records elsewhere), and had, with other children,
Rachel, who married Henry Gordon,† and was mother of Anne Gordon, who, by her husband Alexander Edgar
(buried in Edinburgh in 1820), had a numerous issue, and who is mentioned in the curious *genealogical* will of her

* His will recorded in Jamaica, 1753. N.B.—The author is only responsible for the above lineage from 1690.
† His will recorded in Jamaica, 1789. (*Vide* "Taaffe Notes.") Alexander Edgar was the son of Alexander Edgar of Auchingra-
mont, by his wife Margaret, daughter of James Edgar. His father (born 1698) was the brother of Peter Edgar, of Bridgelands, Peebles
(father-in-law of Sir H. Raeburn, the celebrated artist). Their mother's maiden name was Priscilla Handasyde. (For a notice of the
latter peculiar surname *vide* Sinclair's "Survey, Parish of Hutton, Berwickshire.")

75.

(*Ab.*) EDWARD CLARKE, HEIR OF THE HON: COLL: JOHN CLARKE, OF ST DAVID'S—OB. 6th DECR. 1731.

B. M.

LONG inscription, much obliterated.

76.

(*Ab.*) MARTHA, THE WIFE OF ALEXR GRANT, OB. NOV. 17 1733, AET. 27—ALSO MICHAEL HAY, ESQ., OF KINGSTON, OB. 12 MARCH—ALSO HER DAUR. ISABELLA, WIFE OF WALTER RICHMOND, OB. FEBY. 1772, AET. 28.

SOME nearly obliterated lines follow.

W. M. ; *Arms*, Three antique crowns.   *Crest*, Over an esquire's helmet a dexter hand holding a branch.

77.

REQUIES . . . . ANN . . . .

G. M. ; *Arms* effaced, a maunch on a canton, however, being apparent, also over an esquire's helmet, a head (?) winged.

78.

HERE LYES THE BODY OF—EDMOND FITZPATRICK—ESQ DOCTOR OF PHYSICK—WHO DEPARTED THIS LIFE—THE 11th ... OF JULY 1732

Stone.

79.

. . . . THIS STONE . . . . BODY OF MR THOMAS . . . . BORN AT LIVERPOOL . . . . 80 . . . .

Stone.

aunt, the late Mrs. Catherine Franklyn, who died in London in 1831.   2. Rachael, the second daughter of John and Susanna Lawrence, married Jeremiah Downer.   3. Mary, the youngest daughter of John and Susanna Lawrence, married Philip Auglin, and had a daughter, Elizabeth, who married, in 1765, Robert Scarlett, and was the mother of James Scarlett, created Baron Abinger.   This very extensive family of Lawrence is necessarily connected with numerous other families,* more or less well known, and the records substantiating the descent of its various branches have been carefully preserved in Jamaica and elsewhere, but are of too voluminous a character to be enlarged upon here.   However, a good account of them is to be found in part iii. of Roby's " History of the Parish of St. James,"† who has, however, omitted several descents.

---

 * Richards, Morris, Walcott, James, &c.
 † After the annotator had made his collection, in 1857, he met with this portion of the work, but failed to discover the others.

80.

HERE L..TH INTERR'D THE BODY OF—WILLIAM PARK—OF YE PARISH OF KINGSTON, MERCHANT :—WHO DEPARTED THIS LIFE—THE 25th OF MARCH 1710, AGED 39 YEARS.

B. M.

81.

HERE LYETH INTERR INTERR'D THE—BODY OF THE HONOURABLE — EZEKIEL GOMESSAL — ESQR — ONE OF HIS MAJESTIES COUNCEL—AND COLONEL OF THE REGIMENT OF HORSE—WHO DEPARTED—THIS LIFE THE 12 DAY—OF APRIL ANNO 1734—AGED 70 YEARS.

B. M. ; *Arms,* A chev. ermine between three dexter gauntlets. *Crest,* Over an esquire's helmet, out of a coronet......a cuffed cubit arm holding a battle-axe.

QUERY, Gomersal ?—*See* No. 88.

82.

HERE LYES THE BODY OF—HENRY SMITHSON—OF KINGSTON MERCHANT WHO DEPARTED—.........AUGUST THE .. 1715 IN THE 51—YEAR OF HIS AGE.

B. M.

HE was probably a son of Hugh, grandson of the 1st Bart., who died in 1670.—*Vide* "Peerage."

83.

HERE LYES INTERR'D THE BODY OF—OF MARY THE WIFE OF CHARLES—BRAYNE OF THIS PARISH WHO—DEPARTED THIS LIFE THE 10th OF—DECEMBER A.D. 1710 AGED 30 YEARS—WITH SEVERALL OF HER CHILDREN

B. M. ; *Arms,* Between seven crosses crosslet, a lion rampant. *Crest,* Over an esquire's helmet, a dove close, with an olive branch in beak.

THERE is, in the will of Alexander Henderson, Attorney-General of Jamaica (ob. 1732), a reference to Mary Brayne, his mother-in-law, as "the unfortunate Mrs. Brayne." The Braynes were connected by marriage, with the families of Willoughby, Moore, Cassan, Scott, Tucker, Long, &c. In their pedigree, however, the husband of Mary is not entered as Charles, but as Thomas.

84.

HERE LYETH THE BODY OF MARY THE——......... OF JOHN HAYNES.... ANT AND DA.......—WHO DEPA.......—DAY ...... FIRST—HER AGE

B. M. ; *Arms*, Two lions rampant combatant, supporting a tower. *Crest*, Over an esquire's helmet an arm embowed grasping a pennon. *Motto*, "Turris fortis est mihi Deus."

85.

No date. Inscription almost entirely effaced; the name "Pratter," however, is distinguishable.

B. M. ; *Arms*, On a chev. between three griffins' (?) heads erased, a lion passant. *Crest*, Over an esquire's helmet, a doe's head.

86.

(*Ab.*) MR. THOMAS WOOLHEAD, LATE OF THIS TOWN, PRINTER, OB. 13 DEC. 1777. AET. 60.

B. M.

87.

(*Ab.*) MRS ANN BRIDGE, OB. DEC. 12, 1761, AET. 60—ALSO REBECCA, WIFE OF CHRISTOPHER SPARKE, ESQ. ...., 1763.

88.

HERE LYETH THE BODY OF THE VIRTUOUS MRS MARY GOMERSALL, WIFE OF COLO. EZEKIEL GOMERSALL, AND DAUGHTER OF FRANCIS AND MARGARET DICKENSON. SHE DEPARTED THIS LIFE, THE 1st OF DECEMBER 1723, IN THE 56th YEAR OF HER AGE, AND IN THE 36th YEAR OF HER MARRIAGE.

B. M.

THERE was a well-known poet of the reign of Charles I. of this rare name.

89.

(*Ab.*) MARGARET, WIFE OF DANIEL MCQUEEN OF KINGSTON, MERCHT., OB. DEC. 1 1757 AET 29, ALSO THE BODY OF HER SISTER, THE WIFE OF GEORGE RICHARDS EQR. MERCHT. OB: 1 JULY, 1755, AET. 30. LIKEWISE THE BODY OF THEIR SISTER ANN, WIFE OF JOHN MINOT, OB. 17 JANY. 1758 AET. 30, ALSO MARY M .... 10 SEP. 1764.

B. M.

90.

FORMER ....
TED THIS LIFE ....
DEC. 1762 AGED 30 YEARS ....
THE LATTER...
FOLLOWING AGED 29 YEARS ....
OF ....
RESURRECTION ....
AND ....
IMMORTALITY ....
OUT OF THE SABBATH OF THE TOMB ....
RAPTURES IN A LIFE TO COME...................

B. M.

Part concealed by communion rail.

91.

(*Ab.*) DANIEL MACKQUEEN, OF KINGSTON PARISH, ESQRE. OB. 8 JULY 1758, AET ...... MARY HIS YOUNGEST DAUR., BY JANE HANBURY MACKQUEEN, HIS 2ᵈ WIFE, OB. 27 JUNE 1760, AET. 2 YRS. 10 MTHS. ALSO JAS. MACKQUEEN, MERCHT. OB. 19 FEB 1765, AET. 49.

G. M.

92.

(*Ab.*) EDWARD COOK, GENT. OF THE PARISH OF ST ANDREW —OB. AET. 25. IN 1716. ALSO HIS DAUR. JOAN COOK, OB. JULY 27, 1715, AET. 2 YRS.

G. M.; *Arms*, 3 eagles displayed. *Crest*, On an esquire's helmet, an eagle's head erased.

93.

HERE LIES THE BODY OF MARY ANN MEAD, DAUR. OF JOHN & ELIZABETH MEAD, WHO DEPARTED THIS LIFE, YE 8ᵗʰ OF JULY 1762, AGED FOUR MONTHS— ALSO—JOHN & ELIZABETH MEAD, WHO DEPARTED THIS LIFE, YE 28 OF DECEMBER, 1766, AGED 3 YEARS & 6 MONTHS.

W. M.

94.

(*Ab.*) ELIZABETH REEVES DIED DECR. 10th 1772, AGED 23V. 4M. & 25D.

W. M.

Eight verses follow.

95.

HERE LYETH THE BODY OF—THOMAS WILSONE, ESQ—
FORMERLY OF THE MIDDLE TEMPLE, LONDON—BUT LATE OF
THE PAR: OF ST CATHERINE—WHO DIED UNIVERSALLY
BELOVED, AND—DESERVEDLY ESTEEMED, THE 29th APRILL
1741—AGED 66 YEARS.

B. M. ; *Arms*, A wolf
rampant ; on a chief, between two bezants, a fleur-de-lys. *Crest*, On an esquire's helmet, a demi-wolf rampant.

96.

AND NOW I HAVE FOUND THE GORDIAN KNOTTED BANDS
OF LIFE UNTIED. O LORD, INTO THY HANDS
I RECOMMEND MY BETTER PARTS, WITH TRUST
TO FIND YOU MUCH MORE MERCIFULL IN LUST—
YET TRUELY LUST, WITH ALL. O WELCOME DEATH,
WITH JOY I MEET YOU WITH MY LATEST BREATH.
SHOULD ALL MY FAULTS BEHIND THE MILK WHITE VEIL
OF THY DEAR MERCY THEN I SHALL NOT FAIL
RECALL'D FROM EARTH,—FOR TO RECEIVE THE CROWN
PREPAR'D FOR VERTUE AND DESERN'D RENOWN—
WHERE NOW I LEAVE YOU, WHILST I, IN FULL POSSEST,
OF ENDLESS PEACE AND EVERLASTING REST.

CHARLES WATKINS, 1721.

B. M.

N.B.—The syntax of the above, is scarcely intelligible.

97.

HERE LIETH THE BODY OF—SAMUELL ...... ORGILL,
ESQ .... LATE OF .... PARISH OF ST MARY—WHO DE-
PARTED .... LIFE, 28 SEPTEMBER 1741, AGED 27 YEARS—
THIS STONE .... LAID BY HIS WIDOW—ANNA PETRONELLA.

B. M. ; *Arms*, ... Three
griffins' heads couped. (An esquire's helmet over the shield.)

98.

HERE LYES THE BODY OF—JAMES RODEN, ESQ—DIED THE 14th DECEMBER 1753—AGED 37 YEARS—

B. M.

99.

HERE LYETH THE BODY OF—ELIZABETH BOSLEY, THE RELICT OF—JOHN BOSLEY, ESQ., DECEASED—WHO DEPARTED THIS LIFE, APRIL 5th 1720.

M. M. ; *Device,* A death's head encircled with shamrocks and palm leaves.

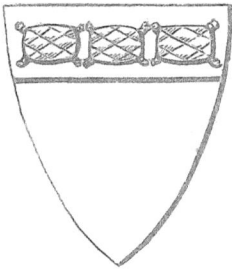

100.

INSCRIPTION entirely obliterated.

G. M. ; *Arms,* On a chief three woolsacks, the under portion effaced ; over the shield, an esquire's helmet. *Crest,* A spur.

101.

HERE LIES THE BODY OF MARY—THE WIFE OF DAVID MONCREIFF ESQ—WHO DIED, THE 14th JUNE 173..

W. M. ; *Arms,* A lion rampant ; a chief ermine. Impaling, on a bend between three wings, three fleurs-de-lys. *Crest,* Over an esquire's helmet, a demi-lion rampant. (The Arms of Moncrieff, Baronet of Tullibole.)

102.

HERE LIES THE BODY OF—MR. PAUNCEFORT MILLER, WHO DEPARTED THIS LIFE, THE—3 OF JANUARY ANNO DOM: 1725—AGED 45 YEARS.

B. M.

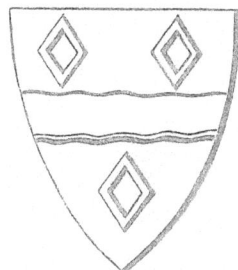

103.

HERE LIES THE BODY OF—MR THOMAS MITCHELL, WHO DEPARTED THIS LIFE, YE 10th OF JUNE—1720, AETATIS SUAE 46.

B. M.; *Arms*, A fess wavy between three mascles. *Crest*, (Esquire's helmet) A crowned, and winged figure, holding a sword—"Vinca."

104.

HERE LIES MARY GRIFF...... WIFE OF LUCOCK GRIFFIN—OF THE PARISH OF KINGSTON—CARPENTER, WHO DIED—THE 17 DAY OF XBER. 1741, AGED 49 YEARS.

B. M.

105.

(*Ab.*) SARAH WYLLYS, WIFE OF WM. WYLLYS, ESQ., OB: 12 FEB, 1716. 17. AET. 27. ALSO BENJAMIN SON TO WILLIAM & MARGARET .... OB: 31 JANR 1761: AET 30—MARGARET DAUGHTER TO BENJAMIN WYLLYS. OB 13 FEB 1762 AGED 3YRS 1M.

G. M.

106.

HERE LYETH THE BODY OF—CAPTAIN CHARLES BROWN—SO...... THE HONOURABLE—CHARLES BROWN, ESQR., COMMISSIONER OF HIS MAJESTIES NAVY, AT CHATHAM—HE DIED, NOVR. 21st 1747, AGED 38 YEARS.

PARENTES PROBOSQUE HONORABAT
UXORUM ET AMICOS AMABAT.

B. M.

107.

(*Ab.*) MR. DANIEL DICKSON, OB. JULY 19 1723, AGED ABOUT 46 YEARS. ALSO, JAMES DICKSON, HIS SON, OB. AUG. 28 1713, AET. 2 MONTHS. ALSO, FRANCES, HIS DAUR. FEB. 28 17$\frac{21}{22}$, AET. 14 MTHS.

B. M.

14

108.

HERE LYETH INTERRED, THE BODY—OF IOHN BENBOW
ESQR., ADMIRAL—OF THE WHITE: A TRUE PATTERN OF—
ENGLISH COURAGE: WHO LOST HYS LIFE—IN DEFENCE OF
HYS QUEENE AND—COUNTRY, NOVEMBER YE 4th 1702—IN
THE 52nd YEAR OF HYS AGE—BY A WOUND IN HYS LEG,
RECEIVED—IN AN ENGAGEMENT WITH—MONS. DU CASSE,
BEING MUCH—LAMENTED.

Arms, King William III.,
as a mark of estimation of his services, granted him an augmentation of his arms, by adding sheaves of arrows, to
the original *bent* bows.

JOHN BENBOW was born at Shrewsbury, in 1650. His gallantry in an action with
    Barbary pirates, gained for him, through the recommendation of the King of
Spain, a commission in the British navy, shortly after which, he was entrusted with the
command of a fleet.*

    In 1702, during an engagement with the French Admiral, Du Casse, he was
struck in the leg by a chain-shot. Of this wound he died, but not before he had
brought to justice the treacherous captains who had abandoned him in the fight.†

109.

HERE LIES—THE HONBLE. EDWARD PRATTER—CUSTOS
ROTULORUM—FOR THE PARISH AND PRECINCT OF KINGSTON
—IN WHOM—THIS ISLAND LOST A TRUE FRIEND—AND AN
EMINENT EXAMPLE—OF COMPASSION TO THE DISTRESSED—
A VIRTUE WHICH NEVER GOES ALONE—HE DYED—AUGUST,
1735, AGED 52 YEARS.

Arms, Three wolves' heads
erased; on a chief, a lion passant.   *Crest*, A greyhound's head, semée of estoiles.

VIDE previous fragment. Pratter was agent to the South Sea Company in Jamaica,
    and Member of Assembly for Hanover in 1723-4; and for Kingston, 1726-7.—
Roby.

110.

HERE LIETH INTERR'D THE BODY OF SMART MAY, WIFE OF THE REVEREND
MR. WILLIAM MAY, RECTOR OF THIS PARISH, WHO WAS KILL'D IN YE 23d YEAR
OF HER AGE, BY YE FALL OF AN HOUSE, IN YE GREAT STORM, AUGUST YE 28th,
A.D. 1722.

    JUSTUS QUACUNQUE MORTE PRÆOCCUPATUS FUERIT IN REFRIGERIO ERIT.
SAP. 4. 7.

SMART *Pennant* was, 1st, married to Thomas Peters, Member for Clarendon, in 1718;
    and, 2ndly, 7th Sept., 1721, to the Rev. W. May.

* *Vide* " Deeds of Naval Daring."
† Deptford churchyard has, generally speaking, been pointed out by tradition as the last resting-place of the
illustrious Benbow. How it came to be so considered, it is difficult to say.—*See* General Notes to this volume.

III.

HERE LIES INTERR'D YE BODY OF THE REVD. MR. WILLIAM MAY, BORN IN YE PARISH OF ASH IN KENT, YE 29th OF AUGUST, 1695. EDUCATED AT ST. JOHN'S COLLEGE, IN CAMBRIDGE, COMMISSARY OF JAMAICA, AND 32 YEARS MINISTER OF THIS PARISH. HIS FIRST WIFE WAS SMART, YE DAUGHTER OF EDWARD AND ELIZTH. PENNANT, OF YE PARISH OF CLARENDON; HIS SECOND WIFE WAS BATHUSA, YE DAUGHTER OF FLORENTIUS AND ANN VASSALL, OF YE PARISH OF ST. ELIZA-BETH, WHO WAS BURIED IN SPANISH TOWN CHURCH BY YE GRAVE OF HER MOTHER ON YE 22 DAY OF JULY, 1746, BY WHOM HE HAD ISSUE SIX SONS AND TWO DAUGHTERS, FIVE OF WHICH ARE ENTERRED UNDER THIS STONE, VIZ. PETER, WILLIAM, ELIZABETH, GEORGE, AND ITHAMAR. TWO DIED AT SEA GOING TO BOSTON FOR YE RECOVERY OF THEIR HEALTH, VIZ. RICHARD, ON YE 28th OF AUGUST, 1745, IN YE 21st YEAR OF HIS AGE, AND FLORENTIUS, YE 4th OF JUNE, 1747, IN YE 16th YEAR OF HIS AGE. HIS SON, ROSE HERRING MAY, IS THE ONLY CHILD THAT SURVIVED HIM, WHO IT IS HOPED WILL INHERIT HIS FATHER'S VIRTUES, AS WELL AS HIS FORTUNE.

THE Revd. William May was buried, 31st January, 1753-4. His only surviving son, Rose-Herring May, born 16th February, 1736-7, was Member of Council, and Custos of Clarendon and Vere. He married, 28th March, 1759, Mary-Trelawny Wigan (she was buried in St. Dorothy's, 18th Nov., 1786), by whom he had nine children, baptized in St. Catharine's. He died, 1st August, 1791, and was buried in Spanish Town.

112.

TO THE MEMORY OF SUSANNA—THE LATE WIFE—OF—COLONEL WILLIAM GORDON—WHO DEPARTED THIS LIFE—31st MARCH 1731—AGED 32 YEARS—MANY DAUGHTERS HAVE DONE VERTUOUSLY—BUT THOU EXCELLEST THEM ALL—

Proverbs xxxi. 20.

Arms, ... An annulet between three boars' heads, 2 & 1, couped. Impaling,...a bend between two birds' wings. *Crest*, A dexter hand grasping a sword.

THESE arms are probably meant for those of the family of Gordon, of Earlston, Kirkcudbright.* The above may have been a son of the 2nd Bart.

---

* It is known, however, that there was a family of this name, in the parishes of St. Elizabeth and St. James, Jamaica, which came from the north of Ireland (Enniskillen), and which was probably derived from the house of Earlston. There are several curious wills of persons of this name, recorded in Jamaica; and others of the usual description. William Gordon, of St. Elizabeth, leaves bequests to Susanna, daughter of Harry Gordon, of St. James. Robert Gordon (1768), then living in *Flanders*, bequeaths his real property, within the

113.

SUB HOC MARMORE REQUIESCIT ANNA—JACOBI KNIGHT ARMIGERI, UXOR—JOANNIS LEWIS ARMIGERI, ET ANNAE— FILIA.—QUAE, UTRASQUE, DUM VIVERET, PARTES [SIVE MATRIS SPECTES, SIVE CONJUGIS]—AMORE ET AFFECTU SUMMO— PRUDENTIA ET PIETATE PARI—JUGITER ADMINISTRAVIT— SUPER OMNIA—FIDE ERGA DEUM ET MORUM SANCTITATE SUMMA—CONSPICUA.—FLEBILIS TANDEM OMNIBUS ET DEPLO-
W. M.; *Arms,......* Three RANDA—FATIS CESSIT NOVEMBRIS DIE 21—ANNO DOMINI pallets gules; on a canton ...within a border.. a spur 1719—AETATIS SUAE 25.
with the rowel downwards
—leathered.... *Crest,* An eagle displayed.

JAMES KNIGHT was Receiver-General in 1716. He left Jamaica in 1737, and died in England, 6th May, 1747. John Lewis was Member of Assembly for Port Royal, in 1701, and for Kingston, in 1704.

114.

HERE LYETH INTERRED THE BODY OF WILLIAM HALL, ESQUIRE, WHO DEPARTED THIS LIFE THE EIGHTEENTH DAY OF SEPTEMBER, 1699, IN THE FORTY-FOURTH YEAR OF HIS AGE.

Arms,...... A chevron en-
grailed between three talbots' heads erased.

HE was the youngest child of Edmund Hall, Esq., of Greatford Hall.*

---

diocese of *Canterbury*, and also in Jamaica, to his brothers John and William, and his daughters Susanna and Rebecca. Thomas Gordon (entered 1748) mentions his wife Anne; his children Susanna, Anne, John, and William; and appoints Dr. William Gordon, M.D., of Bristol, executor. Henry Gordon dated Jan. 18, 1788): this is what may be called a *genealogical* will, and shows the connection between the families of Gordon and Lawrence. Alexander Gordon (dated June 8, 1750) mentions Charles Gordon, of *Blelack,* Aberdeenshire, and his sister Helen, wife of Hugh Ross, of *Fillus* (?).* Charles Gordon (1755) mentions his brothers John of Edinburgh and Thomas of Aberdeen, and his sisters Jane, Susanna, &c. James Gordon (1766) names his "brother Harry Gordon in H.M.'s service." William Gordon (1766) styles his father Robert Gordon of Auchendolly. Robert Gordon, in 1664, mentions his half-sister Catherine Nairn, wife of William Stewart, of *Croft Barn, Glenlivet, Banffshire.* These are only a few of the Gordon wills in Jamaica. Among their estates, was one not far from Kingston, called Gordonstown (where there is now a post-office), also *Armagh,* and St. Andrew's Hill.

 * The Halls of Jamaica, were a reputed branch of the Halls of Greatford Hall, Lincolnshire, a family of great antiquity and high consideration, who were themselves a scion of the Fitz Williams of Clixby, of the same lineage as

---

 * Gordon of Blelack was an old family in Aberdeenshire. Alexander Gordon of Blelack married, Nov. 26, 1604, Katherine, daughter of Gilbert Baird, of Auchmedden.—*Vide* "History of the Baird Family," by W. N. Fraser, Esq., of Tornaveen, a representative of Auchmedden.

115.

THE HONBLE. JAMES IRVING, ESQ.—LATE CUSTOS OF TRELAWNY, DIED—21st NOVEMBER, 1798, AGED 49 YEARS.

THE Irvings, owners of Ironshore and Hartfield, in St. James' parish. James, eldest son of Dr. James Irving, obtained Ironshore, from John Lawrence, in exchange for an estate in South Carolina. James Irving, the younger, was Custos of Trelawny, and represented that parish, in the Assemblies of 1774, 1781, 1787, 1790, and 1796. This was a branch of the family of Irving of Robgill Tower, Dumfriesshire, represented by Sir Paulus Aemelius Irving, Bart.

KINGSTON PARISH CHURCH (YARD).

THE FIRST FOUR ARE FRAGMENTS ON THE CHURCH DOOR-STEPS.

IN front of the principal entrance by the north transept, is a large black marble slab, worn by feet, and without an inscription. The story is, that it is "turned on its face, to conceal the epitaph of an early rector of the parish, who was hanged, for coining counterfeit doubloons in the vestry. It is said he was discovered, in consequence of having issued one from his mint, before it was quite cold." The story is most improbable.

1.

HERE LYETH THE BODY OF ....
LATE WIFE TO JOHN EAST................
OF THIS PARISH WHO DE................
THIS LIFE THE 8th DAY OF F................
1722-3 AGED 45 YRS.

2.

HE.... LYETH YE B................
CASH OF THIS P................
THIS LIFE YE 16 ....
.... AGED 5 ....

Earl Fitzwilliam. William Hall, Esq., born in Lincolnshire, youngest son of Edmund Hall, Esq., of Greatford Hall, by Anne his wife, daughter of John Elmers, Esq., of Swinford. He held first the appointment of British Consul at Bilboa in Spain, and subsequently, in 1687, accompanied to Jamaica, as secretary, Christopher Monk, Duke of Albemarle, Governor of the Island. He married, July 26, 1688, Elizabeth, daughter of William Wyatt, Esq. (lineally descended from the Sir Thomas Wyatt, of Allington Castle, the poet of the time of Henry VIII.), by Elizabeth his wife, daughter of Councillor Edward Heylin; and left at his decease, Sept. 18, 1699, an only son, James Hall, Esq., of Hyde Hall, Jamaica,...who married Elizabeth, sister of Colonel John Cossley* (Aide-de-camp to the Duke of Cumberland at the battles of Fontenoy and Culloden). His second son, Cossley Hall, Esq., married, secondly, Elizabeth Bromley, eldest daughter of Thomas Rose, Esq., of Jamaica, and by her had Thomas James, his successor, and two daughters, the elder of whom, Anne Rose, married William Green, Esq., and secondly, J. Somerville Wood, Esq. By the former, this lady had an only daughter, Elizabeth, Countess Dowager of Harrington, and mother of the sixth Earl of Harrington.

---

* Burke's "Landed Gentry."

3.

.................J OF MR. GEORG...............

................SH WHO DEPA.................

.......................MY ....

..................YE 16..................

4.

LYE ....

THE BODY ....

SWEETING ....

OF THE SUNET.....................

LANCASTER ....

OF THIS LIFE ....

TWENTIETH DAY ....

IN THE TWENTIETH ....

YEAR OF HIS AGE ....

THE YEAR OF OUR L...............

............1720................

SIC TRANSIT GLORIA MUNDI.........

5.

(*Ab.*) JAS: FOTHERINGHAM OB. JUNE 25 1834 AET. 30, ALSO KEITH FOTHER-INGHAM, OB. NOV. 2 1847, AET. 32

6.

(*Ab.*) ELEANOR GIBBONS BULL, DAU. OF JNO. & SARAH BULL, OB: 9 JULY 1792, AET. 14 YRS. & 5 MTHS.

7.

(*Ab.*) PETER WAGSTAFFE, SON OF JOHN & MARY W., OB. 16 DEC: 1759, AET. 16YRS 2MTHS. 29 DAYS : ALSO MARY W., WIFE OF JOHN W., OB. 7 DEC. 1760, AET. 37.

8.

(*Ab.*) JAMES LEWIN, MERCHT. OB. SEP: 1751, AET. 33: ALSO, MRS SARAH CHAP-PELL, NIECE OF THE ABOVE, OB. 29 JUNE 1803, AET. 74. ALSO, ISAAC MUNT, ESQ., OB. FEB. 4 1820, AET. 61 YRS. 29 DAYS.

9.

(*Ab.*) JAS. HANCE, MERCHT. OB. 23 MAY, 1812, AET. 43.

10.

(*Ab.*) JAS DOLLAR, ESQ., MERCHT., OB. 6 JULY 1829, AET. 29.

11.

(*Ab.*) JOHN ATKINSON, ESQ., BURIED 11 FEB. 1798.

12.

(*Ab.*) GEO: CLAYTON, ESQ., OB. 3 APL., 1816, & JOHN MITCHELL, ESQ., OB. 27 AUGT. 1840

13.

(*Ab.*) WM. BROWN, ESQ., REAR ADMIRAL OF THE RED, & COMMANDER IN CHIEF IN JAMAICA OB 20 SEP 1814 AET 50.

IN the " Naval Biographical Dictionary," the date of the admiral's death is given, as in 1816. The latter had been Commissioner of Malta and Sheerness dockyards. His eldest son, C. F. Brown, an officer in the R.N., m. Elizabeth Jane, dau. of John Hawkins, of Byelands ; and his dau., Mary F. Brown, m. Sir G. F. Hampson, 8th Bart., of Taplow, grandson of the 6th Bart., who m. Mary, dau. of Thomas Pinnock, of Jamaica, by whom he had a son, the 7th Bart., and a dau., m. to Samuel Stevenson, of the same island.

14.

(*Ab.*) DAWSON CLOWES, MIDSHIPMAN, HMS. MAIDSTONE, OB. DEC. 3. 1737, AET. 16

15.

(*Ab.*) ANN, WIFE OF ALEXR. BEAN, OB. NOV. 27 1726, AET. 32—ALSO, JAMES BEAN, NEPHEW TO JOHN BEAN OF KINGSTON, OB. 24 DEC. 1802 AET. 24.

16.

HERE LIES THE BODY—OF S. W., AGED 27 YEARS—ALSO THOSE OF TWO CHILDREN OF B. O. W.'S, & ELEANOR HIS WIFE, G. E. W.'S AGED 15 MONTHS—AND—H. W. W.'S, AGED 5 YEARS & 9 MONTHS.

17.

(*Ab.*) CLAUS VAN DOLHERN, OB: 24 OCT. 1807, AET. 47.—ERECTED BY HIS FRIEND, MISS FRANCIS LAMBO.

TWENTY lines follow.

18.

(*Ab.*) D. S. ROBERTS, ESQ., LATE MAJOR, 54th REGT, OB. 12 DEC. 1829, AET. 48.

19.

HERE LYES BURIED—THE BODY OF CAPT—JOHN KENT OF—BOSTON IN NEW ENGLAND—WHO DIED ON THIS ISLAND—SEP. 16 ANNO DOMI. 1732—AGED 37 YEARS 11 MTHS. & 17 DAYS

20.

(*Ab.*) FANNY, CHILD OF JOHN M. TREW CLERK, OB. 24 MARCH 1842.

21.

(*Ab.*) B. C. PATEY, ESQ., MERCHT., OB. 26 JANY. 1837, AET. 57.

22.

(*Ab.*) DONALD ROSS, PLANTER, OF PORT ROYAL PARISH, OB. 18 SEP. 1806, AET. 57.

23.

(*Ab.*) DENNIS BRAUMGAN, ESQ., MERCHT., OB. DEC 9. 1821.

24.

(*Ab.*) MRS. SARAH WARDEN, WIFE OF W. R. WARDEN, OB. 29 AUGT. 1811. AET. 38.

25.

(*Ab.*) EDWARD BAKER, MIDSHIPMAN R.N., BORN SEP. 5 1779: OB. 21 APL. 1796.

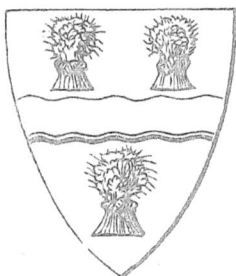

26.

(*Ab.*) THE BODY OF JOHN DRINKWATER, OF THIS PARISH. HE DIED, JUNE 10 1745, AGED 73—ALSO, EIGHT CHILDREN OF THE SAID JOHN, & SARAH DRINKWATER.

Arms, A fess wavy, between three garbs. *Crest,* Over an esquire's helmet, three ears of corn, encircled with a ducal coronet.

27.

INTERR'D YE BODY OF ....
E E HINTON OF LONDON ....
............BRITAIN............................
BORN IN JAMAICA ....
DEPARTED THIS ....
............JUNE ....
...................YEAR OF..................

(Fragment.)

Arms, Per fess indented: three fleurs-de-lys, in chief, and as many in base. *Crest,* Over an esquire's helmet, nil.

28.

(*Ab.*) ANN, WIFE OF JOHN M. TREW—SHE WAS CALLED AWAY SUDDENLY, 29 MARCH 1842, AET. 42.

29.

10th DEC. 1780—DIED AT KINGSTON IN THE 54th YEAR OF HIS AGE, MR. ARCHIBALD CAMPBELL, AUTHOR OF "LEXIPHANES," &C.—(Roby.)

CAMPBELL was a purser in the navy, and is mentioned in Boswell's "Life of Dr. Johnson."

30.

(*Ab.*) FREDK. CHERRY, OB. 22 APL., 1798, AET. 40. FREDK. TREW CHERRY, OB. 24 NOV., 1786, AET. 8 HOURS. MARY ANN CHERRY, OB. 1792, SEPR. 18, AET 3M. 11 DAYS.

31.

INSCRIPTION obliterated.

Old tombstone; *Arms*, On a bend, three double quatrefoils. In sinister chief, a tower, or chess rook. *Crest*, on a demi-chess rook (or mural crown ?) a bird close.

32.

(*Ab.*) MRS. ELIZABETH ARMOUR, OB. OCT. 27, 1827, AET. 35. ALSO HER 3 CHILDREN, JOSEPH, JANE, & CATHERINE WORDIE, AGED RESPECTIVELY $2\frac{5}{12}$, $1\frac{6}{12}$, & 2 YEARS, IN 1825, 7 & 8. LIKEWISE, JOHN BEAN, ESQ., OB. AUGT. 6, 1837, AET. 31.

33.

(*Ab.*) ABNER MELLOR, ESQR., OB. SEP. 11, 1801, AGED 70—& MARY HIS WIFE, OB. 27 JUNE, 1796, AET. 62. ALSO, WM. MELLOR, ESQ., OB. 16 JULY, 1799, AGED 38, SON OF THE ABOVE, AND DOROTHY, DAUGHTER OF ABNER, OB. 7 NOV., 1778, AGED 6 YRS.

On another slab, on same tomb,

4 CHILDREN OF JAMES BROWN, BY HIS WIFE ANN, DAUR. OF ABNER & MARY MELLOR : MARY OB. 1791, ANNE OB. 1794 ; ABNER OB. 1794 ; WILLIAM OB. 1800— AGED RESPECTIVELY, 8 MTHS, 10 MTHS, 2 YRS, & 2 YRS & 3 MTHS.

34.

(*Ab.*) JOHN GRAHAM, ESQR., MERCHT., OB. 15 MARCH, 1799, AET. 74.

35.

BENEATH ARE INTERRED THE REMAINS OF B. S. ROWLEY ESQR., ADMIRAL OF THE BLUE, AND COMMANDER IN CHIEF OF HIS MAJESTY'S FLEET AT JAMAICA, WHO DIED ON THE 7th OF OCTOBER, A.D. MD.CCCXI., AGED 47 YEARS.

36.

(*Ab.*) CAPT. THOMAS STOPFORD, R.N., OB. 10 OCT., 1824.

15

37.

AGNES BAILEY DIED MAY 1st, 1749, IN THE 25th YEAR OF HER AGE.

38.

(*Ab.*) ELIZABETH RUTHERFORD, WIFE OF W. J. RUTHERFORD, OB. 8 OCT., 1837, AET. 38.

On a separate tablet,

MR. RICHARD BURGER, FATHER OF THE ABOVE, OB. 12th JANUARY, 1842, AET. 52.

39.

(*Ab.*) WILLIAM MEREDITH, ESQ., OF GOWICFS (*sic*), MONT-GOMERYSHIRE, NORTH WALES, OB. 13 JULY, 1770, AET. 42.

W. M. ; *Arms,* A lion rampant. *Crest,* Out of a ducal coronet, a wolf's head.

40.

HERE LIES INTERRED THE BODY—OF MR. JOHN EDSOR, LATE OF THE PARISH OF PORT ROYAL, IN THE ISLAND—OF JAMAICA, MERCHANT, WHO DEPARTED THIS LIFE THE 30th OF OCTOBER, 1745—AGED THIRTY—EIGHT YEARS.

W. M. ; On a shield, a rose tree ; the blossom struck by a sunbeam, while a cubit arm, from a cloud on the sinister side, clasps with the fingers the stem.

41.

(*Ab.*) SARAH HOLDEN, WIFE OF ROBERT HOLDEN, SUGAR BAKER, OB. 5 NOV., 1769, AET. 19.

W. M. ; *Arms,* A fess be-tween two chevronels ermine.   Between the fess and upper chev. a covered cup.   *Crest,* a bird (? dove).   *Motto,* " Non est mortali quod optio."

42.

HERE LIETH INTERR'D THE BODY OF ROBERT WATELY, OF KINGSTON, MERCHANT, WHO DEPARTED THIS LIFE, THE 26th OF OCTOBER, 1755, AGED 25 YEARS.

Arms, A lion rampant; on a chief three mullets. *Crest*, Over an esquire's helmet, a stag's head caboshed. *Motto*, " Pello Timorem."

43.

HERE LIES INTERR'D YE BODY OF FRANCIS HARDY, ESQ., WHO DEPARTED THIS LIFE YE 12 OF FEBRUARY, 173⅔.

Arms, A chev. between three griffins' heads, erased. *Crest*, Over an esquire's helmet, a cubit arm in armour, grasping a griffin's head erased.

44.

MRS. PRISILLA WILLIAMS, OB. 1736.

Arms, A chev. ermine be-tween three blackamoors' heads in profile, wreathed. *Crest*, Over an esquire's helmet, a stag's head caboshed.

45.

HERE LIE INTERRED THE BODIES OF MATTHEW HUGHES, LATE OF THIS TOWN, SHIPWRIGHT, (SON OF WALTER HUGHES, LATE OF YE TOWN OF SWANZEY, IN YE KINGDOM OF GREAT BRITAIN, GENTLEMAN, DECEASED) WHO DEPARTED THIS LIFE, THE 1st OF JULY, 1744, AGED 44 YEARS. AND OF MATTHEW, HIS SON, WHO WAS BORN THE 16th OF OCTR., 1734, AND ALSO (*sic*) DEPARTED THIS LIFE, THE 19th OF OCTR., 1737.

Arms, A chev. between three spears' heads imbrued. *Crest*, Over an esquire's helmet, a deer (?) at gaze.

15—2

46.

(*Ab.*) ALDERMAN LAUCHLAN MCLEAN, A NATIVE OF THE ISLAND OF COLL., N.B., OB. 15 OCT., 1829, AET. 43.

47.

(*Ab.*) ALFRED EARLE ROBBINS, OB. 18 MAY, 1852, AET. 48.

48.

NICHOLAS RABB—DIED—11th NOVR., 1833—AGED 61 YEARS.

49.

SACRED TO THE MEMORY OF—PETER WHEELAN—HENRIETTA ARDOUIN— RACHAEL WHEELAN—GEORGE ORRETT—MARY ANN TARRANT—MARTHA ORRETT.

No dates.

50.

(*Ab.*) ROBERT THOMSON, OF LORN, ESQ., DIED AT KINGSTON, JAMAICA, 14th OCT., 1801, AGED 45 YRS. HIS ONLY DAUGHTER, CATHERINE THOMSON, HATH CAUSED ERECT (*sic*) THIS STONE, &C., A.D. 1803.

51.

(*Ab.*) CAPT. JOSEPH EVERETT, OB. AT HONDURAS, 16th JANUARY, AET. 54. HIS FRIEND, MRS. MARY PHILLIPS, HAD HIS REMAINS INTERRED IN THIS VAULT, 22d JULY, 1792.

Also,

MARY SALT STEELE, INFANT DAUR. OF DANIEL STEELE AND SARAH PHILLIPS STEELE, BOTH (*sic*) OF WHOM DEPARTED THIS LIFE 3 OCT., 1797, AGED 6 MONTHS 3 DAYS.

52.

(*Ab.*) MR. SAMUEL RAINFORD, MERCHT., OB. 30 JULY, 1798, AET. 62. HE WAS A NATIVE OF ENGLAND—OF WALEZEY IN THE COUNTY OF CHESTER—(&) A RESIDENT FOR 34 YEARS IN JAMAICA. (ERECTED BY HIS BROTHER, MR. ROBERT RAINFORD.)

On the same tomb,

ALDERMAN ROBERT RAINFORD, OB. 8 SEP., 1803, AET. 46.

53.

HERE LYETH THE BODY—OF CAPT JAMES RAINFORD—OF LEIVERPOOLE WHDIOED (*sic*) NOVBRE. 21, 1734, AGED 32 YEARS.

Slab.

54.

MRS. HELEN ....

....

....

....

....

Covered.

55.

(*Ab.*) MR. EDMOND DENNES, OB. JUNE 15, 1745, AET. 51. ALSO HIS WIFE, MARY HORMSBY, OB. NOV. 12, 1764, AET. 65.

56.

(*Ab.*) MARY CARR, WIFE OF DAWKINS CARR, ESQ., COMMANDER OF THE "JUPITER," WHO DIED JUNE 4th 1798, AGED 28 YEARS.

57.

(*Ab.*) PETER RIENSSETT, ESQ., OB. AUG. 5, 1820, AET. 65. SARAH ALLEN JANE, DAUR. OF THE ABOVE, AND WIFE OF EDWARD CAMPBELL WOODGATE, ESQR., OB. MARCH 4, 1837, AET. 35.

W. M.

58.

(*Ab.*) THE REVD. CHARLES ALFRED COOPER, DURING TEN YEARS MINISTER OF THE DISTRICT OF ST. MARY'S, RURAL HILL, ST. THOMAS IN THE EAST. HE WAS BORN AT NEWPORT, IN THE COUNTY OF SHROPSHIRE, IN ENGLAND, AND DIED OF YELLOW FEVER, IN THIS CITY, 19th JUNE 1853, AGED 34.

Slab.

A TEXT follows.

59.

(*Ab.*) THOMAS CUMMING, ESQ., MERCHT., OB. 29 JULY, 1815, AET. 55. AND ROBT. MCCLELLAND, OB. 15 SEP., 1860.

N. B.—No relationship mentioned.

60.

(*Ab.*) HERE LIETH THE REMAINS OF MRS. ELIZABETH HOWELL, LATE WIFE OF MR. JOSEPH HOWELL, SHIPWRIGHT, OF THE ISLAND OF JAMAICA, OB. 24 JULY, 1779, AET. 42.

G. M.

61.

(*Ab.*) MRS. ELIZABETH SMITH, WIFE OF JOSEPH SMITH, CARPENTER IN KINGS-TON, OB. 24 OCT., 1768, AET. 40.

62.

IN MEMORIAM—PROBI COMMISQ' VIRI ROGERI GRADWELL—DE LIVERPOOLE NAUCLERI QUI FATIS CESSIT—15º JANUII, 1738, AETAT. 28—HUNC TUMULUM EREXIT FRATERNA PIETAS.

W. M.

63.

(*Ab.*) RICHARD NICOL, WHO ARRIVED IN THIS ISLAND, ON THE 7th DAY OF JANUARY, 1819, & DIED 26th JULY FOLLOWING, AGED 16 YEARS, 9 MTHS, 19 DAYS. ERECTED BY HIS ONLY SURVIVING BROTHER, JOHN NICOL.

64.

(*Ab.*) MR. RICHARD MARSDEN, MERCHT., OB. 15 OCTR., 1808, AET. 44 YRS, 3 MTHS, 12 D. ERECTED BY HIS WIDOW.

65.

(*Ab.*) THOS. FISHER, IN MEMORY OF HIS BROTHER, JOHN FISHER, LATE CABINET MAKER IN KINGSTON, OB. 1st NOV., 1804, AET. 67.

69.

MARY, WIFE OF THOS. MARCH, ESQ., OB. 6 NOV., 1820, AET. 19 YRS., 1 M., 8 DAYS.

70.

MRS. ALICE PIERCE WILLIAMS, LATE WIFE OF BARTHOLOMEW OWEN WILLIAMS, ESQ. (*Esq.* has been subsequently chiselled out), OF THIS CITY, OB. 20 OCT., 1805, AET. 39—8—22.

Also,

B. O. WILLIAMS, ESQ., HER HUSBAND, OB. 10 APRIL, 1830, AET. 66.

71.

(*Ab.*) THE REVD. FRANCIS HUMBERSTONE, BORN 16th JULY, 1791; DIED 9 AUGT., 1819.

"HE WAS A BURNING AND A SHINING LIGHT, AND YE WERE WILLING FOR A SEASON TO REJOICE IN HIS LIGHT."

72.

HERE LIETH THE BODY OF—ELIZABETH MASTERS WHO—DEPARTED THIS LIFE THE—14th DAY OF MAY, 1737, AGED 29 YEARS.

73.

HERE LIETH THE—BODY OF ANN, THE—DAUGHTER OF CHARLES AND MARGARET MONK—WHO DIED—THE 27th DAY OF NOVEMBER, 1743—AGED TWO YEARS AND 10 MONTHS.

ALSO SARAH THE DAUGHTER OF THE—ABOVE, DIED THE 30th DAY OF NOV.—1746—AGED 4 YEARS AND 12 DAYS—AND ALSO HERE LIETH THE BODY OF—MARGARET, YE DAUGHTER OF JOSEPH—AND MARGARET HARRIS WHO—DIED THE 29th DAY OF AUGUST 1753—AGED 19 MONTHS—AND ALSO, HERE LIETH THE BODY OF—JOSEPH HARRIS, LATE OF THIS TOWN—WHO DIED THE 6th DAY OF JULY, 1760—AGED 42 YEARS.

74.

(*Ab.*) WILLIAM MUIR MCMURDO, LATE MERCHANT OF THIS PLACE, TRANSLATED INTO THE ABODES OF FELICITY & PERFECTION ON THE 25th DAY OF JULY, 1795, IN THE 36th YEAR OF HIS AGE.

Also,

BARTHOLOMEW WILLIAMS, ESQ., LATE MERCHANT OF THIS CITY, DIED 22 JANUARY, 1847, AET. 60.

ALICE PIERCE WILLIAMS, SISTER OF THE ABOVE, OB. 21st AUGT., 1862, AET. 63.

75.

(*Ab.*) DIED IN THIS CITY—ON THE 7th OF JUNE, 1828—JOHN ALLEN ADAMS, ESQ.—AGED 56 YEARS.

76.

HERE LIES INTERRED—THE BODY OF CAPT. WILLIAM BURNS—LATE OF THIS TOWN, MARINER, WHO—DEPARTED THIS LIFE THE 10th—OF SEPTEMBER, 1800, IN THE 62d YEAR OF HIS AGE.

77.

(*Ab.*) JOHN NICOLL, BORN 27 SEP., 1793. ALSO WILLIAM NICOLL, BORN 24th SEP., 1795, SONS OF JOHN AND ANN NICOLL OF THIS PARISH—THE FORMER DIED 11 OCT., 1793, & THE LATTER, 19th JULY, 1798, &C.

78.

(*Ab.*) CHLOTILDA, WIFE OF ROBERT BARCLAY, OB. 9 JUNE, 1824, AET. 19, &C. ALSO PHILIP LAMBERT, OB. 15 NOV., 1845, AET. 36.

THE name *Clotilda* occurs in the pedigree of Barclay, Bart., of Pierston.

79.

(*Ab.*) JOHN WIGGLESWORTH, ESQR., LATE COMMISSARY GENERAL FOR THE ISLAND OF ST. DOMINGO, OBIIT 21st MARCH, 1800, AETATIS . . . . (the space not filled in). ALSO WILLIAM LANCASTER WHITFIELD, ESQ., MERCHT., OF THIS CITY, MEM. OF ASSLY., &C., OB. 17 OCT., 1824, AETSTIS (SIC) 45 YEAR.

80.

(*Ab.*) WILLIAM PADMORE, BORN OCT. 12, 1811, DIED 7 JUNE, 1812.
GEORGE PADMORE, BORN 26th APL., 1816, DIED AT PORT ROYAL 2 JANY., 1821.
JOHN PADMORE, BORN 4 JUNE, 1817, DIED ON THE 21st OF THE SAME MONTH.
ALEXR. PADMORE, BORN 4 NOV., 1819, DIED 11 FEB., 1820.
GEORGE PADMORE, BORN 15 MAY, 1822, DIED 7 JUNE, 1825.

> " REST, SPOTLESS BABES, BENEATH THIS STONE,
> CROPT LIKE THE FLOWERS IN EARLY BLOOM ;
> SAFE FROM THE ILLS OF WORLDLY STRIFE
> WHICH PLANT WITH THORNS A LENGTH OF LIFE."

ALEXR. PADMORE, BORN 6th FEBY., 1829, DIED 10th JANY., 1830.
WILLIAM ALEXR. PADMORE, BORN 21st SEP., 1785, DIED 25th NOV., 1832, AGED 47 YEARS.
MRS. M. A. PADMORE, DIED 27th JANUARY, 1834, AGED 46 YEARS.

81.

SACRED TO THE MEMORY OF—AGNES LETITIA, INFANT DAUGHTER OF HIS EXCELLENCY, SIR LIONEL SMITH, GOVERNOR & CAPTAIN GENERAL OF THIS ISLAND—DIED 17th NOVEMBER, 1836.

SHE was his daughter, by his second wife, Isabella C. Pottinger.—*See* " Baronetage," " Smith *now* Gordon," and " Pottinger."

82.

JOSEPH DONNELL, ESQUIRE, MANY YEARS A RESPECTABLE MERCHANT OF THIS CITY, OB. 29th NOV., 1828, AET. 62.

83.

(*Ab.*) JOSEPH PIERCY, ESQ., ACTING PAYMASTER TO H.M.'S 85th REGT., OB. 3d DEC., 1807, AET. 35.

FOUR verses follow.

84.

(*Ab.*) ANN SAVAGE, OB. 26 SEP., 1819, AET. 64—WILLIAM SAVAGE, OB. 23 OCT., 1827, AET. 76—MARY TILLY, OB. 11th NOV., 1839, AET. 59—ELIZA ANN, WIFE OF JAMES HEIGHINTON, OB. 14th JULY, 1843, AET. 39. (ERECTED BY HER HUSBAND.) ALSO MR. RICHARD MUNDS, OB. 19 NOV., 1860, AET. 71.

85.

MARK O'SULLIVAN, ESQ., OF THIS CITY, OB. 3 NOV., 1823, AET. 74, & 47 YEARS A RESIDT. IN THIS ISLAND.

86.

(*Ab.*) THOMAS HARTMAN, SON OF THOS. & ELIZA LOUISA FISHER, OB. 10 JANY., 1839, AET. 8 Y. 5 D. ALSO ANNE ELIZA HARTMAN, DAUR. OF THOS. & ELIZA LOUISA FISHER, OB. 30 OCT., 1831, AET. 9 Y. 6 20 D.

VERSES follow.

87.

MRS. ELIZABETH DICKSON, OB. 5 JULY, 1803, AET. 75.

88.

(*Ab.*) MR. PETER MCNEAL, OB. 10th NOV., 1800, AET. 58, — 32 YEARS A RESIDENT IN THIS ISLAND.—A WORTHY MAN AND HIGHLY RESPECTED.

89.

(*Ab.*) GEORGE BEAK, ESQ., ATTORNEY AT LAW, OB. 17 JUNE, 1823, AET. 45,— 20 YEARS A RESIDENT, &C.

90.

(*Ab.*) CAPT. JAMES C. STEWART, LATE HARBOUR MASTER OF KINGSTON, OB. 16 MARCH, 1841, AET. 53.

91.

JAMES EVANS, WIFE OF EDWARD EVANS, SHIPWRIGHT OF THIS TOWN, OB. 7 AUGT., 1795, AET. 24, AND JOHN EVANS, HIS BROTHER, OB. 19 JULY, 1796, AET. 26.

92.

(*Ab.*) ALEXR. FULLERTON, ESQ., OB. 4 JANY., 1850, AET. 62.—ALSO HIS WIFE, ANN FULLERTON, OB. 7 NOV., 1855, AET. 49. ALSO ELIZABETH, WIFE OF ALEXR. FULLERTON, DY. ORDNANCE STOREKEEPER, OB. 9 SEP., 1825, AET. 33.

93.

(*Ab.*) CAPT. PETER COCHRAN, 35 YEARS, HARBOUR MASTER OF KINGSTON, OB. 8 JANY., 1829, AET. 74.

94.

(*Ab.*) JAMES MORRIS, ESQ., MERCHANT, OB. 17 JUNE, 1811, AET. 66.

95.

(*Ab.*) JAMES BRYDON, ESQ., MERCHT., OB. 7 AUGT., 1840, AET. 44: HE WAS AN ALDERMAN OF KINGSTON, AND MEM. OF ASSEMBLY.

96.

(*Ab.*) HUGH WRIGHT, ESQ., MERCHT., OB. 25 NOV., 1819, AET. 38.

97.

A Slab turned on its side, and showing only the name "WILLIAM."

98.

IN MEMORY OF ANN WATER, A NATIVE OF—THIS ISLAND, AND MOTHER-IN-LAW TO JOSEPH NOTT. SHE—DEPARTED THIS LIFE THE 19th—OF APRIL, 1737, IN THE 80th YEAR—OF HER AGE.

ELIZABETH NOTT, WIFE OF JOSEPH NOTT & DAU. OF G. WALTER, OB. 1764, —OCT. 6,—AET. 73, &C., &C.

99.

(*Ab.*) HENRY TURTON, OF THIS PLACE, GENTLEMAN, OB. 16 NOV., 1779, AET. 42. HE WAS A NATIVE OF OLVESTON, GLOCESTERSHIRE IN ENGLAND. ALSO WILLIAM HIS SON, OB. 29 AUGT., 1781, AET. 4—JAMES, HIS SON, OB. 29 MARCH, 1814, AET. 35.—&C., &C., &C.

100.

(*Ab.*) WILLIAM LEADLEY, OB. 21 MAY, 1835, AET. 35. HIS WIDOW, SUSAN BERDOE, OB. 8 JUNE, 1839, AET. 36.

101.

HIC JACET HENRICUS GULIELMUS SMYTH—FRANCISCI GEORGII SMYTH—
ARMIGERI DE GOSHEN, IN—PAROCHIA HUJUS INSULAE—STA ELIZABETHA—FILII
NATU SECUNDI.—LONDINI NATUS—OBIIT KINGSTONAE, DIE NOVEMBRIS VICESSIMO
TERTIO, AN. D. MDCCCXXV. AETATIS SUAE XXII.

102.

HERE LIE THE REMAINS—OF—ALEXR. SINCLAIR, OF MURR, AYRSHIRE, N.B.,
WHO DIED 20th JANY., 1825, AGED 19 YEARS.

·103.

(*Ab.*) GARRET DAGHERTY, OB. 22 AUGT., 1809, AET. 40.

104.

(*Ab.*) JOSEPH HARRIS, SON OF JOHN HARRIS, OF BRISTOL, ARRIVED IN JA-
MAICA 17 MAY, AND DIED JUNE 9th, 1798, AET. 30.

105.

(*Ab.*) MR. ROBERT AGUILAR, OB. 19 FEB., 1859.

106.

(*Ab.*) JOHN GRAHAM, ESQR., MERCHT., OB. MARCH 15, 1799, AET. 74.

107.

(*Ab.*) ROBT. R. P. THURTLE, ESQUIRE, LATE OF LONDON, DIED AFTER A RESI-
DENCE IN THE ISLAND OF TWO MONTHS, APRIL 30, 1835, AET. 44. (ERECTED
BY WIDOW.)

108.

NATHANIEL MARSTON, ESQ., LATE OF THIS CITY, BORN 30 JUNE, 1798, OB.
18 JANY., 1831.—ALSO LOUISA, DAUR. OF NATHL. & SARAH MARSTON, BORN 27
MAY, 1826, DIED 7 FEB., 1840.—ALSO CHARLES ROBERTSON DEWDNEY, BORN 6
DECR., 1831, DIED 29 JULY, 1834.—ALSO EDWARD WEIR DEWDNEY, INFANT SON
OF CHARLES & CHARLOTTE DEWDNEY, BORN 14 JULY, 1834, DIED 25 DEC. 1836.

SEE table of Pedigree, p. 123.

109.

S. M.—CAROLI BLACKWELL, M.D., FIL. ET FRAT. T. T. BLACKWELL, IN ACAD.
MARISCALL. ABREDACENSI, GYMNASIARCHARUM—CUI SUMMUM INGENIUM—SUM-
MA OPE EXCULTUM—PRIMITIAS IN ARTE SUA—DETULIT IMMATURE—RAPTUS BONIS
DOCTISQUE—FLEBILIS SIBI NOMEN SUIS—MOESTITIAM, INSULAE HUIC—DESIDE-
RIUM RELIQUIT—Aº. AETAT. XXXIIX. (*sic*).

MARITO BENE MER., UXOR MOER. P.

(*sic*) ALSO HENRY CROFT PRINCE, SON OF THOMAS & MARY ANN PRINCE,
DEPARTED THIS LIFE 20th NOV. 1798, AGED 3 MONTHS.

110.

(*Ab.*) MR. MICHAEL PARKER, OB. 9 NOV., 1779, AET. 24. ALSO JOSEPH PAR-KER, ESQ., OB. 14 JUNE, 1783, AGED 41. ALSO JAMES WORSFOLD, ESQ., OB. 3 FEB., 1787, AET. 42. ALSO GEO. PARKER, ESQ., OB. 17 OCT., 1787, AET. 48.

111.

(*Ab.*) JOHN POTTER, ESQ., OB. 16 OCT., 1845, AET. 72.

THERE was a family of Potter, supposed to have come from "Ogbourne" at an early period, to Jamaica, whereof was Elizabeth P., 1st w. of Sir N. Lawes (m. 1680, d. 1681).

112.

(*Ab.*) ROBERT MURRAY OF THE PAR. OF VERE, MERCHT., OB. 19 MARCH, 1795, AET. 45. A DUTIFULL SON & A KIND FRIEND.

113.

MAURICE WEST, OB. 16 SEP., 1832—SARAH HIS WIFE, OB. 18 MARCH, 1820—ALSO THEIR SONS, WM. HENRY, OB. 28 JUNE, 1822—STEWART, OB. 12 NOV., 1830. MAURICE, OB. 31 JUNE, 1830. ALSO THEIR NEPHEW WILLIAM HENRY, OB. 17 JULY, 1835.

114.

JAMES PEAKE HUNT, SON OF JAS. & SOPHIA HUNT, OF THIS CITY, OB. 18 JUNE, 1795, AGED 2 MTHS. ALSO HESTER MARY HUNT, HIS SISTER, OB. 30 SEP. 1809, AET. 13 & 1 M. ALSO THEIR BRO. CHARLES GEORGE, OB. 9 NOV. 1809—AET. 2 YR. 9 M. ALSO EDWD. JAMES HUNT, WHO DIED AT BROMPTON, NEAR LONDON, 18 MAY, 1813, AGED 12. ALSO THE SAID SOPHIA HUNT, MOTHER OF THE ABOVE, OB. 26 JUNE, 1835, AET. 73. — LIKEWISE WM. AUGUSTUS HUNT, LATE HEAD MASTER AT WOLMER'S FREE SCHOOL, AND LAST SURVIVING SON OF THE ABOVE, OB. 21 NOV. 1852, AET. 50.

A BRANCH of the Barbadian family of Hunt (whereof was Leigh Hunt, the eminent author, and his son, Thornton Hunt, a highly-esteemed member of the press, &c.) settled in Jamaica, where many notices of it occur in the public records.

In the register of St. Catherine's, Jamaica, is recorded the marriage of a Thomas Hunt and Anne Allen, in 1674. The following is from a MS. of the Hon. Mr. Justice W. D. Bruce :—"John Hunt, of Jamaica (1713), had by his w., Susanna, a son, John of Barbados, and two daurs.; Richard, bro. of John H., senr., was of Barbados, and had two sons, Richard and John."

115.

(*Ab.*) JOHN WILLAN, LATE MERCHT. OF THIS TOWN, OB. 6th MARCH, 1794, AET. 28. ALSO MRS. ELIZAB. JANE NORTON, WIDOW, OB. 6 APL., 1795, AET. 50.

116.

(*Ab.*) JANE, WIFE OF JASPER FARMER CARGILL, BARR. AT LAW, BORN 20 JUNE, 1810, OB. 30, SEP., 1842.

117.

(*Ab.*) CORNELIUS DALY, OB. 6 APL., 1800, AET. 48.

118.

(*Ab.*) WILLIAM ROSEMAN, MERCHT., (ERECTED THIS TOMB) IN MEMORY OF HIS MOTHER, ELINOR ROSEMAN, WHO DIED 30 MAY, 1754, AET. 40.

119.

(*Ab.*) PHILIP MCDONALD, ESQ., MERCHT., DIED AT CASHERE GROVE, PEN., SEP. 5, 1823, AET. 33.—ALSO THOMAS, HIS ELDEST SON, OB. 22 NOV. 1828, AET. 5 YRS. 11 MTHS.

120.

ROBERT STIRLING, ESQ., OF HAMPTON, IN THE PARISH OF ST. JAMES—FIFTH SON OF WILLIAM STIRLING, OF KEIR, IN THE COUNTY OF PERTHSHIRE, SCOTLAND, WHO DIED SEPTEMBER THE 28th, 1808, AGED 36 YEARS.

THIS family is now represented by Sir W. Stirling Maxwell, Bart., of Pollok. The branches of Kippenross and Kippendavie were also connected with Jamaica. Patrick, s. of John S., of the latter, m. a dau. of George Wedderburn, of Par. Westmoreland ; and Wm. S., his yr. bro., m. the dau. and h. of Henry Barrett, of Cinnamon Hill.—*See* "Baronetage."

121.

(*Ab.*) HERE LIETH THE BODY OF CHRISTIANA BETHUNE, DAUGHTER TO JOHN AND MARY ANNE BETHUNE, WHO DEPARTED THIS LIFE THE 15th OCTR. 90, AGED 6 YEARS. ALSO DONCAN JOHN BETHUNE, WHO DEPARTED THIS LIFE THE 29th DECEMR., 90, AGED 13 MONTHS.

122.

(*Ab.*) MR. JOHN EVANS, LATE OF NESTON, IN CHESHIRE, OB. 5 DEC. 1761, AET. 27.

123.

GEORGE CRIMBLE SHERSTONE, SON OF ARTHUR & ELIZABETH SHERSTONE, OB. 7 NOVR., 1746, AET. 2 Y. 8 D. ALSO ELIZABETH PRICE, MOTHER OF ELIZABETH SHERSTONE, OB. 1 SEP., 1754, AET. 53 YEARS, 6 MONTHS, & 19 DAYS. ALSO SAMUEL LEWIS, SON OF JOHN & ELIZABETH LEWIS (FATHER OF THE ABOVE NAMED SAMUEL LEWIS), OB. 14 OCT., 1770, AET. 39 . 11 . 12 DAYS.

124.

(*Ab.*) ROBERT FREDERICK SPEARMAN EPPES, 3D SON OF DY. COMMISSARY GENERAL EPPES, DIED OF YELLOW FEVER 1st AUGUST, 1849, AET. 7 YEARS $\frac{6}{12}$

125.

(*Ab.*) HON. HECTOR MITCHEL, MAYOR, & CUSTOS ROT. OF KINGSTON, MEM. OF ASSLY., &C., OB. 27 MAY, 1853, AET. 74.

126.

(*Ab.*) HENRY ROBARTS HIBBERT, YOUNGEST SON OF GEO. HIBBERT, OF LONDON, AGENT FOR THIS ISLAND, OB. 14 JULY, 1825, AET. 20.

FOR an account of this family, and that of Nembhard, *see* Burke's "Landed Gentry," ed. 1871.

127.

(*Ab.*) HONBLE. GEO. KINGHORNE, ESQ.—CUSTOS ROT. OF KINGSTON, MERCHANT, OB. AFTER AN ILLNESS OF 5 YEARS—SEPTR. 6, 1823, AET. 73.

128.

(*Ab.*) MARY, WIFE OF WALTER BUOR LODGE, OB. 10 FEB. 1745, AET. 32.

129.

(*Ab.*) MR. PATRICK TURNER, MERCHT., OF KINGSTON, OB. 4 FEB. 1767, AET. 28.

130.

MILBE JOHNSON OF THIS PARISH, PLANTER, OB. JUNE 2^d, 1778, AGED 53. LIKEWISE WILLIAM JOHNSON, OB. 12 AUGT., 1755, AGED 5 MTHS—SUSANNA JOHNSON, OB. 18 JUNE, 1757, AET. 9 MTHS. ANN JOHNSON, OB. 31 JANUARY, 1763, AET. 1 YR.—CHILDREN OF THE ABOVE.

131.

(*Ab.*) ANDREW PETERKIN, OB. JULY 26, 1815, AET. 62.
Also,
MR. GEO. CALDER, OB. 14 DEC, 1815, AET. 22. ALSO MISS ELIZABETH BOWIE, OB. 4 NOV. 1818, AET. 18 MTHS. 8 DAYS 12.—MARY ANN BOWIE, OB. 4 MAY, 1820, AET. 15 MTHS. ALSO GEO. CALDER, SENIOR, OB. 15 JUNE, 1821, AGED 64 YEARS. ALSO MR. JOHN MACFEEAT......1824. (Imperfect.)

132.

(*Ab.*) CHARLES WALPOLE GROSSETT, ESQ., OB. 31 MARCH, 1852, AET. 25. YOUNGT. SON OF THE CUSTOS OF ST. GEORGE'S PAR.

SEE " Peerage," " Orford," Robert, 4th s. of Sir Robert, m. in 1780, Diana, d. of W. Grosset.

133.

(*Ab.*) MR. JOHN REIDHEAD, OB. 7 FEB., 1821, AET. 35.

134.

WILLIAM JAMES IRONFOUNDER, OB. NOV. 14, 1816, AET. 52. ALSO THOMAS JAMES IRONFOUNDER, HIS NEPHEW, OB. 9 SEP. 1825, AET. 27, & SON OF HIS BROTHER & COPARTNER THOMAS. ALSO ELIZABETH JAMES, SISTER OF THE ABOVE WILIAM & THOMAS, DIED AT ST. JOHN'S, NEW BRUNSWICK, 28th FEBY., 1829 AET. 23. ALSO THEIR FATHER, WILLIAM JAMES, OB. 9 JULY, 1841, AET. 45.

135.

THE REVD. JOSEPH BETHUNE, A.M., FORMERLY MINISTER OF THE ESTABLISHED CHURCH OF SCOTLAND, AT RENTON, OB. 5th JUNE, 1800. ALSO WALTER REID, OB. DEC. 3^d, 1804, AET. 4 Y., $\frac{5}{12}$. STEPHEN REID, OB. DEC. 7, 1804, AET. 14 MTHS. MARY REID, OB. OCT. 29, 1807, AET. 1, $\frac{10}{12}$. MARGARET REID, OB. MAY 12, 1808, AET. $\frac{8}{12}$. MARY ANN, WIFE OF CHARLES BROWN, OB. 28 OCT., 1814, AET. 30, THEIR BELOVED CHILD CHARLES BEST, OB. 26, NOV. FOLLG , AET. 4 YRS. 8 DAYS.

E. C. BROWN, M.D. OF GLASGOW UNIVERSITY, OB. NOV. 1, 1835, AET. 20, $\frac{4}{12}$. EBEN-EZER REID, OB. 25 MAY, 1843, AET. 66. ELIZABETH, HIS WIFE, OB. 13 MARCH, 1845, AET. 37 & $\frac{10}{12}$, AND WALTER BUCHANAN REID, OB. NOV. 8, 1847, AET 35.

136.

EDWARD, ONLY SON OF WILLIAM .... VIMPANY (?) OF THE PARISH OF ST. JAMES IN THE CITY OF BRISTOL, GENT., BY MARY, HIS WIFE. WHO DEPARTED THIS LIFE THE 17th DAY OF AUGUST, 1736, AET. 17 YEARS, ... (on the same) .... NEPHEW OF CAPT. STOKES.................. DEAR ......HIS PARENTS JOY—BEWAILED...FLIGHT...LIGHT.

137.

MRS. ELIZ................ SMITH, WIFE OF MR. .... W. II.

138.

(*Ab.*) JOHN RIENSSETT, ESQ., OB. 22 DEC., 1826, AET. 47.
(ERECTED BY HIS SON.)

139.

(*Ab.*) EDWARD LYNCH NEMBHARD, OB. 13 MAY, 1779, AET. 5 YRS. 9 MTHS. & 5 DAYS, 5TH SON OF JOHN AND ANN NEMBHARD, OF THE PARISH OF ST. MARY. SEE note to *Hibbert*.

140.

(*Ab.*) ELIZABETH, WIFE OF MR. JAMES STEWART, OF KINGSTON, BLACKSMITH, OB. 29th JANY., 1734, AET. 36. LIKEWISE JAMES, SON OF THE ABOVE, OB. NOV. 15, 1751, AET. 10 YRS.

141.

(*Ab.*) MR. HENRY LANG, OB. MARCH 20, 1739, AET. 31.

142.

(*Ab.*) ELIZABETH WOODCOCK, OB. 30 APL., 1805, AET. 39.

143.

(*Ab.*) WILLM. CARGILL, ESQ., OB. 13 JANUARY, 1819, AET. 49.

Robert Dallas, of Dallas Castle, Jamaica=Elizabeth, d. of Col. T. Cormack.

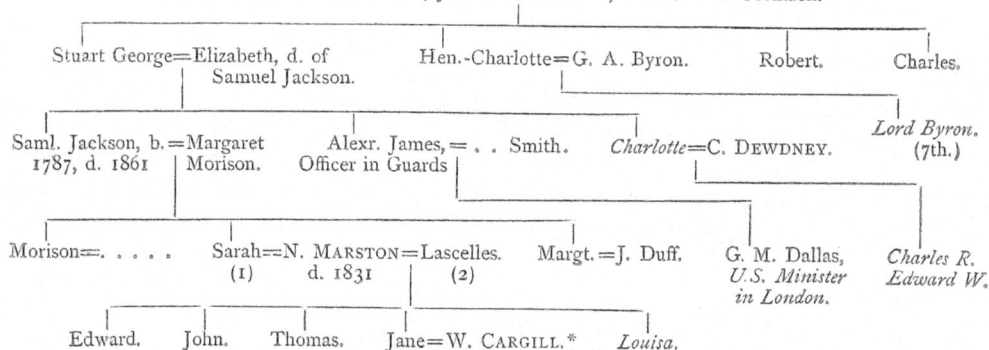

Stuart George=Elizabeth, d. of Samuel Jackson. Hen.-Charlotte=G. A. Byron. Robert. Charles.

Saml. Jackson, b.=Margaret Morison. 1787, d. 1861 Alexr. James, = . . Smith. Officer in Guards *Charlotte*=C. DEWDNEY. *Lord Byron.* (7th.)

Morison=. . . . . Sarah=N. MARSTON=Lascelles. (1) d. 1831 (2) Margt. =J. Duff. G. M. Dallas, *U.S. Minister in London.* *Charles R. Edward W.*

Edward. John. Thomas. Jane=W. CARGILL.* *Louisa.*

---

* Thomas, son of Col. P. Beckford (1731), "slain, it is believed, in an encounter with one, *Cargill.*"—MS. of C. E. Long. This is the earliest notice the author has found of this name in Jamaica.

144.

MRS. MARTHA CARFRAE, WIFE OF JAMES CARFRAE, OF THIS CITY, OB. 17 APL., 1816, AET. 40.

145.

JOHN ROXBURGH, JUNR., OB. 7 SEP., 1770, AET. 18 MTHS.—MARTHA, HIS MOTHER, AND WIFE OF JOHN ROXBURGH, GOLDSMITH, OF THIS CITY, OB. 15 NOVR., 1776, AET. 41, &C., &C.—ALSO, JOHN MOYLE, OB. 24 JANY., 1838, AET. $\frac{9}{12}$.—MARGARET MOYLE, OB. 18 FEBY., 1841, AET. 1 YR.—ANNETTE ORMISTON, OB. 28 JULY, 1841, AET. 3 YRS.—CHILDREN OF THE REVD. T. B. TURNER, ISLAND CURATE, &C., &C.—SARAH ANN TURNER, MOTHER OF THE SAID THREE CHILDREN, OB. 20 JULY, 1856, AET. 38.

146.

(*Ab.*) MR. EDWARD COWELL, MERCHANT OF THIS CITY, OB. 30 AUGT., 1841, AET. 68.—ALSO, CHARLOTTE, HIS WIFE, OB. 22 SEP., 1854, AET. 79.

147.

HENRIETTA S. ABRAHAMS, DIED 1st NOVR., 1857, AGED 4 MONTHS.

148.

(*Ab.*) MRS. E. S. COX, OB. NOV. 8, 1844.

149.

MARY AIKMAN AND LOUISA SUSANNA WELLS......CHILDREN OF JAMES SMITH AND FRANCES, HIS WIFE—BORN AT MONTEGO BAY, 3d DEC. 1840—DIED IN KINGSTON, 10 AUGT., 1844. (The rest covered up.)

150.

(*Ab.*) MRS. PHILLIS SAUNDERS, OB. 11 DEC., 1781, AET. 35.—ALSO TWO OF HER CHILDREN—MARY, OB. 10 APRIL, 1780, AET. 3 MTHS. AND 25 DAYS—SUS-ANNA, OB. 19 NOV. 1781, AET. 3 MTHS.

151.

(*Ab.*) EMMA MARRIOTT PEN[?R]KINS, OB. 16 APL., 1830, AET. 3 Y. 8 M. 17 D., &C., &C.

152.

(*Ab.*) MRS. ELIZABETH DONALDSON, OB. 10 MARCH, 1841, AET. 80. (HER GRANDCHILDREN SURVIVING).

153.

(*Ab.*) MR. WILLM. COUPLAND, OB. 9 JUNE, 1811, AET. 34.

154.

(*Ab.*) WM. P[? B]RANCH, MERCHT., OB. 17 FEB., 1811, AET. 39.

155.

(*Ab.*) JAMES BIGGAR, ESQ., A NATIVE OF DUMFRIES, AND MERCHT. OF KING-STON, OB. 25 JUNE, 1814, AET. 25. HIS AFFECTIONATE UNCLE, JAMES WALKER, ESQ., ERECTED THIS MONUMENT.—IN THE SAME GRAVE, ALSO IS INTERRED HIS YOUNGER BROTHER, JOHN BIGGAR, ESQR., OB. 13 JULY, 1829.

156.

(*Ab.*) HONBLE. JOHN NETHERSOLE, CUST. ROT., BORN 2d JUNE, 1791, OB. 4 JUNE, 1862. HE ARRIVED IN JAMAICA, 9 JUNE, 1808.

157.

(*Ab.*) ELIZA, DAUR. OF BOSWELL MIDDLETON, AND ELIZA, HIS WIFE, DIED 7th JANUARY, 1836, AGED 10 MONTHS.

158.

(*Ab.*) JAMES DYKON, ESQ., OB. 25 NOV., 1801, AET. 30 YRS. 8 MTHS. 10 DAYS.

159.

(*Ab.*) EDWARD NATHANIEL BANCROFT, ESQR., M.D., DEPY. INSPT. GENL. OF ARMY HOSPLS., OB. 18 SEP., 1842, AET. 70—ALSO HIS WIFE, URSULA HILL, OB. 31 JANY., 1830, AET. 40. GEORGE AUGUSTUS B., OB. 11 MAY, 1824, AET. 5 MTHS. CHAS. AUGUSTUS B., OB. 11 APRIL, 183..., AET. 7 WEEKS. URSULA MARIA B., OB. 30 AUGT., 1840, AET. 24.—CHILDREN OF THE ABOVE E. N. B. & U. H.

160.

ELIZABETH SALLY BERRY, DIED 5th NOVR., 1795, AGED ...... (the date not inserted). RICHARD BERRY, DIED 10th FEBY., 1797, AGED 37.

161.

CHARLES ARMSTRONG, INFT. SON OF DAVID & MARY BRANDON, OB. 30 MAY, 1852, AET. $1\frac{11}{12}$. ALSO OLETHIA CONSTANTIA, THEIR DAUR., NAT. OCT., 1857, OB. 21 AUGT., 1858.

162.

(*Ab.*) WILLM. HODGSON, OB. 6 FEB., 1843, AET. 2.

163.

HEAR LYES THE BODY OF ELIZABETH PYICE WACOMB, WHO DEPARTED THIS LIFE SEP. 23d, 1813, AGED 47 YEARS & 6 MTHS. ALSO HER SISTER, SARAH, OB. 3d MARCH, 1822, AET. 53 YRS. 10 MTHS.

N.B.—The letters of the inscription are intermixed capitals and italics.

164.

(*Ab.*) J. C. L. HART, DIED 7th MARCH, 1850, AET. 22.

165.

HERE LIES THE BODY OF MISS ELIZABETH EYEY—WHO DEPARTED THIS LIFE THE 22d DAY OF JANUARY, ...07, AGED 45 YEARS.

166.

(*Ab.*) JUANA, INFT. DAUR. OF ALEXR. NAAR DEGRAFF, ESQR., OB. 4 JULY, 1862, AET. 18 MTHS.

167.

THE FAMILY VAULT OF FRANCIS PITT. 1790.

168.

(*Ab.*) WELLWOOD HYSLOP, ESQR., M. OF ASSLY. FOR PT. ROYAL, OB. 16 FEB., 1845, AET. 65.

169.

IN SPE LAETAE RESURRECTIONIS—SUB HOC MARMORE JACET CORPUS—CLEMENTI HOY FOYSTER—QUI OBIIT 6o DIE DECEMBRIS, 1763—ANNO QUARTO AETATIS SUAE—ITEM (QUI PRIUS INSCRIBI OPORTUIT)

MARIAE ⎫ FOYSTER, ⎧ 9 NOV., 1746, AET. ...
JOSHUAE ⎬ OB. ⎨ 21 NOV., 1752, AET. 4.
MARIAE ⎭ ⎩ 29 SEP., 1758, AET. 5.

Remainder abridged and in English.

170.

(*Ab.*) CLEMENT FOYSTER, OB. 30 JULY, 1765, AET. 2. CALEB FOYSTER, FATHER OF THE ABOVE, OB. 13 MAY, 1777, AET. 69, &C.

171.

(*Ab.*) ELIZABETH LYNCH, OB. 2 APRIL, 1762, AET. 30.

172.

MR. WM. LEWIS, SURGEON, WHO DYED NOVR. 8th, 1753, IN THE 44th YEAR OF HIS AGE.

173.

MRS. ELIZABETH WELLS, WIFE OF MR. RICHARD WELLS, WHO DEPARTED THIS LIFE IN GREAT BRITAIN, THE 4th JANY. 1766, AGED 43 YEARS—ALSO THEIR SONS AND DAURS. :

THOMAS, OB. NOV. 4, 1753, AET. 4.

MARY, OB. JANY. 7, 1754, AET. 2.

SARAH, OB. NOV. 1, 1763.

ELIZABETH, OB. FEB. 26, 1764.

ANN, DIED IN GT. BRIT., FEB. 28, 1769, AET. 13.

ALSO THE CHILDREN OF THE SAID RICHARD, BY HIS SECOND WIFE:

             CHARLES ....

             BERKLEY ....

             RICHARD ....

             JOHN ....

PARTIALLY covered.

174.

(*Ab.*) DAVID BLACK, OB. 23 SEP., 1813.

175.

JOHN CORAM, OB. NOV. 23, ...04, AGED 27 YEARS. MRS. E. H. MANING, OB. JULY 6, 1852, AGED 72. SOPHIA STANLEY PALMES, OB. NOVR. 8, 1853, AET. 15 MTHS.

176.

(*Ab.*) MARY ANNE BERGE, OB. 22 JUNE, 1844, AET. 74.

177.

(*Ab.*) MR. GEO. LEE, OB. 6 OCT., 1813, AET. 43. ERECTED BY HIS FRIENDS.

178.

(*Ab.*) J. G. LORRAIN, OB. 12 DEC., 1812, AET. 47. ALSO HIS WIFE, SUSAN MARGARET, OB. 15 JANY., 1829, AET. 63.

179.

(*Ab.*) JAMES LAWSON, ESQ., OB. 8 DEC., 1803, AET. 38.

180.

LARGE tomb, without any tablet or inscription.

181.

HERE LYETH THE BODY OF ELIZABETH, LATE [WIFE OF WILLIAM GORDON, ESQR.—WHO DEPARTED THIS LIFE—FEBRUY. THE 2nd, 1727, AGED 28 YEARS.— ALSO THE BODY OF THEIR SON—WILLIAM, WHO DEPARTED THIS—LIFE AUGUST YE 10th, 1725, AGED ONE YEAR AND 4 MONTHS. LIKEWISE THE BODY OF

17—2

THEIR SON—JOHN, WHO DEPARTED THIS LIFE—OCTOBER THE 24th, 1725, AGED —14 DAYS.

W. M. Slab.

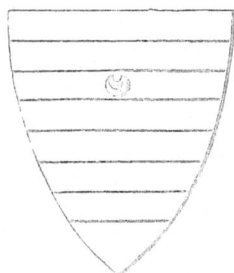

182.

...... LYES THE BODY OF—JOSEPH POVNTZ—OF KINGSTON, IN YE ISLAND—OF JAMAICA—MERCHANT—WHO DEPARTED THIS LIFE ON—... 24 DAY OF SEPTEMBER, 1728— AGED 37 YEARS—

"TEACH US THE NUMBER OF OUR DAYS, THAT WE MAY APPLY OURSELVES TO WISDOM."

Psalm xc. 12.

W. M. Slab ; *Arms*, Barry of eight, on third bar a crescent. *Crest*, Over an esquire's helmet, a dexter hand closed.

183.

(*Ab.*) ARCHIBALD GARBRAND, ESQ., OB. JULY 5, 1798, AGED 36 YEARS.—ALSO JANUARY 25th, 1789, DIED W...... GARBRAND, SON OF ARCHIBALD, AGED 11[?] YEARS, DEC. 15, 1789.—ALSO—MARY ANN GARBRAND, AGED [3 YEARS ?].

Altar Tomb.

184.

(*Obl.*) PHARAOH WHO .... THIS LYFE 27 DEC., 1804, AGED 48 YEARS.

185.

HERE LYETH THE BODY OF—MRS. ANN STEPHENSON—THE WIFE OF—MR. ROBERT STEPHENSON—OF THE PARISH OF KINGSTON—CARPENTER, WHO DEPARTED—THIS LIFE THE 19th DAY OF AUGUST—1783, AGED 37 YEARS.

N. B.—This slab lies on the top of another, of which the only inscribed portion seen bears :—

THE 2d OF AUGUST, 1770, AGED 20 YEARS.

186.

ANN STOUTINBURGH, DIED THE 7th AUGT., 1781, Æ. 80.

187.

MR. JOHN BURROWS, OB. FEB. 12, 1807, AET. 39.—ALSO TWO OF HIS CHILDREN, VIZ., JOHN B., OB. JUNE 9, 1800, AET. 8 M. 13 DAYS; ELIZABETH B., OB. SEP. 13, 1800, AET. 17 YRS. 11 MTHS. 20 DAYS.

188.

(*Ab.*) THE HONBLE. JOHN JAQUES, CUSTOS ROT. AND CH. MAGIST. OF THIS CITY, OB. 5 JAN., 1815, AET. 74.

189.

....Y NOE........ (The remains of the sculptured mantling of a Coat of Arms.)

Fragt. of Slab.

190.

(*Ab.*) ELIZABETH, WIFE OF ANDREW DUNN, M.D., 2d DAUR. OF W. S. TONGE, BARR.-AT-LAW, OB. 26 OCT., 1850, AET. 44 Y. 5 M. 10 DS.—(Two lines follow—then)— WILLIAM SHERRIFFE TONGE DUNN, BORN 19 NOV., 1840, DIED .. JANUARY, 1861.

191.

(*Ab.*) PETER DELMESTRE, SURGEON, OB. 2d NOV., 1746.

HAD ISSUE BY HIS WIFE, MARY, 2 SONS & 2 DAURS., VIZ. :—

JOHN DELMESTRE, BORN 26 DEC., 1745, DIED 24 MAY, 1753, AET. 8 YRS. 5 MTHS.

ANN DELMESTRE, BORN 26 NOV., 1738, DIED 8 MAY, 1760, AET. 20 YRS. 6 MTHS.

PETER DELMESTRE, BORN 6 AUGT., 1741, DIED 26 JUNE, 1763, AET. 21 YRS. 10 MTHS.

MARY DELMESTRE, BORN 13 AUGT., 1746, DIED 13 NOV., 1768, AET. 22 YRS. 3 MTHS.

Also,

MARY BOURQUIN, GRANDMOTHER TO THE ABOVE CHILDREN, OB. 10 AUGT., 1753, AET. 79.

Continued,

SAMUEL GREGORY, MERCHANT IN THIS TOWN, MARRIED MARY DELMESTRE, WIDOW OF THE ABOVE PETER DELMESTRE, BY WHOM HE HAD ISSUE, 3 DAUGHTERS, VIZ. :—

CATHERINE GREGORY, BORN 10th APRIL, 1751, MARRIED TO DOCTOR SIMON MCKENZIE—DIED 31st MARCH, 1771, AGED 20 YEARS.—SUSANNAH GREGORY, BORN OCTOBER, 1762, DIED AN INFANT.—JEAN GREGORY, BORN NOV. 30th, 1753, MARRIED HUGH POLSON, ESQ.—DIED 12th OCT., 1776. BY HER HE HAD ISSUE : MARY DOROTHY POLSON, BORN 4th NOV., 1773, & DIED 5th NOVEMBER, FOLLOWING.

THIS IS PLACED BY ORDER, & AT THE EXPENSE OF THE SAID HUGH POLSON, IN MEMORY OF HIS DEARLY BELOVED WIFE AND DAUGHTER.

SEE pedigree of Gregory, of Jamaica.

192.

HERE LYETH THE BODY OF RICHARD—LAMB, WHO DEPARTID THIS LIFE THE —15 DAY DSEMBER, 1716—AGED 36 YEARS.

ALSO HENRY LAMB, HIS SON, DEPARTED—THIS LIFE THE 22 OF OCTOBER, 1716—AGED FOUR YEARS.

HERE ALSO LYES INTERRED THE—BODY OF MRS. ELIZABETH Thomas, DAUGH-
TER TO THE ABOVE RICHARD—LAMB, WHO DEPARTED THIS LIFE—3^d OF FEBRY.,
1765, AGED 56 YEARS.

193.

. . . . LYETH THE BODY OF
. . . . TH MERCHANT,
. . . . THIS LIFE THE 27th
. . . . 26 YEARS.

Fragment.

194.

(*Ab.*) LEONARD WRAY SENIOR, ESQ., & MARY, HIS WIFE. ERECTED BY THEIR
DAUR., ELIZAB. PARKINSON. THE LATTER DIED 13 AUGT., 1781, AET. 46. THE
FORMER 12th AUGT., 1782, AET. 56.

Altar Tomb.

195.

MARY WHITFIELD, WIFE OF WILLIAM WHITFIELD, OF THIS TOWN, MER-
CHANT, WHO DEPARTED THIS LIFE THE 16th JULY, 1765, IN CHILDBED, OF HER
THIRD SON, &C., &C.

LIKEWISE 3 SONS OF WM. & MARY WHITFIELD.—ALSO, ELIZABETH HILL
WHITFIELD, SECOND WIFE OF THE ABOVE WILLM. WHITFIELD, OB. 3^d AUGT.,
1772, IN HER 65th [?] YEAR.

196.

(*Ab.*) MISS JANE TYNDALL, OF THIS TOWN, BORN 4th AUGT., 1730, OB. 3^d
SEPTR., 1810.—ALSO, MRS. DOROTHY DUCOMMUN, OB. 4th OCTR., 1813, AET. 78.—
ALSO, MRS. ELEONER TYNDALL, OB. 23^d JULY, 1814, AGED (not inserted).

197.

(*Ab.*) MARGARET HILL, WIFE OF STEPHEN HILL, ESQR., MERCHANT, OF THIS
TOWN, OB. 9 SEP., 1798, IN HER 28th YEAR, &C.

PROBABLY of the same family as Colonel Stephen J. Hill, C.B., Governor of New-
foundland.

198.

(*Ab.*) EDWARD ARTHUR, INFT. SON OF CHARLES B. & OLIVIA MOSSE, OB. 6th
MARCH, 1859.—ALSO, ANN RAMOS, WIFE OF DAVID RAMOS, ESQ., MERCHT., OB.
30 MAY, 1858, AET. 51 & 7 M.

Lines commencing :—"DEAR IS THE SPOT WHERE CHRISTIAN," &C.

ALSO, OLIVIA SPREY, THEIR DAUR., OB. 10 MARCH, 1860, AET. 22.

199.

TO THE MEMORY OF MR. JOHN MUZZLE, OB. 5 JANY., 1809, AET. 77.
HE WAS CHARITABLE & COMPOSED IN SUFFERINGS.

200.

I.H.S.

THE FAMILY VAULT—OF—FRANCIS GRANT, A.M., OF THIS TOWN, SCHOOL-
MASTER.—HE DEPARTED THIS LIFE—THE 6th DAY OF SEPTR., 1779—AGED 57 YEARS.
HERE ALSO LIETH INTERR'D—THE REMAINS OF HIS WIFE—HIS SISTER—AND
ELDEST DAUGHTER.

SEE pedigree of Grant, of Kilgraston, Perthshire—Burke's "Landed Gentry."

201.

IN MEMORY OF—MR. JOHN KEISER, WHO DEPARTED THIS LIFE 19th JULY,
1805, AGED 56 YEARS.

202.

ALEXR. THOMPSON, SENR., ESQ., OB. 25th AUGT., 1813, AET. 65.—ALSO—HIS
WIFE, ANN, OB. 2d APL., 1816, AET. 52 & 9 M.—ALSO, MISS SARAH LATHAM, OB.
2d SEPTR., 1818, AET. 44.—ALSO, MRS. ANN WEBLEY, MOTHER OF MRS. ANN
THOMPSON, OB. 28 DEC., 1818, AET. 80, &C., &C.

203.

HERE LIETH THE BODY OF—MR. GEORGE SINDAL—OF THIS ISLAND, GENT.,
WHO DEPARTED—THIS LIFE THE (no date) OF (no date), 17— (the year not in-
serted), ... YS. HE WAS A DUTIFULL SON AND SINCERE—FRIEND—WHICH SHIN-
ING QUALITYES MAID—HIM JUSTLY ESTEEM'D BY ALL WHO HAD—THE PLEASURE
OF HIS ACQUAINTANCE.

204.

(*Ab.*) GEORGE ALDRED, ESQR., PRACTITIONER OF PHYSIC & SURGERY, OB.
23d SEP., 1793, AET. 53.—ALSO, JULIA, HIS WIFE, OB. 15 AUGT., 1808, AET. 70.

Altar Tomb.

205.

(*Ab.*) CHARLES HENRY, INF. SON OF ALEXR. & EMILY BRYMER, OB. AUGT.
10, 1861, AET. I.

VERSES follow.

206.

(*Ab.*) MRS. MARY MARKS, OB. 21 DEC., 1811, AET. 58.

207.

(*Ab.*) ROBERT CHARLES GRUBER, OB. 28 DEC., 1830, AET. 18 M. 4 D.—ALSO,
ROBERT WELLWOOD GRUBER, OB. MAY 6, 1832, AET. 1 Y. 24 DAYS.

208.

MARY STAFFORD, DIED 23d JANY., 1766, AGED 6 M. & 14 DAYS.—ALSO, JAMES McMURTRIE, OB. 13 DEC., 1771, AET. 32.—ALSO, MR. JOHN BURNE, OB. 20 JULY, 1769, AET. 39.—ALSO, ELICHA CHRISTIANA DEDAM, OB. 28 MARCH, 1771, AET. 6 YRS. & 5 MHS.—ALSO, ROBERT RUSSELL DEDAM, SON OF ELICHA CHRISTIANA DEDAM, OB. 21 JULY, 1777, AET. 6 M. 20 DAYS.—ALSO, MR. JOSEPH STAFFORD, OB. 27 JUNE, 1772, AET. 40.—ALSO, THE ASHES OF MR. J. M. R. STAFFORD, OB. 21 OCT., 1784, AET. 24.

209.

FRANCIS V. CHAMBERLAINE, OB. NOV. 20, 1841, AET. 9 YRS.   *   *   IN ME-MORIA EST.   I.H.S.

Probably of the family of Chamberlayne, of Cranbury Park.—Burke's "Landed Gentry."

210.

SACRED—TO THE MEMORY OF—ELIZABETH EDGAR—WHO DEPARTED THIS LIFE ON THE—5th OF MAY, 1842, AGED 82.—"BLESSED ARE THE DEAD WHO DIE IN THE LORD."

M. Altar T. ; A weeping willow sculptured.

211.

(*Ab.*) MRS. CATHERINE GROOMBRIDGE, OB. NOV., 1837, AET. 77 YRS. & 6 MTHS.

212.

(*Ab.*) ALEXR. RITCHIE, ESQR., ATTY.-AT-LAW, J.P., AND ASST. JUDGE OF THE COURT OF COM. PLEAS, OB. 3d APL., 1807, AET. 67.—44 YRS. RESIDENT IN THIS ISLAND.

(HIS WIDOW LAMENTS, &C., AND HIS TWO NEPHEWS, ALEXR. FARQUHARSON & ALEXR. GLENNIE, ERECTED THE TOMB.)

Altar Tomb.

213.

(*Ab.*) WILLIAM SMITH, ESQ., OF THE VINEYARD PEN, OB. 31 AUGT., 1795, AET. 71.—ALSO, SARAH BARNETT, HIS WIFE.

214.

(*Ab.*) GEORGE WARDEN, JUNR., OB. JULY 15, 1788, AET. 51 & 11 MTHS.—ALSO, WILLIAM WARDEN, OB. OCT. 25, 1788, AGED ...—ALSO, GEORGE WARDEN, SENR., OB. SEP. 21, 1793, AET. 50 YRS. 3 MTHS. 17 DAYS.—ALSO, HIS GRAND-DAUGHTER, SUSANNA BAKER, OB. AUGT. 25th, 1798, AET. — MONTHS & 23 DAYS.

215.

WM. REES, ESQ., A NATIVE OF CARDIFF, IN GLAMORGANSHIRE, S. WALES, OB 6 JANY., 182.., AET. 44. (A GOOD HUSBAND).—ALSO, ERECTED BY MRS. ANN

REES, AS A TRIBUTE TO HER BROTHER, JAMES DAVIDSON, ESQR., LATE MERCHANT OF THIS CITY, WHO DIED 25th MARCH, 1814, ON BOARD THE SHIP "INDIAN TRADER," CAPT. LEE, FROM LIVERPOOL, AT THE AGE OF 23.

216.

CHENEY HAMILTON, ESQR.—DIED—THE 17th JANUARY, 1820, IN THE 55th— YEAR OF HIS AGE.

217.

JOHN HUSKISSON, 2d SON OF JOHN HEWITT AND JANE RODON SMITH, OB. I AUGT., 1813.—ALSO, THEIR DAUR., MISS SARAH WHITE, OB. 12 JANY., 1826, AET. I Y. 8 M. & 3 DAYS.

218.

JOHN READER, OB. 15 NOVR., 1801, AGED 45 YEARS.—ALSO, WILLIAM, SON OF WM. MARSDEN, OB. 11th JUNE, 1803, AGED 9 MONTHS & 7 DAYS.—ALSO, WM. MARSDEN, SON-IN-LAW OF THE ABOVE JOHN READER, OB. 15 APRIL, 1805, AGED 33 YRS.—ALSO, OLIVER, SON OF BENJN. BLACKHAM, OB. 16 JUNE, 1811, AGED 15. —ALSO, BENJN. BLACKHAM, ESQ., FATHER OF THE ABOVE, OB. ON BOARD THE BRIG, "LETITIA," CAPT. SLA...

219.

(*Ab.*) HELEN, DAUR. OF H. L. AND E. GARRIGUES, OB. 27 NOV., 1821, AET. 2 M. 21 D.

220.

(*Ab.*) LOUISA NORTON SMITH, DAUR. OF GEO. BURRELL AND ELIZA WHITE, OB. 17 SEP., 1824, AET. 6 M. 3 D.

Altar Tomb.

221.

HERE LIES THE BODY OF—JAMES SMITH, ESQUIRE, LATE OF—THE PARISH OF CLARENDON, WHO—DEPARTED THIS LIFE THE 8th—DAY OCTOBER, 1796— AGED 42 YEARS.

On a side tablet, as follows :—

222.

IN THIS VAULT THE MORTAL REMAINS OF ANNE, WIFE OF MR. WM. SMITH, MERCHT. OF THIS CITY; SHE DIED 11th DEC., 1825, IN HER 21st YEAR, AFTER HAVING BEEN MARRIED ONLY 10 MONTHS & 8 DAYS.—ALSO, WILLIAM TARRANT, SENR., ESQ., OB. 17 MARCH, 1825, AET. 35, & HIS WIDOW, SARAH MARY TAR-

RANT, OB. 18 FEB., 1843, AET. 71 YRS.—AND THEIR DAUGHTER, ANN TARRANT,
OB. 11 FEB., 1822, AET. 20.

On another tablet, on the same :

JAMES ADAMS, GENTLEMAN, OB. 15 NOV., 1717, AET. 37.—ALSO, ANN, HIS
WIFE, WHO DIED THE DAY AFTER, IN THE 37th YEAR OF HER AGE.   SHE ONLY
SURVIVED HIM FIFTEEN HOURS.   BOTH WERE NATIVES OF IRELAND.   JANE
WALLACE TARRANT, DIED 19th AUGT., 1807, AGED 2 MTHS. & 3 DAYS ; & HARRY
WOODS, DIED DEC. 9, 1807, AGED 25 YEARS.

223.

THOMAS, SON OF THOMAS & MARTHA CHADDOCK, OB. JANY. 3, 1734, AET. 6.
—ALSO, BENJN. HEWES, SON OF BENJN. & MARTHA HEWES, OB. JANUARY 11th,
1738, AET. 6.—ALSO, MARTHA HEWES, THE MOTHER OF THE ABOVE CHILDREN,
OB. 5 DEC., 174.., AET. 38.—ALSO, BENJN. HEWES, SON OF BENJN. HEWES &
PRUDENCE HEWES, OB. JULY 21st, 1743, AET. 8 DAYS.

On another tablet, on the same tomb :—

CHRISTIANA ELIZABETH SAYLE, WIFE OF CAPTAIN CHRISTOPHER SAYLE, OB.
28 MAY, 1803, AET. 34.—THEIR DAUR., ELIZABETH, OB. 10 DEC., 1791, AET. 3
YRS.—THEIR SON, WM. SMITH SAYLE, OB. 8 JANY., 1796, AET. 2 YRS. 11 MTHS.
—ALSO, MARY J. EDWARDS, OB. 13 AUGT., 1820, AET. 41.

224.

IN MEMORY OF—MR. ROBERT FYFE—ONLY SON OF MR. BARCLAY FYFE—
MERCHANT IN LEITH.—THIS STONE—IS ERECTED BY HIS UNCLE—DOCTOR WIL-
LIAM FYFE, OF THIS TOWN—AS A MARK OF HIS SINCERE AFFECTION AND RE-
GARD—FOR A NEPHEW—WHO, HAD HIS LIFE BEEN SPARED,—BY HIS PROPRIETY
OF CONDUCT—AND A HIGH SENSE OF HONOUR—PROMISED TO BE AN ORNAMENT
—AS WELL AS AN USEFUL—MEMBER OF SOCIETY.—HE DIED THE 1st OF AUGT.
1794*—IN THE 19th YEAR OF HIS AGE.

On wall of churchyard.

225.

HERE LYETH THE BODY OF—JOHN TURNER, WHO DEPARTED—THIS LIFE
THE 27th OF DECR., A—DOM. 1744, AGED 56 YEARS.

226.

MR. SAMUEL IVERS, OB. 11 JANY., 1807, AET. 25.

---

* This is engraven over a " 5."

227.

. . . . . . WILL . . . .

. . . . BRISTO . . . .

FRAGMENT ; inscription obliterated by the rain dropping from the leaves of an overhanging tree.

228.

(*Ab.*) MR. DANIEL O'HARA, JUNR., A NATIVE OF CHARLESTON, S. CAROLINA,
OB. FRIDAY, 8th JANY., 1808, AET. 20 Y. 2 M.

ALLUSION to a brother.

229.

(*Ab.*) JOHN O'HARA, ESQ., OB. THURSDAY, 20th OCTR., 1808, AET. 34 YRS. &
7 MTHS. HE WAS A NATIVE OF N. AMERICA, AND 14 YRS. A MERCHANT IN THIS
CITY.

NINETEEN eulogistic lines follow.

230.

(*Ab.*) HENRY TIPPET, LATE OF GOOD HOPE, IN THE PAR. OF PORT ROYAL,
ESQUR., OB. AUGT. 7, 1800, AET. 83.

231.

(*Ab.*) MR. THOMAS FISHER, NAT. 23d MAY, 1796, OB. 15 JANUARY, 1847.

232.

(*Ab.*) MARY ANN BETTS, WIFE OF THE REVD. W. K. BETTS, OB. NOV. 4, 1838.

233.

(*Ab.*) JOSEPH JACKSON, ESQR., OB. 20 AUGT., 1850, AET. 79 YRS. & 8 DAYS.

BROTHER of John Jackson, M.P. for Dover, Cr. Bart. in 1815.—"Baronetage,"
"Jackson of Arlsey, Beds."

234.

JOHN HEWITT SMITH, ESQR., OF RIVERSIDE ESTATE, IN THE PARISH OF
VERE, DIED IN THIS CITY 26th APRIL, 1828, AGED 49 YEARS. HE WAS UNITED
TO HIS WIFE, JANE RODON SMITH, UPWARDS OF TWENTY YEARS.—ALSO, E. W.
SMITH, WIFE OF GEORGE BURRELL SMITH, ESQ., OB. 18th JULY, 1853, AET. 65.

235.

HENRIETTA, DAUR. OF H. L. & F. A. GARRIGUES, OB. 22 SEP., 1814, AET.
5 MTHS. & 22 DAYS.

236.

(*Ab.*) HENRY, SON OF JOHN HEWITT SMITH, & OF HER, JANE RODON, HIS WIFE, OB. 19 DEC., 1840, AET. 26.

237.

(*Ab.*) MR. JOHN FEGAN, MERCHT., OB. APL. 8, 1819, AET. 58.

238.

MRS. JANE GREGSON, DIED JULY 21st, 1829, AGED 32 YEARS.

239.

(*Ab.*) CAPT. JAMES LENNY, A NATIVE OF GUERNSEY, OB. 12 JUNE, 1810, AET. 38.—ALSO, GRATEFUL TO THE MEMORY OF SARAH JANE LENNY, BORN IN PORT GLASGOW, SCOTLAND, WIFE OF GEORGE MOREY, ESQ., OF H.M.'S CUSTOMS IN THIS PLACE, OB. 11 APRIL, 1821, AET. 24, 16 OF WHICH WERE IN THE ISLAND. —ALSO, JOHN LENNY, HER BROTHER, A NATIVE OF THE SAME PLACE, OB. 10 JANUARY, 1823, AET. 24, & 18 YRS. REDT. IN JAMCA.

240.

HERE LIES INTERRED THE BODY OF—MR. THOMAS BROCKS—WHO DEPARTED THIS LIFE NOV. 8—1749, IN THE 42d YEAR OF HIS AGE.—ALSO, THE BODYS OF TWO OF HIS CHILDREN—VIZ. : JANE BROCKS, WHO—DIED NOV. 2, 1749, AGED— 4 YEARS AND 10 MONTHS—THOMAS BROCKS, WHO DIED—NOV. 19th, 1749, AGED 2 YEARS—AND 3 MONTHS.

241.

(*Ab.*) SIMON TAYLOR, ESQ., OF PLEASANT HILL PLANTATION, PORT ROYAL, OB. 1 NOV., 1838, AET. 43.

TWENTY-THREE eulogistic lines.

242.

SOLOMON FERRIS, ESQ.—COMMANDER OF HIS MAJESTY'S SHIP—" L'HERCULE " —OBIIT 27th MAY, 1803—ÆT. 54.

243.

IN MEMORY OF MR. MATTHEW PAILLET—OF ROYAN, IN FRANCE ; DIED—THE 6th OF AUGUST, 1821—AGED 48 YEARS.

244.

(*Ab.*) CAPT. JACOB HIND, FROM LIVERPOOL, OB. JULY 9, 1780, AET. 40.

245.

MR. ROBERT HARVIE —DIED THE 30th OF OCT-—BER, 1787, AGED 32 YEARS.

246.

(*Ab.*) BRIDGET COLEAR, WIFE OF MR. THOMAS COLEAR, OF THIS PAR., OB. 20 SEP., 1737, AET. 31.

247.

(*Ab.*) JOHN READ, ESQ., ORDNANCE STONE KEEPER AT JAMAICA, OB. JULY 17, 1832, AET. 47.

248.

(*Ab.*) MRS. SUSANNA BRYAN, OB. 17 OCT. 1804, AET. 20.

VERSES follow.

249.

IN & NEAR THIS VAULT LIE INTERRED THE REMAINS OF THOMAS STEWART, SON OF JAMES STEWART, OF THIS PARISH, MERCHANT, AND ANNE MARY, HIS WIFE, WHO DIED 20th AUGUST, 1794, AGED 20 MONTHS.

On the upper slab :

TALBOT O'BRIEN, ESQ., OF THE PAR. OF ST. DAVID, OB. 24 MAY, 1776, AET. 39.—SARAH BANKS, WIDOW, DIED 10 MAY, 1799, AGED 63.—SARAH KNOT STEWART, WIFE OF JAMES STEWART, OF THIS PAR., MERCHT., & DAUR. OF THE SAID SARAH BANKS, OB. 11 MAY, 1779, AET. 20.—ANNE ELIZABETH O'BRIEN, WIDOW OF WM. O'BRIEN, ESQ., & DAUR. OF E.... BANKS, OB. 3d JULY, 1799, AET. 41.— JOHN STEWART GARNETT, SON OF JOHN GARNETT, OF THIS PAR., MERCHT., AND SARAH ANN, HIS WIFE, DAUR. OF THE SAID JAMES & SARAH KNOT STEWART, OB. 28 DEC., 1798, AET. 1 MONTH.

ANNE , , , , , , , , , , } GARNETT { OB. 24 MARCH, 1803, AET. 11 M.
MARGARET ANNE } { OB. 4 NOV., 1805, AET. 2 YRS. 5 MTHS.

Altar Tomb.

250.

HERE LIES THE BODY OF JOHN STIFF, ESQ.,—BORN IN BRISTOL, UNION STREET—DIED 17 OCTOBER, A.D. 1810—AGED 20 YEARS. (NOT LOST, BUT GONE BEFORE.)

251.

(*Ab.*) JOHN M. ESCOFFERY, ESQ., OB. JULY 17th, 1804, AET. 50.

252.

HERE LIES THE BODY OF GEORGE SKOPP, WHO DEPARTED THIS LIFE, ON THE 30th AUGUST, 1826, AGED 50 YEARS.

253.

(*Ab.*) AUGUSTUS WILLARD, OF PORTSMOUTH, NEW HAMPSHIRE, OB. JULY 7, 1799, AET. 22.

254.

(*Ab.*) EBENEZER EDIE, ESQR., OB. ...., 1802, AET. 44.

255.

(*Ab.*) ROBERT GIBSON, ESQ., PROPRIETOR OF AYTON PLANTATION, IN THE PAR. OF ST. DAVID, OB. MAY 6, 1835, AET. 56 YRS.

EULOGIUM follows. Ayton was afterwards in the possession of the Rev. Samuel Jackson.

256.

GEO. WATSON, ESQ., LATE MERCHT. OF THIS CITY, OB. 3^d APRIL, 1835, IN HIS 55th YEAR. TOMB ERECTED BY HIS SISTER AND CO-PARTNER. (Her name is not given.)

257.

(*Ab.*) ALEXR. SINGER, OF THIS TOWN, OB. 30 JULY, 1799, AET. 35.

HERE rhymes follow, commencing: "This frail memorial to a husband dear."

258.

RICHARD HARVEY—LIEUT. OF THE ROYAL ARTILLERY.—HE DIED AT PORT ROYAL ON THE—29th OF OCTR., 1843, AGED 28 YEARS.

259.

JOHN GRAHAM—DIED—DECEMBER 19th, 1817—AGED 30 YEARS.

260.

SACRED TO THE MEMORY OF—WILLIAM GRAHAM, ESQ., WHO DIED 5th OF MARCH, 1818—AGED 47 YEARS. AND OF HIS—ADOPTED DAUGHTER, ZELIE—DUFFY, WHO DIED 19th—NOVEMBER, 1818, AGED 7 YEARS.—AND OF HIS NEPHEW—THOMAS GRAHAM, ESQ.—WHO DIED 19th AUGUST, 1819, AGED—30 YEARS.

261.

HERE LIES THE BODY OF MISS MITCHELL MUNRO, INFANT DAUGHTER OF JOHN & MITCHELL MUNRO, OB. 21 MARCH, 1805, AGED 14 MONTHS & 7 DAYS.

262.

(*Ab.*) WM. FRANK, ESQ., OB. 16 JUNE, 1825, AET. 86.

263.

IN MEMORY OF—LANCELOT BURTON, ESQ.—ATTORNEY TO CHISWICK—IN THE PARISH OF ST. THOMAS IN THE EAST—THE PROPERTY OF THOMAS & JOHN BURTON—WHO DEPARTED THIS LIFE—30th AUGUST, 1801—AGED 26 YEARS.

THE above was probably a member of the family of Launcelot Burton Archer or Archer Burton, of Woodlands, Hants.—See early editions of Burke's L. G.— Also, "Memorials of the surname Archer."

264.

(*Ab.*) MR. JOHN HENRY, OB. 17 OCT., 1801, AET. 24 YRS. & 3 MTHS.

265.

(*Ab.*) MR. JOHN GORDNER, OB. 9 DEC., 1806, AET. 41. ERECTED BY HIS WIFE.

266.

(*Ab.*) MRS. ELEANOR FREEMAN, WIFE OF CAPT. WM. FREEMAN, OB. 25 SEP., 1810, AET. 32.—ALSO, CAPT. WILLIAM FREEMAN, OB. DEC. 20, 1810, AET. 48.— ALSO, MRS. FRANCIS DOROTHY DREWS, WIFE OF JOHN DREWS, SUGAR REFINER, OB. 17 SEP., 1817, AET. 33.

267.

N. A. GRANT, ESQRE.—ST. THOMAS IN THE—EAST—DIED 18 FEBRUARY—1810.

268.

(*Ab.*) GEO. H. COSENS, ESQ., OF THE PAR. OF PORTLAND, OB. 12 APL., 1817, AET. 49.

EIGHT eulogistic verses follow.

269.

FRANCIS GERARD MAYNE, BORN 25th JUNE, 1839, DIED 21st MAY, 1853.

270.

(*Ab.*) MILO BOURKE, ESQR., LATE OF THIS CITY, DRUGGIST, OB. 6 OCT., 1825, AET. 43. REQUIESCAT IN PACE.

271.

(*Ab.*) MARIA, WIFE OF J. H. SMITH, OF THIS CITY, OB. 10th OCT., 1845, AET. 34.—ALSO, HER HUSBAND, JOHN H. SMITH, STATUARY, OB. 22 OCT., 1848, AET. 48.

272.

(*Ab.*) ANN, WIFE OF ABRAHAM DE PASS OF THIS CITY, OB. 2d SEP. 1863, AET. 40.

273.

(*Ab.*) MR. THOMAS GILLESPIE, LATE MERCHANT, OB. 29 APRIL, 1799, AET. 34$\frac{6}{12}$ YEARS. ERECTED BY FRIENDS.

274.

(*Ab.*) GEORGE LOWDON, ESQR., OF KINGSTON, MERCHANT, OB. 14 FEB., 1801, AET. 47.—ALSO, ARCHIBALD LOWDON, HIS BROTHER, OB. 4 DEC., 1795, AET. 95, WHO BOTH HE INTERRED UNDER THIS STONE.

275.

(*Ab.*) MR. GEO. USHER, OB. 4 NOV., 1813.—ALSO, HUGH USHER, ESQ., OF LONDON, LOST AT SEA IN THE "LADY PELEW" PACKET, WHICH FOUNDERED ON HER PASSAGE HOME, IN THE YEAR 1812, AGED 40 YEARS.—ALSO, MR. JAMES, USHER, THEIR YOUNGER BROTHER, WHO UNHAPPILY MET A SIMILAR FATE IN THE BRIG "MARGARITTA," IN HIS PASSAGE FROM MONTE VIDEO TO THIS ISLAND, IN 1807.

276.

HERE LIE THE REMAINS—OF—WILLIAM DAWSON HOOKER, M.D.—ELDEST SON OF—SIR WILLIAM JACKSON HOOKER, K.H., L.L.D.—BORN AT HALLESWORTH, SUF-FOLK—APRIL 4th, 1816—DIED IN THIS CITY—1st JANUARY, 1840—AGED 23 YEARS.

THE late Sir W. J. Hooker, Kt., Director of the Royal Gardens, Kew—an eminent botanist and author—and father of Dr. J. D. Hooker, F.R.S. (also an eminent botanist and author), his only surviving son.

277.

(*Ab.*) JOHN, INF. SON OF DR. JACOB ADOLPHUS & ESTHER, HIS WIFE, BORN 7th FEB., 1813, AND AS A NASCENT FLOWER, DROOPED, AND DIED ON THE FIRST OF APRIL, IN THE SAME YEAR.

278.

(*Ab.*) CAPT. JOHN GRANT, OB. 9 APL., 1840, AET. 51$\frac{6}{12}$ M.

279.

(*Ab*) CAPT. THOS. WALKER, OB. 2 DEC., 1836, AET. 61.

280.

(*Ab.*) JOHN HOLCOMBE, ESQ., 1799, AGED 42 YEARS.

Also

MRS. MARY HAY—DIED DEC. 5th, 1859, AGED 66 YEARS.

281.

(*Ab.*) MRS. CATHERINE LEIGHTON, OB. 31 MARCH, 1823, AGED 62.—ALSO, MRS. SARAH MANNING SMITH, OB. 23^{d} JULY, 1808, AGED 23 YEARS.

LINES follow.

Also on a third tablet :

(*Ab.*) JAMES JACKSON SEWELL, ESQ., LATE MERCHT., OB. 6 NOV., 1815, AET. 49.

EULOGISTIC lines.

Altar Tomb.

282.

(*Ab.*) MISS ELIZABETH WILLS, OB. 6 NOV., 1839, AET. 45. ERECTED BY HER FRIEND, MARY THOMPSON, WITH WHOM SHE LIVED, UPWARDS OF 20 YEARS, ON SISTERLY TERMS.

283.

(*Ab.*) CAPT. JOHN MOSES, OB. 9 DECR., 1751 (remainder underground).

284.

(*Ab.*) MR. JOHN PENNYCOOK, OB. 31 OCT., 1813, AET. 60.

285.

(*Ab.*) MARGARET CROOKS, SPOUSE OF HENRY DRYSDALE, OB. 11 SEP., 1812, AET. 24.—ALSO, HENRY DRYSDALE, OB. 16 AUGT., 1819, AET. 43.—ALSO, WILLIAM PHILLIPS, FARMER, OB. 9th DEC., 1832, AET. 37.

286.

(*Ab.*) ROBERT JOHN ROBINSON, A YOUTH OF EXEMPLARY DUTY, &C., OB. 9 JANY., 1782, IN HIS 20th YEAR. "MORS OMNIA AUFERT—RESTITUITQ. NIHIL."

287.

(*Ab.*) DRUMMOND SIMPSON, OB. 19 JANY., 1802, AET. 49. 10. 10.

288.

(*Ab.*) MRS. FRANCES BARKER DRUMMOND, WIFE OF JAMES DRUMMOND, DIED 26 SEPT., 1803, AET. 25.—ALSO, MR. ARCHIBALD DRUMMOND, OB. 2d FEB., 1811, AET. 28.—ALSO, MR. JAMES DRUMMOND, OB. 2d FEB., 1815, AET. 40.—ALSO, ALEXR. MENZIES, OB. 20 JULY, 1815, AET. 13.—ALSO, ALEXR. MENZIES (abruptly terminated here).

289.

MRS. JOSEPH EMANUEL.

OBLITERATED fragment.

290.

(*Ab.*) SON OF JOHN WEEKE*—LATE CAPTAIN 7th REGT., OR R. F. ...... 23 JUNE, 1809.

OBLITERATED fragment.—N.B. R.F., *i.e.*, Royal Fusileers.

---

* Qy. Weekes?

291.

(*Ab.*) DANIEL O'HARA, SON OF DANIEL O'HARA, ESQ., OF CHARLESTON, S. CAROLINA, AND REBECCA, HIS WIFE, OB. 10 JANY., 1808, AET. 20.

292.

(*Ab.*) SUSANNA MANBY WIFE OF MR. AARON MANBY, OF KINGSTON, IRON-MONGER, OB. 21 NOV., 1762, AGED 22 YEARS.—ALSO, MR. AARON MANBY, OB. 21 JANY., 1763, AET. 32.—ALSO, ZACHARY MANBY, SON OF THE ABOVE—OB. 19 SEP., 1796, AGED 34.

293.

(*Ab.*) JUDITH, WIFE OF JOHN HALLS, APOTHECARY, IN KINGSTON, OB. 1 JULY, 1752, AET. $18\frac{9}{12}$ YEARS.—ALSO, MRS. MARY TRUXTON, OB. 5 NOV., 1755, AET. 53.—ALSO, THE ABOVE JOHN HALLS, OB. 15th DEC., 1756, AET. 36.—ALSO, DR. ROBERT HALLS, BROTHER OF THE ABOVE, OB. 11 JUNE, 1760, AET. 39.

294.

(*Ab.*) HERE LAYS INTERRED, &C., MR. JOSEPH SPROTSON, BORN AT MIDDLE-WICH, IN CHESHIRE, AND SINCERELY REGRETTED BY A NUMEROUS ACQUAINT-ANCE, OB. 1st MARCH, 1769, AET. 55 & $\frac{7}{12}$ YEARS.

295.

(*Ab.*) WILLIAM GREGORY, LATE OF KINGSTON, OB. SEP. 5th, 1744, AET. 56. VERSES follow.

296.

JOHN SCOT, SON OF THE LATE ROBERT SCOT, BANKER, IN GLASGOW, SCOT-LAND; DIED 26th OCTOBER, 1815, AGED 40 YEARS.

297.

W. X. W. (*sic.*) BENEATH THIS STONE—RESTETH THE REMAINS OF—WILLIAM WILLSHIRE, WHO—WAS A TENDER AND AFFECTIONATE—FATHER. HE LIVED RE-SPECTED—& DIED LAMENTED, ON THE 31—DECR., 1757, AGED 47 YEARS.

298.

(*Ab.*) WILLIAM CALDWELL, ESQ., ALDERMAN OF THIS CITY—MEM. OF ASSLY. FOR ST. DOROTHY. BORN MAY 15, 1771, AT BEVINGTON BUSH, NEAR LIVERPOOL, AND DIED JANY. 29, 1819, IN HIS 45th YEAR, AFTER A RESIDE CE OF 26 YEARS IN THIS ISLAND. AN eulogium follows.

299.

(*Ab.*) MR. PETER JOHNSON, CARPENTER, OF THIS TOWN, OB. 22 DEC., 1766, AET. 32. HE WAS AN AFFECTE. HUSBAND & TENDER PARENT. HERE ALSO ARE THE BODIES OF MASTER WILLIAM WELLS, SON OF WM. & FRANCES WELLS, OB. 4 JANY., 1771, AET. 2.—ALSO, MR. W. WELLS, UPHOLSTERER, OB. 31 JULY, 1773, AET. 33, &C.

300.

(*Ab.*) 1. HANNAH KIESSELBACK, A NATIVE OF HESSEE CASSEL, OB. 17 DEC. 1841, AET. 53. ERECTED BY HER SINCERE FRIEND, ISAAC PINTO, SENR. VERSES follow.

2. MATILDA, YOUNGT. DAUR. OF ROBT. KIESSELBACK, OB. 28 DEC., 1841, AET. 12. 6. 21.

3. MR. GEO. KIESSELBACK, OB. 18 JUNE, 1844, AET. 29.

Altar Tomb ; three slabs conjoined.

301.

(*Ab.*) ISABELLA, WIFE OF ALEXR. MILLER, ESQ., OF KINGSTON, OB. 7 MAY, 1831, AET. 32.—ALSO, TO THE MEMORY OF THE ABOVE ALEXR. MILLER, ESQ., WHO DIED ON THE 15th OF JUNE, FOLLOWING, OF GRIEF, IN THE 45th YEAR OF HIS AGE.—ALSO, MARGARET, WIFE OF JAMES MAC FAADYEN, M.D., OF THIS CITY, AND COUSIN OF THE ABOVE ISABELLA MILLER, BORN 3d MAY, 1812, DIED 21 JUNE 1843.

N. B.—Another slab lies under this.

302.

(*Ab.*) WILLIAM JENNINGS, INF. SON OF JOHN & ELIZA CATER, OF THIS CITY, OB. 7 OCT., 1834.—ALSO, SAMUEL BARCLAY CATER, 4th SON OF THE ABOVE, OB. 12th APRIL, 1840, AET. 17 MONTHS.

303.

(*Ab.*) GREGORY BAKER, OB. 20 JANY., 1815, AET. 45 ; AND HANNAH, HIS WIFE, OB. APL. 2d, 1836, AET. 67 ; & THEIR DAUR., ELIZABETH P. TOWNSHEND, OB. JANY. 24, 1841, AET. 36.—ALSO, HER DAUR., ELIZABETH TOWNSHEND, OB. 28 FEB., 1848, AGED 18 YEARS, 3 MONTHS, & 16 DAYS.

304.

(*Ab.*) ROBERT MATHIAS KIESSELBACK, INF. SON OF DAVID, & EMMA AGUI-LAR, & GRANDSON OF ROBT. KIESSELBACK, ESQ., OB. 4 MARCH, 1852, AET. $1\frac{9}{12}$ YRS.

305.

MR. BENJM. BLACKHAM, ... 16 JUNE, 1811, ...

Fragment ; broken.

306.

On Tablet on north side of Tomb.

THE BELOVED CHILDREN OF MICHAEL AND ELIZABETH HUGHES, VIZ.:
JAMES, OB. 27 JUNE, 1803, AET. 13 MONTHS, & 5 DAYS. ANN, OB. 25 SEP.,
1804, AET. 4 MTHS., & 3 DAYS. RICHARD MICHAEL, OB. 23 MAY, 1808, AET. 10
MTHS., 28 DAYS. ELIZA JANE, OB. 16 FEB., 1810, AET. 8 MTHS.—ALSO, MRS. E.
HUGHES, THEIR MOTHER, OB. 20th APRIL, 1812, AET. 36.

On the top.

JOHN HERRING, MARINER, OF WHITEHAVEN, GREAT BRITAIN, OB. 5 DECR.,
1753, AET. 38.—ALSO, HANNAH FRANCE, OB. 3d JANY., 1789, AET. 46 (WIFE OF
JOHN FRANCE, OF THE SAME PLACE).—ALSO, THOS. FRANCE, OB. 31 JULY, 1796.
—HENRY FRANCE, OB. 14 DEC. .... MARY ...... 1795.—GUANHOC [?], AGED
54 YEARS.—................. BORN APL. 12th, ... OB. 1767, AGED 19 YEARS.
VERY indistinct and confused inscription.

Lofty Altar Tomb.

307.

(*Ab.*) MARIA, DAUR. OF THOS. & MARIA PAPPS, OB. SEPTR. 13, 1797, AET. 19
DAYS.—ALSO, THOMAS PAPPS, OF THE PARISH OF KINGSTON, MERCHT., OB. SEPTR.
30, 1790, AET. 39, &C.
"AN HONEST MAN IS THE NOBLEST WORK OF GOD."

308.

HERE LIETH THE BODY OF MISS—MARY TAYLOR, THE DAUGHTER—OF
GEORGE HANBURY TAYLOR—ESQR., WHO DEPARTED THIS LIFE THE—26th OF
JULY, 1745, AGED 14 YEARS.—ALSO, HERE LIETH THE BODY OF—GEORGE TAYLOR,
THE SON OF—PATRICK TAYLOR, ESQ., WHO DEPARTED THIS LIFE, THE 9th OF—
JUNE, 1749, AGED ONE YEAR.

309.

(*Ab.*) CHARLES, SON OF MR. CHARLES MITCHELL, OF KINGSTON, MERCHANT,
OB. ... OCTR., 1754, AET. ... MONTHS & 20 DAYS.—...... GEORGE ...... MIT-
CHELL, ... 3 YEARS...................

310.

(*Ab.*) HOPPER BRANFOOT, ESQR., OF NEWFIELD, PARISH OF MANCHESTER,
OB. 4 JULY, 1838—AFTER FOUR DAYS' ILLNESS OF YELLOW FEVER—AGED 21
YEARS.

311.

(*Ab.*) ELIZABETH ROBINSON, OB. 9th JUNE, 1816, AET. 58, OF WHICH SHE WAS 37 A RESIDENT IN THE ISLAND.

312.

(*Ab.*) MRS. SARAH WIFFETT, OB. JULY 7th, 1812, AET. 58.

313.

(*Ab.*) DANIEL GULLY, OB. 18th OCT., 1823, AET. 54.—ALSO, FOUR OF HIS CHILDREN :—JAMES, OB. 30 JANY., 1796, AET. 14 MONTHS.—ELEANOR, OB. 31 OCT., 1803, AET. 4 YRS.—SUSANA, OB. 20 JANY., 1808, AET. 6 YRS.—DANIEL, OB. 29 MAY, 1809, AET. 3 YRS. $\frac{4}{12}$ M.

314.

(*Ab.*) MR. JONATHAN JONES, SHIPWRIGHT, OB. SEP. 21, 1790, AET. 44.—ALSO, FOUR OF HIS CHILDREN :—PHILIP, OB. FEB. 18, 1782, AET. 7.—PHILIP JOHN, OB. NOV. 15, 1784, AET. $\frac{8}{12}$ Y.—ELIZABETH, OB. SEP. 8, 1786, AET. 1 YR.—MARY REBECCA, OB. JUNE 1, 1789, AET. $\frac{8}{12}$ Y.—ALSO, MR. AARON EDWARD MANBY, OB. JUNE 27, 1792, AET. 23.—ALSO, MR. JAS. MANBY, FATHER OF THE ABOVE A. E. M., OB. JUNE 11, 1794, AET. 57.

315.

(*Ab.*) MRS. ELIZABETH MOWAT, WIFE OF EDWARD C. MOWAT, ESQ., SOLICITOR, OB. 1 MAY, 1859.

316.

HERE LIES INTER'ED THE BODY OF—MRS. MARY DALLAS—THE WIFE OF MR. PETER DALLAS—OF THIS TOWN, WHO DEPARTED THIS LIFE—YE 6 DAY OF MAY, IN YE YEAR OF OUR LORD—1761, AGED 26 YEARS—EIGHT MONTHS AND 11 DAYS.

317.

(*Ab.*) CHARLES JAMES, AGED 8 YRS., & SARAH AINSLIE, AGED 4 YEARS, THE BELOVED CHILDREN OF ROBERT & JANE METCALFE, OB. 10 JANY, 1842.

Also,

WM. BEEL, OB. 9 JULY, 1853, AET. $4\frac{3}{12}$ YEARS.

318.

(*Ab.*) WM. FRY, OF THIS CITY, OB. 12 OCT., 1814, IN HIS 52d YEAR.—ALSO, MARY, HIS DAUR., OB. JULY 18, ..., AET. $2\frac{3}{12}$ YRS.—ALSO, HIS SON, MR. GEO. FRY, OB. 24th OCT., 1825, AET. $29\frac{9}{12}$ YRS.

319.

(*Ab.*) CHARLES METCALFE, ESQR., OB. 2^d FEB., 1826, AET. 45.—ALSO, FREDE-RICK AUGUSTUS, HIS GRANDSON, OB. 22^d JUNE, 1856, AET. 20$\frac{6}{12}$ YEARS.

320.

(*Ab.*) JOHN, SON OF THE LATE JOHN & ELIZABETH GLEGG, OB. 2 JANY., 1815, AGED 13 YEARS, & 6 MONTHS.—ALSO, MARIA, WIFE OF MR. GEO. MANUEL, OB. FEB. 5, 1830, AET. 32.

LINES follow.

321.

(*Ab.*) WM. ROBERTSON, OB. SEP. 17., 1827, AET. 53.

322.

JAMES STEEL.

NOTHING more.

323.

THE BODY OF JAMES SLO...., OB. 26 AUGUST, 1807

Fragment.

324.

(*Ab.*) MR. JAMES MURUSS, OB. 17 MARCH, 1804, AET. 39.

325.

(*Ab.*) EDWARD CODD, JUNR., OB. 25 NOV., 1813, AET. 3$\frac{11}{12}$ YRS.—ALSO, MARY ANNE CODD, OB. 10 JULY, 1821, AET. $\frac{9}{12}$ YR.

326.

(*Ab.*) MISS CATHERINE CAMPBELL, OB. 16 MAY, 1852, AET. 76.

327.

(*Ab.*) JAMES ROBERTSON, M.D., OF THE NAVAL HOSPITAL, BARBADOS, AND MEDICAL STAFF OF THIS ISLAND, OB. IN KINGSTON BARRACKS, 12 JANY., 1812, AET. 42.

328.

MRS.
AITKEN'S
TOMB.

NOTHING more.

329.

(*Ab.*) ON THE 9th JANUARY, 1838, WAS BURIED, &C., ALDERMAN ADAMS.—
ERECTED BY THE CORPORN. OF KINGSTON.

330.

(*Ab.*) CHARLES BERNARDI, ESQR., BORN AT TURIN, IN PIEDMONT, 19th SEPT.
1812, DIED 7th MARCH, 1848. ERECTED BY HIS WIDOW.

331.

WILMOT ...... 25 OF JULY ...... 26 ......
Ponderous Slab broken into fragments.

332.

(*Ab.*) WM. MOUNCER, ESQR., OF ST. MARY'S PAR., OB. 24 MARCH, 1836, AET.
38.

333.

(*Ab.*) MRS. LUCY TITTLE, WIFE OF MR. EDWARD TITTLE, OB. 11 NOV., 1744,
AET. 65.

334.

(*Ab.*) MRS. JANE NIVEN, OB. 6th JANY., 1818, AET. 59.

335.

(*Ab.*) SAMUEL WILLIAM CARPENTER, ESQ., OF ST. ANDW. PAR., OB. 18 OCT.,
1818, AET. 37.

336.

(*Ab.*) HANNAH SMITH, OB. 24 NOV., 1810, AET. $3\frac{6}{12}$ YRS.—ALSO, RACHEL SMITH,
OB. 3d AUGT., 1811, AET. $\frac{4}{12}$THS.

337.

(*Ab.*) WM. GEO. WRIGHT, SON OF THE LATE GEO. WRIGHT, OF GREENWALL,
PAR. ST. DAVID, OB. 2 FEB., 1860, AET. 39.—ALSO, JESSIE LOUISA & ALICE MARY,
DAUGHTERS OF WILLIAM WRIGHT, MERCHT., OF KINGSTON, AGED RESPECTIVELY
$7\frac{8}{12}$ & $5\frac{11}{12}$ YEARS. THESE BELOVED CHILDREN WERE CARRIED OFF IN ONE
WEEK BY DIPHTHERIA, OCTOBER, 1862, &C. ALSO, WILLIAM WRIGHT, A NATIVE OF
LONDON, MERCHT. OF THIS CITY, AND VICE-CONSUL OF FRANCE, OB. 11 MAY,
1864, AET. 54.

338.

SACRED TO THE MEMORY OF—THOMAS HIGSON, ESQUIRE—WHO WAS FOR
MANY YEARS A MERCHANT IN THIS CITY, & FOR SOME TIME ISLAND BOTANIST,

HE DEPARTED THIS LIFE ON THE 21st DECEMBER, 1836, AGED 63 YRS. & 10 MONTHS. THIS TOMB IS PLACED OVER HIS MORTAL REMAINS BY HIS AFFLICTED WIDOW, DELAFITTE HIGSON.

339.

SACRED TO THE MEMORY OF VIRGINIA FAIRFAX, THE BELOVED WIFE OF PETER ALEXANDER ESPEUT, ESQR., OF THIS CITY, AND DAUGHTER OF COLONEL ROBERT MUNRO HARRISON, CONSUL-GENERAL OF THE UNITED STATES OF AME- RICA FOR THIS ISLAND, BORN 28th AUGUST, 1821, DIED 5th NOVEMBER, 1841, AGED 20 YEARS AND 69 DAYS.—ALSO, VIRGINIA MARGARET GROSETT, DAUGHTER OF THE ABOVE, BORN 25th OCTOBER, 1839, DIED 7th JANUARY, 1841, AGED 14 MONTHS, & 15 DAYS. THIS MONUMENT IS ERECTED BY HER AFFECTIONATE SUR- VIVING HUSBAND.

An elegant and classic Marble Tomb, enclosed by a railing, overgrown with flowers.

VERSES follow. The Espeut family came to Jamaica with the French refugees from St. Domingo, in 1798.

340.

(*Ab.*) THOMAS CARPENTER, ESQ., OB. FEB. 8, 1801, AET. 52.—ALSO, HIS TWO WIVES :—ANN, OB. 18 FEB., 1786, AET. 34, & MARY, OB. 23d APL., 1801, AET. 49.— ALSO, FREDERICK CARPENTER, SON OF THE ABOVE, OB. AUGT. 8, 1806.—ALSO, CATHE. MC NAUGHTON, HIS WIDOW, OB. 12 MARCH, 1811, AET. 31.

341.

PETER ESPEUT, ESQR., OBT. DECR. 4th, 1790, AGED 49 YEARS.

342.

(*Ab.*) AUGUSTA MARIA, INFT. DAUR. OF MOSES & ELIZABETH PENELOPE RA- MOS, OB. 9 OCT., 1850, AET. 17 M. 20 DAYS.—ALSO, HENRY FIDDIS TAYLOR, THEIR INFT. SON, OB. 16 AUGT., 1856, AET. 7 M. 3 D.

343.

(*Ab.*) ELIZABETH SANDERSON, OB. 8 AUGT., 1754, AET. 53.

VERSES.

ALSO, THE BODY OF ELIZABETH CODRINGTON, RELICT OF DR. WILLIAM COD- RINGTON, DECEASED, OB. 19 APL., 1810, AET. 61, &C.

A BRANCH of the Barbadian family. William Codrington, Planter, mentions in his will [recorded in Jam. 1745], a decree in Chancery, relating to the property of Sir Wm. Codrington. He also names his wife—Ann—and his children, John, Christopher, George, William, Richard ; and Frances, Ann, Hannah, Mary, and Catherine.

344.

(*Ab.*) CAPTAIN JOSEPH WOOD, LATE OF ST. ANDREW, OB. 28 SEP., 1791, AET. 64.

345.

(*Ab.*) WM. ATKIN, SON OF LIEUT. WM. ATKIN, 77th REGT., OB. 5 JULY, 1830, AET. 8.

346.

(*Ab.*) ROSETTA HUGHES, LATE OF THIS CITY, AND OF ROSEMOUNT PLANTA-TION, PAR. ST. ANDREW, OB. 17 APL., 1836, AET. 75, OF WHICH SHE SPENT 55 IN THE ISLAND (JAMAICA). ERECTED BY HER HUSBAND, CAPT. WM. HUGHES.

347.

(*Ab.*) JOHN DOUGLAS, ESQR., OB. FEB. 12th, 1812, AET. 47.

348.

(*Ab.*) ABRAHAM GIBBS, OB. 15 FEB., 1789, AET. $20\frac{6}{12}$ YRS.

349.

(*Ab.*) MRS. CHRISTIAN STANTON, WIFE OF MR. ROBERT STANTON, MERCHT., OF KINGSTON, OB. 9th AUGT., 1737, AET. 22 YRS.—ALSO, MR. WILLIAM STANTON, OF KINGSTON, MER-CHANT, BRO. OF THE SAID ROBERT, OB. 12 DEC., 1751, AET. 40.—ALSO, GEORGE STANTON, BRO. OF THE ABOVE ROBT. & WM., OB., IN ST. ELIZAB. PAR., JANY. 5, 1745, AET. 28.

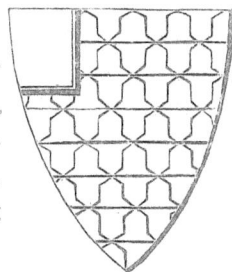

Slab ; *Arms*, Vair, a canton dexter. *Crest*, On a wreath, over an esquire's helmet, a twisted ring, fillet, or wreath, surmounted by a sheep's [?] head couped.

350.

(*Ab.*) WM. ROSS, ESQ., OF KINGSTON, JAMAICA, BORN IN SCOTLAND, APL. 28, 1753, OB. JULY 10, 1815. ERECTED BY HIS BROTHERS.

351.

(*Ab.*) LIEUT.-COLONEL HAFFEY, LATE OF THE 18th REGIMENT OF FOOT, NEPHEW TO MAJOR-GENL. STEVENSON, OF THE E. I. C. S., & TO HENRY HAFFEY, OF THE CITY OF BATH, ESQR., OB. JULY 6, 1814, AET. 41 YEARS.

352.

JAMES BOYLE, ESQUIRE, MANY YEARS A MOST RESPECTABLE MERCHANT IN THIS PARISH. HE DIED, LAMENTED BY ALL WHO KNEW HIM, ON THE 10th OF MAY, 1774, AGED 42 YEARS.

353.

HERE LIES THE BODY OF MR. THOMAS STARROW, LATE OF THIS PARISH, CARPENTER, DIED NOVR. 5th, 1762, AGED 34 YEARS.—ALSO, THE BODY OF MR. JAMES STARROW, LATE OF THE PARISH OF ST. ANDREW, BROTHER OF THE ABOVE THOMAS STARROW, DIED NOVEMBER 29th, 1760, IN THE 29th YEAR OF HIS AGE.—LIKEWISE, THE BODY OF JAMES STARROW, SON OF THE ABOVE THOMAS

STARROW, DIED AUGUST 24th, 1761, AGED 11 MONTHS AND 29 DAYS.—ALSO, YE BODY OF ROBERT LAREY, LATE OF THIS TOWN, WHO UNFORTUNATELY WAS DROWNED IN ENDEAVOURING TO CROSS THE YALLAHS RIVER, BY FALLING FROM HIS HORSE, DECEMBER 1st, 1763, AGED 35 YEARS.

THE Yallahs, a beautiful river in the Parish of St. David, abounding in red mullet and other fish.

354.

JOHN SCOT, SON OF THE LATE ROBERT SCOT, BANKER IN GLASGOW, SCOTLAND, DIED 26th OCTOBER, 1815, AGED 40 YEARS.

355.

(*Ab.*) IMOGENE AUGUSTA, DAUR. OF AUGUSTUS & ROSALIN MORAIS, OB. SEP. 21, 1862, AET. $12\frac{11}{12}$ YRS.

356.

MR. ROGER READING, DIED—AUGUST YE 8th, 1731, AGED 37 YEARS.—ANN READING, DAUGHTER TO MRS. ROGER READING, DIED NOVBR.—THE 24th, 1734, AGED 2 YEARS.—HANNAH COX, WIFE TO DOCTR.—SAMUEL COX, DIED YE 25th OF OCTR.—1735, AGED 19 YEARS.—ELIZABETH PALMER, WIFE OF PHILIP PALMER, DIED AUGST. 18, 1770, AG'D 45 YEARS.—ALSO, THE REMAINS OF MRS. FRANCES INGLIS, WIDOW, WHO DIED 9th JANUARY, 1791, AGED 65 YEARS.—AND JAMES SUTHERLAND, ESQR., WHO DIED 12th FEBRUARY, 1796, AGED 62 YEARS.

357.

(*Ab.*) JANE FORSYTH, OB. AUGT. 23, 1841, AET. 24.

Also, on a separate slab :

(*Ab.*) MISS ELIZABETH PARNELL, OB. JANY. 3, 1842, AET. $65\frac{4}{12}$ YRS.

358.

THIS SARCOPHAGUS, TO THE MEMORY OF WILLIAM JAMES STEVENSON, ESQUIRE, LATE RECEIVER-GENERAL OF THIS ISLAND, WHO DEPARTED THIS LIFE, ON THE 15th DAY OF APRIL, 1830, AGED 66 YEARS—IS ERECTED BY THE MERCHANTS OF KINGSTON—IN TESTIMONY OF THEIR RESPECT AND ADMIRATION—OF HIS CHARACTER, ADORNED AS IT WAS, BY ALL THE VIRTUES—WHICH RENDER A MAN REALLY ESTIMABLE, BOTH IN—PUBLIC AND PRIVATE LIFE.

HE was son of Wm. Stevenson [by his wife, Mary, daughter of Samuel Jackson], and married, in 1796, Mary, daughter of J. R. James [by his wife, Mary, daughter of J. Lawrence, of Fairfield], and had, with other issue, a son, William, father of the late Sir W. Stevenson, Governor of Mauritius.

359.

(*Ab.*) WILLIAM BUTT WRIGHT, ESQR., LATE MERCHT. OF KINGSTON, OB. 20th FEB., 1821, AET. 30. ERECTED BY HIS WIDOW.

Altar.

360.

PIERRE MARCELIN SAMBOUR AÎNÉ—BORN AUX CAYES (HAITI), 1824—DE-CEASED 3ᵈ AUGUST, 1863.

Wooden.

361.

(*Ab.*) MR. WM. PANTON, JUNR., OB. AUGT. 2ᵈ, 1780, AET. 18.

362.

(*Ab.*) REBECCA DALMAHOY, OB. JUNE 13, 1819, AET. 43 & $\frac{7}{12}$ YEARS.

Altar.

363.

(*Ab.*) MARY WYNTER, OB. 5 APL., 1822, AET. 37, AFTER AN ILLNESS OF 3 MONTHS.

Altar.

364.

HERE LIES THE BODY—OF MR. DAVID GORDON—LATE LIEUT.—IN HIS MAJESTY'S 79ᵗʰ REGT. OF FOOT—HE DIED DECR. 6ᵗʰ, 1781, AGED 37 YEARS.—HIS LOSS IS SINCERELY REGRETTED BY ALL HIS ACQUAINTANCE—BOTH IN THE MILITARY AND CIVIL LINE.—HE WAS A LOVING HUSBAND,—A TENDER FATHER, AND SINCERE FRIEND.

Slab.

365.

(*Ab.*) MRS. ELIZABETH CHILDS, OB. 10ᵗʰ DECR., 1836, AET. 21$\frac{10}{12}$ YEARS.

366.

(*Ab.*) CHARLES MIDDLETON, ESQ., ORDNANCE STORE-KEEPER, OB. 22ᵈ NOV., 1848, AET. 63. (On another tablet:) CATHERINE ELIZA CAMPBELL, INFT. DAUR. OF CAPTN. CAMPBELL, BARRACK MASTER, OB. 15 MARCH, 1850, AET. 8 M. 10 D.

367.

ANN LISTEN.

Altar Tomb—on a wooden slab.

368.

JOHN READER .... 15 NOV., 1801, ... 45 YEARS.—ALSO, WILLIAM MARS-DEN. THIS HAS BEEN COPIED & RESTORED........

Fragment.

369.

(*Ab.*) MRS. CATHERINE CAMPBELL, OB. 26 OCT., 1816, AET. 80.—ALSO, MISS ISABELLA CAMPBELL, DAUGHTER OF THE ABOVE, OB. 18 MARCH, 1852, AET. 74.

370.

(*Ab.*) MASTER JOHN WHYTE, OB. SEP. 9, 1800, AET. $\frac{5}{12}$ YRS. 9 DAYS.—ALSO, MASTER ALEXR. WHYTE, OB. 18 FEB., 1805, AET. 11 M. 11 D.

371.

(*Ab.*) JHN. BINNIE, A NATIVE OF EDINBURGH, OB. 6 DEC., 1830, AET. 37.

372.

(*Ab.*) JAMES FORSYTH, JUNR., OB. 21 OCT., 1846, AET. 27.

373.

SACRED—TO THE MEMORY OF—MATILDA, WIFE OF CAP—TAIN ROBERT WIN-CHESTER—92d HIGHLANDERS—WHO DEPARTED THIS LIFE—THE 10th SEPTR., 1819—BELOVED AND LAMENTED.

MATILDA, first wife of Captain, afterwards Colonel Winchester, K.H., whose sister, Garden Winchester, married F. Fraser, of Findrack, Commander R.N.—*See* "An Account of the Surname Baird," Edited by W. N. Fraser; also, Burke's "Landed Gentry," &c.

374.

BENEATH ARE DEPOSITED THE REMAINS OF—GEORGE INNES, WHO WAS KILLED IN A DUEL—ON 9th NOVR., 1784, AGED 22.—WILLIAM INNES, WHO DIED ON 11th JULY, 1791—AGED 19.—PETER INNES, 17 JUNE, 1801, AGED 34.—HUGH INNES, 6 OCT., 1803, AGE 40, GENTLEMEN.—MUCH RESPECTED, THEY WERE SONS OF THE LATE—ALEXANDER INNES, ESQ., OF ABERDEEN, N.B.—THIS STONE IS INSCRIBED TO THEIR MEMORY, BY—THEIR AFFLICTED MOTHER.

375.

HERE LIETH THE BODY OF—PETER WALLACE, ESQR.—WHO DIED THE 15th JULY, 1782—AGED 28 YEARS.—ALSO, THE BODY OF HIS SON—THOMAS STOAKES WALLACE—WHO DIED THE DAY FOLLOWING—AGED 4 YEARS AND 5 MONTHS.

376.

IN MEMORY OF—JOHN GEORGE HUNT REYNOLDS, SON—OF JOHN AND ESTHER REYNOLDS, DIED THE—4th DECR., 1795, AGED 3 MONTHS & 11 DAYS.—MARY ANNE REYNOLDS, DAUGHTER—OF JOHN AND ESTHER REYNOLDS, DIED THE 3d AUGUST, 1797, AGED 5 MONTHS & 12 DAYS.—ESTHER REYNOLDS, WIFE OF— JOHN REYNOLDS, DIED 12th DECEMR., 1797.—SAMUEL JONES, SON OF SAMUEL— JONES, OF WREXHAM NORTH ....—DIED AT PORT ROYAL, 9th FEBRY., 1805— AGED 31 YEARS AND 12 DAYS.

A WIDELY connected family.—*See* will [recorded 1800] of H. Archer, second husband of Amy Boyd Reynolds.

377.

THE HONBLE. JAMES IRVING, ESQR., LATE CUSTOS OF TRELAWNEY, DIED— 21st NOVEMBER, 1798, AGED 49 YEARS.

378.

BENEATH THIS SIMPLE TOMB—ON THE XXXth DAY OF DECEMBR.—A.D. MDCCXCIX.—WAS INTER'D THE PERISHABLE—PART OF PETER FRANCKLEN, ESQUIR. —LATE CULLECTOR OF HIS MAJESTY'S CUSTOMS—IN THE PORT OF KINGSTON,— A MEMBER OF THE LEGISLATIVE ASSEMBLY OF JAMAICA, AND—SOMETIME OF THE PRIVY COUNCIL—OF TOBAGO.

PROBABLY Peter Ramsey Francklin, or Franklyn [convertible]—will in Jamaica, died 1794, recorded 1800—and brother of John F. [will 1808], whose armorial seal has been noticed.

379.

HERE LYETH—THE BODY OF THOMAS—HERRING, OF THE CITY OF BRISTOL, —WHO DEPARTED THIS LIFE NOV.—THE 19th, 1751, AGED 27 YEARS.—ALSO, YE BODY OF WM. ANDERSON—ESQ., WHO DIED DECR. 14, 1770—AGED 43 YEARS.

THE family of Herring was connected with those of Beckford, Ellis [Seaford], &c.

380.

HERE LIETH INTERR'D THE BODY OF—MRS. PRISELLA WILLIAMS—DAUGHTER OF MR. HUGH & MRS. MARTHA WIL-LIAMS—OF THE PARISH OF KINGSTON, MERCHANT—WHO DIED THE 7th DAY OF DECEMBR.—ANNO 1735—AGED FOUR YEARS AND SIX MONTHS.—ALSO THE BODY OF MR. HUGH WILLIAMS—SON OF THE ABOVE SAD, WHO DIED—THE 19th— DAY OF DECEMBER, ANNO 1736—AGED FOUR YEARS AND ONE MONTH.

*Arms,......*On a chevron, between three Moors' heads in profile, five ermine spots. *Crest,* On a wreath, over an esquire's helmet, a stag's head caboshed.

381.

HERE LIES THE BODY OF—MARY SADLER—WHO DEPARTED—THIS LIFE THE 9th DAY—OF SEPTEMBER, 1744, AGED—3 YEARS AND ONE MONTH.

382.

(*Ab.*) MRS. ANN JOY, OB. 14 APL., 1818, AET. 70.

Also

EDWARD DELPRATT, ESQUIR., NEPHEW OF THE ABOVE, OB. 10 NOV., 1841, AET. 52. ERECTED BY HIS WIFE & CHILDREN.

THE Delpratts were extensive produce merchants of Kingston, in the eighteenth century.

383.

D. O. M.

GEORGE STEWART,

DIED THE 20th DAY OF MA...,

1755,

AGED 33.

Handsome Marble Slab.

384.

(*Ab.*) MRS. MARGARET ...., WIFE OF MR. PAUL ...., 32 YRS. 1 M.
11 DAYS......

Fragment.

385.

(*Ab.*) JOHN HANBURY TAYLOR, ESQR., OB. 15 FEB., 1781, AET. 51.—ALSO, HIS
DAUGHTER, MARIANNE HANBURY TAYLOR, OB. 25th FEB., 1778, AET. 20.

Vault.

PROBABLY a near relative of Wm. Taylor, Chief Justice of Jamaica.—*See* Burke's
"Landed Gentry," vocë Taylor.

386.

(*Ab.*) ROBERT CALVERT, OB. JUNE, 1832, AET. 80.

QUERY of the family of Calvert, of Ockley Court.—*See* Burke's "Landed Gentry."

387.

(*Ab.*) MR. THOMAS HOLT, OB. JANY. 21, 1797, AET. 36.

388.

(*Ab.*) JOHN WALLIS, OF KINGSTON, MERCHT.—OB. 7 NOV., 1746, AET. 29.—
ALSO, ANN PRUDENCE GLOUG, DAUR. OF THE SAID JOHN & ELIZABETH WALLIS,
& WIFE OF THOMAS GLOUG, DIED IN CHILDBED OF HER SECOND CHILD, ANDREW
GLOUG, 12th JULY, 1764, AGED 18 YRS. & 6 MONTHS.—ALSO, THE ABOVE-NAMED
ANDREW GLOUG, OB. 19 JULY, 1764, AET. 14 DAYS.—ALSO, ELIZABETH CHRIS-
TIAN GLOUG, OB. 17 APL., 1771, AGED 8 YRS.—ALSO, THOS. GLOUGH, HUSBAND
OF PRUDENCE, OB. 12th JULY, 1771, AGED 47 YRS.

M.

389.

(*Ab.*) MRS. ANN JONES, WIFE OF MR. THOS. JONES, TAYLOR, OF KINGSTON,
OB. 30 SEP., 1804, AGED 37 YEARS.

390.

(*Ab.*) ALEXR. WILLSON, OB. 4 DEC., 1812, AET. 46.

391.

(*Ab.*) MR. PETER DEMETRES, OF CORFU, & MERCHT. OF KINGSTON, OB. 1815,
JUNE 26th, AGED 80 YRS.

On another slab or tablet :

(*Ab.*) MR. JOHN BLAY, A NATIVE OF ZANTE, IN THE MEDITERRANEAN SEA,—
BORN 4th APRIL, 1743,—CAME TO THIS ISLAND 1772, & DIED 24th APRIL, 1821,
AGED 78 YRS. & 20 DAYS.

392.

(*Ab.*) THOMAS HAYLE,—OB. 27th JUNE, 1732, AGED 27 YEARS.—ALSO, SIX OF THE CHILDREN OF WILLIAM & PRISCILLA HAYLE, VIZ. :—

ELIZABETH		JANUARY 1, 1736.
CATHERINE		AUGT. 9, 1737.
JAMES	DYED.	DECR. 27, 1738.
MATTHEW		JANY. 12, 1740.
JAMES		JANY. 24, 1740.
JAMES		JULY 11, 1742.

393.

(*Ab.*) SAMUEL BARRETT HYLTON, ESQ., OB. 19 MARCH, 1856, AET. 22.—ALSO, UNA, AGED 15 MTHS., OB. 7th JULY, 1856.

394.

(*Ab.*) SUSANNA MANBY, WIFE OF MR. AARON MANBY, OF KINGSTON, IRON-MONGER,—OB. 21 NOV., 1762, AGED 22 YRS.—ALSO, MR. AARON MANBY, OB. 21 JANY., 1763, AET. 32.—ALSO, ZACHARY MANBY, SON OF THE ABOVE, OB. 19 SEP., 1796, AET. 34.

Marble.

395.

(*Ab.*) THE BODY OF MR. DONALD ROBINSON, WHO DIED SEP. 1, 1811, AET. 30.

396.

(*Ab.*) C. CARDE, ESQ.—OB. 8 JANY., 1823, AET. $39\frac{6}{12}$ YRS.—HIS DAUR., JANE CARD, DIED 16 JUNE, 1815, AET. 17 YRS. ; & C. M. CARD, OB. 4 MAY, 1816, AET. 11 MONTHS.

397.

(*Ab.*) LIEUT. JOHN N. FRASER, LATE 37th REGT., & BARRK. MR. FOR KINGSTON, STONY HILL, & PORT ROYAL, OB. 26 DECR., 1842.

398.

HERE LIETH THE BODY OF FRANCIS—SLICKER, WHO DEPARTED THIS LIFE THE—20th DAY OF APRIL, ANNO DOMINI 1728,—AGED 88 YEARS.—ALSO, THE BODY OF MARY, HIS LATE WIFE, WHO DEPARTED THIS LIFE THE 18th DAY OF JULY, ANNO DOMINI 1744, AGED—95 YEARS.—THEY LIVED TOGETHER A VIRTU-OUS MARRIED—LIFE, 50 YEARS, AND CAREFULLY EDUCATED—THEIR CHILDREN IN THE FEAR OF GOD.

Altar.

399.

(*Ab.*) JOHN HORN, ESQ., PAR. OF ST. ANDREW, OB. 27 MAY, 1788, AET. 48.—ALSO, MRS. ELIZABETH ECTOR, LATE HORN—WIFE OF ALEXR. ECTOR, OF KING-

STON, MERCHT.,—OB. 15 JUNE, 1796, AET. 38.—ALSO—LUCY MARSHALL, OB. JULY 30, 1797, AET. 24.

400.

(*Ab.*) JOHN REID, ESQ., MERCHT. OF THIS CITY, OB. 6th JUNE, 1833, AET. 47.

401.

(*Ab.*) ISAAC WILLASEY, ESQ., LATE OF CITY OF KINGSTON, MERCHT., OB. OCT. 11, 1804, AET. 36—ALSO, GARNETT WILLASSEY, HIS BRO., OB. AUGT. 13, 1807, AET. 20.

402.

(*Ab.*) MR. JOHN D. GALLAGHER, OB. NOV. 15, 1807, AET. 25 YRS.—ALSO, MR. WM. B. JACKSON, OB. JULY, 1810, AET. 22.

403.

(*Ab.*) MR. JOHN ROSS, PARISH OF ST. ANDREW, PLANTER, FORMERLY OF THE CITY OF KINGSTON, OB. 8 AUGT., 1807, AET. 48.—ALSO, EXPERIENCE ROSS, HIS WIFE, OB. 9th JANY., 1816, AET. 63 YRS.; & OF JOHN ROSS MILNE, SON OF THEIR NEPHEW & NIECE, OB. 29 MARCH, 1810, AET. 8 MTHS. 7 DAYS.

404.

(*Ab.*) THOS. EDWARD, SON OF ADAM & SARAH DOLMAGE, OF ST. CATHERINE PARISH, NAT. 2d FEB., 1784, OB. 4 AUGT., 1817.

405.

(*Ab.*) ALEXR. MACKINTOSH, ESQ., OF SPICEY HILL, ST. ANN'S, OB. SEP. 17, 1824, AGED 35.

406.

(*Ab.*) DONALD MCDONALD, SADLER, OF KINGSTON, OB. 20 JUNE, 1810, AGED 28 YEARS.

407.

(*Ab.*) JOHN SWARBREEK, SENR., OB. ON CHRISTMAS-DAY, 1781. HE WAS A NATIVE OF LANCASHIRE, IN GREAT BRITAIN.

408.

(*Ab.*) WILLIAM VREDENBURG, ESQ., OB. 8 FEB. 1822, AET. 38. HE LEFT A WIDOW & CHILDREN.

THE above was Wm. John Vredenburg, who married Mary Lawrence, daughter of John Carmichael Walcott [son of Henry Walcott, by his wife, Love Archer], by his wife, Mary Anne, daughter of Benjamin Lawrence [died 1784], son of Benjamin Lawrence, second son of John Lawrence, by his wife, Susanna Pelgrave.

409.

(*Ab.*) ANN, WIFE OF JOHN SWARBRICK, MERCHT., FROM POOLTOWN-IN-THE-FIELD, IN ENGLAND, OB. 5th SEP., 1769, AET. 27.

410.

(*Ab.*) ELLEN ANN MUNRO, NAT. 13 MAY, 1823, & OB. 4th JUNE, 1824.

411.

(*Ab.*) MR. ROBT. BOGLE, 3d SON OF ROBT. BOGLE, ESQ., MERCHANT, OF GLASGOW, FORMERLY OF KINGSTON, OB. 21 DEC., 1819, AET. 18.

412.

(*Ab.*) MISS JANET SCOTT, 4th DAUR. OF ALLAN SCOTT, ESQ., OF GLASGOW, OB. 4th JANY., 1819, AET. 32.

413.

(*Ab.*) MARIANNE DALY, DAUR. OF EDWARD C. LEWIS, OB. 15 SEP., 1839, IN 6th YEAR.

414.

(*Ab.*) JAMES FORSYTH, ESQ., MERCHT., OB., IN 53d YR., ... JUNE, 1836.

415.

(*Ab.*) CHARLES BINNEY, 4th SON OF HONBLE. H. N. BINNEY, OF NOVA SCOTIA, OB. FEB. 8th, 1822, IN HIS 20th YEAR.

416.

(*Ab.*) JESSY MARSHALL, WIFE OF GEO. MARSHALL, ESQ., OF SPANISH TOWN, WHO AFTER MANY SEVERE TRIALS, &C., OB. 23 MARCH, 1828, AET. 48.

417.

(*Ab.*) MARGARET ANN MUNRO, DAUR. OF JAS. MUNRO, ESQ., OF ST. ANN'S, OB. 5 SEP., 1831, AET. 17.

418.

(*Ab.*) FRANCIS TREADWAY, ESQ., 30 YRS. MERCHT. OF THE PARISH (KINGSTON), NAT. 13 NOV., 1771, OB. JANY. 29, 1836.

419.

(*Ab.*) JOHN LEAKE, ESQR., ATTORNEY-AT-LAW, KINGSTON, OB. 22 MAY, 1810, AET. 32.

21

420.

(*Ab.*) SARAH JORDAN, OB. 9 MARCH, 1859, AET. 21.—ALSO, ADELAIDE CLERMONT, OB. 27 JULY, 1862, AET. 25.

421.

(*Ab.*) ROBERT HAMILTON, ESQUIRE, OF ST. ANDREW'S PARISH, OB. 30 OCT., 1826, AET. 68.

Sculptors, Neilson & Galbraith, Glasgow.

422.

(*Ab.*) CATHERINE GARDNER, DAUR. OF WM. & REBECCA GARDNER, OB. 3 FEB., 1779, AET. 18 MTHS. 23 DAYS.—ALSO ANNABELLA SOPHIA PHILBIN, DAU OF RICHARD & CATHERINE JANE PHILBIN, OB. 29 APRIL, 1804, AET. $2\frac{9}{12}$ YRS. 17 DAYS.

423.

(*Ab.*) SARAH JANE KING, ONLY DAUR. OF ADAM DOLMAGE, ESQ., & WIFE OF WILLM. BROOKS KING, ESQUIRE, OF THIS CITY (KINGSTON), ATTORNEY-AT-LAW, DIED ON MONDAY MORNING, 9th DECR., 1816, AFTER A FEW HOURS' INDISPOSITION, HAVING BEEN PREVIOUSLY DELIVERED OF A STILLBORN FEMALE CHILD, BEING THEN IN THE EIGHTH MONTH OF HER PREGNANCY.

424.

(*Ab.*) JOHN, SON OF HUGH JOHNSTON, MERCHT. OF ST. JOHN, N. BRUNSWICK, OB. 19 SEP., 1801, AET. 21 YRS.—ALSO, CHARLES J., SECOND SON OF HUGH J., OB. 27 APRIL, 1808, AET. 25 YRS.

425.

HERE LYETH THE BODY OF ELIZABETH, LATE WIFE OF WILLIAM GORDON, ESQ., WHO DEPARTED THIS LIFE, FEB. THE 2d, 1727, AGED 28 YEARS.—ALSO, THE BODY OF THEIR SON WILLIAM, WHO DEPARTED THIS LIFE, THE 10th OF AUGUST 1725, AGED 1 YEAR AND 4 MONTHS.—LIKEWISE, THE BODY OF THEIR SON JOHN, WHO DEPARTED THIS LIFE OCT. THE 24th, 1725, AGED 14 DAYS.

SCULPTURED device of three skulls and two roses.

EBENEZER BURIAL-GROUND (KINGSTON).

1.

(*Ab.*) ...... MARY, THE BELOVED WIFE OF HENRY SOLOMON, OB. 30th NOVEMBER, 1862, AGED 48 YEARS.

2.

(*Ab.*) ...... WILLIAM PRIESTLY, WHO DIED 18th JUNE, 1853, AGED 56 YEARS.
"A LOVING FRIEND, A HUSBAND DEAR,
A TENDER FATHER SLEEPETH HERE."

3.

MRS. SUSANNAH GORDON, DIED ON THE 2d APRIL, 1854, AGED 36 YEARS.

4.

(*Ab.*) ...... WILLIAM NELSON, OB. 9th MAY, 1856, AGED 54 YEARS.

5.

(*Ab.*) ...... MRS. MARY ANN DELPRATT, WHO DIED 18th MARCH, 1856, AGED 16 YEARS.

6.

SACRED TO THE MEMORY—OF—MR. JOHN SURJEON,—BORN ON THE 18th NOVR., 1770, & INTERRED ON THE 18 NOVR., 1829. THE DECEASED('S) CAREER ON THIS TERRITORIAL (*sic*) SCENE TERMINATED ON THE IDENTICAL DAY OF THE MONTH WHICH GAVE BRATH (*sic*) TO HIS EXISTANCE (*sic*).

7.

(*Ab.*) SACRED—TO THE MEMORY OF—JOHN HENRY FEURTADO,—DIED 23 APRIL, 1856,—AGED 33 YEARS & 2 MONTHS.
VERSES follow.

8.

ARABELA—URSULA—PHILLIPPS,—DIED—FEBRUARY, 1848.

9.

STEPHEN PEYNADO,—DIED—14 DECEMBER, 1843,—AGED—43 YEARS.

10.

(*Ab.*) ...... MR. EDWARD FOLLIUS, OB. 13 AUGT., 1853, AGED 29 YEARS. HE WAS KIND AND AFFECTIONATE AS A HUSBAND, & SINCERE AS A FRIEND.

11.

(*Ab.*) ...... MRS. ELIZABETH YATES, OB. 2d JANY., 1857, AGED 97 YEARS.

12.

DOROTHY N. CALLENDER,—DIED—29th JANUARY, 1863, AGED—63 YEARS.

13.

CATHERINE GREEN,—DIED—18 DECEMBER, 1863,—AGED 83 YEARS.

14.

(*Ab.*) ...... MISS FRANCES WRIGHT,—DIED—17th NOVEMBER, 1850,—AGED 34 YEARS.

15.

(*Ab.*) ...... MISS MARTHA YOUNG,—OB. 24th OF MAY, 1853,—AGED 33 YEARS.
"WHAT IS THE BRIGHT REWARD WE GAIN?
THE GRATEFUL MEMORY OF THE GOOD."
CONS ... RE POSTE[A] SPERAV....T.[*]

16.

(*Ab.*) ...... MRS. SARAH WATT,—THE WIFE OF—MR. JOHN WATT, OF THIS CITY, OB. 26th OF JANUARY, 1833—AGED 33 YRS. & 11 MTHS.
SHE DIED AS SHE LIVED, AN EXAMPLE OF EVERY MORAL WORTH, WHICH ADORNS THE CHRISTIAN. REQUIESCAT IN PACE.

17.

(*Ab.*) ...... JENNETTE MARIE,—WIFE OF—MR. JOHN PHILLIPPS,—OF THIS CITY,—OB. 27th AUGUST, 1832,—AGED 46 YEARS.
VERSES follow.

18.

(*Ab.*) ...... JOHN FARRIER,—BORN IN LONDON,—ON THE 20th OF JULY, 1797,—AND DIED AT MONALTREE, ST. ANDREW'S,—ON THE 5th OF OCTOBER, 1860. (Eight lines in verse follow, and then :) ALSO, TO THE MEMORY OF—GEORGE & WILLIAM, CHILDREN OF THE ABOVE.

19.

(*Ab.*) ...... HARRIETT ANN,—WIFE OF—J. J. OLIVER,—WHO EXCHANGED THIS LIFE OF MORTALITY—FOR THAT OF IMMORTALITY—ON THE 15th DAY OF OCTOBER, 1842,—AGED 39 YEARS.
SEVEN lines in verse follow.

---

[*] The Latin inscriptions are frequently ungrammatical.

20.

(*Ab.*) ...... DAVID MENDES, OB. 6 NOVR., 1850, AGED 35 YEARS. FOUR lines in verse follow.

21.

DEPARTED THIS LIFE—ON THE 21st OF NOVR., 1842,—MRS. ANN BROWN,—AGED 31 YRS.—AND—ELVENIA BROWN,—HER DAUGHTER,—ON THE 28th JANY., 1843,—AGED 6 YRS.—" HAPPY ARE THE FAITHFUL DEAD.—AMEN."

22.

(*Ab.*) ...... S. A. SMITH,—THE BELOVED WIFE OF—D. SMITH, OB. 10th MARCH, 1835,—AGED 64 YEARS 5 MONTHS.

23.

REBECCA CHRISTIE,—DIED 10th APRIL, 1864,—AGED 19 YEARS 7 MONTHS.

24.

(*Ab.*) ...... JULIET, LATE WIFE OF—DAVID MENDES, OF THIS CITY,—DIED —17th MARCH, 1848,—AGED 27 YEARS—AND 7 MONTHS.

25.

(*Ab.*) ...... MR. THOMAS CAMBELL, WHO—DIED 15 OCT., AGED 45 YEARS. (Qy. in what year.)

26.

IS. GIBSON,—DIED—JUNE 8th, 1843,—AGED 25 YEARS.

27.

GEORGE BONNER,—DIED—8 JANUARY, 1832.

28.

(*Ab.*) ...... FRANCIS ELLIS, WHO DIED 25th MAY, 1864, AGED 49.

29.

(*Ab.*) ...... EVANGELINE,—INFANT DAUGHTER OF JAMES & SUSAN REID, OB. 13 JULY, 1854, AGED 16 MONTHS.

" THIS LOVELY BIRD—SO YOUNG, SO FAIR—
NOW CALLED TO EARLY TOMB,
JUST CAME TO SHOW HOW SWEET A FLOWER
IN PARADISE COULD BLOOM."*

---

* Given as an example of the general style of verses in many of these epitaphs.

Also,

TO THE MEMORY OF—EVELYN MCGREGOR REID,—BORN 2d DECR., 1855,—DIED 8th JANY., 1856.

30.

(*Ab.*) ...... MRS. GRACE BLUNDELL,—AN OLD AND RESPECTABLE INHABITANT OF THIS CITY,—OB. 16th OF AUGUST, 1855,—AGED 67 YEARS.

31.

(*Ab.*) ...... MARY ANN WOOLFRYS FORD,—DIED 28th FEBY., 1857.—AGED 92 YEARS.

32.

(*Ab.*) ...... MRS. ELEANER DAVIS,—DIED 25 JUNE, 1834, AGED 52 YEARS.

33.

(*Ab.*) ...... MRS. ELIZABETH LAUDERDALE,—WHO DEPARTED THIS LIFE—ON THE 12th APRIL, 1847,—IN THE EIGHTY-FIFTH YEAR OF ... AGE.

A FEW lines from the Apocalypse.

34.

SACRED TO THE MEMORY—OF THE—REVD. W. B. WILDISH,—WHO DIED OF YELLOW FEVER,—APRIL 9th, 1853,—AGED 28 YEARS.

35.

(*Ab.*) ...... REVD. JAMES ATKINS,—OB. JANUARY 24th, 1854,—AGED 45 YEARS—AND 30 DAYS.

36.

(*Ab.*) ...... CATHERINE N. PEARCE,—FOR SEVERAL YEARS A MEMBER—AND CLASS LEADER IN THE—WESLEYAN METHODIST SOCIETY—AT PORT ROYAL.—SHE DIED IN THE LORD DECEMBER 9th, 1843,—AGED—27 YEARS & 24 DAYS.

37.

SAMUEL FRASER,—SON OF HERBERT AND MARY JANE CARTER,—DIED JUNE 22d, 1853,—AGED 2½ YEARS.

38.

(*Ab.*) ...... HENRY CLARKSON FOSTER,—WHO DIED OCT 6th, 1843,—AGED—16 MONTHS.

39.

(*Ab.*) ...... JAMES WAVELL MATTHEWS,—OF—NEWPORT, ISLE OF WIGHT,—WHO FELL A VICTIM TO YELLOW FEVER—ON THE 30th MAY, 1853,—AFTER A RESIDENCE OF 23 DAYS,—AGED 26 YEARS.

40.

(*Ab.*) ...... REVD. THOMAS PROTHEROE,—WESLEYAN MINISTER,—OB.—SEPTEMBER 5th, 1856,—AGED 28 YEARS.
"THE MEMORY OF THE JUST IS BLESSED."

41.

(*Ab.*) ...... MARTHA, OB. FEBR. 22, 1857,—AGED 10 MONTHS;— .... HANNAH, OB. MARCH 4, 1857, AGED 2 YRS.;—INFANT CHILDREN OF THE REVD. J. WEBSTER, WESLEYAN MINISTER.

42.

(*Ab.*) ...... LYDIA MORIATY (*sic*) KELLY, OB. 6th DAY OF—OCTOBER, 1855,—AGED 43 YEARS.

43.

(*Ab.*) ...... DAVID MAC PHERSON,—OB.—16th AGUST, 1856,—IN THE 53d YEAR OF HIS AGE.

44.

HERE SLEEPETH,—BENEATH THIS TOMB,—MRS. GEO. DA COSTA,—WHO DEPARTED THIS LIFE—19th OCTOBER, 1856,—AGED 66 YEARS & 6 MONTHS.—PEACE, &C........

45.

(*Ab.*) ...... MRS. WM. STEUART, OB. 14th DECR., 1861, AGED 45 YEARS, AND HER FOUR INFANTS.

46.

(*Ab.*) ...... LOUISA JOSEPHINE, INFANT DAUR. OF FREDERICK BAIN (&) SARAH STARRIDGE (?), DIED 14th FEBY., 1857, AGED 6 MTHS. & 8 DAYS. "OF SUCH," &C........

47.

(*Ab.*) ...... MISS R. E. SPIGHT, OB. 19th NOVR., 1837, AGED 60 YEARS.

48.

(*Ab.*) ...... MRS. REBCA. COLLINS, OB. 12th JULY, 1854, AGED 52 YEARS.

49.

(*Ab.*) .... ELIZABETH MARSHALL,—DIED 28th AUGUST, 1856,—AGED 58 YEARS.

50.

(*Ab.*) ...... MARY A. WILLIAMS,—DIED 12th MAY, 1850,—AGED 90 YEARS.— AND—LUCY A. FITCH, DIED 22d JANUARY, 1858,—AGED 58 YEARS.—ALSO, RICHARD, HER GRANDCHILD,—SON OF R. LANGLEY, DIED 24th NOVR., 1850,— AGED 1 YEAR & 15 DAYS.

51.

(*Ab.*) ...... HANNAH,—LATE WIFE OF DAVID TODD, OB. 22d JANY., 1853, AGED 39 YEARS.

A DISTICH follows.

52.

(*Ab.*) ...... PHILLIS FRASER, OB. JUNE 1st, 1832, AGED 106 YEARS.

53.

(*Ab.*) ...... WALTER WALKER, OB. 21st DECR., 1841,—AGED—53 YEARS.

54.

(*Ab.*) ...... MRS. MARY NAPIER REATTO,—WHO AFTER A PAINFUL & LIN-GERING ILLNESS .... BREATHED HER LAST ON THE 9th DAY OF JULY, ANNO DOMINI 1820,—IN THE 71st YEAR OF HER AGE, ... LEAVING A LARGE CIRCLE OF RELATIONS ....

TWELVE lines in verse follow, in praise of the deceased, as "the tender grand-mother," &c.

55.

(*Ab.*) ...... SARAH, THE WIFE OF THE REVD. ROBT. GRAHAM, OB. 9th JUNE, 1853,—AGED 85 YEARS, AND 7 MONTHS.

56.

(*Ab.*) ...... MRS. MARY BECKFORD,—DIED AUGUST 21st, 1829,—AGED 40 YEARS.

57.

(*Ab.*) ...... MRS. ELIZABETH CROSSLEY, OB. 3d OF AUGUST, IN THE YEAR OF OUR LORD, ONE THOUSAND EIGHT HUNDRED & THIRTY-NINE, AGED 85 YEARS.—ALSO, HER GRANDSON, HENRY JOHN STEUART, OB. 21st OF JANUARY, 183..., AGED 19 YEARS. THIS TABLET IS ERECTED .... BY THOMAS BYNDLOSS, & CHARLOTTE RUSSEL GRAY, HER TRUSTEES.

58.

(*Ab.*) ...... G. HARVEY, WHO DIED 9th OF MAY, 1842, AGED 20 YEARS.—ALSO, J. MCCLAHLIN, DECD. 2d AUGUST, 1843,—AGED 51 YEARS, MOTHER OF THE ABOVE.

59.

(*Ab.*) ...... MISS ANN ELIZABETH WOOLFRYS, OB. 23d SEP., 1830,—AGED 10 MTHS.

60.

(*Ab.*) ...... ELIZA GOLDSON WHITE, OB. DECR. 15th, 1835, AGED 29 YEARS.

61.

(*Ab.*) ...... ELIZABETH BYSFIELD, OB. 17th MAY, 1856, AGED 95 YEARS.

62.

(*Ab.*) ...... ANN TAYLOR, OB. 30th MARCH, 1830, AGED 33 YEARS.

63.

(*Ab.*) ...... MISS ELEANOR FRANKLIN, OB. 15 MAR., 1832, AGED 46 YEARS.

64.

(*Ab.*) ...... HENRY MILLS, OB. 7 OCTOBER, 1856, AGED 38 YEARS.

65.

(*Ab.*) ...... JAMES MOREAU, OB. 13th MAY, 1850, AGED 64 YEARS.

66.

(*Ab.*) ...... EDMUND WELSH, OB. 12th NOVR., 1850, AGED 55 YEARS.

67.

(*Ab.*) ...... SUSANNA WRIGHT, OB. MAY 15th, 1857,—AGED 90 YEARS.

68.

(*Ab.*) ...... GEORGE FORTEATH, OB. 9 JULY, 1853, AGED 53 YEARS.

69.

(*Ab.*) ...... MRS. MARY BRISTOW, OB. 23d OCTOBER, 1841, AGED 55 YEARS.

22

70.

(*Ab.*) ...... MARY ANN GREEN, OB. 23^d NOVR., 1850,—AGED 36 YEARS 9 MONTHS AND 4 DAYS. TABLET ERECTED BY HER AFFECTIONATE HUSBAND, ROBERT GREEN....

71.

(*Ab.*) ...... MRS. ELIANER COOK,—DIED THE 26th SEPTR., 1857,—AGED 55 YEARS.

72.

(*Ab.*) ...... MRS. ADALAIDE SMITH, DAUGHTER OF MRS. JOHN BERKLEY,—OB. 30th DECR., 1854, AGED 30 YEARS,—LEAVING AN ONLY SON. (Six lines follow, and then :) THIS TOMB IS ERECTED .... BY HER AFFECTIONATE MOTHER.

73.

(*Ab.*) ...... OLIVIA SPRING, OB. APRIL 7th, 1850, AGED 32 YEARS,—THE WIFE OF STEPHEN SPRING.—ALSO, HER INFANT BOY.

74.

JOHN FORO, DIED 9th OF SEPTR., 1848, AGED 63 YEARS.

75.

(*Ab.*) RICHARD MOORE,—DIED—13 NOVEMBER, 1850,—AGED 23 YEARS & 6 MONTHS.

76.

(*Ab.*) ...... ELIZABETH STREDWICK, OB. APRIL 7th, 1851,—AGED 36 YEARS. —"HAPPY IN JESUS."

77.

(*Ab.*) EMILY HENRY,—DIED 21st MARCH, 1863, AGED 9 YEARS.

78.

(*Ab.*) ...... MATILDA CAMERON, OB. NOVR. 21st, 1850,—AGED 16 YEARS & 8 DAYS....

79.

(*Ab.*) ...... ROBERT SHERLOCK, OB. 3^d JANUARY, 1860, AGED 41 YEARS & 3 MONTHS....

80.

(*Ab.*) ...... WILLIAM CARR,—DIED 6th DECR., 1862, AGED 77 YEARS. ERECTED BY HIS AFFECTE. WIDOW.

81.

(*Ab.*) ...... ARCHIBALD MONTGOMERY,—DIED—16 MARCH, 1863,—AGED 63 YEARS.

82.

(*Ab.*) ANN MARIA DARLY,—DIED 16 APRIL, 1863,—AGED 70 YEARS.

83.

(*Ab.*) CHARLOTTE THOMAS COX,—DIED 29 NOVEMBER, 1861.

84.

MRS. LEAH LINGING,—DIED 14 DECEMBER, 1861, AGED 60 YEARS.

85.

(*Ab.*) ...... ELLEN EAST,—DIED 24th AUGT., 1860,—AGED 75 YEARS.

86.

(*Ab.*) CECILE ELIZABETH BACKEY.

87.

(*Ab.*) ...... MRS. ANN SCOLLEY, OB. NOV. 15, 1861. (Four lines follow.)

88.

(*Ab.*) ...... REBECCA ... WIFE OF THOMAS PITT,—DIED 13 JUNE, 1848, —AGED 46 YEARS .... (SHE HAD SERVED) AS A LEADER FOR THIRTEEN YEARS.

FOUR lines in verse follow.

89.

(*Ab.*) ...... MRS. ANN JOHNSTON, OB. 25th JULY, 1860,—AGED 59 YEARS.

90.

(*Ab.*) JOHN JOSEPH,—DIED AUGUST 5th, 1860,—AGED 22 YEARS.

All the following are abridged :

91.

ELLENNA DAVIDSON,—DIED NOVR. 6, 1863, AGED 57 YEARS.

92.

HANNAH JOHNSON, DIED 2d OCTR., 1863, AGED 48 YRS.

22—2

93.

MARY H. THOMAS,—DIED 22^{d} OCTR., 1862, AGED 74 YEARS.

94.

MARIA SPENCER,—DIED 19th SEPT., 1862,—AGED 39 YEARS.

95.

LEWIS BERWICK,—DIED THE 6th OF A....., 1864, AGED 60 YEARS.

96.

EWD. LAWRENCE,—DIED 24th DECR., 1863, AGED 34 YEARS.

97.

ADAM NEWLANDS,—OB. 19th MAY, 1864, AGED 60 YEARS.

98.

CAROLINE DICK,—DIED MAY 30th, 1864, AGED 36 YEARS.

99.

ALEXR. WRIGHT,—DIED 30 JUNE, 1864, AGED 23 YEARS.

100.

VICTORIA PEARCE,—OB. 24 JULY, 1860, AGED 11 YEARS 6 MONTHS.

101.

ELIZA HENDERSON,—DIED AUGT. 28, 1864, AGED 32 YEARS.

102.

MARY SAUMERS,—DIED 23 NOVR., 1862,—AGED 68 YEARS.

103.

SAMUEL DOUGLAS,—DIED FEBRY. 9th, 1863, AGED 40 YRS.

104.

CHARLOTTE DOUGLAS,—DIED NOVR. 21st, 1862, AGED 31 YRS.

105.

ANN WILLOCKS,—DIED 21 FEBRY., 1862,—AGED 24 YEARS.

106.

MISS MARIA DAVIS,—DIED 2 MAY, 1850, AGED 23.

107.

ALEXR. TODD,—DIED—MAY 26, 1860, AGED 26 YEARS.

108.

JAMES I. TRUEMAN,—DIED JANUARY (*sic*), 1861.

109.

ELLEN GORDON, DIED 8 JUNE, 1839, AGED 72 YEARS.

110.

EMANUEL MUDGE, OB. 21 JUNE, 1859, AGED 2 YEARS.

111.

JULIA B. CURTIS, OB. OCT. 29, 1858, AGED 20 YEARS & 8 MTHS.

112.

MISS MARY ANN SHEA,—DIED—12th FEBY., 1860,—AGED 73 YEARS.

113.

...... MRS. SARAH JACKES, OB. 13th FEB., 1859,—AGED 28 YEARS.

114.

...... MARY EDWARDS, OB. 27 JANUARY, 1859,—AGED 37 YEARS.

115.

...... JOHN AUTHUR ROBERTS, OB. 20 DECR., 1857,—AGED 53 YEARS.

116.

...... MRS. ELEANOR BECKFORD.........

SCULPTURE and inscription left unfinished.

117.

...... HENRY THOMAS, OB. JUNE 4, 1861, AGED 23 YEARS. BY HIS FOND MOTHER THEIR REMAIN—A REST FOR THE PEPPLE (*sic*) OF GOD.

118.

MARTHA VIRGINA WIGNALL,—DIED 30th AUGUST, 1864,—AGED 1 YEAR & 8 MONTHS.

119.

...... G. DASON, DIED 25th JULY, 1861,—AGED 44 YEARS.

120.

...... CHARLES BAILEY,—OB.—1st OCTOBER, 1859,—AGED 24 YEARS.

121.

FRANCES TERISSA,—DIED 7th JUNE, 1861,—AGED 4 YEARS. "THY WILL BE DONE."

122.

...... MARIA GILROY, OB. 18th JUNE, 1860,—AGED 74 YEARS....

123.

...... EDUARD GOOD, OB. 19th APRIL, 1857,—AGED 44 YEARS.

124.

...... FRANCES JAVARES, OB. 25th MARCH, 1861, AGED 25 YEARS & 6 MONTHS. THIS TOMB IS ERECTED BY HER SINCERE FRIEND, J. A. C. "THERE REMAINETH A REST TO THE PEOPLE OF GOD."

125.

...... LOUISA LODGE, OB. 29 JULY, 1846, AGED 26 YEARS & 4 MONTHS.

126.

...... JANE ANN, THE BELOVED WIFE OF THOMAS CLARKE, OB. 20 JUNE 1848, AGED 29 YEARS.

127.

MARY ROAM, DIED 24th NOVR., 1861, AGED 101 YEARS.

128.

ELIZA BURKE,—DIED 1858.

129.

...... ADELAIDE J. DOYEN,—DIED 26 JULY, 1852,—AGED 6 MONTHS.—ALSO, —ROSALVINA H. DOYEN, OB. 12th NOVR., 1852, AGED 4 YEARS & 9 MONTHS.

130.

SACRED TO THE MEMORY OF DOROTHY DAVIS BRAVO. NOTHING more.

131.

MRS. MARGARET EVANS,—DIED 2d APRIL, 1862,—AGED 52 YEARS.

132.

...... SERGT. JAMES SHARP,—2d W. I. REGT., OB. 6 SEPTR., 1864, AGED 36 YEARS.—ALSO,—SOPHIA SHARP,—WIFE OF THE ABOVE,—DIED 12 DECR., 1860 (OR 6?), AGED 25 YEARS.

133.

MRS. MERCY WILLIS,—DIED 26th FEBY., 1842, AGED 33 YEARS ...

134.

...... JANE BROMF..., DIED 10th JANY., 1842, AGED 13 YEARS & 7 MONTHS.

135.

MR. ROBERT LAING, OB. JANY. 18th, 1842.

136.

...... SARAH DE LION THOMPSON, OB. 30 NOVR., 1841, AGED 24 YEARS & 7 MTHS.

137.

...... JOHN CAMPBELL, DIED 8 NOV., 1836, AGED 52 YEARS.

138.

MRS. JANE GILBANKS,—DIED 1 SEPTR., 1845,—AGED 40 YEARS.

139.

...... ISABELLA TINKER GREEN, OB. 18 MAY, 1858, AGED 28 YEARS.

140.

HERE LIES ANTHONY LOWRY,—AGED 4 YEARS.

141.

...... ALFRED TAYLOR,—DIED 29 JANY., 1853,—AGED 2 YRS. 10 MTHS. 9 DAYS.

142.

...... PENELOPE BROWN,—2d DAUGHTER OF SAMUEL PRYCE, ESQ., SPECIAL JUSTICE, OB. 21 APRIL, 1851 (OR 7), AFTER 7 HOURS' ILLNESS, OF MALIGNANT CHOLERA,—AGED 23 YEARS & 4 MONTHS.

143.

MRS. SUSANNA BECKFORD,—DIED 7th APRIL, 1862, AGED 57 YEARS.

144.

MRS. MARY ANN DANCER, OB. 30 JULY, 1862,—AGED 86 YEARS.

145.

...... MISS JANE HOYES .... OB. 31 MARCH, 1846, AGED 75 YEARS & 3 MONTHS.

146.

ELIZA CATO, DIED I JANUARY, 1862,—AGED 29 YEARS.

147.

ROSANNA MORLY (?)

NOTHING more.

148.

JAMES MUNDS,—DIED 1844.

149.

ELIZABETH RENNALLS,—DIED 9th OCTOBER, 1863.

150.

ROSANNA MILLAR, OB. AUGT., 1841, AGED 82 YEARS.

151.

MR. JAMES MONTAGUE,—DIED 26th MARCH, 1839,—AGED 70 YEARS,—ALSO,— MRS. ELIZTH. MONTAGUE, DIED 13 MARCH, 1843,—AGED 75 YEARS.

152.

...... DIANNA E. NUGENT, OB. 20 JUNE, 1846, AGED 57 YEARS.

153.

...... JANE M. DAVIS,—OB.—MARCH 29, 1860,—AGED 20 YEARS & 3 MONTHS.

154.

...... MARY J. MORE, OB. 26 JANY. 1839,—AGED 75 YEARS.

155.

...... MRS. ELIZABETH MILLS,—DIED 31 JULY, 1857,—AGED 93 YEARS.

156.

...... ABRAHAM HENRY,—DIED AUGUST 13, 1852, AGED 26 YEARS.

157.

ELIZABETH MURPHY, OB. 29th OF MAY, 1845,—AGED 36 YEARS.

158.

WILLIAM JAMES WISEMAN, OB. 29 MAY, 1845,—AGED 39 YEARS.

159.

...... ARMERY DIAS,—DIED JUNE 16, 1844, AGED 3 YEARS & 5 MONTHS.

160.

...... MRS. MARY ANN CONOLLY, OB. 24 OCT., 1836,—AGED 44 YEARS.

161.

...... MISS SUSAN NOWLAN, OB. MAY 28, 1837,—AGED 31 YEARS.

162.

...... WILLIAM DICK, OB. 4th FEBY., 1836,—AGED 50 YEARS.

163.

MISS ELIZABETH RICHARDS, DIED 2d FEBRY., 1839.

164.

...... HURSELINA, DAUR. OF JAS. & ELIZABTH. BROWN,—DIED 13th OCT., 1839, AGED 3 YRS.

165.

...... THOMAS STEVENSON ROSS, OB. 27th SEPTR., 1832, AGED 30 YEARS & 7 MONTHS.

166.

ALEXR. DALLACE COLLIAN, DIED MARCH 10, 1864, AGED 47 YRS.

167.

...... MR. JOSEPH BENJAMIN, OB. 15th FEBY., 1831,—AGED 53 YEARS.

168.

THOS. H. STAPLES,—DIED 27th FEBY., 1864,—AGED 56 YEARS & 6 MONTHS.

169.

ELIZA BROWN, DIED 14th JANUARY, 1849.

170.

...... MR. HAMILTON BARCLAY,—OB. FEBY. 19, 1831, AGED 86 YEARS.—ALSO,—MRS. ELIZ. (OR ELSIE, OR ELIN) BARCLAY—OB. JUNE 2d, 1831, AGED 26 YEARS.—ALSO, HER INFANT, HENRY BARCLAY, DIED THE 1(5th?) OF THE SAME MONTH.

171.

MR. H. LAURANCE, DIED 4th MARCH, 1842, AGED 26 YRS. 6 MONTHS & 24 DAYS.

172.

REBECCA CHRISTIE, DIED 10th APRIL, 1864,—AGED 19 YRS. & 7 MONTHS.

173.

...... RICHARD GILBORNE, DIED MARCH 14, 1832, AGED 41 YEARS.—AMELIA CHRISTIAN, DIED JUNE 6th, 1839, AGED 2 YRS. & 7 MONTHS.—ALSO, SUSANNA CHRISTIAN, DIED DEC. 5, 1840, AGED 25 MTHS., DAURS. OF PETER & CATHERINE C.

174.

...... LOUISA DEMETRIOUS,—THE BELOVED WIFE OF WM. GOLDEN MCKENZIE, OB.—10 JANY. 1848,—AGED 33 YEARS.

Lines follow.

175.

...... CATHERINE B. GILCHRIST, OB. 11th AUGT., 1844,—AGED 17 YEARS.

176.

...... CHARLES H. SMITH,—DIED OCT. 25th, 1830, AGED 71 YEARS.

177.

...... ANN ABRAHAMS, OB. 1st NOVR., 1847,—AGED 20 YEARS.

178.

CATHERINE GOLDEN,—DIED—AUGUST 11th, 1831,—AGED 68 YEARS.

179.

...... SUSAN RICHARDS, DIED JUNE, 1857,—AGED 1 YEAR.

180.

...... ELIZABETH LOWES, OB. 4th OCT., 1832, AGED 63.

181.

THOMAS NEPPEN, OB. 22d AUGUST, 1830,—AGED 50 YEARS.

182.

MRS. MARY BECKFORD, DIED AUGUST 21, 1829, AGED 40 YEARS.

183.

RICHARD DURRANT,—DIED—24th OCTR., 1859, AGED 49 YEARS.

184.

DOROTHY FRANCES, OB. 17th AUGT., 1844, AGED 50 YEARS.

185.

MRS. SARAH AIKENHEAD, OB. 3d MAY, 1832, AGED 14 YEARS.

186.

JULIANA GEOGHEGAN, DIED 13th JANRY., 1848, AGED 39 YEARS.

187.

ELEANOR NICHOLAS.

188.

MRS. BUTLER, BORN—12th MACH., 1834; DIED 30 SEP., 1861.

189.

MRS. LUCY AUSTIN, DIED APRIL 3d, 1862.

190.

MRS. ELIZABETH REEFE, DIED 19th NOVEMB., 1864, AGED 26 YEARS & 6 MTHS.

191.

...... ADAM EVANS.

NOTHING more.

192.

HERE LIES THE BOY—OF—ANN JONES,—DIED 27 JANUARY, 1836, ... AGED ..6 YEARS.

193.

MRS. JULIET DAVIS,—DIED—DECR. 25, 1844, AGED 70 YEARS.

194.

ELIZABETH MORRISON, DIED THE 18th JUNE, 1864.

195.

...... EDWARD COLTH..T, DIED 18 AUGT., 1847, AGED 70 YEARS.—ALSO, HIS BELOVED WIFE, ABIGALE.

196.

...... JAMES BAILEY, DIED JANY. 1, 1844, AGED 37 YEARS.

197.

...... ELIZA ANN, THE BELOVED WIFE OF THE REVD. HENRY BLAIRE FOSTER,—WHO DIED AT GUY'S HILL, IN THE FULL—TRIUMPH OF FAITH, ON THE 25th AUGUST, 1842,—IN THE 30 YEAR OF HER AGE—(three lines follow). ALSO, OF HENRY CLARKSON, THEIR SON,—WHO DIED AT PORT ROYAL, OCT. 6, 1842, AGED 16 MONTHS.

FOUR verses follow.

198.

...... THE REVD. THOMAS PROTHEROE,— WESLEYAN MINISTER,— WHOSE PIETY, ZEAL, AND DEVOTEDNESS—SECURED THE STRONG AFFECTION—AND HIGH REGARD—OF ALL WHO KNEW HIM.—ARRIVED IN THIS ISLAND NOVR. 6th, 1855.— HE DIED OF YELLOW FEVER SEPTR. 8th, 1866.

THIS TABLET, A MEMENTO OF—THEIR LOVE, IS ERECTED BY—THE LEADERS OF THE EBENEZER SOCIETY.

Sculptured Bible.

NEW WEST GROUND (KINGSTON).

1.

...... CATHERINE FRANCES BURKE, ... BORN MARCH 13th, 1771, & DIED AUGUST 13th, 1823 (an eulogium on her virtues). .... HER DISCONSOLATE SISTER, FRANCES C. BURKE, INSCRIBED THIS MONUMENT TO HER MEMORY.

2.

...... GILBERT ELLIOTT, WHO DEPARTED THIS LIFE ON THE 5th (or 8th?) OF SEPTEMBER, 1830, AGED 41 YEARS & 8 MONTHS.

3.

...... MRS. ANN HACKET,—THE WIFE OF JOHN HACKET, ESQR., KINGSTON, OB. 18th OCTR., 183., AGED 51 YEARS.

4.

...... MR. JOHN CONSTANTINE,—AN OLD INHABITANT OF THIS CITY,—OB. MARCH 25th (or 28th), 1843,—AGED 81 YEARS & 3 MONTHS.

5.

SACRED TO THE MEMORY OF—MASTER WILLIAM BERRY, SON OF MISS JENNETT BERRY,—DIED 13th DAY OF APRIL, 1826,—AGED 11 YEARS.

6.

...... JOHN ORRETT, INFANT SON OF G. E. & SARAH ALDRED.—DIED 21 OCTOBER, 1841,—AGED 3 YEARS.

7.

SACRED TO THE MEMORY OF MISS JANET BERRY,—DIED JUNE 22d, 1833, AGED 38 YEARS.—ALSO HER GRANDCHILDREN, JANE G. SMITH & G. W. SMITH.— THE FORMER DIED JULY 29, 1836, AGED 5 YEARS & 10 MONTHS, AND THE LATTER DEC. 22, 1836, AGED 4 YEARS & 3 MONTHS.

8.

IN MEMORY OF GEO. D. MURCADO,—DIED 30 NOVEMBER, 18.., AGED 13 YEARS.

9.

LOUISA SUXAS—DIED 16th FEBY., 1861, AGED 32 YEARS.—ALSO, RANDOLPH EUSTACE, INFT. SON OF ANDREW & SUSAN R. LYON,—DIED 4th OCTOBER, 1861,—AGED 2 YEARS & 4 MONTHS.

10.

MARY STEUART, DIED ON THE 4th, JANY., 1819, AGED 77 YEARS. ALSO,—LUCRETIA ANDREWS, DAUGHTER OF THE ABOVE, OB.—4 MAY, 1826, AGED 46 YEARS.

11.

...... MRS. CLEMENTINA WATSON, WIFE OF MR. WM. WATSON,—DIED 24th OCTOBER, 1825, AGED 30 YEARS.

12.

.... AND HIS DAUGHTER, CLEMENTINA, BY CHARLOTTE, HIS WIFE, AGED 5 MONTHS.

13.

...... CHARLOTTE BYRON, WHO DIED 6 DECR., 1820, AGED 26 YEARS.—ALSO,—JOSEPH WYNTER, DIED 4th OF MARCH, 1825, AGED 45 YEARS.

14.

...... MRS. ROSANNAH WEST, THE WIFE OF JAMES WEST, WHO DIED ON 16th OF JULY, 1826, AGED 43 YEARS.

15.

...... MR. JOHN CUBBISON, OB. MARCH 8, 1827, AGED 29 YEARS 3 MONTHS.

16.

...... MR. JAMES MAY, OB. SEP. 7, 1820, AGED 37 YEARS.

17.

...... MASTER ALEXANDER HINE, OB. 17 APRIL, 1826, AGED 14 YEARS.

18.

...... MR. JACOB BEN...., ELDEST SON OF ANN ELLIS, WHO DEPARTED THIS LIFE ON THE 2d SEPTEMBER, 1830, IN HIS 28 YEAR.

19.

...... MR. THOMAS ASHBURN, OB. 4 OCTOBER, 1829, AGED 55 YEARS. THIS TOMB IS NEVER TO BE OPENED,—WHICH WAS THE REQUEST OF THE DECEASED.

20.

...... THE EARTHLY REMAINS OF JOHN ELBY,—FORMERLY OF THE PARISH OF CLARENDON,—HE DIED AT THE RESIDENCE OF MRS. CHRISTIAN, IN THE CITY OF KINGSTON,—IN THE FIFTY-FIFTH YEAR OF HIS AGE,—ON THE 4th OF AUGUST, 1841. .... THE REMAINS OF HIS SONS,—ROBERT & BENJAMIN,— WHO DIED MANY YEARS AGO,—LAY ALSO IN THIS GRAVE.—THIS TOMB IS ERECTED BY MRS. CHRISTIAN, 18..2.

21.

...... MR. LOUIS C. RAYMOND, OB. 29 OF JANUARY, 1826, AGED 36 YEARS.— AND—MISS SUSANNA SIVRIGHT,—OB. JULY THE 19th, 1836, AGED 43 YEARS.

22.

GEORGE THOMPSON,—DIED 6 MARCH, 1864, AGED 6 DAYS.

23.

...... JESTINA VERLEY, ... WIFE OF LOUIS FRANCOIS VERLEY, ESQR., OF THIS CITY. .... AS A MOTHER, ... SUBSEQUENTLY TO THE UNTIMELY DE- PARTURE OF HER TWO INFANT SONS, LOUIS & EUSTACE, WHO WERE SUMMONED FROM LIFE, DURING THE BRIEF SPACE OF 11 DAYS, PRIOR TO HER DEATH..... SHE ALSO FELL A VICTIM TO THE RAVAGING INFLUENCE OF A FEARFUL EPI- DEMIC .... ON THE 30th JULY, 1852, AT THE AGE OF 26 YEARS, LEAVING A .... HUSBAND, ... MOTHER, & 3 INFANT CHILDREN.

SEVERAL lines of lamentation follow.

24.

.... LOUIS LOUIS VERLEY, THE INFANT SON OF LOUIS FRANCOIS VERLEY, ESQR., & HIS LAMENTED WIFE, JESTINA VERLEY, ... (OB.) 26 JULY, 1852, AGED 3 YEARS & 7 MONTHS.

FOUR verses follow.

25.

...... EUSTACE LOUIS VERLEY, INFANT SON (OF THE ABOVE) (OB.) 19 JULY, 1852, AGED 19 MONTHS.

FOUR verses.

26.

...... CHARLES W. PIERCE, ESQR.,—A NATIVE OF BARBADOES, WHO DIED ON THE 14th FEBRY., 1856, AGED 29 YEARS.

27.

...... MRS. MARIA NUNIS, DIED 9th APRIL, 1856, AGED 84 YEARS.

28.

...... JOHN SIMPSON, SON OF SERGT.-MAJOR SIMPSON, R.B. 99th REGT.—
.... (OB.) 16th MARCH, 1851, (AET.) 1 YEAR & 10 MONTHS.

29.

...... PHILIP SANCHES, (OB.) 14th FEB., 1842, AGED 75 YEARS.

30.

...... MARIA SANCHES,—WIDOW,—DIED 21 JANY., 1849, AGED 80 YEARS.

31.

...... SAMUEL C. PARKINSON, (OB.) 31 JULY, 1863, (AET.) $2\frac{9}{12}$ YRS.
FOUR verses.

32.

...... JANE MCGREGOR, WHO DIED 14th DECR., 1863, AGED 28 YEARS.

33.

...... MISS MARGARET PALMER, (OB.) APRIL 2, 1833, AET. 15Y. 5M. 3D.

34.

...... RICHARD, SON OF JAMES M. & MARY DA SILVA, (OB.) OCTR. 2, 1834,
AGED 8 YEARS & 6 MONTHS.

35.

FANNY A. DESDUNES.

On a cross.

36.

...... M. E. MCNAUGHTON, (OB.) 21 APRIL, 1836, AGED 50 YEARS.

37.

...... MR. BURNSIDE.

38.

..... ALEXANDER H. MCRAE, (OB.) 8 FEBY., 1825, AGED 19 YEARS.

39.

...... WALTER BRETT, ESQUIRE, LATE OF THIS CITY,—ATTORNEY-AT-LAW,
(OB.) 22d OCTR., 1835, AGED 75 YEARS.

40.

...... EDWARD BARTHOLOMEW THOMAS,—SOLICITOR,—A NATIVE OF TEWKES-BURY, ENGLAND, WHO, AFTER A RESIDENCE OF 20 YEARS IN THIS CITY, (OB.) 13 JANUARY, 1846, AGED 44 YEARS.

41.

DANIEL W. DELVALLE,—DIED—3 MAY, 1863, AGED 9 MONTHS.

42.

...... ELIZABETH ANN SAUNDERS,—DIED 28 SEPT., 1846, AGED 7 MTHS. & 3 DAYS.—ALICE SAUNDERS,—DIED 13th JUNE, 1855, AGED 7 YRS. 6 MTHS.

43.

...... MARY AUGUSTA FARQUHARSON, (OB.) 14 AUGT., 1845, AGED $2\frac{3}{12}$ YRS.

44.

...... PRISCILLA WELCOME, (OB.) 15th NOVR., 1850,—AGED 69 YEARS.

45.

...... THOMAS ELLIS, ESQRE.,—DIED—10 SEPR., 1863, AGED 56 YEARS.

46.

CHARLOTTE E. STEUARD.

47.

...... THOS. EDWD. MILES, (OB.) 16 NOV., 1821, AET. 10 MTHS.

48.

...... LIEUT. WM. A. ANDERSON, LT. W. I. RANGERS,—DIED 10 FEBY., 1822.

49.

...... SOPHIA, THE BELOVED WIFE OF JOHN DAVIS, ESQR., WHO DIED 7 SEPTR., 1852, AGED 44 YEARS.

50.

...... MRS. ANN THOMAS,—WHO DEPARTED THIS LIFE—ON THE 5th OCTOBER, 1847,—AT THE ADVANCED AGE—OF 91 YEARS.

51.

EDWARD PHILLPS, DIED 28 DECR., 1849, AGED 44 YRS.

52.

ANN THOMAS SCOTT, DIED 27th JULY, 1853, AGED 2 YRS. & 3 MTHS.

53.

...... JOHN E. MC CREA, ESQR., DIED 12th JANUARY, 1848, AGED 43 YRS.

54.

MRS. JULIANA THOMPSON, DIED 9th MAY, 1849, AGED 69 YEARS.

55.

...... AGNES CAMPBELL,—INFANT DAUGHTER OF—MR. ALEXR. CAMPBELL, (OB.) 16 DECR., 1816, AGED 25 DAYS.

56.

...... JOHN MORCE, ESQUIRE,—FOR MANY YEARS—AN EMINENT MERCHANT OF THIS CITY,—LATTERLY SERJEANT-AT-ARMS—OF THE HONBLE. HOUSE OF ASSEMBLY,—AND ACTING—DEPUTY POSTMASTER-GENERAL OF THIS ISLAND.—HE DIED ON THE 19th FEBY., 1834,—AGED 53 YEARS.—...... ALSO, OF MISS ELIZA FLEMING,—MRS. REBECCA D..ANY,—MRS. ANNE MORCE,—JAMES MORCE, A CHILD, —RICHARD MORCE, ESQR.,—WM. MORCE, ESQR. ;—ALSO, GEORGE MORCE, ESQR.,— LATE NOTARY PUBLIC &—CASHIER IN THE TREASURY; ELIZA MORCE,—SONS & DAUGHTERS OF JOHN & ANNE MORCE.

57.

MR. JAMES GUNTER,—DIED 3 JUNE, 1853, AGED 44 YEARS.

On a cross.

58.

...... MRS. CHARLOTTE BOGLE,—WIFE OF G. O. BOGLE, DIED 7th OCTOBER, 1841,—AGED 39 YEARS.—ALSO,—THEIR DAUGHTER,—A.... ROSAMOND, 1841,— DIED 5th SEPTR., 1840, AET. 8 M. 27 DAYS.

59.

...... MR. GEORGE WM. HAMILTON, OB. 17th NOVEMBER, 1818, AET. 1Y. 6M. 24D.

60.

...... RICHARD RANCE, OB. 8 SEPTEMBER, 1856,—AGED 33 YEARS.

61.

...... MARIE ANTOINETTE,—THE WIFE OF ALEXANDER SHAW, ESQUIRE, DIED 8 NOVEMBER, 1845,—AGED 48 YEARS..... ALSO, ... ALEXANDER SHAW, ESQUIRE, ... DIED 3d MARCH, 1851,—AGED 64 YEARS.

DEVOTIONAL sentiment.

62.

ELIZABETH STEPHENS, DIED 2 MAY, 1859, AGED 3 MONTHS.

63.

D. O. M. SUB HOC MARMORE CONDUNTUR RELIQUIÆ CAROLI HUTCHINGS,—QUI AETERNAM EXPECTANS—BEATITUDINEM—RECESSIT,—OBIIT 25 DIE JUNII, A.D. 1839, AETATIS SUAE 28.—"MORTUI IN CHRISTO—RESURGENT PRIMI."

64.

HENRY, SON OF HENRY & JULIA HUTCHINGS,—DIED 23ᵈ FEBRUARY, 1842,—AGED 6 YEARS....

MR. HENRY HUTCHINGS' collection of relics of the earlier families of note, in Jamaica, deserves to be noticed, as does also his MS. of " Jamaica Worthies," &c.

65.

...... ROBERT PIKE, OB. 5th SEPTR., 1852, AET. 36.

66.

MR. RICHARD KING,—DIED—5th FEBRY., 1858, AGED 16 YEARS.

67.

...... MARY ELIZABETH .... WIFE OF ... JOHN DAVIS, ESQUIRE,—H.M. CUSTOMS, WHO DIED 6th MAY, 1848,—AGED 34 YEARS 2 MONTHS.—ALSO, CHARLES MOIR,—WHO DIED 3ᵈ AUGT., 1844,—AND MARIA ELIZABETH,—DIED 3ᵈ MAY, 1848,—CHILDREN OF THE ABOVE.

68.

...... HENRY GEORGE DAVIS,—ELDEST SON OF—JOHN DAVIS, ESQ.,—H.M. CUSTOMS,—WHO DIED 8 NOVR., 1850, AGED 8 YEARS.

69.

...... MAS.* PERCY K. ARNOLD, OB. 26 APL., 1844, AET. 9 YRS.

70.

...... ELIZA CATHERINE BAILEY, OB. 12 FEB., 1846, AET. 39, LEAVING 3 SONS, WHO SINCERELY LAMENT HER LOSS.

71.

...... WILLIAM GEORGE DAVIS, OB. 12th DECR., 1852, AET. 38.

72.

...... THOMASINE,—THE BELOVED WIFE OF CHRISTOPHER STEPHENSON, DIED 11 JANUARY, 1844, AGED 30 YEARS.—ALSO, CHARLES GEORGE,—SON OF THE ABOVE, WHO DIED 9th MAY, 1844.

---

* For *Master* (?).

73.

...... MARY MEACHER, SPINSTER, WHO DEPARTED THIS LIFE ON SATUR-DAY, THE 19th OF MARCH, 1808, AGED 31 YEARS.

74.

...... ROBERT DEWHURST,—WHO DEPARTED THIS TRANSITORY STATE & HONORABLE LIFE OF THIRTY-FIVE YEARS, THREE MONTHS, & TWENTY DAYS.—HE WAS RESPECTED IN LIFE,—AND REGRETTED IN DEATH.

75.

MRS. MARY ANN LEPEALT (?), DIED JULY 9th, 1861, AGED 85 YEARS & 4 MTHS.

76.

...... SOLOMON DELEON, DIED 17 MAY, 1847, AGED 39 YEARS.

77.

...... JOHN D. HARNETT,—CAPTAIN OF THE BRIG—"LAWTON," OF CORK,—OF WHICH PLACE—HE WAS A NATIVE, WHO DEPARTED THIS LIFE ON THE 24th MAY, 1841, AGED 26 YEARS.

78.

...... JA.... MAXWELL,—DIED JUNE, 1863, AGED 25 YEARS.

79.

SILVESTER TILLY.

80.

.... EDWARD BAKER CONYEAR,—CHIEF OFFICER OF THE "HENRY DAVID-SON,"—DIED OF FEVER—JUNE 8th, 1838, AGED 40.

81.

...... GEORGE PARKER, ESQR.,—OF CLAREMONT, PORT ROYAL,—LATE CLERK OF THE VESTRY FOR ST. DAVID'S—DIED ON THE 23d NOVR., 1850,—AGED 66 YEARS,— .... CHOLERA.

82.

...... MISS SELINA MATRO,—DIED—25 OCT., 1844, AGED 34.—AND .... HER .... CHILD, CHRISTIANA COLLINGS, AGED 2 YRS. & 6 MTHS.

83.

LOUIS OTTO,—DIED APRIL 16, 1864,—AGED 3 MONTHS.

84.

...... EDWARD TAYLOR, DIED 5th APRIL, 1859, AGED 28 YEARS.

85.

...... JOHN JEOFFERY, JUNR., OB. 3 OCT., 1855, AET. 87.

86.

...... THOMAS POWELL, ESQUIRE,—OF THE PARISH OF MANCHESTER, WHO DIED IN THIS CITY—NOVR. 29, 1840(?), AGED 29 YEARS. HE WAS DEVOTED TO HIS WIFE & CHILDREN....

87.

...... FREDERICK T. PRESCOTT,—SON OF EUSTIS & M. A. PRESCOTT, & A MEMBER OF THE FIRM OF E. & F. T. PRESCOTT,—NEW ORLEANS,—BORN IN NEW YORK,—2 NOVEMBER, 1819,—DIED ON THE 21 MARCH, 1843.

88.

...... MRS. ELIZABETH DICK,—DIED 4 MAY, 1839, AGED 40 YEARS.

89.

...... HENRIETTA,—WIFE OF JOHN PHILLIPS, SOLICITOR, DIED .... 19 JUNE, 1843, AGED 31 YEARS.

FOUR verses.

90.

...... MISS REBECCA NUNES,—SISTER-IN-LAW OF—JOHN PHILLIPPS, SOLICITOR, DIED 30 JANUARY, 1852, AGED 48 YEARS.—ALSO, OF HIS DAUGHTERS,— MARIA MARGARET .... DIED 13 JULY, 1852, AET. 13 YRS. 3 MTHS. & 20 DAYS. —AND JEANETTE ELIZABETH .... DIED 9 AUGUST, 1853, AGED 15 YRS. 6 MTHS. & 13 DAYS.

FOUR verses.

91.

...... MARY HILL,—DAUGHTER OF R. B. BERRY, ESQ.,—CONTROLLER OF H.M. CUSTOMS, KINGSTON.—AND JANE HENRIETTA, HIS WIFE,—WHO DIED 19 MAY, 1842, AGED 4 YEARS & 4 MONTHS.—ALSO, OF THEIR INFANT SON,—HENRY, —WHO DIED 5th SEPTR., 1855, AGED 1 YEAR & 8 MONTHS.—......MARY FRANCES BERRY, ANOTHER BELOVED DAUGHTER, DIED 29 AUGT., 1857, IN THE 14 YEAR OF HER AGE.

92.

EZEBELLE THOMAS,—DIED SEP. 5th, 1864,—AGED 38 YEARS.—DIED IN THE LORD.

93.

MRS. A. MC GHEE,—DIED 18 NOVR., 1850, AGED 62 YEARS.

94.

JAMES M. CUNTRA,—DIED 27 NOVR., 1850,—HIS SON, J. C. MATCHUM,—DIED 8 DECR., 1862,—MONTHS 27—DAYS 23.

95.

...... JULIUS HENRY PLACK, ESQR.,—MERCHANT OF LONDON,—WHO DIED IN THIS CITY ON THE 2d OF NOVEMBER, 1843,—AGED 45 YEARS,—ON HIS RETURN TO ENGLAND FROM NEW GRANADA, LEAVING A BEREAVED WIFE WITH TWO INFANT CHILDREN....

96.

...... ANGELINA, ... WIFE OF GEORGE SILVERA, ESQUIRE, (OB.) .... 23d OF JUNE, 1851, AGED 37 YEARS,—LEAVING A .... HUSBAND & SIX CHILDREN....

EULOGISTIC lines, and texts from Scripture.

97.

...... MRS. ELIZA WRAY (?), DIED .. NOVR. 18, 1830, AGED 56 YRS. ..

98.

...... LIEUT. ALBERTO GRIFFITH,—OF THE U.S. NAVY,—WHO DIED IN THIS ISLAND—ON THE 20th DAY OF DECR., 1842, Æ. 36.—THIS MONUMENT IS ERECTED BY HIS DEVOTED WIFE,—VALUED AS AN OFFICER,—& BELOVED AS A MAN,—HE DIED IN THE FAITH OF THE GOSPEL,—& RESTS IN THE BOSOM OF JESUS.

99.

...... GEORGE H. HOPKINS,—DIED—10th JUNE, 1863, AGED 44.

100.

JAMES BREMAND SMITH,—DIED 9 MAY, 1842, AGED 28 YEARS.

101.

THIS STONE COVERS THE BODY AND RECORDS THE DEATH OF MATHEW BARTOLOZE, ESQR.,—WHO DEPARTED THIS LIFE THE 16th OF APRIL, 1808, AGED 49 YEARS.

EIGHT lines follow.

102.

LOUISA PINNOCK,—DIED—17th DECR., 1844.

103.

...... CHARLES BRITTLEBANK, (OB.) 24 JUNE, 1848, AGED 43 YEARS.... ERECTED BY HIS....WIFE....AN ONLY SON LEFT TO MOURN.

104.

...... GEO. MC LENNAN,—OF PORT MARIA,—WHO DIED IN THE LORD—4 NOVR., 1856, AGED 38 YEARS.

105.

...... HENRY DA COSTA,—WHO DIED—31st OCTR., 1836, AGED 7 MONTHS. FOUR lines follow.

106.

.... FREDERICK HAYMAN,—DIED 10 APL., 1846, AGED 56 YEARS.

107.

MR. B. COOK KENT,—DIED FEBRY. 26th, 1812, AGED 25 YEARS.

108.

.... JOHN WEBBER HASSELL,—OF PORTLAND,—DIED 8 AUGUST, 1827, AGED 47 YEARS.

109.

...... WILLIAM PARRY, ESQUIRE,—OF THE PARISH OF PORTLAND, DIED 23d ... JANUARY, 1833, AGED 32 YEARS.

110.

MARY ANN SALEM,—DIED JUNE 30th, 1847,—AGED 47. LINE: Prov. xiv. 32.

111.

...... MISS MAIRTHER LIFELY, DIED 28. ... MARCH, 1844, AGED 65 YEARS. —ALSO,—MISS CHARLINE L. WALLS, DIED 15 ... FEBRUARY, 1853, AGED 38 YEARS. —AND,—MISS JANE DUNNETT, DIED 19 ... OCTOBER, 1854, AGED 51 YEARS.

112.

ANN ELIZA STONE,—BORN 10 OCTOBER, 1860,—DIED 12 FEBY., 1861. FOUR verses.

113.

MR. CHRISTIAN OTTO—POTTER, DIED ... JULY 25th, 1817, AGED 56 YEARS & 8 MTHS.

114.

...... ELIZABETH BENNETTO,—DIED 3d JUNE, 1854,—AGED 6 YEARS & 6 MONTHS.

115.

LOUISA ELIZABETH HENRY,—DIED 29 JULY, 1863,—AGED 30 YEARS.

116.

...... THOMAS GILSON (OR GIBSON ?), OF LIVERPOOL, ENGLAND, COM-
MANDER OF THE SHIP "JAMAICA," BELONGING TO THAT PORT,—WHO DIED IN
THIS CITY—ON THE 25th DAY OF OCTOBER, 1846 (OR 1844 ?), AGED 41 YEARS
....ERECTED BY HIS WIDOW....

117.

WILLIAM CEPHAS,—DIED 14 DEC., 1862, AGED 38 YEARS.

118.

ANGELINA SEPHAS,—DIED 11 JANY., 1863, AGED 33 YEARS.

119.

...... JANE WAUGH, THE BELOVED WIFE OF JAMES WALSH .... OB. 10th
FEBRY., 1845, AET. 37....

120.

ANN E. BARLOW,—DIED—1 MAY, 1864.

121.

CAROLINE WILLIAMS,—DIED—DECR. 28, 1862, AGED 44 YEARS.

122.

HENRY BERNALL JOHNSTON, DIED APRIL 24, 1864, AGED 17 YRS. & 11 MONTHS.

123.

WILLIAM H. PHILLIPPS,—DIED 1 JANY., 1849.—JEANETTE M. PHILLIPPS,—
DIED MARCH 8, 1864.

124.

...... MR. GEORGE OGILVIE, DIED .... FEBY. 29, 1824, AGED 30 YEARS.

125.

...... WILLIAM HARRIS, DIED .... JUNE 2d, 1811,—AGED 23 YEARS.

126.

...... JAMES TINDALL,—LATE OF THE CITY OF KINGSTON,—CARPENTER,
(OB.) .... 7 FEBY., 1809,—AGED 54 YEARS.

127.

...... CLARISSA DELEON,—DIED THE 6th JANUARY, 1842, AGED 62 YEARS
—HE SLEPT IN THE ARMS OF JESUS.

128.

THOMAS TROUTMAN.—DIED OF CHOLERA—THE 6th NOVR., 1850,—AGED 51
YEARS.—MUCH REGRETTED BY AN AGED MOTHER.

129.

JAMES GILLESPIE,—SHIP-MASTER,—A NATIVE OF GREENOCK, ... DIED HERE 19th OCTR., 1827, AGED 31 YEARS.—ERECTED BY HIS WIDOW.

130.

MR. SAMUEL KUCKAHN,*—DIED 6th JANY., 1864, AGED 85 YEARS.

131.

...... EMMA, THE ENDEARED WIFE OF—CAPTAIN THOMAS REAY,—OF THE—SCHOONER, "BLACK-EYED SUSAN," OF LIVERPOOL.

DATE gone.

132.

...... DR. AARON GARSIA,—BORN THE 23d OCTOBER, 1785,—DIED THE 3d JULY, 1848.—HE WAS A GOOD SAMARITAN,—THE POOR MAN'S FRIEND,—AND THE SICK MAN'S COMFORTER.

133.

EDWARD A. USHER.

134.

...... STEPHEN SHEFFIELD,—A NATIVE OF CORNWALLIS, NOVA SCOTIA,—LATE CHIEF MATE OF THE BRIG, "THOMAS," OF ST. JOHN, N.B. .... PROMISING YOUTH,—DEPARTED THIS LIFE ON THE 5th AUGUST, 1827, IN THE 22d YEAR OF HIS AGE.

135.

...... MARY ISABELLA DUGALD .... BELOVED .... WIFE OF MR. GEORGE GARSIA, WHO DIED ON THE 22d MAY, 1861, AGED 33 YEARS.— .... ALSO, ... MARY CATHARINE ELIZE, THEIR INFANT DAUGHTER, ... DIED ... 13th APRIL, 1861, AGED 2 MONTHS.

136.

IN MEMORY OF MY BELOVED HUSBAND,—JAMES TAYLOR,—WHO DIED—FEBRUARY 6th, 1853, AGED 29 YEARS.

EIGHT verses follow.

137.

...... FRANCIS MARCAUD, WHO OBIT (*sic*) APRIL 29th, 1826, AGED 77 YEARS.

138.

...... MARY ARNOTT, DIED ... 26 JANY., 1845, AGED 84 YRS.

---

* Qy. Cockayne?

139.

...... JAMES OTTLEY,—SHIPWRIGHT, OB. .... JANUARY 28th, 1824, AET. 39 YEARS & 3 MONTHS.

140.

...... JACOBA PAULINE HILL,—RELICT OF AWDRES OTTING, DIED 9 SEP., 1825, AGED 58 YEARS.

141.

...... ALICE MC CORMACK,—DIED 26 JULY, 1858,—AGED 6 MONTHS.

142.

CI GIT LOUIS RENE MALATRE,—AGE DE 45 ANS, DECADE—LE 30 NOVEMBRE, 1814.

143.

...... MRS. H. S. DALLAS,—WHO DEPARTED THIS LIFE ON THE—11th OF MAY, 1845, AGED 78—YEARS & 6 MONTHS.

144.

...... JULIUS SHERBROOK BRICE,—DIED 24th OCTOBER, 1851, AGED 11 YEARS & 11 DAYS.

145.

...... CAPTAIN JOHN PEACOCK,—OF THE BRITISH BRIG—ISABELLA,...... DIED 7th AUGUST, 1853, AGED 42 YEARS.—THIS TOMB IS ERECTED BY HIS DISCONSOLATE WIDOW, WHO ACCOMPANIED HIM TO THIS ISLAND........

146.

...... MISS FELICIA LASELVA, ELDEST DAUGHTER OF THE LATE BERNARD LA SELVA, OF SAINT GEORGE, ... OB. 22 JUNE, 1852, ... AET. 27.

147.

...... CHARLES LAMBERT, ... OB. 15th JUNE, 1852, AET. 53 YEARS & 6 MONTHS.

148.

...... JESSY MARIA FORD,—BORN IN LONDON 23d JULY, 1844, DIED IN KINGSTON 23d MARCH, 1862,—AGED 17 YEARS & 8 MONTHS .... REGRETTED BY BROTHERS.....

149.

...... CORDELIA HENRIQUES FORD,—BORN 3d FEBY., 1859,—DIED 30 JULY, 1862,—AGED 3 YRS., 5 MTHS., & 27 DAYS.—

150.

ALEXANDER SOWLEY,—DIED 10th JUNE, 1852, AGED 20 YEARS.

Not abridged.

151.

...... JOHN TAYLOR, ESQR., ... DIED 8th FEBY., 1815, AGED 40 YEARS.

152.

...... MASTER FREDERICK WILSON,— .... DIED OCT. 20, 1827, AGD. 11 MONTHS.—ALSO,—ALEXR. C. WILSON, ESQR., BROTHER TO THE ABOVE, WHO DEPARTED THIS LIFE ON THE 7 APRIL, 1848,—AGED 25 YEARS.

153.

MRS. JANE M. HURST,—DED—5th JANRY., 1859,—AGED 40 YEARS.

154.

MRS. ANN BUCKNOR,—DIED 6 NOVR., 1851, AGED 35 YEARS.

155.

...... GEORGE S. APPLEBY,—A NATIVE OF EAST POST,—STATE OF MAINE, U.S.—DIED MAY, 1853,—AGED 20 YEARS.

156.

.... MR. JAMES MC KAILL, CARPENTER, WHO DIED ON 2d JULY, 1818, AGED 60 YEARS.

157.

MRS. CAROLINE THOMAS DUFFUS, ... DIED 19 JUNE, 1853, AGED 84 YEARS.

158.

...... MR. JOHN FARLEY, ... DIED 18 APRIL, 1813,—AGED 34 YEARS.

159.

...... CAPTAIN OWEN LEWIS, OF THE—BRIG ACORN, OF LIVERPOOL,—WHO DIED ON THE 19th JULY, 1818, IN THE 43d YEAR OF HIS AGE.—AND,—THE REVD. JOHN HODGSON, WHO FOR 12½ YEARS—FAITHFULLY DISCHARGED THE DUTIES OF CHAPLAIN—TO THE GENERAL PENITENTIARY—IN THIS CITY.—HE DIED ON THE 5th OF JULY, 1861,—AGED 55 YEARS. (Verse, Matthew xxiv. 46.) .... AND OF MARY LEWIS MILNE,—BORN MAY 28, 1862,—DIED JULY 16th, 1863,—THE BELOVED DAUGHTER OF THE REVD. A. MILNE, & GRANDDAUGHTER OF THE REVD. J. HODGSON.

160.

.... SUSANNAH BROWN, ... DIED 13 MARCH, 1857, AGED 28 YEARS.

Two lines.

161.

...... GEORGE DEANS CODRINGTON,—ELDEST SON OF GEORGE CODRINGTON, ESQR., OF ST. THOMAS IN THE EAST, BORN ON THE 8th DAY OF JUNE, 1821, & DIED AT KINGSTON, ON THE 4th DAY OF NOVEMBER, 1854.

$\int$EE a notice of this family elsewhere.

162.

...... THOMAS GROOM, ESQR.,—OF THIS CITY, ... DIED DECR. 4, 1854, AGED 61 YEARS. THIS TABLET ERECTED BY HIS .... CHILDREN....

163.

...... MR. THOMAS JOHN GROOM,—WHO DIED OF CHOLERA,—DECEMBER 10th, 1850,—IN HIS 32d YEAR.

164.

MRS. ELIZA LOUISA FISHER,—BORN 5th APRIL, 1797,—DIED 31st OCTOBER, 1850.

165.

...... JOHN THEODORE MEYER, ... DIED 24th DECEMBER, 1857 (or 1), AGED 12 YEARS.

166.

...... CAPT. WM. DONOLDSON,—OF THE—BRIG HIBERNIA, OF BELFAST,— WHO DIED OF A MALIGNANT FEVER—IN KINGSTON, ON 25 OCTOBER, 1816, Æ. 33 YEARS, ... BEST OF HUSBANDS & FONDEST OF FATHERS, ... LAMENTED BY WIDOW & CHILDREN.

167.

...... JACOB J. ATHIAS,—SON OF DAVID ATHIAS & REBECCA CORRA,—BORN 16 MARCH, 1848, DIED 25 APRIL, 1853.

168.

...... GEORGE ....Y, THOS. & SUSANNA TINLEY, OF DOCK..AY SQUARE, NO.... SHIELDS, NORTHUMBERLAND, ... DIED .. YELLOW FEVER, OCT. 4, 1816, 1 DAY SHORT OF COMPLETING HIS 25th YEAR.

169.

...... MISS JANE ELIZTH. COUNTESS, ... DIED MAY 25, 1848, AGED 27.

170.

...... FRANCIS CLARKE, ... DIED 6th OCT., 1862, AGED 38 YRS. 8 MTHS.

171.

...... JAMES M. DAYES, ... DIED 25 NOVR., 1854, AGED 15 M. & 19 DAYS, AND OF JOHN W. DAYES, ... DIED 30 APRIL, 1856, AGED 4 M. & 6 DAYS.

25—2

172.

JOHN ROCKE,—DIED MAY 3, 1862, AGED 52 YEARS.

173.

MISS ANN WHITE,—DIED 11 JULY, 1858, AGED 27 YEARS.

174.

...... LUCY ANN, ... WIFE OF ALVION* TOLMON, OF THE BARQUE M. H. KENDALLUS (?), ... DIED 15 APRIL, 1853, ... YEARS & 3 .... (obliterated).

175.

...... ELIZABETH JUMP, ... DIED 28 MARCH, 1852, AGED 42 YEARS.

176.

...... JESSIE B. SMITH, DIED 9th JUNE, 1854, AGED 23 YEARS.

177.

...... JOHN HEEKS, DIED APRIL 8th, 1848, AGED 32 YEARS.

178.

...... JOSEPHINE JANE, ... WIFE OF MR. GEORGE BURGER, ... DIED 3 DAY OF JANRY., 1838, AGED 30 YEARS.

179.

...... GODFREY JOHN GOODMAN, ... DIED 25 DECR., 1839, AGED 49 YEARS.

180.

...... MISS ELLIN LEENAN,—DIED JANY. 8, 1859, AGED 24.

181.

...... MISS FRANCES PRINCE, ... DIED MAY 5th, 1825,—AGED 29 YEARS ;—AND ELIZA MUIR, DAUGHTER OF THE ABOVE,—DIED SEPTR. 28th, 1825,—AGED 9 YEARS & 3 MONTHS ;—AND WILLIAM DARBY, HER NEPHEW,—DIED OCTOBER 7th, 1818, AGED 3 YEARS & 4 MONTHS.—ALSO, THE SISTER OF THE ABOVE,—K RUSEL, DIED 29 JUNE, ... AGED 33.—HERE ALSO THE REMAINS OF WILLIAM THERE (?), FATHER-IN-LAW, WICH DIED DBER. 20,—1830.

J. Cox Thomas.

182.

...... MR. WILLIAM FRANCIS, ... DIED A.D. 1813, AGED 29 YEARS.

---

* Qy. *Oliver* (?).

183.

...... F. C. S. E. HORTON, ... DIED 1 APRIL, 1861, AGED 7 YEARS & 9 DAYS.....

184.

MARIE HIBGAME,—DIED 5 MARCH, 1864.

185.

...... ELLEN HALL, ... OB. 8 NOVR., 1854.

186.

OLIVIA GRETTY.

On a cross.

187.

JULIA DA SILVA,—AGED 18 YEARS.

188.

...... MATTHEW TRICKETT, ... SON OF MATTHEW AND ELEANOR TRICKETT, OF CARISBROOK, IN THE ISLE OF WIGHT, & A NEPHEW OF THE LATE CAPT. WILKINSON, R.N., K.C.T.S., WHO DIED OF YELLOW FEVER,—AUGUST 23^d, 1853,— AGED 26 YEARS.—ALSO,—ENTOMBED IN THE SAME,—MARY,—THE BELOVED WIFE —AND DAUGHTER OF THE LATE RICHARD & AMELIA SMITH, OF LANDGUARD, ISLE OF WIGHT,—WHO DIED AUGUST 21st, 1853,—AGED 23 YEARS.....

189.

...... CAPT. BRYAN H. RUMLEY,—OF THE SCHOONER, WALTER J. DOIL, U.S. —....DIED 4 JUNE, 1853, OF YELLOW FEVER,—AGED 45 YEARS.

190.

.... CHARLES & MARY THERESA CUSHNIE, CHILDREN OF JANE MC LEOD,— DIED 5th JUNE, 1855, AGED 4 YRS. 7 MTHS., & 25th FEBY., 1857, AGED 1 YR. 3 MTHS.

191.

WILLIAM FINLISTER.

192.

...... MR. JAMES SPENCER, ... DIED 22^d FEBY., 1862, AGED 56 YEARS.

193.

...... JANE GILLIN, ... WIFE OF NEIL MC DOUGAL, ... OB. 16th AUGUST 1856, AET. 40.

194.

...... MR. ANDREW MILLAR, ... DIED 11 JANUARY, 1826, AGED 64 YEARS

195.

.... MRS. SUSANNA HOYS, ... DIED 20th FEBRUARY, 1840,—AGED 95 YEARS.

196.

...... GEORGE RICHARD HAMILTON,—DIED 7 APRIL, 1837,—AGED 50 YEARS.

197.

THOMAS BELL,—DIED—DECR. 21st, 1839, AGED 68 YEARS.

198.

...... MR. JAMES HENRY, ... OB. 13th MAY, 1816, AET. 39.

199.

.... MARY A. L. BAPTISTE, ... DIED 15 DECR., 1841, AGED 21 YEARS & 4 MONTHS.

200.

MARY ANN SMITH, DIED 15 DECR., 1840, AGED 2 YEARS & 4 MONTHS.

201.

ELLEN FORTEATH,—DIED OCT. 16th, 1858, AGED 26 YEARS.

202.

MISS ELEANOR WILLIAMS, ... DIED 31st MARCH, 1816, AGED 35 YEARS.

203.

MRS. CECILIA STRADWICK.

204.

...... FREDERICK—& ALSO WILLIAM CHARLES,—THE SONS OF—DUNCAN & MARY [?] HAMILTON,—DIED OF CHOLERA, NOVR., 1850.

205.

...... CATHERINE SARAH PRESCOTT, ... WIFE OF WILLIAM W. PRESCOTT, ESQR., ... OB. 11 NOVR., 1850.

206.

JAMES CARTER,—DIED—26 AUGUST, 1843.

207.

.... MARTHA HAMILTON, ... WIFE OF DUNCAN HAMILTON, ... OB. 13 NOVR., 1850.

208.

.... JANETTA CODD, ... OB. 12 NOVR., 1863.

209.

.... WILLIAM HEWETT, ESQUIRE,—A MERCHANT OF THIS CITY,—AND FORMERLY OF ST. THOMAS IN THE EAST,—DIED 20th NOVR., 1841, AGED 39 YEARS. —ALSO, DOROTHY, HIS WIFE, ... DIED 15 SEPTR., 1844, AGED 38 YEARS.

210.

THOMAS WILMOT,—DIED—21 JULY, 1861, AGED 57 YEARS.

211.

ALFRED WRIGHT,—DIED—JULY 5,—1862,—AGED 1 YEAR.

212.

MISS SCOTT.

213.

CAPT. J. S. SPICER,—DIED—9 OCT., 1864,—AGED 66 YEARS AND 3 MONTHS.

214.

HENRIETTA MC INTOSH,—DIED—OCTR. 9th, 1864, AGED 16 YEARS 9 MONTHS.

215.

.... JOHN PHIL WIGNALL,—DIED—18 JULY, 1850, AGED 64 YEARS.

216.

.... SARAH CROASDALE,—DIED AUGUST 10th, 1834, AGED 53 YEARS.

217.

.... ISABELLA JARRATT,—WIFE OF—JOHN JARRATT,—WHO DIED NOVR. 24th, 1834, AGED 52 YEARS.—FAREWELL, FRIENDS AND RELATIONS,—WEEP NOT FOR ME BUT YOURSELVES,—I AM ASLEEP & IN HEAVEN,—I HOPE WE SHALL MEET AGAIN.

218.

J. B. BARKER,—DIED—31 MARCH,—1862,—AGED 26 YEARS.

219.

...... MR. ANDREW NICHOLL,—DIED JULY 2ᵈ, 1833, AGED 19 YEARS & 7 MONTHS.

220.

JAMES MC CREA,—DIED—JULY 10ᵗʰ, 1834, AGED 46 YEARS.

221.

CHARLES J. D. WRIGHT,—DIED 16 JANUARY, 1841, AGED 5 YEARS & 3 MONTHS.

222.

...... MISS MARGARET WALLICE, ... DIED 13 DECR., 1813, AGED 78 YEARS.

223.

...... J. J. HENDERSON, M.D., DIED 6 DECR., 1861,—AGED 45 YEARS.

224.

...... MRS. ANN DENTON, ... OB. 20 AUGT., 1839, AET. 72 YRS.

225.

...... MR. THOMAS FREEMAN, ... DIED MAY 13ᵗʰ, 1834, AGED 74 YEARS.

226.

ALEX. HIX, ALSO HIS BELOVED WIFE, SARAH,—.... DIED 22 APRIL, 1848, AGED 68 YEARS.

227.

MRS. MARY ANN TAYLOR,—DIED—AUGT. 16, 1864,—AGED 31 YEARS.

228.

...... ATWELL SMITH,—DIED OF CHOLERA,—24 NOVR., 1850, AGED 36 YEARS.

229.

EDWARD ALDRIDGE,—DIED—2 DECR., 1860.

230.

CAROLINE LEVEN,—DIED—10 JULY, 1863,—AGED 24 YEARS.—THE CHILD, WM. MC CREA,—DIED—27 JULY, 1863, AGED 1 MONTH 19 DAYS.

231.

NICHOLAS LOPEZ,—DIED ON THE 22ᵈ OCTOBER, 1863, AGED 61 YEARS.

232.

...... SUSAN JANE COOMBS, ... DIED DECR. 1, 1860, AGED 21 YEARS.

LINE from 1 Cor. xx. 57.

233.

JAMES M. MC CAN.

234.

DANIEL FENTON, DIED 29 AUGT., 1864, AGED 7 MONTHS.

235.

ANNA WALKER, DIED JULY 24th, 1860,—AGED 46 YEARS.

236.

MRS. SUSAN COOMBS.

237.

FRANCIS W. MC CARTHY,—DIED 24th FEBY., 1863, AGED 49 YEARS 5 MONTHS.

238.

SHIRLEY ALLEN,—DIED 7 SEPTR., 1861, AGED 23 YEARS.

239.

WM. M. OGG,—DIED 28th OCT., 183..., AGED 11 MTHS. & 13 DAYS.

240.

MAY EDWARD.

241.

ELIZABETH SANCHES,—DIED—28 DECR., 1863,—AGED 37 YEARS.

242.

...... CHARLES BABSON,—OF BROOKLYN, MAINE,—SEAMAN OF THE AMER. BRIGT., "PRONCESLON (?), WHO DIED JANY. 1, 1860,—OF CONGESTION OF THE BRAIN,—AGED 20 YEARS.

243.

STELMAN A. PIKE,—DIED 8 FEBY., 1864, AGED 18 YEARS.

244.

ROBERT R(OR K)ITSON,—DIED AUGT. 7, 1863, AGED 22 YEARS.

245.

RICHARD WHITE,—DIED—AUGT. 29, 1863, AGED 25 YEARS.
...... W. H. LAWSON ......

246.

FREDRICK WILMOT,—DIED 29 MARCH, 1864, AGED 32 YRS. & 5 MTHS.

26

247.

MISS MARY EARDY,—DIED 29th MARCH, 1864.

248.

ALEXR. DAWSON,—DIED—19 FEBY., 1864,—AGED 66 YEARS.

249.

MRS. ELIZA CARR,—DIED 11 NOVR., 1859,—AGED 55 YEARS.

250.

MARY MADLIN BURK, ... DIED 8 MAY, 1864, AGED 7 YEARS.

251.

C. W. TYMON,—DIED 6 JULY, 1859.

252.

...... HENRY FRANKLIN, ESQUIRE, ... DIED 8th NOVR., 1857, AGED 46
YEARS.

253.

...... THOS. POOLE, DIED 19th OCTR. 1863, AGED 32 YRS.

254.

FREDERICK W. NETHERSOLE, DIED 9 NOVR., 1861, AGED 43 YEARS.

255.

MISS JANE MURRAY,—.... DIED 25 DECR., 1839, AGED ... YEARS.—ALSO,—
MISS ANN EVANS, ... DIED 26 DEC., 1840, AGED ... YEARS.

256.

...... ELLEN HALL,—OB. .... 8 NOVR., 1854.

257.

...... WILLIAM EBENEIZA TURNBUL, ... DIED 11 APRIL, 1858, AGED 40
YEARS.

258.

MR. GODFREY NUGENT,—DIED 4 JULY, 1858, AGED 57 YEARS.

259.

GEORGE DAVIS,—DIED 31 JANY., 1864, AGED 30 YRS.

260.

...... WILLIAM HANRY,—DIED 4 DEC., 1861, AGED YEARS 43.

261.

CAROLINE GRANT,—DIED 4 OCT., 1862, AGED 42 YEARS.

262.

...... JANE ELIZABETH TURNNER,—DIED MARCH 14, 1860, AGED 14 ....

263.

WILLIAM FITCH,—DIED AUGUST, 1862, AGED 60 YRS.

264.

DANIEL THEOPHILUS DEAN,—DIED JANY., 1862, AGED 1 M. 20 DAYS.

265.

MARY ANN JANE EDWARD,—BORN ON THE 12 OF MAY, 1839,—DIED ON THE 5^h OF AUGUST, 1862.

266.

...... SOPHIA REALLO, ... DIED 26 DEC., 1862, AGED 85 YEARS.

A TEXT.

267.

ELIZABETH C. WISEMAN.

268.

...... GEORGE ADOLDPHUS BENJAMIN, ... DIED 1 NOV., 1863, AGED 45 YEARS.

A TEXT follows.

269.

ROBERT BATTY, ... DIED 8 NOVR., 1862, AGED 34 YEARS.

270.

EBENEZAR CHARLES GOOD, DIED 23 JULY, 1864, AGED 10 YRS. & 8 MONTHS.

271.

FREDRICK R. BOLTON,—DIED—24 MAY, 1864.

272.

REBECCA MATILDA JACKSON, DIED 29th JUNE, 1864, AGED 1 YEAR, 10 MONTHS, & TWO WEEKS.

273.

NATHANIEL GRIFFITHS,—DIED 29th JUNE, 1864, AGED $1\frac{6}{12}$ YRS.

274.

...... CAROLINE GRANT,—.... DIED 4th OCTR., 1862, IN THE 42d YEAR OF HER AGE....

275.

ALEXANDER MITCHEL,—BORN 1 OCTR., 1864.   D. B. F., 1864.

276.

DANIEL BAILEY, FRIEND (?) .... DIED SEP. 13, 1864, AGED 29 YEARS.

277.

...... ELIZABETH FORTE,—ELDEST DAUR. OF HENRY W. & MARGARET FO-DERINGHAM, OF THE ISLAND OF BARBADOS, ... DIED NOVR. 18, 1850, AGED 26 YRS.   POOR, POOR BESSIE.

278.

SYLVESTER GENIN,—OF THE—OHIO BAR,—DIED APRIL 4, 1850,—AGED 28 YEARS, 2 MONTHS,—AND 13 DAYS.—A JURIST, ORATOR, ARTIST, AND POET.

279.

MARGARET RAFFINGTON GRAHAM, DIED 31 DECR., 1862,—AGED 23 YEARS.

280.

...... THOMAS RODGERS, ESQR., DIED JANRY. 4th, 1838,—AGED 60 YEARS, —& HIS GRANDCHILDREN,—THOMAS,—DIED JANY. 1, 1864, AGED 4 YEARS,—CHARLOTTE BOLTON,—DIED MARCH 25th, 1853, AGED 3 MONTHS,—ALICE MARIA, DIED NOVR. 24,—1855,—AGED 11 YEARS.—AND ALSO THOMAS RODGERS, ESQRE., —LATE MERCHANT OF THIS CITY,—AND FATHER OF THE ABOVE CHILDREN,— DIED OCTOLER 21st, 1856, AGED 40 YEARS.

281.

...... MRS. ADELAIDE HESSE, ... DIED 20th APRIL, 1857,—AGED 25 YEARS.
Schlaf mohn ein Hieh !
Schlof mohn ein im Krioh !

282.

...... WM. JOHNSON,—DIED 28 NOVR., 1846, AGED 9 MTHS. & 2 DAYS.

283.

MR. THOS. WM. BLAKE, ... DIED 23 JULY, 1852, AGED 75 YEARS.

284.

ELIZABETH, DAUGHTER OF B. & M. MILWARD,—DIED SEPTR. ..., 1813,—AGED, 1 YEAR.—JUDITH MILWARD, SISTER OF Y^e ABOVE BENJAMIN,—DIED ... MARCH 1814,—AGED 49 YRS.—ALSO, ... MR. BENJAMIN MILWARD,—FATHER OF THE ABOVE ELIZA,—WHO DIED 23^d SEPTR., 1826,—AGED 64 YEARS.

285.

PATRICK WILKINSON, DIED 8 DECR., 1863, AGED 13 YRS.

286.

SARAH WINTER, ... DIED 30 APRIL, 1858.

287.

EVELINE MARD DA COSTA,—DIED 6th AUGT., 1864, AGED 7 YRS. & 3 MONTHS.

288.

EDWARD COLIN SONLEY,—DIED 10 AUGUST, 1864, AGED 8 MONTHS & 12 DAYS.

289.

...... MR. JOHN SMITH, ... DIED 9th AUGUST, 1846, AET. 80 YRS.

290.

...... MR. RICHARD THOMAS,—DIED 24th SEPTR., 1844,—AGED 32 YEARS.

R. W. Willshire, Sculp.

291.

FRANCES R. COLECLOUGH,—DIED 14 FEBRY., 1863, AGED 33 YEARS.

292.

MATTILDER ROSE ANARHARIS,*—DIED 1st OF MAY, 1862,—AGED 40 YEARS.

293.

ANN MOORE GUTZMER, DIED 14 APRIL, 1855, AGED 25 YEARS & 10 MONTHS. —ALSO,—ANTHONY ALEXIS SIMON,—DIED 23 OCT., 1856, AGED 9 YRS. & 3 MONTHS.

294.

WILLIAM CHANDLER,—DIED THE 19 APRIL, AGED 72.

Qy. Anno?

295.

THOS. R. PEYNADO,—DIED 24th OCTR., 1864, AGED 2 YRS. & 8 MTHS.

296.

GEORGE KILDEAR,—DIED 15 JUNE, 1862, AGED 18 MONTHS.

---

* Qy. Matilda Rose Anna Harris?

297.

THOMAS AUGUSTUS JONES,—DIED 15 MARCH, 1861,—AGED 50 YEARS.

298.

THIS MONUMENT WAS ERECTED BY THE OFFICERS AND CREW OF THE R. M. S. "CONWAY," IN MEMORY OF ALBERT MOORE,—STOREKEEPER OF THAT VESSEL,—WHO DEPARTED THIS LIFE—MAY 21st, 1863, AGED 21 YEARS. HE MET HIS DEATH BY AN ACCIDENT,—WHILE BATHING IN THE HARBOUR. "REQUIESCAT IN PA...."

An anchor.

299.

CHARLES LEGERE,—DIED 22d APRIL, 1863.

300.

HENRY BONNER, DIED 7th JUNE, 1863, AGED 40 YRS.

301.

JOHN A. JACOBS,—DIED THE 6th OF JUNE, 1863.

302.

...... MISS REBECCA MC KAY, ... DIED 7 SEP., 1855, AGED 16 YRS. & 7 MTHS.

303.

WILLIAM D. MORRISON,—DIED 8th OCT., 1863, AGED 33 YEARS.

304.

MISS JANE DA COSTA, DIED 24 DECR., 1863, AGED 54 YEARS.

305.

MARY ANN DRUSILLA MYERS,—DIED JULY 22, 1864, AGED 4 YRS.

306.

DANIEL BALLIN,—DIED 5th JULY, 1863,—AGED 53 YEARS.

307.

WILLIAM HENRY RICKETT,—DIED 11 JUNE, 1860, AGED 72 YEARS.

308.

...... PHADE, THE .... WIFE OF PETER BENJAMIN, DIED 10 SEPTR., 1858, AGED 88 YEARS.

309.

...... MRS. ANN BISH,—.... DIED OCT. 1, 1848, AGED 61 YEARS. (Four verses.) .... ERECTED BY HER .... DAUGHTER, ELOISA.

310.

.... REBECCA TINKER, ... DAUR. OF JOHN & ELIZATH. TINKER, ... DIED SEP. 2, 1825, ... AGED $2\frac{6}{12}$ YEARS.

311.

...... JAMES D. SCOTT, ... DIED DECR. 11th, 1842, AGED 6 YRS. & 8 MTHS.

FOUR rhymes follow.

312.

REBECCA (broken off), DIED MARCH 20th, 1863, AGED 46 YRS.

313.

...... EVAN EVANS,—LATE COMMANDER—OF THE BRIG "COURIER,"—OF LIVERPOOL,—.... DIED 2d APRIL, 1843, AGED 48 YEARS.

THIS IS ERECTED, AS A TOKEN OF RESPECT & ESTEEM, BY HIS BROTHER SHIPMASTERS.

314.

EVELINA BROUN,—DIED ON THE 17 APRIL, 1863, AGED 33 YEARS.

315.

ELLEN COLE,—DIED 6th MAY, 1864,—AGED 27 YEARS & 7 MONTHS.

316.

...... DAVID BARROW,—OF THE UNITED STATES,—WHO ARRIVED IN THIS ISLAND,—FROM CALIFORNIA,—& DEPARTED THIS LIFE—FEBRY. 8th, 1853, AGED 44 YEARS.

317.

THOMAS BLYCHENDEN.

NO date.

318.

MARY ANN JACKSON, DIED 12th APRIL, 1858, AGED 32 YEARS.

319.

GEORGE ASHURST,—DIED MARCH 15th, 1863, AGED 1 YEAR & 2 MONTHS.

320.

...... MASTER HENRY STINES, ... DIED 27 SEP., 1839, AGED 9 MONTHS, 3 WEEKS, & 10 DAYS.

321.

FREDERICK AUGUSTUS SILVERA, DIED 25th FEBY., 1853, AGED 3 YRS. & 10 MONTHS.

322.

JAMES MC CLOD,—DIED SEP. 14th, 1861, AGED 23 YEARS.

323.

MISS MARY MC KIE,—DIED 23 JUNE, 1856.

324.

ROBERT WILES.

No date.

325.

...... MRS. CATHERINE WILLIAMS, ... DIED 6th AUG., 1858, AGED 69.

326.

DAVID ALEXR. CAMBLE,—BORN 7th JANY., 1855, DIED 15 OCT., 1855.

327.

ELIZABETH DAVIS,—DIED 6th FEBY., 1862.

328.

DAVID THEOPLUS. CAMBLE,—BORN 14th JANY., 1858,—DIED 27th JANUARY, 1858.

329.

...... MARY WHITE, ... DIED 10th FEBRUARY, 1852,—AGED 46 YEARS.

330.

......MARY ANN,—DAUGHTER OF MR. JOHN COLMAN,—BY MARY ANN, HIS WIFE,—BORN 28 DECR., 1823,—DIED 26 NOVR., 1825.—ALSO,—SARAH MC DONALD, DAUGHTER OF MR. JOHN MC DONALD,—BY PRISCILLA HENRIQUES, HIS WIFE,— BORN 29 NOVR., 1827,—DIED NOVR. ..., 1829.—ALSO,—MRS. MARY ANN COLMAN, —DIED OF CHOLERA,—NOVR. 4th, 1850,—AGED 64 YEARS.

331.

...... CHARLES VERLEY, ... DIED 21st MAY, 1832, AGED 2 YRS. & 8 MONTHS.—ALSO,—.... EMILY VERLEY, ... DIED 12 NOVR., 1834, AGED 2 YRS. & 8 MONTHS.—.... REBECKER, BORN .... 9 NOVR., 1855, ... DIED .... 21st OCTR., 1856,—AT THE AGE OF 18 MONTHS 12 DAYS OLD (*sic*).—CHARLES HENRY RUSSELL, DIED 22 MARCH, 1860, AGED 7 MTHS. 2 WEEKS.

332.

.... CHRISTIAN SIMPSON,—WIFE OF MR. THELLAMONT DA SILVA, OF THIS CITY,—GENTLEMAN,—WHO DIED SEPTR. 12th, 1827.—ALSO, HIS TWO SONS, STEVENS JOHN HILL, DIED MARCH 27th, 1822, & CHARLES MC DERMENT, DIED NOV. 16, 1825.

333.

...... MISS ELIZA ANN MC KINSIE, ... DIED 5th DEC., 1838, AGED 24 YEARS.

334.

SUSANNAH PUSEY, DIED 9th MARCH, 1862,—AGED 36 YEARS.—SARAH ELIZABETH HAYMEN, DIED 17th MARCH, AGED 5 MONTHS & 12 DAYS.

335.

.... SARAH JACKSON,—.... DIED 11th JANY., 1852.—ALSO, MARGARET REID, ... DIED 27 APRIL, 1863.

336.

...... HENRY DE PASS, ... DIED 7th JUNE, 1861, AGED 28 YEARS & 10 MONTHS.

337.

CHAS. JAS. DUFF,—PORT ROYAL.

No date.

338.

...... MR. WILLIAM EMBLETON, ... DIED 18th JUNE, ANNO DOMINI, 1832, IN THE 32d YEAR OF HIS AGE,—LEAVING A FOND MOTHER AND OTHER RELATIONS....

339.

FREDERICK BRYAN,—DIED 11th JULY, 1819, AGED 9 MONTHS & 11 DAYS.

340.

...... GEORGE PYSHELL, ... DIED 19th JANY., 1817, AGED 29 YEARS & 7 MONTHS.

341.

...... MR. SOULANGE NARCISSE SAVARIAU (?), ... DIED 9th JUNE, 1845, AGED 38 ...., LEAVING .... WIFE AND THREE CHILDREN....

342.

...... CHARLES CHIPPS, ... DIED 3d APL., 1843, AGED 32 YEARS.

343.

...... MR. JOHN CRAWLEY WHITE,—.... DIED 6th MARCH, 1813, AGED 61 YRS. ...

344.

EDWARD SOMERS, JUNIOR,—.... DIED 9th DECR., 1827, AGED 2 YRS. & 5 MONTHS.

345.

HENRY JAMES ANDREWS,—DIED 13th APL., 1839, AGED 2 MONTHS.

346.

...... MRS. CHARLOTTE B. HAMILTON,—WIFE OF JAMES HAMILTON,—.... DIED 5th FEBY., 1849, IN THE 28th YEAR OF HER AGE.... ERECTED BY HER .... HUSBAND.

347.

MISS ANN E. DARLEY,—DIED 23d SEPTR., 1860, AGED 72 YEARS.

348.

...... MISS SUSANNAH SIMPSON, ... DIED 18th MARCH, ANNO DOMINI 1833,—IN THE 22d YEAR OF HER AGE,—LEAVING A FOND MOTHER AND AN IN-FANT CHILD....

349.

...... MRS. ELIZA MUNT MC CREA.—SHE DIED OF MALIGNANT CHOLERA—ON THE 29th OCTR., 1850,—IN THE 40th YEAR OF HER AGE.... ERECTED BY HER .... CHILDREN.

350.

...... MARY,—WIFE OF GEORGE HAMILTON,—DIED 27th JULY, 1849, AGED 23 YEARS.

VERSES follow.

351.

EMILIA HAMILTON,—AGED—49 YEARS.

352.

...... CHARLES DADDS, WHO DIED 4 SEP., 1864, AGED 57 YEARS.

353.

MRS. SARAH MC BEAN,—AND HER INFANT TWINS,—WHO DEPARTED THIS LIFE ON THE 4th MARCH, 1838, AGED 28 YEARS.

354.

...... INTERRED BESIDE HER BELOVED DAUGHTER, ARE THE REMAINS OF MRS. MARY ASKEW, WHO .... DIED 17th JANUARY, 1847, AGED 50 YEARS. .... TABLET ERECTED BY HER SURVIVING CHILDREN.

355.

...... MRS. ANN HAMILTON,—WIFE OF W. A. HAMILTON, ... DIED 22^{d} SEPTEMBER, 1834, AGED 17 YEARS & 7 MONTHS. (HER PARENTS,—HUSBAND, & AN INFANT BOY SURVIVE.)—ALSO, THE REMAINS OF HER TWIN SISTER, JANE ANDREWS,—WHO DIED—ON THE 5th NOVR., 1818, AGED 1 YEAR & 9 MONTHS.

356.

HELEN BOGLE, ... DIED 25 MARCH, 1831, AGED 15 MTHS.

357.

...... WILLIAM CARTER WORTHINGTON, ... DIED 3^{d} MARCH, 1860,— AGED 42 YEARS.—.... ERECTED BY HIS WIFE....

358.

...... MISS SARAH TAYLOR, ... DIED FEB. 1st, 1827, AGED 81 YEARS.

359.

...... JANE F. THANE,—DIED AUGT. 3^{d}, 1846, AGED 50 YEARS.

360.

...... MR. JAMES BARNALL,—DIED 22^{d} FEB., ..., AGED 38 YEARS.

361.

...... MRS. ARABELLA BOOTH, ... DIED 15th JUNE, 1837,—AGED 70 YEARS.

362.

...... MRS. SARAH GREER, ..., DIED 23^{d} JUNE, 1834, AGED 60 YEARS.

363.

...... MISS ANN CYRUS, ... DIED 30th NOVR., 1811, AGED 70.—.... ALSO, ... MRS. ANN RUGLESS,* WIFE OF MR. WM. L. RUGLESS, ... DIED MAY 12th, 1853, AGED 36 YEARS.

364.

...... MISS ISABELLA MARGARET MC LEAN, DIED 18th SEPTR., 1812,—AGED 10 MONTHS & 18 DAYS.

365.

MISS MENDES,—DIED 2^{d} MARCH, 1863, AGED 5 YEARS.

---

* Qy. Ruggles?

366.

...... ANN DURRANT, ... DIED 5th AUGT., 1834, AGED 37 YEARS.   THIS LAST TRIBUTE .... BY A SINCERE FRIEND, IN TESTIMONY OF HIS GRATITUDE.

367.

...... MARY ANN BURKE, ... DIED 18th JANUARY, A.D. 1824, AGED 38 YEARS.

368.

...... CORNELLIA,—WIFE OF HENRY HUNTER, ... DIED 30th AUGUST, 1827,—AGED 45 YEARS.

369.

...... MR. WILLIAM ANDERSON, ... DIED JANY. 28th, 1833, AGED 64 YEARS.

370.

MARY ANDERSON,—WIDOW,—DIED .... 14th MARCH, 1847, AGED 80 YEARS.

371.

...... FRANCES HARDY, ... DIED JANUARY 28th, 1831, AGED 48 YEARS. —ALSO,—HENRIETTA HARDY,—DIED JULY 24th, 1833, AGED 16 YEARS & 8 MONTHS.

372.

...... JOANNAH HARDY,—DIED ON THE 25th OF MAY, 1852, AGED 74 YEARS. FOUR verses follow.

373.

...... MISS ESTHER EAVES, ... DIED AUGT. 6th, 1821, AGED 40 YRS.— ALSO,—MISS ANN WICKINSIN (*sic*), DIED 30 NOVR., 1817, AGED 13 MTHS.—AND MASTER WILLIAM WILKINSON, DIED AUGT. 9th, 1821, AGED 7 MONTHS.

374.

MISS MARY WILLIS,—DIED SEPTR. 4th, 1821, Æ. 48 YEARS.—ALSO, OF MRS. ELLIN FAVIE,—DIED—9th JANY., 1842, AGED 34 YEARS.

375.

JOHN DANIEL BOYD.

376.

JOHN SIBBIT SMITH, ... DIED 19th MARCH, 1846, AGED 26 YEARS & 5 MONTHS.—ALSO, HIS NEPHEW,—FRANCIS ST. LEGER SMITH, ... DIED 21st NOVR., 1846,—AGED 3 YEARS & 5 MTHS.

377.

CAROLINE MENDES,—DIED AUGUST 8th, 1861, AGED 49 YEARS.

378.

JANE ELIZABETH PINNOCK.

No date.

379.

ELIZA ROAN,—DIED APRIL 21st, 1864, AGED 48 YEARS.

380.

CHARLES AUGUSTUS DAVIS, DIED 14th OF OCTOBER, 1864, AGED 3 YRS. & 7 MTHS.

381.

...... JAMES FORBES COLTHIRST,—BORN NOVR. 13th, 1796,—DIED JULY 23, 1841.—FANNY ANN, HIS DAUGHTER,—BORN NOVR. 22d, 1838,—DIED NOVR. 30th, 1842.—ALSO,—JAMES FORBES, BORN SEPTR. 22d, 1847,—DIED JANUARY 30th, 1848. —AND HENRY CHARLES,—BORN DECR. 21, 1851,—DIED AUGT. 19, 1852, CHILDREN OF HENRY FORBES & THERESA MARIA COLTHIRST.

382.

...... MARY NICHOLSON, DIED SEPTR. 5th, 1824, AGED 10 YEARS.

383.

...... MR. JOHN P. CROSS,—DIED 8th JUNE, 1821, AGED 49 YEARS. A SCRIPTURE text.

384.

...... MR. ROBERT POPE MYRS, ... DIED DEC. 1st, 1821, AGED 61 YRS., 5 MTHS., & 28 DAYS.

385.

...... MR. PETER SPENCER, ... DIED 31st MAY, 1829, AGED 96 YEARS.... ALSO, MRS. EDWARD MITCHEL, ... DIED 25 SEP., 1829, AGED 80 YEARS.

386.

HERE LIETH THE BODY—OF MISS ELIZABET HORABL (*sic*),—DIED ON THE 29 OF JUNE,—1829, AGED YARS.........

387.

...... RICHARD HARCHIN, ... DIED 16th MAY, 1863, AGED 34 YEARS.

388.

MARY SMITH,—DIED—JULY 11th, 1827, AGED 55 YRS.—ALSO, HER DAUGHTER, CATHE. ARCHER, ... SEP. 5th, 1825, AGED 29 YEARS.—AND HER THREE CHIL- DREN :—MARY JANE,—AGED 2 YEARS & 2 MONTHS—SUSAN, 1 YEAR & 3 WEEKS —AND GILBERT NANCE,—9 MONTHS.—IT IS REQUESTED BY THE LAST DECEASED THIS VAULT SHOULD NOT BE OPENED.

389.

...... MRS. ANN H. HUNTER,—WHO DIED JUNE 9th, 1836, AGED 23 YRS.,— 6 MONTHS.

390.

MR. JOHN NICOLSON,—DIED—NOVR. 2d, 1837, AGED 93 YEARS.—CATHERINE HOUELL, DIED 3d MARCH, 1863.

391.

MR. W. ENGLETON,—DIED ON MONDAY MORNING, 21st NOVR., 1836, AGED 62 YRS.

392.

...... MR. JOHN MOORE, ... DIED 18th AUGUST, 1834, AGED 61 YEARS.

393.

...... MRS. MARY WILLIAMS, ... DIED 20th JUNE, 1826, AGED 57 YEARS.

394.

...... EBENEZER TAYLOR, DIED 30th SEPTR., 1833, AGED 25 YEARS.

395.

HENRY CLARKE,—DIED 9th JANY., 1821, AGED $1\frac{1}{13}$ YEARS.

396.

...... MISS MARY LAMBERT, ... DIED 5th AUGT., 1830, IN HER 21st YEAR. VERSES.

397.

.... JANE CLIFF,—DIED 20 JANY., 1838, AGED 54 YEARS.—ALSO, HER SON, ROBERT MILLWOOD, DIED 27th DECR., 1841, AGED 23 YEARS & 2 MONTHS. EULOGISTIC lines.

398.

...... MRS. GRACE GRANT, ... DIED 30th JULY, 1819, AGED 70 YEARS.

399.

...... MRS. ANN MOON, ... DIED JANY. 19th, 1822, AGED 49 YEARS, ...
AFFECTIONATE MOTHER, ... KIND SISTER.

400.

THOMAS BINNIS, DIED 14th OCTR., 1864, AGED 27 YEARS.

401.

...... JOHN WALTERS, DIED 18th JUNE, 1827, AGED 40 YEARS.

402.

...... MASTER JOHN CAMPBELL,—INFANT SON OF ALEXR. CAMPBELL, DIED
10th APRIL, 1826, AGED 5 YEARS.

403.

...... JOHN CAMPBELL, INFANT SON OF ALEXR. CAMPBELL, DIED 11th
AUGT., 1821, AGED 12 DAYS.

404.

DIED AT KINGSTON, ON SATURDAY, THE ...rd DAY OF OCTOBER, 1821 (7?),
MRS. ANN HUNTER, AGED 66 YEARS & 4 MONTHS.

405.

...... JOHN DARLING JOHNSTON,—SON OF COLONEL JOHN JOHNSTON, ...
DIED 5th ... FEBRY., 1836, AGED 1 YEAR & 6 MONTHS.

406.

MORTIMER GORDON,—DIED .... 15th JANRY., 1833, AGED 50 YEARS.—THIS
.... TRIBUTE IN TESTIMONY OF .... FAITHFUL .... SERVITUDE .... OF 20
YEARS, ... BY HIS LATE MASTER, G. B. SMITH, ESQR., OF KINGSTON.

407.

...... MRS. JANE CLARKE,—DIED 24th SEPTR., 1839, AGED 56 YEARS.

408.

...... MISS LOUISA MILLS,—DIED 3d JULY, 1829, AGED 29 YEARS.

409.

...... CHARLES DEMETRIOS,—DIED 26th DECR., 1837, AGED 59 YRS.

410.

...... ISABELLA I. TURNER, WIFE OF THOMAS LORIOS, DIED 2d JULY, 1860,
—AGED 45 YEARS & 8 MONTHS....

411.

...... MARY HAY COWELL, WHO DIED OF CHOLERA, 28th NOVR., 1850,—
AGED 32 YEARS.

412.

...... ELIZABETH,—WIFE OF THE LATE RICHARD WEBB PANLING,—DIED—
5th NOVR., 186..., AGED 63 YEARS....ERECTED BY HER CHILDREN, WALTER M.
AND ISABELLA TURNER....

413.

M. J. CURTIS,—AGED—10 MONTHS,—&—A. A. BROWN, AGED 3 YEARS & 5
MONTHS....

414.

HENRIETTA CHARLES.

415.

T. W. S. H., DIED NOVR. 29th, 1863.

416.

...... MISS JANET LINDSAY,—OF ST. THOMAS IN THE EAST, ... DIED 21st
FEBY., 1826, AGED 33 YEARS.

417.

...... AMELIA, THE .... WIFE OF JOSE A. FIGUERICE, WHO DIED OF
MALIGNANT CHOLERA,— .... 7th NOVR., 1850,—AGED 28 YRS. & 14 DAYS.

418.

...... MR. JOHN FRITH, ... DIED 20th DECR., 1821, AGED 32 YRS. & 9
MTHS.,—ALSO,—BARBARA,—HIS MOTHER, ... DIED 28th NOVR., 1841, AGED 73
YEARS.

419.

...... MISS ANN HUGHES, ... DIED 16th MAY, 1816, AGED 2 YRS., 2 MTHS.,
& 4 DAYS,—ALSO, SUSANNAH COLEMAN,—(HER) MOTHER, DIED 17th OCT., 1816,
AGED 36 YEARS.

420.

...... SARAH PARKE, ... DIED 29th SEPR., 1820, AGED 40 YEARS, 4 MTHS.,
AND 25 DAYS, ... ALSO, ... HER TWO GRAND-DAUGHTERS, SARAH PARKE DA
COSTA, & SARAH PARKE DA MERCADO,—THE FORMER AGED 8 MONTHS & 24
DAYS,—THE LATTER, ON THE 11th FEBRUARY, 1822, AGED 13 MONTHS & 26
DAYS.

421.

...... EDWARD LUKE STEIBEL, ... DIED 31st JULY, 1831, AGED 3 YEARS.

422.

...... JULIA & EDWARD,—THE CHILDREN OF—HENRY FRANKLIN, OF THIS CITY,—SOLICITOR, & ELIZABETH, HIS WIFE,—THE FIRST WAS BORN .... 8th NOVR., 1835, & DIED .... 17th APRIL, 1836,—THE SECOND WAS BORN .... 6th SEPR., 1844, & DIED .... 15th MARCH, 1848.

423.

THOMAS JAMES, DIED—28th MAY,—1853,—AGED 29 YEARS.

424.

MR. WILLIAM SUZZY, DIED FEB. 15th, 1860, AGED 25 YRS.

425.

...... FRANCES ANN DICK,— .... DIED 30th ......, 1856,—AGED 27 YRS. & 2 MONTHS.

426.

...... ROBERT AITKEN, DIED 11th SEPR., 1841, AND JANE, HIS WIFE, DIED 13th APRIL, 1863, AGED 68 YEARS.

427.

BENJAMIN LOPES ALVER, DIED 16th MARCH, 1862.

428.

...... MRS. ELIZABETH HARRIS, ... MRS. MARY HARRIS, ... MRS. MARY MITCHELL,—THE LATTER DIED ON THE 18th OF MARCH, 1826, AGED 36 YRS. & 10 MTHS.—ALSO,—EDMUND B. LYON, ESQ., ... DIED 22d AUGT., 1841, AGED 40 .... —EDWD. E. LYON, ... DIED 30th JUNE, 1841,—AGED 16 MTHS. .... MAY M. LYON, DIED 2 JULY, 1843, AGED 14 MTHS.

429.

...... SAMUEL HENRY, ... DIED 23d APRIL, 1839, AGED 21 YEARS.

430.

...... JOHN K. MONTGOMERY,—OF THE PARISH OF CLARENDON, ... DIED 4th DECR., 1861.

431.

.... MARGARET CAMERON, ... DIED 8th APL., 1821, AGED 49 YEARS.

432.

...... MISS JANE CREIGHTON, ... DIED 18th SEPTR., 1825, AGED 25 YEARS.

433.

...... MISS FRANCIS THOMAS, ... DIED 16th AUGT., 1818, AGED 46 & 8 MTHS.

434.

...... MISS ELIZABETH CREIGHTON, ... DIED 24th DECR., 1834, AGED 5 YRS. & 9 DAYS.

L INES follow.

435.

...... PRISCILLA BYNDLOSS, DIED 28th JANRY., 1862, AGED 50 YRS. & 8 MTHS.

436.

...... MRS. MARY SMITH, DIED 29th MARCH, 1862, AGED 52 YEARS.

437.

...... MISS ANN GRAHAM, ... DIED AUGT. 11th, 1823, AGED 31 YRS. & 9 MTHS.

438.

...... EDMUND SNARE, ... DIED 1st JANRY., 1822, AGED 27 YRS. & 8 MTHS.

439.

...... THOMAS BLACAS, ESQR.,—LATE A MEMBER OF THE CORPORATION OF KINGSTON,—DIED 25th SEPTR. (1837 ?), AGED 46 YRS., (HIS) WIDOW FRANCES & AN ONLY DAUGHTER, ALSO, ... FRANCES BLACAS HAMILTON, HIS .... GRAND-DAUGHTER, DIED 30th NOVR., 1834, AGED 11 MONTHS & 8 DAYS.

440.

...... MRS. MARY MORGAN, ... DIED NOVR. 10, 1808, AGED 75 YRS. & 7 MTHS.

441.

MR. ELIZABETH WAITE,—DIED 26th DECR., 1861, AGED 59 ....

442.

JAMES NEWLAND DAWSON, DIED MARCH 18th, 1863, AGED 57 YEARS.

443.

MR. WILLIAM BARNETT,—DIED—APRIL 6th, 1833, AGED 36 YEARS.

444.

MRS. HAYMAN,—THE FORMER WIFE OF [MR. WM. BARNETT], DIED 9th FEBY., 1845, AGED 59 YEARS.

445.

...... JAMES .... AUSTIN, DIED 12th MAY, 1831, AGED 20 YEARS.

446.

...... MARY D. WILLIAMSON, ... DIED 20th APL., 1837, AGED 36 YEARS.

447.

C. M., 1856.

448.

MR. GEOE. DAWSON, DIED DECR. 19th, 1833, AGED 40 YEARS, 4 MONTHS, & 17 DAYS.

449.

...... MRS. ELEANOR DRUDD (*sic*), WIFE OF JOHN DRUDGE, DIED JANRY., 1815.

450.

...... CHARLES LOVEMORE,—DIED NOVR. 18th, 1828, AGED 48 YEARS.

451.

MRS. GRACE JOHNSON, ... DIED FEBY. 3d, 1863, AGED 34 .. ARES.

452.

GRACE BREWSTER, DIED 20th SEPTR., 1808.

453.

ANN MC VIGOR, DIED 13th SEPTR., 1863, AGED 21 YEARS.

454.

NICHOLAS REID,—DIED—MAY 22d, 1863, AGED 30 YRS. & 7 MONTHS.

455.

SAMUEL TAYLOR.

No date.

456.

...... FRANCES ELIZA,—WIFE OF R. W. BUCK, OF THIS CITY, ... DIED 11th FEBY., 1835,—AGED 23 YEARS, ... MONTHS, ... A TENDER MOTHER. .... LIKEWISE .. HER BROTHER, EDWARD MORISON, ... DIED 11 ...., 1831, AGED 10 (or 16 ?) YEARS & 6 MONTHS.—ALSO, THEIR MOTHER,—MARGARET HORNBY, WHO DIED .... 4th FEBY., 1837, AGED 49 YEARS & 5 MONTHS.

457.

...... SOPHIA BRICE, BORN MARCH, 1768,—DIED JUNE, 1808, AGED 40 YEARS.

458.

...... MR. SAMUEL CODOT, ... DIED 29th MAY, 1808,—THE GRANDSON OF DR. WILLIAM MC DONALD.

459.

...... WILLIAM BADLEY, ... DIED 13th JANRY., 1822, AGED 1 MONTH & 7 DAYS.— .... GEORGE GLADSTONE BADLEY, ... DIED 1 APRIL, 1832, AGED 1 MONTH & 12 DAYS.—ANNE WATSON BADLEY, ... DIED 8th APRIL, 1836, AGED 6 YRS., 5 MTHS., & 8 DAYS.—THIS CHILD WAS BEAUTIFUL IN PERSON,—OF AN EXTRAORDINARY CAPACITY OF MIND.....

460.

...... WILLIAM KELLY, — SON OF — JOHN KELLY, ESQUIRE, — DIED IN KINGSTON, ... 18th NOVR., 1839,—AGED 25 YEARS.

461.

...... MR. THOMAS RAYMOND, ... DIED JULY 27th, 1835, AGED 41 YRS. &
7 MTHS. MISS ELLINOR PHILLIP, WHO DIED JULY 1st, 1836, AGED 60 YEARS.

462.

...... MRS. SARAH LEWIS, ... DIED 22d JANUARY, 1858, AGED 63 YEARS.

463.

...... ELIZA PARKE, ... DIED 15th DECR., 1818, AGED 16 YEARS.

464.

...... ALBERT GEORGE PARKER, DIED 6th SEP. 1864, AGED 18 MONTHS.

465.

...... EMILY,—WIFE OF MR. T. S. HARVEY,—DIED OF MALIGNANT CHOLERA,
.... 10th NOVR., 1850,—AGED 41 YEARS—(long eulogium). ALSO, ... CHILDREN
OF THE ABOVE, NAMED .... EMILY BAINES, DIED 6th JULY, 1847, AGED 20 MTHS.
—EMMA MATILDA, DIED 23d JULY, 1847, AGED 1 DAY.—EDWARD CHARLES, DIED
5th SEP., 1848, AGED ONE WEEK.—HENRY JOHN, DIED 30th JANUARY, 1850, AGED
TEN DAYS.

S CRIPTURAL lines follow.

THE STRANGERS' BURIAL GROUND, KINGSTON.

1.

...... CHRISTOPHER BENTHAM (LATE CAPT. OF THE BRIG SARAH, OF LAN-
CASTER). THIS STONE PLACED BY HIS .... WIDOW .... NATUS AUGUST 9th,
1754; DENATUS MAY 2d, 1794.

2.

...... MASTER JAMES EWING, ... DIED 22d DECR., 1815, ... 11 MTHS. &
3 WEEKS.

3.

...... MASTER GEORGE & MISS CHARLOTTE DANIELL,—THE FORMER DIED
30th JUNE, 1810, AGED 11 YRS. & 9 MTHS., THE LATTER 14th NOVR., 1817, AGED
17 YEARS.

4.

...... MISS ANN MCCARTHY, ... DIED 13th .... AUGUST, 1797,—AGED
40 YEARS,—ALSO, ... MISS LUCRETIA CURTIS, MOTHER OF THE ABOVE, ...
DIED 28th JANRY., 1812, .. AGED 79 YRS. & 6 MTHS.

5.

JAMES KETTLE, SON OF MR. JOSEPH KETTLE, OF BIRMINGHAM, IN WARWICK-
SHIRE,—ENGLAND,—DIED 26th JULY, 1760, AGED 19 YEARS.

6.

...... ELIZABETH STORER ROOMS, LATE OF THIS TOWN, ... DIED 8th JUNE, 1796, AGED 39 YEARS.

7.

.... TERESA LONE, ... DIED JULY, 1813, AGED 18 MONTHS.

8.

...... JOHN, YOUNGEST SON OF WILLIAM AND MARGARET HUNTER,—OF FRODSHAM, IN THE COUNTY OF CHESTER,—ENGLAND,—WHO DIED IN THIS ISLAND OF JAMAICA, ON THE 15th DAY OF MARCH, 1812, AGED 15 YEARS.....

9.

...... MADEMOISELLE ANNE VIRGINIA STEUART, DIED 28th OF MAY, 1801, AGED 3 YEARS.

10.

MARY HOWARD,—DIED JUNE 27th, 1804, AGED 1 YEAR, 8 MONTHS, & 17 DAYS.

11.

...... MR. JOHN MUZZLE, DIED .. 26th FEBY., 1814, AGED 23 YEARS.

12.

MRS. JANE MC DONALD,—DIED—JANY. 20th, 1809.

13.

ESPERANCE EN DIEU, ... GEORGE ELLIS DAVIS, ESQR., ... DIED 1st AUGT., 1806, AGED 22 YEARS.—ALSO,—ELIZABETH SARAH CASSAN, ... DIED 1st SEPTR., 1809, AGED 37 YEARS. WILLIAM NATHAN DAVIS, ESQR., ... DIED 7th APRIL, 1810, AGED 28 YRS. HAMPSON RICE DAVIS, ESQ., ... DIED 1st SEPTR., 1814, AGED 29 YEARS.

14.

...... GEORGE WASHINGTON BUCHANAN,—SON OF JOHN & DEBORAH BUCHANAN,—OF THE CITY OF—NEW YORK, ... DIED JANY. 8th, 1806, AGED 22 YEARS, 1 MONTH, & 27 DAYS.

15.

SARAH FRANCES EDWARDS, ... DIED JULY 17th, 1796, AGED 19 YEARS.

16.

...... MR. HENNERY WEATHERS, .. DIED JULY 31st, 1804, AGED 29 YEARS, 7 MTHS., & 3 WEEKS.

17.

...... MR. WILLIAM STEWART, ... DIED AUGUST 1st, 1800, AGED 29 YEARS.

18.

...... MASTR. JOHN DUBUISSON, ... DIED 29th OCTR., 1809, AGED 3 YRS. ALSO, MISS ELLEN DUBUISSON, ... OB. 1st NOVR., 1812, AGED 3 YRS. & 10 MTHS.

19.

...... ROSANNA SIMPSON,—.... DIED 27th .... JANY., 1797, AGED 50 YEARS.

20.

...... MISS ELIZABETH DURE,* .... DIED JANY. 7th, 1802, AGED 28 YEARS.

21.

...... WILLIAM BURKE, ... DIED APRIL 13th, 1801, AGED 2 YRS., 9 MTHS., & 12 DAYS.—ALSO, ... JULIET MA...CE BURKE, DIED 9th SEPTR., 1804,—AGED NEAR 11 MONTHS & 26 DAYS.

22.

...... DOROTHY BOGLE, DIED APRIL 29th, 1802, AGED 3 YRS., 11 MTHS., & 11 DAYS.

23.

MISS GRACE WELLING, DIED MARCH 18th, 1785, AGED 40 YEARS.

24.

...... MARY COSSLEY, ... DIED MARCH 14th, 1805, AGED 40 YEARS.

25.

...... ELIZA DUNNING, ... DIED 19th NOVR., 1785, AGED 87 YEARS.

26.

SUSANNAH BARGE, ... DIED 4th APRIL, 1790.

27.

HANNAH HOWELL, DIED MAY 11th, 1802,—AGED 12 YEARS.

28.

...... CHARLES VALLANCY, ... DIED 16th JUNE, 1814, AGED 1 MONTH & 2 WEEKS.

29.

MR. CHARLES WILLIAM BARRETT, DIED 7th JULY, 1815, AGED 79 YRS.

30.

...... WILLIAM EDWARDS, DIED .... 21st NOVR., 1813,—AGED 17 YEARS & SIX MONTHS. ERECTED BY WILLIAM ROWLAND.

31.

MRS. HANNAH COLLETT, DIED 28th FEBY., 1812, AGED 52 YRS., 10 M., 16 D.

32.

...... FRANCIS GAYTON HARRIS, DIED 15th OCTOBER, 1787, AGED 2 YEARS & 6 MONTHS.—ALSO, ... REBECCA KNOWLES, MOTHER OF THE ABOVE ...., DIED 20th APRIL, 1788, AGED 36 YEARS & 6 MONTHS.

33.

OLIVER SPARKS,—DIED—JANUARY 19th, 1798, AGED 5 MTHS. & 9 DAYS.

---

* Qy. Dewar?

34.

ANN STEPHENS,—BORN DECR. 7, 1776, ... DIED JUNE 26h , 1797.

35.

MR. JOSEPH HARVEY, ... 19th JANRY., 1797, AGED 20 YEARS.—ALSO, ...
HENSON HARVEY, HIS .... BROTHER, ... DIED 12th NOVR., 1798, AGED 24
YEARS.—ALSO, HENSON ALEXR. HARVEY, NEPHEW OF THE ABOVE,—DIED APRIL
24th, 1803, AGED 3 YEARS.—ALSO, ROBERT GILBERT HARVEY, DIED MARCH, 1803,
AGED 25 YEARS.

36.

...... SARAH LINDO,—DIED 24th JANY., 1808.

37.

...... MARY JOSEPH EMILLA CHAVANIES, DIED THE 9th OCTOBER, 1814,
AGED 18 YEARS ; & ELIZABETH MARIA HIGSON, DIED 16th MAY, 1815, AGED 2 YRS.
& 1 MONTH.

38.

MISS CECILIA KENT,—DEPARTED LIFE, 25th NOVR., 1812,—AGED 2 YEARS &
11 MONTHS.

39.

...... ROBERT FAIRBAIRN, OF THIS CITY,—CARPENTER, ... DIED 11th
AUGUST, 1810, AGED 30 YEARS....

40.

...... MASTR. SAMUEL NORTON F. NORTON, WHO DIED DECR. 30th, 1803,
AGED 5 YEARS & 2 MONTHS.

41.

...... JAMES SALAS, DIED FEBY. 20th, 1798, AGED .... 9 MONTHS.

42.

MASTER WILLIAM YOUNG,—DIED 20th SEPTR., 1801, AGED 8 YRS. & 8 MONTHS.

43.

MASTER WILLIAM DUFFUS, ... DIED 14th MAY, 1810, AGED 1 YEAR., 4
MONTHS, & 25 DAYS.

44.

MR. AMNON TODD, DIED 13th AUGUST, 1814, AGED 44 YEARS.

45.

...... DOROTHY GREGORY, ... DIED 21st JULY, 1806, AGED 90 YEARS.

46.

...... MR. BRYAN MANNING, OF THIS TOWN,—MERCHANT,—WHO DIED 28th
JUNE, 1777, AGED 43 YEARS. .... A FATHER .... A HUSBAND....—ALSO, ...
DOROTHY MANNING, DAUGHTER OF THE ABOVE, WHO DYED THE 16th MAY,
1770, AGED 5 MONTHS.

47.

...... WILLIAM BEAL, SON OF THE DECEASED ANN GOLDSON BURTON, ...
DIED 10th FEBY., 1807, AGED 32 YRS. & 3 MONTHS.

48.

...... BUTCHER, WHO .... JUNE 28th, 1809, ... 15 YEARS.

49.

...... MISS ANN GOLDSON, ... DIED 24th OCTR., 1794, AGED 25 YEARS.—
ALSO, MISS ANN GOLDSON, DIED 28th APRIL, 1802, AGED 59 YEARS.

50.

...... CHARLES PARKEY, ... DIED JUNE 18th, 1819, AGED 1 YEAR & 2
MONTHS.

51.

...... MDM. MARIE JOSEPHE DALLIER, ... DIED JUNE 20th, 1804,—AGED
40 YEARS.—ALSO, HER GRANDDAUGHTER, ADELLE BRODHURST, WHO DIED AUGT.
28th, 1814, AGED 21 MONTHS.

52.

...... PHILIP GARTHWAITE, ... DIED 1st MAY, 1753,—AGED 42 YEARS.—
ALSO, HIS WIFE, ELEANOR GARTHWAITE, ... DIED 29th NOVR., 1754, AGED 40
YEARS.—ALSO, RACHEL RICHARDSON, DAUGHTER OF RALPH & ALICE, WHO DIED
5th APRIL, 1756, AGED 5 MONTHS & ....—RALPH RICHARDSON, DIED 29
JANUARY, 1758, AGED 32 YEARS. (Four verses.) HERE ALSO LIETH .... WM.
LOYD, SON OF WILLM. LOYD, MERCHANT, ... DIED OCTR. 3d, 1763, AGED 13
MONTHS.—ALSO, THOMAS GARTHWAITE, ... DIED OCT. 1st, 1758, AGED 23 YEARS.

53.

...... MASTER DAVID AIRD, ... DIED SEPTR. ..., 1813, AGED 2 MTHS. &
15 DAYS.

54.

...... WILLIAM WEDDERBURN VERNON (?), ESQR.,—LATE OF CHARLOTTE
STREET, FITZROY SQUARE, LONDON, ... DIED .... 1st DAY OF SEPTEMBER,
1802, AGED 29 YEARS.

55.

...... REBECCA BARNES SILVA, ... DIED FEBY. 6th, 1795, AGED 32 YEARS.

56.

...... MR. BREDDIE PARK,—A NATIVE OF GREENOCK, IN SCOTLAND, WHO
DIED AT KINGSTON,—WHERE, UNDER THE PRESSURE OF A FATAL DISEASE,—HE
HAD SOUGHT REFUGE FROM THE SEVERITY OF THE BRITISH CLIMATE,—ON THE
20th JUNE, 1811,—IN THE 27th YEAR OF HIS AGE.
EULOGISTIC lines.

57.

...... AGNES MC MICKAN, ... DIED 26th OCTR., 1806, AGED 70 YEARS.

58.

...... GEORGE FURTADO,—AGED 11 MONTHS,—21 SEPTR. 1810.

59.

...... MISS FRANCES COOFN (?), ... DIED 27th JULY, 1807, AGED 74 YEARS.

60.

...... ALEXR. BIGGAR, ... DIED ... NOVR., 1802,—AGED 5 YRS. & 11 MTHS.

61.

...... ADELLA PELRIN, ... DIED .... 10th OCT., 1813, AGED 29 YEARS.

62.

...... MISS ANN WAKEFIELD, ... DIED 11th OCTOBER, 1805, AGED 30 YRS. & 6 MTHS.

63.

...... MARTHA DEMETRIES,—.... DIED JUNE 1st, 1802, AGED 30 YEARS.

64.

MR. WILLIAM FYFE, ... DIED JULY 20th, 1802, AGED 23 YEARS.

65.

...... DOROTHY HENDLEY, ... DIED .... 23d FEBY., 1805, ... AGED 36.

66.

...... JANE BROWN BATTY, ... DIED JULY 13th, 1808, AGED 26 YEARS. MAY SHE SLEEP—IN PEICE.—KINGSTON,—JAMAICA, S.S., APRIL 2nd, 1809.

67.

...... WILLIAM CATHARWARD, DIED J.... 2d, 1808, AGED 5 MTHS. & 26 DAYS.

68.

...... MR. WILLIAM AIKMAN, OF THE PARISH OF KINGSTON,—STATIONER. —HE ARRIVED IN THIS ISLAND THE 21st OCTOBER, 1775, & .... DIED 6th .... NOVR., 1784, AGED 33 YEARS, 3 MONTHS, & 6 DAYS.

69.

...... THREE INFANTS,—OFFSPRING OF ALEXR. AIKMAN & LOUISA SU-SANNA, HIS WIFE :—ANNE, DIED OCTR. 26th, 1785,—AGED 9 MTHS.—ROBERT, DIED OCT. 31st, 1786, AGED 9 MTHS.—LOUISA SUSANNA,—DIED AUGT. ..., 1791, AGED 7 MTHS.

MARK, 10 chap., 14 v.

70.

...... WILLIAM SUTHERLAND GRANT,—DIED MAY 13th, 1802, AGED 52 YEARS.

71.

...... THREE INFANTS, OFFSPRING OF ALEXR. AIKMAN & LOUISA SUSANNA, HIS WIFE :—MARY, BORN MAY 12th, 1794,—DIED MAY 3d, 1796.—JANE, DIED SEPT. 29h, 1799, AGED 3 YRS. & 6 MTHS.—LOUISA, DIED OCT. 11th, 1799, AGED 3 MTHS.

72.

AMELIA ROBERTSON, BORN 31st JANY., 1805, DIED 19th NOVR., 1809, AGED 4 YRS., 10 MONTHS.

73.

...... MARY ANN REEVES, ... DIED 19th MARCH, 1800, AGED 5 YRS.

74.

...... JANE WHITE MC LEAN, ... DIED 5th JUNE, 1798, AGED 41 YEARS.

75.

...... MISS DANSEL DAWES, DIED FEBY. 14th, 1802, AGED 55 YEARS.

76.

...... MRS. CATHERINE NEIL NOTT, ... DIED 7th JANY., 1806, AGED 41 YEARS.

77.

...... PETER SANCHES, ... DIED OCT. 1st, 1802, AGED 55 YEARS.

78.

...... CAROLINE DEVANY, ... DIED 5th OCTR., 1811, AGED 2 YEARS, 8 MTHS., & 4 DAYS.

79.

ESTHER HOLLAND,—DIED, 12th OF JUNE, 1809, AGED 13 YEARS.

80.

A. W. THOMBS,—DIED 3d FEBY., 1800 (or 6 ?), AGED 61 YEARS.

81.

...... JANE LAING, DIED 9th JANRY., 1803, AGED 12 YRS., 11 MTHS., & 22 DAYS.—ALSO, ... SARAH NIMO, ... DIED 3d MAY, 1803, AGED 77 YEARS & 5 MONTHS.

82.

...... MARY SEPH...S, ... DIED NOVR. 22d, 1809.—ALSO, MASTER GEORGE NICOLL, ... DIED 10th .... JANRY., 1811, AGED 3 YRS. & 4 MONTHS.

83.

...... CHARLES DRURY, ESQR.,—ONLY SON OF ADMIRAL T. DRURY, WHO DEPARTED THIS LIFE ON THE 20th OCTOBER, 182..., AGED 21 YEARS.

84.

...... JAMES MUIR, DIED THE 27th JANY., 1809,—AGED 16 YRS. & 9 MONTHS.

85.

DOROTHY BROOKS,—DIED—4th OCTR., 1799, AGED 2 YEARS & 5 MONTHS.— ELEANOR BROOKS,—DIED—18th SEPTR., 1806,—AGED 8 YEARS & 6 WEEKS.— GEORGE BROOKS,—DIED 7th NOVR., 1806, AGED 5 YRS. & 6 MONTHS.—BROOKS & MARY MOR...K HALL.

86.

...... GEORGE THOMAS & ROBERT MILLERS.

87.

..... GRIFFITH MORGAN, OF THIS CITY, DIED .... 23d APRIL, 1805, AGED 36 YEARS.

88.

...... MRS. ELIZABETH HULL,—LATE WIFE OF MR. WILLIAM HULL, OF KINGSTON, IN THIS ISLAND, ... DIED OCT. 25th, 1813,—AGED 36 YEARS, 3 MONTHS, & 24 DAYS....

A HUSBAND, ... 2 SONS, AND A DAUGHTER, TO MOURN HER LOSS....

89.

MASTER F. B. HULL,—DIED NOVR. 17th, 1801, AGED 15 MONTHS & 17 DAYS.

90.

MASTER B. J. HULL,—DIED MAY 17th, 1805,—AGED 2 YRS. & 10 MONTHS.

91.

MASTER J. HULL, DIED SEPTR. 17th, 1805, AGED 10 DAYS.

92.

MISS MARGT. TO...H...D HULL,—DIED FEB. 12th, 1808, AGED 2 YRS. & 10 MONTHS.

93.

SARAH MASTER,—DIED—9th JULY, 1801,—AGED 40 YEARS.

94.

FRANCIS DONNEL,—DIED DECR. 21st, 1810,—AGED 4 YEARS.

95.

...... MISS DOROTHY FLEET, ... DIED 15th SEPTR., 1793, AGED 50 YEARS. —ALSO, ... HER 4 GRANDCHILDREN, VIZ. :—MICHAEL KEVAN, SON OF JANE SMITH, & GRANDSON OF THE ABOVE-NAMED DOROTHY FLEET,—DIED 20th JULY, 1789, AGED 1 YR. & 11 MTHS.—MARY ANN VERDON, DAUR. OF SUSANNA SMITH, ... DIED 8th MARCH, 1808, AGED 25 YEARS, 1 MONTH, & 2 DAYS.—JAMES GRANT PRINGLE, SON OF GRACE SMITH, ... DIED 30th SEPTR., 1806, AGED 21 YEARS, 8 MTHS., & 14 DAYS.—JANE SCOTT GRAY, DAUR. & ONLY SURVIVING CHILD OF THE ABOVE .... JANE SMITH, ... DIED ... MAY, 1807, AGED 24 YRS. & 1 MONTH.... ERECTED BY THE DAUGHTERS OF DOROTHY FLEET.

96.

...... MASTER ROBERT WHAIR,—DIED 8th JULY, 1811, AGED 1 YR. & 3 M.

97.

...... MISS JANE LUCRETIA IBBOTT, ... DIED 12th JUNE, 1808, IN THE 9th YEAR OF HER AGE. (Many verses follow.) .... ERECTED BY .... HER FATHER.

98.

...... MISS ANGEL & MIGHEY* ROBERTSON THOMPSON,—DAUGHTERS OF ELEANOR PLEASURE,—BORN 14 JULY, 1786,—THE FORMER, ... DIED 22^d OCTR., THE LATTER, ON THE 29th OF NOVR. FOLLOWING, 1802.

99.

MISS AMELIA MANUEL,—DIED JUNE 13th, 1803, AGED 9 YRS. & 5 MONTHS.

100.

MRS. JOHANNA BARTLET,—DIED APRIL, 1808, AGED 65 YEARS.

101.

MISS CECELIA MILES,—DIED NOVR. 10th, 1812, AGED 76 YEARS.

102.

MISS BARBARA THOMAS,—DIED JULY 1st, 1814, AGED 20 YEARS.

THE ROMAN CATHOLIC YARD, KINGSTON.

1.

MARIE JUSTINE,—DIED—20th OCTR., 1815,—AGED 45 YEARS.

2.

MLLE. ULALIE ROX ROSES,—DECEDÉE LE 10 FEVRIER, 1810,—AGÉ 28 ANS.

3.

MARIE FRANÇOIS FANNY MARTEL,—DECEDÉE—LE 1 MARS, 1814,—52 ANS.

4.

MARIE JUSTINE MERIMERCE COUPON,—DECEDÉE 21 OCTOBRE, 1815,—AGÉE DE 45 ANS.

5.

JANE MOREAU,—DIED—3 SEP., 1815, AGED 43 YEARS.

6.

DON JUAN DE FRANCISCO MARTIN,—DIED 9th MARCH, 1813,—48 ANOS.

THE BAPTIST GROUND, KINGSTON.

1.

MRS. ELIZABETH GRAHAM,—DIED 25th NOVR., 1810, AGED 46 YEARS.

2.

ELEANOR SAMUEL,—DIED—JUNE 20th, 1801, AGED 63 YEARS.

---

* Qy. Maggy?

THE WESLEYAN METHODIST CEMETERY, ELLETSON ROAD, KINGSTON.

1.

S. R. HOOPER, DIED—MARCH 15th, 1814, AGED 70 YEARS.

2.

MR. WILLIAM WILSON,—DIED—4th SEPTR., 1815, AGED 59 YEARS.

3.

THE REVD. JOHN DAVIES,—DIED OCTR. 13th, 1814.

4.

JOHN SHIPMAN, INFANT SON OF JOHN AND ANN SHIPMAN,—DIED—NOVR. 18th, 1815.

5.

MR. WILLIAM WILSON,—DIED SEPTR. 4th, 1811, AGED 59 YEARS.

6.

A. M. WILSON,—DIED JUNE 11th, 1811.

7.

THE REVD. THOMAS WERRIL,—DIED—15th NOVR., 1791.

8.

THE REVD. JAMES RICHARDSON, DIED 7th APRIL, 1799.

9.

MRS. PHILS. GY. DEMETRUS, DIED 9th JUNE, 1814, AGED 50 YEARS.

10.

MISS MARY BROWN,—DIED APRIL 5th, 1797.

11.

MISS SUSANNAH CAMPBELL,—DIED—APL. 6th, 1807, AGED 56 YEARS.

12.

JOHN LODGE DEFOSE,—1809.

13.

MRS. DIANA JERDON RODGERS, DIED 14th MAY, 1795, AGED 21 YEARS.

14.

MISS SUSANNAH JURDON,—DIED—12th NOVR., 1815, AGED 79 YEARS.

15.

MRS. SARAH SIMPSON, DIED 13th MAY, 1802, AGED 70 YRS.

16.

CASTELL WALKER,—DIED APL. 4th, 1808, AGED 70 YRS.

17.

FRANCES POLSON,—DIED—NOVR. 11th, 1808, AGED 51 YEARS.

18.

JOHN HARRIS CONSTANT,—DIED MAY 17th, 1796, AGED 45 YRS.

19.

ELIZABETH ISRAEL,—DIED 4th JUNE, 1815, AGED 48 YRS.

20.

CHARLOTTE SAUNDERS, DIED 28th NOVR., 1827, AGED 100 YEARS.

21.

ROBERT OAKES,—DIED AUGST. 21st, 1796, AGED 42 YRS.

22.

MR. ROBERT WILSON LAMB, DIED 28th MARCH, 1812, AGED 39 YRS.

23.

LUCY GREEN,—DIED 22d JUNE, 1816, AGED 31 YEARS.

24.

MRS. ROSY BENNETT,—DIED APRIL, 1814, AGED 40 YEARS.

SCOTCH BURIAL GROUND, KINGSTON.

All abridged.

1.

...... JOHN WATT, ESQUIRE,—A NATIVE OF IRELAND,—AND FOR MANY YEARS A HIGHLY RESPECTED MERCHANT OF THIS CITY, ... OBIIT 2d DAY OF OCTOBER, 1862, AETATIS 46.

2.

...... EDWARD TATE,—ENGINEER,—WHO DIED AT KINGSTON—ON THE 26th OCTOBER, 1862, AGED 37 YEARS........

3.

HERE LIES THE BODY OF—MRS. ELIZTH. CHRISTIE,—BORN JUNE 4th, 1764,— DIED SEPR. 21st, 1850,—AGED 86 YEARS, 3 MONTHS, & 12 DAYS.

4.

...... DR. SILVESTER TUTHILL,—OF NEW YORK,—WHO DIED IN THIS CITY MARCH 13th, 1841,—AGED 32 YEARS & 8 MONTHS.

5.

...... ANDREW SUTHERLAND, ESQR., DIED 24th DAY OF DECEMBER, 1840, AGED 83 YEARS.—PLACED OVER HIS REMAINS BY HIS .... SONS & DAUGHTERS.

Sculptured Sarcophagus.

SEVERAL eulogistic lines follow.

6.

...... JOHN MC INTYRE, MASON, WHO WAS BORN IN THE PARISH OF GLEN-ORCHY, IN THE COUNTY OF ARGYLE, N.B., THE 29th DAY OF MARCH, 1768,—ARRIVED IN THIS ISLAND ON THE 4th DAY OF JUNE, 1789,—WHERE HE LIVED MUCH RESPECTED UNTIL THE 15th DAY OF JUNE, 1842, WHEN HE DIED,—MAKING HIM 74 YEARS OF AGE, & 53 A RESIDENT IN JAMAICA.

7.

...... WILLIAM SCOTT—SAIDLER (*sic*),—A NATIVE OF BELL'S HILL, NEAR GLASGOW, DIED 30th NOVR., 1838, AGED 31.

8.

...... JOHN WILLIAM & JAMES SCOTT, THE FORMER BORN 23d JANY., 1832, —DIED 16th JULY, 1833,—THE LATTER, JAMES S. SCOTT,—SOLICITOR,—BORN HERE 28 JULY, 1826,—DIED AT RIO B. (RIO BUENO?) 3d DECR., 1856.

A DISTICH.

9.

...... WILLIAM DOUGLAS, ESQR., DIED 15th OCT., 1837, AGED 59 YEARS & 7 MONTHS.

10.

...... JANE,—WIFE OF RALPH TURNBULL, SENIOR,—OF THIS CITY,—WHO DIED ON THE 28th DAY OF MAY, 1838, AGED 43 YEARS.—ALSO, ... — RALPH TURNBULL, JUNIOR,—ELDEST SON OF THE ABOVE,—WHO DIED 30th JULY, 1844, AGED 27 YEARS. (Eulogistic lines.) ALSO, IN MEMORY OF—ROBERT, SECOND SON OF THE ABOVE, WHO DIED ON THE 23d OF NOVEMBER, 1844, AGED 21 YEARS.

E ULOGISTIC lines.

11.

...... ELIZABETH WILHELMINA COOPER, DIED 30th MARCH, 1850,—AGED 22 YEARS.—WHILST ON THEIR JOURNEY TO ...., THE VESSEL STRUCK ON THE ROCK—OFF PORT MORANT,—AND SHE, WITH SIX OTHERS, HER FRIENDS & COM-PANIONS,—LOST THEIR LIVES.

"WATCH & PRAY, FOR YE KNOW NOT WHEN THE TIME IS."

12.

...... MARY JANE AND FANNY BASCOM,—THE BELOVED CHILDREN OF NATHANIEL & SELINA DARRELL,—THE FORMER OF WHOM DEPD. THIS LIFE ON THE 7th OF NOVR., 1839, AGED 9 MTHS. & 3 DAYS,—AND THE LATTER, THEIR ONLY SURVIVING CHILD, ... ON THE 24th OF THE SAME MONTH, JUST SEVEN-TEEN DAYS AFTERWARDS, AGED 2 YEARS & 3 MONTHS.

13.

...... JOHN HOYES FINLAYSON, ESQR.,—MERCHANT OF THIS CITY, & ONLY SON OF THE LATE REVD. JOHN FINLAYSON CROMARTY, SCOTLAND, WHO DEPD. THIS LIFE ON THE 9th DECR., 1840, AGED 29 YEARS.

14.

...... FRANCIS ELIOTT, ESQR., WHO DEPARTED THIS LIFE ON THE 2d OF JUNE, 1854, AGED 75 YEARS.—ALSO, ... MARY JANE ELIOTT, HIS WIFE, DIED 24 OCTR., 1859, IN 76th YEAR OF HER AGE.

15.

...... ANDREW MURRAY, ESQUIRE,—A NATIVE OF DUMFRIES, NORTH BRITAIN,—DIED—18th DAY OF DECEMBER, 1841,—AGED 47 YEARS, 23 OF WHICH HE HAD RESIDED IN THIS ISLAND,—LEAVING WIDOW & EIGHT CHILDREN.

16.

RT. GRAHAM,—A NATIVE OF GREENOCK, N.B., SON OF MR. JOHN GRAHAM, MERCHANT THERE,—WHO DIED AT KINGSTON ON THE 5th MARCH, 1836,—IN THE 21st YEAR OF HIS AGE.

17.

C. W. CLYMOUTH,—1843.

18.

...... CHARLOTTE DRUMMOND, DAUGHTER OF MAJOR THOMAS MENZIES,— LATE 79th REGT., AND WIDOW OF JOHN JENNINGS DRUMMOND, ESQUIRE, DECEASED,—BORN AT ST. JOHN'S, NEW BRUNSWICK,—28th DECEMBER, 1804,—AND DIED—AT ST. ANDREW'S, JAMAICA,—2d DECEMBER, 1858.

19.

...... ELIZABETH MARY DRUMMOND,—DAUGHTER OF JOHN JENNINGS DRUMMOND, ESQUIRE,—DECEASED, & CHARLOTTE, HIS WIFE,—BORN 13th DECEMBER, 1825,—DIED 4th NOVR., 1857.

20.

J. J. DRUMMOND,—DIED—JANY. 29th, 1836,—AGED 43 YEARS.

21.

...... ANNA MARIA, ... WIFE OF—MR. ROBERT B. LORD, DIED—12th JULY, 1845, ... REGRETTED BY HER HUSBAND, DAUGHTER, & SON.

22.

...... MR. JOHN LORD, DIED 10th AUGUST, 1838, IN THE 25th YEAR OF HIS AGE.... ERECTED BY HIS PARENTS.

23.

CAPTAIN JOHN NEWLANDS, SR. .... ERECTED BY AN AFFECTIONATE RELATIVE.—THE ENTOMBED FOR MANY YEARS—TRADED TO THIS ISLAND—AS COMMANDER & OWNER, AND—HE HAS STRUCK HIS FLAG—AMONG MANY (WHO ARE) ACQUAINTED WITH, & APPRECIATE HIS WORTH.—CAPTAIN NEWLANDS WAS BORN IN GLASGOW, SCOTLAND, & DIED ON THE 31st JULY, 1836,—IN THE 55th YEAR OF HIS AGE.

Sculptured anchor and cable.

24.

MR. JAMES CHALMERS, DIED 15th JANY., 1840, AGED 38 YEARS.—ALSO,—MASTER JAMES, SON OF JAMES CHALMERS,—WHO DIED 23d DECR., 184 (0 ?), AGED 8 YEARS & 14 DAYS.

25.

...... JOHN PALMER, ESQ.,—DIED, 30th DECR., 1839, AGED 47.—(Seven lines follow.)—TABLET ERECTED BY HIS WIDOW.

26.

...... WM. GEO. NUNES,—DIED, 3d APRIL, 1854, AGED 65 YEARS. SCRIPTURE texts.

27.

...... MISS SUSAN TALBOT, ... 19th JULY, 1841, AGED 26 YEARS....

28.

JOHN HOYES PANTON,—DIED 7th SEPTEMBER, 1850,—AGED 39 YEARS.

29.

...... ROBERT URQUHART, ESQR., MERCHANT OF THIS CITY, DIED, 26th OCT., 1851, AGED 45.

30.

...... ALFRED EDWD. MACLAREN, DIED 14th NOV., 1855, AGED $3\frac{8}{12}$ YRS.

31.

MR. P. TURNBULL,—DIED, JULY 20th, 1833.

32.

...... WILLIAM STUART,—A NATIVE OF GLASGOW, DIED, 6th MAY, 1832, AGED 32.—ERECTED BY HIS SURVIVING BROTHER.

33.

...... JAMES MC CANN, ESQUIRE,—LATE MERCHANT OF THIS CITY,—BORN AT GREENOCK, IN SCOTLAND, 4th OF FEBRY., 1799,—& DEPD. THIS LIFE, 13th OF MARCH, 1832.—ERECTED BY—SURVIVING RELATIVES.

34.

...... HENRY MICHELL,—DRUGGIST,—AND HIS FOUR CHILDREN,—1856.

35.

...... MRS. ISABELLA LEIGHTON,—DIED, 27th OCTR., 1855, AGED 25 YEARS.

36.

...... GEORGE GIBSON,—BORN AT GLASGOW ON THE 18th OF JULY, 1818,—DIED HERE 30th APRIL, 1839.—ALSO, ... WILLIAM FRASER, MERCHANT, KINGSTON,—BORN AT FORFAR ON THE 27th (or 29th) JULY, 1799,—DIED ON THE 12th JUNE, 1839.—ALSO, ... LAURENCE GIBSON, MERCHANT,—BORN AT UDDINGSTON, NEAR GLASGOW, ON 15th FEBRY., 1791 (or 6),—DIED AT ST...L...D, RAE TOWN, ON 7th JANY., 1851, IN THE 66 YEAR OF HIS AGE.

37.

PETER HILL,—DIED ON THE—16th OCTOBER, 1840, AGED 54 YEARS.

38.

...... WILLIMA RAE, ESQUIRE,—OF SHERWOOD FOREST & OTHER ESTATES, IN THIS ISLAND,—A NATIVE OF DUMFRIES, IN SCOTLAND,—&—FOR FIFTY-FIVE YRS. RESIDENT IN KINGSTON, WHERE HE DIED ON THE 7th OF MAY, 1837, AGED 75 YEARS.—ERECTED BY ADAM, DAVID RAE,—JANE & CATHERINE NEUART, OF DUMFRIES, THE CHILDREN OF HIS SISTER....

39.

HENRY G. MALLISON,—DIED—19th FEBY., 1864, AGED 29.

PSALM xxxi. 5—7.

40.

...... ISABELLA BOGLE, DIED 8th MAY, 1847, AGED $12\frac{7}{12}$ YRS.

Sculptured book.

41.

...... MRS. ELIZABETH ANN GREEN, DIED 12th MAY, 1837, AGED 65....

42.

...... SIMON NOYES, ESQR., OF STOAKESFIELD, ST. THOMAS-IN-THE-EAST, DIED 19th MAY, 1852, AGED 62 YEARS.

EULOGIUM.

43.

...... JOHN DONALDSON, DIED 9th MARCH, 1848, AGED 50. A NATIVE OF KIRKCUDBRIGHT, N.B., & RESIDENT FOR MANY YEARS IN THE PAR. OF ST. THOS.-Yᵉ-EAST, IN THIS ISLAND.

44.

...... ALEXANDER MACKINTOSH, DIED 24th NOVR., 1857, AGED 24 YEARS.

45.

...... JOHN RENWICK, ESQR.,—A NATIVE OF DUMFRIES, IN SCOTLAND, & FOR UPWARDS OF FIFTY YEARS IN THIS ISLAND, DIED 24th APRIL, 1847, AGED 76 YEARS.

46.

...... HENRY WILLIAMS, ESQR.,—DIED—6th APRIL, 1859, AGED 47 YEARS & 6 MONTHS, LEAVING A WIDOW,—FIVE CHILDREN, AND OTHER RELATIVES....

47.

...... HENRY MAC LEAN WOOD, DIED 18th MAY, 1858, AGED 30.

48.

JOHN MC DONALD, ESQR.,—DIED—23d DECR., 1844,—AGED—43 YEARS.

49.

OVER THE REMAINS OF A DUTIFUL & MERITORIOUS SON, JOHN MUIR,—MERCHANT IN KINGSTON,—WHO DIED THERE,—19th MARCH, 1849,—AGED 30 YEARS,—HIS SORROWING PARENTS—AT ST. VIGEAN'S, SCOTLAND,—PLACED THIS MEMORIAL,—1849.

50.

...... JANE,—WIFE OF THE REVD. J. RADCLIFFE,—MINISTER OF THE SCOTCH CHURCH, KINGSTON,—BORN IN IRELAND, MDCCXXVI*, DIED IN KINGSTON, MDCCLVI.—ALSO, TWO OF THEIR CHILDREN :—ELIZABETH, AGED NINE MONTHS, —HENRY, AGED 10 DAYS....

51.

ELIZA,—RELICT OF THE LATE ADMIRAL DRURY,—1845.

SEE "Naval Biographical Dictionary."

52.

MARATAN RICHARDSON,—BORN AT MEMPHIS, U.S.,—18th OCTOBER, 1830,—DIED, 2d APRIL, 1864.

53.

ISABELLA CLARKE,—DIED, 21st NOVR., 1858, AGED 12 YEARS....

54.

...... CAPT. WM. CARMICHAEL, OF STRANRAER,—SCOTLAND,—WHO DIED NEAR KINGSTON, ON THE 25th AUGUST, 1858,—AGED 34 YEARS.

Sculptured anchor.

55.

...... ANDREW HUNTER WOOD,—MERCHANT IN KINGSTON,—YOUNGEST SON OF—WM. WOOD, OF WOODFIELD, NEAR AYR, SCOTLAND,—WHO DIED, 28th NOVR., 1858, AGED 25 YEARS.

56.

...... JOHN WRAY, DIED, 18th MAY, 1864, AGED 64....

57.

CHARLES MC LEOD.

No date.

58.

JAMES G. MC CLELLAND, DIED, 11th OF APRIL, 1861, AGED 63.

59.

ROBERT ALVES,—DIED—16th OF APRIL, 1863, AGED 55 YRS. & 3 MTHS.

60.

...... EDWARD RECUSSET,—DIED—17th JULY, 1858.

61.

...... JANE MARGARET, WIFE OF THE LATE JOHN FINLEY, ESQ., DIED 24th OCTR., 1859, AGED 60 YEARS. ERECTED BY HER DAUGHTER, MRS. HENRY KINKEAD.

---

* Qy. MDCCC.

62.

...... JOHN HORNE,—MERCHANT OF KINGSTON, JAMAICA,—A NATIVE OF EGLESHAM, RENFREWSHIRE, SCOTLAND, DIED, SEPR. 9th, 1847,—AGED 65(?) YEARS.

A sculptured urn.

63.

...... FELIX HARRISON, DIED AT PAPINE, 23d OCT., 1860, AGED 25. ERECTED BY HIS BROTHER, THOS. H.

64.

...... ELIZABETH JANE EDWARDS, OF TOP HILL PLN., ST. THOS.-Ye-VALE, DIED, 26th FEB., 1854, AGED 79.

65.

...... HELEN BLUDGEN, WIFE OF COLIN CAMPBELL, DIED, 28th APL., 1854, —AGED 38.

Sculptured skull and cross-bones.

SPRING PATH CONSECRATED GROUND, KINGSTON.

"SPRING PATH," or "The Consecrated Ground," is one of the oldest graveyards in the Parish of Kingston, and faces the railway station. Its appearance is very remarkable, for each tomb, being covered with a dense green mantle of a small hardy plant—like a robust chickweed—the crabweed*, its general contour is preserved, although softened, so that the whole, chequered by the shadow of the light foliage of the cashaw-tree, presents the appearance of groups of verdant little hillocks.

1.

AQUI—YACEN LOS RESTOS INANIMADOS—DE—DN. GASPAR CAMP FONOLL,— NATURAL DE LA CIUDAD DE VIE, EN—EL PRINCIPADO DE CATALINA, EN—ESPANA, —NACIO EL 6 DE ENERO DE 1776,—Y FALLICIO EL 31 DE ENERO DE 1829 (2 ?), —A LOS 52 ANOS DE EDAD.

VERSES follow.

2.

HERE LIETH THE BODY OF MR. WILLIAM RUGLESS, OF THE PARISH OF ST. ANDREW, PLANTER, DIED, JANUARY 11th, 1796, ENT. WITH MILITARY HONOURS IN THE CONSECRATED GROUND, IN THE PARISH OF KINGSTON, AGED 39 YEARS, 9 MONTHS, AND 9 DAYS.

CONTINUATION to the effect, that he left a wife and seven children.

---

* Conyza minor.

3.

𝕴. ℭ. 𝕴.—REPOSE LE CORPS DE—CHARLES SMITH,—DÉCÉDÉ À KINGSTON LE 11 JUIN, MDCCCXXVIII.,—AGE DE XXIV. ANS.—CE SIMPLE MONUMENT EST CONSACRÉ À LA MÉMOIRE D'UN FILS QUI SA DEPLORABLE—MÈRE NE CESSERA DE REGRETTER.—REQUIESCAT IN GLORIA DEI.

Sculpture : a dove descending on △, supported by two flying angels in clouds.

4.

IN THIS TOMB ARE DEPOSITED—THE REMAINS OF CHARLES PETERS, —WHO DEPARTED THIS LIFE—ON THE 22 DEC., 1814, AGED 15.

5.

(*Ab.*) ICI—REPOSE LE CORPS DE—MARIE ANGÉLIQUE DUROCHER,—DÉCÉDÉ À KINGSTON LE 13 MAI, 1833, AET. 24.—ET, MDE. HENRIETTE FRANÇOISE BELL, —DEC., 25 OCT., 1837, AET. 26.

6.

(*Ab.*) JOANES GUION,—NATIVE OF CURAÇOA, OB. 1 JUNE, 1827, AET. 53.

7.

(*Ab.*) MARIE SIMMONIE, OB. 4 MARCH, 1828, AET. 70.

Marble tablet : dove holding a scroll, inscribed, "Mors omnibus communis."

8.

(*Ab.*) ANN, WIFE OF JACOB BROMFIELD, ESQ., OF THIS CITY, OB. 28 JUNE, 1837, AET. 49.

Tablet.

9.

HERE LIES INTERRED MR. EDWARD BURKE, OB. 8 APL., 1807, AET. 48.—ALSO —MR. PETER MATTHEWS, OB. 24 DEC., 1818, AET. 53 & 7 MONTHS.—ALSO, ANN, DAUR. OF JACOB & ANN BROMFIELD, OB. 26 SEP., 1819, AET. 10 MONTHS.

10.

(*Ab.*) MARIA LUCY JOSEP CHARLES, NAT. JANY. 8, 1833, OB. 12th OF SAME MONTH.—MARIA LOUISE GASPARD, AGED 90 YEARS,—DIED THE 29th JULY,— 1818.

11.

(*Ab.*) EMILE CATHERINE, SPOUSE OF HENRY DRYSDALE, OB. 27th JANY., 1842, AGED 23 YEARS & 6 MTHS.—ALSO, HER SISTER, HENRIETTA MARCELL, DIED 1st FEBY., 1842, AGED 22 YEARS.—ERECTED BY THEIR MOTHER.—ALSO, THEIR MOTHER, ROSELLA PRATT, DIED 10th NOV., 1844, AGED 48.

12.

(*Ab.*) EMILY RICHMOND, OB. 23 JULY, 1842, AET. 2 YEARS & 2 WEEKS.

13.

SANITTE FRESENEAUX,—16th OCT., 1845.

14.

(*Ab.*) ADELAIDE LEGER,—NATIVE DE LEOGANE DE ST. DOMINGUE, OB. 26 AUGT., 1828, AET. 76.

15.

(*Ab.*) GEORGE LAMARTILLIÈRE, OB. 10 JUNE, 1831, AET. 10 MTHS.

16.

(*Ab.*) MR. ABRAHAM SANDERS, LATE OF THIS CITY, SHIPWRIGHT, OB. 25th JULY. 1815, AETATIS 53. ERECTED BY HIS WIDOW.

Pretty sculpture of an angel conducting a soul upwards.

L INES follow.

17.

HERE LIES THE BODY OF—MARY MORRIS, WHO DIED 31st MAY, 1814, AGED 20 YEARS AND 8 MONTHS.

B ROKEN.

18.

CATHE. DRYSDALE,—OBIIT—10th AUGUST,—1794,—AGED 36 YEARS.

19.

(*Ab.*) ELIZABETH S. MARES, OB. 2d NOV., 1832, AET. 4.

20.

IN MEMORY OF—ELIZABETH DELPRATT,—WHO DIED ON THE 18th OF MARCH, 1828, AGED 23 YEARS.

T HE Delpratts were wealthy produce merchants of Kingston.

21.

(*Ab.*) HERE LIES—THE BODY OF—MORRIS PEAT BULKLEY,—WHO DEPARTED THIS LIFE—MAY 24, 1808,—AGED 17 YEARS—AND 9 MONTHS.—ALSO, SUSANNAH FRENCH, HIS MOTHER, OB. 9 SEP., 1818, AET. 74.

22.

(*Ab.*) MRS. M. L. PAVAGEAU, OB. 21 OCT., 1812, AET. 68.

23.

HENRY JOHN CLERMONT,—AGÉ 16 MOIS,—DÉCÉDÉ LE 14 MAI, 1817.

24.

(*Ab.*) MISS PICTERNELLE, CORNELIA BROOK, OB. 17th JULY, 1826.—SHE WAS A NATIVE OF CURAÇOA.

V ERSES follow.

25.

LUIS MARTINES, NATU .... CARTAGA.,* ÆDAD 17 AÑOS, 11 MESES, 20 DIAS, MURIO EL DIA 30 DE SEP., DE 1826.—REQUIESCAT IN PACE.

26.

C'EST ICI OU L'AME D'ANTOINE EUGENE VEAU,—AGÉE DE 4 MOIS, MORT LE 20 SEPT., 1827.

---

* Qy. Carthagena.

27.

(*Ab.*) JEANNE BRILLOUET, WIDOW, OB. 3ᵈ NOV., 1832, AET. 60.

28.

(*Ab.*) MARIE CELESTINE CHARRIER, OB. 27ᵗʰ AUGT., 1823, AET. 40.

29.

CI GIT—EULALIE VVE. DE JEAN,—DÉCÉDÉE 6 SEPTRE.,—1842.—RÉPOSE LE CORPS DE SA DEFUNTE, REINE ELIZABETH HEURLELOUX,—DÉCÉDÉE À KINGSTON—23 JUILLET, 1830.

30.

(*Ab.*) VICTOIRE ADÈLE COLETTE,—OB. 12 SEP., 1827, AET. 26.

M. F. M.

31.

MARGUERITE DESDUNES,—AINSI QUE SA FILLE—MARIE ANTOINETTE LLADO, EPOUSE DE MR. J. E. MORIN,—OB. 6ᵗʰ JANY., 1833, AET. 28.

M. F.

32.

(*Ab.*) MARY JOSEPHINE MONTOYA, OB. 4ᵗʰ OCT., 1826, AET. 7 YRS., 3 WEEKS.

E.

33.

(*Ab.*) MRS. ELIZABETH HALL, WHO DEPARTED THIS LIFE THE 17ᵗʰ DAY OF NOVEMBER, 1807,—AGED 40 YEARS, SEVEN MONTHS, AND 17 DAYS.

34.

(*Ab.*) MISS ELEANOR BROWN, DIED MARCH 18ᵗʰ, 1808, AGED 39 YEARS & 11 MONTHS.

35.

(*Ab.*) MISS KATHARINE HALL ROBERTSON, WHO WAS BORN ON THE 24ᵗʰ MAY, 1801,—DIED ON THE 1ˢᵗ APRIL, 1821.

THE three last tombs are so placed, as to indicate family connection.

36.

(*Ab.*) MARY ANN ROPER,—OB. 25ᵗʰ APRIL, 1833, AET. 34. 4. 28.

37.

MISS ELIZABETH HUMMELL, DIED, 9ᵗʰ NOV., 1821, AGED 65 YEARS.

38.

(*Ab.*) GEORGE HARDY, DIED, OCT. 31ˢᵗ, 1831, AGED 52 YEARS.—ALSO, HIS GRANDSON, GEORGE—HAYMAN, DIED JUNE 25ᵗʰ, 1831, AGED 8 YRS., 11 MONTHS.

39.

THOMAS HARDY, MASTER BRICKLAYER, BUILDER, OB. 6 AUGT., 1837, AET. 86.—ALSO, FRANCIS HARDY, FATHER OF THE ABOVE, OB. FEB. 2, 1790.—ALSO, MARY T. HARDY, OB. 4ᵗʰ OCT. 1792.—ALSO, MARY CARR, OB. 22 NOVR., 1802.—ALSO, WILLIAM MOODY, OB. 29ᵗʰ MARCH, 1808.

40.

SACRED TO THE MEMORY OF JOHN DARBY, WHO DIED, APRIL 5th, 1799, AGED 55 YEARS.

41.

(*Ab.*) SARAH ANTONETE PHILIBERT, OB. 18 DECR., 1811 (?),—AET. 7 YRS., 11 MTHS.

F.

42.

(*Ab.*) JOHN BAPTIST PHILIBERT, OB. 7 JANUARY, 1842, AET. 46.

43.

(*Ab.*) MARYAN JANE, OB. 15th AUGT., 1831, AET. 20.

44.

(*Ab.*) SOUS CE MARBRE—REPOSE—MLLE. BELDAM LAMOUSIER, NATIVE DES CAILLES, ST. LOUIS,—DÉCÉDÉE À KINGSTON, LE 10 DE JUIN, 1838, AGÉE DE ANS 50.

F.

45.

(*Ab.*) MR. JEAN VRIGNEAUX,—NATIVE OF ROCHFORT, IN FRANCE, OB. 20 SEP., 1835, AET. 70.

46.

(*Ab.*) VICTORIN MAYAN, OB. MAY 17th, 1816, AET. 21 YRS., 6 MTHS.

F.

47.

M. JANNE PIERRE DE L'ONGRAIS,—OB. 5th DECR., 1822, AET. 45. (Also on the same tomb, but in English :) JEAN LOUIS CELESTIN, OB. 16th JANY., 1830, AET. 23.

F.

48.

JOHN CHAPLIN, 17th SEP., 1823, AET. 58.

49.

EPITAPH.—CATHERINE GUILLEAUMEAU DE JLAVILLE, VEUVE DE FRANÇOIS GREGOIRE DE LA BICHE, DÉCÉDÉE 12 SEPTEMBRE, 1826, AGÉE DE 68 ANS.

F.

50.

(*Ab.*) CI GIT—MESSIRE BOUIS VENDRYES, OB. JANY. 10th, 1820, AET. 60. ET DE MARIE ANTOINETTE ADARE VENDRYES, SON EPOUSE,—OB. 21 FEB., 1830.

F.

61.

(*Ab.*) MISS REBECCA TAV(or N)ARTS, OB. 25 APL., 1833, AET. 7 YRS.

PARISH OF ST. ANDREW'S.

ST. ANDREW'S PARISH CHURCH.*

INTRAMURAL.

1.

HERE LYETH THE BODY OF CAPT. ROBERT PHILLIPS, WHO DEPARTED THIS LIFE, THE 29th OF SEPTEMBER, ANNO DOMINI, 1702.

HERE RESTS YE BODY OF THE—SOUL NOW BLEST, WHO, —WHILST ON EARTH,—WITH VARIOUS CARES OPPREST,—TO GOD HIS KING AND COUNTRY—STEDFAST TRUE,—JUST TO'S NEIGHBOUR,—RENDERING ALL THEIR DUES,—MAUGRE DETRACTION OF HIS FOES,—THO' FEW.

VADE, ET TU FAC SIMILITER.

St. Luke ye 10th, vr. ye 37.

Black Marble Slab; *Arms*, No tinctures; a lion rampant. *Crest*, Over an esquire's helmet, a lion rampant.

2.

HERE LYETH TH . . . .

THOMAS HARRIS . . . .

THIS LIFE THE 28 . . . .

DOM., 1718, IN THE . . . .

HERE ALSO LY . . . .

ELIZA HARRIS . . . .

HARRISON AND . . . .

WHO DEPARTED . . . .

OF FEBRUARY, 17 . . . .

MONTHS . . . .

Black Marble Slab, with Arms, partly concealed by a pew.

PROBABLY members of the same family as Thomas Harrison, Chief Justice of Jamaica, who died in 1792.

There were several families of this name in Jamaica, and notably one, said to be descended from the regicide.

---

* Commonly called *Half-Way-Tree* Church.

3.

I KNOW THAT MY ....
HE SHALL STAND ....
THE EARTH & THE.........................
DESTROY THIS ....
I SEE GOD WHO ....
AND MINE EYES ....
IN HOPES OF.............................
RECTION RES.............................
LEAH THE W.............................
ZACHARIA ....
DYED THE 29............................
170$\frac{6}{7}$, AGED 8............................
    HERE ALSO, ...
THE BODY ....
ZACHAR ....
WHO DEPART.............................
19th OF JULY, ...
HERE ALSO LYETH ....
WIFE OF DANIEL ....
DEPARTED THIS ....
171$\frac{4}{5}$, AGED 49 ....

Black Marble Slab, partly concealed by a pew.

ZACHARIAH BAYLY is the name now covered by the pew flooring.

4.

HERE LYETH THE BODY OF CHARLES HOLMES, ESQ., REAR-ADMIRAL OF THE WHITE, WHO DEPARTED THIS LIFE, THE 21st OF MARCH, 1761, AGED 50 YEARS.

Slab.

SEE " Naval Biographical Dictionary."

5.

IN THE NAME OF GOD AMEN.—HERE RESTETH THE BODY OF—EDWARD HARRISON, ESQ.,—WHO DEPARTED THIS LIFE THE 29th DAY—OF AUGUST, IN THE YEAR OF OUR LORD,—1695, AND IN THE 41st YEAR OF HIS AGE.—HERE ALSO RESTETH THE BODY OF—EDWARD, SON TO THE SAID—EDWARD, & DOROTHY, HIS—WIFE, WHO DEPARTED THIS LIFE THE—23d DAY OF FEBRUARY, 1696,—AGED 7 YEARS, AND—6 MONTHS.

Black Marble Slab, partly covered.

6.

......LIES THE BODY OF THE ....

......RABLE MAJOR JAMES GARTH..........

......DEPARTED THIS LIFE THE 18th........

......OF OCTOBER, 1734, ...

......AGED 37 YEARS.....................

......WAS MAJOR TO THE RIGHT ....

......RABLE LORD SHANNON'S ....

......OOP OF HORSE GUARDS ....

Slab, partly covered.

7.

...... OF PHILIP BECKET, ESQ.; SHE DEPARTED THIS LIFE THE VI. DAY OF JULY, MDCCXXII., IN THE XIVth YEAR OF HER AGE. SOLA VERTUS (*sic*) SERVIRA DEO. IN HOPES OF A BLESSED RES—URRECTION—TO ETERNAL LIFE.—HERE LYETH INTERRED AMONG THIE (*sic*)—ANCESTORS, THE BODY'S OF MRS. ELIZA—PHIPPS, LATE WIFE OF MR. JOSEPH PHIPPS, OF THE PARISH OF KINGSTON, MER—CHANT, WHO DEPARTED THIS LIFE—JUNE 30th, 1764, AGED 31 YRS.—ALSO, YE BODY OF HER BROTHER, MR.—JOHN BLAIR, LATE OF THIS PARISH, PLAN—TER, WHO DIED JULY 3d, 1764, IN THE—THIRTIETH YEAR OF HIS AGE.

Slab.

8.

...... OF OUR LORD, 1719, ...

BEING 24 YEARS & EIGHT MONTHS OLD ....

HERE ALSO LYES THE BODY OF—JAMES PINNOCK,—SON OF JAMES AND MARY PINNOCK, WHO DEPARTED—THIS LIFE THE 20th DAY OF—JUNE, IN THE 23d YEAR OF HIS AGE, 1736.

Black Marble Slab, partly covered by pews.

James Pinnock, *=Anne Powell,
Quaker, of Reading; emigrated to Barbados, | married in Barbados.
and thence to Jamaica.

Anne Becket,=James, b. July 6,=Mary Seaward, 2nd wife,=Elizabeth Traxton, 3rd wife, dau. of
1st wife, m. Septem- | 1660, d. 1733. | b. August 9, 1694; m. Oc- | Col. Wm. T.; b. August 27, 1705;
ber 29, 1690. | | tober 30, 1711; d. 1719. | m. December 10, 1719.

James | A Son, | Thomas,=Mary Lawrence, | Philip, Chief Justice of Ja-
(see epitaph), | d. unmarried. | b. March 26, 1714; | m. 1736; d. 1780. | maica; b. October 20, 1720;
ob. 1736. | | d. 1758. | | m. and had issue.

James,=Elizabeth, dau. of | George, Pres.=Grace, dau. of | Dau.=Lewis Cuthbert. | Dau.=Geo. Cuth-
b. 1740; | George Dehany; | of Council; b. | Philip Pinnock | | bert.
d. 1811. | m. 1772. | 1749; d. 1834. | (his cousin). |

Daughters. | Issue. | George, d. 1789.

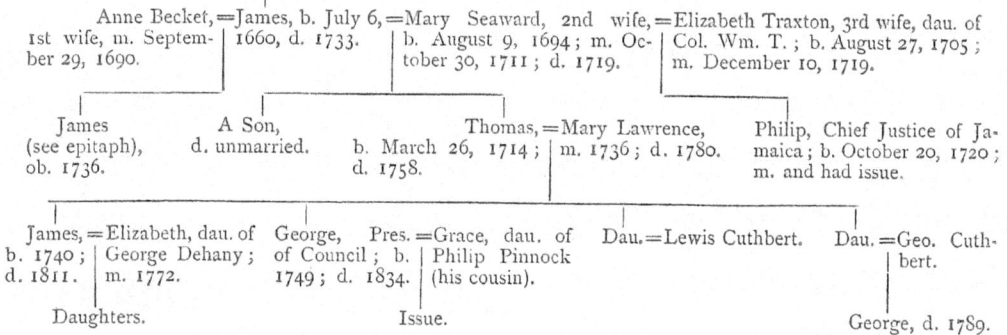

* N.B.—This is a different family from that mentioned in Kent's "Banner Display'd," London, 1728, p. 780. See also *Notes and Queries*, 3, s. vii. 419.

9.

TO THE ....
MARY ELIZAB..............................
DAUGHTER OF ....
AND MANY..............................
DYED ....
ALSO THEIR ....
BORN NOVR. ....
AND SWAINE..............................
BORN SEP. 2, ...

Two lines in rhyme.

LIKEWISE, THOMAS CROASDAILE, THEIR NEPHEW, DIED OCTOBER 10th, 1752, AGED 23 YEARS.

Black Marble Slab, partly covered.

10.

Mural Monument of Gray and White Marble; richly gilt, and bearing on a bracket a fine marble bust by John Sheere; *Arms*, Or, on a chief azure, three estoiles, of eight points, of the first; on an escutcheon of pretence, or, a lion rampant, sable, debruised of a bend gules, charged with three escallops of the first.

HIC, JUXTA RELIQUÆ POSITÆ SUNT, HONORABILIS VIRI, —JACOBI LAWES, HUNC PRIMOGENITUM HABUIT EX UXORE SUA—SUSANNA TEMPLE, NICOLAUS LAWES, EQUES, ET INSULÆ PRÆFECTUS:—ELIZABETHAM, UNICAM, GULIELMI GIBBONS, ARMIGERI, FILIAM—ET HÆREDEM, DUXIT UXOREM, TUM JUVENIS, ADMODUM, VIX—ANNOS QUATER NOVENOS EMENSUS, SUMMUM PENE—FASTIGIUM HONORIS, APUD SUOS ASSECUTUS EST: NEMPE—VICARIAM, EX REGIS MANDATO PRÆFECTURAM: SED PRIUSQUAM—INGRESSUS, EST, IN IPSO FLORE AETATIS, PROH DOLOR! INTERIIT 4—CAL: JAN: A. Æ. C. 1733.

IN EO DESIDERATUR CIVIS PROBUS ET EXIMIUS, AMICUS FIDUS,—ET STRENUUS. CONJUX AMANTISSIMUS, IN OMNES ÆQUUS ET—BENEVOLUS, IN DEUM HAUD FUCATA PIETATE RELUCENS, IN PERPE—TUAM CONJUGIS DILECTI MEMORIAM, HOCCE MONUMENTUM—UXOR SUPERSTES, EXTRUENDUM CURAVIT.

SIR N. LAWES was appointed Governor of Jamaica, and received the honour of Knighthood in 1717. He was succeeded by the Duke of Portland in 1722, and died in 1731. He was an enterprising planter. Of his parentage little is known, and, like many self-made men, he is somewhat reserved on the subject. In his will (1 Aug., 1730), he styles himself, "late of Isleworth, in Middlesex," and states that he "was born in the year of our Lord, 1632, of honest and loyal parents, who suffered considerably for their loyalty."

Amongst his estates in Jamaica, may be enumerated Snowhill, Mount James, Swallowfield, and Temple Hall.*

He was five times married :—1. To Elizabeth Potter (St. Andrew's Register, May 20, 1680) ; 2. To Frances, daughter of Paul Godwyn Carter, son of Francis, Bishop of Hereford (May 23, 1685) ; 3. To Elizabeth, daughter of Sir T. Modyford, and widow of Col. S. Barry (July 2nd, 1693) ; 4. To Susanna Temple, by whom he had two sons :—1. James (above), baptized 1697, Mem. of A. in 1721–2. Temple, baptized Feb. 26, 1699 ; 5. Elizabeth, daughter of Sir Thos. Lawley (3d Bart.), by his wife, Catherine, daughter and co-heiress of Sir H. Winch, Bart., and widow of Thos. Cotton, great-grandson of Paul Beilby, Lord Wenlock.—By this wife Sir N. Lawes had a daughter, Maria, married in 1737, to Simon Luttrell, created Baron Irnham, and, in 1785, Earl of Carhampton.

The following epitaph, on a slab in the church of Isleworth, further explains these family connections :—

"In the name of God, Amen.—Here lieth the body of Susanna, late wife of— Nicholas Lawes, Esq. She was 5th daur. of—Thomas Temple, of Franckton, in the county of Warwick, Esq.

" She was first married to Samuel Bernard,—to whom she left one son, Thomas Bernard,—now of the Inner Temple, Esquire ;—to the said Nicholas Lawes, two sons, James—and Temple, whom God preserve.—She departed this life for a better the 20th—day of April, in the year of the Lord, 1707,—in the 47th year of her age."

From MSS. of the late C. E. Long.

II.

SACRED TO THE MEMORY OF THE HONBLE. THO-MAS DANVERS, ESQRE., VICE-ADMIRAL OF THE RED ; SECOND SON TO SIR ROBERT DANVERS, BART., & OF DAME MARY, ELDEST DAUGHTER & CO-HEIRESS OF THOMAS JER-MYN, BARON OF BURY, SEATED AT RUSHBROOK PARK, IN THE COUNTY OF SUFFOLK. SHE WAS, LIKEWISE, CO-HEIRESS TO HER UNCLES, HENRY JERMYN, EARL OF ST. ALBANS, & HENRY JERMYN, EARL OF DOVER.

THE SAID THOMAS DANVERS DYED OF YE YELLOW FEVER, IN THIS ISLAND OF JAMAICA, YE 16th DAY OF SEPTR., IN THE YEAR 1746, WHEN COMMANDER-IN-CHIEF OF HIS MAJESTY'S SQUADRONS IN THE WEST INDIES—THEN AT WAR WITH FRANCE AND SPAIN—AFTER 40 YEARS' FAITH-FULL & ESSENTIALL SERVICE TO HIS COUNTRY, HAVING PERFORM'D ALL TRUST PLACED IN HIM, WITH GREAT HONOUR, ALACRITY, & COURAGE, Wch GAIN'D HIM THE

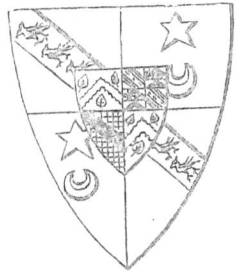

Mural Monument of White and Coloured Marbles; *Arms*, Quarterly ; 1 & 4, Or, on a bend gules, three martlets(?) of the f.; 2 & 3, azure, be-tween a mullet in chief. and in base, a crescent, or; on an escutcheon of pre-tence : Gr. quarterly, 1 & 4, Or, a chev. engrailed be-tween three leaves slipped; 2 & 3...; 2d Gr. quarter, 1 & 4, Or, on a bend azure, cotised gules, three lions passant of the field ; 2d & 3d, Or, on

---

* In St. Andrew's Church there is a brass chandelier, inscribed :—" Anno, 1706.—The Gift of Nicholas Lawes, Esq.,—For St. Andrew's Church."

a fesse sable, between two chevronels, sable, three crosses patée, of the field ; a canton gules, thereon a lion passant guardant of the first. 3d Gr. quarter, chequy or and gules, a bend sable.

FAVOUR OF HIS ROYAL MASTER, AS WELL AS THE JUST AP-PLAUSE AND ESTEEM OF ALL GOOD AND GENEROUS MINDS, THEY BEING CONVINCED THAT WHAT APPEAR'D MOST CON-DUSIVE TO THE INTEREST OF HIS KING, AND THE GOOD OF HIS COUNTRY, WOULD BE THE SOLE GUIDE OF HIS CON-DUCT.

HE MARRIED KATHARINE, THE ONLY DAUGHTER OF WM. SMITHSON, OF YORKSHIRE,—AN HEIRESS, NIECE TO LORD JERMYN, AND LORD DOVER, BY WHOM HE HAD THREE SONS & TWELVE DAUGHTERS, WHEREOF ONLY ONE SON & THREE DAUGHTERS SURVIVED HIM. IN THE 58th YEAR OF HIS AGE, HE YIELDED UP HIS SOUL INTO THE MERCIFULL HAND OF HIM WHO GAVE IT.

"THOUGH HE SLAY ME, YET WILL I TRUST IN HIM."

Job 13th & 15th.

THIS MONUMENT WAS ERECTED BY HIS TRULY AFFEC-TIONATE WIDOW, OUT OF A JUST & FAITHFULL REGARD TO HIS MEMORY. ANO. 1748.

SEE Burke's *Extinct and Dormant Peerage.*

12.

GRACE PINNOCK, LAST SURVIVING DAUGHTER OF HONBLE. GEO. PINNOCK, & TWIN SISTER TO ELIZABETH, OB. 2 FEB., 1818, AET 32.

Mural, White Marble.

13.

ELIZABETH PINNOCK, DIED OCTOBER 5th, 1804, AGED 18 YEARS.

Mural, White Marble.

LINES follow.

14.

IN THE NAME OF GOD, AMEN............HERE RESTETH THE BODY OF ....DOROTHY, THE WIFE OF EDWARD HARRISON, WHO DEPARTED THIS LIFE, YE 5th DAY OF NOVEMBER, IN THE YEAR OF OUR LORD, 1696, & IN THE 28th OF HER AGE.—HERE ALSO RESTETH THE BODY OF LANCELOT, 2d SON OF THE SAID DOROTHY & EDWARD HARRISON, WHO WAS BORN THE 14th OF SEP-TEMBER, 1694, AND DEPARTED THIS LIFE, YE 10th DAY OF APRILL, 1697.

Black Marble Slab, partly covered.

15.

(*Ab.*) MARGARET, WIFE OF LOVELL PENNELL, DEPUTY COMMISSARY GENERAL, OB. 7th JANY., 1851, AET. 47.

Mural, White Marble.

16.

(*Ab.*) THE HONBLE. JAMES STEWART, CUSTOS OF THIS PARISH, & MEMBER OF ASSEMBLY, OB. 25 MARCH, 1824, AET. 74.

Mural, White Marble.

17.

SACRED TO THE MEMORY OF—JOHN HOLLAND, ESQR.,—JUDGE OF—THE VICE-ADMIRALTY COURT IN JAMAICA.—HE DIED ON THE 12th OF JANUARY, 1804, —IN THE 47th YEAR OF HIS AGE.

Mural, White Marble ; Sculpture.

18.

(*Ab.*) THE HONBLE. ZACHARY BAYLY, ESQRE., CUSTOS & CHIEF MAGISTRATE OF THE PRECINCT OF ST. MARY, & ST. GEORGE, OB. 18 DEC., 1769, AET. 48. HE WAS A MEMBER OF THE PRIVY COUNCIL OF JAMAICA.—ALSO, NATHANIEL BAYLY EDWARDS, OB. 28th JANY., 1771, IN THE 21st YEAR OF HIS AGE. ERECTED BY BRYAN EDWARDS, HIS SURVIVING BROTHER.

Very Handsome Mural Monument of Coloured Marbles.

THIS family was distinguished through the literary merits of the historian of the West Indies—Bryan Edwards.

19.

HERE LIETH THE BODY OF—MASTER HENRY BUSHMAN,—SON OF JAMES BUSHMAN,—WHO DEPARTED THIS—LIFE ON THE 21st JUNE,—1810, AGED 6— MONTHS.

Plain Stone Slab, in Vestry.

20.

(*Ab.*) RICHARD SPEAR, ESQ., SECRETARY TO REAR-ADMIRAL DOUGLAS, OB. 14 NOVR., 1815, AET. 27.

Mural, Black Marble, and gold letters (indistinct).

21.

(*Ab.*) CHRISTIAN AND MARY ANNE DA SILVA, THE BELOVED WIVES OF SHELLAMONT DA SILVA, OB. 12 SEP., 1827, & 27 MARCH, 1854.

Mural, White Marble (indistinct).

22.

(*Ab.*) CATHERINE, JEMIMA, & EMMA, THE CHILDREN OF WM. BROOKES KING, ESQ., & CHRISTIAN, HIS WIFE.

Mural, White Marble (indistinct).

23.

(*Ab.*) THE REVD. ALEXANDER CAMPBELL, M.A., FOR 45 YEARS RECTOR OF THIS PARISH, OB. 8 DEC., 1858, AET. 81.

Mural, W. Marble on Gray.

SEE Pedigree.

24.

(*Ab.*) CHARLES MACKGLASHAN, ESQ., FORMERLY A SURGEON IN THE ROYAL NAVY, OB. 27 JUNE, 1834, AET. 74.

White Marble Mural, small Mosaic of arms (indistinct).

25.

MAJOR GENERAL LAMBERT,—COMMR. OF H.M.'S FORCES,—OB. JANY. 4, 1848, AET. 62.

Mural, White Marble.

26.

(*Ab.*) JOHN NICHOLLS, OF THE WAR DEPARTMENT, DIED AT BALACLAVA, 3d NOV., 1855, AET 35.

White Marble, Mural.

27.

(*Ab.*) HONORA WATSON POPHAM, DAU. OF SIR HOME & LADY POPHAM, OB. ON BOARD H.M.S. "SYBILLE," AT PORT ROYAL, MARCH 30, 1820, AET. 22.

White Marble, Mural.

SEE "Naval Biographical Dictionary."

28.

(*Ab.*) ELEANOR, WIFE OF DAVID DUNCOMB, & DAU. OF JOHN & ELIZABETH WINTER, OF WATCHET, CO. SOMERSET, IN THE U. K. OF G. B., OB. 7 SEP., 1786, AET. 37.

White Marble, Mural.

29.

(*Ab.*) MRS. CHARLOTTE AIKMAN, WIFE OF ALEXR. AIKMAN, ESQ., JUNR., PRINTER TO H.M., &C., & 2d DAU. OF ROBT. CORY, ESQ., ATTORNEY-AT-LAW, OF GT. YARMOUTH, CO. NORFOLK, ENGLAND,—OB. 8 NOV., 1810, AET. 29.

White Marble, Mural ;
Arms, Argent, issuing from clouds, at sinister base, a hand proper, holding a rod upright sable, bearing at the top two sprigs of leaves—en surtout, a baton sinister engrailed gules. Impaling, sable, on a chevron or, between three griffins' heads erased, of the second, three estoiles gules.

30.

(*Ab.*) CHARLES HOPE KERR, 2d SON OF THE RIGHT. HONBLE. LORD ROBERT KERR, AND MARY, HIS WIFE,—LIEUT. 61st REGT., & A.D.C. TO M. GENL. SIR WM. MAYNARD GOMM, K.C.B.,* COMMANDER OF THE FORCES IN THIS ISLAND, OB. 31 DEC., 1840, AET. 23.

White Marble, Mural.

SEE Burke's "Peerage," *voce* "Lothian."

---

* Now Field-Marshal & G.C.B.

31.

(*Ab.*) SACRED TO THE MEMORY OF CHARLOTTE MARY,—THE BELOVED WIFE OF JOHN CAMPBELL, ESQUIRE, OF THIS PARISH,—WHO DEPARTED THIS LIFE ON THE 7th SEPTR., 1817,—AT THE DECOY IN ST. MARY'S, WHERE SHE WAS INTERRED, IN THE 51st YEAR OF HER AGE, &C.

JOHN CAMPBELL was a merchant of Kingston, and Colonel-in-Chief of its Militia. He was also a Member of Assembly.

32.

(*Ab.*) THE HONBLE. EDWARD FOORD, ESQR., MERCHANT OF KINGSTON, OB. 13th MARCH, 1777.

White Marble, Mural.

33.

(*Ab.*) JOHN FALCONER, M.D., NATIVE OF THIS ISLAND, & LATE MASTER OF THE ST. ANDREW'S KILWINNING LODGE, OF THIS PARISH, OB. 24th AUGT., 1857, AET. 59.

KILWINNING, in Ayrshire, gives its name to several Masonic Lodges.

34.

(*Ab.*) JOHN WALLACE HARRIS, ESQ.,—CLERK OF THE PEACE, &C., OF THIS PARISH, FOR 25 YEARS, OB. 15th OCT., 1857, AET. 53.

35.

IN MEMORY OF—LUCAS BARRETT, ESQ., F.G.S., F.L.S.,—DIRECTOR OF THE WEST INDIAN GEOLOGICAL SURVEY,—WHO WAS DROWNED* NEAR PORT ROYAL,— DECR. 19, 1862.

SEE notes on " Barrett."

36.

(*Ab.*) EDWARD WARWICK HARVEY,—YOUNGEST SON OF LIEUT.-GENERAL SIR JOHN, & THE—HONBLE. LADY ELIZABETH HARVEY,—OB. 15 FEB., 1846, AT SEA, NEAR KINGSTON.

LT.-GENERAL SIR JOHN HARVEY, K.C.B., A.D.C. to the King, married, in 1806, Elizabeth, daughter of the first Baron Lake.

37.

(*Ab.*) CAROLINE BROUGHTON, WIFE OF THE REVD. GEO. B. BROOKS, OB. 14th DECR., 1857, AET. 23.

38.

(*Ab.*) CHARLES MITCHELL JOPP, OB. SEP. 8, 1861, AET. 56.

39.

(*Ab.*) JOHN GARDINER CLARKE, ESQ., H.M. CUSTOMS, OB. 26 JUNE, 1850, AET. 23.

White Marble, Mural Tablet.

---

* While in a diving-bell, through the negroes in the boat neglecting the breathing apparatus.

40.

(*Ab.*) AT STONY HILL, ... REPOSE THE REMAINS OF THE FOLLOWING OF-
FICERS .... OF THE 36th REGT. :

LIEUT. TUCK, OB. 15th DECR., 1855, AET. 23 YRS. & 10 MONTHS.

LIEUT. MAHON, OB. 16th JUNE, 1856, AET. 26 YRS. & 5 MONTHS.

LIEUT. SCARLETT, OB. 29th JUNE, 1856, AET. 23 YRS. & 2 MONTHS.

White Marble, Mural Tablet.

41.

(*Ab.*) EDWARD STAINES HARRISON, LIEUT. 1 W.I. REGT., & OF SCARBOROUGH,
YORKSHIRE, OB. 13th SEP., 1856.

White Marble, Mural Tablet.

42.

(*Ab.*) GENL. WM. ANNE VILLETTES, 2d SON OF ARTHUR VILLETTES, ESQR.,
MINISTER PLENIPOTENTIARY AT THE COURT OF TURIN, &C.,—COLONEL OF THE
64th REGT. OF INFANTRY,—LIEUT.-GOVERNOR & COMMR. OF THE FORCES IN
THIS ISLAND,—OB. 13th JULY, 1808, AET. 54.

Underneath :

CAPTAIN ALBERT TURRETTINI, 2d SON OF ALBERT TURRETTINI, ESQR., &
MARY, HIS WIFE, SISTER OF GENERAL VILLETTES,—OB. 15th JULY, 1808, AET. 24.
—BURIED AT FORT ANTONIO.

Mural Monument, White Marble.

43.

(*Ab.*) THE HONBLE. RICHARD GUSSEN, MEMBER OF THE PRIVY COUNCIL OF
JAMAICA, ... CUSTOS OF METCALFE, ... OB. 8th AUGT., 1860, AET. 58. HE
WAS 39 YEARS & 11 MONTHS RESIDENT IN JAMAICA.

44.

(*Ab.*) THE HONBLE. GEO. PINNOCK, PRESDT. OF P. C. OF JAMAICA, OB. 1
DEC., 1834, AET. 87.—GRACE, HIS WIFE, OB. 11th MAY, 18..., AET. 58.—MRS. MARY
STEVENSON, THEIR NIECE, ERECTED THE MONUMENT.

INDISTINCT.

White Marble, Mural;

45.

M.S. ....

HEN. CROASDAILE, ...

ARMIG. QUI ....

VIRI MARITI, ...

PARENTIS, CIVIS ....

INNOCUE, FIDELITER ....

JUSTE ET HONESTE...............

MUNIA .. PLEBAT ....

OBIIT AN. DOM. LXX., ...

AETAT. L. . . . .

MÆRENS CONJUX, HOC POSUIT, ...

MDCCLXXII. . . . .

partly obliterated ; *Arms*, Argent, a chevron sable, between three cocks, gules, on an escutcheon of pretence, azure, a fesse, or, fretty gules, between three deer trippt. *Crest*, Over an esquire's helmet, a cock, gules.

46.

DORMITORIUM MITE* HUMANIS—EXUTÆ LABORIBUS FRANSCISCÆ,—NUPERÆ UXORIS CLARISSIMÆ—PIETATIS, ET CONSUETUDINIS HON^{is},—NICHOLAI LAW[ES], AR-MIGERI . VIRGINIS—NOMEN FUIT GODWYN,* ARMIGERO RELI—GIONIS, ET REGIÆ CAUSÆ FORTITER—STUDIOSO, OBTINUIT [?] QUI PATERNIS—FRANSCISCI GODWYNI, HEREFORDIENSIS—EPISCOPI, THOMÆ GODWYNI—BATHONENSIS, ET JOHANNIS WOOTTON,—EXONIENSIS EXEMPLIS ET INSTITU—IS DOCTUS, FIDE ET CONSTAN-TIA—CLARUIT.—HÆ ETIAM RUINÆ MEMORIAM—DANT SEMPITERNAM—OBIIT DIE 7 MO., MARTIJ, ANNO 169⅔,—FILIUS HORUM, VIX NATUS E—ITA DISCEDENS CUM MATRE—CONTUMULATUS JACET.

Slab, Black Marble.

47.

"WITH THE PURE—THOU SHALT SHOW THYSELF PURE."

TO THE MEMORY OF ELIZABETH DALLING, AN INVALUABLE WIFE ; AND HER LOVELY INFANT DAUGHTER, NAMED AFTER HER.

THIS MONUMENT WAS ERECTED BY THEIR AFFLICTED & AFFECTIONATE HUSBAND, & FATHER, LIEUT.-COLL. JOHN DALLING, IN 1768.

ELIZABETH DALLING, DEPARTED THIS LIFE, JULY THE 6, 1768, IN THE 22 YEAR OF HER AGE. SHE WAS THE ELDER DAUGHTER OF PHILLIP AND GRACE PINNOCK, OF THIS ISLAND, AND HEIRESS OF HER UNCLE, COLL. HENRY DAW-KINS. THE INFANT DAUGHTER DIED MAY 1, 1768, IN THE THIRD YEAR OF HER AGE.

White Marble Mural, elegantly Sculptured.

SIR JOHN DALLING, created a Baronet in 1783, was son of John Dalling, of Bun-gay, Suffolk, and Governor of Jamaica. By Louisa Lawford, his second wife, he had surviving issue. See the "Baronetage," and also the "Peerage," and "Extinct and Dormant Peerage," *voce* "Penrhyn."

48.

SACRED TO THE MEMORY—OF—ANN DELAPIERRE LITTLE-JOHN, THE WIFE OF—ALEXR. LITTLEJOHN, AND DAUGHTER OF GEORGE BENNETT, ESQR.,—BY HIS WIFE, ANN DELA-PIERRE.—SHE WAS AN UNPARALLELLED EXAMPLE OF—FILIAL DUTY, AND CONJUGAL AFFECTION.—SHE DEPARTED THIS LIFE ON THE 10th SEP., 1771,—15 DAYS AFTER THE DE-LIVERY OF TWIN MALE INFANTS,—WHO FOLLOWED HER, ON THE 3^d SEP. & 5th OCTR., 1771.—THEY WERE BAPTIZED White Marble, Mural.

* Qy. *morte ?*   † Qy. [Quod patre nata Joanne Godwyn.]

Monument, elegantly Sculptured; *Arms,* Argent, three arrows, two in saltire, and one in pale, crossed, between six trefoils sable. *Crest,* A bow bent, and stringed, with arrow drawn to the head, point upwards. "Olim sic erat," 6 Nov., 1771.

AT THE FUNERAL OF THEIR MOTHER,—BY THE NAMES OF :—

ALEXANDER }
                } DELAPIERRE BENNETT,
AND DAVID }

AND THEIR REMAINS ARE HERE INTER'D WITH THOSE—OF —THEIR MOTHER.

"BLESSED ARE THEY WHO DIE IN THE LORD."

THE Bennetts (of Dorsetshire origin) were settled, soon after the capture of Jamaica, at Barbican, in Liguanea. The founders of the family appear to have been Henry Bennet (will, 1666) and the Honble. George Bennett (will, 1678). The latter was Member of Assembly for Kingston, and colonel of militia, as were also his son and grandson, of the same name.

An interesting narrative, concerning the assassination of a member of this family, is given in the "Gentleman's Magazine," for May, 1751. [See also *Notes and Queries,* 5th ser. ii. 349.]

BENNETTS OF JAMAICA.

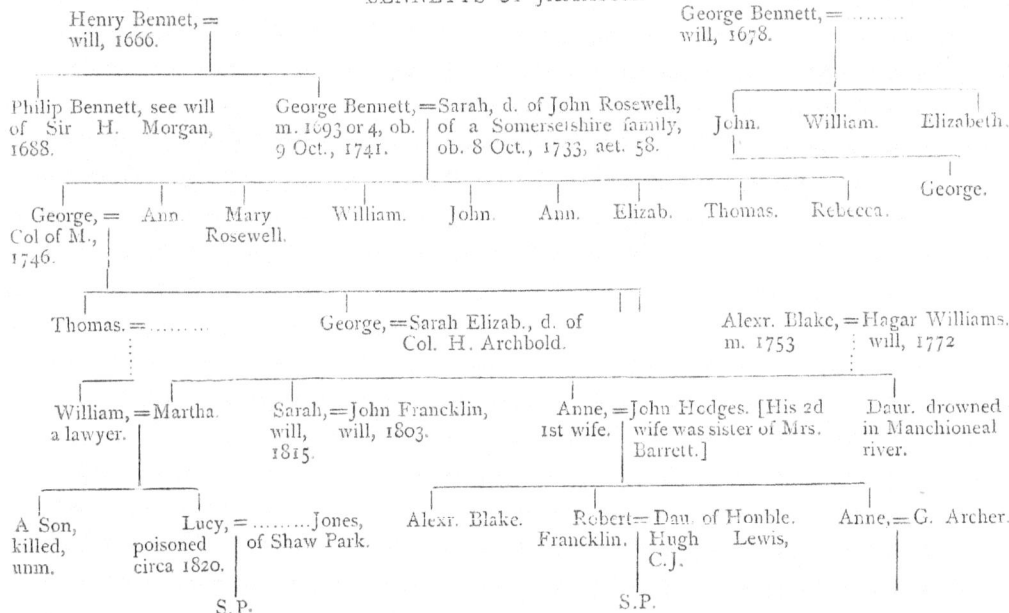

Henry Bennet, = will, 1666.

George Bennett, = ... will, 1678.

Philip Bennett, see will of Sir H. Morgan, 1688.

George Bennett, = Sarah, d. of John Rosewell, m. 1693 or 4, ob. 9 Oct., 1741. | of a Somersetshire family, ob. 8 Oct., 1733, aet. 58.

John.   William.   Elizabeth.

George.

George, = Ann. Col of M., 1746.

Mary Rosewell.

William.   John.   Ann.   Elizab.   Thomas.   Rebecca.

Thomas. = ...

George, = Sarah Elizab., d. of Col. H. Archbold.

Alexr. Blake, = Hagar Williams, m. 1753 | will, 1772

William, = Martha. a lawyer.

Sarah, = John Francklin, will, | will, 1803. 1815.

Anne, = John Hedges. [His 2d 1st wife. | wife was sister of Mrs. Barrett.]

Daur. drowned in Manchioneal river.

A Son, killed, unm.

Lucy, = ...Jones, poisoned | of Shaw Park. circa 1820.

Alexr. Blake.

Robert = Dau. of Honble. Francklin. | Hugh   Lewis, | C.J.

Anne, = G. Archer.

S.P.   S.P.

49.

THIS STONE IS PLACED NEAR THE REMAINS OF CAPT.— JAMES RENTON, TO PRESERVE TO POSTERITY, THE MEMORY OF THAT—GALLANT OFFICER, WHO WAS BORN IN SCOTLAND, OCT., 1702.—HE WENT EARLY TO SEA, AND BY HIS EXPERIENCE IN MARITIME AFFAIRS,—WAS SIGNALLY USEFULL TO THE BRAVE VERNON, AT THE TAKING OF—PORTO BELLO, WHERE HE SERVED AS A VOLUNTEER, & WAS REWARDED Wth THE—COMMAND OF A FRIGATE, ADDED TO THE BRITISH

Mural, White Marble, Bas

NAVY, BY THAT GLORIOUS CONQUEST.—HE WAS CAPTAIN OF THE "STRAFFORD," WHEN PORT LOUIS WAS TAKEN BY— REAR-ADMIRAL KNOWLES, MARCH 8, 18⁷₄,* & MORTALLY WOUNDED IN THE ATTACK,—DYING WITHOUT REGRET, IN THE SERVICE OF HIS COUNTRY, AND IN THE—ARMS OF VICTORY.—ELIZABETH RENTON, HIS WIDOW, FROM DUTY AND AFFECTION, INSCRIBED—THIS, TO TESTIFY A JUST SENCE (*sic*) OF HER LOSS, AND HIS MERIT.

relief of a naval engagement; *Arms*, Argent, within an orle ingrailed, a lion rampant, sable: impaling, argent, between two lions rampant, combatant, sable, a tower gules.

50.

H. S. E.—ANTONIUS LANGLEY SWYMMER, ARMR., VIR SI QUIS ALIUS AD AMICORUM UTILITATEM ATQUE COMMODA PROMOVENDA,—ALACER, ET FIDELIS—AD PATRIÆ JURA ATQUE PRIVILIGIA—TUENDA ET VINDICANDA, VIGIL. ACER STRENUUS. HISCE ACCEDEBAT OPTIMA INDOLES—MIRA MORUM ELEGANTIA, COMITAS SUAVISSIMA. UXOREM DUXIT ARABELLAM FILIAM NATA QUINTAM — Dⁿⁱ JOANˢ. ASTLEY, BARTᵗ. DE PATSHULL IN AGRO STAFFORD.—OBIIT PRID. NON. MENSIS JANUARIJ,—ANN. DOM. MD.CCXL. AETAT XXXIV., AMICIS PATRIÆ VIDUÆ. DESIDERATISSIMUS.

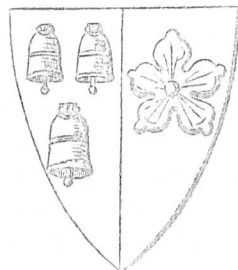

Mural Monument of handsome Coloured Marbles: *Arms*, Gules, three bells, or: impaling, az., a cinquefoil, argt.

Sᴇᴇ "Baronetage."

51.

SACRED TO THE MEMORY OF—THE REVD. JOHN CAMPBELL.—WHO DEPARTED THIS LIFE IN LONDON—13ᵗʰ OCTOBER, 1813, AGED 64 YEARS.—THE JUSTICES AND VESTRY—HAVE CAUSED THIS MONUMENT TO BE ERECTED AS A TRIBUTE TO HIS MERIT—AND EXEMPLARY GOOD CONDUCT DURING A RESIDENCE OF THIRTY-THREE YEARS—AS RECTOR OF THIS PARISH—ST. ANDREW, 1814.

W. M. on Gray Mural Tablet.

Hɪs son became Chaplain-General to the Forces, and had with other issue—1. John, Rector of St. Thomas yᵉ Vale, married Anne, only child of J. F. Archer; 2. Duncan, Rector of Kingston, married Emily P., daughter of Dr. A. G. Spencer, Bishop of Jamaica; 3. Charles, M.D., married Isabel M., daughter of .... Edwards, Receiver-General.

52.

MARY ANNE ISABELLA, DAUR. OF MARY ANNE, AND DR. WILLIAM GORDON, OB. 27 MAY, 1858, AET. 21 YRS. & 5 MTHS.

In the Churchyard—nearly all abridged.

53.

ANN EUPHEMIA DARRELL, INF. DR. OF W. G. ASHWOOD, & EUPHEMIA FRANCES, HIS WIFE, BORN IN BERMUDA JANY. 1, 1854; DIED IN JAMAICA 21 JANY., 1855.

---

* Mauritius was taken from the French in 1810.

54.

ROBT. FRANCIS JOHN EDEN, INF. SON OF LOUISA, & LT. COLL. C. M. EDEN, WHO WAS BORN AT DINAN, BRITTANY, AUGT. 4th, 1836; & DIED AT VILLA MEDICI, 6th JUNE, 1837.

55.

WILLIAM MATTCOCKS, ESQ., A NATIVE OF LANCASHIRE, ENGLAND, OB. 20th FEB. 1835, AET. 74.

56.

NICOL CUNNINGHAM GRAHAM, OB. 22d JULY, 1860, AET. 9 MTHS.

57.

JAMES FALCONER, ESQ., OB. 5th MARCH, 1828, AET. 69.

58.

HUGH MC LACHLAN, ESQ., OB. 22d AUGT. 1823, AET. 37 YRS. 2 MTHS.

59.

JOHN ARNETT CATOR, OB. 10 th JUNE, 1862, AET. 52.

60.

CHARLES ISAACS, SON OF GEO. & ELIZA ISAACS, OB. 8 AUGT. 1838, AET. 7 MTHS.

61.

FRANCES HARRIS, OB. 5 NOV. 1820, AET. 42 Y. 2 MTHS., & JOHN TOWNSHEND HARRIS, HER HUSBAND, OB. 16th FEB. 1836, AET. 66 YRS. 7 MTHS.—JANE, THEIR DAUR., OB. 19th APL., 1836, AET. 22 YRS. 23 DAYS, & JAMES TURNER HARRIS, INF. SON OF GEO. HARRIS, OB. 11 NOV. 1831,—FRANCES HARRIS, WIFE OF JNO. T. HARRIS, ESQ. OB. 5 NOV. 1820, AET. 42.

62.

CHARLOTTE AIKMAN, OB. 8th NOV. 1810, AET. 29.

63.

ALEXR. AIKMAN, SENR., ESQ., OB. 6th JULY, 1838, AET. 83.

64.

ESTHER ELIZAB. DAVIS, OB. 17th DEC. 1834, AET. 59.

65.

LUCY, WIFE OF REVD. DR. MAGRATH, RECTOR OF TRELAWNEY, OB. 30th MAY, 1852, AET. 44.

66.

FRANCIS HARRIS, DIED OF MALIGNANT CHOLERA, DECR. 3, 1850, AET. 42.

67.

ISAAC MC CORKELL, OB. 12 FEB. 1842.—ANN LONGMAN HARRIS, OB. 14th DEC. 1849, AET. 16 MTHS.

68.

HANNAH MOORE, WIFE OF ROBERT SMITH, ESQ., OB. 22d SEP. 1846, AET. 64.

69.

NEAR THIS SPOT LIE INTERR'D, WILLM. CUMMING & JAMES WADDELL—MRS. MARY DUNBAR WADDELL—RACHAEL CUMMING WADDELL, & MARY ROSE—1826.

70.

JOHN EDWARDS, OB. 8th JANY. 1863, AET. 39. ERECTED BY HIS WIDOW.

71.

ANN TINLING, OB. 12th JANY. 1791, AET. 50; ALSO HER DAU. & GR.-DAU.

Red Granite.

72.

SARAH FRANCES GEDDES, WIFE OF ALEXR. GEDDES, & ELDT. DAUR. OF THE LATE THOS. WM. HORLOCK—BORN, 6th APRIL, 1802; DIED, 15 JANY. 1840.

73.

FRANCES ELIZA NELSON, 3d DAU. OF THE LATE DR. WM. F. NELSON,—DIED OF YELLOW FEVER, 29th OCT. 1841, AGED 19.

74.

ARTHUR MARSHALL, SON OF JAMES MARSHALL, & HELEN HIS WIFE, OB. 3 NOV. 1841, AET. 2.

75.

MISS REBECCA STEUART........ AET. 54 YS. 2 MTHS. DIED 16th MARCH, 18..

Fragment.

76.

ALEXR. GRAHAM.

No date.

77.

MISS ELIZABETH CORRELL, OB. 16th SEP. 1852, AET. 36.

78.

MARY CAMPBELL, OB. 3d FEB. 1767, AET. 22.

79.

JOHN GRAHAM MCKAY, NAT. 28th DEC. 1776—OB. 12th SEP. 1779.—ALSO HIS MOTHER, MARY MCKAY—OB. FEB. 7th, 1706.

80.

JOHN FISHER, ESQ., OB. 9th AUGT. 1841, AET. 58.

Crest, An arm in armour, embowed, holding in the hand a cross crosslet.

81.

BENEATH THIS STONE ARE DEPOSITED THE MORTAL REMAINS OF A CLERGYMAN, WHOSE NAMES ARE IN THE LAMB'S BOOK OF LIFE, &C. 1849.

No name.

Crest, An arm in armour, embowed, holding in the hand a cross crosslet.

82.

NEAR THIS PLACE ARE DEPOSITED, THE REMAINS OF MARGARET ELIZA-BETH BAKER, DAUGHTER OF JOHN PROCULUS BAKER, ESQ., AND ANN SU-SANNA, HIS WIFE. THIS LAMENTED INFANT WAS BORN THE 6th OF NOVR. 1778, AND DIED THE 23d OF NOVR. 1779.

83.

JOHN READ, ESQ. OF KINGSTON, OB. 28th AUGT. 1822, AET. 44 YEARS, 7 MONTHS.

84.

MISS SUSANNA G. COX, AN AFFECTIONATE & ENGAGING CHILD, DEPARTED THIS LIFE 13th MAY, 1822, IN HER SEVENTH YEAR.

85.

THE BODY OF BENJAMIN HEAD,—WHO DEPARTED THIS LIFE—THE 28th DAY—OF MARCH, 1753, AGED 55 YEARS.

86.

HERE LYETH THE BODY OF SAGE HARRIS, WIFE OF OF DOCTR. NICHS. HARRIS, OF LEGUANEA, WHO DEPARTED THIS LIFE, FEBY. 12th, $17\frac{13}{14}$. — ALSO,—MARY HARRIS, HIS DAUGHTER, WHO DEPARTED THIS LIFE, SEP. 22, $17\frac{13}{14}$, AGED 2 YEARS,—ALSO, THOMAS HARRIS, HER SON, WHO DEPARTED THIS LIFE, DECEMR. 7th, 1736—AGED 29 YEARS.

HERE LYETH INTERR'D, THE BODY OF DOCTR. NICHS. HARRIS, OF LEGUANEA, WHO DEPARTED THIS LIFE, DECEMR. 18, 1736, AGED 57 YEARS. HE LIVED IN THIS ISLAND 44 YEARS, AND WAS ESTEEMED A MAN OF VIRTUE & PROBITY.

Sculpture ; a Rose, Escallop, and Hour Glass.

87.

HERE LIETH INTERR'D, YE BODY OF JOHN MARTIN, WHO DEPARTED THIS LIFE, THE 27th OF DECEMBER, 1710, AGED 32 YEARS. HERE LIETH INTERR'D, THE BODY OF FRANCES MARTIN, THE WIFE OF YE SAID JOHN MARTIN, WHO DE-PARTED THIS LIFE, THE 16th OF SEPTEMBER, 1714, AGED 33 YEARS.—ALSO THEIR TWO SONS AND THREE DAUGHTERS.

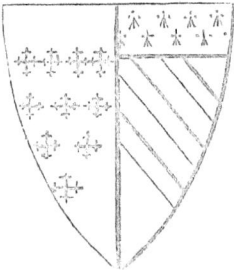

Arms, 10 crosses crosslet (4, 3, 2, and 1): impaling, three bendlets, a chief erm.

88.

HERE LIETH INTERR'D THE BODY OF RICHARD MOORE MERCHANT, WHO DEPARTED THIS LIFE YE 29th OF JULY, 1738, AGED 29 YEARS AND SEVEN MONTHS.

89.

GEORGIANA JOHNSON LYNCH, WIFE OF JOHN LYNCH, ESQ., OB. 23 JUNE, 1832, AET. 40.—WM. HYLTON, ESQ., OB. 20th FEB. 1837, AET. 88. — GEORGIANA, NAT. JUNE 28, 1811, OB. 13th OCT. 1819 ;—MARY, NAT. 15 OCT. 1814, OB. 16th OCT. 1819 ;—JULIA, NAT. 13th MAY, 1819, OB. 30th MARCH, 1822 ; —LAWRENCE.... CHILDREN OF ELIZABETH & JOHN HYLTON.

90.

THE BODY OF .... JOHN WADE .... JULY, 1807....

Fragment.

91.

CHRISTOPHER WARD..AGED 78 YEARS..OB. SEP. 9th, 1798.

92.

CORNELIA, WIFE OF CAPT. WM. STUBBS, BORN AT GRAND TURK'S ISLAND, 27th MAY, 1828 ; DIED DECR. 8th, 1860.

93.

MISS JANE DANIEL.... 11th MARCH ....

94.

MISS CLARISSA HENRY, OB. 21st NOV. 1819, AET. 48....

95.

MARY BLOOM, OB. NOV. 1802, AET. 25......

96.

JAMES MASSI, DIED FROM THE CHOLERA, 20th NOV. 1850, AET. 39...... ERECTED BY HIS WIFE SARAH.

97.

CHARLES C. PRESCOTT, OB. 10th MAY, 1855, AET. 36. — ALSO, MRS. JOHANNA PRESCOTT, OB. 21 JUNE, 1841, AET 61.

98.

MARY COCKBURN, RELICT OF THE LATE WILLIAM TITLEY, OB. 5th MARCH, 1857, AET. 57.

99.

NEAR THIS ....—LYES THE RE....—AGNES ROB....—DAUGHTER OF ALEX-ANDER AND JEAN ROBINSON—OF THIS PARISH, DIED OCT.—YE 14th, 1756, AGED 2 ....—YEARS AND 7 MONTHS.

Fragment.

100.

ANN, DAUR. OF ROBERT & MARTHA FRANCES STOKES, OB. 10 DEC. 1816, AET. 3 YEARS & 5 DAYS.

101.

CHARLES HOPE KERR, OB. 31 DEC., 1840, AET. 23.

SEE "Peerage."

102.

FRANCES EVES, WIFE OF CHRISTOPHER, LORD-BISHOP OF JAMAICA, DIED APRIL 27th, 1825, IN THE 30th YEAR OF HER AGE.

"HEU FUGAX SICUT FLOS ANGELI."

103.

CHRISTOPHER, THE FIRST BISHOP OF JAMAICA, OBIIT PRID. NON. APRIL IV., —ANNO—DOM. MDCCCXLIII.,—AETAT LXI.,—EPISCOPAT. XIX.

Arms.

DR. CHRISTOPHER LIPSCOMB was educated at New College, Oxford; B.A. 1804, M.A. 1811, B.D. 1824, D.D. 1824. He was appointed first Bishop of Jamaica, on the erection of that see, in 1824. He married Anna Maria, daughter of Francis Eves, & relict of Ebenezer Pope. This lady was first married (second wife) to the Honble. John Coventry, son of the sixth Earl of Coventry, who died 12th Nov., 1829 (?).

104.

SARAH, THE WIFE OF ALEXR. FORBES, ESQ., OF KINGSTON, DIED JULY 17th, 1823, AGED 33 YEARS.

EULOGISTIC lines.

105.

TIMOTHY D. C. SHARPE, OB. 31st MAY, 1845, AET. 40.

106.

JOHN FISHER, ESQ., OB. 9th AUGUST, 1845, AET. 58.

107.

MISS ANN BROWN TYRELL, DAUR. OF JOSEPH EYRE, ESQR., OB. 8th JUNE, 1835, AET. 20.

108.

WILLIAM JUNOR, ESQR., OF EDINBURGH, LATE MANAGER OF THE BRANCH OF THE COLONIAL BANK, IN THIS ISLAND,—OB. 9th MAY, 1853, AET. 63.

109.

JOSEPH BARTON PHIPPS, OB. 30th JUNE, 1793, AET. 30 Y., 1 M., 29 D.

JOHN PHIPPS, DIED 9th MARCH, 1798, AGED 29 Y., 8 M., 5 D.

110.

SACRUM MEMORIAE—JACOBI TOWNSON ARMIGER,—IN HAC INSULA MERCA-TORIS—QUI POST VITAM BENE PERACTAM DECESSIT.—CONJUX AMANS, BENEVO-LUS PATER,—FIDELISSIMUS AMICUS.—FAMILIAE PARITER AC—SODALIUM.—AMOR

ET DELICIAE — OBIIT DIE OCTAVO MENSIS JULII, — AERAE CHRISTIANAE, MDCCCXLVII.—ANNUM AGENS LXII.—QUAE EST ENIM VITA ?—EHEU ! VAPOR EST —AD MODICUM PARENS DEINCEPS—EVANESCENS !—VIATOR—A MOMENTO, PENDET AETERNITAS.

III.

HIC SITUS EST, QUI FUIT, SAMUEL ALEXANDER, HUJUS PAROCHIAE MEDI-CINAE STUDIOSUS,—VIR HOSPITALIS, ALACRIS ET URBANUS.—IN DELICIIS AMICIS —DECIDIT EX HAC VITA, DECMO. SEPMO. NOV.,—ANNO DOM. 1716,—ANNO AETATIS, TRIGESIMO PRIMO—ILLE OBIIT SED NON OBIIT, SOLUM ILLE FACETUS —RISUS OBIT—GRATIA LUSUS OBIT.

112.

WILLIAM TITLEY, LATE MERCHANT OF KINGSTON, OB. 5th NOV., 1851, AET. 70.—ERECTED BY HIS CHILDREN.

Red Granite Obelisk.

113.

WILLIAM MC INTYRE, OB. JULY 1st, 1853, AET. 22.

114.

MARIANNE WILLIAMS, WIFE OF JOHN JAMES VIDAL, ESQ., OB. 25th JANUARY, 1857, AET. 26.

115.

CHARLES ASTWOOD PAINE, OB. 28th JANY., 1858, AET. 2 YRS., 11 MTHS.

116.

THOMAS GEORGE SHORTLAND, ESQR., POST-CAPTAIN IN THE NAVY, & H.M.'S COMMISSIONER AT PORT ROYAL,—OB. 23d NOVR., 1827, AET. 57.—ALSO,—HIS DAUGHTER, ELIZA-BETH SHORTLAND, OB. 25th NOVR., AET. 25.

Arms, Gules, an inescut-cheon, argent. In chief, three birds close : impaling, azure, an eagle displayed, argent. *Crest*, Over an esquire's helmet, a bird close. *Motto*, " Nec sorte nec fato." The impalement in the engraving is transposed.

117.

ERECTED BY THE 2nd BATTN. 60th RIFLES, TO THE ME-MORY OF LIEUT.-COLONEL AUGUSTUS FREDERICK ELLIS, SECOND SON OF LORD SEAFORD, WHO DIED IN THIS ISLAND IN COMMAND OF THAT REGIMENT, 16th AUGUST, 1841, AETAT. SUAE 41.

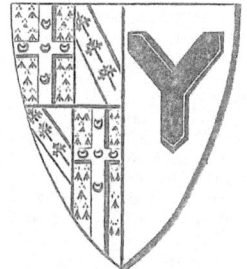

Arms, Quarterly ; 1 & 4, [or], on a cross sable, five crescents [argt.] ; 2 & 3, gules, on a bend, [argt.], [3 trefoils, slipped vert.] : im-paling, argent, a shake fork [between 3 fleurs-de-lys] sable. *Crest*, A goat's head erased. *Motto*, " Non modo sed quo-modo." (A Sarcophagus.)

VIDE Burke's "Peerage," *voce* "Howard de Walden." The family of Ellis was originally from Wrexham, county Denbigh, and it is asserted, in the Peerages of Lodge, Burke, and De Brett, that John Ellis was a colonel in the army at the taking of Jamaica, in 1655, and married Grace, sister of Wm. Nedham, Speaker of Assembly. But these statements are incorrect, as there was no officer of that name and rank in Venable's force. A John Ellis, captain in 1685, was Member of Assembly in 1688, and many years subsequently. He settled on the estate known as "Ellis' Caymanas," and was buried 1st Sept., 1706, being then, according to the Parish Register of St. Catherine, a "maiger." It was his eldest son, John, who married *Elizabeth Grace* Nedham. The son of the latter was Chief-Justice George Ellis, who introduced the valuable Guinea grass into Jamaica. Charles Rose Ellis, elder son of the Chief-Justice, was created Baron Seaford 15th July, 1826, and died in 1845, when his elder son, Charles Augustus (in right of his mother, Baroness Howard de Walden), succeeded.

Lord Seaford's younger son, Augustus Frederick, married 25th June, 1828, a daughter of Sir David Cunynghame, Bart., and died Lt.-Colonel of the 60th regiment,* as above stated in his epitaph.—See Peerage, "Howard de Walden."

118.

ERECTED BY THE 2nd BATTN. 60th RIFLES, TO THE MEMORY OF LIEUT.-COLONEL CHARLES MARKHAM, FIFTH SON OF WILLIAM MARKHAM, ESQ., OF BECCA HALL; WHO DIED IN THIS ISLAND, IN COMMAND OF THAT CORPS, ANN. AETATIS SUAE 39,—1842.

Arms, Per fesse, or ; and azure, in chevrons, a demi-lion rampant : impaling, gules, a cross moline...in dexter chief an escallop. *Crest,* A winged lion, holding a lyre. (A Sarcophagus.)

119.

HERE LIES THE BODY OF MR. JOHN CARTER, MERCHANT, WHO DEPARTED THIS LIFE THE 24th DAY OF APRIL, IN THE YEAR OF OUR LORD, 1731, IN THE 40th YEAR OF HIS AGE.

Arms,...A cross moline, on a chevronel...three buckles...*Crest,* Over an esquire's helmet, a demi-eagle, wings displayed.

120.

HERE LYES THE BODY—OF WILLIAM CUMMING, ESQ.,—WHO DEPARTED THIS LIFE DECEMBER THE...., ...24, AGED 63 YEARS.

Old and much effaced.

No date.

---

* "King's Royal Rifles"—one of the *corps d'élite* of the British army.

121.

DANIEL BRIDGES, JUNIOR, OB. 21 AUGT., ... AETATI (*sic*) 29.

Fragment.

No date.

122.

MRS. SARAH WATT, OB. 3 MARCH, 1837, AET. 56.

123.

SACRED—TO THE MEMORY OF—JAMES CORNE POWNELL, ESQ.,—PROPRIETOR OF SILVER HILL PLANTATION—....—ONE OF THE ASSEMBLY—OF THE SUPREME COURT—OF JAMAICA, AND A MEMBER OF THE HONORABLE HOUSE OF ASSEMBLY. —HE DEPARTED THIS LIFE ON THE 4th DAY OF SEPTEMBER, 1823,—AGED 49 YEARS.

124.

MRS. RACHAEL LAWFORD,—DIED 10th MARCH, 1785, AGED 60 YEARS.

A large Mausoleum, containing the coffins (lead and cedar) of two adults and a child. *

THIS family was connected with the Caymanas. (The above is on the coffin-lid.)

125.

MISS MARY W. WILSON, OB. MAY 7th, 1806, AET. 7.

126.

MISS HENRY WILKINSON, OB. 13th SEP., 1807, AET. 30 Y., 8 M., 17 D.

127.

ELLEN MARIA, ELDT. DAUR. OF GEO. & ELLEN MATILDA FISHER, OB. OCT. 29, 1859, AET. 20 YRS., 4 MTHS.

128.

FANNY SUSANNA GROOM, OB. 2d NOV., 1845, AET. 1 Y., 17 D.

129.

MR. JOHN CROSS, OB. FEB. 10th, 1808, AET. 66.

130.

CHARLES POULTON HICKS, NAT. 16th APL., 1832, OB. 25th SEPT., 1850.

131.

GENERAL WILLIAM ANNE VILLETTES, OB. 13th JULY, 1808, AET. 54.

132.

AML. RICHD., SON OF THE REVD. S. JOHNSON, OB. 9th SEP., 1830, AET. 8 MTHS.

133.

LIEUT. HENRY BERESFORD, 2d BATTN. 60th RIFLES, DIED AT UPPARK CAMP, 16th NOVR., 1841, IN HIS 29th YEAR.

SEE "Peerage," *voce* Waterford.

---

* N.B. A circular pane of glass had been placed over the latter's face, so that it could be viewed after death.

134.

MAJOR-GENL. SAMUEL LAMBERT, OB. 4th JANY., 1848, AGED 62,—WHILE IN COMMAND OF H.M.'S FORCES.

135.

ANNA MARIA, WIFE OF JAMES WALLACE, OF KINGSTON, ESQR., OB. 5th JANY., 1854, AET. 31.—ALSO,—CHARLOTTE BROOKS, HER SISTER, OB. 25th SEP., 1833, AET. 21.

136.

JAMES BECKETT SHEPPERD, OB. 7th SEP., 1798, AET. 55. (ERECTED BY HIS WIDOW.)

137.

JOHN HOWLETT, ESQ., LATE MERCHANT OF KINGSTON, OB. 12th NOV., 1826, AET. 45.—ELIZA, HIS WIFE, OB. 6th JANY., 1826, AET. 39.

138.

PETER MC QUHAE, ESQR., COMMODORE OF THE 2d CLASS, & CAPTAIN OF H.M.S. "IMAUM," DIED OF YELLOW FEVER, AT PORT ROYAL, JUNE 9th, 1853.

139.

MAJOR HENRY BOONE HALE, & SARAH, HIS WIFE.

No date.

140.

JAMES RUTHERFORD, OB. 29th MAY, 1791, AET. 59.—JOHN RUTHERFORD, ESQ., HIS NEPHEW, OB. 5th APL., 1816, AET. 68.—JEANETTE, DAUR. OF JOHN R., OB. 6th OCT., 1819, AET. 19.

141.

ELEANOR, WIFE OF DAVID DUNCOMB MARCH, OB. 7th SEPTR., 1786, AET. 37.—ALSO, THEIR YOUNGEST SON, BENJAMIN DUNCOMB, OB. 1st OCT. FOLLOWING, AET. 11 MONTHS.

142.

CAROLINE BROUGHTON, WIFE OF THE REVD. G. B. BROOKS.

See *ante.*

143.

MRS. LUCIA ANDREWS, OB. JULY 13th, 1801, AET. 88.

144.

HERE LIETH MRS. FRANCIS WILLIS, OB. 4th DEC., 1804, AET. 72.

145.

ALICIA, ELDEST DAUR. OF WM. HACKETT, INSPR. GENL. OF HOSPLS.

146.

BATHIA, YOUNGEST DAUR. OF ALEXR. BARCLAY, RECEIVER-GENL., OB. 10th FEB. 1849, AET. 15 YRS.

147.

THOS. MORTON, ESQ.,—OB. 16th JULY, 1817.

148.

PRISCILLA, WIFE OF FRANCIS CLARK, OB. 29th DEC., 1816, AET. 53.—FRANCIS CLARK, MEM. OF ASSLY., OB. 31st JULY, 1830, AET. 65.

149.

WM. STAKER CARVER,—CLK. OF VESTRY,—OB. 3d SEP., 1846, AET. 51.

150.

BERNARD MAHON, SPECIAL MAGISTRATE OF VERE PARISH, &C. OB. DEC. 23d, 1845, IN HIS 36th YEAR.

151.

ANDREW LUNAN, ESQ., MAGISTRATE, OB. 14th APL., 1831, AET. 52.

152.

JOHN SATCHELL, ESQ., OB. 11th OCT., 1830, AET. 50.—ANN SATCHELL, HIS WIFE, OB. 24 JULY, 1845, AET. 52.

153.

JAMES FALCONER, ESQ., OB. 5th MARCH, 1828, AGED 69.

154.

JOHN ROSE, BORN 31st OCT., 1846, DIED 7th JULY, 1856.

155.

WILLM. MATTOCKS, ESQ., AET. 74, OB. 20th FEB., 1835.

156.

CAPTAIN DANIEL PRING, ROYAL NAVY,—OF IVEDON PENN, IN THE COUNTY OF DEVON, ENGLAND, WHO FELL A VICTIM TO THE CLIMATE, AT PORT ROYAL, WHILE FILLING THE POST OF COMMODORE OF THE JAMAICA STATION,—29th NOV., 1846, AGED 59 YEARS.

157.

MASTER CALEB LOUIS LITTLEJOHN, DIED 5th DEC., 1818, AGED FIVE YEARS.

158.

SELINA FANNY WETHERALL, WIFE OF FREDERICK AUGUSTUS WETHERAL, LT.-COL. I.W.I.R.,—BORN AT BANGALORE, 17 NOV., 1827,—MARRIED AT MONT-REAL, 29th AUGT., 1848, DIED AT PORT ROYAL, 26th APRIL, 1850.

159.

FREDERICK GEORGE NUTTALL CLARKE, ESQ., MAJOR 3d W.I. REGT., DIED AT (*sic*) JAMAICA, 21st OCT., 1861, AET. 31.—(ERECD. BY HIS WIDOW.)

160.

CECIL CHARLES, INFANT SON OF CHARLES HERRIES JONES, OF THE NAVAL YARD, PORT ROYAL, OB. 29th JUNE, 1855, AET. 10 MONTHS.

161.

CAPTAIN SAMUEL MORRISH, WHO DIED WHILST IN COMMAND OF H.M.S. "IMAUM," AT PORT ROYAL, 30th SEPTR., 1861, AGED 47.

162.

CHARLES LE POER, INFANT SON OF D. P. FRENCH, ESQ., OB. 12th OCT., 1861, AET. 1 Y., 4 M.

163.

CHRISTIAN ELLA, DAUGHTER OF ALEXR. & ANN CAMPBELL, OBIIT MAY 31st, 1860.

164.

CHA. MITCHELL JOPP, OB. SEP. 8th, 1861, AET. 56.

165.

MARY ANN FANNY AGNES JOPP, OB. 30th JULY, 1862, AET. 7 MTHS., 8 DAYS.

166.

GEO. JAS. MACQUEEN, ESQ., COLLR. OF TAXES, OB. 14th FEB., 1859, AET. 65.

167.

THE HONBLE. RICHD. CUSSEN BURKE, MEMBER OF THE PRIVY COUNCIL & LEGTE. COMMTEE., & CUSTOS ROT. OF METCALFE, OB. 8th AUG., 1860, AET. 58, & 39 YRS. A RESIDENT.

168.

ROBERT MUNROE HARRISON, FROM VIRGINIA, OF THE AMERICAN NAVY, CONSUL FOR THE U.S., OB. DECEMBER, 1857, AET. 70 YRS., 1 MONTH, & 10 DAYS.— MARGARET, HIS WIFE, OB. 17th DEC., 1857, AET. 70 Y., 1 M., 10 D.

169.

ELIZA JAMES, INF. DAUR. OF ROBT. & ELIZA TAYLOR, BORN 4 APRIL, 1843, —DIED 8th AUGT., 1846.

170.

CI GIT,—EDMOND BEGEL,—NE AUX CAYES—LE 3 NOVEMBRE, 1818,—DÉCÉDÉ À KINGSTON,—JAMAÏQUE, LE 14 NOV......, 1850,—AGÉ DE 32 ANS.

171.

CHARLOTTE OLIVIA, LAST SURVIVING DAUR. OF THE LATE CAPT. CHANDLER, 17th LANCERS, & MARGARET, HIS WIFE, BORN IN THE CITY OF GLOUCESTER, 3d AUGT., 1832—DIED AT PORT ROYAL—7th APRIL, 1860.

172.

LT. VINCENT WELLS, R.A., WHO DIED AT UP PARK CAMP, FROM THE EFFECTS OF AN ACCIDENT, MARCH 24th, 1862, AET. 22.

173.

HERE LYETH THE BODY OF—MUSGRAVE YEAMANS, ESQ.,—LATE OF THIS PARISH,—WHO DEPARTED THIS LIFE JULY THE 11th, 1728,—AGED 36 YEARS.— HERE ALSO LYETH THE BODY OF HIS MOTHER,—MARY ELLICOTT,—WHO DE-

PARTED THIS LIFE JUNE THE 10th, 1722.—ALSO, HER DAUGHTER,—MARY ELLI-
COTT, WHO DEPARTED THIS LIFE MAY THE 25th, 1708.—HERE ALSO LYETH THE
BODY OF MARY YEAMAN'S, DAUGHTER OF MUSGRAVE AND ANGELINA YEAMANS,
—WHO DEPARTED THIS LIFE JULY THE 12th, 1720,—AGED 4 YEARS & 4 MONTHS.
—HERE ALSO LYES THEIR SON, JOHN YEAMANS, WHO DEPARTED THIS LIFE
SEPTR. THE 4th, 1723, AGED 2 YEARS.—HERE ALSO LYETH THE BODY OF THEIR
DAUGHTER, ANGELINA YEAMANS,—WHO DEPARTED THIS LIFE JUNE THE 4th,
1723, AGED 5 YEARS.

YEAMANS of Bristol.   Created baronet 12 Jan., 1665 : extinct 19 Feb., 1788.   John,
the first baronet, wedded in Barbados.   By his second wife, Margaret, daughter
of the Revd. John Forster, he had a son, Robert, father of 1. Robert, = Sarah,
daughter of Jno. Trent, of Barbados ; 2. John,=Mary, daughter of (Judge) Alexr.
Walker, of Barbados ; 3. Philip,=Mary, daughter of Joseph Gibbs, of Barbados.

The author has not identified these two families as of common origin, but has no
doubt of the connection.

174.

JOHN EDWARDS, RECEIVER-GENERAL, ... HERE BY HIS MOURNING WIFE &
FAMILY.   HE DIED JANY. 18th, 1848, AGED 58.

Red Granite.

175.

ALEXANDER CAMPBELL, M.A., 45 YEARS RECTOR, DIED ON THE 8th DECR.,
1858, IN HIS 81st YEAR.

176.

CHARLES HAMILTON BATTEN, B.A., OF ST. JOHN'S COLL., CAMBRIDGE, OB. 14th
NOV., 1852, AET. 26.

177.

WILLIAM BEARD MOSS, WHO DIED ON HIS 24th BIRTHDAY, AT THE RESI-
DENCE OF HIS COUSIN, AUGUSTUS MILES, ESQ., MOUNT MOSES, ST. ANDREW'S
(PARISH),—BORN 15th DEC., 1839,—DIED 15th DECR., 1863.—4th SON OF WM.
MILES MOSS, & ESTHER, HIS WIFE, BOTH OF LIVERPOOL, ENGLAND.

178.

MR. THOMAS NIMMO, OB. 8th FEB., 1774.—(ERECTED BY HIS NEPHEW, ROBERT
STEWART.)

179.

TO THE MEMORY OF ROBERT NIMMO, OF EDINBURGH, WHO WAS BORN 22d
MARCH, 1741 . . . .

THE rest obliterated.

180.

HERE LIETH THE BODY OF ELIZABETH CHURCHILL, WIFE OF MAJOR-GENERAL
CHURCHILL, OB. 12th MARCH, 1820.

181.

HUGH MACHLACHLAN, OB. AUGT. 22ᵈ, 1826, AET. 37 YRS., 2 MTHS.

182.

DONALD CAMPBELL, ESQ., OB. 29ᵗʰ OCT., 1859, AET. 58.—
ALSO, HIS CHILDREN, SARAH FIELDING, & JOHN, AN IN-
FANT.

Arms, Campbell,* on the
mast of a galley. *Crest,* A boar's head.

183.

JAMES HARTLEY, OB. 14ᵗʰ MARCH, 1861, AET. 38.

184.

FRANCES DAVIES, OB. 7ᵗʰ JULY, 1810, AET. 43.—(LEAVING BEHIND HER
SEVERAL CHILDREN.)

185.

MR. EDWD. NEWLAND, OB. 19ᵗʰ NOV., 1850, AET. 29.

186.

JOHN DONALD, OB. 22ᵈ SEP., 1798, AET. 50.—ALSO, HIS SON, DONALD, OB.
30ᵗʰ SEP., 1798, AET. 9.

187.

MR. HENRY HARGREAVES, OB. 23ᵈ JANY., 1729, AGED 63 YRS.—ALSO,—ANN
HARGREAVES, DAUR. OF SAID HENRY, & ELIZABETH, OB. 27ᵗʰ OCT., 1717, AET. 8.
—ALSO,—MRS. ELIZABETH HYDE, WIFE OF EDMUND HYDE, ESQ., & RELICT OF
MR. H. HARGREAVES,—OB. 21ˢᵗ JUNE, 1735, AET. 55.

188.

WILLIAM TINKER, ESQ., AN EMINENT MEDICAL PRACTI-
TIONER, OB. FEB. ..., 1817, AET. 72.—ALSO,—MRS. SERENA
HESELTINE, OB. 3ᵈ DEC., 1822. JUST 18 YEARS A VIRGIN
TRUE,—AND 17 DAYS A WIFE,—SHE BADE HER WEEPING
FRIENDS ADIEU,—AND BREATHED HER LAST OF LIFE.—ALSO,
—ANDREW BARCLAY, OF KINGSTON, DRUGGIST, UNCLE OF
THE ABOVE,—OB. SEP. 22ᵈ, 1829, AET. 58.—SUSANNA BAR-
CLAY, OB. MAY 23ᵈ, 1857, AET. 86.

Arms, Argent ; two chevronels, gules. On dexter can-
ton, gules, a spur. *Crest,* A tower.

189.

WM. JNO. JAMES, ESQ., ATTY.-AT-LAW, OB. 16ᵗʰ NOV., 1821.

---

* Crescent, for difference.

190.

JOHN CAMPBELL, ESQ., OB. AT PORT HENDERSON, 3d SEP., 1820, AET. 57.—ALSO, JAMES JOHN CHARLOTTE BARNES, & MARY, HIS CHILn., OB. INF.—ALSO, —JOHN, HIS SON, OB. 4th APL., 1833, AET. 31.

191.

MARY JANE POPE, DAUR. OF JNO. CAMPBELL, ESQ., & WIFE OF EDWD. POPE, ARCHDEACON OF JAMAICA, OB. MAY 27, 1834.

192.

MARY DOROTHY, WIFE OF MAJOR OTTLEY, 2 W. I. REGT., & DAUR. OF THE REVD. CHARLES TOPPING, VICAR OF WEST BRADENHAM, IN THE COUNTY OF NORFOLK, WHO DIED, AFTER ONE DAY'S ILLNESS, 19th AUGUST, 1805, AGED 37. —ALSO,—OLIVIA CAMILLA DEVEREUX, NIECE OF MRS. OTTLEY, DIED 5th AUGT., 1803, AGED 17.

193.

THE HONBLE. DAVID SHERIFF, OB. 4th SEP., 1805, AET. 54.

194.

LIEUT. JAMES MC DOWALL, R.N., OB. 4th AUGT., 1827, AET. 34.

195.

DR. BENJAMIN SILVERA, OB. SEP. 3, 1813, AET. 23.

196.

ELINOR HENRY, DIED 30th MARCH, 1852, AET. 73.

197.

ELIZA FRANCES, WIFE OF MAJOR LONGDEN, H.M.'S 33d REGT., DIED AT UP PARK CAMP, 22d OCT., 1823, IN HER 32d YEAR.

198.

ADELEINE MARY, DAUR. OF MR. JAS. BROWN, OB. 18th MARCH, 1854, AET. 18 MTHS.

199.

ANN JANE, DAUR. OF WM. JOHNSTON, ESQ., OF THE 65th REGT., & STEP-DAUR. OF ALEXR. CHILD, ESQ., BARRACK MR.,—DIED AT UP PARK CAMP, 15th JUNE, 1835.

200.

SUSAN EMILY, DAUR. OF JOHN GEGG, CLERK,—BORN 6th DEC., 1844,—DIED 17th SEP., 1845.

201.

HENRY GRIFFIN, ELDEST SON OF JEREMIAH AND AGNES JANE LEAYCRAFT, NAT. 15th MARCH, 1851, & OB. 23d.

202.

WILLIAM MARTIN JOHNSTON, M.D., ELDEST SON OF DR. LEWIS JOHNSTON, OF SAVANNAH, GEORGIA,—DIED AT KINGSTON, 9th DEC., 1807,—BORN MAY 24th, 1754.—ALSO,—HIS 3 CHILDREN : JANE, DIED 1793.—JANE, DIED 1794.—ANDREW LIGHTENSTONE JOHNSTON, OB. DEC. 2d, 1806. — ALSO,—ELLA MACK GLASHEN ALYMON, DAUR. OF THE LATE WILLIAM BRUCE ALYMON, M.D., OF HALIFAX, NOVA SCOTIA,—OB. AT KINGSTON, FEB. 3d, 1843.

203.

CATHERINE BROWN, OB. NOV. 16th, 1850, AET. 23 YRS., 25 DAYS.

204.

EDWARD BAINBRIDGE THOMAS, ESQR., OB. 4th JUNE, 1849.

205.

WM. DANIEL, ELDEST SON OF FRANCES AMELIA & MARK MATTHEWS, ESQ., PAY-MR. I W. I. R., ACCIDENTALLY SHOT AT STONYHILL, SEP. 1st, 1845, AGED 5 YRS.

206.

EMILY M. CLEMENTS, OB. 20th JANY., 1852, AET. 39.

207.

HERE LYETH THE BODY OF SUSANNAH CASS, WIFE OF JOHN CASS, WHO DEPARTED THIS LIFE YE 12th DAY OF FEB., 1730,—AGED 23 YEARS, 10 MONTHS, AND 7 DAYS,—WHO DIED IN CHILDBED.

208.

ALICIA, DAUR. OF WILLIAM MACKAY, ... INSPECTOR-GENERAL OF HOS-PITALS, IN JAMAICA, ... JANUARY ..., 184...

On an Iron Plate.

OBLITERATED.

209.

BROOKS.

On an Iron Plate, on a railing, bearing simply the name.

210.

...... MRS. LUCIA ANDREWS, ... 13th JULY, 1805, AET. 88 ....

Slab.

211.

(*Ab.*) MRS. FRANCES WILLIS, OB. 4th DEC., 1804, AET. 72.

Slab.

212.

ANN ARCHER.

Marble.*

---

* The author afterwards saw the tombstone in an office in Kingston.

THIS was removed some years ago, but whether since restored to its place, the author is not aware.

The lady was the daughter of John Hodges, of Maxfield, by his first wife, Ann Blake, and married George Archer, M.D.

HUNT'S BAY, ST. ANDREW'S PARISH.

JEWS' BURIAL GROUND.

1.

IN MEMORY OF MR. JACOB HIZRIAHU DE LUZENA, MERCHANT, WHO DEPARTED THIS LIFE JANUARY ..., 1686.

2.

IN MEMORY OF DOCTOR JACOB RODRIGUES DE LEON, WHO DIED ON THE 5th OF JUNE, 1703, BEING THE SIXTIETH YEAR OF HIS AGE.

3.

IN MEMORY OF JACOB BRANDAO, WHO DIED ON THE 7th DAY OF JANUARY, 1711, AGED 46 YEARS.

4.

IN MEMORY OF MR. ISAAC NARBEUS, MERCHANT, WHO DEPARTED THIS LIFE ON THE 10th OF MARCH, 1686,—THAT IS THE FIFTH OF NISAN, 5447, FROM THE CREATION OF THE WORLD.

5.

IN MEMORY OF ESTER BARUCH ALVANS, THE WIFE OF MR. ABRAHAM ALVANS, WHO DEPARTED THIS LIFE 30th OF JANUARY, 1692.

N.B.—The Jewish burial ground is full of tombs, but with the above exceptions, the inscriptions are in the Hebrew characters.

CEMETERY—"NEWCASTLE"—OF ST. ANDREW'S PARISH.

1.

SACRED TO THE MEMORY OF MARY ANNE,—THE DEARLY BELOVED WIFE OF MAJOR & BT. LIEUT.-COLONEL—EDWARD RICHARD KING,—H.M. 36th REGIMENT,—WHO DEPARTED THIS LIFE,—SUDDENLY,—AT NEWCASTLE, JAMAICA,—ON THE 29th DAY OF AUGUST, 1856,—IN THE 47th YEAR OF HER AGE.—ALAS! MARY.

Altar Tomb. On the panel, "Alas! Mary." On the ledger, "Spes tutissima cœlis."

SHE was poisoned through the mistake of a druggist.

2.

SACRED TO—THE MEMORY OF—JOHN BLAND SAWYER,—LIEUT. H.M. 4th W.I. REGT.,—WHO DEPARTED THIS LIFE—29th OCTR.,—1863,—AGED 28 YEARS.—THY WILL BE DONE.

Altar Tomb, of Porphyry.

3.

SACRED TO THE MEMORY OF—WILLIAM RANDOLPH EPPES,—DEPUTY COMMISSARY GENERAL,—DIED—OF YELLOW FEVER,—AUGUST 11, 1849,—AGED 55 YEARS.—ALSO,—WILLIAM ISHAM EPPES,—ELDEST SON OF THE ABOVE,—DIED OF YELLOW FEVER,—AUGUST 13th, 1849,—AGED 15 YEARS & 4 MONTHS.

Marble Slab.

4.

SACRD—TO THE MEMORY—OF—LIEUTENANT & ADJUTANT—WILLIAM G. BINDON,—RES. BATT. 97th REGT,—DIED MAY 13th, 1849,—AGED 25 YEARS.—ERECTED BY HIS BROTHER OFFICERS, IN TOKEN—OF THEIR REGARD AND ESTEEM.

M. Altar Tomb.

5.

SACRED—TO THE MEMORY OF—WILLIAM BURNS,—LATE—SERGEANT IN THE 38th REGIMENT,—WHO—DEPARTED THIS LIFE—THE—4th JULY, 1847,—AGED 27 YEARS.—THIS STONE WAS ERECTED TO HIS—MEMORY BY THE SERJEANTS OF THE—38th REGIMENT,—AS—A TOKEN OF ESTEEM.

M. Slab.

6.

SACRED—TO THE—MEMORY—OF—SERGEANT GAVIN FINNIE,—NO. 8 COMPANY,—1st BATTN. 14th REGT.,—WHO DEPARTED THIS LIFE—ON THE 28th DAY OF AUGUST, 1860,—AGED 28 YEARS AND 4 MONTHS. (*Ab.* Four lines, &c.) THIS TABLET IS ERECTED,—AS A TOKEN OF RESPECT, BY THE SERGTS. OF THE REGIMENT—AND MEN OF HIS COMPANY.

M. Altar Tomb.

7.

ERECTED—TO THE MEMORY—OF—ARMOUR[ER]-SERGT. JNO. FRY, — AND — SERGT. PR. DAFFEY,—BY THE SERGTS. OF THE 1st BN. 14th REGT.,—1863.

M. Altar Tomb.

8.

(*Ab.*) IN MEMORY OF DOUGLAS, THE BELOVED SON OF REVD. H. MAC DOUGALL, M.A. "HE WAS TAKEN FROM THE EVIL TO COME" (IS. 57, 1) 6th SEPT., 1857.

On another face :

FRANCES HALE, DAUR. OF REVD. H. MAC DOUGALL, M.A., OB. 20th MAY, 1857.

On third face :

FRANCES HALE, THE BELOVED WIFE OF REVD. H. MAC DOUGALL, M.A., CHAP-
LAIN TO THE FORCES AT THIS STATION. THE LORD JESUS RECD. HER SPIRIT
ON THE 5th MARCH, 1858.

TEXTS and verses.

Wooden Tablets.   A triangular pyramidal Tomb.

9.

THIS MONUMENT—HAS BEEN ERECTED BY THE OFFICERS,—NON-COMMIS-
SIONED OFFICERS,—AND PRIVATES OF THE 36th REGIMENT,—TO THE MEMORY
OF THEIR COMRADES,—WHO DIED DURING—THE EPIDEMIC OF YELLOW FEVER
—-AT—NEWCASTLE & STONY HILL,—IN THE YEAR 1856.

On the opposite face :

36th REGIMENT.

FIRM.

LIEUT. TUCK.	SERGT.-MAJOR WILDBORE.
„ MAHON.	COLOR-SERGT. CATTON.
„ SCARLETT.	„ KIEMAN.
	„ LANE.
	„ MC GARRY.
SERGT. BENNETT.	DR. BOYLE.
„ BROUGH.	PRIVATE KELLY.
„ PRICE.	„ SPLANE.
CORPL. CREAM.	„ GREEN.
„ JACOB.	„ YOUNG.
„ ORAM.	

(Privates continued :)—DISLEY, QUINYAN, SAINT, TURNER, SAVAGE, WOOD, KEN-
NEDY, HOWARTH, PERCIVAL, KILDARE, BROWN, JAMES, TAYLOR, COLLYEAR,
GRIFFITHS, ANDERSON, ROSSEN, SMITH, MELONEY, WILD, WILKINS, MONK, HICKEY,
LEATHER, WINTER, CRIBBIN, CAFFREY, WRIGHT, HARDWICK, BOX, SHARPLEY,
HART, LITTLEWOOD, FIELDHOUSE, HANNON, MARRIOTT, GORDON, SOLLIS, BEARD,
TUER, PRICE, HOGAN, BUTLER, TAYLOR, NEEDHAM, HEARSEY, WARREN, CONNOR,
JONES, ROSTRON, ECKWORTH—MRS. BELL, MRS. MAHONEY—CHILDREN :—BROCK,
BRADISH, HINES—STAFF ASST. SURGN. GORDON, LT. LEGALLAIS, R.E., ENSN. GUN.
REQUIESCANT IN PACE.

10.

MARY MAUDE HARVEY, CHILD OF J. E. HARVEY, ESQ., CAPT. 41 REGT.,
& OCTAVIA, HIS WIFE, OB. 20 MARCH, 1860, AET. 11 MTHS.

Stone Pyramid and Marble Slab.

11.

WILLIAM GORDON, M.D.,—DIED 7th DECEMBER, 1856,—AGED 22 YEARS.

M. Tablet.

12.

Porphyry Altar Tomb.

No inscription.

13.

IN MEMORY—OF—HARRIET—M. WILLIAMS,—DAUGHTER OF—H. WILLIAMS, ESQ., OF—THE WAR DEPT.,—WHO DIED—ON—CHRISTMAS DAY,—1857,—AGED 3 YEARS.

Obelisk Porphyry.

14.

SACRED—TO THE MEMORY—OF—JOHN EDWARD HALL,—LATE—CAPTAIN H.M. 48th REGT.,—DIED MAY 19th, 1844, AGED 30 YEARS.—ERECTED,—AS A TOKEN OF REGARD,—TO HIS MEMORY,—BY HIS BROTHER OFFICERS.

Marble.

15.

SACRED TO THE MEMORY OF—W. FRD. F. SHIRLEY,—DIED 2d JULY, 1862,— AGED 3 YEARS & 1 MONTH.—"SUFFER LITTLE CHILDREN & FORBID THEM NOT TO COME UNTO ME."

Marble Altar Tomb.

16.

MATTHEW IFIELD . . . .

Wooden Tablets.

DATES, &c., obliterated.

17.

CHARLES HEN. DENT, SON OF QUARR.-MR.-SERGT. R. DENT, DIED 4th MAY, 1552, AGED 18 MONTHS.

18.

T. JENNING, LATE PRIVT. SOLDIER, IN H.M. 97th REGT., DIED 22 AUGT., 1848, AGED 27. (Verses follow.) ERECTED BY LIEUT. VICARS,* THE OFFICER OF HIS COMPANY, AS A TOKEN OF RESPECT.

19.

MS. HEALE, 97th REGT., DIED 2d OCT., 1849, AGED 29 YEARS.

20.

EDWD. TURNER, 97th REGT., DIED 6th MAY, 1848, AGED 26 YEARS.

21.

CORPORAL JAMES BELTS,—MASTER SHOEMAKER, 2nd BATTN. 60th RIFLES.

DATES gone.

22.

CAROLINE DAUR. OF SERGT. ON. BARRY, 1 BN. 14th RT., DIED 6th DEC., 1861, AGED 4 MTHS.

---

* Who afterwards died in the Crimea, and whose biography is well known.

23.

ANDW. WILLM., INFANT SON OF JOHN KIERNAN, & AGNES MARY DELANEY, DIED 1 MAY, 1851, AGED 2 YRS., 2 MTHS., 20 DAYS.

24.

EDWD. FITZ-SIMONS, 97th REGT., DIED, 2d SEP., 1850, AGED 26 YEARS.—ALSO, PATK. DEVANEY, DIED AT U. P. CAMP, 24th NOV., 1850, AGED 27 YEARS.

25.

WM. MOSS, GN. COMPY., 36th REGT., DIED 16th AUGT., 1855, AGED 28 YEARS —ALSO, T. BRYANT, 25th JULY, 1855, AGED 23 YEARS.

26.

W. WARBOYS, PTE., GR. COMPY., 36th REGT., DIED, 16th NOV., 1855, AGED 22 YRS. —ALSO, W. GREEN, 2d JULY, 1856, AGED 28 YRS.

27.

SIMON SEXTON, PTE., 16th REGT., DIED OF CHOLERA, 10th AUGT., 1851, AGED 24 YEARS. (ERECTED BY N.-C.-O. & MEN OF THE COMPANY.)

Wooden.

28.

THOS. QUILTY, I BN. 14th REG., DIED, 2d FEB., 1862, AGED $28\frac{7}{12}$.

29.

CHAS. CHAPMAN, 16th REGT., DIED, 31st AUGT., 1857, AGED 28 YEARS.

30.

CHAS. LENNON, LT. COMPY., 16th REGT., DIED OF CHOLERA, 13th AUGT., 1861, AGED . . . .

31.

MICHL. KEARNEY, 48th REGT., DIED, 14th DEC., 1845, AGED 24 YEARS.

32.

THOS. NORREY, PTE., 14th REGT., DIED 18th OCT., 1860, AGED 23 YRS., 6 MTHS.

33.

WILLM. SMITH, CORPL., 48th REGT., DIED ... SEPR., 1846, AGED 32 YEARS.

34.

JAS. ELLIOTT, PTE., 48th REGT.

No date remains.

35.

JOHN, SON OF JNO. & AGNES BROWN, I BN., 14th REGT., DIED, 31st MARCH, 1861, AGED 15 MONTHS.

36.

GEO. WILSON, PRIVATE, LATE MUSICIAN, 48th REGT., DIED 22d JULY, 1845, AGED 25 YEARS.

HIS EARLY DEATH WAS MUCH REGRETTED BY HIS COMRADES.

37.

JOSEPH, SON OF DORA & JOHN MC DONALD, 14th REGT., DIED, 17th SEP., 1861, AGED 1 YEAR & 10 DAYS.

38.

SARAH JANE, DAUR. OF SERGT GEO. BAKER, 41st REGT., DIED AUGT. 20, 1857, AGED 7 M.

39.

ANNE JANE, WIFE OF ROBT. MOORE, COMMT. STOREKEEPER, DIED, 8th DEC., 1847, AGED 29 YEARS.

40.

MARGARET, WIFE OF SCHOOLMASTER SERGT. JNO. CULLEN, RES. BATTN., 97th REGT., DIED, 17th OCT., 1848, AGED 40 YRS. & 7 M.—ALSO,—CHARLOTTE, HIS DAUR., DIED, 14th OCT., 1848, AGED 10 YRS. & 8 MTHS.—ALSO,—ROBERT, THEIR SON, DIED, 8th OCT., 1848, AGED 8 YRS. & 2 MTHS.—ALSO,—JOHN, THEIR SON, DIED, 23d OCT., 1848, AGED 2 YRS. & 6 MTHS.

Verses and texts follow.

41.

JAS. IDDENDEN, PTE., 48th REGT., DIED, 29th JUNE, 1844, AGED 29 YEARS.

42.

JNO. WHITE, PTE., LT. COMPY., 48th REGT. DIED, 5th NOVR., 1841.

43.

MICHL. ELLIS, PTE., 48th REGT., DIED, 25th SEP., 1844, AGED 21 YEARS.

44.

W. BERRY, CORPL., 16th REGT., DIED, 24th NOV., 1853, AGED 23 YEARS.

45.

HENRY, SON OF JOHN & MARY HARNEY, 48th REGT., DIED, 18th DECR., 1844, AGED $3\frac{9}{12}$ YEARS.

46.

EDWD. VINCT. BRADISH, DIED, DEC. 8d 1856, AGED 4 YRS. & $\frac{8}{12}$ M.

47.

RICHD. WILSON, DIED AT U. P. CAMP, OCT. 6th, 1850, AGED 24 YRS.—ALSO, JAMES JACKSON, DIED AT U. P. C., 24th NOV., 1850, AGED 30 YEARS. BOTH PRIVATES OF THE 97th REGT.

48.

J. DONOVAN, PTE., 97th REGT., DIED, 30th JULY, 1848, AGED 26 YEARS. Verses.

49.

PAK. DALEY, PRIVATE, 1st BN., 14th REGT., DIED, 17th JULY, 1860, AGED 26 YEARS.

Wooden.

50.

MARY ANNE, DAUR. OF MICHAEL & ANN DOYLE, DIED, 5th JANY., 1861, AGED I YR., $\frac{2}{12}$.

51.

GEORGE, SON OF SERGT. GEO. & ELIZABETH SHADBOLT, 14th REGT., DIED, 17th SEP., 1860, AGED 2$\frac{5}{12}$ YRS.

52.

CORNELIUS GILLASPIE, PRIVATE, 48th REGT. . . . .

53.

JOHN WHITE, PRIVATE, 48th REGT.

54.

MICHAEL ELLIS, PTE., 48th REGT., DIED, 23d SEP., 1844, AGED 21 YEARS.

55.

GEO. DARBY, DIED, 16th JANY., 1843, AGED 17 YRS. ERECTED BY HIS MASTER, MAJOR CROMBIE, 60th RIFLES.

56.

G. WHITING, PTE., 1st BN., 14th REGT., DIED, 30th OCT., 1860, AGED 24 YEARS.

57.

MARGARET, WIFE OF THOS. LONICAN, PTE., 97th REGT., DIED, 13th APL., 1848, AGED 31 YEARS.

58.

J. GREGORY, PTE., 1st BN., 14th REGT., DIED, 8th JULY, 1860, AGED 34 YEARS.

59.

DRUMMER MC CARBERRY, 41st WELCH REGT. DIED, 1st AUGT., 1857, AGED 22 YEARS.

Stone.

60.

THOS. NORREY, PTE., 14th REGT., DIED, 18th OCT., 1860, AGED 23 & $\frac{6}{12}$ YEARS.

61.

ELIZA MARY CAMPBELL, OF THE ROYAL ARTILLERY, DIED 30th APL., 1844, AGED 3$\frac{6}{12}$ YEARS.

62.

CORPORAL W. BERRY, 16th REGT., DIED, 24th NOV., 1853.

63.

LCE.-SERGT. JOB. BEAUCHAMP, 16th REGT., DIED, 29th OCT., 1853, AGED 30 YEARS.

64.

THOS. WRAITH, PTE., 2d BN., 60th RIFLE CORPS, DIED, 30th MAY, 1842, AGED 42 YEARS.

65.

CORPORAL EDWARD WALSH, 2d BN., 60th RIFLES, DIED, 17th AUGT., 1842, AGED 36$\frac{3}{12}$ YRS.

66.

BARRACK-SERGT. THOS. VALE, LATE SERGT. 32d REGT., DIED, 26th JANY., 1844, AGED 47 YEARS.

67.

SAML. SMITH, PTE., 48th REGT............

68.

JAMES DELF, BARRK.-SERGT., DIED, 6th JULY, 1853, AGED 36 YEARS.

69.

ROBERT DIBBLE, 8 CO., 6 BY., R.A., DIED, 3 JULY, 1850, AGED 24 YEARS.

70.

JAS. FRANCOM, PTE., 97th REGT., DIED, 10th MAY, 1848, AGED 33 YEARS.

71.

SAML. CASTLEDINE, PTE., 38th REGT., DIED, 30th MARCH, 1847, AGED 27 YEARS.

72.

ELIZABETH, DAUR. OF JOHN WOOD, 9th BN., R.A., DIED 3d AUGT., 1845.

73.

JOHN TORPY, PTE., 48th REGT., DIED, 20th FEB., 1846, AGED 24$\frac{7}{12}$ YEARS.

74.

ALEXR. PENTLAND, GUNNER, R.A., DIED, 30th JULY, 1846, AGED 24 YEARS.

75.

JAS. EDGE, PTE., 97th REGT., DIED, 7th NOV., 1848, AGED 31. ERECTED BY HIS COMRADE, SAML. CANDLING.

"MAN, LIKE A SHADOW, VAINLY WALKS,—WITH FRUITLESS CARES OPPRESS'D,
    HE HEAPS UP WEALTH, BUT CANNOT TELL—BY WHOM 'TWILL BE POSSESS'D."

76.

JAS. HOLDEN, BOMBR., 1 CO., 6 BY., R.A., DIED, 6th JULY, 1844, AGED 25 YEARS.

77.

MARY ANN, DAUR. OF WM. & MARY ANN WATTS, R.A., DIED, 31st MAY, 1848, AGED 13 YRS., 7 D.

78.

HOSPITAL-SERGT. WM. PRICE, 36th REGT., DIED, 15th OCT., ..., AGED ...—ALSO,—COMPY.-SERGT.-MAJOR A. JORDAN, W. I. REGT., LATE 36th REGT., DIED AT UP PARK CAMP......

DATES obliterated.

Wooden.

79.

WILLIAM, SON OF T. & JANE IRWIN, 97th REGT., DIED 2^d JUNE, 1850, AGED 1 $\frac{2}{12}$ YEAR.

80.

I. INGHAM, PTE., 97th REGT., DIED 11th MAY, 1850, AGED 28 YEARS.

81.

MICHAEL MULLINS, PTE., 48th REGT., DIED SEP. 20th, 1846, AGED 35 YRS. ERECTED BY JAS. KENNEDY.

82.

ANDW. MC QUADE, PTE., 97th REGT., DIED 14th DEC., 1850, AGED 27 YRS.— ALSO,—MICHL. MC LOUGLIN, PTE., 97th REGT., DIED 7th OCT., 1850, AGED 32 YRS., AT U. P. CAMP.

THIS TABLET WAS ERECTED BY LIEUT. VICARS, THE OFFICER OF THEIR COMPANY, AS A TOKEN......

SEE previous note.

83.

JOHN REGAN, LATE BASS DRUMMER, H.M.'S 97th, DIED 20th NOV., 1850, AGED 29 YRS.

84.

RACHEL, WIFE OF PTE. HUGH POLAN, 48th REGT., DIED 30th DEC., 1846, AGED 27 YEARS.

85.

DANIEL MAGHEE, LATE 60th RIFLES.

DATE effaced.

86.

KATHERINE, WIFE OF ROBT. CAPS, 2nd BN., 60th RIFLES......

87.

ARTHUR SHIELDS, PTE., 97 REGT., DIED 22^d JUNE, 1848, AGED 30 YEARS.

88.

MARY, WIFE OF R. COE, PTE. 97th REGT., DIED 16th JANY. 1849, AGED 31 YEARS.

89.

....COX, 10 COMPY, 97th REGT., DIED 11th DEC. 1848, AGED 25 YEARS,—ALSO,— PTE. S. CLARKE, DIED 26th NOV., 1848, AGED 28 YRS. (AT PORT ROYAL, — ALSO,— PTE. J. BALLIN, DIED 25th JUNE, 1849, AGED 30 YEARS.

90.

JAS. HOYLE, PTE. 97th REGT., DIED NOV. 9th, 1848, AGED 29 YRS.

91.

BARTHW. CONNORS, PTE. 97th REGT., DIED SEPT. 25th, 1848———

92.

J. MC DONALD, PTE. 97th REGT., DIED 28th JANY., 1851, AGED 27 YRS.,—ALSO,—
R. FITZ PATRICK, DIED 12th JANY, 1851, AGED 29 YEARS.

93.

SACRED TO THE MEMORY OF THE UNDERMENTIONED MEN OF THE BAND,
36th REGT., WHO DIED DURING THE EPIDEMIC OF YELLOW FEVER, IN THE
MONTHS OF NOVEMBER & DECEMBER, 1856.

M. O'CONNOR.......... 🎵 AGED 27

M. HOGAN .... 🎵 AGED 28

E. JONES .... 🎵 AGED 28

D. TUER.............. 🎵 AGED 19

J. WARREN............ 🎵 AGED 21

GLORIA PATRI

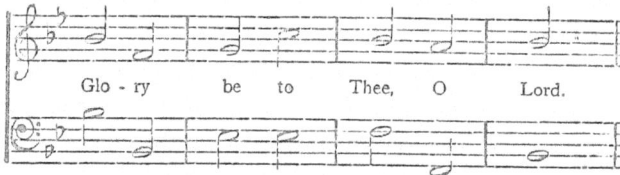

Glo - ry   be to Thee, O Lord.

THIS is probably a rare instance of musical notation appearing on a tomb.

94.

FRAS. NELSON ......

No dates remaining.

95.

C. HOGAN, I B. 14th REGT., DIED 8th MAY, 1860, AGED 22 YRS. 6 MTHS.,—ALSO,
J. MORIARTY, CORPORAL, DIED 26th AUGT, 1860, AGED 22 YRS. 6 MTHS.
VERSES.

ERECTED BY N. C. OFFRS. AND MEN OF COMPY.

96.

ANN SCARROTT, WIFE OF SERGT. THOS. SCARROTT, 16th REGT., DIED 11th AUGT.
1851, IN HER 29th YEAR.

97.

LCE. CORPL. DUNDON, I B. 14th REGT., DIED 27th JUNE, 1861, AGED 27
YEARS.

98.

GEO. RAMSDEN, PTE. 16th REGT., DIED 17th AUGT, 1851, AGED 30 YRS. & 4
MTHS.

99.

JOHN COLLOPY, 16th REGT., DIED OF CHOLERA, 10th AUGT., 1851, AGED 24
YEARS.

100.

JAS. ARMSTRONG, PTE. 48th REGT., DIED 23d MAY, 1846, AGED 26 1/8 YEARS.

101.

MICHL. MC KEARNEY, PTE. 48th REGT., 14th DEC., 1845, AGED 24 YEARS.

102.

JAS. ROGERS, PTE. 48th REGT., ...

103.

SERGT. JOS. BENNETT, 36th REGT., DIED 13th OCT., 185.. AGED 36 YRS.
ERECTED BY HIS WIFE, MARY ANN.

104.

WM. BURFORD, PTE. 97th REGT., 23d NOV., 1849, AGED 29 YEARS.

OLD BURIAL GROUND, TWO MILES BEYOND HALFWAY TREE—
ST. ANDREW'S PARISH.

1.

HERE LYETH THE BODY OF DAVID BECK, WHO WAS BORN, THE . . . . XI FEB-
RUARY, ANNO DOM . . . . MD. DYED YE X DAY OF JUNE, ANNO DOM. 1712.

2.

HERE LYETH . . . . BODY . . . . MARY MARTIN, WIFE OF
THOS. MARTIN, COOPER, WHO DIED . . . . 10th OF FEBRUARY,
1710, IN THE THIRTY-SECOND YEAR OF HER AGE.

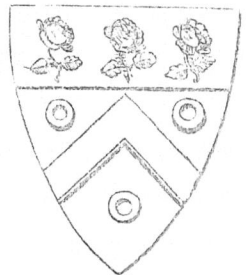

Arms, A chev. between 3
annulets: on a chief, 3 roses slipped and leafed, ppr. *Crest,* a demi eagle displayed, with a rose, leafed and
slipped, in its beak.

3.

HERE LYETH THE BODY OF MAJOR GUY, ESQ., WHO
DEPARTED THIS LIFE, YE 6th DAY OF DECEMBER, 1736;
AGED 56 YEARS AND 4 MONTHS.

THIS was Major Samuel Guy, son of Nathaniel Guy, by his
wife, Dorothy Wood. He was bapt. 16 Nov. 1681, and
married 6 Dec. 1704, Priscilla Long.

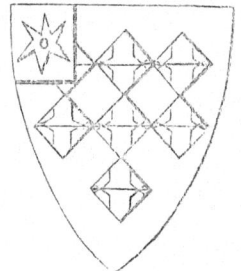

Arms nearly effaced.

4.

HERE LIETH INTERRED THE BODY OF MR. GEORGE BENNETT, WHO CAME HERE A SOLDIER UNDER GENERAL VENABLES, THE 10th DAY OF MAY, ANNO DOMINI 1655, AND ONE OF THE FIRST SETTLERS.   HE WAS OF A DORSETSHIRE FAMILY.

HERE ALSO LIETH INTERRED THE BODY OF MRS. SARAH BENNETT, LATE WIFE OF HIS GRANDSON, THE HONBLE. GEORGE BENNETT, ESQR., WHO DEPARTED THIS LIFE THE 8th DAY OF OCTOBER, ANNO DOMINI 1733, AGED 58 YEARS, AND MARRIED 39 YEARS AND 2 MONTHS.   SHE WAS A WISE GOOD WIFE, AND ALL THAT KNEW HER WILL SAY THE SAME, AND THE ONLY DAUGHTER OF MR. JOHN ROSEWELL, A SOMERSETSHIRE FAMILY.

ALSO THE BODIES OF SEVEN CHILDREN, (vizt.) ANN AND MARY ROSEWELL, WILLIAM, JOHN, ANN, ELIZABETH, AND REBECCA BENNETT.

SEE previous note.

5.

HERE LYETH INTERR'D THE BODY OF—JUNIA YOUNG, WHO DYED THE 20th APRIL, 1753—AGED 42 YEARS.

6.

(ANOTHER monument, with inscription effaced, except "CARTWRIGHT FECIT.")

7.

IN MEMORY OF

JACOB WADE		1759, AGED 70 YEARS.
JOHN FITZGERALD	DIED	APRIL 16, 1782, AGED 66 YEARS.
MARY CHRISTIAN		APRIL, 1784, AGED 70 YEARS.

8.

HERE LIETH THE BODY OF—MISS ELIZABETH DISTON, WHO DEPARTED THIS LIFE—THE 22d OF AUGT. 1796, AGED 69 YEARS.

9.

SAMUEL MURPHY, ESQ., OB. 21 OCT., 1863, AET. 76.

MARY ANNE, WIFE OF SAMUEL MURPHY, ESQ., OB. 17 SEP. 1863, AET. 76.

10.

HERE LIE THE REMAINS OF—THOMAS MURPHY, ESQUIRE, FORMERLY OF THE RAMBLE AND DECOY ESTATES—IN THE PARISH OF ST. MARY.   HE WAS BORN ON THE 24th DAY OF JUNE, 1741,—AND DEPARTED THIS LIFE—ON THE 2d DAY OF NOVR., 1826,—IN THE 83d YEAR OF HIS AGE.—HE WAS FOR MANY YEARS—CUSTOS ROTULORUM OF THIS PARISH—AND FORTY-FOUR YEARS—ONE OF ITS REPRESENTATIVES TO THE—HONORABLE HOUSE OF ASSEMBLY.

SEE *Lawrence* Pedigree.

11.

HERE LYETH INTERR'D THE BODY OF MRS.—ANNE SLEIGH, WIFE TO MR. SAMUELL SLEIGH,—WHO DEPARTED THIS LIFE, THE X DAY OF MAY—ANNO DOMINI MDCLXXXVII, AND—THE XLIX YEARE OF HER AGE.

Arms, A chev....between 3 owls, close ...... *Crest,* Over an esquire's helmet, a horse salient.

12.

HERE LYES INTERR'D THE BODY OF—WILLIAM WILLIAMS, ESQ., WHO—DEPARTED THIS LIFE, THE FIRST DAY OF JULY —ANNO 1733, AGED SIXTY FIVE YEARS—AND SIX MONTHS.

3 moors' heads, couped, 5 ermine spots.   *Crest,* On a wreath over an Esquire's helmet, a deer's head caboshed. *Arms,* On a chevron, between

13.

HERE LYETH THE BODY OF—HENRY DAKINS, SENIOR, ESQ.—WHO DEPARTED THIS LIFE—THE FIRST DAY OF AUGUST, 1683—AGED 43 YEARS—AND LEFT BY HIS WIFE ELIZABETH, FIVE SONS—VIZ., HENRY, CHARLES, JOHN, PHILIP —AND RICHARD.

HERE ALSO LYETH THE BODY OF—HENRY DAKINS, JUNIOR,—WHO DEPARTED THIS LIFE—THE 29th DAY OF AUGUST, 1737—AGED FIVE YEARS AND TEN MONTHS—THE SON OF DOCTOR RICHARD DAKINS—AND GRANDSON OF THE ABOVE—HENRY DAKINS, ESQ.

Arms, ... between 2 flanches, each charged with a lion rampant. ... a lion statant, between a mullet in chief, and one in base.   *Crest,* Over an Esquire's helmet, on a wreath, an arm embowed, grasping in the hand a battleaxe-spike turned to dexter.

14.

TO THE IMMORTAL MEMORY OF THE—DECEASED:—UNDER THIS STONE DOTH LIE TRUTH......

THE rest covered.

15.

HERE LYETH THE BODY OF—WILLIAM COLBERT—WHO DEPARTED THIS LIFE, MARCH 2d—1760, AGED 51 YEARS.

16.

ERECTED TO—HIS MEMORY BY—ELIZABETH MARKS, THE...... —JAMES....
......LIFE ON THE—.... OF JULY, 18.... AGED 32 YEARS......—THIS ......

Fragment.

17.

HERE LIE THE REMAINS—OF—DOROTHY SHEA, SPINSTER, — ELDEST DAUGH-
TER OF RICHARD SHEA, ESQUIRE,—AND—DOROTHY, HIS WIFE—BOTH DECEASED—
AND FORMERLY OF THIS ISLAND—BORN, 30th SEPT., 1786—DIED, 7th JULY, 1826.

18.

IN MEMORY OF—WILLIAM STEVENSON, ESQ.—BORN THE 12th AUGUST, 1720—
OB. 14th APRIL, 1790, AGED 69—YEARS 8 MONTHS & 2 DAYS.

SEE Lawrence pedigree.

19.

HERE LIE THE REMAINS—OF—THOMAS MURPHY, ESQ.,—BARRISTER AT LAW—
SON OF—THOMAS & ELIZABETH MURPHY—OF THE PARISH OF ST. MARY—IN THIS
ISLAND—BORN THE 22d OF OCTOBER, 1781—AND DEPARTED THIS LIFE—THE 30th
OF DECEMBER, 1805,—AGED 24 YEARS.

20.

(*Ab.*) THIS STONE—AT THE REQUEST OF A—GREATLY AFFLICTED MOTHER
—IS PLACED OVER THE REMAINS OF—HER BELOVED SON—JOHN BARNETT SHAW
—BY A FRIEND—.......... HE WAS THE ELDEST MALE ISSUE OF—JOHN SHAW,
OF SHAW PARK, ESQUIRE—AND ELIZABETH HIS WIFE—BUT WAS SEVERED FROM
—HIS DISCONSOLATE PARENTS BY THAT — BANEFUL DISEASE — THE YELLOW
FEVER, ON THE 5th DAY OF JULY, 1810—IN THE 18th YEAR OF HIS AGE.

SHAW PARK is romantically situated near Ochorios, in the parish of St. Ann's.

21.

(*Ab.*) HERE LYETH THE BODY OF MRS. ELIZABETH DRURY, MOTHER OF
COLONEL HENRY DAKINS, OB. MARCH 31, 1733, AET. 76. — ALSO, — CHARLES
DAKINS, SON OF ELIZABETH DRURY, OB. JUNE 12, 1711, AET. 34. — ALSO, — JOHN
DAKINS, SON OF ELIZABETH DRURY, OB. 21 JUNE, 1725, AET. 16 & 4 D. — ALSO, —
DR. RICHARD DAKINS, SON OF ELIZABETH DRURY, OB. 1 NOV. 1732, AET. 48 &
10 M.

22.

(*Ab.*) ELIZABETH, WIFE OF JAS. PINNOCK, ESQ., OB. 8 NOV. 1722, AET. 18.—ALSO,
—DAKINS PINNOCK, SON OF HONBLE. PHILIP PINNOCK, BY GRACE HIS WIFE, AND
GRANDMOTHER OF THE SAID ELIZABETH PINNOCK, BORN 3 OCT. 1753, DIED NOV.
1756.—ALSO,—ELIZABETH WYNDHAM DALLING........ DIED 1st MARCH, 1768, ON
HER VOYAGE FROM ENGLAND. — ELIZABETH DALLING, HER MOTHER, WIFE OF

COLL. JOHN DALLING, & DAUR. OF SAID PHILIP AND GRACE PINNOCK, WHO DIED 6 JULY......IN THE 22 YEAR OF HER AGE. — ALSO, THE SAID GRACE PINNOCK, OB. 11 AUGT., 1771, AET. 42. HER ...... NAME WAS DAKINS, &—SHE WAS— NIECE AND HEIRESS OF THE LATE COLL. HELLIRY.

SEE previous note.

Arms, Azure, a fess chequy, betweeen 3 greyhounds courant.

23.

HERE RESTETH THE BODY OF—MISS DOROTHY DOUCE, —WHO DEPARTED THIS LIFE THE 1st DAY OF—AUGUST, 1736, IN THE 15 YEAR—OF HER AGE.

24.

ANN GRAHAM GRAY, DAU. OF WILLIAM AND DOROTHY GRAY, OB. 30th JUNE, 1764, AET. 20.—ALSO,—ELIZABETH CAROLINE GRAY, DAUR. OF WM. & DOROTHY, OB. 13 APL. 1766, AET. 17 Y. 5 M. 23 D.

25.

E........EDWARD, THE SOVEN (*sic*) OF WILLIAM & ANNE BEESTON, WHO....
........AUGUST............1676........................
Fragment.

NEW BURIAL GROUND, UP PARK CAMP,—ST. ANDREW'S PARISH.

1.

.... THIS TOKEN OF RESPECT WAS PLACED OVER HIS REMAINS BY HIS CAPTAIN, WHO BEST KNEW HIS WORTH.
Wood.

2.

ARCHIBALD RANDOLPH, ESQ., LIEUT. ROYAL ENGINEERS, OB. 14 MAY, 1841, AET. 21.
Marble Tablet.

3.

GEORGE MARSHALL, K.H., LATE LT.-COLL. COMG. H. M.'S 82d REGT. OF FOOT, WHO, AFTER 42 YEARS' MERETORIOUS SERVICE, DIED OF FEVER, 2d JUNE, 1841, AT U. P. C., AGED 58.

4.

JAMES PRESTON, ESQ., OF EMSWORTH, IN THE COUNTY OF HAMPSHIRE, LATE OF H. M.'S 10th ROYAL HUSSARS, IN WHICH HE SERVED 22 YRS., AND THEN WAS APPTD. BARRACK MASTER AT U. P. C., JAMAICA, WHERE HE DIED OF FEVER, APRIL 9th, 1842, AET. 50, LEAVING A WIDOW TO DEPLORE HIS LOSS.

5.

LT. JOHN MARYON WILSON, 3 W. I. R., OB. AUG. 12, 1853, AET. 26.

6.

WM. D'ESTERRE TAYLOR, 3 W. I. R., & OF KINSALE, IRELAND, DIED OF YELLOW FEVER, AT U. P. C. 4 SEPT., 1856, AET. 30.

7.

MATTHEW RECHLEY BURKE, ASST.-SUR., OB. 6 AUGT., 1837, AET. 24.

8.

WM. HOGG ANDERSON, M.D., ASST.-SURGEON 8th FOOT, OB. 26 JUNE, 1837, AET. 26.

9.

JAS. HUNTER CARDIERE, M.D., SUR. 8 FOOT, OB. 5 DEC. 1836, AET. 49.

10.

HENRY PALMER HILL, PAYMR. 8th FOOT, OB. 26 MAY, 1836, AET. 45.

11.

WILLM. ST. LEGER, ENS. 8th FOOT, OB. DECR., 1836, AGED 21 YRS. & 9 MONTHS.

12.

SELINA HINGSTON, & LOUISA HER INFANT, AGED 3 MONTHS.

13.

ELIZ. CHANCELLOR WILSON.

14.

CAROLINE, WIFE OF CAPT. CARY, BARRACK MASTER, OB. 11 DEC. 1843, AET. 27.

15.

JOHN ALEXR. BUTCHER, 3 W. I. R., OB. 19 DEC. 1850, AET. 26.

16.

JAS. THOMPSON, INFANT SON OF MAJOR ALLEN, 2 W. I. R., OB. APRIL, 1842, AET. 1 YR.

17.

WM. BOND LEWIS, ENSN. 56 REGT., OB. 25 SEP. 1837, AET. 18.

DISUSED GRAVE YARD AT UP PARK CAMP.

1.

LIEUT. EVERETT, ADJUTANT OF THE 33d REGT., DIED AT U. P. C., 8th JANY. 1829, IN THE 29th YEAR OF HIS AGE. ERECTED BY HIS BROTHER OFFICERS.

2.

THOMAS JOSEPH FURLONG, ORDNANCE DEPARTT., DIED 19th APRIL, 1829, AGED 27.

3.

LT.-COLL.—P. C. TAYLOR, 22d REGT.—DIED AT KINGSTON—7 DECEMBER, 1827, AGED 37.

4.

SACRED TO THE MEMORY OF CAPTAIN ANDREW DONALDSON—THE 93d REGIMENT—DIED IN CAMP ON THE 16th JULY, 1825, IN THE 34th YEAR OF HIS AGE—BELOVED AND RESPECTED.—ERECTED BY HIS WIDOW.

5.

WM. HENRY VINICOMBE, PAYMASTER OF THE 50th REGT., DIED 27th DEC. 1824, AGED 30.

6.

W. J. BOWEN, CAPT. 77th REGT., DIED 3d APL., 1825, AGED 27 YEARS.

7.

SACRED TO THE MEMORY OF ENSIGN THOMAS EDWARDS, LATE OF HIS MAJESTY'S 50th REGIMENT, WHO, AT THE EARLY AGE OF NINETEEN YEARS, FELL A VICTIM TO THE FEVER WHICH PROVED SO FATAL TO THE TROOPS, IN THE YEAR 1819.—THIS STONE IS ERECTED BY HIS FATHER, LIEUT.-COLL. EDWARDS, OF THE 17th FOOT, TO MARK HIS AFFECTION FOR ONE WHO, AS LONG AS SENSE AND REFLECTION SHALL REMAIN, WILL NEVER BE FORGOTTEN BY HIM.

8.

JOHN MONTGOMERY, PAYMR. 50th REGT., DIED 19th AUGT., 1819, AGED 64.— ELIZAB. HIS WIFE, DIED 25th AUGT., AGED 52. THEIR SON BT. MAJOR MONTGOMERY, DIED 11 AUGT., 1819, AGED 35. — BT. MAJOR ROWE DIED 3d AUG., 1819, AGED 34, & HIS WIFE, DAUR. OF PAYMR. MONTGOMERY, EXPIRED THE SAME DAY, AGED 26. — JOSEPH BROWN, PAYMR. M.'S SON-IN-LAW, DIED 6 AUGT., 1819, AGED 31. — ELIZABETH, HIS CHILD, DIED.... SAME MONTH, AGED 6 WEEKS, & .... AGED 33 YRS.

DETACHED CEMETERY, UP PARK CAMP.

ABOUT 200 yards N.E. from the present Burial Ground, Up Park Camp, there is a very small Cemetery, quite hidden by a fence of penguin, and the surrounding bush, and, without very precise directions, one might be searching for hours and not find the exact spot.

An altar tomb of brick, with a marble slab bearing the following inscription underneath a compass and rule within a circle :—

1.

(*Ab.*) TO THE MEMORY OF—JAMES ARNOLD—REGTL. SERGT.-MAJOR 3d W. I. REGT. —WHO DIED OF YELLOW FEVER—ON THE 25th — SEPT., 1856, AGED 40. — THIS RECORD IS PLACED HERE BY THE—LT.-COLONEL OF HIS REGIMENT, WHO DEEPLY —FEELS THE LOSS OF SO GOOD A SOLDIER. — HAD HE LIVED 23 DAYS LONGER HE WOULD — HAVE KNOWN THAT HE WAS COMMISSIONED — BY THE SOVEREIGN HE SERVED SO WELL. — AS LONG AS MEMORY LASTS HIS BROKEN-—-HEARTED WIDOW WILL REMEMBER—HIS VIRTUES & AFFECTION.

VERSES follow.

2.

COMPANY SERGEANT-MAJOR A. JORDAN, 3 W. I. REGT., OB. 20 DEC., 1855, AET. 29. BY HIS WIFE.

3.

SACRED TO THE MEMORY OF—CORPORAL FRANCIS STANFORD—3 W. I. REGT. —WHO DEPARTED THIS LIFE—ON THE 30th FEBRUARY—A.D. 1862—AGED 38 YEARS.—MAY HIS SOUL REST IN PEACE.

4.

ISAAC FOSTER, OB. DEC. 8, 1861, AET. 14.

5.

FRANCIS PARRY, OB. 25 AUG., 1862, AET. 86.

6.

SERGT. THOS. BURKE, 3 W. I. R., OB. 28 JULY, 1853, AET. 26.

7.

J. W. FITZPATRICK, OB. 30 DEC., 1853, AET. 34.

BURIAL GROUND, UP PARK CAMP.

All abridged.

1.

JOHN WILSON, ESQ., LATE MAJOR IN HER BRITANNIC MAJESTY'S 36th REGT., OB. 4th JULY, 1837, AET. 50.

2.

CAPT. R. H. MINTY, 1st W. I. REGT., OB. AT PORT ROYAL, 19th NOV. 1848, AET. 48.

3.

MAJOR HENRY BOONE HALE, OB. AT U. P. C., 26th APL., 1834, AFTER 38 YEARS' SERVICE. HE HELD THE APPOINTMENT OF MILITARY SECRETARY ON THE STAFF OF JAMAICA.

4.

FANNY JANE O'CONNOR, ELDT. DAUR. OF THE LATE EDWARD HIGGINS, ESQ., OF EDEN & OLD MANOR HOUSE, NEVIS, & WIFE OF MAJOR LUKE SMITH O'CONNOR, 1st W. I. REGT., OB. AT U. P. C., 5th JANY., 1848.

5.

COLONEL HENRY CAPADOSE . . . .

REMAINDER indistinct. *Vide* KINGSTON Monumental Inscriptions.

6.

THOS. INCE WEBB BOWEN, ESQ., LATE LIEUT. 64th REGT., OB. 13 MAY, 1839, AET. 27.

7.

MAJOR FREDERICK IM-THURN, OB. OCT. 2, 1831, AET. 52.

8.

JOHN GEORGE STREACHEY, ESQ., LATE CAPT. 56th REGT., OB. AT U. P. C., 24 JUNE, 1837, AET. 28.

9.

MRS. ADELAIDE MATILDA MORRIS, DIED ON PASSAGE FROM ENGLAND, OF A DEEP DECLINE, 20th FEB., 1836, AGED 29 YEARS. — ALSO HER HAPLESS INFANT, ADELAIDE SOPHIA MORRIS, DIED 20th MARCH, 1836, AGED 5 M.

10.

CAPT. HAMMOND A. TAPLE, RL. ENGNRS., OB. 13 SEPT., 1831, AET. 40.

11.

RALPH MITFORD PRESTON INGILBY, CAPT. 84th REGT., OB. 29 AUGT., 1831, AET. 34.

12.

E. A. S. MOORE, SON OF LT. & ADJT. MOORE, 3d W. I. REGT., OB. FEB. 28, 1862, AET. 9 M.

13.

JOSEPH WM. HALEMAN, LT. 2d W. I. REGT., ELDT. SON OF LATE COLONEL HALEMAN, E. I. C. S., OB. 20 NOV. 1858, AET. 31.

14.

On a black marble tablet, on a small upright altar tomb, engraven thereon :

TO THE MEMORY OF ELIZABETH, WIFE OF WILLIAM WHITE, CAPT. WAR DEPARTMENT, DIED 11 AUGUST, 1856, AGED 39 YEARS.

VERSES follow.

15.

CHARLES SWEETLAND, SON OF JOHN & MARY SWEETLAND, H. M. 56th REGT., OB. 20th MAY, 1832, AET. 1. — ALSO, — SARAH GEORGIANA, DAUR. OF JAMES AND SARAH DEBENHAM, OF THE SAME REGT., OB. 4th JUNE, 1832, AET. 6 MTHS.

16.

GEORGE MEEKLY, LATE BARRACK SERGEANT, DIED 12th JUNE, 1845, AGED 50 YRS.

17.

JAS. POLLITT, CR.-SERGT. 56th REGT., DIED 20th MAY, 1832, AGED 36 YRS. 9 M. LEAVING A WIFE—AND 3 SMALL CHILDREN—TO LAMENT THEIR LOSS.

18.

JAMES MESSENGER, CR. SERGT. 56th REGT., DIED 31st YR.............

DATE concealed by earth and plants.

19.

SACRED TO THE MEMORY OF ELIZABETH, WIFE OF LIEUT. BEVERHOUDT, 58th REGT., WHO DIED 1st OCTOBER, 1820, AGED 27 YEARS.—ALSO THEIR INFANT CHILD, WHO DIED SHORTLY AFTER HIS BIRTH, 27th SEPTEMBER.

20.

SACRED TO THE MEMORY OF MRS. MARY WARREN, WIFE OF CAPTAIN JOHN WARREN, OF THE 18th ROYAL IRISH REGT., WHO DEPARTED THIS LIFE THE 6th DAY OF JUNE, 1816, AGED 26 YEARS, LEAVING TWO FEMALE CHILDREN TO DEPLORE THE LOSS OF A TENDER AND AFFECTIONATE MOTHER. THIS STONE IS ERECTED BY CAPT. JOHN WARREN, AS THE LAST MARK OF RESPECT DUE TO A BELOVED AND AFFECTIONATE WIFE.

21

On a solitary tomb within the Barrack enclosure, Up Park Camp, is this nearly obliterated inscription—

HIC JACET
SACRA LA..MITISS ....
.......FELIA.....................
MAGISTRO.........RICI LICT ....
JO.........UA .........LEGES..R..
...........E ....
UXORIS S......................
....VXIII R ....
CL..M....FEBRIS............XXVII
....SIS.. A ....
REQUIESCAT IN CŒLIS.

STONY HILL, ST. ANDREW'S PARISH.

1.

(*Ab.*) LIEUT. H. R. COLLINSON, LATE OF THE 61st REGT., DIED, MAY 8th, 1840, AGED 25 YRS.—ERECTED BY HIS BROTHER OFFICERS.

Altar Tomb.

2.

(*Ab.*) RICHD. DISLEY, 36th REGT., DIED 30th JUNE, 18..7, AGED 24 YRS.

3.

(*Ab.*) SAL (?) PEGG, DIED JULY 8, 1833, AGED 24 YRS.

4.

THE OFFICERS OF THE YORK CHASSEURS, AS A MARK OF THEIR ESTEEM, HAVE ERECTED THIS STONE TO THE MEMORY OF LIEUTENANT FRANCIS MCMORRAW OF THAT REGIMENT, WHO DIED, ON THE 26th DAY OF DECEMBER, 1818, IN THE THIRTIETH YEAR OF HIS AGE.

Altar Tomb.

THIS is the common grave of two Officers, who fell by each other's hands, in a duel, as some say ; but the real circumstances are these. The deceased, above commemorated, was forced into the duel and fell by the challenger's pistol. The latter, however, being seized with remorse, committed suicide, whereupon both were interred in the same grave. Beside this tomb is another without any tablet or inscription. They are erected outside the ordinary cemetery, and in a secluded spot.

5.

CAPTN. T. R. THOMSON, 8th (THE KING'S) REGT., DIED AT SLO............

BROKEN off.

PORT ROYAL PARISH.

INSCRIPTIONS,
PORT ROYAL PARISH CHURCH.

(At the Vestry),

GEORGIUS REX—

THIS CHURCH WAS REBUILT

UNDER THE DIRECTION OF

LEWIS GALDY, ⎫
JAMES CLARK, ⎬ ESQRS. Church Wardens,

IN THE YEAR ⎱ 1725
⎰ 1726 „

Organ Loft,

THIS LOFT WAS ERECTED

BY THE DIRECTION OF

JNO. WOODRUFF
&
WM. CHISHOLM,

IN THE YEAR.

⎱ ESQRS.,
⎰ Church-
wardens
1743.

THE Church, in an architectural point of view, is very poor and inelegant; and like most of the older parish churches of Jamaica, is in the style so prevalent after the time of Sir C. Wren, whose preference for classical models, in inferior copyists, led to the general corruption of taste, which reached its culminating point during the reign of George the Third.

I.

SACRED—TO THE MEMORY OF—LIEUTENANT PHILIP FROWD, OF THE—ROYAL NAVY,—WHO DIED HERE OF THE YELLOW FEVER, APRIL 15th, 1804,—IN HIS TWENTY FOURTH YEAR.—THIS IS PLACED AS A TOKEN OF AFFECTION—BY HIS — DISCONSOLATE SISTER HARRIOT FROWD OF — WEYMOUTH, DORSETSHIRE ENGLAND.

2.

SACRED TO THE MEMORY OF — WILLOUGHBY J. SMITH, LIEUTENANT.—MAURICE H. TREVILIAN, MIDSHIPMAN.—JAMES H. COOK.—CHARLES MC CARTHY·—HENRY ROBINSON.—HENRY BENNETT.—GEORGE DUNN, SEAMAN. — OF HER MAJESTY'S SHIP "DARING," — COMMANDER, GERARD J. NAPIER. — WHO WERE DROWNED ON JUNE 23^d, 1853,—BY THE UPSETTING OF ONE OF HER BOATS,—IN CROSSING THE BAR OF TAMPICO.—

WATCH THEREFORE FOR YE KNOW NOT WHAT HOUR YOUR LORD DOTH COME.
Matt. xxiv. 42 v.

3.

SACRED—TO THE MEMORY OF—GEORGE EDWARD OUGHTON—GENTLEMAN' R.N.—ELDEST SON OF GEORGE V. OUGHTON, ESQUIRE, R.N., K.T.S., — WHO DEPARTED THIS LIFE — 4th AUGUST, 1832,—AGED 28 YEARS. — THIS TABLET IS ERECTED TO THE MEMORY—OF THE DECEASED—BY HIS AFFECTIONATE FATHER.

4.

SACRED—TO THE MEMORY OF—THOS. J. GRAHAM, M.D.,—AND 16 SEAMEN OF H. M. SHIP "PANTALOON,"—WHO DIED FROM FEVER — BETWEEN BELIZE AND JAMAICA.—ERECTED OUT OF RESPECT, BY THE CAPN. & OFFICERS, 1847.
M. Tablet.

5.

SACRED — TO THE MEMORY OF—BREVET MAJOR—HENRY PEIRCE—ROYAL REGT. OF ARTILLERY—WHO DIED AT PORT ROYAL—23^d SEPTR., A.D. 1824, AGED 41 YEARS.
M. T.

6.

TO THE MEMORY OF EBENEZER SCOTT, M.D., SURGEON OF H. M. S. "CORNWALLIS," WHO DIED OF FEVER AT PORT ROYAL, DECEMBER 30th, 1838. — THIS TABLET IS ERECTED, AS A SMALL TRIBUTE OF ESTEEM AND RESPECT, ACCORDING TO THE WISH OF HIS COMMANDER IN CHIEF — VICE ADMIRAL THE HONORABLE SIR CHARLES PAGET, G. C. H., WHO WAS DESTINED, WITHIN ONE MONTH, TO FOLLOW HIS LAMENTED FRIEND TO THE GRAVE, CUT OFF BY THE SAME FATAL DISORDER.—REQUIESCANT IN PACE.
M. T.

7.

(*Ab.*) JOHN MACNAMARA, ESQ., M.D., SURGEON OF THE ROYAL NAVAL HOSPITAL AT PORT ROYAL, DIED, AUG. 3, 1820, AGED 33 YEARS. — ERECTED BY HIS WIDOW.
M. T.

37—2

8.

(*Ab.*) HORACE BAYFIELD, ESQ., OF H. M. S. "CONFIDENCE," DIED 23ᵈ DECR., 1819,—AT PORT ROYAL, JAMAICA, OF THE FEVER OF THE COUNTRY. — ERECTED BY HIS MOTHER, BROTHER, & SISTER.

Six lines follow.

Oval, encircled by a snake.
M. T.

9.

(*Ab.*) GEORGE BLOOMFIELD GARVEY, LT. & ADJT. ROYAL ARTILLERY, DIED AT PORT ROYAL, OF YELLOW FEVER, NOV. 19ᵗʰ, 1853, AGED 23 YEARS.—ALSO,— LIEUT. ROBERT LEONARD, RL. ARTLLY., DIED ON THE FOLLOWING DAY, OF THE SAME FATAL MALADY, AGED 22 YEARS.

M. T.

10.

(*Ab.*) LIEUT. JAMES WILCOX, H. M. SLOOP "WOLVERINE," DIED AT PORT ROYAL 14ᵗʰ OCT., 1855, AGED 24 YEARS. — ALSO, — THOMAS BOUGLARE,—PRIVATE, ROYAL MARINE LIGHT INFANTRY. — THIS TABLET IS ERECTED AS A MARK OF ESTEEM & RESPECT, BY THE CAPTAIN & OFFICERS OF THE SHIP.

M. T.

11.

(*Ab.*) JAMES WILLIAMS, ESQ., BORN 6ᵗʰ MAY, 1803, DIED 4ᵗʰ AUGUST, 1857. —HE WAS CLERK OF THE VESTRY, AT PORT ROYAL, FOR 25 YEARS. — DIED LA-MENTED—A PUBLIC LOSS—LEAVING A WIDOW AND TWELVE CHILDREN.

M. T.

12.

(*Ab.*) ARCHIBALD LANG, M.D., SEVERAL YEARS SURGEON OF THE NAVAL HOSPITAL, PORT ROYAL, DIED, 21ˢᵗ APL., 1826. — ERECTED BY VICE ADMIRAL SIR LAWRENCE W. HALSTED, K.C.B., COMMANDER IN CHIEF, AND THE CAPTAINS AND OFFICERS EMPLOYED UNDER HIS COMMAND, ON THE JAMAICA STATION. — COM-MISSIONER T. G. SUTHERLAND AND OFFICERS OF THE CIVIL DEPARTMENT, R.N, &C.

Six verses follow, commencing—

OF FIRST RATE TALENT IN THE HEALING ART.

13.

(*Ab.*) LIEUT. THOS. MARRIOTT, COMMR. OF H. B. M.'S SCHOONER, "UNION," DIED, 17ᵗʰ SEPT., 1823, OF YELLOW FEVER, IN HIS 26ᵗʰ YEAR.—ERECTED BY CAP-TAIN GRAHAM, H. B. M.'S SHIP "ICARUS," & LIEUTENANT HOBSON, H. B. M. SCHOONER "LION."

M. T.

14.

SACRED—TO THE MEMORY OF—LIEUT. JOHN LOVE HAMMICK, ROYAL NAVY—
WHO DIED HERE, OF THE YELLOW FEVER, THE 11th—OF JULY, 1810, IN HIS TWENTY-
THIRD YEAR—MOST SINCERELY AND DESERVEDLY LAMENTED—BY HIS AFFLICTED
FATHER AND FAMILY—OF THE ROYAL NAVAL HOSPITAL, PLYMOUTH—ENGLAND.
M. T.

JOHN LOVE HAMMICK, Lieut. R.N., who died unmarried, in Jamaica, was second son
of Stephen Hammick, Esq., Alderman of Plymouth [father of the 1st Baronet],
by his wife, Elizabeth Margaret, only child of John Love, Esq., of Plymouth.

15.

SACRED TO THE MEMORY OF THE OFFICERS AND MEN OF H. M. S. "IMAUM,"
WHO DIED OF YELLOW FEVER, IN OCTOBER & NOVEMBER, 1860 :—

MR. F. D'AGUILAR, LIEUT.

   „ JOHN JARVIS, MASTER.

   „ WM. MC COMBIE, ASSIST. SURGEON.

   „ N. G. SIMMONDS, ASSIST. PAYMASTER.

   „ WM. ALBIN, CLERK.

   „ JAS. GOWLLAND, ASST. CLERK.

   „ WM. CLIFT, BOATSWAIN.

THOS. BENNETT
WM. WRIGHT } SEAMEN.

GEO. W. LYALL.
EDWD. BARBER.
JAS. CLAMP.
JNO. DEA.
GEO. MC LEAN. } BOYS. {

THOS. FLYNN.
JNO. MARKHAM.
JNO. TIMOTHY.
ROBT. LEGGETT.
JNO. WYATT.
EDWD. HOLMES.

M. T.

16.

(*Ab.*) LIEUT. ROBERT LLOYD, RL. ARTLLY., 2d SON OF THE LATE EDWARD
LLOYD, OF 12, UPPER MOUNT STREET, DUBLIN, & ANNE, HIS WIFE, DIED, AT PORT
ROYAL, NOVR. 9th, 1857, AGED 22 YEARS.
M. T.

17.

(*Ab.*) ANNA W. ST. JOHN, DIED 30th JULY, 1836, AGED 24 YRS, & 3 MTHS.—
ERECTED BY HER HUSBAND.
M. T.

18.

(*Ab.*) MISS CHARLOTTE CASTLES, ONLY CHILD OF REBECCA HOLMES, OF THIS
TOWN, DIED 12th JUNE, 1843, AGED 15 YEARS.
M. T.

19.

(*Ab.*) ERECTED BY COMMODORE DUNLOP, C.B., & OFFICERS H. M. S. "IMAUM," IN MEMORY OF CAPT. SAMUEL MORRISH, LATE OF THAT SHIP, WHO DIED 30th SEP., 1861, & WAS BURIED AT HALF WAY TREE CHURCH, IN THE PARISH OF ST. ANDREW'S.

20.

(*Ab.*) THE REVD. CHAS. F. HALL, RECTOR OF PORT ROYAL, DIED, SEP. 28th, 1855, AGED 54 YEARS.—ERECTED BY THE PARISHIONERS.

21.

SACRED — TO THE MEMORY OF—SARAH ANN—WIFE OF THE REVEREND THOMAS BRYETT TURNER—RECTOR OF THIS PARISH—AGED 39 YEARS—DIED 20th JULY, 1856.—BELOVED AND RESPECTED.

22.

(*Ab.*) THE REVD, GEO. W. GARROW, CHAPLAIN IN H. M.'S SERVICE, BORN OCT. 27th, 1817—DIED 16th OCT., 1847.

23.

(*Ab.*) BY CAPT. WM. HOBSON, OF H. M.'S SLOOP "FERRET."—TO THE MEMORY OF HIS NEPHEW, MR. THOMAS MC GWIRE, LATE MIDSHIPMAN OF THAT SLOOP, WHO DIED OF YELLOW FEVER, 23d SEP., 1825, AGED 15 YEARS.

24.

(*Ab.*) LIEUT. JOSEPH ANDREW BAINBRIDGE, LATE COMG. H. M. SCHOONER "PICKLE,"—SERVED HIS COUNTRY 50 YRS., & DIED OF YELLOW FEVER, 9th FEB. 1846, AGED 49 YEARS.—ERECTED BY HIS SHIPMATES, BROTHER OFFRS. & FRIENDS, AS A TRIBUTE TO HIS HONEST WORTH.

25.

IN AFFECTIONATE REMEMBRANCE OF—EDWARD—YOUNGEST & BELOVED SON OF REAR ADMIRAL HORATIO T. AUSTEN, C.B., — WHO DIED OF YELLOW FEVER— WHILE SERVING AS A MATE—ON BOARD H.M.S. "HYDRA,"—AT PORT ROYAL—27th OCTOBER, 1860, AGED 20. — HIS BODY WAS INTERRED—IN THE PALISADES.—THE LORD GRANT UNTO HIM THAT HE MAY — FIND MERCY OF THE LORD IN THAT DAY.

M. T.

26.

(*Ab.*) TO THE OFFICERS AND SEAMEN OF H. M. S. "RAINBOW," WHO DIED OF FEVER, AT PORT ROYAL, BETWEEN 31 JULY & 28th OCTR., 1835. — EDWD. GREY, LIEUT. — WM. HEN. RUDLAND, SURGEON. — FRAS. W. MEREWHETHER, MATE.— HEN. F. DAVIES, MIDSHIPMEN.—EDWD. W. BENNETT, MID.—ROBT. ELLIS, CLERK.— WM. CLEMENTS, JNO. O'DONNELL, WM. CROWTHER, THOS. COX, SEAMEN. — HEN. THOMPSON & WM. PORCH, MARINES.—JAS. GOUBUN, JAS. HALSTEAD, GEO. SWELLING & GEO. PATIENCE, BOYS.—ERECTED BY THE CAPT. & SURVIVING OFFICERS.

M. T.

27.

(*Ab.*) H. M. STEAM SLOOP "MEDI[E?]A," COMMR. AUGUSTUS PHILLIMORE, DIED BETW. AUGT. 8, & SEP. 22, 1854 (THE FOLLOWING) — JOHN CANTER, CAPTAIN'S COXWAIN, OFF HAVANNAH. — JOHN WHITE, ARMOURER, & ROBT. LUCAS, ORD. SEAMAN, AT SEA.—HEN. SPARKES, O. S.,—WM. WHAYPOOL, LEADING STOKER, JOSEPH WARN & WM. SMITH, BOYS, AT PORT ROYAL. — WILLM. ROBERTS, ROYAL MARINE, SAMANA, AUGT. 5, 1855.

M. T.

28.

(*Ab.*) OFFICERS & MEN OF H. M. S. "LEOPARD."—E. FRANCIS, A.B., DROWNED AT BLEWFIELDS, 6th JANY., 1858, AET. 28. — MR. R. SMIRKE, NAV. CADET, WHO FELL FROM ALOFT, AT BELIZE, — 13th APRIL, '58, AET. 15. — DIED OF FEVER, AT BELIZE, MR. H. BAYFIELD, MID., 15 APL., AGED 17 — MR. E. W. R. EVERARD, MID., 16 APL., AET. 18—MR. H. COLE, CLERK, APL. 17, AET. 20—W. WILLIS, (O. S.) APL. 17, AET. 17—H. WHITFORD, MUSICIAN, 18 APL., AET. 29—H. BOARD, BOY, 24 APL., AET. 17. — DIED AT PORT RL. : — P. HUNT, GUNNER, R. M. A., 19 MARCH, AET. 27—S. CHOLWICH, SEAMANS SCHOOLMASTER, 20 MAY, AET. 23--F. CUNDAY, CAULKER, 25 MAY, AET. 48.

M. T.

29.

NEAR LYE INTER'D THE REMAINS OF—WILLIAM STAPLETON, ESQR. — LIEU-TENANT OF HIS MAJESTY'S SHIP "SPHINX," — NEPHEW TO THE EARL OF WEST-MORELAND—AND BROTHER OF SIR THOS. STAPLETON, BARONET, — WHO, IN AT-TEMPTING TO FIRE OFF A CANNON — IN THE FORT AT PORT MORANT—WAS SO TERRIBLY WOUNDED BY ITS BURSTING — THAT HE EXPIRED A FEW HOURS AFTERWARDS —ON THE EIGHTH DAY OF MAY, 1754—IN THE 28th YEAR OF HIS AGE.

Gray and white Marble Monument.   Sculptured in relief,—a representation of the fatal accident. Naval trophies, &c.

TWELVE lines, in verse, follow.   See "The Peerage."

30.

SACRED TO THE MEMORY OF — AUGUSTUS JAMES DE CRESPIGNY, 3d SON OF SIR W. CHN. & LADY SARAH DE CRES-PIGNY, WHO DIED ON BOARD H. M. SHIP "SCYLLA," OCT. 24th, 1825.

CAPT. DE CRESPIGNY WENT FIRST TO SEA UNDER THE— PATRONAGE OF LD. ST. VINCENT, & SERVED UNDER THE FLAG —OF NELSON, AT TRAFALGAR. FROM THENCE HE WAS TAKEN UNDER THE PATRONAGE OF LD. COLLINGWOOD, WHO MADE HIM STUDY THE DUTIES OF A SEAMAN, UNDER HIS PAR-TICULAR CARE—

M. Mural Mont. Crespigny; impaling......a fleur de lys —a canton erm. *Crest,* A helmet. *Motto,* "Mens conscia recti."

THE ABOVE GALLANT OFFICER

SAVED NO LESS THAN SIXTEEN LIVES OF HIS FELLOW CREATURES,—DURING HIS NAVAL CAREER, FOR WHICH HE WAS PRESENTED WITH A SERVICE OF PLATE, FROM HIS SHIP'S CREW, AS WELL AS A MEDAL FROM THE R. H. S., IN THE ANNUAL REPORT OF WHICH SOCIETY AN ACCOUNT IS GIVEN. THE LAST PARAGRAPH IS AS FOLLOWS—

THESE ARE TO CERTIFY TO THE PRINCIPAL OFFICERS OF THE ROYAL HUMANE SOCIETY—THAT LIEUTENANT AUGUSTUS C. DE CRESPIGNY—SERVED WITH ME AS A VOLUNTEER MIDSHIPMAN, FROM HIS—MAJESTY'S SHIP "TONNANT," IN THE GUN-BOAT SERVICE AT CADIZ, IN—1810, DURING WHICH TIME I HAD OPPORTUNITIES OF SEEING HIS—NOBLE CONDUCT, ON THREE VERY PARTICULAR OCCASIONS. FIRST, IN JUMPING—FROM A BOAT, IN A VERY STRONG TIDE WAY, AND SAVING A MARINE,—SECOND, A BOY IN THE SAME WAY, AND, THIRDLY, IN TAKING TO A SMALL—BOAT, & PULLING INTO THE VERY MUZZLES OF THE ENEMY'S GUNS, AND—EVIDENTLY SAVING FIVE MEN THAT WERE NEAR DROWNING, BY THE —ACHILLES BARGE BEING SUNK : HIS CONDUCT WAS ON THIS LAST OCCASION— SO TRULY NOBLE, THAT HE NOT ONLY GAINED THE ADMIRATION OF THE— WHOLE FLOTILLA, BUT THE ENVY OF THE FRENCH COMMANDING—OFFICER, WHO AT LAST ORDERED HIS MEN TO CEASE FIRING ON HIM.—GIVEN UNDER MY HAND, THIS 12th DAY OF JULY, 1815, WEST COWES.　　　　　　　　G. W. SARMON.

THIS TRIBUTE TO A FATHER'S MEMORY WAS ERECTED BY HIS ELDEST SON, SIR CLAUDE CHN. DE CRESPIGNY, BT., 1841.

SEE "The Baronetage."*

THE PALISADES—PORT ROYAL.

I.

MISS RACHAL THOMAS, WHO DEPARTED THIS......ON THE 21st OF DEC.... 1820, AGED 41 Y ....

Fragment.

2.

HERE LIETH THE—BODDY OF EST. LOW.... DEPARTED THIS LIFE, NOVR. 13, 1771, AGD 60 YERS.

Large Initials, Small Capitals.

3.

TO THE IMMORTAL MEMORY OF ELIZA CARVALLO, WHO DEPARTED THIS LIFE, SEPT. 7, 1780, AGED 65 YEARS. &c.—ALSO,—(*Ab.*) THOS. DAWKINS, WHO DEPARTED THIS LIFE, JANY. 18th, 1760, AGED 51 YEARS.—ERECTED BY HIS YOUNGEST SON.

* N.B. The impalement in the escutcheon is not that of Smijth, although Capt. De Crespigny's wife was a daughter of Sir W. Smijth, 7th Bart.

4.

(*Ab.*) LIEUT. JOHN DOUGLAS, 64th REGT., DIED OF FEVER, AT PORT ROYAL, 20th AUGT., 1834, AGED 31.

5.

(*Ab.*) MR. JOSEPH TODD MOXEY, LATE ASST. SUR. H. M. S. "VICTOR," DIED OF FEVER, AT PORT ROYAL, 14th NOV., 1840, AGED 21.

6.

(*Ab.*) GEO. SMITH—JOHN WEST—WM. BARTON, SEAMEN, — AND GEO. RADFORD—JOSEPH CURETON—CHARLES MILLS, — MARINES, WHO DIED DURING 1849, & 1850.

7.

....C. H. N. RUSSELL,—DIED, FEB. 1807—AGED 30—YEARS—

8.

THE BURYING PLACE OF—MR. JOHN FERRON—AND FAMILY—1853.

On a marble tablet over entrance to a vault.

9.

(*Ab.*) ELIZABETH ADELINE FERRON, BORN 20th JULY, 1805, DIED 2d AUGT., 1821, AGED 16 YEARS, & 14 DAYS, THE DAUR. OF JNO. FERRON, ESQ., LATE MERCHT. IN PORT ROYAL.

Within vault.

10.

LIEUT. THOS. MARRIOTT, LATE OF H. M. SCHOONER, "UNION."
NOTHING more.

11.

(*Ab.*) HENRY HOPKINS, DIED, 15th FEB., 1798, AGED $3\frac{3}{12}$ YRS.—ALSO MARY, HIS MOTHER, WIFE OF THOS. HOPKINS, SHIPWRIGHT, IN H. M. N. YARD, PORT ROYAL, DIED, 8th MARCH, 1799, AGED 22 YEARS.

12.

MRS. MARGARET MARQUIS, WIFE OF ALEXANDER MARQUIS, DIED, THE 29th DAY OF AUGUST, 1795, AGED 30 YEARS. — ALSO, — (*Ab.*) ALEXR. MARQUIS, A NATIVE OF SCOTLAND,—CARPENTER, ... HE DIED, THE 22d OF JULY, 1799, AGED 40 YEARS. THIS IS DONE BY A SURVIVING FRIEND, AS A MEMORIAL OF HIS MERIT, & HER ESTEEM.

13.

(*Ab.*) JOHN ALLARDICE, DIED 19 FEB., 1823, AGED 25 YEARS, &C.

14.

MEMENTO MORI — HERE LIETH THE BODY OF JOHN JENNINGS, ESQR., LATE PURSER OF HIS MAJESTY'S SHIP "MAIDSTONE," OBT. 3 DECEMBER, 1797, AETAT 29 YEARS.

BROTHER, NOW YOU ARE GONE,

NEVER SHALL I AGAIN MEET

SO AFFECTIONATE A FRIEND.

BENJ. JENNINGS.

15.

JAMES DEANE, ESQRE., CORONER MAGESTRATE, (*sic*) AND ASSISTANT JUDGE— FOR SEVERAL YEARS CHURCH WARDEN OF THIS PARISH, DIED 11th MAY, 1802, IN HIS 51st YEAR.

Slab of black and yellow veined marble, on an altar tomb of brick.

MARY, WIFE OF JAMES DEANE, ESQ., CORONER OF THIS PARISH, IN HER 49th YEAR...........1800....

On another slab, in fragments.

16.

HERE LIETH THE BODY OF — MR. JAMES BURROWS,—DEPT. THIS LIFE, DEC. 6, 1811,—AGED 71 YEARS, & 8 MONTHS........OF HIS—MAJESTY'S DOCK YARD, JAMAICA.

17.

HERE LIES THE BODY OF STEPHEN HOWE, ESQR., BRIGADR.—GENL. AND COLL. OF THE 5th WEST INDIA REGT., DIED 19 DAY OF—JULY, 1796, AGED 33 YEARS.

18.

MEMENTO MORI—HERE LIETH THE BODY OF—MR. JOHN RIDLEY, LATE COL- LECTING CONSTABLE OF THIS PARISH, WHO DEPARTED THIS LIFE, THE 6th DAY OF NOVEMBER, ANNO DOMINI 1796, IN THE 43d YEAR OF HIS AGE. VERSES follow.

19.

(*Ab.*) THOMAS CULLENAN, SHIP WRIGHT — IN H. M.' YARD, DIED APL. 1st, 1795, AGED 51 YEARS. — ALSO,—HIS WIFE, MARY, DIED 27th JULY, 1798, AGED 56 YEARS. — ALSO, — SUSANNAH, DAUR. OF THE ABOVE, BY HER FORMER HUSBAND, WILLIAM PETTY, & WIFE OF EDWARD TYRREL, OB. 8 NOV., 1830, AET. 54.

On the same double Altar Tomb.

HERE LIES THE BODY OF JOSEPH HARPER HEARN, SHIPWRIGHT IN HIS MAJY'S. YARD, PORT ROYAL, WHO DEPARTED THIS LIFE, JULY 20, 1792, AGED 32 YEARS.

20.

CHARLES THOMPSON, SON OF VICE ADMIRAL ...... CHARLES THOMPSON, BART.,......D. 13th APRIL, 1801......

Fragment.

SEE "Baronetage"—*Thompson of Virhæs.* Sir C. Thomson, Vice Admiral of the Blue, was created Bart. 23rd June, 1797, for his services in Jervis' action, off Cape

St. Vincent, where he was second in command. He married Jane, only daughter and heiress of Robt. Selby, &c.

21.

TO THE MEMORY OF—ROBERT HAMILTON—MASTER'S MATE OF HIS MAJESTY'S —"RAISONABLE,"—SON OF ROBERT HAMILTON, M.D. OF LYNN, NORFOLK........ ANE, HIS WIFE, WHO, IN CONSEQUENCE........AT KINGSTON—.... MAJESTY'S SERVICE....GIVEN HIM, 20th JUNE, 1795, AGED 23...... HE FELL A VICTIM TO ASSASSINS, AFTER NEAR SIX YEARS' SERVICE IN THE ROYAL NAVY, DURING WHICH, ON BOARD THE "TREMENDOUS," HE HAD BEEN A FORTUNATE SHARER IN THE ENGAGEMENTS OF 29th MAY, & 1st JUNE, 1794, BETWEEN THE BRITISH & FRENCH FLEETS.

A ponderous broken Slab, in fragments.

22.

(*Ab.*) MR. JOHN LINN, DIED, APL 15th, 1805, AGED 38 YEARS. HE WAS OF H. M. YARD.

23.

(*Ab.*) GEORGE FURNISS PADMORE, SON OF WM. & MARY ANN PADMORE, DIED, 2d JUNE, 1825, AGED $4\frac{9}{12}$ YEARS.

24.

(*Ab.*) JOHN FREEMAN......SON OF MARY FREEMAN...... DIED, 18 FEB..... 15 YEARS.—WILLIAM....RY JOHN FREEMAN.........

Altar Tomb, Sandstone Slab.

Dates gone.

BELLE VUE, IN THE PORT ROYAL MOUNTAINS,

Two tombs, in a thicket of rose apples, on one of which, is the following inscription :—

I.

HERE LIE DEPOSITED — THE REMAINS — OF — FRANCES MASSEY STRUPAR, SPINSTER,—WHO DEPARTED THIS LIFE, ON THE—30th DAY OF DECEMBER, 1824,— AGED 36 YEARS. — THIS TOMB WAS ERECTED BY HER MOTHER—AS A TESTIMONY OF THE WORTH OF, — AND HER AFFECTIONATE REGARD FOR — A DUTIFUL DAUGHTER.

THE Strupar family appears to have been obscure, and connected with another, named Jackson, of more note in the island.

PARISH OF ST. THOMAS IN THE EAST.

OLD CHURCH, MORANT BAY.

1.

HERE LYES THE BODY OF LIEUTENT. COLONEL — MARMADUKE FREEMAN,— WHO DEPARTED THIS LIFE, IN THE EIGHT (*sic*) YEAR—OF THE REIGN OF OUR SOVEREIGN LADY ANNE—AND IN THE 63rd YEAR OF HIS AGE—1709.

Slab.

FOR a notice of this family, see Epitaphs of St. Catherine's Parish.

2.

HERE LYETH THE BODY — OF THE HONBLE. — ANTHONY SWYMMER, ESQ.,- WHO DEPARTED THIS LIFE—THE 23rd OF JANUARY,—ANNO DOMINI, 1729.

Slab.

3.

RELIQUÆ MARIÆ LYTTLETON,

GULIELMI HENRICI LYTTLETON,

HUJUS INSULÆ PRÆFECTI.

UXORIS DELECTISSIMÆ,

A.D. 1765.

Slab.

4.*

BLANDA HIC SPONSA JACET, BREVIOR CUI VITA, SED OMNI

VIRTUTUM STUDIO CULTA PERENNIS ERIT.

HEU DOLOR ! INDULGENS SPONSO, SPONSO IPSA NOCEBAT,

ET LACRYMIS LACRYMAS ADDIDIT IPSA NOVAS.

EREPTUM, SED ENIM, NATUM PUERILIBUS ANNIS

(DUM TACUIT) TACITA MENTE SECUTA FUIT.

TO THE PERPETUAL AND JUST MEMORY — OF ELIZABETH — LATE WIFE TO EDWARD LASCELLS, ESQ. ,— AND DAUGHTER — TO ROBERT STRACHAN, ESQ., AND FRANCES, HIS WIFE. —AS ALSO,—OF ROBERT STRACHAN LASSCELLS,—LATE AND ELDEST SON — TO SAID EDWARD AND ELIZABETH, — WHO DEPARTED THIS LIFE — THE 16th XBER, 1747, — AGED 5 YEARS 4 MONTHS AND 3 DAYS.—SHE BEING AT HER DECEASE,—AGED 29 YEARS 1 MONTH AND 1 DAY.

Slab.

---

* Communicated by the Rev. J. G. Richards.

E DWARD LASCELLS was the third son of Captain James Lascells [St. Andrew's Reg., ob. Feb. 4, 1693], by his wife, Rebecca, [ob. Oct. 20, 1691]. The baptisms, and burials of several other children of the latter, are entered in the Reg. of St. Andrew's Parish.

There is a coat of arms over the above epitaph, but the blazon of it has not been obtained. This family is a branch of that, of the Earls of Harewood.

5.

HERE LYETH ANNE FREEMAN, WHO WAS WIFE TO YE HON. COLLONELL THOMAS FREEMAN, OF BELLVEDER, DAUGHTER TO RICHARD BELLTHROPP, ESQ., AND GRANDAUGHTER TO SIR JOHN COLT. SHEE LEFT FIVE SONNS, AND ONE DAUGHTER,—VIZ., THOMAS, JOHN, CHARLES, RICHARD, AND HOWARD, AND ANNE ; AND TWO SISTERS, IN THE ISLAND.—HESTER MARIED TO THE HON. COLLONELL JOHN COPE, AND MARGARET UNMARIED. SHE DEPARTED THIS LIFE, AUGUST YE 3rd, 1681. ÆTATIS SUÆ, 30.

SHE LIV'D A VERTUOUS AND RELIGIOUS LIFE,
AND WAS A TENDER MOTHER, AND MOST LOVEING WIFE.

Tomb.

S EE "Baronetage:"—"COLT." The pedigree of Sir J. D. Colt, 2nd Bart., is not fully stated in any of the Baronetages.

LYSSON'S ESTATE, NEAR MORANT BAY.

I.

On the South side :

HERE LIE THE REMAINS OF—SIR JOHN TAYLOR, OF LISSONS, BARONET,—AMIABLE IN HIS MANNERS, STEADY IN HIS ATTACHMENTS—AND EXEMPLARY IN THE PRACTICE OF THE SOCIAL AND DOMESTIC DUTIES. — HE DIED—DURING A VISIT TO HIS ESTATES IN THIS ISLAND,—MAY 6th, 1786,—AGED 41.

On the North side :

HERE LIE THE REMAINS OF — THE HONORABLE SIMON TAYLOR, — A LOYAL SUBJECT, — A FIRM FRIEND, AND AN HONEST MAN. — WHO AFTER AN ACTIVE LIFE, — DURING WHICH HE FAITHFULLY AND ABLY FILLED THE HIGHEST OFFICES—OF CIVIL AND MILITARY DUTY IN THIS ISLAND,— DIED APRIL 14th, 1813,—AGED 73.

On the East side :

TO THE MEMORY OF — A BELOVED AND HONOURED — FATHER AND UNCLE.

THIS MONUMENT WAS ERECTED — SIR SIMON RICHARD BRISSETT TAYLOR,—BARONET,—1814.

M. Altar Tomb, Sculpture. *Arms*, Two escutcheons. 1. Argent, a saltire sable, between two human hearts, in pale gu., and 2 cinquefoils [Q. trefoils] in fesse, vert. Baronet's badge in the fesse point. *Crest*, Out of a ducal coronet, a cubit arm holding a cross crosslet. 2. The same arms with supporters—Two leopards chained and collared. *Motto*, "In hoc signo vinces."

ON the death of the second Baronet, Sir S. R. B. Taylor, who died unm. 18th May, 1815, his extensive estates descended to his eldest sister, Anna Susanna, whose husband, George Watson, Commissioner of Excise, assumed the name of Taylor, and soon ran through his fortune. (*See* BURKE'S " Dormant and Extinct Baronetage.")

" Simon Taylor," says Dr. Miller, " probably exercised greater influence in Jamaica, and for a longer period than any other individual, not even excepting the Prices. His father is said to have been a Scotchman, who came to Jamaica to follow his trade as a carpenter, which he did with such effect, as to leave £20,000 to each of his two sons. Simon Taylor died at Port Royal, leaving behind him the greatest fortune which, perhaps, any West Indian had ever accumulated. He was buried at his pen in Liguanea, where his brother had been previously interred, but from a subsequent sale, it was thought proper to remove the bodies afterwards to Lysons, in St. Thomas in the East. This was done in not a very decent manner, on a common mule cart."—*Memoir of Lt. Gov. Morrison, in Kingston Chronicle newspaper.*

There was another, and distinct, family of this name in Jamaica, descended from one of the Pilgrim Fathers, and which intermarried with many well-known old families in the island.

PARISH OF VERE.

VERE CHURCH.

I.

UNDERNEATH, AMIDST THE ASHES OF — HER FATHER, MOTHER, BROTHERS AND SISTERS—LYES THE BODY OF—ELIZABETH, DAUGHTER TO YE HONBLE.—JOHN GALE, AND ELIZABETH, HIS WIFE,—WHO DYED, APRIL THE 30th, 1761,—IN THE 34th YEAR OF HER AGE,—IN MEMORY OF WHOSE MANY AMIABLE QUALITIES, HER HUSBAND,—DANIEL McGILCHRIST, ESQ.,—HATH ERECTED THIS MONUMENT OF HIS LOVE AND REGARD—TO ONE OF THE BEST OF WIVES.

2.

BENEATH THIS MARBLE—IN THIS PEW, LIETH INTERRED THE BODYS OF — THE HONORABLE JOHN MORANT,* ESQ.,— WHO DEPARTED THIS LIFE, OCTOBER THE 3d, ANNO DOMINI 1723,—IN THE 44th YEAR OF HIS AGE.— AND HIS SON, JOHN MORANT, ESQ.,—WHO DEPARTED THIS LIFE—FEBRUARY THE 6th, ANNO DOMINI 1734, IN THE 38th YEAR OF HIS AGE.— AND ALSO, ELIZABETH, — THE WIFE OF JOHN GALE, ESQ.,— DAUGHTER OF JOHN MORANT THE ELDER, WHO DEPARTED THIS LIFE — JANUARY THE 10th, 1740, IN THE 34 YEAR OF HER AGE.

Arms, Gules, a fess lozengy argent and sable, between three talbots rampant or.

3.

NEAR THIS PLACE ARE DEPOSITED—THE REMAINS OF—JOHN MORANT—WHO DIED, THE 9th AUGUST, 1741, AGED 18. — WILLIAM MORANT, WHO DIED, THE 9th OF NOVEMBER, 1744, AGED 19.—SAMUEL MORANT, WHO DIED THE . . . . OCTOBER, 1752, AGED 18. — ELEANOR ANGELINA MORANT,— WHO DIED, THE 5th FEBRUARY, 1756, AGED 24.—MARY MORANT—WHO DIED, THE 9th AUGUST, 1756, AGED 60.

Arms (same as last).

---

* " In England," Miller* adds, "it is generally believed that Morant Bay, and Port Morant, were named after this family, but the agreement in name is accidental, as the district from White Horses to Morant Point was named ' Hato de Morante,' by the Spaniards."—*Roby.*

This family, now represented by J. Morant, Esquire, of Brockenhurst, Hants, is distinguished by its noble alliances, for which the reader is referred to *Burke's* " Peerage," " Dictionary of Landed Gentry," &c. See *Pedigree.*

* Sheridan's Magazine, vol. ii., p. 86.

Edward Morant, son of John, baptized 10th December, 1730, represented Vere in 1752, 1754, in both the Assemblies of 1755, and in 1756. He was called up to the Council, in 1757; left Jamaica in 1760, and in the following year was elected M.P. for Hindon. On the 16th July, 1791, as he was driving in Kensington, his horses took fright, when he was precipitated from his carriage, carried home senseless, and died four days afterwards. He married, firstly, in Clarendon, 10th June, 1754, Eleanor-Angelina, widow of William Dawkins, Member for Portland in 1749, and St. Thomas in the Vale, in 1752, whose tombstone in Clarendon old church is inscribed:

Arms, ... on a fess ...... between three bull's heads erased ..... (each with a ring in its nose ......) a fret between two eagles close...

4.

D.O.M.L.

IN PIAM MEMORIAM DNI DNI ANDREÆ, KNIGHT, ROTU-LORUM CUSTODIS ET SUPREMI JUDICIS COMMUNIUM PLACI-TORUM IN PROVINCIIS CLARENDON ET VERE IN JAMAICA, ET TURMÆ PEDESTRIS CENTURIONIS, QUI OBIIT 42° ÆTATIS ANNO, 19° JULII, 1683.

EPITAPHIUM.

DIVES OPUM ANDREAS : FAMÆ VIRTUTIS ET ARTIS
DITIOR ; HOCQUE MAGIS DIVES HONORIS ERAT.
PLURA DARENT SUPERI, NI FATA INVICTA NEGARENT
STERNENDO HUMANI FUTILE MOLIS ONUS.
NI SUPERI TAMEN HUIC ET SORS SIBI FIDA DEESSENT
URNA TENET CORPUS, MEUS HABET ALTA POLUM,
DICAT, VOVET, DEDICAT
JA. BARCLAY.

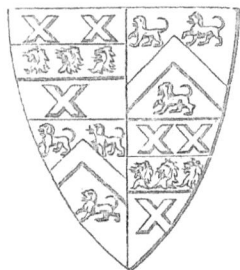

Arms, Quarterly, 1 and 4, On a fesse, between three saltires as many lions' heads erased ; 2 and 3, A chevron between three talbots passant.

5.

NEAR THIS PLACE ARE DEPOSITED THE REMAINS OF— JOHN GALE, ESQUIRE, — WHO DEPARTED THIS LIFE ON THE 24th JUNE, 1743—AGED 24 YEARS. — SARAH GALE, WHO DIED ON 29th AUGUST, 1748,—AGED 14 YEARS.—THE HONBLE. JOHN GALE, ESQUIRE, WHO DIED ON 27th FEBRUARY, 1749-50,— AGED 52 YEARS. — AND ELIZABETH, THE WIFE OF WILLIAM GALE, — AND DAUGHTER OF JOHN MORANT, ESQUIRE, WHO DEPARTED THIS LIFE THE 14th OF JUNE, 1759, — AGED 31 YEARS.

William Gale was the son of John Gale, who first (in 1747) settled his estate, which he named York, and died in 1749-50. The family held a high position, and were members of Council, of Assembly, &c.

PARISH OF CLARENDON.

CHAPLETON.

1.

BENEATH THIS STONE LIE THE REMAINS OF THE HONOURABLE JOHN MOORE, WHO DIED JULY 17th, 1733, AGED 51, AND OF PRUDENCE, HIS WIFE, WHO DIED OCTOBER 8th, 1733, AGED 87.

COLONEL JOHN MOORE, from Barbados, was the founder of his family in Jamaica. He was Member of Council in the latter island, in 1718. His second son. Samuel, by his wife Prudence Weymouth, was father, by Elizabeth Smart his wife, of Henry Moore, Member of Council, Island Secretary, and in 1756 Lieutenant-Governor of Jamaica, &c.; who was raised to the Baronetage in 1764, and appointed Governor of New York, where he died in 1769, leaving issue by his wife Catherine Maria, d. of Samuel Long, a dau.; and, his successor, Sir John Henry Moore, 2d Bart., who dying *s. p.* in 1780, the Baronetcy expired.

2.

HERE LYETH THE BODY OF MRS. ELIZTH. PENNANT, AGED 56 YEARS—WHO DEPARTED THIS LIFE JANRY. 13th, 1735. — SHE HAD BEEN MARRIED TO THE HONBLE. EDWARD PENNANT, ESQ., ABOVE 40 YEARS, BY WHOM SHE HAD A VERY NUMEROUS ISSUE.

THE remainder of the inscription is a record of the excellent qualities of the deceased.

EDWARD PENNANT (son of Gifford Pennant,—will pr. Sep. 19, 1676,—married Elizabeth, relict of Thomas Aldwinkle — will pr. Aug. 19, 1669, — by whom he had two children, Edward and Elizabeth), born in 1672, was Chief-Justice of Jamaica, and married Elizabeth, daughter of Colonel John Moore, and aunt of Sir Henry Moore, Bart. John Pennant, his second son, married Bonella Hodges, and had two sons, the second of whom (Richard) was created Baron Penrhyn of the Kingdom of Ireland. Dying without issue in 1808, he was succeeded in his estates by his cousin, George Hay Dawkins, who thereupon assumed the surname and arms of Pennant.

Bonella Hodges was the daughter of Joseph Hodges, Member for the parish of St. Elizabeth, Jamaica, in 1711.

One of the present representatives of this family is the Right Hon. Lady Penrhyn. (*See* "Peerage;" also M. Ins. of the w. of C. J. *John* Lewis.)

3.

HERE LIETH THE BODY OF — WILLIAM DAWKINS, ESQ, — OF THIS PARISH, WHO DIED—THE 14th OF DECEMBER, 1752, AGED 26 YEARS.

His wife's maiden name was Yeamans. *Vide* PENNANT.

4.

IN MEMORY OF — THE HONBLE. THOMAS BEACH — FORMERLY ATTORNEY-GENERAL AND LATE CHIEF JUSTICE — OF THIS ISLAND, — BEING A DESCENDANT OF THE ANCIENT FAMILY—OF THE LORD DE LA BECHE—OF THE KINGDOM OF GREAT BRITAIN—HE DIED 29th JUNE, 1774.—ALSO OF HELEN, HIS WIFE, — DAUGHTER AND COHEIRESS OF JOHN HYNES, ESQ. — OF THE PARISH OF WESTMORELAND. — SHE DIED IN THE YEAR 1771.—AND OF ROSE, THEIR THIRD SON—WHO DIED AN INFANT,—1770. — THIS TOMB IS ERECTED AT THE EXPENCE OF — THOMAS BEACH JARRETT GOWLAND, ESQ., — GRANDSON OF THE ABOVE THOS. AND HELEN BEACH—FROM RESPECT TO THEIR MEMORY, 1804.

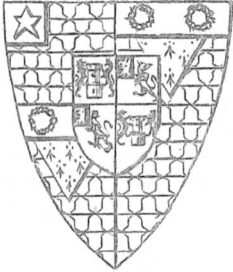

Arms, Quarterly, 1 and 4, Vaire, argent and gules, on a canton azure, a mullet of the first ; 2 and 3, Vaire, (argent and azure), a pile ermine : on a chief of the first, two chaplets of the second. On an escutcheon of pretence, Quarterly, 1 and 4, Vert, a tower argent supported by two lions rampant ; 2 and 3, Or, a lion rampant regardant gules : on a canton sable a griffin's head erased argent. *Crest*, A demi-lion rampant ducally gorged, holding within his paws an escutcheon charged with a pile. *Motto*, "Garde La Foy."

THOMAS BEACH was succeeded by his eldest son, Lieutenant-Colonel Thomas Beach, who assumed, in 1790, the name of De la Beche, from a supposed connection with the ancient family of that name. He was father of the eminent geologist, Sir Henry de la Beche.

Vide "Notes and Queries :" *voce* BEKE.

I.

IN MEMORY OF JOHN SULTAN, SON OF JOHN SULTAN, ESQ., OF THIS PARISH, DIED 23 AUGT., 1745.

2.

HERE LYETH WM. RAND, WHO DEPTD. 18 SEP., 1760, AGED 50.

3.

HERE LIETH THE BODY OF WM. DOUCE, THE SON OF JOHN AND ELIZABETH DOUCE, WHO DEPTD. THIS LIFE 27 MAY, 1720, AGED 22 MOS.

TENNANTS' ESTATE, CLARENDON.

I.

HERE LIES THE BODY OF LAURENCE WEDDERSPOON,—WHO DEPARTED THIS LIFE—APRIL 25, 1788,—AGED 87 YEARS.

OLD PLANTATION ESTATE.

I.

HERE LIES THE BODY OF — THE HONOURABLE—HENRY DAWKINS, ESQUIRE, OF THIS PARISH, WHO DIED—THE 30th JUNE, 1744,—AGED 46 YEARS.

2.

HERE LIES THE BODY OF JAMES DAWKINS, ESQUIRE., JUNIOR, OF THIS PARISH, WHO DIED THE 16th SEPTEMBER, 1757, AGED 35 YEARS.

3.

HERE LIES THE BODY OF — MRS. ELIZABETH DAWKINS, — WIDOW OF THE HONOURABLE HENRY DAWKINS, ESQUIRE, WHO DIED, THE 19th OF AUGUST, 1857.

PRIVATE BURIAL GROUND, HALSE HALL.*

I.

HERE LYETH THE BODY OF MAJOR THOMAS HALS, WHO DEPARTED THIS LIFE THE 27th OF FEBRUARY, 170$\frac{1}{2}$, IN THE SIXTY EIGHT YEARE OF HIS AGE.

HE was a "Major of Horse," and came from Barbados, with Penn and Venables. He married (18 Dec. 1697,) Mary, daughter of John Rose, of London, but predeceasing her, she married secondly, Charles Sadler, Member of Council in 1701.

Arms, ... a fess between 3 griffins' heads erased...... : a label for diff. *Crest*, A griffin's segreant...

---

* The estate of Halse Hall, agreeably to the will of the third Thomas Hals, after the death of his son, Thomas Richard Hals, became the property of his half-brother, Francis Sadler, who thereupon assumed the name of Hals in addition to Sadler, by Act of the Island Legislature, 15th May, 1746. In 1739, Captain Francis Sadler obtained five patents, for three hundred acres each, in this parish, and established the noble estate of Montpelier. He represented St. James in 1745-6, and again as Francis Sadler Hals, in 1749, and dying in 1750, without issue, left Halse Hall to his widow Jannet, who by her first husband, John Hynes, had two daughters, Elizabeth, who married Goodin Elletson, and Helen, who married Thomas Beach, Chief Justice. Both ladies were buried at Halse Hall.

2.

HERE LYETH BURIED THE BODIE OF THOMAS HALSE, ESQ., WHO WAS GREAT GRAND SONN OF SR. NICHOLAS HALSE, OF VENLON COLLUNN, IN CORNWALL, IN ENGLAND. HE DIED THE 24th DAY OF AUGUST, 1702, IN THE 27th YEARE OF HIS AGE.

The same paternal arms as the preceding.

3.

HERE LYES THE BODY OF THE HONBLE. THOS. HALS, ONE OF HIS MAJESTY'S COUNCIL FOR THE ISLAND OF JAMAICA, WHO DEPARTED THIS LIFE NOV. THE 20th, 1737, AGED 38.

ELIZABETH, widow of the third Thomas Hals, married secondly, Benjamin Hume, Member for Port Royal 1735-6 ; called to the Council 1745 ; Receiver-General 1746 ; but dismissed from that office and his seat in the Council, 27th October, 1753.

Arms, Hals as before, but omitting the label, impaling, on a chevron between three lions' heads erased, three pheons.

4.

IN MEMORY OF ELIZABETH ELLETSON, DAUGHTER OF JOHN & JANNET HAYNES, DIED AUGUST 31st, 1760. — JANNET HYNES, WIFE OF THE ABOVE JOHN HYNES, AND MOTHER OF HELEN BEACH, WAS ELDEST DAUGHTER & CO-HEIRESS OF JAMES GUTHRIE OF WESTMORELAND, AND WAS SECONDLY, MARRIED TO FRANCIS SADLER HALS, ESQRE., BY WHOM SHE HAD NO ISSUE.

HELEN, THE SECOND DAUGHTER & COHEIRESS OF THE SAID JAMES GUTHRIE, WAS MARRIED TO THOMAS STORER, ESQRE., OF WESTMORELAND, BY WHOM SHE HAD ISSUE OF ELIZABETH THE 3RD DAUGHTER & COHEIRESS OF THE SAID JAMES GUTHRIE, WHO WAS FIRST MARRIED TO — HAUGHTON, ESQRE., OF WEST-MORELAND, BY WHOM SHE HAD A SON NAMED WILLIAM, AND BY HER 2ND HUSBAND, MAJOR EDWARD CLARKE SHE HAD ISSUE GEORGE HYDE & OTHER ISSUES.

SHECKLE'S ESTATE, CLARENDON.

I.

HONBLE. JOHN SHECKLE, ESQ., CUSTOS ROTULORUM OF THE PARISH OF CLARENDON & VERE, AND BRIGADIER GENERAL OF MILITIA, WHO DEPARTED THIS LIFE IN THE 70th YEAR OF HIS AGE, 17th JUNE, 1782. — DURING A RESIDENCE OF 55 YEARS IN THIS ISLAND, HE ACQUIRED AND CONSTANTLY PRESERVED THE LOVE & ESTEEM OF VERY NUMEROUS ACQUAINTANCES, & DIED UNIVERSALLY LAMENTED.

2.

HERE LIES THE BODY OF JOHN HAYES, WHO DEPARTED THIS LIFE 5th SEPTR., 1766, AGED 30 YEARS. — ALSO NEAR THIS PLACE ARE INTERRED RICHARD AND HANNAH HAYLE, FATHER & MOTHER OF THE SAID JOHN HAYLE. — AS ALSO MARY AND SAMUEL HAYLE AND ELIZABETH BOWEN, BROTHERS AND SISTERS TO THE SAID JOHN HAYLE. — AND HIS NIECE, ELIZABETH BOWEN, DAUGHTER OF FRANCIS & THE ABOVE MENTIONED ELIZABETH BOWEN.

3.

ADAM SMITH, THE SON OF ADAM & ELIZABETH SMITH, WHO DEPARTED THIS LIFE THE 18th OF APRIL, 1799, AGED 14 MONTHS & 13 DAYS. — ALSO ROBERT SMITH, THE SON OF ADAM & ELIZABETH SMITH, WHO DEPARTED THIS LIFE THE 15th OF AUGUST, 1799, TO THE INFINITE REGRET & AFFLICTION OF THEIR FOND PARENTS, WHO CAUSED THIS MARBLE TO BE PLACED OVER THEIR GRAVE AS THE LAST INSTANCE IN THEIR POWER TO SHEW THEIR PARENTAL LOVE & AFFECTION TO THE REMAINS OF THEIR EVER DEAR AND BELOVED CHILDREN.

4.

IN MEMORY OF ELIZABETH AYREY, DIED 27th MARCH, 1839, AGED 16 YEARS.

5.

IN MEMORY OF CHARLIANNA AYREY, DIED 17th FEBRY., 1839, AGED 15 YEARS.

DENBIGH ESTATE.

Coat of Arms, with the following device inscribed—"RECTVS INDEX SUI."

BLACK RIVER CHURCH.*

1.

IN MEMORY OF—THE HONOURABLE HENRY GALE, ESQ.,—CUSTOS AND COLO-NEL OF THE PARISH — OF ST. ELIZABETH IN THIS ISLAND, — BORN THE 19 OF FEBUY., 1737,—DIED THE 8th OF MARCH, 1767.

2.

SACRED TO THE MEMORY OF THE REVD. THOMAS WARREN [THIRTY-THREE YEARS RECTOR OF THIS PARISH] BORN THE 31ST OF JANUARY, 1738—DIED THE 22d OF FEBRUARY, 1807, AGED 69 YEARS—AND OF MARGARET, HIS WIFE, BORN THE 6TH OF AUGUST, 1747, DIED THE 15TH OF MAY, 1807, AGED 59 YEARS. THIS MONUMENT IS ERECTED BY THEIR SURVIVING SON AND FOUR DAUGHTERS.

THE above lady was Margaret Broadbelt [m. 13th Jany., 1772]. Their son, Thomas Fullerton Warren, of Brompton, County Middlesex, died in 1816.

———

TOMBSTONE near the Roadside, on the way to Black River :—

1.

THOMAS JORDAN SPENCER,—BORN 14 OCT., 1723,—DIED 17 SEPT., 1738.

---

* Now pulled down.

PARISH OF ST. DOROTHY.

I.

HERE LYETH YE BODY OF COLLONEL JOHN COLBECK, OF COLBECK, IN ST. DOROTHYES, WHO WAS BORN YE 30th MAY, 1630, AND CAME WITH YE ARMY THAT CONQUERED THIS ISLAND, YE 10th DAY OF MAY, 1655, WHERE HAVEING DISCHARGED SEVERAL HONBLE. OFFICES, BOTH CIVILL AND MILITARY, WITH GREAT APPLAUSE, HE DEPARTED THIS LIFE YE 22d DAY OF FEBRUARY, 1682.

SEE PAR. OF ST. CATHERINE.

CHURCH OF ST. DOROTHY.

I.

HERE LYETH THE BODY OF COL. THOMAS FULLER, ONE OF THE FIRST TAKERS OF THIS ISLAND, WHO DEPARTED THIS LIFE THE 6th DAY OF JUNE, 1690.

COLONEL THOMAS FULLER, a soldier of fortune, under Venables, was amongst the earliest settlers in Jamaica. His son Charles, [bapt. 24 June, 1677, buried 15 Feb., 1706,] married Catherine Maria, second daughter of Colonel Byndloss, 21 Nov., 1695, and had a daughter Mary, married 31 March, 1719, to Edmund Kelly, Attorney-General of Jamaica, and probably related to John Kelly, Clerk of the Grand Court, and Charles Kelly, Registrar in Chancery, who married respectively, Margaret, and Sarah, daughters of Colonel James Risbie, who died aged 63, in 1740. (*Roby.*)

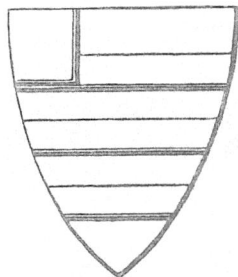

Arms, Argent, 3 bars and a canton gu. *Crest*, A fire beacon.

2.

HERE LYETH THE BODY OF CATHERINE FULLER, WHO DEPARTED THIS LIFE, THE 27th DAY OF AUGUST, 1706.

SEE PAR. OF ST. CATHERINE.

PARISH OF ST. MARY.

AT DECOY.

I.

HIC JACET—CAROLUS PRICE, BARONNETTUS — MULTIS VIR ORNATUS VIRTU-
TIBUS—IN OMNIBUS ENIM VITÆ OFFICIIS—ITA SE PROBAVIT—UT ET CIVIBUS
ET SOCIIS—GRATISSIMA ESSET EJUS INTEGRITAS—ET FIDES—MEMORIÆ TANTI
VIRI—CAROLUS PRICE—FILIUS NATU MAXIMUS—ET QUATUOR SOLUS SUPERSTES
FORTUNÆ ET HONORIS,—UTINAM AC VIRTUTUM,—HAERES—HOC MONUMENTUM
—POSUI.

THE monument is covered with eulogistic inscriptions.

See also PAR. OF ST. CATHERINE.

PARISHES OF ST. GEORGE, AND METCALFE.*

PARISH OF ST. GEORGE.
PRIVATE BURIAL GROUND NEAR CEDAR VALLEY.

I.

SACRED TO THE MEMORY OF — WILLIAM WILLIAMSON, ESQRE. — OF MOUNT HOLSTEIN, — A NATIVE OF ELGIN, SCOTLAND, — WHO DIED ON THE 28th NOVR., 1855, AGED 68 YEARS.

PARISH OF METCALFE (formerly part of St. George's).
TABLETS IN THE CHURCH AT ANNOTTO BAY.

I.

SACRED TO THE MEMORY OF HERBERT, FIFTH SON OF ISAAC WESTMOR-LAND, ESQUIRE, OF LONDON, AND BROTHER OF HENRY WESTMORLAND OF THIS PARISH, WHO DEPARTED THIS LIFE AT ETINGDON ESTATE, TRELAWNY, THE 10th DAY OF MARCH, 1846, IN THE 18th YEAR OF HER AGE.

EULOGISTIC lines.

2.

SACRED TO THE MEMORY OF .... MRS. CHARLOTTE CLEMENTS, WHO DEPARTED THIS LIFE, JULY 18, 1844, AGED 37 YEARS.—GRATEFUL FOR THE MANY YEARS FELICITY HER SOCIETY AFFORDED HIM, THIS TABLET IS ERECTED BY HER HUSBAND.

The following are Inscriptions on Tombstones in THE CHURCHYARD :

I.

BENEATH THIS ARE DEPOSITED THE MORTAL REMAINS OF MRS. CHARLOTTE CLEMENTS, WHO DEPARTED THIS LIFE, 18th JULY, 1844, AGED 37 YEARS.

Prov. xxxi., verse 28.

2.

SACRED TO THE MEMORY OF EDMUND LEA(M?)Y, WHO DEPARTED THIS LIFE ON THE 14th DAY OF NOVEMBER, 1855, AGED 26 YEARS.—THIS TOMB IS ERECTED TO HIS MEMORY BY HIS AFFECTIONATE BROTHER.—REQUIESCAT IN PACE.

---

* Originally one parish ;—viz., St. George.

3.

IN MEMORY OF WILLIAM MELBOURNE FOX, ESQUIRE.—FOR MANY YEARS COLLECTOR OF CUSTOMS AT THIS PORT.—HE WAS BORN IN LONDON, ENGLAND, OCT. 25th, 1798.—DIED JULY 8th, 1847.—ALSO OF ———————

HERE follow two verses of a hymn.

———————

The following are on Tombstones in Private Burial Grounds (*communicated*),
ANNOTTO BAY.

1.

A TRIBUTE OF AFFECTION TO THE MEMORY OF CHARLES MEMELL, ESQUIRE, WHO DEPARTED THIS LIFE, SEPTR. 23rd, 1823, IN THE 40th YEAR OF HIS AGE.—READER, PREPARE TO MEET THY GOD.

2.

SACRED TO THE MEMORY OF MR. THOMAS PHILLIPS, LATE HARBOUR MASTER OF THIS BAY, AND MANY YEARS RESIDENT IN THE PARISH. HE DIED, 18th AUGUST, 1822, AGED 47 YEARS.

3.

SACRED TO THE MEMORY OF SYLVESTER JEPSON, WHO DEPARTED THIS LIFE THE 25th JULY, 1812, IN THE 18th YEAR OF HIS AGE.

4.

SACRED TO THE MEMORY OF * PHILLIPS, WHO DEPARTED THIS LIFE THE 20th JUNE, 1816, AGED TWO YEARS. AND ANOTHER OF SAME FAMILY * (?)

5.

SACRED TO THE MEMORY OF CAPTAIN MATTHEW LEVY, UPWARDS OF 38 YEARS A TRADER OF THIS PORT, WHO DEPARTED THIS LIFE JULY 8th, 1823, AGED 53 YEARS. — LIKEWISE IN MEMORY OF MATTHEW, HIS ONLY SON, WHO WHILST IN THE BLOOM OF LIFE, AT QUEBEC ESTATE, IN SAINT MARY'S, OCTOBER 8th, 1820,—AGED 21 YEARS.

6.

IN A VAULT NEAR THIS PLACE LIE DEPOSITED BY HIS OWN DIRECTION THE REMAINS OF—THOMAS HIBBERT,* ESQ., — LATE A MERCHANT IN THE TOWN OF KINGSTON—AND PROPRIETOR OF THIS AND THE TWO ADJOINING ESTATES. HE WAS THE ELDEST SON OF ROBERT AND MARY HIBBERT, OF MANCHESTER, IN THE COUNTY OF LANCASTER, IN THE KINGDOM OF GREAT BRITAIN — FROM WHENCE HE FIRST ARRIVED IN THIS ISLAND IN 1734—AND AFTER RESIDING IN IT, WITH LITTLE INTERRUPTION, ALMOST FORTY-SIX YEARS—DIED UNMARRIED AT THIS ESTATE, ON THE 20th OF MAY, 1780,—IN THE 71st YEAR OF HIS AGE.

THE remainder of the inscription is a panegyric in general terms.

———————

* Thomas Hibbert was Judge of the Grand Court, and also Member of Assembly for Portland in 1754-5.

PARISH OF ST. JOHN.

CHURCH AND CHURCHYARD OF ST. JOHN.

I.

HERE LYETH BURYED THE BODY OF — RICHARD GUY, ESQ., WHO DYED THE 10th — DAY OF JUNE, 1681, AGED 63 YEARS. — HE HAD BY HIS BELOVED WIFE 4 CHILDREN — MARY THE ELDEST, RICHARD AND KATHERINE, TWINS, — AND SUSANNA THE YOUNGEST. — RICHARD DYED YOUNG, AND LYES BURYED IN THIS GRAVE. — SUSANNA ALSO DYED YOUNG IN ENGLAND, — WHITHER SHE WAS SENT TO BE EDUCATED,—AND LIES BURIED IN HACKNEY—CHURCH, NEAR LONDON.

M.—Arms.

HE was a Captain, Member of Assembly, &c. He married, in St. Catherine's, 27 Dec. 1669, Frances Bedle ; and 2ndly, 12th Feb., 1674, Mary Davenport. He patented in 1676, 1000 acres, of which the present estate of Latimer forms a part. His daughter Mary, married 24th July, 1690, Richard Lloyd, a Member of Council in 1693. His other daughter, Katherine, married John Freeman, Member of Assembly for St. John, 1695, 1701-4.

See St. Catherine.

2.

HERE LYETH THE BODY OF — GEORGE MODD, ESQ., — WHO DIED JULY 14th, 1724,—AGED 45 YEARS. — ALSO — ANNE MODD, YE ONLY SURVIVING — CHILD OF GEORGE MODD, ESQ. AND MARGARET† HIS WIFE,—BORN AUGT. YE 7th, 1718, DIED AUGT. YE 5th, 1724.

C. Y.

3.

HERE LYES THE BODYS OF—GEORGE MODD, JUNR., — WHO WAS BORN FEBY. YE 6th, 1712-13 : — AND ALSO MARY MODD,—BORN JANY. 14th, 1713-14, — DIED. DECEMBER THE 10th, 1719.

C. Y.

4.

HERE LYES THE BODY OF MARY, YE WIFE OF GEO. MODD, DAUGHTER OF LAURCE. AND SARAH CHARNOCKE. SHEE WAS A DUTIFULL CHILD, A TRUE

---

* Moulsworth, Colonel Guy, petition against Sir James Drax, for things done in Barbados. Laid aside.—Jour. House of Lords, 3 July, 1661.

† Mrs. Modd remarried (27 Sep., 1724) Rev. Richd. Marsden, Rector of St. John.

FRIEND, AND A FAITHFULL LOVING WIFE, BUT BEING SEIZED WITH AN INVIDI-
ENT FEAVOUR, SHE DEPARTED THIS LIFE THE 10th DAY OF FEBY., AETAT SUAE
26 ANO SALUTIS, 1709.

GEO. MODD was thrice Speaker of Assembly. His death should have been recorded
in 1723.

5.

(*Ab.*) UNDER THIS TOMB ARE DEPOSITED THE BODYS—OF 2 SONS AND 6
DAUGHTERS, THE CHILDREN—OF COLL. CHARLES PRICE—AND SARAH HIS LADY.

DEBORAH		13th JUNE, 1716,	2 YEARS.
KATHERINE.........		23 NOV., 1717,	7 YEARS.
ELIZABETH		25 NOV., 1717,	12 YEARS.
FRANCIS	DIED 10 JULY, 1720,	AGED 4 MONTHS.	
SARAH		„ 1721,	14 YEARS.
DEBORAH............		„ 1721,	5 YEARS.
PHILLIP		JANY., 1722,	3 WEEKS.
ELIZ. KATHERINE		25 AUGT., 1727,	9 YEARS.

SARAH, his wife, was a daughter of Philip Edmunds. Colonel Price had three surviving sons: Charles (Bart.), Thomas, and John.

M.—Arms.

See ST. CATHERINE.

6.

HERE LIES THE BDY. OF MADAME JOYCE AYLMER, THE WIFE OF THE
HONBLE. COL. WHITGIFT AYLMER, WHO DEP: THIS LIFE, 18 (Q. 19?) SEP: 1702, AET.
52 YEARS.

M.—Arms.

7.

HERE LIES THE BDY. OF THE HONBLE. COL. WHITGIFT AYLMER, WHO AFTER
HE HAD LIVED IN THIS ISLAND 46 YRS. 2 M. 10 D., DEPTD. THIS LIFE 20 JULY,
BEING SUNDAY, 1707, AET. 67 YRS. 4 M. 3 D.....

M.—*Arms*, A cross between 4 birds, close.

CATHERINE, daughter and heir of Major Whitgift Aylmer, [a supposed descendant
of Dr. John Aylmer, Bishop of London, and from Dr. Whitgift, Archbishop of
Canterbury], and relict of a Mr. Hamilton, of .... co. Galway, married John,
8th Viscount ....(illegible).

[*MSS. of the late C. E. Long, Esq.*]

8.

HERE LYETH THE BODY OF HESTER BALTHROPP, DAUG. OF SIR JOHN COLTE
KNT., & THE LATE WIFE & RELICT OF RD. BALTROPP, OF GRAY'S INN ESTATE, BY
WHOM SHE HAD ISSUE, 3 SONS & 3 DAUGHTERS, AS FOLLOWETH:— RICHARD,—
JOHN AND ALBERICUS GENTILLS, —MARGARET, ANN & HESTER. — THE 3 SONS
DEAD, BUT THE 2 DAUGHTERS LIVING. — OBIJT. 3rd OCT., 1679, AETATIS SUAE—

58— ANN BEING MARRIED TO THE HONBLE. COL. THOS. FREEMAN, & HESTER TO THE HONBLE. COL. COPE.

M.—Arms.

9.

HERE LYETH THE BODY OF ED. (RD. ?) HARRIS, ALSO DEPTD. THIS LIFE, 4 JULY 1723, AET. 57 YR. 2 M. I D. — ALSO, THE BODY OF ELIZ. HARRIS, WIFE OF THE ABOVE, & DAU. OF WM. WEBB, OF THE PARISH OF ST. DOROTHY'S, BY EMMA, HIS WIFE.—ALSO, DEPTD. THIS LIFE, 30 MAY. M.D.CXCII. — AND ALSO THE BODY OF ELIZABETH HARRIS, DAUGHTER TO THE ABOVE ED. & ELIZ. HARRIS, WHO DEPTD. THIS LIFE, 9 AUGT., MDCXCIII, AGED 2 MOS. IO DAYS.

10.

UNDER THIS STONE LIES THE BODY OF MRS. DEBORAH CORKER, THE WIFE OF T. CORKER, ESQ. — THE DAUGHTER OF DR. JOHN BURNELL, WHO DIED IN CHILDBED OF HER FIRST CHILD, HAVING BEEN MARRIED 4 YRS. 8 MOS., 5 DAYS,— BORN 4 NOV., 1707, & DIED 29 OCT., 1727, AGED 19 YRS. II MOS. & 7 DAYS.— GOD EXECUTES JUDGMENT.

M.—Arms.

II.

(*Ab.*) JOHN CHARNOCK, M.D., D. SEP. 30, 1730,—AND HIS 2 DAURS. — BY HIS W. FRANCES, D. OF CAPT. JOHN ROSE, OF LONDON, DECD.—ELIZABETH, D. AUG. 19, 1720, AGED 9 YRS. ; MARY, D. 27 OCT. 1720, AGED 4 YEARS.

M.—Arms.

12.

(*Ab.*) FRANCIS, S. OF FRAS. & ELIZABETH ROYKES, — D. 6 NOV., 1708, AGED 14 YRS. & 3 MTHS. — ALSO FRANCIS ROYKE, ESQ., THE FATHER, — D. 5 MARCH, 1709, AGED 68 YRS. & 4 MTHS.

M.—Arms.

13.

(*Ab.*) WINKWORTH TONGE, ESQ., DY. J. ADV. OF THE FORCE IN JAMAICA,— D. 12 JULY, 1820.

C. Y.

14.

(*Ab.*) ELIZABETH, D. OF DR. JOHN CHARNOCK & FRANCES, HIS W. — D. AUG. 19, 1720, AGED 9 YEARS.

C. Y.

15.

(*Ab.*) ROBT. MC CULLOCH, D. 4 FEB. 1864, AGED 33 YEARS.
C. Y.

16.

(*Ab.*) J. R. RICHARDSON, D. 21 NOV., 1857, AGED 46 YEARS.
C. Y.

17.

(*Ab.*) DAVID TOBOIS, D. 5 AUG., 1869, AGED 27.
C. Y.

18.

(*Ab.*) LOUISA EDITH, D. OF JOHN & LAURA STONA,—D. 16 DEC., 1870, AGED
1 YEAR.

IN A WOOD NEAR AYLMER.

I.

(*Ab.*) NEAR TO THIS MOURNFULL MARBLE, LIES INTERR'D
THE BODY OF THE HON. COLL. CHARLES PRICE, WHO WAS
DIVESTED OF THE ROBE OF MORTALITY, ON THE 23^{d} DAY OF
MAY, 1730, AGED 52 YEARS.

MANY lines of eulogy follow.

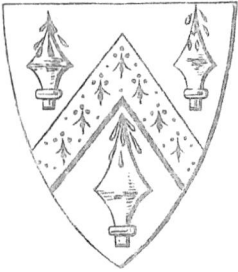

Arms, A chev. erminois
(colour added) between 3 spear heads argent embrued at points, ppr. *Crest*, A dragon's head erased, holding in
its mouth a sinister hand erect, couped, dropping blood, ppr.

M. Slab.

PARISH OF ST. ANN.

IN AN OLD ORCHARD,* AT SPRING MOUNT.

Marble Altar Tomb (now in fragments).

I.

VITÆ SUMMA BREVIS SPEM NOS VETAT INCOHARE LONGAM.

SACRED TO THE MEMORY OF MARY, THE .... WIFE OF JAMES HENRY ARCHER, M.D., WHO DEPARTED THIS LIFE ON TUESDAY MORNING, OCTOBER† 11, 1831,—AGED 29 YEARS AND 9 MONTHS.

SHE was the third daughter of Alexr. Edgar, (son of Alexr. Edgar, of Auchingrammont, Lanarkshire), by his wife, Ann, daughter of Henry Gordon, by his wife, Rachel, daughter of Lawrence Lawrence.‡ Henry Gordon was the grandson of Christopher Taaffe (1723), "generosus in com. Derriæ".

WINDSOR ESTATE BURIAL GROUND.

I.

BENJAMIN SANFORD, M.D, BORN AT RIDGE IN THE STATE OF CONNECKCOUT, 15 MARCH, 1798, DIED AT WINDSOR ESTATE, 20 APRIL, 1832.

2.

MARY COLE, DIED 11th FEB., 1799, AGED 64.—HER NEPHEW, JOHN TAYLOR, CAUSED THIS STONE TO BE ERECTED.—ALSO TO THE MEMORY OF TABITHA COULBOURN AND CATHERINE ANN TAYLOR.

SHAW PARK BURIAL GROUND.—(*Communicated.*)

I.

HERE LIETH INTERRED THE BODY OF MRS. JANE ABRAHAM,—WHO DEPARTED THIS LIFE THE 30th DAY OF JANY., ANNO DOM. 17$\frac{17}{18}$ AGED 63 YEARS.—ALSO,—

---

* There are other mutilated tombs in the same orchard, but the tablets have been removed. Likewise altar tombs on Great Pond Estate, of others of *this* family of Archer. See *The Lyon Register;* " Notes and Queries," 11th July, 1874, &c.

† Qy. *Dec.?* Letter of her husband, dated 24 Dec.

‡ By Susanna, eldest daughter, and third child of Jno. Lawrence and his wife Susa. Pelgrave. See "Notes and Queries," 4th S. xii., 489, 511.

ELIAS ELY, YE ELDEST SON OF THE SAID JANE ABRAHAM, BY HER FIRST HUS-
BAND, WHO DEPARTED THIS LIFE IN THE 31 YEAR OF HER AGE.

Arms,......a fess indented between six fleur de lis, three in chief, and three in base.

2.

THIS STONE CONSECRATED BY ELIZABETH ANN SHAW, TO THE MEMORY OF
HER BELOVED MOTHER SUSANNAH KNIGHT, WHO DIED 20 JANY., 1794,—AGED
52 YRS.

3.

MARGARET & SUSANNAH SHAW, TWIN SISTERS; THE FIRST DIED 10 JAN.,
1799, AGED 1 YEAR,—THE LATTER, ON THE 7 JULY, 1802, AGED FOUR YEARS &
7 MONTHS. — THIS STONE WAS PLACED OVER THEM BY THEIR DISCONSOLATE
PARENTS.

4.

MRS. ELIZABETH KING, WIFE OF CAPT. GEORGE KING, WHO DIED 2 MAY,
1811, AET. 38.—ALSO ONE SON OF THE ABOVE, WHO DIED IN INFANCY.

5.

CAPT. GEORGE KING, OF THE MERCHANT SHIP "JAMES LAING," DIED JULY,
1823, AET. 27 ; ALSO CAPT. GEORGE KING, SENIOR, DIED AT SEA, AUGT., 1822,
AET. 58.

6.

ELIZABETH OLIVIA, WHO DIED AT SHAW PARK, 2 MARCH, MDCCCXXVII.,
WIFE OF JAMES WALKER, ESQ., & DAUGHTER OF JOHN SHAW, DECEASED.

PARISH OF ST. JAMES.*

MONTEGO BAY—CHURCH AND CHURCHYARD.

1.

(*Ab.*) MRS. ROSA PALMER—OB. 1 MAY, 1790—

Marble Mont. Sculpture in bas relievo, by Flaxman.

THE family of Palmer was one of the oldest in Jamaica, and intermarried with those of Modyford, Ellis, &c.

Mrs. Palmer was three times married. She met her death by strangulation, at the hands of a negress, according to tradition, in an arbour, at her residence, Rose Hall.

2.

(*Ab.*) WILLIAM FOWLE, ESQ., OF WILTSHIRE ESTATE,— DIED JULY 6th, 1796.

Westmacott, Junr., Sculpt.

HE was a native of Charlton, co. Wilts. Monument erected by his nephew, W. Fowle, Esq., of Durrington, co. Wilts.

M.M. Arms, Gules, between 3 roses, a lion passant.

3.

(*Ab.*) GEORGE MC FARQUHAR, ESQ., AFTER 22 YRS. RESIDENCE IN THE ISLAND, IN THE PRACTICE OF THE HEALING ART, DIED DEC. 25th, 1786, IN THE 45th YEAR OF HIS AGE.

G.M.—*Arms*, Quarterly: 1. Arg. a lion rampant, gu. ; 2. Or, a raven close, ppr. ; 3. Or, a lymphad, ppr. ; 4. Gu., a fish naiant in fess, argt.

4.

(*Ab.*) ELIZABETH MINTO, DAUGHTER OF JACOB AND ISABELLA FLETCHER, OF LIVERPOOL,—OB. 1783.

M.½M.

5.

(*Ab.*) THOMAS REABURN,—OB. 1844.

M. M.

6.

(*Ab.*) RACHAEL ANGLIN MORRIS,—NAT. 1789,—OB. 1814.

SHE was the daughter of Philip Anglin Morris, by his wife Amelia Barrett, daughter of William Waite, a supposed descendant of the Regicide, Thomas Wayte.

M. M.

---

* St. James' and St. George's parishes were, in 1711-12, exempt from taxation, "they having no towns, few inhabitants, and little commerce."—Jour. House of Assembly.—*Roby, &c.*

7.

(*Ab.*) THE HON. JOHN PERRY, ESQ., MEMBER OF ASSEMBLY, AND FORMERLY OF BRISTOL—OB. 1809, AET. 58.—ALSO, ELIZABETH AND ANNE, HIS DAUGHTERS, AND ANNE, HIS WIFE.

M. M.

8.

(*Ab.*) BERNARD BIRCH,—BORN AT LIVERPOOL,—OB. 1782, AET. 22.

M. M.

9.

(*Ab.*) JOHN HUGHES, BARRISTER AT LAW,—OB. 1802, AET. 27.—ERECTED BY HIS FRIEND, JOHN CUNNINGHAM.

M. M.

10.

(*Ab.*) DUNCAN ANDERSON, — BORN AT SHENTON, EAST LOTHIAN, N.B.—1757, —OB. 1796—

M. M.

11.

(*Ab.*) MRS. MARGARET BERNARD,—OB. 1781.

M. M.

12.

(*Ab.*) DAVID BERNARD,—OB. 1804.—ERECTED BY HIS WIFE JUDITH.

M. M.

13.

(*Ab.*) JOHN, ELDEST SON OF JOHN AND ELIZABETH CUNNINGHAM,—OB. 1804.

M. M.

14.

(*Ab.*) JOHN THARP, OF GREENPOND,—OB. 1811, AET. 59.

M. M.

15.

(*Ab.*) JANE, WIFE OF EDWARD MONTAGUE,—OB. 1819.

M. M.

16.

(*Ab.*) SARAH NEWTON KERR, DAUGHTER OF HERBERT NEWTON JARRETT,— NAT. 1762,—OB. 1814.

M. M.

17.

(*Ab.*) THE HON. JOHN CUNNINGHAM, ESQ., MEMBER OF ASSEMBLY,—BORN AT KIRKNEWTON, SCOTLAND IN 1738.—HE MARRIED ELIZABETH, RELICT OF ROBERT WESTLAND, — AND DIED IN 1812.—ERECTED BY HIS SONS, JAMES, SAMUEL, AND GEORGE.

M. M.

HE acquired Maxfield Estate, of which he had been the Attorney for the Hodges family.

18.

(*Ab.*) MRS. ELIZABETH CUNNINGHAM,—OB. 1806.

M. M.

19.

(*Ab.*) ELIZABETH ROCHFORT, — OB. 1783, AET. 58. — ERECTED BY HER HUS-
BAND, ROBERT ROCHFORT, M.D.

20.

(*Ab.*) SAMUEL LABERT, ESQ.,—NAT. 1713,—OB. 1786.

HE married Mary Poole, only daughter of Lemon Lawrence Lawrence, and Elizabeth Rachel, his wife, daughter of Jno. Lawrence of Ironshore.

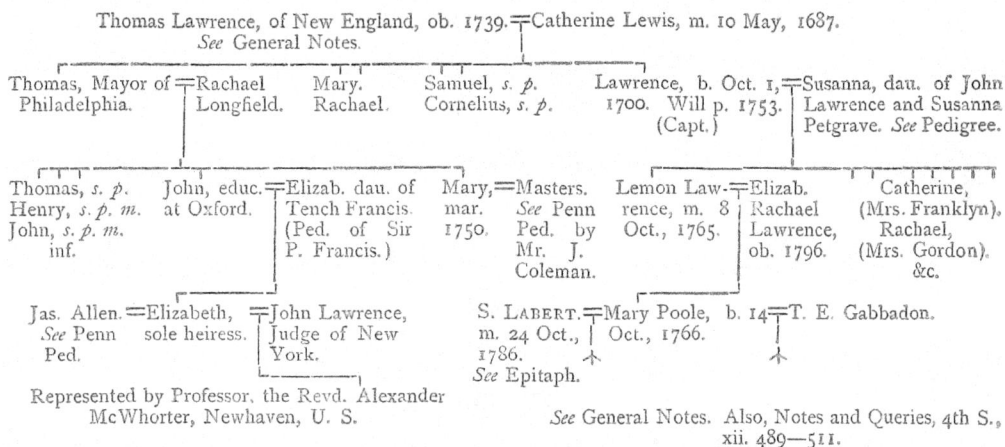

Thomas Lawrence, of New England, ob. 1739.⹀Catherine Lewis, m. 10 May, 1687.
    See General Notes.

Thomas, Mayor of ⹀Rachael	Mary.	Samuel, *s. p.*	Lawrence, b. Oct. 1,⹀Susanna, dau. of John
Philadelphia. Longfield.	Rachael.	Cornelius, *s. p.*	1700. Will p. 1753. Lawrence and Susanna
			(Capt.) Petgrave. *See* Pedigree.

Thomas, *s. p.*	John, educ.⹀Elizab. dau. of	Mary,═Masters.	Lemon Law-⹀Elizab.	Catherine,
Henry, *s. p. m.*	at Oxford. Tench Francis.	mar. *See* Penn	rence, m. 8 Rachael	(Mrs. Franklyn),
John, *s. p. m.*	(Ped. of Sir	1750. Ped. by	Oct., 1765. Lawrence,	Rachael,
inf.	P. Francis.)	Mr. J.	ob. 1796.	(Mrs. Gordon),
		Coleman.		&c.

Jas. Allen.═Elizabeth, ⹀John Lawrence,	S. LABERT.⹀Mary Poole, b. 14⹀T. E. Gabbadon.
See Penn sole heiress. Judge of New	m. 24 Oct., Oct., 1766.
Ped.	York.	1786. ⋏ ⋏
	See Epitaph.

Represented by Professor, the Revd. Alexander
McWhorter, Newhaven, U. S.

See General Notes. Also, Notes and Queries, 4th S.,
xii. 489—511.

21.

TO THE MEMORY OF CHARLES O'CONNOR, ESQ., OF CHARLEMOUNT IN THIS
ISLAND, WHO DIED AT MONTEGO BAY ON 4th MARCH, 1839, IN THE 68th YEAR
OF HIS AGE. — THIS TABLET WAS ERECTED BY HIS FRIENDS IN TESTIMONY OF
HIS MANY VIRTUES AND OF THEIR SENSE OF HIS SERVICES IN THE MANAGE-
MENT OF THEIR ESTATES DURING A PERIOD OF UNPARALLELLED DIFFICULTY.

HE was the son of Philip O'Connor, Lieut. 89th Regt., by his wife, Susanna, daughter of James Lawrence, of Fairfield.

22.

(*Ab.*) CHARLES MORTON,—OB. 1796.

23.

(*Ab.*) ROSA, WIFE OF THE HONBLE. JOHN PALMER,—OB. 1 MAY, 1790, AET. 72.

See *ante.*

24.

(*Ab.*) SAMUEL BERNARD,—OB. 1792.—

25.

(*Ab.*) WILLIAM RENWICK,—OB. 1795.

26.

(*Ab.*) WILLIAM THARP,—OB. 1809, AET. 47.

41—2

27.

(*Ab.*) VALENTINE WARD.....................

THIS is one of the most defaced tombstones in the Churchyard.   Nothing of the inscription remains, but the name.*

28.

(*Ab.*) CAPTAIN HENRY BENNETT, OF THE SHIP "W....LONG,"—OB. 1801.

FOR an account of this family, see *ante.*

29.

SACRED TO THE MEMORY OF JOHN CAMPBELL, ESQ., OF MONTEGO BAY, WHO DIED 21st DEC., 1834, AGED 46. — THIS STONE IS PLACED OVER HIS MORTAL REMAINS, AS A TOKEN OF REGARD, BY HIS RESPECTED FRIEND, PATRICK NEILSON, GLASGOW, 1835.

30.

(*Ab.*) JOHN HAMILTON DALRYMPLE, ESQ., LATE COLLECTOR OF THE CUSTOMS HERE....DIED 7th AUGUST, 1804, IN THE 28th YEAR OF HIS AGE.... HIS DEEPLY AFFLICTED RELATIVES IN SCOTLAND ERECTED THIS MONUMENT OF THEIR GRIEF, 1806.—MULTIS ILLE BONIS FLEBILIS OCCIDIT.

Crest, On a wreath a rock.   *Motto,* "Firm."

N.B.—The short stay of the author in the northern parishes of Jamaica, precluded his copying their monumental inscriptions *in extenso.*

PRIVATE BURIAL GROUNDS.

RUNNING GUT ESTATE.

I.

IN MEMORY OF—BENJAMIN LAWRENCE,† SENR.,—WHO DEPARTED THIS LIFE, —THE 2d DECR. 1776, AGED 72.

HE was the second son of John and Susanna Lawrence, and was Member of Assembly for St. James', in 1735-6.   The male line continues.   A female line is represented by the Walcott and Vredenburg families.

2.

SACRED TO THE MEMORY — OF JAMES LAWRENCE, — WHO DIED, — JULY 2d, 1798, AGED 47.

HE was the younger son of Colonel James Lawrence, by Mary, his wife, daughter of George Brissett.

---

* In the Methodist Chapel, Montego Bay, there is a marble tablet to "the Reverend Valentine Ward, Wesleyan Methodist Minister, who died March 26th, 1835." He was born 4th Jany., 1781.

† In the Will of another (?) Benjamin Lawrence, of Running Gut, (quoted by Roby, as of date 24th Jany., 1784,) the testator desires "that my body be laid on the ground in my garden, and a pillar of stone be built thereon, and on no account my body to be interred in the earth."

SPRING MOUNT ESTATE.

I.

IN MEMORY OF — MRS. SARAH HEATH, — BORN 15th NOVEMBER, 1731, — OBT. 12th OCT., 1818,—AGED 86 YEARS, 11 MONTHS.

2.

(*Ab.*) BENJAMIN HEATH, ESQ., OB. 10th MARCH, 1788, AET. 56. — MULTIS ILLE BONIS FLEBILIS OCCIDIT.

3.

(*Ab.*) RICHARD HEATH, ESQ., DIED 12th JANUARY, 1823, AGED 62 YEARS AND 4 MONTHS ○○○ ○○○○○○ HE WAS THE FOURTH SON OF BENJAMIN HEATH, ESQ. [AND SARAH, HIS WIFE,] PROPRIETOR OF THIS ESTATE. ○○○○○○○○○○

CATHERINE HALL ESTATE.

I.

(*Ab.*) SACRED — TO THE MEMORY OF — JANE STONE,—WHO DEPARTED THIS LIFE,—OCT. 3rd, 1774, AGED 80.—A LADY OF SINCERE PIETY.

EIGHT eulogistic lines follow.

2.

NEAR THIS PLACE—LYES INTERR'D THE BODY OF—COLONEL JONATHAN BARNETT,—AN HONEST, BRAVE,—AND HUMANE MAN,—ON WHOM REST THE—MERCIES OF HIS—CREATOR.—HE DIED IN MARCH, 1744,—AGED 67 YEARS.

IN 1730—March 28—Colonel Jonathan Barnett, Richard Haughton, John Lawrence, Senr., and Hugh Kirkpatrick, Junr., were appointed Commissioners, for a party to be raised in Hanover, to reduce rebellious slaves.

3.

IN MEMORY OF MRS. ANN CURTIS, — DAUGHTER OF COLONEL JONATHAN BARNETT,—DEPARTED THIS LIFE, THE 11th DAY OF FEBRUARY,—IN THE YEAR OF OUR LORD, 1700,—AGED 42 YEARS.—A DUTIFUL CHILD, AN AFFECTIONATE WIFE, —A TENDER MOTHER, & A SINCERE FRIEND.—

ADELPHI ESTATE.

MARIA — INNOCENT—LOVING—BELOVED, — DYED A.D. 1798. — HOW READ'ST THOU ?—DYED ?

(Sixteen verses, the reputed composition of Peter Pindar, follow.)

MARIA was the natural daughter of Isaac Lascelles Winn, of Marley Estate.

PARISH OF TRELAWNEY.

(FORMERLY A PART OF THE PARISH OF ST. JAMES.)

FALMOUTH CHURCH AND CHURCHYARD.

1.

(*Ab.*) CAPTAIN HERMAN B. MORRIS, OF NEW HAMPSHIRE, NORTH AMERICA,—OB. 1795.

M.

NOT improbably a member of the family of Morris, of Keldgate Gate, Yorkshire; the elder branches of which, on the breaking out of the second American war, lost their hereditary property in New England.

The founder of this family in the New World, appears to have been Captain Lewis Morris, a servant of the Providence Island Company, in 1633.

In 1652, when Prince Rupert was threatening the British colonies, the Governor of Barbadoes recommends to the Council of State the appointment to the command of a squadron, to oppose him, "Colonel Lewis Morris, whose personal valour at Scilly was taken notice of."

2.

(*Ab.*) THOMAS REID, M.-GENL. OF MILITIA, OB. 1793 [8 ?].

M.

SEVERAL members of this family held a high position in Jamaica, during the eighteenth century. The name occurs frequently in the pedigrees of the principal families in the northern and western parishes of the island.

3.

(*Ab.*) JAMES, SON OF THOMAS LEAMEY, OB. 1785.

M.

4.

(*Ab.*) THOMAS CHRISTIE, OB. 1798.—SUSANNA CHRISTIE, OB. 1798.

M.

5.

(*Ab.*) NEAR THIS PLACE, LIE INTERRED, THE REMAINS OF JOHN, THE BELOVED SON OF PRESTON AND REBECCA EDGAR, OF THE CITY OF BRISTOL, ENGLAND, WHO DIED, MAY 16th, 1805, AGED 22......

(Verses follow.)

THIS family appears to have been of Scottish origin—probably from Peffermyln, near Edinburgh, of which Alexander Edgar was a subscriber to the Darien scheme. On the failure of the latter several of those emigrants settled in Jamaica. Amongst the refugees were—Colonel Blair, Colonel Dowdell, who had served under William III., at the Boyne, and Colonels Guthrie and Campbell, &c.

See "An Account of the Sirname Edgar."—Hotten, London, 1873.

6.

KOSIUSKO TERRELL, SON OF WILLIAM AND MARY TERRELL, OF THE CITY OF BRISTOL, ENGLAND,—OB. 1821.

M.

OF the origin of this family in the West Indies, little is known. A Nicholas Terril occurs in the list of officers and soldiers engaged in the American Expedition of 1665-6.—(*Cal. S. P.*, Col. S.)

Usher Tyrrell, who had been expelled the Assembly, by Governor Beeston, was re-elected Member for St. James' Parish, in 1700.

7.

(*Ab.*) ALEXANDER MC CARTHY, ESQ.,—AN OFFICER IN THE .... REGIMENT,— OB. 1820.

M.

8.

SACRED TO THE MEMORY OF JOHN HODGES, ESQ., WHO DEPARTED THIS LIFE, THE 27th OF FEB., 1787, AGED 53 YEARS.

M.

THE name of Hodges is frequently met with in the earlier history of our West India colonies.

In 1690, Anthony Hodges was Lieutenant-Governor of Montserrat; and about the same period, there was an Anthony Hodges, Judge of the Admiralty Court. The name is found also in connection with warlike expeditions from the Island of Nevis.

The Hodges' of Jamaica, appear to have descended from Francis Hodges, Secretary of Nova Scotia, who became Treasurer of the former island in the time of Charles II., where he may have acquired estates named Acadia, and Luana, in the parish of St. Elizabeth. This gentleman was probably related to the Rev. Dr. Hodges, Chaplain to the House of Lords, at the Restoration.

A writer in "Notes and Queries," seems to be of opinion, that the family in question sprang from Sir Nathaniel Hodges, of Middlesex.

Of the same family was, probably, Sir W. Hodges, created a Baronet in 1697, but his line became extinct on the death of Sir Joseph Hodges, in 1722.

Nathaniel Hodges, an eminent physician, and son of Dr. Thomas Hodges, Dean of Hereford, distinguished himself in his professional capacity, during the Great Plague of London. He was author of a work intitled "Loimologia;" but getting into difficulties, he died in Ludgate prison, in 1684.

The will of Joseph Hodges (1718, I. S. Off. Jamaica), of St. Elizabeth, tends to throw some light on this subject. He mentions his sons Nathaniel and Joseph, and his daughter Bonella—so named after her mother. The subsequent letters of administration of Andreise Joseph Hodges, brother of Nathaniel Hodges, show that he was then lately of Eaton, in Berks., of the Inner Temple, and of Lacovia plantation, Jamaica. In this document (entered Sept. 22, 1733) is mentioned, among other relatives, his cousin John Hodges, progenitor of Hodges of Maxfield, Member of Assembly in 1795.*

There are many other wills of Hodges' and Blakes, bearing on the family connections, which are interesting in a genealogical point of view; while the "Renunciation" of John Hodges, of Maxfield (whose first wife was Anne Blake), of his executorship, under the will of Richard Haughton James (1781), grandson of Samuel Williams Haughton, by his wife, Margaret Bonella, daughter of William and Elizabeth Blake, still further elucidates a connection of which present limits forbid a lengthier discussion. This John Hodges was a cousin of Bonella Hodges, who married the father of the first Lord Penrhyn; his father, Captain John Hodges, having been the son of Thomas Hodges, uncle of Joseph the father of Bonella.

See General Notes. Also, M. I. of Lt.-Col. B. Andreiss, of Lacovia, ob. 1710.

9.

TO THE MEMORY OF THE SEVEN BELOVED CHILDREN AND ONE GRANDCHILD OF THE REVD. WM. FRASER, A.M., RECTOR OF THIS PARISH, AND ELIZABETH LUCY, HIS WIFE. THIS WAS ERECTED BY HIM IN THE EIGHTIETH YEAR OF HIS AGE, 1843.

THE Rev. William Fraser, Rector of Trelawney, second son of Francis Fraser, Esquire of Findrack, co. Aberdeen, was born at Findrack, Dec. 22d, 1763, and died at Falmouth, Jamaica, April 1st, 1844. He was educated at Aberdeen, and subsequently at Oxford. He married Elizabeth Lucy, daughter of .... James, of Jamaica. (*See* Notice of the family of James.)

The family of Findrack show a descent from Sir Alexr. Fraser of Durris, Lord High Chamberlain of Scotland, in the reign of King Robert the Bruce. The Revd. W. Fraser's mother was, Henrietta, daughter of William Baird of Auchmedden, Chief of that name, and great grand-daughter of Lady Katherine Hay, daughter of George, 2d Earl of Kinnoull, through whom the family of Findrack represents the heirs of line of George, 1st Earl of Kinnoull, and as such, the *dormant* Viscounty of Dupplin, of date 4th May, 1627. (*See* Burke's "Peerage," *voce* Kinnoull: "Landed Gentry *v.* Fraser;" and "An Account of the Family of Baird"—Edinb. 1856.)

---

* His son and heir, Robert Francklin Hodges, married a daughter of Chief Justice John Lewis. There was a connection also with the Barretts and Moultons. C. J. John Lewis was a relative of M. G. Lewis.

10.

(*Ab*). NICHOLAS SMITH, OB. 1831.

M.

Arms, On a saltire, between 3
crescents, and a camel's head in base, an escallop—the whole within a border. *Crest*, A padlock (Q. escallop?)
between a sword and a pen in saltire.

11.

(*Ab.*) JOHN MARNOCH,—OB. 1815.

M.

12.

(*Ab.*) JOAN GIBBES,—OB. 1817.

M.

13.

(*Ab.*) SAMUEL EARNSHAW,—OB. 1824.

M.

14.

(*Ab.*) THE HON. JAMES STEWART,—OB., 1828,—AET. 66.

M.

THE Hon. James Stewart, Esq., a Justice of the Bench,
Jamaica, a reputed descendant of a Stewart of Appin,
married a lady named Law, by whom he had issue, two sons:
Robert, the younger, and James Law Stewart, (viv. in 1869,
æt. 86,) who married Anne Williamina Brisset, by whom he
had—1. James, of Shaw Park, late Lieut. in the Army, who
married Dorcas, daughter of .... Norcott, 4th D. Guards;
2. Alexander; and three daughters, viz.,—Emma, married
1st, H. Spooner, and 2nd, Col. Eyre; Margaret Ann, married
Revd. T. Niblet; Josephine, married R. Ewell.

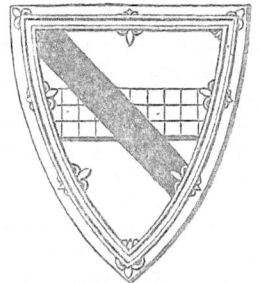

Arms, Or, within a border flory
counter flory, a fess checquy, az.
and arg. surmounted of a bend
sable. *Crest*, A pelican feeding
her young.

15.

(*Ab.*) MISS MARY ATKINS,—OB. 1813.

M.

16.

(*Ab.*) JAMES HOLMES,—OB. 1816.

M.

17.

(*Ab.*) ROBERT HOLMES,—BORN AT GREENOCK, 1744, OB. 1807.

REGINALD sixth son of Christopher Wilson, Esq., of Broomhead, Yorkshire, was with his only son, swallowed up in the earthquake of 1692, at Port Royal, Jamaica.

Anne, sister of Reginald, was married to Robert Holmes, of Alfreton, but it is not quite clear that these families were identical.

18.

(*Ab.*) JAMES LYON, ESQ., OB. 1807, AET. 47.

19.

(*Ab.*) MISS MARY LAMONT, DAUGHTER OF FREDERICK AND JANE LAMONT, OB. 1801.

SHE was aunt, by marriage, of the mother of the late William Dauney, Esq., Adv. and Solicitor General of British Guiana, an accomplished musician, and author of a work on Ancient Scottish Music, &c.

20.

(*Ab.*) LIEUTENANT WILLIAM WARBURTON, 60th REGIMENT, OB. 1801, AET. 45.

21.

(*Ab.*) WILLIAM BELLFLOWER,—OB. 1801.

22.

(*Ab.*) HENRIETTA PIDGEON,—NAT. 1784,—OB. 1843.

23.

(*Ab.*) WILLIAM BROWN,—OB. 1798.

24.

TO THE MEMORY OF JAMES BLAKE.—ERECTED BY HIS WIDOW.—BORN, MARCH 4th, 1753,—AGED 48 YEARS.

(For a notice of this family, see *ante*.)

OF this family was Anne Blake, who married John Hodges of Maxfield, and her sisters, Sarah (Mrs. Francklin, ob. 1815), and Martha (Mrs. Bennett).

25.

(*Ab.*) JAMES GALLOWAY,—OB. 1833, AET. 75.—A RESIDENT FOR FIFTY-SIX YEARS IN JAMAICA.

M. M.

Arms, A lion rampant, ducally crowned. Impaling, Quarterly, 1 and 4, A cross crosslet ; 2 and 3, Three battle-axes, or hatchets, in pale. *Crest,* A grenade. *Motto,* " Altior."

26.

(*Ab.*) JANE MC CONNELL, DAUGHTER OF DAVID & ANNE MC CONNELL, — OB. 1798.

27.

(*Ab.*) MARY ANN BROWN,—OB. 1819, — WIFE OF DANIEL BROWN. — ERECTED BY AN UNKNOWN FRIEND.

M. M.

28.

(*Ab.*) MARY ELIZABETH, WIFE OF WILLIAM CAMPBELL, MERCHANT, — OB. 1802.—

M.

29.

...... WALTER .... OB. 1798.

Fragment – oblit.

30.

(*Ab.*) JAMES TELFER, SON OF PATRICK AND ANNE TELFER,—OB. 1788.

31.

(*Ab.*) JAMES GAYNER, — OB. 1796, AET. 37.

32.

(*Ab.*) THOMAS WHITESIDE,—OB. 1850.—

33.

(*Ab.*) ROBERT CHRISTIE,—OB. 1847.

?4.

(*Ab.*) JOSEPH HODGSON,—OB. 1843.—

35.

(*Ab*). ROBERT ELLISON, LIEUTENANT 60th RIFLES,—OB. 1843.

36.

(*Ab.*) MISS GRACE THARP, DAUGHTER OF CAPTAIN JOHN THARP, MARINER, AND MARGARET THARP, HIS WIFE, OB. 1796.

THE family of Tharp, or Tharpe, was of considerable local distinction. (*See* Burke's " Landed Gentry.")

William Tharpe, of Tap River Estate, (eldest son of Joseph Tharpe, of Bachelor Hall, first settler of the name, in Jamaica,) married Ann, daughter of Jonathan Haughton (from Barbados), by his second wife, Mary Dehany. Mary, the elder sister of Ann Haughton, married John Brissett, of Hampshire estate, also the first settler of his family in Jamaica.

37.

(*Ab.*) JOHN THARP CHAMBERS, SON OF EDWARD CHAMBERS, ESQ,—OB. 1795.

42—2

38.

(*Ab.*) THE REVEREND GRIFFITH GRIFFITHS, RECTOR OF TRELAWNEY, — OB.
1845.

M.

39.

(*Ab.*) DR. WILLIAM ELLIS, OF FENCHURCH STREET, LONDON,—OB. 1802.

IT does not appear whether Dr. Ellis was of the old Jamaica family, said by Roby,
and others, to have been originally from Denbighshire, and which was founded by
Captain John Ellis, an officer in the expedition under Venables, in 1655, and who was
ancestor of the present Lord Howard de Walden, and Seaford.

There was also a Colonel Gershom, Gerthon, or Gershon Ely, or Elys. He represented the parishes of St. Mary, St. James, St. Thomas in the Vale, and St. Ann (in which
latter he died, in 1738) from 1711 to 1737. He seems to have possessed much local
influence, and it is recorded that, at his marriage with Mary Willis [10 June, 1712],
"his Excellency my Lord Archibald Hamilton," was present.

These names, Ellis and Elys, may possibly have been one and the same family,
hence the introduction of this note.

40.

(*Ab.*) JOHN JAMES LEAMY, OB. APRIL 2, 1783,—AND, MARY JAMES LEAMY,—
OB. FEBRUARY 19, 1784,—THE CHILDREN OF JOHN HODGES, BY HIS WIFE, MARY
ANNE.

(The inscription concludes with grotesque rhymes.)

THE above were the grandchildren of John Hodges, of Maxfield (see *ante*), and
appear to have been named after the family of Houghton *James*.

PRIVATE BURIAL GROUNDS.

MAXFIELD ESTATE.

I.

IN MEMORY OF — JOHN SPENCE, — BORN AT YARM. (*sic*) YORKSHIRE, — LATE
COMMANDER OF THE "TABETH VIGILANT," MERCHANTMAN, FROM — LONDON TO
MARTHA BRAE ;—OBT. 3rd JANUARY, 1785, Æ. 31.—HIS ISSUE BY THE DAUGHTER
OF—JOHN HODGES, ESQUIRE, OF THIS ISLAND,—WERE, MARTHA,—WHO DIED IN
LONDON, AN INFANT.—ELIZABETH ANN, WHO LIETH HERE,—OBT. 25th FEBRUARY,
1788, Æ. 3 YEARS.—AN AFFECTIONATE BROTHER PLACETH—THIS TESTIMONY OF
RESPECT.

THE daughter of John Hodges, was probably the widow of a Mr. Bennett, when she
married John Spence, as the latter name does not occur in the will of John
Hodges of Maxfield, or in that of his son of the same name.

2.

[ANNE BLAKE, 1st WIFE OF JOHN HODGES, OF MAXFIELD (OB. 1787), WAS BURIED AT MAXFIELD. But, in the absence of a copy of her epitaph, the author places this note upon record.]

ROSLIN CASTLE ESTATE.

1.

(*Ab.*) ROBERT MINTO,—OB. MAY 3rd, 1803,—AET. 63. — AND,—ROBERT MINTO, HIS GRANDSON'S ELDEST BORN, CHILD OF—HIS SON WALTER MINTO AND—MARY, HIS WIFE,—OB. AUGT. 24th, 1814,—AGED 4 YEARS, 8 MONTHS, & 11 DAYS.

2.

(*Ab.*) WALTER MINTO,—OB. 18th DECEMBER, 1830,—AET. 51. . . . .

3.

(*Ab.*) MRS. MARY VIRGO, RELICT OF THE LATE COLL. WILLIAM VIRGO, OB. 21 NOVEMBER, 1787,—AET. 67.-

GOLDEN GROVE ESTATE.

1.

TO THE MEMORY OF THE DECEASED WIFE OF REBECCA REID, WIFE OF COL. THOMAS REID, WHO DEPARTED THIS LIFE, ON THE 11th DAY OF APRIL, 1747, AGED 24 YEARS.

SHE was daughter of Col. R. Houghton, by his second wife, Elizabeth, daughter of Geo. Goodin. Mary, younger daughter of Colonel Richard Haughton, by his wife, Elizabeth Goodin,* married (29th March, 1743) Colonel John Reid, elder brother of the above.

Of the same family was Maj.-Genl. Peter Reid, who married Elizabeth Barrett relict of Ezekiel Lawrence, of "The Spring" Estate. [*Lawrence* Pedigree.] Also, Maj.-Genl. Thomas Reid, who married Elizabeth, daughter of James Lawrence, of Fairfield.

---

* Goodin, erroneously spelled *Goodwin* and *Godwin*, in the pedigrees of *Ricketts*, *Lawrence*, &c. (See Burke's "Landed Gentry," &c.) The two surnames are quite distinct.

PARISH OF HANOVER.

ST. LUCEA CHURCH AND CHURCHYARD.

I.

IN THIS CHURCH IS DEPOSITED THE MORTAL PART—OF SIR SIMON CLARKE BART.,—WHO WAS BORN IN THIS ISLAND, — A.D. 1727, AND DIED ON THE 2d OF NOVEMBER,—1777,—HAVING THAT DAY COMPLETED—HIS 50th YEAR.

M. M.—Sculptured by Flaxman.

(The remainder of the inscription is a general character of the deceased.)

SIR SIMON was 7th Baronet ; he married Anne Haughton.* He was the eldest of six children of Sir Simon, 6th Baronet, by his wife Mary, daughter of Philip Bonny, of Jamaica.

Philip Clarke, a younger son of the 3rd Baronet of that name and family, held the office of Patent Clerk of the Crown, in Jamaica, in 1722.

The 5th Bart. was an officer in the Navy, in 1730, but was transported to Jamaica, for a highway robbery committed by him and another man, near Winchester, and died in the former island, without issue, in 1736, whereupon the eldest son of Philip, Clerk of the Crown, above mentioned, succeeded to the Baronetcy.

2.

HERE LIES THE BODY OF WINSTON ELIZA ROSE, THE DAUGHTER OF THE REVD. D. W. ROSE, BY ANN, HIS WIFE, BORN 13 NOV., 1802 ; AND DIED 25th AUGUST, 1806.

HERE LIES A ROSE, A BUDDING ROSE,
  BLASTED BEFORE ITS BLOOM :
WHOSE INNOCENCE DID SWEETS DISCLOSE
  BEYOND THAT FLOWER'S PERFUME.
TO THOSE WHO FOR HER LOSS ARE GRIEV'D,
  THIS CONSOLATION'S GIVEN :
SHE'S FROM A WORLD OF WOE RELIEV'D,
  AND BLOOMS A ROSE IN HEAVEN.

* By his wife, Anne Haughton, who died in 1800, he left two sons, Philip Haughton, and Simon Haughton, and one daughter, Catharine Haughton, born 1773, married 20th May, 1801, Lieut.-General the Honble. William Fitzroy, brother of George, 2nd Lord Southampton, and died 6th May, 1808, having had issue five sons. Her husband re-married, 4th July, 1811, Elizabeth, daughter of Augustus-Henry Fitzroy, 3rd Duke of Grafton, K.G., first Lord of the Treasury, Junius's Duke.

3.

THE REVD. DANIEL WARNER ROSE, SON OF JNO. ROSE, PROVOST MARSHAL GENL. OF ANTIGUA, WAS EDUCATED AT CHARTER HO., LONDON, & JESUS COLL., CAMB.

THE preceding epitaph is inserted in Webb's Collection, as " on Miss Rose, niece to Hugh Rose, of Kilravach, in Ireland (*sic*)."

N.B.—THERE are many more inscriptions in this Church and Churchyard, which have not been obtainable.

PRIVATE BURIAL GROUNDS.

ORANGE BAY ESTATE.

1.

HERE LYETH INTER'D THE BODY OF COLOL. JAMES CAMPBELL, WHO DEPARTED THIS LIFE THE 13th OF JULY, 1744, AGED 47 YEARS.

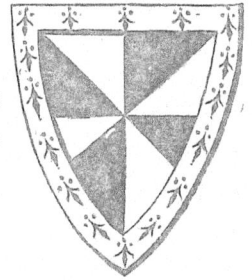

Arms, Gyrony of eight, a bordure ermine. *Crest*, A dexter hand holding a spur.

2.

IN MEMORY OF—CAPT. JOHN CAMPBELL,—WHO DEPARTED THIS LIFE—JULY THE 29th, 1766, IN THE 66th YEAR OF HIS AGE.

Arms, As the preceding. *Motto*, " Forget Not."

3.

(*Ab*.) TO THE MEMORY OF — JOHN CAMPBELL, OF ORANGE BAY, ESQUIRE,—FORMERLY CUSTOS ROTULORUM—OF THE PARISH OF HANOVER IN THE COUNTY OF CORNWALL,—WHO DIED THE 16th OF MAY, 1808, AGED 76 YEARS.

Arms, As the preceding.

(A record of his virtues follows.)

THIS monument was erected by his dutiful and affectionate nephew, John Blagrove, Esq.

SALT SPRING ESTATE.

I.

(*Ab.*) TO THE MEMORY OF JOHN CAMPBELL, ESQ., OF SALT SPRING, WHO, IN HIS PASSAGE TO ENGLAND, FOR THE RECOVERY OF HIS HEALTH, WAS TAKEN BY AN AMERICAN PRIVATEER, AND CARRIED INTO NEW LONDON, WHERE HE DIED ON THE 2d OF NOVEMBER, 1782, IN THE 53rd YEAR OF HIS AGE.

HE FOR MANY YEARS REPRESENTED THE PARISH OF HANOVER IN THE ASSEMBLY OF THIS HIS NATIVE ISLAND, HAD BEEN LONG, AND WAS AT THE TIME OF HIS DEATH, CUSTOS OF THAT PARISH. THE DUTIES OF THESE STATIONS HE DISCHARGED WITH DISTINGUISHED APPLICATION, ABILITY, AND PATRIOTISM. . . . .

THIS MONUMENT WAS ERECTED BY ORDER OF HIS BROTHER-IN-LAW, DUNCAN CAMPBELL, ESQ., OF LONDON, AS A LASTING MARK OF THE FRIENDSHIP AND AFFECTION WHICH FROM EARLY YOUTH EVER SUBSISTED BETWEEN THEM.

THIS John Campbell was Member for Hanover, 1755, 1761, 1768, 1770, and 1773.

A John Campbell "of Spotfield," represented Trelawny, 1779. A John Campbell "of Hope," was Member of Council, 1785.

HAUGHTON COURT—PREVIOUSLY "UNITY" ESTATE.

I.

HERE LIES THE BODY OF THE HONBLE. COLONEL RICHARD HAUGHTON, WHO DEPARTED THIS LIFE THE 15th JANUARY, 1740, AGED 49.

HE was the eldest son of Jonathan Houghton (from Barbados), by his second wife, Mary Dehany, of Vere Parish. He was Custos Rotulorum of Hanover, a Colonel of Militia, and Member of Assembly for the former parish, in 1726.

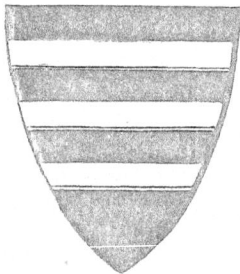

Arms, ...3 bars...... *Crest,* A bull passant.

2.

HERE LIETH THE BODY OF — JONATHAN HAUGHTON. — HE WAS BORN—17th DECEMBER, 1694,—AND DIED—18th FEBRUARY, 1767,—AGED 72 YEARS 2 MONTHS AND 2 DAYS.

TWO brothers, Jonathan and Valentine Haughton, with their wives and families, came from Barbadoes, and settled on the north coast of Jamaica, in 1670. Jonathan, who was thrice married, had by his second wife, Mary Dehany, or Dehaney of Vere, three sons and two daughters, who intermarried with the families of Brissett and Tharpe, &c.

The ramifications of this family were very extensive ; *vide*—Blake, Hodges, Terrick (Bishop of London), Reid (Sir Simon), Taylor, Malcolm of Poltolloch, Ricketts, Guthrie, and other families.

3.

HERE LIETH THE BODY OF JOHANNA, WIFE OF JONATHAN HAUGHTON, WHO DEPARTED YS LIFE THE 2d OF SEPTEMBER, 1733, IN THE 31st YEAR OF HER AGE.

4.

(*Ab.*) THE REMAINS OF LYDIA HAUGHTON, BORN THE SECOND DAY OF MAY, 1710. MARRIED JONATHAN HAUGHTON, ESQR., THE NINTEENTH DAY OF JUNE' 1734. AND LEAVING TWO SONS AND TWO DAUGHTERS RESIGNED HER LIFE ON THE TENTH DAY OF SEPTEMBER, 1755.

EULOGISTIC lines follow.

5.

ROBERT HAUGHTON, NAT. 29 AUGT., 1733, OB. 25 JUNE, 1766; RICHARD HAUGHTON, NAT. 2 JULY, 1747, OB. 14 JANY., 1779; RACHEL HAUGHTON, NAT. 22 DEC. 1739, OB. 23 FEB., 1778 ; LYDIA HAUGHTON, NAT. 3d FEB., 1745, OB. 19 JULY, 1746.

THE above were the offspring of Jonathan and Lydia Haughton.

6.

(*Ab.*) HERE LIES ALL THAT IS MORTAL OF MR. JONATHAN HAUGHTON JUNR., WHO WAS KILLED BY A FALL FROM HIS HORSE, ON THE 24th OF JUNE, 1753, IN THE 26th YEAR OF HIS AGE.

SISTE VIATOR.

TO THIS SAD TOMB, WHOE'ER THOU ART, DRAW NEAR, ETC.

JONATHAN HAUGHTON, second son of Jonathan, the first settler in Jamaica, married, firstly, Johanna Violet, by whom he had an only son Jonathan, who was killed by a fall from his horse, and five daughters ; the eldest, Mary, married Dr. Wood, of Hanover ; the second, Sarah, married Colonel Edward Chambers, of Prosper Estate in the said parish ; the third and fourth, Frances and Elizabeth, died unmarried ; and the youngest, Rebecca, married John Waller, nephew of John Terrick, Bishop of London.

Jonathan Haughton married secondly, Lydia, daughter of Robert Bowen, of Westmoreland, by whom he had two sons : Robert, who married, 2nd June, 1763, Sarah Garbrand Barrett, and died 25th June, 1766 ; Richard, who died unmarried, 14th January, 1779 ; and three daughters : Elizabeth, who married John Patterson, M.D., but had no issue ; Rachel, who died unmarried, and Lydia, who died an infant.

7.

HERE LIETH THE BODY OF REBEKAH, WIFE OF COL. RICHARD HAUGHTON, WHO DEPARTED THIS LIFE JANUARY 27th, 1722, AGED 26 YEARS.

SHE was a daughter of Thomas James.

8.

HERE LIETH THE BODY OF ELIZABETH, SECOND WIFE OF COL. RICHARD HAUGHTON, WHO DEPARTED THIS LIFE, DECEMBER 25th, 1734, AGED 34 YEARS.

HE was the eldest son of Jonathan Haughton, and she the daughter of George Goodin.

9.

JOHN HAUGHTON JAMES,—ESQUIRE,—PROPRIETOR OF BURNT GROUND PEN, AND HAUGHTON HALL ESTATE,—AGED 72 YEARS,—NAT. 23 SEPT., 1763, OB. 29 JUNII, 1835.

FAT HOG QUARTER ESTATE.

1.

HERE LIETH THE BODY OF PHILIP HAUGHTON, ESQUIRE, WHO DEPARTED THIS LIFE ON THE 22d OF FEBRUARY, 1765, AGED 64 YEARS, 2 MONTHS, AND 10 DAYS.

PHILIP HAUGHTON of Fat-Hog-Quarter Estate in Hanover. third son of Jonathan the first of the Jamaica Haughtons, married Catherine, daughter of Joseph Tharpe, of Bachelors'-Hall, by whom he had issue, three sons : two Philips and a Jonathan, who died infants ; and five daughters, three of whom, two Sarahs and a Catharine, died young, and two, Mary and Ann, who survived him and became his coheirs.

2.

BENEATH THIS MARBLE ARE DEPOSITED THE REMAINS OF MRS. CATHERINE HAUGHTON, WIFE OF PHILIP HAUGHTON, ESQ. DURING A SPACE OF NEAR 40 YEARS, SHE PERFORMED WITH CREDIT THE DUTIES OF AN AFFECTIONATE WIFE, AND A GOOD MOTHER, AND ON THE 7th DAY OF MAY, 1775, IN THE 60th YEAR OF HER AGE, SHE YIELDED TO THAT FATE TO WHICH ALL MORTALS MUST ONE DAY SUBMIT.

3.

THIS IS THE EARLY TOMB OF MISS SARAH HAUGHTON, FIFTH DAUGHTER OF PHILIP AND CATHERINE HAUGHTON, WHO QUITTED THIS WORLD ON THE 10th DAY OF NOVEMBER, 1766, AGED 19 YEARS.

(Eulogistic lines follow.)

ALSO TO THE MEMORY OF HER BROTHERS AND SISTERS—PHILIP HAUGHTON, OB. 9th MARCH, 1745, ÆT. 8 YEARS ; PHILIP HAUGHTON, OB. 20th FEB. 1755, ÆT. 5 YEARS ; JONATHAN HAUGHTON, OB. 30th APRIL, 1746, ÆT. 24 DAYS ; SARAH HAUGHTON, OB. 11 MARCH, 1745, ÆT. 10 YEARS ; CATHERINE HAUGHTON, OB. 20 AUGT., 1756, ÆT. 16 YEARS.

POINT ESTATE.

I.

TO THE MEMORY OF MR. DAVID DEHANY, WHO DEPARTED THIS LIFE THE 11th DAY OF MARCH, IN THE YEAR OF OUR LORD, 1701, AND 46th YEAR OF HIS AGE.

2.

TO THE MEMORY OF MR. PHILIP DEHANY, WHO DEPARTED THIS LIFE THE FIRST DAY OF MAY, ANNO DOMINI, 1711, AGED 22 YEARS.

3.

TO THE MEMORY OF MRS. MARY DEHANY, WHO RESIGNED HERSELF TO DEATH, THE 15th DAY OF DECEMBER, 1722, AND IN THE 51st YEAR OF HER AGE.

4.

IN REMEMBRANCE OF SARAH DEHANY, WHOM IT PLEASED GOD TO TAKE UNTO HIMSELF THE 23d DAY OF AUGUST, 1729, AND IN THE FIRST YEAR OF HER AGE.

5.

(*Ab.*) HERE LIETH THE BODY OF DAVID DEHANY, ESQ., OF THIS PARISH WHO AFTER A WELL SPENT LIFE OF 53 YEARS AND 24 DAYS, CHANGED IT FOR A BETTER, MAY 23d, 1754. . . . .

6.

DAVID DEHANY, ESQ., BORN 20th APRIL, 1724. DIED 22d JUNE, 1761.—MARY, WIFE OF DAVID DEHANY, ESQ., BORN 22d JANUARY, 1702. DIED 14th JULY, 1761.

7.

HERE LIETH THE BODY OF GEORGE DEHANY, ESQ., SON OF DAVID* AND MARY DEHANY. HE MARRIED MARY, DAUGHTER OF MATTHEW GREGORY, ESQ., OF WHOM HE LEFT THREE DAUGHTERS, LUCRETIA-MARY, FAVELL, AND ELIZABETH, AND ONE SON, GEORGE, AND DEPARTED THIS LIFE APRIL 1st, 1767, AGED 46 YEARS AND 3 MONTHS.

TRINITY CHAPEL, GREEN ISLAND.

(*Ab.*) TO THE MEMORY OF HUGH MUNRO, ESQ., WHO DEPARTED THIS LIFE THE 23d DAY OF APRIL, 1829, IN HIS 79th YEAR. — DURING A PERIOD OF 45 YEARS RESIDENCE IN THIS ISLAND HE MAINTAINED THE CHARACTER OF AN HONEST MAN. — ERECTED AS A TESTIMONIAL OF ESTEEM AND GRATITUDE BY ONE WHO HAS TO LAMENT THE LOSS OF THE BEST OF UNCLES.

---

* According to the Kingston B. Reg., he was buried in a garden in that town. "It is said that the Dehanys *claim* descent from the Dehennins Counts de Bossu."—*Roby.* Such a claim was to have been expected.

PARISH OF WESTMORELAND.

CROSS PATH.

1.

SACRED TO THE MEMORY OF THE HONOURABLE JOHN GUTHRIE — CUSTOS ROTULORUM AND COLONEL OF THE MILITIA OF THIS PARISH,—WHO BY HIS COURAGE, CONDUCT, AND PERSEVERANCE EFFECTED THE REDUCTION OF THE REBELL NEGROES THAT FOR MANY YEARS MISERABLY HARRASS'D THIS ISLAND, AND AGAINST WHOM ALL FORMER ATTEMPTS HAD BEEN MADE IN VAIN.

THEREFORE LET HIS MEMORY BE DEAR, AND HIS REMAINS SACRED TO POSTERITY. LET NONE WITH IMPIOUS HANDS DISTURB HIM DEAD, TO WHOM THE LIVING OWE THEIR QUIET, PEACE, AND SAFETY. HE DIED THE 13th DAY OF JUNE, IN THE YEAR OF OUR LORD 1739, IN THE 52d YEAR OF HIS AGE.

Arms, Quarterly, 1 and 4, Or, a lion rampant reguardant gules; 2 and 3, Azure, three garbs or.

(Eight eulogistic lines in verse follow.)
Altar Tomb.

COLONEL JOHN GUTHRIE married Mary, daughter of George Williams, of Spanish Town, and of Old Hope, Westmoreland. On the 16th April, 1740, the Assembly, on petition, granted her a pension of £100 per annum, for her life, in consideration of the services of her late husband, who lost his life in an expedition against the Windward rebels, and because the sum of £1500 granted to him for his services against the Leward rebels (Trelawny Town Maroons), not having been paid, had become the property of his creditors.—*Journals*, vol. 3, p. 513.

She married, secondly, 15th November, 1741, Robert Delap, Member for Westmoreland, 1745-6, and Provost-Marshal, 1750. He died 11th November, 1751. She was a third time married.

2.

HERE LIETH THE BODY OF JAMES GUTHRIE, WHO DEPARTED THIS LIFE THE 10th DAY OF JULY, 1728.

SAVANNA LA MAR.

I.

(*Ab.*) IN MEMORY OF THE HONOURABLE GEORGE MURRAY, WHO DEPARTED THIS LIFE, ON THE 14th DAY OF APRIL, 1804, AGED 75 YEARS, FIFTY-SIX OF WHICH HE RESIDED IN THIS ISLAND......HE WAS UPWARDS OF TWENTY YEARS ASSISTANT JUDGE OF THE SUPREME COURT OF JUDICATURE........

Arms, Azure, 3 mullets arg. *Crest*, A cubit arm, surmounted by a star of 8 points. [N.B. On his book-plates he bore—Azure a chev. between 3 mullets arg. within a tressure flory counter flory, or.]

HE married 5th April, 1775, Catherine Gordon, spinster, of St. James' Parish.

DEAN'S VALLEY—DRYWORKS ESTATE.

I.

.... LIETH INTERR'D THE BODY........WILLIAMS, LATE OF THE PARISH OF WESTMORELAND, ESQ.,......OF THE REDGIMENT OF YE M......AND CUSTOS ROTULORUM. A PERSON DESERVING SUCH HONOURS FROM THE GOVERNMENT, FOR AFFECTION TO HIS COUNTRY AND BENEVOLENCE TO THE POOR, ESPECIALLY THOSE WHO SUFFERED IN THE LATE DREADFUL HURRICANE WHICH......ON YE 28th OF AUGUST, 1722, GREAT NUMBER OF WHOM HE SUPPORTED IN THEIR NE-CESSITIES.—HE DEPARTED THIS LIFE NOVEMBER YE 19th, 1723, AGED 35 YEARS.

HERE ALSO LYETH THE BODY OF WILLIAM WILLIAMS, SON OF THE AFORE-SAID COLL. WILLIAM WILLIAMS, WHO DEPARTED THIS LIFE OCTO. YE 23d, 1719, AGED ALMOST FIVE YEARS.

2.

HERE LIETH THE BODY OF—MRS. JANE LEWIS,—LATE THE WIFE OF THE HONOURABLE WILLIAM LEWIS, ESQ., AND ELDEST DAUGHTER OF MATTHEW GREGORY, ESQ.,—WHO DEPARTED THIS LIFE—ON THE 19th DAY OF FEBRUARY, 1765,—AGED 39 YEARS AND 10 MONTHS. — SHE WAS MARRIED 22 YEARS AND 5 DAYS......(Eulogies follow.)

WILLIAM LEWIS,—WHO DIED THE 27th OF APRIL, 1774, — AGED 53 YEARS.— HIS REMAINS WERE BROUGHT FROM ENGLAND—ACCORDING TO HIS OWN REQUEST —AND DEPOSITED IN THIS PLACE — NEAR THOSE OF HIS — AFFECTIONATE AND BELOVED WIFE.

M. G. LEWIS, grandson of the above, thus refers to another member of his family: " Breakfasted with the Chief Justice, who is my relative, an l of my own name." *W. I. Journal*, 4th Feb., 1816.

HARMONY HALL.

1.

TO THE MEMORY OF THE HONOURABLE JOHN LEWIS, WHO DEPARTED THIS LIFE, ON THE 17th SEPTEMBER, 1820, IN THE 71st YEAR OF HIS AGE. HE WAS FOR MANY YEARS, A REPRESENTATIVE IN THE HOUSE OF ASSEMBLY, AND CUSTOS ROTULORUM OF THE PARISH OF WESTMORELAND, — CHIEF JUSTICE OF THIS ISLAND, AND PRESIDENT OF HIS MAJESTY'S COUNCIL.

THE above was the relative of M. G. Lewis.—N.B. It was *this* C. J. Lewis, and not C. J. *Hugh* Lewis, whose daughter married into the family of Hodges, as erroneously stated elsewhere.

2.

TO THE MEMORY OF MRS. MARY LEWIS, WHO DEPARTED THIS LIFE, NOVEMBER 18th, 1813, AGED 61 YEARS: — A TENDER MOTHER, AN AFFECTIONATE WIFE, AND FAITHFUL FRIEND, BELOVED AND LAMENTED. — THIS MONUMENT IS ERECTED AS A TRIBUTE OF AFFECTION, BY HER DUTIFUL CHILD, ANNE KATHERINE HODGES.

THE above had a son, John Goodin Lewis, attorney-at-law. — At the beginning of the eighteenth century there seem to have been two distinct families of the name of Lewis.* The more distinguished, was that settled in the parish of Westmoreland, whereof was John Lewis, Member of Assembly for St. Elizabeth, in 1702; Odoardo Lewis, Member of Assembly for the parishes of Westmoreland and St. Elizabeth, 1702-7; and an Andreiss Lewis, named probably after Colonel B. Andreiss, of Lacovia, who was buried 28th Oct., 1733, and was succeeded by his son Odoardo Lewis, bapt. in 1732.

We next find William Lewis, who, by his wife, Jane, daughter of Dr. Matthew Gregory, had one son and four daughters.†

Matthew Lewis, the son, became Under Secretary of State for War, and married a daughter of Sir T. Sewell, Knt., Master of the Rolls, &c., by whom he had two sons and two daughters:—1. William, who died young; 2. Matthew Gregory Lewis, who succeeded to the family estates, and was better known as the author of " The Monk." Dying unmarried, "Monk" Lewis bequeathed his estate of *Cornwall* to his elder sister, Frances Maria, wife of Sir Henry Lushington, 2d Bart., and a moiety of *Hordley* to his younger sister.

---

* Chief Justice Hugh Lewis was the first of his family in Jamaica, and came originally to the island as a merchant's clerk.

† Two of these married men of note, on the same day, [April 8th, 1783, in St. Catherine's parish]—Elizabeth Catherine, to Genl. Robert Brownrigg, Captor of Kandy; and Mary, to Genl. John Whitelocke, vanquished a Buenos Ayres.

PARISH OF ST. ELIZABETH.

BLACK RIVER CHURCH.

I.

IN MEMORY OF — THE HONOURABLE HENRY GALE, ESQ.,—CUSTOS, AND COLONEL OF THE PARISH — OF ST. ELIZABETH, IN THIS ISLAND — BORN THE 19th OF FEBUY., 1737,—DIED, THE 8th OF MARCH, 1767.

THIS Henry, who was also a Member for St. Elizabeth in 1760, 1765, and 1766, and married, 25th October, 1764, Elizabeth Williams, (she remarried 24th May, 1770, William Harvie of St. Dorothy, Member for St. Elizabeth, 1774 and 1781) was great-grandson of Jonathan Gale, who patented, 28th April, 1673, five hundred and thirty-three acres, in Wel. Savanna, in St. Elizabeth's, with other lands in that parish. His son, Jonathan, was Colonel and Custos of St. Elizabeth, Member for that parish in 1708-9 and 1711 ; for Westmoreland, 1715 to 1726-7, and was buried in St. Elizabeth's in 1727 ; and his elder son, a third Jonathan, was father of Custos and Colonel Henry.

Arms, Azure, on a fess between 3 saltires or, 3 lions' heads erased, gules.

John Gale, an uncle of Henry, was Member for St. Elizabeth, in 1731 and 1732-3, and was buried in that parish, 14th June, 1738, being then a Major.

Eleanor Gale, an aunt of Henry, so named after her mother Eleanor, wife of the second Jonathan, (she was buried in St. Elizabeth's, 16th October, 1725), married in St. Catharine's, 22nd August, 1727, Colonel Robert Phillips of St. Andrew's, Member for that parish in 1738 and 1745-6. Eleanor Phillips was buried in St. Andrew's, 25th February, 1759 ; her husband, the Colonel, 17th November, 1763.—*Roby.*

2.

HERE — LYES INTERRED THE BODY OF — ELIZABETH, DAUGHTER TO YE — HONBLE. JOHN GALE, AND ELIZABETH HIS WIFFE, — WHO DYED APRIL THE 30th, 1761,—IN THE 34th YEAR OF HER AGE.—IN MEMORY OF WHOSE MANY AMIABLE QUALITIES, HER HUSBAND, DANIEL M'GILCHRIST, ESQ., — HATH ERECTED THIS MONUMENT OF HIS LOVE AND REGARD—TO ONE OF THE BEST OF WIVES.

PRIVATE BURIAL GROUNDS.

1.

HERE LIES THE HONOURABLE JOHN CAMPBELL, BORN AT INVERARY IN ARGYLESHIRE, NORTH BRITAIN, AND DE-SCENDED OF THE ANTIENT FAMILY OF AUCHENBRACK : WHEN A YOUTH HE SERVED SEVERAL CAMPAIGNS IN FLAN-DERS. HE WENT AS CAPTAIN OF THE TROOPS SENT TO DARIEN, AND ON HIS RETURN BY THIS ISLAND, IN 1700, HE MARRIED THE DAUGHTER OF COLLONEL CLAYBORN, BY WHOM HE HAD SEVERAL CHILDREN. IN 1718 HE MARRIED ELIZABETH, NOW ALIVE, RELICT OF COLLONEL GAMES. HE WAS MANY YEARS MEMBER OF THE ASSEMBLY, COLONEL, AND CUSTOS OF ST. ELIZABETH'S. IN 1722 HE WAS MADE ONE OF THE PRIVY COUNCILL. HE WAS THE FIRST CAMP-BELL WHO SETTLED IN THIS ISLAND : AND THRO' HIS EXTREAM GENEROSITY AND ASSISTANCE, MANY ARE NOW POSSESSED OF OPULENT FORTUNES. HIS TEM-PERANCE AND GREAT HUMANITY, HAVE ALWAYS BEEN VERY REMARKABLE. HE DIED JANUARY THE 29th, 1740, AGED 66 YEARS, UNIVERSALLY LAMENTED.

Arms, Gyrony of eight, within a border. *Crest*, A cubit arm holding a spur. *Motto*, "Forget not."

2.

HERE LIES KATHERINE, WIFE TO JOHN CAMPBELL, AND DAUGHTER TO COLONEL CLAYRORN, AND JOINT HEIRESS WITH HER SISTER. SHE DIED 1715, AGED 34 YEARS. — THIS TOMB THEIR ELDEST SON COLIN HAS CAUSED TO BE ERECTED AS HIS FILIAL DUTY AND AFFECTION, DECEMBER 25th, 1740.

THE first person of this name in the Island, married the daughter of Leonard Clay-borne, Member for St. Elizabeth in 1698, and Colonel of its regiment, who was slain, while opposing the invasion of the French, under Du Casse, in 1694.

He was a Darien refugee.

These Campbells are supposed to have been a branch of the Scottish house of Auchenbrack.

There were several Campbells who rose to eminence in Jamaica, and intermarried with some good families. Donald Campbell, private Secretary to Governor Campbell, and Speaker of the House of Assembly after William Blake, married Frances Gent, widow of Ballard Beckford, eldest son of Thomas, second son of Governor Peter Beckford.

LACOVIA ESTATE.

HERE LYETH THE BODY OF BARNARD ANDREISS, ESQ., LIEUT.-COL. OF YE LEEWARD REGIMENT, AND CUSTOS ROTULORUM OF ST. ELIZABETH'S PARISH, WHO DIED THE 23d DAY OF JULY, 1710, AGED 70 YEARS 3 MONTHS AND 26 DAYS.

HE was proprietor of *Lacovia*, which probably passed to the Hodges family, by the marriage of his daughter [?] Bonella, with Joseph Hodges, Member of Assembly in 1711.

SUPPLEMENTARY.

PARISH CHURCH OF ST. DOROTHY.

I.

NEAR THIS MONUMENT LIES INTERRED THE BODY OF JOHN PUSEY, ESQ., WHO DIED ON THE 24th DAY OF JANUARY, 1767, AGED 75 YEARS.

EULOGY.

Arms, Gu. 2 bars, or.   *Crest*, A cat-o'-mountain.

2.

SACRED TO THE MEMORY OF WILLIAM PUSEY, ESQ., REPRESENTATIVE IN ASSEMBLY FOR THIS PARISH, AND COLONEL OF THE MIDLAND DIVISION OF THE HORSE MILITIA ; WHO DIED, THE 11th DAY OF JUNE, 1783, AGED 42 YEARS ; AND OF ELIZABETH,* HIS WIFE, WHO DEPARTED THIS LIFE, THE 8th DAY OF JUNE, 178.. IN HER FORTIETH YEAR.

VERSES follow.

PARISH CHURCH OF VERE.

I.

HERE LYETH INTER'D THE BODY OF COLL. THOMAS SUTTON, WHO DE-PARTED THIS LIFE, THE 15th DAY OF NOVEMBER, IN THE SEVENTY-SECOND YEAR OF HIS AGE, AND IN THE YEAR OF OUR LORD GOD, 1710.

B. M. Slab.

IT was on his plantation in Clarendon, that the first serious servile revolt occurred, in 1669.

Sutton was a gallant soldier, and defended Carlisle Bay breastwork against the French, under Du Casse, in 1694.

---

* RULE was her maiden name—married 11th March, 1715.

2.

(*Ab.*) IN MEMORY OF JOHN SUTTON, SON OF JOHN SUTTON,* ESQ., OF THIS
PARISH......(Eulogium.) POST TAM ILLUSTRE DILUCULUM QUALIS EXPECTAN-
DUS ESSET MERIDIES? SED NUBES—SED TENEBRÆ—SED UMBRA MORTIS—HE
WAS CUT OFF IN THE FLOWER OF HIS AGE, BY THE VIOLENCE OF A FEVER,
23d AUGUST, ANNO 1745.

W. M. Slab.

H E was grandson of Colonel Thomas Sutton, before mentioned.

CHAPLETON—PARISH OF CLARENDON.

HERE LYETH THE BODY OF THE HONOURABLE EDWARD PENNANT, ESQ.,—
WHO DEPARTED THIS LIFE, THE 11th OF JUNE, 1736,—AETAT 64.

H E was Chief Justice, Custos Rotulorum of Clarendon and Vere, &c. ; and father
of Samuel, Henry, Smart, [a daughter], and —— John, eldest surviving son, who
married in St. Catherine's, 22d Oct., 1734, Bonella, daughter of Joseph Hodges, of
Lacovia, Member of Assembly in 1711, and whose name survives in a large pen near
Black River. Richard, their son, was created a peer of Ireland, on the 19th Nov.,
1783, by the title of Lord Penrhyn. *See* "The Peerage."

---

* At page 304 of this work, there is an epitaph, communicated by a gentleman [W. D. B.] in Jamaica, in
which the *coincidence* of dates, if no more, is suggestive.

BARBADOS.

BARBADOS.

THERE are probably few of our colonies more carefully *mis*represented, and consequently less known, than those in the Caribbean Sea. For many years past, public attention has been so slightly directed to the West India Islands, that an apology
seems required when one introduces the subject. No good artist has as yet made
familiar to Northern eyes, the grandeur and marvellous beauty of those tropical
scenes, although, now and again, some thin volume about our neglected interests
slightly stirs the surface of popular attention, with "governmental theories," and "colonial practice,"—the "decay of the *white*," and the "*growth* and claims of the *brown*
man," &c.

But the West Indies, although they may have lost much of their political and
commercial importance, retain their historic interest, and offer to the genealogist, in-
terested in the seventeenth century, an almost totally unexplored field of investigation.
Their parish registers, wills, and monumental inscriptions,* would probably afford
much valuable information, on the subject of social and family history, during that
century, when, as is well known, men of birth and distinction left the mother country,
to avoid religious and political intolerance, or to repair their fortunes.†

A cursory glance at the "Peerage and Baronetage" will probably suffice to show,
that at least thirty hereditary titles have originated in these islands; while the landed
gentry are largely recruited from the same locality,—facts the more remarkable, when
we consider the prejudices of the present generation.‡

The parochial and other records of Barbados are especially rich in historical
names, and it is to be regretted that no arrangement has ever been made to have
copies of them (at any rate up to the year 1750) deposited in England, where they
would form a valuable addition to existing records, at the State Paper Office, and be
preserved against the recurrence of such destruction as overtook many of them, during
the hurricanes of Barbados; and elsewhere, from the yet more insidious dangers of
the Vestry.

---

* A few of these were contributed by the author, to the "Gentleman's Magazine."
† Macaulay.
‡ In 1661 the following Barbadian gentlemen were created Baronets, viz., John Colleton, James Modiford,
James Drax, Robert Danvers, Robert Hacket, John Yeamans, Timothy Thornhill, John Witham, Robert Legard,
John Worsum, John Rawdon, Edwyn Stede, and Willoughby Chamberlayne. [See "Baronetage."]

Of these islands, the most important are Jamaica and Barbados.

The former, even to the present day, has managed to retain its English tone to a much greater extent than the others ; a peculiarity due possibly, in some measure, to the attention which has invariably been bestowed on those institutions which are more peculiarly characteristic of the mother country. The architecture of her churches is assimilated to models familiar at home, and the quaint tower and belfry of St. James', rising above clumps of leafy trees, are quite worthy of some old-fashioned rural parish in one of our counties.

There is scarcely one of the eleven parishes* of Barbados, that does not contain, at least a few, interesting fragments of the past ; at the same time, the greater number of monuments are of course to be found in the cathedral church of St. Michael,—Christ Church is also remarkable for its monuments,—not indeed the present church, but the old burial-ground, between it and the sea. St. John's is noted, as being the burial-place of the supposed last of the Palæologi ; the other parishes are more or less interesting.

As nothing can be uninteresting, which is connected with the misfortune and wanderings of so illustrious a race as the Palæologi, some digression may be permitted on the present occasion, although the scope of this work renders it unnecessary, and indeed out of place, to discuss the opinions of the many able writers, who have treated the subject in its many bearings, and especially with reference to the lineage and descendants of *Theodore Palæologus*, whose remarkable monumental inscription at Landulph, professes to give both :

Theodore, of Pesaro, was son of Camillo—son of Prosper—son of Theodore—son of John—son of Thomas, youngest brother of Constantine XIII., the last reigning sovereign of the Byzantine empire.

After many vicissitudes, this Prince came to England, in 1628, and was received by the English minister—the celebrated Duke of Buckingham—as befitted his birth.†

Before this, however, Theodore appears to have been married to Eudoxia Comnena, by whom he had a daughter named Theodora,‡ [born at Scio, 6th July, 1594, and married, October 10th, 1614, at the Greek Church of SS. Peter and Paul, Naples, to Prince Demetrius Rhodocanakis],

During his residence in England, Theodore Palæologus had, by Mary Balls,§ the following issue : — 1. Theodore, [buried in Westminster Abbey, in 1644?] ; 2. John ; 3. Ferdinand [the Barbadian] ; 4. Mary, [d. unm.] ; 5. Dorothy, [wife of William Arundel].

The earlier writers on Barbados seem to have an indistinct idea of the pretensions

---

* St. Michael, St. George, St. Philip, St. Peter, St. James, St. Lucy, St. Andrew, Christ Church, St. John, St. Joseph, St. Thomas.

† See Cal. S. P. Dom. Ser., 1628-9, vol. 96, No. 47, p. 27.

‡ See "Life of Leo Allatius," Athens, 1872, &c.

§ Their *marriage* record has never been found, but the fact of the marriage is generally accepted.

of Ferdinand Palæologus, but recent inquiries have thrown a considerable light on the question of his origin.

Ferdinand Palæologus appears to have settled in Barbados between 1628 and 1645, and to have become proprietor of a plantation in the parish of St. John, where, between 1649—1669, he was surveyor of highways, &c. 1678 and 1680 have both been assigned as the year in which he died, a discrepancy that ought certainly not to exist. The late Sir J. Emerson Tennant has stated that Palæologus is described "in the *register of his interment*," as "Lieutenant Ferdinand Palæologus." But this is at variance with the entry in the *burial register* of the Cathedral Parish of St. Michael in the same island, (a transcript of an older one, of which nothing is known), wherein the entry is made without either military title or baptismal name; and that this is substantially the case, is evident from the fact, that earlier writers who were aware of the burial register, have not mentioned the *baptismal* name of the deceased.*

There is doubtless some explanation of these apparent discrepancies. Possibly the errors of copyists, and the sanguine speculation of the Barbadians themselves, may have led to the inadvertent occurrence of oversights; for on the whole, there seems to be no doubt, that these accounts sustain the belief of the identification of Ferdinand as the son of Theodore Palæologus of Pesaro and Landulph.

Amongst the ruins of the Parish Church of St. John, which was destroyed in the hurricane of 1831, was discovered in the vault under the organ loft, the leaden coffin of Ferdinand Palæologus, in the position adopted by the Greek Church, which is the reverse of others. It was opened on the 3rd of May, 1844, and in it was found a skeleton of remarkable size, imbedded in quicklime—thus showing, that although Ferdinand may have accommodated himself to the circumstances of his position, he had died in the faith of his own Church.†

---

* Lygon, Oldmixon, Schomburgak.

† WILL OF F. PALÆOLOGUS.

"In the Name of God, Amen. — I Ferdinand Palæologus, of the parish of Saint John, being sick in body, but in perfect memory, commit my soul into the hands of Almighty God, my most merciful Creator, and my body to be interred in a Christian burial there to attend the joyful resurrection of the just to eternal life by Jesus Christ, my most blessed Saviour and Redeemer. Imp. I give and bequeath unto my loving wife, Rebecca Palæologus, the one half of my plantation, with·all the profits thereof arising, during the term and time of her natural life. Item. I give and bequeath unto my son Theodorus Palæologus, the other moiety of my plantation, with all profits, stock, and goods thereunto belonging, which moiety is to be employed for his maintenance and education, together with the increase of his estate, until he attains the age of 14 years, the other moiety given as aforesaid after the death of my wife, Rebecca Palæologus, my will is, that her said moiety return, with all the profit, unto my son Theodorus Palæologus. Item. I give and bequeath unto my sister, *Mary Palæologus*, twenty shillings sterling. I give and bequeath unto my sister *Dorothy Arundel*,‡ twenty shillings sterling. Item. I give and bequeath unto Ralph Hassell my godson of Ralph Hassell, my black stone colt. Item. I give and bequeath unto Edward Walrond, son of Henry Walrond, Jun., one grey mare colt. And for executrix of this my last will and testament, I do constitute and appoint my loving wife Rebecca Palæologus. In witness whereof I have hereunto set my hand and seal, this 26 of September, in the year of our Lord, 1670.

"FERDINAND PALEOLOGUS (L.S.)

‡ On the tomb of Palæologus, at Landulph, occur the names of his children by Mary Balls, viz., "Theodore, John, Ferdinando, Maria, and Dorothy." The latter was married in 1656 to William Arundel.

It is said, that during the last conflict for Grecian independence and deliverance from the Turkish yoke, an application was made by the Provisional Greek Government, assembled at Nauplia, to the authorities of Barbados, respecting any male descendants of Ferdinand Palæologus, who might still exist, but it was ascertained that there was none. This assertion, it may be added, has been denied. (*See* " Notes and Queries.") The truth is, the mere name of *Palæologus* suffers, with others of Royal origin, in this country, and is of no particular significance amongst the Greeks, many of whom adopted it, *propria motu*, and appear to have brought it here, where its rarity has attracted notice to many individuals, who, in consequence, have been erroneously accredited with an Imperial origin.

The early landowners, or "planters," used to be particular in their funeral arrangements; and most of the better families interred their dead in leaden coffins, cased in cedar or mahogany.

Family vaults were also common. That of the Chase family, at Christ Church, just mentioned, is the locality of a very remarkable (so-called) *spiritual* phenomenon.* The mausoleum of the Colepepper family, in a quiet recess on the brink of Hacklestone's Cliff, in the parish of St. John, is singularly picturesque, and commands one of the most beautiful of sea views.

Many of these tombs have, from time to time, been broken up and rifled—particularly those in private cemeteries. In Jamaica, more especially, where estates often lie at an inconvenient distance from the parish church, there was always a private place of sepulture, generally near the mansion, but screened by trees, where, even now, one may frequently catch glimpses of old tombs, matted with ferns and a flowery undergrowth, among the deep shades of mango, wild tamarind, and pimento trees.

Jamaica, although, in some respects, as careful and imitative as her rival, was always more or less deficient in *amour propre;* and her population having absorbed the greater portion of the " roughs " then afloat in the Spanish waters, seems to have offered few social inducements to the higher order of settlers to remain, after accom-

---

" Signed, sealed, and delivered, in the presence of Tobias Bridge, George Hammer, Thomas Kendall. And upon further consideration it is my Will and Testament, that in case ...... should happen, my son Theodorus Paleologus should die before my wife, without issue, lawfully begotten by him, that then, my said wife shall have the whole estate equally divided, as before mentioned, to her heirs and assigns for ever. As witness my hand and seal, this 2 day of October, 1670.

" Ferdinand (F. P. his mark) Paleologus (l.s.)

" Signed, sealed and delivered in the presence of us—

" Tobias Bridge.
" George Hammer.
" Thomas Kendall.
" Abraham Pomfrett."

Theodorus was a mariner on board the ship " Charles II." He died at sea, 1693, (Will Doct. Com.) when the property in Barbados went to his mother, although he appears to have had a wife named Martha, for her children are referred to in his will.

* The " Grave Disturbance," described in *Once a Week*, March 11th, 1865, &c.

plishing the grand object of securing wealth, sufficient for the settling, or re-establish-ing, of their families in England.

Sometimes, death overtook those prudent worthies, and the well-paid servants of Government; and there being no lack of means in the hands of the executors, the island gradually became enriched with costly monuments. In many instances, par-ticularly of later dates, the armorial sculptures on these monuments are not to be de-pended on; consequently, although the epitaphs are useful records, as regards dates and names, they are too often illusory in respect of family descent. In annotating, therefore, one ought not to forget that very excellent *names** are common in the lists of rebels of an inferior grade, sent from England, and sold to the loyal settlers.

The following pages comprise all the monumental inscriptions of Barbados, from the earliest period, to the year 1750; after which date, it seemed unnecessary, with a few exceptions, to pursue the task of copying; the object being to secure the preservation of the much effaced inscriptions of the preceding century.

These monumental inscriptions generally, have been carefully collected, down to the above date, subsequent to which limit, they have been more or less abbreviated, as they gradually lose the interest attached to antiquity, and acquire a complimentary character, which, being quite conventional, ceases to answer any useful purpose.

A few extracts from the valuable collection of papers relating to Barbados, at the State Paper Office, may tend to throw a light on some of the accompanying Monumental Inscriptions.

There is a curious account of the order of march, from Fontabell to the "towne of St. Michael's," on the 23rd April, 1685, "for proclaiming our Gratious King James the Second." The regiments of foot were commanded and led as follows :

" 1. Major Phillip ——, Colonels Ricd. Elliot and Jno. Fryer (Frere ?)

" 2. Major Geo. Lillington and Colonel Thomas Holmes.

" 3. Major Abell Alleyne, Lt.-Col. Wm. Sandiford, and Col. Jno. Waterman.

" 4. Major Wm. Lewgar (Legard ?) and Col. Jno. Sampson.

" 5. Major Samuell Smith and Col. Thos. Colleton.

REGIMENTS OF HORSE.

" 1. Major Jno. Berringer, Lt.-Col. Ml. Terrill, and Col. Jno. Farmer.

" 2. Capt. Jno. Leslye and Major Richard Winter.

" The Justices of the Peace.

" The Clergy.   The Lawyers in their gowns.

" Next, a noise of trumpetts, &c.

" His Excellency the Governor of the Island.

---

* Amongst other remarkable names to be found in the registers of Barbados, are the following : — Evelyn, Walpole, Hoadley, Atterbury, Sancroft, Oates, Dangerfield, Cornish, Sarsfield, Ginkell, Sidney, Bedloe, Vane, Fauconbridge, Fleetwood, Claypole, Syndercombe, Ireton, Penderell, Levelis, Vere Byron, De la Warr, Talbot, Tudor, Stafford, Michelbourne, Hacker, Breakspeare, Walcot, Venner, Sheldon, Shirley, Rumbold, Ayloffe, St. Quentin, Bullen, &c.

" The King's Life Guards of Horse.

" His Maj'ies Regiment Royall of Foot Guards,* commanded by the Honble. Coll. Edwyn Stede.

" George Hannay, Provost Marshall."

H.M.'s ship "Diamond,"† in Carlisle Bay, saluted during the ceremony.

In connection with Monmouth's Rebellion, we find, dated Nov. 25, 1665, an " Invoice of the Western Rebells shipt from Weymouth," (for Barbados), "in which occur some peculiar names, such as Gaich, Cumet, Mader, Follett, Jewell, Dolbeard, Duck, Pine, Forcey, Estmond, Guppy, Bovell, Pester, Cordelion, Venner, Osborne, &c. The invoice is signed by " George Penne."‡

It was customary to sell such persons as slaves for ten years or longer.

There is also on record, about the same period, a receipt granted by Mr. John Rosse, for one hundred prisoners, to be transported from Taunton. The latter were persons in humble life, and yet (showing how deceptive are genealogies based on mere *nominal* and *local* coincidences) we find among them Austin, Chamberlayne, Osborne, Mountstephen, Bellamy, Pearce, Bennet, &c.

On March 25, 1685, there is the account of the sale of sixty-seven rebels, who were delivered by Capt. Gardner, of " The Jamaica Merchant," to the following masters in Barbadoes, viz., Colonel T. Colleton, Mr. Nicholas Prideaux, Mr. Abel Allen, Mr. Edward Harlestone, Captain Thomas Morris, &c. Among the former were Walter Taaffe, Peaceful Knowles, &c.

The following is a specimen of the style of information connected with contemporaneous history. In the examination of Christianus Gardner (Barbados, Aug. 8, 1688), the witness states :—

" That about 8 months ago, being at the Coffee house in St. Michael's towne kept by the widow Hales, with severall in company......they talked of the tryal of Mr. Cornish of London, amongst which one of the Company sayed, that one of the persons summoned to be of the said Cornish's jury, desired to be excused, for that he had had great dealings with the said Cornish, but the said Cornish desired he might be one of the jury. The Attorney General thereupon declared that he ought not to be of the jury, and that the king had liberty to except against him. .... It was also said by one of the Company, that one John Price summoned of the said Jury, urged that he was on my Lord Russell's tryall."

---

* It seems probable that a portion of the Body-Guard of Charles I. found their way, with Lord Willoughby, to Barbados, and were perhaps at the defence of Carlisle Block house, in that island, when attacked by Sir George Ayscue. Amongst other records bearing on this question, may be mentioned No. 161, May 12th, 1639—State Papers—Home Series. See also *The Broad Arrow* of Aug. 15th, 1874.

† See Treasury Papers, [S.P.O.], Oct. 4, 1694.

‡ For further particulars, *vide* Locke's History of the Rebellion of James Duke of Monmouth, in 1685.

CHRONOLOGICAL TABLE.

Date.	Events.	Governor.
1600.	The exact date of the discovery of Barbados is unknown ; but in this year it is first indicated in charts. It was first visited by the Portuguese, who found it uninhabited, and named it " Los Barbados," or the *bearded*, from the trees fringing parts of the coast.	
1625.	Sir William Courteen, merchant of London, under the protection of the Earl of Marlborough, who had a grant of the island, fitted out two large ships, one only of which, however, arrived at Barbados, with about thirty persons, who formed a settlement at James' Town, and elected Captain William Deane, Governor.	Captain William Deane.
1627.	Settled under a charter granted to the Earl of Carlisle, on his indemnifying the Earl of Marlborough.	
1628.	Charles Wolferstone, a native of Bermuda, appointed Governor. Sixty-four immigrants arrive in Carlisle Bay, and found Bridgetown. The Leeward and Windward settlers opposed to each other—triumph of the latter.	Charles Wolferstone.
1629.	Eleven parishes. Chancery Court established. Barbados declared *not* one of the Caribee islands. The Council composed of eleven settlers.	John Powell. Robert Wheatly.

Date.	Events.	Governor.
1636.	Six thousand English inhabitants.* About this time, Capt. Holdip is said to have introduced the sugar-cane from Guinea.	Henry Hawley.
1649.	Royalist refugees arrive—probably amongst them, officers, &c., of the late King's body guard.	Francis Lord Willoughby.
1650.	Refusal of Barbados to submit to Cromwell's Government.	
1652.	Vigorous repulse of Sir George Ayscue, by the Royalists under Lord Willoughby. (Jan. 12.) Capitulation of Barbados to Sir G. Ayscue. Force in the island, 10,000 foot and 2000 horse.	Sir George Ayscue.
1653.	Design to make Barbados a free state.	
1655.	Prisoners taken at Dunbar, &c., sent to Barbados.	Daniel Searle. (Dy.)
1656.	*Christian* population, 25,000.	
1660.	Charter granted to the Company of Merchant Adventures. Proposal to banish the sect of Quakers from the island. Chief products — sugar, indigo, tobacco, cotton, aloes, &c.	Thomas Modiford.
1662.	The proprietary Government of Lords Carlisle and Willoughby abolished, and the island annexed to the Crown.	
1671.	George Blake and others have a patent to erect Lighthouses.	Christopher Codrington. (Dy.)
1683.	358 sugar works in operation.	Sir John Witham. (Dy.)
1693.	Several Barbadians carried prisoners to France. *See* Cal. S.P.	James Kendall.
1710.	Death of General Codrington, founder of Codrington College.	Metford Crowe.
1780.	Hurricane—loss of 4000 lives.	James Cunninghame.

* In 1638, in a list of the inhabitants, we find these names—Weekes, Yeamans, Vaughan, Tracey, Walcot, Stanhope, Talbot, Tudor, Drax, Drake, Lawrence (John), &c,

Date.	Events.	Governor.
1784.	Remarkable shifting of land, by which many lives were lost.	David Parry.
1795.	Inundation.	George Poyntz Ricketts.
1796.	Great fires.	
1824.	Bishopric erected. (*See* Antigua.)	Sir H. Warde.
1831.	Great hurricane, 10th Aug.	Sir J. Lyon.
1833.	Abolition of slavery.	Sir Lionel Smith.
1835.	Police force established.	
1841.	First Chief Justice appointed. (*See* Colonial Office List.)	Sir C. E. Grey.
1851.	Population, 135,939.	K. B. Hamilton. (Adm.)
1852.	Inland Post Office established.	Sir W. M. G. Colebrooke.
1854.	Epidemic of Cholera, 17,000 perished.	
1860.	Destructive fire at Bridgetown.	Francis Hincks.
1869.	A Staff-Colonel substituted for a Major-General to command the Forces.	R. W. Rawson.

GOVERNORS, DEPUTY-GOVERNORS, AND LIEUT.-GOVERNORS OF BARBADOS.

WITH THE YEARS WHEN THEY COMMENCED THEIR ADMINISTRATION.

Governors.	A.D.	Deputy-Governors and Presidents.	A.D.
William Deane	1625	(D.G.) Richard Peers	1633
Charles Wolferstone	1628	(D.G.) Richard Peers	1634
John Powell	1629	(D.G.) William Hawley	1638
Robert Wheatly	1629	(D.G.) Daniel Searle	1652
Sir William Tufton	1629	(P.) Humfrey Walrond	1660
Henry Hawley	1630	(D.G.) Christopher Codrington	1668
Henry Hawley	1634	(D.G.) Sir Peter Colleton, Bart.	1673
Henry Hawley	1636	(D.G.) Sir John Witham	1683
Henry Hawley	1639	(D.G.) Edwin Stede	1685
Sir Henry Hunks	1640	(P.) Francis Bond	1696
Philip Bell	1641	(P.) John Farmer	1701
Francis Lord Willoughby	1650	(P.) William Sharpe	1706
Sir George Ayscue	1652	(P.) George Lillington	1710
Thomas Modiford	1660	(P.) William Sharpe	1714
Francis *Lord* Willoughby	1663	(P.) John Frere	1720
Henry Willowby		(P.) Samuel Cox	1720
Henry Hawley	1666	(P.) Samuel Barwick	1731
Samuel Barwick		(P.) James Dotin	1733
William *Ld.* Willoughby	1667	(P.) James Dotin	1735
William *Ld.* Willoughby	1669	(P.) James Dotin	1740
William *Ld.* Willoughby	1672	(P.) Ralph Weeks	1753
Sir Jonathan Atkins	1674	(P.) Samuel Rous	1766
Sir Richard Dutton	1680	(P.) Samuel Rous	1771
Sir Richard Dutton	1684	(P.) John Dotin	1783
James Kendall	1690	(P.) Henry Frere	1790
Francis Russell	1694	(P.) William Bishop	1793
Ralph Grey	1698	(P.) William Bishop	1800
Sir Bevill Granville	1703	(P.) John Ince	1803
Metford Crowe	1707	(P.) John Spooner	1806
Robert Lowther	1711	(P.) John Spooner	1814
Robert Lowther	1715	(P.) John Foster Alleyne	1817

The three names Henry Willowby, Henry Hawley, Samuel Barwick are bracketed together as *interim* 1666.

GOVERNORS, DEPUTY-GOVERNORS, AND LIEUT.-GOVERNORS—*continued.*

Governors.	A.D.	Lieut-Governors and Presidents, &c.	A.D.
Henry Worsley*	1722	(P.) John Brathwaite Skeete	1820
Scroop, *Visct.* Howe	1733	(P.) Samuel Hinds	1821
Hon. Robert Byng	1739	John Brathwaite Skeete	1825
Sir Thomas Robinson	1742	John Brathwaite Skeete	1827
Hon. Henry Grenville	1747	John Brathwaite Skeete	1830
Charles Pinfold	1756	John Brathwaite Skeete	1832
William Spry	1768	John Alleyne Beccles	1834
Hon. Edward Hay	1772	John Alleyne Beccles	1835
James Cunninghame	1780	John Alleyne Beccles	1836
David Parry	1784	J. Brathwaite	1841
David Parry	1790	(L.G.) H. C. Darling	1841
Geo. Poyntz Ricketts	1794	J. R. Best	1846
Francis *Lord* Seaforth†	1801	J. S. Gaskin	1848
Francis *Lord* Seaforth	1804	J. S. Gaskin	1849
Sir Geo. Beckwith, K.B.	1810	J. R. Best	1856
Sir James Leith, K.B.	1815	(ADM.) K. B. Hamilton	1851
Stapleton *Lord* Combermere	1817	J. S. Gaskin	1852
Sir Henry Warde, K.C.B.	1821	Grant E. Thomas	1856
Sir Henry Warde, K.C.B.	1826	(ADM.) James Walker	1859
Sir James Lyon, K.C.B.	1829	(ADM.) R. M. Mundy	1865
Sir James Lyon, K.C.B.	1829		
Sir James Lyon, K.C.B.	1830		
Sir Lionel Smith, K.C.B.	1833		
Sir Lionel Smith, K.C.B.	1834		
Sir Lionel Smith, K.C.B.	1835		
Sir Lionel Smith, K.C.B.	1836		
Sir E. J. M. McGregor, Bart., K.C.B.	1836		
Sir Charles E. Grey	1841		
William Reid, C.B.	1846		
William Reid, C.B.	1847		
Sir W. M. G. Colebrooke	1848		
Sir W. M. G. Colebrooke	1849		

* Henry Worsley was M.P. for the Isle of Wight, and Envoy to the Court of Portugal in 1714. He was second son of Sir R. Worsley, Bart., of Appuldercombe, by his wife Mary, daughter of James, second son of Philip, Earl of Pembroke. Sir Francis Worsley was a Captain in the second Squadron of K. Charles I.'s Guards, in 1639.

† Francis Humberstone Mackenzie, created in 1797, Baron Seaforth. A remarkable account of his Lordship (who was born deaf and dumb) is to be found in Burke's "Vicissitudes of Families," *voce* "The Warlock of the Glen."

Governors.	A.D.
Sir W. M. G. Colebrooke	1852
Francis Hincks	1858
Francis Hincks	1860
James Walker, C.B.	1862
James Walker, C.B.	1865
R. W. Rawson, C.B.	1869

MEMBERS OF COUNCIL.

(THE EARLIEST ON RECORD.)

1629.

Samuel Andrews.
Capt. Talbot.
Thomas Peers.
Anthony Marbury.
Thomas Gibbes.
William Birch.
Capt. Richard Leonard.
Capt. Robert Hall.
Henry Brown.
Capt. Heywood.
Daniel Fletcher.

1636.

Capt. George Bowyer.
Capt. William Hawley.
Thomas Gibbes.
Edward Cranefield.
Theodore Stevens.
William Fortescue.
Capt. James Holdip.*
William Sandiford.
Samuel Andrew.
Richard Peerce (P.).

CIVIL ESTABLISHMENT.

1 Governor and Commander-in-Chief. 1 Private Secretary, and A. D. C.
2 Chief Clerks, &c.; 1 Colonial Secretary, and 2 Clerks; 1 Colonial Treasurer; 1 Auditor-General and Clerk; 1 Controller of Customs, and 1 Landing Surveyor, and 13 Clerks. 1 Inspector-General of Police; 1 Inspector of Prisons; 1 Provost-Marshal; 1 Colonial Postmaster; 1 Superintendent of Public Works; 1 Harbour-Master, &c.

---

* Said to have planted the first sugar-cane (from Guinea) in Barbados. See "Memoirs of the First Settlement of Barbados." (Brit. Mus. 1196, b. 33.) — 1741.—The model of the Barbados sugar-mill was introduced from Holland, by Sir Jas. Drax.—Richard Holdip, of Barbados (Will P. C. 1622 ?) was of the family of Colonel Richard Holdip, who went to Jamaica with the expedition in 1655, and was probably descended from Simon Holdip, incumbent of Ash, near Basingstoke, 1606—32.

ECCLESIASTICAL ESTABLISHMENT.

1 Bishop Coadjutor ; 1 Chancellor of Diocese ; 1 Archdeacon (Bishop Coadjutor) ; 1 Registrar ; 11 Rectors.

JUDICIAL ESTABLISHMENT.

1 Chief Justice ; 1 Attorney-General : 1 Solicitor-General ; 1 Queen's Solicitor and Proctor ; 2 Masters in Chancery ; 1 Registrar in Chancery ; 1 Official Assignee ; 1 Escheater-General ; 1 Crown Clerk ; 1 Casual Receiver ; 1 Registrar in Admiralty ; 1 Marshal in Admiralty ; 6 Probate Commissioners ; 3 Assistant Judges ; 14 Police Magistrates ; 6 Coroners, &c.

ARMY.

(Military Establishment— Windward and Leeward Islands.)

1 Major-General ; 1 Officer Commanding Artillery ; 1 do. Engineers ; 1 Brigade-Major, &c.

Troops—Artillery, Engineers. Head Quarters of Regiment of the Line. Detachment of Colonial Corps.

PARISH OF ST. MICHAEL.

ST. MICHAEL'S CATHEDRAL CHURCH.

1.

PHILIP ALLEN........TAMASIN ALLEN......OB. 1669.

Fragmentary.

2.

(*Ab.*) FRANCIS BOND, ESQ., BORN IN BODMYN, CORN-
WALL, 1636 ...... OB. AUG. 3, 1699.

Probably a son or near relative of Dennis Bond, Esq., of
Lutton,—a staunch Parliamentarian, and M.P. for Weymouth from 1654 to 1656.

Francis Bond was President of the Council in 1696.

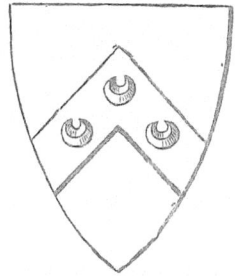

Arms, On a chev. 3 crescents.

N.B. Where tinctures are omitted, they are not shown on the sculpture.

3.

RICHARD B.............(obliterated).. OB. 1685.

(A reference to the Burial Registers would doubtless supply many of these obliterated names.)

4

(*Ab.*) HUMPHREY BROCTON, MERCHANT,—OB. 1673.

5.

(*Ab.*) CAPTAIN CHRISTOPHER BRADBURY,—OB. 14th AUGT., 1685.

6.

(*Ab.*) DORA BOELLE, OB. AUGT. 6th, 1723.

7.

SUSAN BARRETT, DAUGHTER OF RICHARD AND MARTHA
BARRETT,—OB. 9th APRIL, 1665. — ALSO, — JOHN PENNELL,
SONNE OF THOMAS & SUSAN PENNELL,—OB. JULY 9th, 1665.

The arms on this monument are probably inaccurate. The
Barretts of Shortney, Notts., bear "three spear-heads."

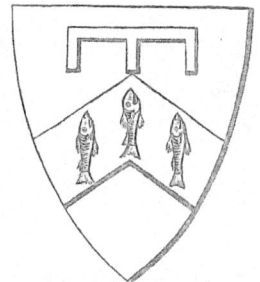

Arms, Or, on a chev.... 3 fishes hauriant......

46—2

8.

(*Ab.*) JOSEPH BOULSTROD, SON OF EDWARD BOULSTROD, AND MILDRED HIS WIFE, — BORN 18th FEB., 1644, IN THE PARISH OF LITTLE ST. BARTHOLOMEW, LONDON,—OB..... 1675.

Partly obliterated.

9.

(*Ab.*) SAMUEL LAROQUE BRUCE,—OB. 1799.

HE was third son of the Honble Joseph Osborne Bruce, Judge of the Court of Common Pleas from 1756 to 1761, by Jane, his wife, daughter and heiress of Samuel Barwick, son and heir of Governor Samuel Barwick, and grandson of the Honble. James Bruce,* Esq., of Garlet, grandson of Robert Bruce, of Kennet. [See "The Peerage," *voce* Burley ; Burke's " Landed Gentry," *voce* Walrond, Bruce, &c. ; Gentleman's Magazine, 1749 ; Scott's Magazine, 1749 ; Claim to the Peerage of Kinloss, before the Committee of Privileges, 1866, &c.]

Mr. Justice W. D. Bruce is now the representative of this branch of the House of Bruce. (See Pedigree.)

10.

..........MAJOR GENERAL ....
................................LORD CLARINA ....
........1796.......

The Inscription is nearly obliterated.

THE above was, Nathaniel Massey, 2nd Baron Clarina, born 23rd May, 1773. He commanded the troops in Barbados ; and left issue, three sons and two daughters. In Burke's "Peerage," it is stated that Lord Clarina was married in 1796, and died in 1810, but the former date only appears (without context) on the slab. The Barony of Clarina, in the Peerage of Ireland, was created, 27 Dec., 1810, in the person of Eyre Massey, a General in the Army, Commander of the Forces in Ireland, and who had served at the Battle of Culloden. Dying in 1804, he was succeeded by his second and only surviving son, Nathaniel William, 2nd Baron, and Major-General, who died in Barbados, while Governor and Commander-in-Chief of that Island, leaving three sons and two daughters, by his wife Penelope. (See " Peerage.")

Arms, Arg. on a chev. between 3 lozenges, sa. a lion passant or.   *Crest*, Out of a ducal coronet or, a bull's head gu., armed sa.   (Crest, only, on slab.)

11.

(*Ab.*) HENRY CARTER,—OB. 1753.

12.

....EXUVIÆ MARIÆ UXORIS ED. CHEARNLEY, 2 DECEMBRIS, ANNO 1723, ..
......

---

* This gentleman held many important offices under Government.

13.

.... ELIZABETH CROUCH..... OB. 25 MAY, 1747, AET. 52....

THERE was a well-known family of this name, in the seventeenth century, whereof was Alderman Giles Crouch. (See Pedigrees, Harl. MSS.)

On the tomb of John Bargrave, at Patrixbourne, is commemorated his wife, daughter and coheiress of Giles Crouch, of London. (Bank's "Baronia A. C.")

14.

(*Ab.*) MR. EDWARD CRISP, MERCHANT, ELDEST SON OF NICHOLAS CRISP, MERCHANT IN BRED STREET, LONDON, IN YE KINGDOM OF ENGLAND .... OB. 14th JENVARY, 1678, AET. 50.—ALSO, MR. THOMAS YEATS. OB. 2nd MARCH, 168½. — ALSO, MRS. MARY YEATS, WIFE TO THE ABOVE-MENTIONED PERSONS....OB, 25th AUGUST, 1682....

*Arms,......*On a chev. 5 horse shoes points downwards. (The arms are properly, Arg. on a chev. sa. 5 horse shoes or.)

THE founder of this family was Sir Nicholas Crispe, Knt., of London, great grandson of Ellis Crispe, Esq., of Marsefield, Gloucestershire, Alderman and Sheriff of London in 1625.

Sir Nicholas had a son, Ellis, who, by his wife Anne, daughter of Sir G. Strode, was father of Sir Nicholas Crispe of Hammersmith, who was created a Baronet in 1665. This latter gentleman was a merchant of vast fortune, and great consideration ; he was a staunch Royalist, and advanced large sums to King Charles I. "All the succours which the king had from beyond seas, came through his hands." He raised, at his own expense, a regiment of horse, and on the failure of the Royal cause, retired to France, but subsequently returned. Sir Nicholas died in 1665, and the baronetcy continued in his family until the death of his great grandson Sir Charles Crispe, in 1740, when it became extinct.

In one of the Parish Registers of Barbados, the marriage is recorded (Dec. 8, 1643) of a Thomas Crispe, and Sarah Archer. There is also a bequest to his cousin, J. Archer, in the will* of a T. Crispe, later on, in the same century, of "a ring with this poesy of love—A S I S T C, so shall thee," *i.e.*, As is now T. Crispe, so shalt thou be.

---

* At Doctor's Commons.

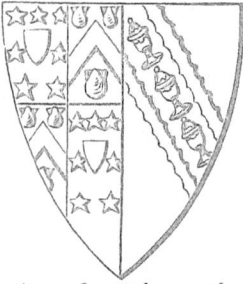

Arms, Quarterly, 1 and 4, An inescutcheon between seven stars ; 2 and 3, A chevron between three escallops: Impaling, between two bendlets engrailed, three covered cups. *Crest*, Out of a ducal coronet an ass's head.

15.

HERE LIES INTERRED COLONEL EDWARD CHAMBER-LAINE, WHO WAS BORN IN THE COUNTY OF LEICESTER IN ENGLAND, AND MARRIED MARY, DAU. OF EDWARD BUTLER, OF STRATFORD, IN THE COUNTY OF BEDFORD, ESQ., OB. 23 JULY, 1673, AET. 50.

COLONEL EDWARD CHAMBERLAIN was father of Butler Chamberlain, whose son, Sir Willoughby Chamberlain, of Barbados, was knighted 1695, and died 1697. Mary, his widow, married George Greene, Esq., of Barbados, and, secondly, Sir John Witham, Bart., and died in 1687, leaving a numerous issue.

Sir Richard Dutton, in 1684, complains to the King, that Sir John Witham detained cargoes and imprisoned merchants for purposes of extortion ; and that he also at a public-house, *threatened to hang* a member of council *by court marshal* in time of peace.—(S. P. O.)

March 10, 1684. Sir John Witham's wife declares that she has made over her estate to her children by her former husband, " Colonel Edward Chamberlaine, deceased."—(S. P. O.)

16.

. . . . CAPTAIN JEREMIAH EGGINGTON, MERCHANT OF SALOP . . . .
Fragment.

DATES effaced, but apparently about 1650—80.

17.

JOHN FREWEN,—OB. 1669, AET. 44.

AMONG the licences to go abroad (S. P. O.), Feb. 1633, Francis T(F?)rewin, aged 26, is named, as one of the passengers on board the " Bonaventure," for St. Christopher's. He appears to have been a native of Plympton, of which locality was also his companion, Matthew Archer. The suggestion may be thrown out, that John Frewin was son of Francis. It is quite possible that the latter may have been a member of the Worcestershire family of the same name.

18.

. . . . JONATHAN EVILER (Q. FULLER?), ... OB. . . . 1682.
Fragment.

ROBERT FULLER was settled in Barbados, prior to 1657, and died there in 1666. He came from Kinsale, co. Cork, and left issue in Barbados, Robert, *Jonathan*, and William.

19.

MR. WILLIAM GODMAN, MERCHANT, SON OF REV. HENRY GODMAN, OF THE KINGDOM OF GT. BRIT., OB. AUGUST 1, 1710, AET. 37 ; 22 YEARS A RESIDENT.

GODMAN, of Leatherhead, Surrey, granted 1571, bore, Per pale ermine, and ermines, on a chevron indented or, a lion passant vert. *Crest,* On a mount, a black cock with wings displayed, all proper.

Arms, Ermine on a chief a lion passant.   *Crest,* A bird rising.

20.

(*Ab.*) GARRETT.. OB. OCTOBER .... 1729, AET. 60.
Oblit.

21.

(*Ab.*) ....ROBERT HOOPER, ARMIGER.... OB. 1700....

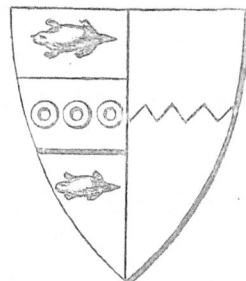

Arms, ... on a fesse, between 2 moles proper, 3 annulets.   Impaling..... per fesse indented.

22.

(*Ab.*) .... ROBERT HOOPER....OB. 1700.
Fragment.

23.

(*Ab.*) CHRISTOPHER HALKETT.... OB..... 1678,.... HIS DAUGHTER ELIZA-BETH.... OB..... 1679. — CAPTAIN GREGORY HALKETT, BORNE AT LYME REGIS, DORSET. —ALSO, MARTIN BENTLEY, SON OF MARTIN & MARY BENTLEY, ... OB. .... 1724, AET. 30.

24.

(*Ab.*) ....MR. BARNARD HANNINGTON, ... OB. JULY .... 1755 ....
Fragment.

25.

(*Ab.*) .... ROBERT HOYLE, ... OB. 1698...
Fragment.

26.

(*Ab.*) .... COLONEL JOHN HASSITT ....
Fragment.   No date.

27.

(*Ab.*) .... EDWARD JURDAIN, ORGANIST, — OB. DEC. 28, 1722. — ELIZABETH JORDAN, HIS WIDOW, OB. SEP. 30, 1737, AET. 65 ....

28.

LT.-COLL. CHRISTOPH. JACSON, ESQ., LIES HERE UNDERNEATH INTERRED, WHO DEPARTED THIS LIFE THE 9th DAY OF JAN., 169⅚, AET. 87.....

SEE Burke's "Landed Gentry,"—Jacson of Barton.

29.

....JACOB KOPKEE, OB. .... 1722 .... AET. 36.

30.

ALLAN LYDE, MERCHANT, 17 JAN., 1680.

LYDE (Ayot St. Lawrence, Herefordshire), descended from Cornelius Lyde, of Staunton Wick, Somerset, born in 1641; the last male heir, Lionel Lyde, was created a baronet in 1772.

Allen Lyde was probably of this family, which had many connections with the Western colonies, in the seventeenth century.

Stephen Lyde, fourth son, and Lyonel, fifth son of Cornelius above mentioned, were planters in Virginia.

Three Lydes (Edward, John, and Sylvester,) were transported for participation in the rebellion of 1685.

31.

.... ROBERT MOORE, OB. 8, SEP..... [16..?], AET. 37 ...

Fragment.

THIS name, in Barbados, is said to have been altered from More, to Moore, by Colonel John More, said to have been the son of Thomas, (by his wife, Mary Longueville) a younger son of Sir Edward More, 1st Bart. of More Hall, co. Lancaster, and who subsequently removed to Jamaica, early in the eighteenth century, or late in the seventeenth. (See Notes to Moore, &c., *Jamaica.*)

32.

CAPTAIN JOHN MOODY, OB. 1673.

SIR HENRY MOODY, second and last Baronet, sold the family estate of Garresdon, Wilts., and emigrated to New England, where he is supposed to have died, *s. p.*, in 1662.

33.

LIEUT.-COL. JOHN MERRING, ESQ., ONE OF THE BARONS OF HER MAJESTY'S HON. COURT OF EXCHEQUER, OB. 28 AUG.. 1711, AET. 49.

34.

(*Ab.*) ....ROBERT MILN, SON OF DAVID MILN.... OB... 1619 .. — ALSO .. DAVID, SECOND SON OF DAVID MILNE..OB... 1705.

THERE was an extensive and influential family of this name in Edinburgh, in the seventeenth century, whereof was Sir Robert Milne, and Milne, the King's architect, whose curious monument in the old Greyfriars' Churchyard still exists. The name very frequently occurs throughout the records of the Scottish metropolis, wherein David and Robert are the prevailing baptismal names.

Sir Robert Milne had a numerous issue, and it is probable that the Barbadian Miln (for the name is indifferently spelt with a *y* or an *i*, and with or without the final *e*) was one of his sons.

Of this family, there are monuments in the picturesque churchyard of Inveresk —namely, of Admiral Sir David Milne, &c.

James Milne, Esq., of Trinity Grove, near Edinburgh, represents one branch of the family ; while another has been distinguished in the naval service, and of which, is the present Admiral Sir Alexr. Milne, G.C.B.

35.

MARY MILES, WIFE OF JOHN MILES....OB.....1695.

36.

HONORABLE JOHN PEERS, ESQ, ... HESTER, DAU. OF SIR THOMAS...... OF HEREFORDSHIRE......FRANCES, DAU. OF HIS EXCELLENCY SIR JONATHAN ATKINS, OB, 1685.

SIR RICHARD PEERS, of Barbados, married a daughter of James Hawley, Esq. of Brentford, and sister of Henry Hawley, Governor of Barbados. Sir Richard was Governor of Barbados in 1631 ; he was afterwards a Member of the Provisional Council in 1639—1651, and 1660. John Peers, who died in 1685, was a son of Sir Richard ; he was, with Colonel S. Barwick, appointed a Commissioner to take oaths in the Plantation. In 1673 he held no less than 1000 acres of land in Barbados. By his first wife, Hester, he had issue, John, Richard, Margaret, and Elizabeth ; and by his second, Thomas, Frances, and Anne wife of Capt. Hale. Henry Peers was a member for St. George's in 1706 ; Speaker of Assembly in 1733; Lieutenant-General and Governor of the island in 1740, in which year (Sept. 4) he died.

In 1649, Samuel Atkins had a warrant to ship horses to Barbados.—(C. S. P.)

37.

(*Ab.*) ...... EDWARD PEARCE......OB. DEC. 19, 1725....

38.

HELEN RICH, NATA 25 JULY, 1664,—DIED 20 NOV. 1665. — WILLIAM RICH, NATUS 25 DEC., 1666, DIED .... 1667. — ROBERT RICH, NATUS 21 NOV. 1668, DIED 17 SEP. 1670.

ROBERT RICH of Barbados, living in 1682, married Helen, daughter of the Rev. — Thornborough, son of the Rt. Rev. John Thornborough, Bishop of Worcester.

Probably of the family of Rich, of London, [*see* Lord Rich--in which, Jany. 24, 1676, a Baronetcy was created]. Sir Charles, great grandson of the 2nd Lord Rich, had an uncle Robert Rich, who married Elizabeth, daughter of Sir Adam Felton, and is said to have died without issue, but whether this is a mistake or not, it is difficult to say.

39.
(*Ab.*) CAPTAIN JOHN RAINSFORD......OB. FEB. 3, 1710....

40.

...... ALEXANDER SANDFORD ....
Obliterated.

Arms, Semée of nine cross crosslets, 3 falcons' (?) heads, erased, two and one. Impaling......a fesse nebulée, between 3 mullets. *Crest,* A talbot's head.

41.
...... THOMAS SHAWE, OB. 1713, AET. 42, ... AND ELIZABETH SHAWE .... — ALSO ELIZABETH BOOTH, WIDOW, ... OB. FEB. 12, 1721, AET. 67.

THESE arms indicate a Scottish origin. James Shawe of Ayrshire, and merchant of London, was uncle to John Shawe, father of James, merchant, and Lord Mayor of London, (born 1764), who was created a Baronet in 1809, and is now represented by Sir — Shaw, Bart., of Kilmarnock, whose *Arms* bear 3 *covered cups,* with a chief, &c., for augmentation.

Arms, A chev. between 3 covered cups. *Crest,* A chough.

42.
...... THE HON. COLONELL WILLIAM SHARPE, ESQ. ... .ANNO 16... AETATIS SUÆ 53......
Partially effaced.

HIS son William, of Waltham Abbey, died Oct. 7th, 1724. He had been twice Governor of Barbados. His will was proved in London.

Mrs. Barbara Sharpe, wife of William Sharpe (the son), was daughter of Sir Thomas Mompesson. Their son, Thomas Sharpe, married Elizabeth, daughter of Joseph French, Esq., whose sister, Keturah French, married the Hon. James Bruce, Chief Judge of Barbados.

Arms, Within a bordure engrailed, 3 eagles' (?) heads erased. *Crest,* A scimetar erect.

43.

DOROTHY, WIFE OF MR. JAMES SHEPHERD, MERCHANT, OB. 7 JULY, 1736, AET. 53, 2 M. 23 DAYS.

H IS son, James Shepherd, married, 1743, Barbara, daughter of William Jones, Esq., son of Nathaniel Jones, by Barbara, his wife, daughter of Robert Stroud. He was Baron of the Exchequer in Barbados. She died March 11, 1768, leaving an only child, Dorothy, born 1744, and married Jan. 12, 1762, to Alexander Bruce, Esq., M.D., third son of the Hon. James Bruce, Esq., of Garlet, N.B. [*See* " Peerage," *voce* Burley.]

44.

...... ELIZABETH, DAU.... OF...... SMITH, WIFE OF ...... OB. 1680, AET. 15...

T HERE was an Elizabeth Smith, wife of Colonel John Forster, of Egham House, Surrey, who died in 1731. She married, secondly, Dr. H. Barham, of Jamaica, and had, with other issue, Samuel Warren Forster, who married Sarah Warren Walrond, daughter of Thomas, second son of Anthony Walrond, of Barbados. (See will of the latter.)

In Ligon's History of Barbados, 1657 [Q. 1675 ?], there is a pleasing account of the almost exceptional kindness of Colonel Walrond, to his servants and slaves.

45.

(*Ab.*) AGNIS, WIFE OF JOSEPH WARD, OB. JAN. 12, 1713. — JAMES PEMBERTON, "SON OU THIS MERCHANT," OB. JUNE 29, 1736.

" A ZURE, a cross patonee, or," is given, in the peerage, for Ward, Visct. Bangor.- Joseph was possibly one of the three younger surviving sons of Bernard Ward, ancestor of the present peer, who was killed in a duel, in 1690 ; and this supposition is strengthened by finding the main line connected although at a much more recent period with Barbados.

There is an example of a somewhat similar cross and annulet, engraved in Edmonston's Heraldry.

Arms, ... a cross moline, charged with a mullet. Impaling, On a fesse voided (?) wavy, 3 bulls passant between 3 crosses potent, each ensigned with an annulet.

46.

.........SON OF THOMAS AND MARY WITHER............ ALSO THOMAS WITHERS, MERCHANT,...... OB. FEB. 18, 1755, AET. 43.........

47.

.........JOHN (surname obliterated), OB.......1715...... AET. 63......

48.

IN GRATEFUL REMEMBRANCE OF JOHN BRATHWAITE, ESQRE., OF "THREE HOUSES," IN THE PARISH OF ST. PHILIP. MANY YEARS AGENT OF THIS COLONY, IN GREAT BRITAIN. WHOSE COMPREHENSIVE VIEWS AND CONSUMMATE KNOWLEDGE OF ITS VARIOUS INTERESTS WERE ONLY TO BE EQUALLED BY THE MASTERLY ADDRESS WITH WHICH HE CONDUCTED, AND THE INFLEXIBLE PERSEVERANCE WITH WHICH HE PURSUED THEM. — THE LEGISLATURE OF BARBADOS ERECT THIS MONUMENT, ANXIOUS THAT POSTERITY SHOULD KNOW HOW HIGH HE STOOD, THROUGH HIS DISTINGUISHED SERVICES, IN THE ESTIMATION OF HIS COUNTRY. — HE WAS BORN IN THIS ISLAND ON 25th OCT. 1722, & DEPARTED THIS LIFE IN GREAT BRITAIN, ON 21st SEPT., 1800, AT EPSOM, IN THE COUNTY OF SURREY, WHERE HIS REMAINS WERE INTERRED.

49.

(*Ab.*) IN MEMORY OF THE FOLLOWING OFFICERS OF THE 69th REGT. — LT. COL. PAXTON, AND SURGEON CLELAND, WHO DIED IN 1853, IN TRINIDAD. — LIEUTENANTS DORRINGTON, & ALLEN, WHO DIED IN BARBADOS, IN 1855.—ALSO CAPTAIN J. CARMICHAEL, WHO DIED IN ENGLAND.

THE SAVANNAH OF ST. ANN.

I.

West Panel.

AROUND THIS TOMB,—REST THE REMAINS OF—FIFTEEN OFFICERS—AND THE CAPTAIN'S STEWARD—OF H. M. SCREW FRIGATE "DAUNTLESS,"—WHO, TOGETHER WITH THIRTY-EIGHT SEAMEN, — TEN MARINES, AND TEN BOYS, — BURIED IN THIS GARRISON; — AND ONE OFFICER, THREE SEAMEN, — SIX MARINES, AND ONE BOY,—COMMMITTED TO THE DEEP; ALL PERISHED BY YELLOW FEVER,—WHICH BROKE OUT AT SEA, — ON LEAVING THE HARBOUR OF ST. THOMAS, — ON THE 10th OF NOVEMBER, 1852.

South Panel.

AT THIS ISLAND—A GENEROUS REFUGE WAS AT ONCE AFFORDED,—AND BY THE UNCEASING CARE OF ITS CIVIL, MILITARY AND MEDICAL AUTHORITIES,—THE SHIP, WITH HER SURVIVING CREW RESTORED TO HEALTH,—WAS ENABLED TO SAIL HOMEWARDS ON—THE 21st MARCH, 1853.—COL. SIR WILLIAM M. G. COLE-BROOKE, C.B., K.H., GOVERNOR IN CHIEF.—LIEUT.-GEN. WILLIAM WOOD, C.B., COMMANDING THE TROOPS. — THE THIRTY-FOURTH REGIMENT. — THE SIXTY-NINTH REGIMENT.—WILLIAM MUNRO, ESQRE., INSPECTOR GENERAL OF HOSPITALS.—REVD WILLIAM W. JACKSON, M.A., CHAPLAIN OF THE FORCES.—WILLIAM DENNY, ESQRE., SURGEON 34th REGIMENT. — ALEXANDER B. CLELAND, ESQRE, M.D., SURGEON 69th REGIMENT.

East Panel.

THIS HALLOWED SPOT—WAS PURCHASED AND ENCLOSED,—AND THIS MONUMENT INSCRIBED—IN HONOURED MEMORY TO ALL,—BY THE LORDS COMMISSIONERS OF THE ADMIRALTY, — THE CAPTAIN, — AND SURVIVING OFFICERS — OF THE SHIP,—AND BY THE SORROWING RELATIVES AND FRIENDS—OF THOSE WHO REST BELOW—THAT THEIR—SACRED AND BELOVED REMAINS—SHOULD ASSIST IN UNDISTURBED REPOSE — FOR THE COMING OF THAT GREAT DAY, — WHEN ALL GRAVES SHALL BE SUMMONED—TO GIVE UP THEIR DEAD.

North Panel.

		ÆTAT.	OBIIT.
ROSS MOORE FLOUD	FIRST LIEUTENANT	37	28th NOV. 1852.
CHARLES KENT	SECOND LIEUTENANT	28	2nd DECR. ,,
ALFRED NEALE...........................	THIRD LIEUTENANT	25	22nd NOV. ,,
WILLIAM SIMPSON	LIEUTENANT	23	17th NOV. ,,
ALEXANDER LANGLANDS	CHIEF ENGINEER ...	32	22nd NOV. ,,
ARTHUR C. COUPER (*buried off the port*)	MATE	21	17th NOV. ,,
HENRY I. NUTTALL.......................	SECOND MASTER	28	23d NOV. ,,
EDWIN DEATH	CAPTAIN'S CLERK ...	27	6th DEC. ,,
GEORGE GORDON BUSHBY	MIDSHIPMAN............	20	14th DEC. ,,
JOSEPH CRISPIN	MIDSHIPMAN............	15	1st DEC. ,,
FLEETWOOD PELLEW HASWELL	MASTER'S ASSISTANT	18	14th DEC. ,,
CHARLES MARTIN.........................	ASSISTANT ENGINEER	28	25th DEC. ,,
ST. GEORGE G. S. DAVIS	ASSISTANT ENGINEER	25	2nd DEC. ,,
JAMES T. HENWOOD	ASSISTANT ENGINEER	21	18th NOV. ,,
WALTER W. H. RICHARDS	ASSISTANT ENGINEER	21	24th NOV. ,,
WILLIAM WELMAN	CARPENTER	40	15th DEC. ,,
JAMES VENABLES	CAPTAIN'S STEWARD	23	12th DEC. ,,

BLESSED ARE THE DEAD WHICH DIE IN THE LORD.

PARISH OF ST. GEORGE.

I.

.... THE HON. THOMAS APPLEWHAITE, ... OB. JUNE 14, 1749 (7 ?) AET. 59°
—ALSO MRS. ELIZABETH, HIS WIFE, ... OB. 11 APRIL, 1750 (9 ?)

2.

ALEXANDER, SON OF ALEXANDER ANDERSON, OB. OCT. 11, 1730, AET. 32.

3.

(*Ab.*) SARAH BASCOMB, OB. 30 OCT., 1777, AGED 74 ; ALSO, SARAH, WIFE OF
GRIFFIN BASCOM, OB. 12 OCT., 1798, ÆT. 52.

4.

.... FRANCIS BUTCHER, ... OB. 1777, AET. 65.

5.

(*Ab.*) .... DR. JOHN BATTYN, .. OB. JAN. 7, 1692. .... ALSO WILLIAM BATTYN,
ESQ., HIS GRANDSON, ... AND ELIZABETH, DAUGHTER OF DR. JOHN BATTYN,
AND WIFE OF EDWARD PERCE, ESQ. ....

D R. J. BATTYN was father, also, of A. Dottin Battyn, who married Mary, daughter
of William Dottin, great-grandfather of the late Captain A. R. Dottin, 2nd Life-
guards.

6.

.... EDWARD CLAYPOOL, .. OB. SEP. 11, 1699, ALSO, SARAH AND ELIZABETH,
HIS DAUGHTERS.......

T HE Claypole family, so powerful during the Commonwealth—Elizabeth, daughter
of Oliver Cromwell, having married John Claypole, Esq., of Norborough, Master
of the Horse to the Lord Protector—is noticed elsewhere in these pages.

7.

(*Ab.*) .... THE REVD. JOHN CARTER, ... OB. .... 1796.

8.

.... EDWARD DAYRELL, ... OB. .. SEP. 16, 1789.

M ARMADUKE DAYRELL, of Antigua, married, in 1784, a daughter of Warner
Tempest, of that island, and had issue. Perhaps the above was their son.
(Burke's "Landed Gentry"—Dayrell.)

John Keyt, ancestor of Keyt, Baronet of Ebrington (Cr. 29 March, 1660 ; Ext. 1699), married, 1st, Jane Porter, by whom he had a fifth son, Thomas Keyt, baptized 27th Oct., 1622, who married Mary, daughter of *William Dayrell*, Esq., of Abingdon, and relative of Professor John Morris, of Oxford.

Mr. John Keyt married, 2ndly, Margaret, daughter of Mr. William Harrison, and widow of Mr. Bovey, of Coughton, Warwickshire.

9.

(*Ab.*) GRANT ELLCOCK, OB. DEC. 11, 1774, ÆT. 60.

IN 1688, in a "list of papers delivered to ye Gov'r per Ben. Skutt," we find the following names in connection with a charge against William Pendleton for threatening the life of his "Unkle Skutt :"—affidavits of S. Bateman and Mr. Hollingsworth ; mittimus of Justice Wiseman ; depositions of Messrs. Ellison, Richard Turner, John Howlett, Rowland Tryon, *Cholmeley Elicock*, Jonathan Osborne, &c.   (See *Hayne's* family.)

Robert Archer, of Barbados (married to Elizabeth, daughter of Provost-Marshal Ellisson, or Elletson) was styled, in 1679, "Provost-Marshal of the Army."

10.

MRS. DOROTHY FREERE, DAUGHTER OF RICHARD AND MARY ...., OF KENT CHURCH COURT, HEREFORDSHIRE, BORN JAN. 26, 1734, MARRIED SEPT. 13, 1756, DIED JUNE 11, 1789.

11.

(*Ab.*) HON. JOHN FREERE, ESQ., OB. JAN. —, 1766, ÆT. 60.

THIS distinguished family being well known to the public, a few remarks only are necessary.

There was a Baronetcy conferred, in 1620, on Edward Frere, of Water Eyton, Oxfordshire, but leaving no issue by his wife Mary, daughter of John Stafford, of Blatherwick, it became extinct on his death, in 1630.

The Freres of Barbados came originally from Suffolk.   Mary, daughter of John Frere, who was Governor of Barbados in 1720, married Joseph Pilgrim, Chief Judge of the Common Pleas, who died in 1734, left issue (the Rev.) John, of New Windsor, Berks, who married Keturah, daughter of the Hon. James Bruce.

Government House in Barbados, is called "Pilgrim," after the family of the same name ; and, about the middle of last century, a branch of the Barbadian family of Archer settling in Jamaica, probably, so named one of their estates there, although there were also Pilgrims in the latter island.

12.

(*Ab.*) SUSANNA FREERE, OB. .. JAN. .. 1759.

13.

THE HON. BURY FRERE.........

Arms, ... 2 leopards' heads affrontée, or, between 2 flaunches of the second. N.B.—In Boutell's "Popular Heraldry," in one of the illustrations, the Arms of Guy Frere are given as, three hatchets, but the same escutcheon in the text, p. 44, is assigned to Wm. de Hursthelve (13th century).

14.

(*Ab.*) .... THE REVD. THOMAS FALCON, ... OB. .... 1762, AET. 33.

15.

.... CHRISTIAN, WIFE OF JOHN GIBBES, AND DAUGHTER OF REYNOLD ALLEYNE, ... OB. .. 1780, ÆT. 77.......

THE Baronetcy of Gibbes, of Barbados, was created in the person of Philip Gibbes (30th May, 1774), great-grandson of Philip Gibbes, who settled in Barbados in 1635.

16.

(*Ab.*) .... GEORGE HALL, .. OB. NOV. 20, 1742, AET. 31. .... ALSO, HANNAH SPOONER, WIFE OF JOHN SPOONER, AND DAUGHTER OF GEORGE HALL, ... OB. JAN. 5th, 1759.

17.

(*Ab.*) MRS. FRANCES JORDAN, WIFE OF MR. THOMAS JORDAN, BORN 27 JUNE, 1757, OB. 18....

18.

(*Ab.*) .... JOSEPH JORDAN, ... OB. 29 MARCH, 1752, AET. 63. .... ELIZABETH, HIS WIFE, ... OB. SEPT. 6, 1761, AET. 66. .... EDWARD, SON OF DR. JOSEPH JORDAN, .. OB. AUG. 5th, 1780. MR. WALKER JORDAN, OB. .... 1781.

19.

.... EDMUND KEYZAR, ... OB. .. 1795.....

EDMUND KEYZAR was farmer of the Customs in 1667.

20.

.... DURD LEWIS, PHYS. .... OB. .... 1692, AET. 40.

21.

.... ARABELLA, WIFE OF GEORGE PE......

(Very old fragment.)

48

22.

(*Ab*) .... THE HON. HENRY PEERS, .. OB. SEP. 4, 1740, AET. 57......

HENRY PEERS left two daughters, one of whom married Tobias Freere, and the
other, John Lyte. Sir Richard Peers, D. Governor in 1633, was probably his
ancestor.

23.

.... MARY PARTRIDGE, WIFE OF SAMUEL YARD PARTRIDGE. ...... JAMES
GRASSELL....

A BRANCH of this family was settled in Jamaica, where Mary Partridge married
Richard Houghton James, about the middle of the eighteenth century.

24.

ANN SAWYER, OB. 1691, ÆT. 30; ALSO HER BROTHER, VALENTINE WILEE,
OB. NOV. 10, 1691, ÆT. 29; ALSO, ROBERT WILEE, OB. 1691.

25.

.... CHARLES SAWYER,* SON OF ANN SAWYER, ... OB. 2ᵈ NOV., 1701, AET. 18.

26.

.... THE HON. RICHARD SALTER, ... OB. AUGUST 6,
1776, AET. 66......

RICHARD SALTER was the son of the Hon. Timothy Salter, of
St. George's Parish.

Arms, On a chev. engr.
between 3 birds close, 3 crescents. An escutcheon of pretence; quarterly, 1 & 4, a saltire between 4 spears erect,
2 & 3, 3 fishes hauriant.

27.

THE TOMB OF DR. SEDGWICK AND HIS FAMILY.

M.

NO date.

28.

.... DRAX SHETTERDEN, ... OB, MAY .., 169.., AET. 29........
(Fragment.)

DRAX of Yorkshire. "Colonel Drax, Colonel Modiford, and Colonel Walrond con-
verted their estates into money, and retired to Barbados, where Colonel Drax
married a daughter of the Earl of Carlisle." (Burke's "Landed Gentry"—Drax.)

29.

(*Ab*.) ANN TRUSSLER, DAU. OF JACOB MERCY TRUSSLER, OB. JUNE 15, 1780,
ÆT. 23; ALSO, HER FATHER, 1785.

30.

.... KATHERINE, WIDOW OF THE HON. RICHARD WORSUM, .. OB. AUGUST
25ᵗʰ, 1769, AET. 52.

* See note elsewhere in this volume.

PARISH OF ST. THOMAS.

I.

MR. WILLIAM ALUMBY, AGED ABOUT 72 YEARS, OB. 4 OCT., 1678.

2.

WILLIAM BRIANT, ESQ., AND MARY HIS WIFE, A NATIVE OF THIS ISLAND. AFTER AN EXEMPLARY DISCHARGE OF YE DOMESTIC VIRTUES, WITH TEMPER AND WITH HEALTH, BY DILIGENCE WITH PROSPERITY, DURING A MOST TENDER UNION OF FIFTY-EIGHT YEARS, WERE BY DEATH SEPARATED 4 MONTHS AND 11 DAYS ONLY, SHE DYING NOV. 6, 1756, AGED 74, HE THE 16th MARCH, 1757, AGED 78. TO WHOSE BLAMELESS MEMORY THIS STONE WAS DEPOSITED BY THEIR GRATEFUL AND AFFECTIONATE GRANDSON, J. WORRELL.

Arms, A chev. between three escallops. *Crest*, A dexter arm in armour, brandishing a sword.

WILLIAM BRIANT, and Mary his wife, were living in Barbados in 1715, and had three children, William, Ann, and Mary.

Leigh Hunt, the eminent author, was grandson of the Rev. Dr. Hunt, a member of this family.

3.

A VAULT OF THE OSBORNES OF SPRINGHEAD.—NO TABLET.

THE family of Osborne is mentioned in the Gibbes' pedigree. (*Vide* " Baronetage.")

4.

HERE LIES C. SKEET, OB. FEB. 3, 1758.

ON a lead coffin.

5.

M.S. SUB HOC MARMORE POSITÆ SUNT RELIQUÆ EPHRAIM SMITH DE AGRO LINCOLNIENSI ORUNDI MATHESEOS SCIENTIA CELEBRIS MENSURANDI ARTIS ÆQ. PROFESSIONE AC USI LONGE PRIMARII. GUBERNANTE RADULPHO DOM. GREIO BARONE DE WORK ILLUSTRI CHILIARCHA ET FRANCISCO RUSSELLO PRECESSORI BARBADIS FACILITATE PERQUAM BENEFICI—EX HAC VITA SPE BEATORIS EXCELSIT OCT. 27. 1701. PARITER VITAM CUM SANGUINE FUDIT POSUIT G. LILLINGTONUS IN HAC INSULA REGIÆ MAJESTATIS CONSILIIS.

SIR WILLIAM GREY, of Werke, was created Lord Grey of Werke, a dignity that expired with Ralph, fourth baron, in 1706.

The Hon. Ralph Gray (afterwards Lord Grey of Werke) was appointed Governor of Barbados in 1701.

Captain George Lillington, living in Barbados, 1680, was a Member of Council, at the age of 60, in 1708. His son, of the same name, was of the Inner Temple, London. (S. P. B. I., vol. 74.)

The Lillingstons were intermarried with the Barbadian families of Dottin, and Alleyne.

Colonel Henry Lillingston, born in 1620, served under General Monk. He had two sons, Henry and Luke, the latter of whom became a General, and commanded an expedition to the West Indies in 1695.

6.

CAPTAIN EDWARD THOMPSON, ESQ., OB. 6th OF APRIL, 1659; ALSO, CAPTAIN SAMUEL THOMPSON, OB. .... MARCH, 1655. "FROM HENCE WE SHALL RISE AGAIN."

Arms, A lion statant guardant.   *Crest*, A wyvern passant.

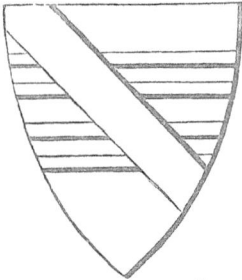

7.

MAJOR-GENERAL TIMOTHY THORNHILL, OB. AUG. 1, 1681; ALSO, HIS TWO WIFES, BOTH NAMED SUSANNA, AND HIS ELDEST SON TIMOTHY; DAU. ELIZABETH, AND HIS BROTHERS, JOHN AND ISAAC.

SOME curious disclosures respecting his habits are to be found in the State Papers, S. P. O. (*See* Burke's "Extinct and Dormt. Baronetage.")

Arms, Two bars gemelles, a bend dexter. *Crest*, A bush.

8.

(*Ab.*) THE BODY OF JEAN WOOD, WIFE OF MR. THOMAS WOOD, AND DAU. OF MR. ROGER AND JANE PIGGOTT, OB. APRIL 21, 1733.

PARISH OF CHRIST CHURCH.

I.

(*Ab.*) BENJAMIN ASHEHURST, GENT., WHO DEPARTED THIS LIFE OCT. 22, 1718, AGED 60.—ALSO, MAGDALEN, HIS WIFE, OB. FEB. 21, 1715, AET. 50.—ALSO, CAPT. JOHN ASHEHURST, OB. 27 SEPT., 1729, AET. 39, 11 M. 16 DAYS.

THIS was probably a branch of the family of Ashurst, of Waterstock, in which a Baronetcy was created, on the 21st July, 1688, and which expired in 1732.

Arms, A fesse between 3 fleur-de-lys: Impaling, ... on a bend wavy, 3 swans statant. *Crest*, A dexter cubit arm, grasping an imperial crown.

2.

HERE LIES INTERRED THE BODY OF—REYNOLD ALLEYNE, OF MOUNT ALLEYNE,—IN THE PARISH OF ST. JAMES, ESQRE. —WHO DEPARTED THIS LIFE THE—THIRTIETH DAY OF JUNE, ANNO DOMINI—1740 (9 ?) AETATIS 49.—

IT is stated in Burke's "Baronetage" that Reynold Alleyne, the first known of this family, commanded the Cromwellian forces in Barbados; and that his great-grandson, Sir John Guy Alleyne, was created a Baronet, on the 6th April, 1769.

Arms, Per chev. ... and erm., m. ch. 2 lions' heads erased. *Crest*, A horse's head.

Captain Reynold Alleyne was one of those officers whose estates were forfeited, by order of Lord Willoughby of Parham, in 1657.

3.

HERE LIES THE REMAINS—OF—THE REVD. ROBT. BOWCHER, RECTOR OF THIS PARISH 22 YEARS,—HE DIED 25th NOV., 1795,—AGED 63 YEARS.—IN GRATITUDE TO HIS MEMORY—THIS STONE IS PLACED BY—HIS NEPHEW—ROBT. B. CLARKE.

4.

HERE LYETH THE BODY OF JOHN CHASE, SENIOR, ESQRE., OB. FEB. 9, 1736, AETATIS 31 YEARS, 1 MONTH, & 20 DAYS.—ALSO, JOHN CHASE, SON OF JOHN & CHRISTIAN CHASE,—OB. 11 APRIL, 1737.—

THERE is a curious *Spiritualist* story connected with this family. (*See* "General Notes"—"Once a Week," March 11, 1865, &c.)

The Chase family of Maldon, and the Brewsters of Halsted Lodge, Essex, were connected; both seem to have possessed estates in Barbados, and the latter, also in Jamaica. There was at least *one* intermarriage between the Brewsters and Archers in Barbados.

5.

HERE LYETH INTERR'D, YE BODY—OF DOC^R. JOHN DURANT, SON OF THOS. DURANT, AND MARY HIS WIFE, WHO DEPARTED THIS LIFE, YE 4th DAY OF MARCH, 1726,—AGED 23 YEARS, 9 MONTHS, & 12 DAYS.

6.

HERE LIES THE BODY OF—THE HONBLE. JAMES ELLIOT, ESQRE.—HE MARRIED ELIZABETH, DAU. OF THE HONBLE. THOMAS WALROND, ESQ.—HE WAS SNATCHED AWAY FROM US—THE 14th DAY OF MAY, ANNO DOM. 1724.—IN THE 24th YEAR OF HIS AGE.—

JAMES ELLIOT was a Member of Council, and, probably, was the James Elliot stated in the "Peerage" to have died unmarried in 1742, and if so, his uncle, who succeeded him, was father of the 1st Lord St. Germains.

For particulars of the *Walrond* family, *see* Burke's "Landed Gentry," &c.

Arms, Within a bordure compony, ... three barrulets wavy; on an escutcheon of pretence, ... 3 bulls' heads cabossed. *Crest*, an elephant's head.

7.

(*Ab.*) ELIZABETH EVERSLEY, WIFE OF WILLIAM EVERSLEY, ESQ.,—OB. 6th OCT., 1813.

8.

SACRED TO THE OBSEQUIES—OF DOROTHY—CONSORT OF THE HONORABLE HENRY FREERE.

9.

HERE LYETH INTERR'D THE BODY OF SAMUEL GRAEME, SON OF GEORGE GRAEME, ESQ.,—WHO DEPARTED THIS LIFE THE 28th JULY, 1728, AGED 11 YEARS.

10.

HERE LIES THE BODY OF ELIZABETH — SEAWELL, WIDOW OF RICHARD—SEAWELL, ESQR,, WHO DIED THE 1st SEPTR., 1728, AGED 78 YEARS.

Arms, ... On a bend, 3 sea (?) birds close.   *Crest*, A sea-bird close, holding a ring in its bill.

OLD CHURCHYARD, CHRIST CHURCH.

IN the Old Churchyard there is a monument of classic design, with ovals of grey marble, on which are the following inscriptions :

I.

QUOD RELIQUUM EST DOROTH. FRANCESS ET JOANNÆ JARMAN FILIÆ. DANIELIS GILBERT......CONJUGIS, HIC JACET INHUMATUM, QUÆ OBIT, 12º DIE JAN. 1661.—IDEMQUE TUMULUS, PETRI UNI CUM FRANC. RISLEY FILIOLO CONDIT CONSECRATQUE ADIACENTES CINERES.

Arms, A double headed eagle displayed. Impaling, ... a chev. between three roundles.

HERE LYETH THE BODY OF THE HONBLE. JOSEPH BROWNE, ESQRE., WHO DEPARTED THIS LIFE, JUNE YE 28, 1728, IN YE 69th YEARE OF HIS AGE.

JOSEPH BROWNE may have been a member of the noble family of Oranmore. At the same time, the following is not unworthy of notice. A baronetcy was conferred on James Brown, of Barbados [Extinct Baronetage], and Willoughby, a daughter of Sir Jas. Brown, married Sir W. Yeamans, Bart. of Barbados. We also find that Colonel Joseph Brown, born 1665, had issue:—1. Joseph, aet. 25 in 1715 ; William, James, John, and Damaris.*

2.

HERE LYETH ...... BODY OF MRS. MARY ADDAMS, YE WIFE OF SAMVELL ADDAMS, WHO DECEASED......12 OF DECEMBER, 1672.—(ALSO)......SISER LOYD......

SAMUEL ADAMS was living in Barbados so early as 1638. He was probably a brother of Lieutenant Geo. Adams. (*See* Burke's "Landed Gentry," *voce* Ap-Adam.)

3.

HERE LYES WILLIAM BALSTON, ESQ., DEd TH...26 OCTOB. ANO. DOM. 1659.

A FAMILY of Balston intermarried with that of Ricketts, of Jamaica, now of Combe. (*See* Burke's "Landed Gentry.")

4.

J. W. GILES,—DIED JUNE 14th, 1854, AGED 56 YEARS.

5.

(Fragment).........S...P.....................

6.

(*Ab.*) ROBERT FARRER,—OB. JULY 23, 1691.

---

* Damaris is a name found also in the Prideaux family. Vide the will of Elizabeth Blake, of Barbados, 1694.

7.

(*Ab.*) DOCTOR JAMES HOLMES, OB. AUG. 31, 1728.

8.

(*Ab.*) HERE LIES THE BODY OF JOHN KIRTON, M.D., WHO DEPARTED THIS LIFE, JULY 15th, 1738.

(Eulogistic lines.)

HERE ALSO LIES—ANN HIS WIFE—WHO DIED—AUGUST 7th, 1765, AGED 65 YEARS.—SHE WAS A PATTERN OF DOMESTIC ŒCONOMY—AND TO HER CHILDREN —SHE AMPLY SUPPLIED THE LOSS OF THEIR FATHER, [&c.] THIS HUMBLE MONUMENT IS RAISED BY HER SURVIVING DAUGHTER.

FEW notices of this name are to be found in pedigrees. It occurs in one of the early wills of *Archer*, in Barbados, where also, in 1713, is recorded the marriage of Nathan Kirton and Mary Archer. In England [K. 6, p. 136, Her. Coll.], in the pedigree of Richard, brother of Sir Simon Archer, Katherine, the former's daughter, appears to have married in 1640, Edmund *Kirton*, of Thorpe Mandeville.

ADAM'S CASTLE ESTATE.

I.

IN OBITUM CHARISSIMA PATRIS SUI, DOMINI ROBERTI HACKETT, MILITIS, QUI EX HAC VITA MIGRAVIT ULTIMA DIE CALENDARUM MARTIS, ANNO DOMINI, 1679.

HIC JACET EFFIGIES SACRÆ VIRTUTIS OPIMA
    NOBILIS ET PRUDENS CANDITA SARACOPHAGO,
QUIS VALEAT LACHRYMAS MANENTES SISTERE GUTTAS!
    QUIS COHIBERE POTEST! VIR PIUS ECCE JACET!
TE PLORANT NATI PLORANT CHARISSIMA CONJUX
    MÆSTA DOMUS PUERI LUGET ET OMNIS INOPS.
FLERE NEFAS RAPTUM CÆLESTI SEDE BEATUM
    INDIGENUS NOBIS QUI JOVE DIGNUS ERAT
NON DECET ELYSIUM MISERIS IMPLERE QUERELIS,
    HOC BONA MEUS VIRTUS, HOC PIETASQUE DEDIT
VIRIDA PERPETUUM DURABIT FAMA PER ÆVUM,
    PENSABIT VITAM GLORIA LONGA BREVEM.

B. M. S.—(Now forms the doorstep of an overseer's house.)

THE barony of Hackett is one of the dormant peerages of Ireland. Lineage— Paganus de Hachett, a knight of King Henry the Second's suite, at the conquest of Ireland. He was father of Reginald and William, which latter gave his infant son, Peter, to King John, in 1204, as hostage for John de Courcy, Earl of Ulster. Lords

Robert, John, and William, followed in succession. In the certified list of peers who sat in the parliament of Edward I., the Barons de Hackett are included. 1307, Sir Henry Fitz Geoffrey Hackett, after whom came Lord Peter Hackett, Lord John Hackett, Lord Richard Hackett, Lord Peter Hackett (a kinsman of the Geraldines), joined in the Desmond revolt.

This family decayed under Queen Elizabeth, but having risen again, risked all for King James II., under Lord James Hackett, who left a son named Pierce Hackett. (Lodge—seriatim.)

Sir Robert Hackett, the subject of the epitaph, was one of the gentlemen of Barbados, raised to the baronetage by King Charles II., in 1661.

HANNAY'S PLANTATION.

A Tomb, with the following inscription :—

I.

GEORGE INCE, SON OF JOHN & MARGARET INCE, BURIED MARCH 9, 172... 11 MONTHS OLD : AND MARGARET, DAUGHTER OF JOHN & MARGARET INCE, BURIED, JULY 13th, 1734— ...13 YEARS, 2 MONTHS, AND 21 DAYS.

JOHN INCE, President of Council in 1803, was probably grandson of John and Margaret.

BANNATYNE ESTATE.

Two fragments of an old Tombstone, *circa* 1680.

I.

```
. . . . . . . . . . E. MORIAM
. . . . . . . . . . CAREW CHIRARGO
. . . . . . . . . CHARISSIMVS FRATER
. . . . . . . . . RISTOPHERVS CAREW
. . . . . . . . . AXEAM  HANC MOLEM
. . . . . . . . .  OS VIT PIETATIS ERGO
. . . . . . . . . TVMVLOS STRVIMVS
. . . . . . . . . . AMICA GADAE A
. . . . . . . . . . . MOR SIC.

. . . . . . . . . . FATA
. . . . . . . . . REVI MARMOR
. . . . . . . . . . FVNVS  HAB
. . . . . . . . . SVOS  CINERES
. . . . . . . . . . AXARIDACTAA
. . . . . . . . . . IN ÆTERNOS
. . . . . . ST FATA SVOE PER
. . . . . . . . . . RTVTE
. . . . . . . . . . ITE.
```

PARISH OF ST. JOSEPH.

OLD CHURCHYARD.

1.

HERE LYES INTERRED THE BODY OF EDWARD BENNEY, ESQ., WHO WAS BORN IN THE TOWN OF SHREWSBURY, THE 24th DAY OF JUNE, 1619, AND DEPARTED THIS LIFE THE 16th DAY OF SEPTEMBER, 1701. HE WAS AN INHABITANT OF THE PARISH SINCE THE YEAR 1647, AND SERVED IN THE ASSEMBLY AS ONE OF THE SAID PARISH SEVERAL YEARS.

2.

IN MEMORY OF DANIEL McCLOUD. DIED JULY 13, 1751, AGED 50 YEARS.

3.

HERE LYETH INTERRED THE BODY OF LIEUT.-COLL. JOSEPH SHENE, MERCHANT, IN BRIDGETOWN. DIED THE 20th OF AUGUST, 1709, AGED 44 YEARS.

PARISH OF ST. ANDREW.*

1.

HERE LIES THE BODY OF JOHN FOORD, GENT., WHO WAS B......... OVTº (*sic*) THE ...... 1617, AND DIED......

HE was probably ancestor of Thomas Ford, Esq., of Barbados, great grandfather of Sir Francis Ford, created a Baronet in 1793.

2.

HERE LIES THE BODY OF MRS. LUCY JOHNSTON, THE WIFE OF CAPTAIN ARCHER JOHNSTON, WHO DEPARTED THIS LIFE, ON THE ...... OF 9BER, 1680...... ABOUT 22 YEARS OF AGE.

3.

... EDWARD LAMING......OB. JAN. 17......AET. 59......

4.

MRS. MARY MORRIS, YE DAUGHTER OF MAJOR ROBERT MORRIS, — BORN 14 MARCH, 1694, — MARRIED TO JAMES DOTHIE, ESQ., — 7th OF FEBRUARY, 1713, — AND DIED 12 JULY, 1720.

5.

(*Ab.*) ... THE HON. JOHN MILLES, ESQ., MEMBER OF COUNCIL,—OB. 30th AUG. 1718, AET. 65.—ALSO, JANE MILLES, HIS WIFE,—OB. 4th MARCH, 1722,—AET. 57.

6.

(*Ab.*) ... ANNE POOLE ...... OB. .... JAN. 5, 1740, AET. 56.
Fragment.

7.

.... MARGARET RUDDER, DAUGHTER OF DAVID AND ELIZABETH RUDDER...... OB. JUNE 16, 1752......ALSO DAVID RUDDER, HER FATHER, OB. APRIL 17, 1753.

8.

... TURPIN WILLOUGHBY, OB. MARCH 2, 1741, AET. 61.........

HE may have been a member of the noble family of Willoughby. Francis, Lord Willoughby, was Governor of Barbados, and died, April 10th, 1673. By his will, dated July 17th, 1666, he appointed executors, his nephew, Henry Willoughby, Esq., Samuel Barwick, his secretary, Haughton, &c. ; and bequeathed his property to his brother William Willoughby, &c.

---

* There are no Registers of this Parish, prior to the present century.

49—2

Francis, 5th Lord Willoughby of Parham, was drowned at Barbados, in 1666.

There was a Captain Martin Turpin, whose grandson Captain Thomas Denton, served in the Duke of Newcastle's regiment during the Civil War of Charles I., but the name is comparatively rare.

9.

N.........G......... OB.......... 1758 ....
Fragment.

10.

...... VAUGHAN, 1733 ....
Fragment.

IN 1715, there was an act of the local legislature passed, to break the entail of Thomas Somers, Esq., to the lands of *James* Vaughan, for the latter's creditors.*

---

* John Vaughan, Francis Smith, and Samuel Cox, appear as witnesses to the will of Lucie Blackman, of Barbados, in 1710. *Lucie* was of the *male* sex. (Oliver MS. Papers.)

PARISH OF ST. PHILIP.

1.

(*Ab.*) .... JAMES AYNSWORTH, ESQ., ... OB. 7th MARCH, 1723.....

AINSWORTH of Smithill's Hall, Lancashire, bore : Gules, 3 battle-axes argent, with a crest the same as the above, and motto, " Spero Meliora."

In a letter from Henry Palmer, of London, 3rd Nov., 1727, to Mrs. Dixon, at Ather House, Maidstone, the writer mentions a lease granted in Barbados, in 1710, to " Mr. Aynsworth, and Mr. Rous." In the same, is a reference to Mr. Ashley of Barbados, and Dr. Dod. ("Oliver Papers," privately printed—*voce* Samuel Pasfield.)

Arms, ... 3 battle-axes. *Crest,* A knight in full armour standing, with a battle-axe in dexter hand, resting on shoulder.

2.

.... JOHN ARCHER, ESQ., WHO DIED OCT. 30, 1786.—AND OF ANN, HIS WIFE WHO DEPARTED THIS LIFE MAY 18, 1794, BOTH AGED 50.—ALSO, MRS. MILLICENT WHITE, SISTER TO THE ABOVE ANN ARCHER,—OB. .... 1798. .. WILLIAM STENHOUSE, .. OB. 1780. .. SARAH WARD STENHOUSE, .. OB. 1785. .. ALSO, JOSEPH STENHOUSE, .. OB. 1797...

THIS MARBLE SLAB IS PLACED TO THE COMMEMORATION OF THEIR ...... (obliterated.)

M. S.

SEE the "Gentleman's Magazine," Aug., 1861, p. 191; "Memorials of surname Archer," &c. John Archer must have been of a junior branch of Archer, of St. Lucy's and St. Philip's Parishes.

3.

(*Ab.*) .... ROBERT BOUCHIER, .. BORN SEP. 3, 1707, .. OB. MARCH 17, 1739.

4.

.... ROBERT BISHOP, ESQ., OB. SEP. 16, 1715, AET. 35.—ALSO, MARY FORBES, RELICT OF ROBERT BISHOP, ESQ., OB. MAY 26, 1724, AET. 48.—ALSO, MARY MORRIS, THEIR DAUGHTER, OB. MAY 25th, 1743, AET. 33.

Arms, A saltire indented ; an escutcheon of pretence charged with a St. George's Cross ; Impaling, three lions rampant, ducally crowned.

5.

.... JOHN BEST, ... OB. 21 AUG., 1758, AET. 50...

6.

J. B. .... OB. 1743.

J. B. .... OB. 1745.

8.

.... WILLIAM COX, .. OB. 1766....

SAMUEL COX was President of Council in 1701.

9.

A. C. .... OB. .... 1752.

10.

.... TEMPERANCE CARTER, WIFE OF TIMOTHY CHESSMAN CARTER, .. OB. .. 1780.

11.

.. HENNINGHAM CARRINGTON, WIDOW OF PAUL CARRINGTON, ... OB. JAN. 28, 1741, AET. 69.

12.

.... ISAAC GITTENS, .. OB. 1819.....

THERE was a family named Gytyng, at Wrexham, about the middle of the seventeenth century.

13.

.... JOHN H..DY (probably Hardy), OB. 1790.

A fragment.

14.

.... MARY, WIFE OF HENRY HERNE, OB. .... 1725.

Fragment.

15.

.... ROBERT HAYNES, ESQ., OB. 9th OCT., 1727. ....

HE married Annie Elcock, and had issue Robert. (Burke's " Landed Gentry.")

Several persons of this name, are found in the West Indies at an early period. A Colonel Haynes was killed at Hispaniola, April 13, 1655.

16.

(*Ab.*) .... JOHN HALL, ESQ., OB. 22 MARCH, 1729.....

Arms, ... A fesse indented, between 3 griffins segreant. *Crest*, On a ducal crown, a lion sejeant.

17.

.... LAETITIA MOE, .. OB. 1735.—JAMES MOE. .... SAMUEL MOE. .... CHRIS-
TIAN MOE. ....

Dates effaced.

18.

A.... M...., OB. .... 1743.
Fragment.

19.

J..... M....., OB. .... 1743. (Obliterated.)
Fragment.

20.

(*Ab.*) .... JAMES MAPP, ESQ., OB. 1757. ....

21.

HIC SEPULTA JACET M..RITA NOKE, X^ROP. RICHARD NOKE NUPER.... HUJUS
INSULÆ, SECRETA .. R. .. II. .. ET FELIA GULIELMI BULLONEX—ANTIQUA FA-
MILIA. E. B..TSON DE DVFFVN CUJIS OPTIME MERETIS MEMORIA TRISTIS.
DOLENS QUÆ CONJUX. HOC POSUIT OBIIT XXIIII. JVLY 16, 1677.

22.

MR. JOHN PERRATT, OB. JUNE 7, 1729, AGED 74 ; ALSO,
MRS. ANN PERRATT, HIS WIFE, OB. MARCH 16, 172⅝,
AGED 63.

Apparently the same arms as those borne by Sir John
Perrott, Lord of Haroldston, and Laugharn Castle ; also
Lord of Carew Castle, Lord Deputy, Lieutenant-General, and
Governor of the Kingdom of Ireland, Admiral of England,
Lord of the Privy Council, and Knight of the Bath, who died
Nov. 3, 1599.

Arms, Three pears, on a chief
a demi-lion rampant ; Impaling, ... a fesse : in chief three
roses or cinquefoils. *Crest,*
A raven holding a flower,

Sir James, a younger son of Sir John, had a warrant for
a patent (but never signed) creating him a Marquis.

23.

.... RICHARD PAYNE, .. OB, 1769.
Fragment.

He was probably of the Antiguan family, of which Lord Lavington was the head.
This is a distinguished Anglo-Norman name, and is to be found in the various
rolls of Battle Abbey. *See* Burke's "Extinct and Dormant Peerage," &c., *voce* "Lavington." "The Armorial of Jersey," &c., and "The King of Arms," London, 1873.
Nathaniel Payne, grand-uncle of Lord Lavington, had an only daughter, who
married William Woodley, Governor of the Leeward Islands.

24.

W. P. .... 1741 ......
Fragment.

25.

I. P. .... 1772 ......
Fragment.

26.

.... 1732 ......
Fragment.

27.

R..R, ... OB. 1755 ......
Fragment.

28.

.... MRS. MARY ROGERS, WIFE OF HENRY ROGERS, ESQ., OB. SEP. .., 1753,
AET. 57. ....

29.

.... HENRY SCOTT, .. OB. .. FEB. 6, 1793. ....

30.

T.... S...., 1777.....

31.

.... K.... W...., 1730.....
Fragment.

32.

.... C.... W.... (WHITE ?), 1757.........
Fragment.

A CAPTAIN W. WHITE, of Barbadoes, married Ann, daughter of Philip Gibbs, who
died 1697.

33.

WILLIAM ....
OF THE KINGDOM OF ....
THIS LIFE YE 8th ....
YEAR OF HIS AGE........................
DYED YE 19th OF........................
EAR OF HER AGE........................
RTHERS. ....
MILLESAUNT .... (WHITE ?)............
INFANCY. ....
Obliterated.

PARISH OF ST. LUCY.

CHURCH AND CHURCHYARD.

This parish has suffered severely from hurricanes, and particularly in that of 1831.

JAMES BUTLER......1696.

THE above fragments have been used in repairing the wall of the churchyard.*

James Butler may have been of the family of the 7th Lord Cahir, outlawed in 1691. *See* "Peerage," *voce* Glengall.

2.

.... 18, YEARS. SHE WAS A.... AL CHILD, A TENDER, KIND DA...... AFFECTIONATE WIFE. SINCERE IN FRIENDSHIP; MILD, PRUDENT, AND DISCREET IN ALL HER ACTIONS; MUCH BELOVED BY HER ACQUAINTANCE.... HER DEATH LAMENTED BY HER FRIENDS AND RELATIONS......

THE above fragment has been *utilised* like the preceding.

3.

JAMES, SON OF CAPT. JAMES GRAHAM, OB. 20 DEC., 1729, AET. 38. — CAPT JAMES GRAHAM, FATHER OF THE ABOVE, OB. 12 JULY, 1730, AET. 77. — ELIZA-BETH, DAUGHTER OF SAID JAMES, OB. JULY 16, 1730, AET. 19. — MARY, WIFE OF THE ABOVE JAMES, OB. MAY 22, 1747, AET. 51.

---

* During the repairs after the hurricane of 1831, many of the old tombstones were laid on their *faces* (it is to be hoped), in the formation of the present paved way, from the outer gate, to the church door.

4.

HERE LIES COLONEL JOSEPH PICKERING,—OBIIT 14 MARCH, 1715.

Pickering, of Tichmarsh, descended from Gilbert Pickering, who purchased the Manor of Tichmarsh (*temp.* Elizab.) from William Earl of Worcester.

Gilbert, who was son of John Pickering of Gretton, and grandson (by Margaret his wife, daughter of Lascells of Esrick, Yorkshire,) of James Pickering, of the County of Westmoreland, married Elizabeth, daughter of John Stanbank, and was great grandfather of Sir Gilbert Pickering of Tichmarsh, created a Baronet of Nova Scotia.

Arms, Ermine, a lion rampant, ducally crowned...... *Crest*, A lion's jamb, erased.

Dorothy Pickering, probably a daughter of the 1st Bart., married in 1724, George, eldest son of Theodore Walrond.

5.

HERE LYETH THE BODY OF ELIZABETH GIDY, WIFE OF MATTHEW GIDY, WHO WAS BORN JANUARY YE 6, 1687, AND DEPARTED THIS LIFE, THE 1st DAY OF APRIL, 1726.—HAD ISSUE BY THE SAID MATTHEW GIDY, FOUR SONS AND FIVE DAUGHTERS.

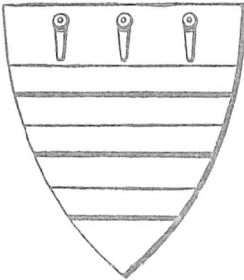

A REFERENCE to the local records might enable the genealogist to throw some light on this family. Its arms bear a close resemblance to those of Grey, Earl of Stamford.

Arms, Barry of seven, in chief 3 *buckle* tongues. *Crest*, The sun in splendour·—thereon a bear or goat statant.

6.

...... THOMAS WHITECOTE, ESQ......OB. 17 JULY, 1796......

Old, fragments.

7.

....I. I. SEALS...... (date effaced).

8.

(*Ab.*) MICHAEL BOYCE, SENIOR, OB. MAY 9, 1750, AET 63, O. 3.
M.

9.

.... W. M. BROWN (date effaced—very old.)

10.

......SALMON............

Fragment.

11.

.... GRISSEL MACKAY..OB. 10 SEP. 1787,..AET. 37....

12.

R... I....... 1750. ....

Tombs of the family of Archer of St. Lucy [and St. Philip] (destroyed, or displaced, during the hurricane of 1831).

The following appeared in *Notes and Queries*, July 11th, 1874 (abridged):—

"My attention has lately been drawn to the question of the origin of the Archer family of Barbados in the seventeenth century from having seen a work on this surname. In this work frequent suggestions are thrown out in favour of the Worcestershire origin of this family. A careful analysis of the contents, and collation, with other sources of information, will, I think, show that there were Archers in Barbados from London, Suffolk, and Lincoln, but that Edward Archer, of St. Philip's and St. Lucy's parish,—will proved 1693,—who died there in 1693, was none of these, but was of a distinct and Worcestershire origin. I am well aware how little reliance can be placed on family traditions, yet, to a certain extent, they possess some value as clues. The descendants of this Edward Archer are still to be found, not only in Barbados, but in Jamaica,† where two of his grandsons settled about 1753. In both branches of the family, notwithstanding the lapse of time since their separation, the tradition still exists that their English progenitors were Royalists, and of Umberslade descent ; [and this, too, in face of the facts, that Sir John Archer of the De Boys, or Essex, family was himself in Barbados, and that he had relatives in Jamaica, in the seventeenth century,] and they still treasure an heirloom transmitted from generation to generation, which would seem to strergthen the first part of the tradition, viz., a locket, set in gold of the period, containing a portrait of Charles I. reading.

"That the Worcestershire Archers were Royalists, there can be no doubt ; the children of Edward Archer of Hanley Castle, eldest son of John Archer of Welland, by his wife Eleanor, daughter of Richard Frewen of Hanley Castle, were dispossessed of their estates by Cromwell. We find, about 1652, ' William Archer and William Walter petitioning on behalf of the children, *being minors*, Thomas, George, and Anne, of the late Edward Archer of Hanley Castle.' There is no mention of his elder children in this petition ; they, no doubt, had equally incurred the Protector's displeasure. Thomas, George, and Anne, being minors, might be presumed to be guiltless of political sympathies. These Welland Archers appear to have broken up entirely, about 1649, and to have dispersed in all directions, their large possessions passing into the hands of their Cromwellite neighbours—the Lechmeres* and others. Presumably, the Frewens—maternal ancestors of Edward of Hanley—were also Royalists, for we find them settled in Barbados, at the same period as Edward Archer, of 1693, as well as the Thornes, Moores, and other families, and *Kirtons*, with whom the [Umberslade] Netherthorpe Archers had intermarried. It is a curious and suggestive fact, that the first Barbadian ancestor of Edward Archer of 1693, called his estates ' Cleobury,' and ' Oldbury.' Now, if we refer to Dugdale's ' Pedigree of Archer of

---

* With whom they intermarried once.   † Now in the female line—*Walcott, Campbell*, &c.

Umberslade,' we find that Thomas le Archer—(*temp.* Edward III.)—married Marga-
rita, daughter of—— Cleburie, and Rowland Archer [grandson of Archer] of Umberslade, quartered the arms of the Mortimer-Cleburie family. His sister was Mrs. Walrond, and his aunt, Mrs. Kirton. Again, Oldbury is a town in Worcestershire. I cannot
but think that a deep significance lies in the names chosen by this branch of Barbadian
Archers, for the first properties held by them, in the land of their [choice]. They would
serve, not only to keep alive the cherished memory of the mother country, but act as
landmarks to their posterity, showing the *line* of Umbersdale from which they derived,
as in the case of *Cleoburie*, and their Worcester origin from *Oldbury*.

"The earliest Archers mentioned in the Parish Registers of Barbados, are Richard,
Leonard, and Nicholas.* They were undoubtedly sons of Nicholas Archer of Hus-
tropp, co. Lincoln, and of "foreign p^{ts}." His will is recorded in London. Sons,
Richard, Leon (qy. cont. Leonard), *Nicholas,* and *Christopher.* That they were also
Cromwellites and Puritans, I think we may infer, from the baptismal names of their
children, when we consider the mania, at that period, for Biblical appellations among
the followers of the Protector. Nathaniel, Joseph, Joshua, and Peter, are the Christian names we find bestowed on the offspring of these *early* Archers, and they were
perpetuated in their descendants. The name of *Edward* appears but once amongst
them ; one Peter Archer, grandson of Leonard, called his son by this name, but *he*
was born in 1703, *ten years after the death of Edward Archer of* 1693.

"It is morally impossible that the latter could be descended from either of the
three brothers, *Richard, Leonard,* or *Nicholas,* since the only member of their respective
families who bore the name of Edward was born after his demise.

At the present time, baptismal designations have no signification ; it was not
thus, however, in the days of our forefathers. Let us, then, turn from these Lincoln
Archers to Edward Archer, of 1693, and his descendants. In no single instance do
we find a Scriptural name amongst them, but in their stead we *do* find the baptismal
names borne for centuries by the Umberslade Archers—*Thomas, Edward, Robert,
John,* and *William*—names, moreover, borne by the sons of John Archer of Welland,
from whom I claim descent for Edward Archer, who died in Barbados, in 1693, either
through his eldest son, Edward, of Hanley Castle, or through Robert, a younger son,
born 1616. We know that the former's eldest son, John, was in 'foreign p^{ts}' (see
Nash) ; it is possible, nay, probable, that his other 'dispossessed' elder sons were also
emigrants. Edward, of Hanley Castle, was born June, 1600. Allowing thirty years
for a generation, Edward Archer, of Barbados, might clearly have been his son ; were
he born about 1630, he would only have been sixty-three at the time of his death
in 1693. That some members of the Worcestershire Archers did emigrate, is an
undoubted fact ; for among the wills of Archers in 'foreign p^{ts}' we find those of

---

* There are no Archers named in the List of Inhabitants of Barbados, in 1638 ; but about 1640—80, there
were Archers from Hampshire, in addition to those from the other counties mentioned. The Archers of Wainfleet
[1684] were evidently a branch of Umberslade, as were also the earlier Norfolk and Suffolk Archers.

'John of Worcester,' Humphrey Archer, &c. The former, I presume, was the son of Edward of Hanley. I am more disposed, however, to think that Edward Archer of Barbados was the son of the younger brother Robert, son of John Archer of Welland and Eleanor Frewen of Hanley.

"Robert Archer was baptized at Hanley, April, 1616. He married Anne Skinner of Ledbury, and was the father of many children. His son Robert was 'Parson of Castle-Morton': he married, 1677, Hannah Moore, daughter of Edward Moore, of Suckley Court. Two short tabulations will show more clearly than I can do by words, my reason for believing that this younger Robert was a brother of Edward of Barbados. That Edward Archer's father was named Robert, I myself believe, though I readily admit that my reasons for this preference will not satisfy genealogists; but, in the absence of proof, let the following fact weigh for what it is worth. During the hurricane of 1831, in common with many other ancient mansions of the old settlers (or 'Planters,' as they were called), the ancestral home of this branch of the Barbadian Archers was destroyed; beneath the foundation-stone was found, by Mr. Edward Archer (the owner), an exquisite porcelain* cup, on which were the initials R. A. in gold. It is necessary to explain, that Mr. Edward Archer was innocent of all genealogical precise information, and, like many others, merely relied on a family tradition, without any misgiving, and, at the same time, without any interest in such questions.

R. C."

=Robert Archer, son of=Anne John Archer and Elea- | Skinner. nor Frewen, b. 1616.	Edward Archer† of Barbados, =Elizabeth. ob. 1616.
The Rev. Robert Archer,=Hannah, dau. of Parson of Castle Morton. | Edw. Moore of 1677. | Suckley Court.	Robert Edward.= Tho- Eliza- Hannah, pro-= --Ashby. disin- | mas. beth. bably called herited. | after his bro- | ther's wife.
Timothy. Edward. Elizabeth, Hannah name of his ob. an brother's wife. infant.	Other children, Edward. John."‡ names unknown.

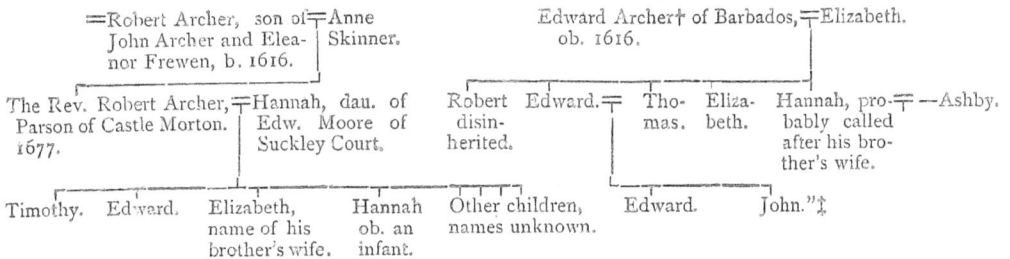

* It was apparently of *Sèvrse*.

† Qy. *Brother* of Rev. Robert.

‡ The author of the above remarks might be equally critical with the pedigrees of, at least, two-thirds of the families whose origin is not less doubtful, although unquestioned. The arguments advanced by R. C. as above, still leave untouched the hypothesis of the descent of E. A. [1693] from a Suffolk descendant of Edward [mat. at Oxon], son of Miles [2nd son of Richard Archer, by his wife, Maud Delamere], who lived at Ambleside, co. Westmoreland, towards the close of the 16th century. The Plantations, or estates, of the families of Archer [E. A. 1693], Brathwaite [Miles], and Gretton of St. Philip, were contiguous. The latter intermarried with that of Toppin, present representatives of which are, the Revd. G. P. Toppin, and Capt. Toppin, 18th Regt. [Royal Irish].

PARISH OF ST. JAMES.

PARISH CHURCH.

I.

SAMUEL BARWICK, COMMANDER IN CHIEF OF HIS NATIVE COUNTRY, OB. JAN.
I, 1732, AET. 63.—WILLIAM, HIS ELDEST SON, PLACES THIS STONE, OVER SAMUEL
HIS YOUNGEST BROTHER,—OB. JUNE 4, 1741, AET. 39.

SAMUEL BARWICK, appointed, in 1665, Governor and Commander-in-chief of Barbados, was the son of Christopher Barwick, of Andover, who died in 1624.

His son Samuel, born in 1669, was also afterwards Governor and Commander-in-
chief of Barbados, and died in 1733, leaving an only daughter and heiress, Jane, married to J. O. Bruce, Esq., grandson of Alexander Bruce, Esq., of Garlet, Clackmannan-
shire, which family is now represented by W. D. Bruce, Esq., F.S.A., &c., Recorder of
Wallingford, &c., and now a Judge in Jamaica.

2.

ANN, WIFE OF JOHN COLLINS, OB. NOV. 27, 1763; ALSO, ANNE, WIFE OF
REYNOLD GIBBES, ELDEST DAU. OF THE ABOVE JOHN AND ANN COLLINS, OB.
1766, AET. 45.

3.

MRS. MARY GIBBES, RELICT OF HON. THOS. GIBBES, OB. 24 DEC., 1770, AET. 42
—MRS. MARGARET ELIZABETH GIBBES, WIFE OF REV. HAYNES GIBBES, OB. 9 MARCH
1775, AET. 50.—SARAH GIBBES, OB. JUNE 24, 1783, AET. 56.

4.

MAJOR EDWARD HARRISON, OB. 16 FEBRUARY, 1669,
AET. 63. HE WAS BORN IN THE COUNTY OF DARBY.

Arms, (no tincture), On a chief 3 eagles displayed. — N.B. Arms of Harrison of Hurst and Finchhamstead,
Berks., granted 1623 : Or, on a chevron sable three eagles displayed of the field. *Crest*, Out of a ducal coronet
or, a talbot's head of the last, guttèe de poix.

5.

THE HON. WILLIAM HOLDER, OB. AUG. 11, 1705, AET. 48.—HIS WIFE, MRS.
SUSANNAH HOLDER, OB. 12 MARCH, 1725, AET. 57.—ALSO, WILLIAM HOLDER, THEIR
GRANDSON, OB. 14 AUG., 1752, AET. 31.

6.

MR. EDWARD JORDAN, OB. FEB. 16, 170⅘.—ALSO MRS. ANN JORDAN, WIFE TO
MAJOR EDWARD JORDAN, OB. 17 AUG., 1726, AET., 41. — ALSO MAJOR EDWARD
JORDAN, SON OF THE AFORESAID EDWARD JORDAN, AND HUSBAND OF AFORE-
SAID ANN, OB. APRIL 16, 1728. AET. 41. — ALSO, JOSEPH DOTIN, ESQ., SON IN
LAW TO MAJOR EDWARD JORDAN, OB. MARCH 30 1735, AET. 45.—ALSO EDWARD
JORDAN DOTIN, SON OF JOSEPH, BY HIS WIFE, ANN JORDAN, OB. MAY 21, 1736,
AGED 11.—ALSO ANN, RELICT OF JOSEPH DOTIN, AND WIFE TO THE REV. DUDLEY
WOODBRIDGE. — ALSO ANN WOODBRIDGE, HER DAUGHTER, OB. JULY 27, 1740.

D UDLEY WOODBRIDGE was probably a son of Dudley Woodbridge, Judge Advocate
of Barbados, and agent there of the celebrated *South Sea Company.*

7.

EDWARD JORDAN, OB. OCT. 25, 1787, AET. 67 ; — ALSO,
ANN JORDAN, HIS WIFE, CO-HEIRESS OF JOSEPH DOTTIN
AND ANN JORDAN, OB. JAN. 30, 1791, AET. 69. — ALSO,
EDWARD JORDAN, THEIR SON, OB. 17 DEC., 1799, AET. 58.

Arms, Quarterly, 1 and
4, Azure, on a bend cotised or, an alyrion displayed of the second—a canton sinister or ; 2 and 3, Argent, two
lions passant gules.

8.

THOMAS LITTLETON, EDWARDI LITTLETON, ARMIGERI, FILIUS UNICUS.

DII ADAMI LITTLETON, BART., NEPOS.
[… ?] CII ANNIS SEPTENIS NOVEOS MENSES.

S IR ADAM LITTLETON, of Stoke Milburgh, was created a baronet in 1642. He
married the daughter and heiress of Thomas Poyntz, leaving a son, Sir Thomas
Littleton, who died in 1681, and whose son was Speaker of the House of Commons,
temp. William III.

9.

ELIZABETH, WIFE OF WILLIAM SPARKE, ESQ., AND
DAU. OF JOHN KELLOND, OF PANGSFORD, IN THE
COUNTY OF DEVON, ESQ., OB. OCT. 15, 1672; — ALSO,
JOANNES SPARKE.

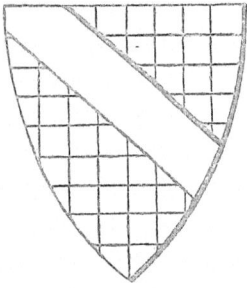

JOHN KELLOND, of Pangsford, Devon, married Margaret,
daughter of Thomas Drewe, by his wife, a daughter of
Sir Peter Prideaux, Bart. The Drewes were connected
with the Walronds of Ile-Brewers.

Arms, Chequy, a bend.... *Crest*, Out of a mural crown a demi-fox or, issuant rampant.

10.

(*Ab.*) ROWLAND WILLEY. OB. 2nd JAN., 1762, AET. 80.

11.

ELIZABETH HANNAH WILLING, RELICT OF CHARLES WILLING, LATE OF THE
CITY OF PHILADELPHIA. SHE WAS BORN 12 MARCH, 1739, OB. 12 OCT., 1795.

12.

BOY OF . . . . . . N . . . . . . GODWARD, WHO DEP . . . . . . JUNE, 1670.
Fragment.

13.

(*Ab.*) JOSEPH GIBBES, OB. 30 SEPT., 1700, AET. 51, 5 M. 7 D.

PARISH OF ST. PETER.

CHURCH AND CHURCHYARD.

1.

JOHN BOVELL, OB. 10 MAY, 1700, AET. 28.

2.

ROBERT BELLGROVE, OB. 25 NOV., 1741, AET. 51 : ALSO, SAMUEL BELLGROVE, HIS SON, OB. 7 JUNE, 1736; ALSO, KATHERINE BELLGROVE, OB. 17 MARCH, 1743.

PROBABLY a descendant of the Cromwellian partizan of that name.

3.

DREIDUIZ....(much obliterated) 1710 .... 1713 .... 1716 .... 1718.

4.

MARY, WIFE OF ROBERT EWING, 28 MAY, 1770; ALSO, ELIZABETH FORD, OB. 24 JUNE, 1776.

5.

WARD HARRIS, ESQ., OB. 2 JUNE, 1761, AET. 49 ; ALSO, ELIZABETH, HIS WIFE, OB. 13 JAN., 1791, AET. 70.

ELIZABETH, daughter of John Harris, Esq., of Barbados, was mother of Sir Philip Gibbs, created baronet in 1774. *Vide* Walrond, Bruce, and Osborne pedigrees, —"Landed Gentry."

6.

EDWARD LANG, SENIOR, AGED 50, AND HIS GRANDDAUGHTER KATHERINE LANG, YE DAU. OF HIS SON JOSEPH, OB. 22 JAN., 1736.

7.

EDMUND SKINNER, OB. 1794, AET. 50.

8.

WILLIAM POOL SMITH, OB. 1729, DEC. 6, AET. 30 ; ALSO, WILLIAM BEND, OB. DEC. 19, 1745, AET. 56.

9.

WILLIAM WALKER (a child), OB. 1752.

ALL SAINTS' CHAPEL

(One of the oldest places of worship in the island, if not the very oldest.)

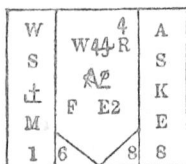

1.

MONOGRAM, WILLIAM ARNOLD, 1688.

THE "Olive Blossom" was fitted out in 1605 by Sir Olive Leigh (whom Purchas styles a "worshipful Knight of Kent") for Barbados.

Lord Ley, afterwards Earl of Marlborough, obtained the first grant of the island, but the first regular settlement was planned and accomplished by Sir William Courteen, who fitted out, in 1624, the ship "William and John" (John Powell, Master), which, arriving at its destination with forty emigrants, founded, in 1625, the present colony.

Popular tradition assigns to William Arnold the distinction of having been the first Englishman to set foot on this island, but such a belief can scarcely be reconciled with the date on his tomb.

In 1628, Charles Woolferstone and sixty-four emigrants, under a company of London merchants, embarked for Barbados, where on arrival each "took up" one hundred acres. The names of these merchants were, Marmaduke Brandon, Robert and Henry Wheatley, Alexander Banister, Edmund Forster, Robert Swinnerton, John Charles, and John Fairingdon.

2.

SARAH BELL, DAU. OF FRANCIS AND MARY BELL, OB. 23 AUG., 1736.—ALSO, FRANCIS BELL, ESQ., OB. 6 APRIL, 1739, AET. 57.—ALSO, FRANCIS, SON OF THE ABOVE FRANCIS AND MARY, OB. 16 AUG., 1747, AET. 14.—ALSO, SARAH, WIFE OF FRANCIS BELL, OB. 14 FEB., 1747, AET. 35.—ALSO, HON. FRANCIS BELL, ESQ., OB. ...., 1760, AET. 56.

THE founder of this family was, probably, Philip Bell, Governor of Barbados in 1641.

3.

.... THOMAS FOX AND HIS TWO WIFES, PRUDENCE AND RACHEL FOX,— TWO SONS, JOHN AND WILLIAM,—TWO DAUS., SARAH AND ESTHER.—

ALSO, THOMAS, JOSEPH, WILLIAM, AND MARY, WILLIAM BEING YE LAST, AGED 27, DYED SEPT. 14, 1754, CAPTAIN WILLIAM FOX.

4.

HERE LYETH INTERR'D YE BODY OF MRS. ELIZABETH FORSTER, WHO DEPARTED THIS LIFE YE 18th DAY OF JANUARY, 1717, IN THE 62 YEAR OF HER AGE.—

SHE was twice married. Her first husband was Colonel William Sandiford, Esq. and her last, Captain John Forster, Esq.

5.

(*Ab.*) SIR WILLIAM GIBBONS, BART., OB. 11 APRIL, 1766.

Crest, Gibbons.

6.

IN MEMORY OF ROBERT GIBBONS, SECOND SON TO SIR WILLIAM GIBBONS, BARONET. HE DIED JULY 13, 1744, AGED 28 YEARS.

Arms, Gibbons, with a crescent for difference. *Crest*, Gibbons.

7.

(*Ab.*) DAME FRANCIS GIBBONS, DAUGHTER OF ROBERT HALL, ESQ., AND WIFE OF SIR WILLIAM GIBBONS, OB. 1757, AET. 64.

Arms, A lion rampant debruised by a bend dexter, charged with 3 crosses patée fitchée. In dex. ch. the baronet's badge. On an escutcheon of pretence, ... 3 griffins' heads erased. *Crest*, On a baronet's helmet a lion's jamb erect holding a cross fitchée.

8.

HERE LYETH THE BODY OF PHILIP GINKINS, DECEASED IN THE YEAR OF OUR LORD, 1663, THE 9th OF JULY.

SEE genealogical additions to the " History of Stockton-upon-Tees," by W. Downing Bruce, Esq., *voce* Raisbick.

9.

HERE LIETH THE BODY OF GILES HALL, LATE OF THIS ISLAND, ESQ., BORN IN YE PARISH OF WHITMINSTER IN THE COUNTY OF GLOCESTER, WHO DEPARTED THIS MORTAL LIFE THE 26th DAY OF JANUARY, ANNO DOM. 1686, AGED 84 YEARES.

GILES HALL was a considerable proprietor, and held, in 1679, one hundred and ninety-five acres in the parish where he died.

Arms, Three talbots' heads erased.

10.

Another " Hall " slab, nearly obliterated, and apparently older than the former.

11.

(*Ab.*) RICHARD HAYNES,—OB. 1768.

SON of Robert Haynes and Ann Elcock, now represented by Haynes, of Thumbeley Lodge, co. York.

12.

.... ELIZABETH KENRICK, SECOND DAUGHTER OF REV. DR. SCAWEN KENRICK, SUB-DEAN & PREBEND OF WESTMINSTER, AND NIECE TO SIR WILLIAM GIBBONS, BART., OB. AUG. 17, 1744, AET. 16.—ALSO, THE ELDEST SON OF JOHN GIBBONS, ESQ., AND GRANDSON OF SIR W. GIBBONS, OB. SEP. 16, 1746, AET. 7 YEARS.

THERE was a family named Kendrick of some note. *See* " Extinct and Dormant Baronetage."

13.

MR. MICHAEL MAHON, OF THE KINGDOM OF IRELAND, AND MARGARET, HIS WIFE, OF BARBADOS, WITH SEVERAL OF THEIR CHILDREN AND GRANDCHILDREN, AND IN MEMORY OF THEM THIS MONUMENT HAS BEEN ERECTED BY MR. JAMES MAHON, SON OF THE ABOVE MICHAEL AND MARGARET MAHON.—

THERE is no date, but the style is that of the latter part of the seventeenth century.

Arms, ... 3 lions passant, in pale.
Crest, A dexter arm embowed, brandishing a scimetar. *Motto,* " Signos sic sacra tuimur."

14.

JAMES PRAT, SON OF DR. HENRY PRAT, & DOROTHY, HIS WIFE, OB. APRIL 23, 1738, AET. 2.—ALSO, HENRY PRAT, SON OF DR. HENRY PRAT. .... ALSO, DOROTHY PRAT, WIFE OF DR. HENRY PRAT, OB. 19 OCT., 1749.

15.

UNDER THIS STONE LYES THE BODY OF KATHERINE, LATE WIFE OF JOHN ROKEBY, MERCHANT, DAU. AND CO-HEIRIS OF CHRISTOPHER THOMPSON, LATE OF THIS PARISH, GENT., AND KATHERINE HIS WIFE, WHO DEPARTED THIS LIFE YE 15th OF APRIL, 1666, IN YE 19th YEAR OF HER AGE.

ROKEBY, of Rokeby and Mortham, Yorkshire, a family of great antiquity and distinction, of which was Sir Thomas Rokeby, a gallant warrior of the reign of Edward III., emi-nently distinguished at the battle of Neville's Cross, who be-came eventually Lord Justice of Ireland.

Arms (above the epitaph), On a chevron between three ravens close a mullet.   Underneath, the same arms, impaling, On a fess (dancetté') three estoiles wavy of six ; a dexter canton charged with a sun in splen-dour......

The line of Rokeby, of Rokeby and Mortham, continued until the time of Sir Thomas Rokeby, who disposed of the domain to W. Robinson, Esq.

Arms, Argent, a chevron sable between three rooks proper. *Crest,* A rook proper.

William Rokeby, of Skiers, Yorkshire, created baronet in 1661, was eldest son (by Dorothy, his wife, daughter of William Rokeby, Esq., of Skiers) of William Rokeby, Esq., of Hotham, who was son of Thomas Rokeby, Esq., third son of Thomas Rokeby, Esq., of Mortham.

Rokeby, of Arthingworth, Northants., derived from Thomas Rokeby, Esq., of Barnby, youngest brother of Sir William Rokeby, Bart., of Skiers.

Thompson (Haversham, Bucks.) descended from Maurice Thompson, of Cheston, Herts. Sir John Thompson, Bart., of Haversham, a distinguished member of the House of Commons, was created Baron Haversham in 1696, a title which expired with his son Maurice, second lord, in 1745, who left two daughters, his co-heirs : the younger, Anne, wife of Richard Reynolds, Esq., son of the Bishop of Lincoln, died *s. p.* in 1737 ; the elder, Elizabeth, married, in 1724, John Carter, Esq., of Weston Colvile, and had one daughter, Elizabeth Anne Hall, wife of John Morse, Esq., of Sprowston Hall, Norfolk, whose only daughter, Elizabeth Anne Ella, is married to Simon Digby, Esq.*

16.

HERE LYETH INTERRED YE BODY OF THE HON. WILLIAM SANDIFORD, ESQ., —ONE OF YE JUDGES OF THIS ISLAND.—BORN IN BRISTOLL, DYED YE 30th OF DECEMBER, 1668, AGED 80 YEARS. ALSO, CAPTAIN HENRY SANDIFORD, HIS SON, AGED 33 YEARS, DYED YE 7th OF SEPT., 1685,—ALSO, ELIZABETH SANDIFORD, HIS WIDOW, AGED 82 YEARS, DYED YE 29th OF MARCH, 174..

17.

HERE LYES YE BODY OF CAPTAIN EDWARD SKEETE,—BORN YE 13 JUNE, 1639,—AND DIED MAY 14, 1727, AGED 88 YEARS.

18.

TIMOTHY ROBERTS, OB. 13 OCTOBER, ... AET. 57.

Very old.

19.

JOSEPH WATERMAN, OB. 1763, AET. 26.

---

* *Arms*, Or, on a fesse dancetté azure, 3 estoiles argent. On a canton of the second, the sun in splendour proper. *Crest*, An arm erect, vested gules, cuff argent, holding in the hand proper, 5 ears of corn or. *Motto*, " In lumine lucem."

ANTIGUA.

ANTIGUA.

FEW of our older colonies have a more eventful and romantic history than Antigua, and its vicissitudes have been comprehensively narrated in a work entitled "Antigua and the Antiguans," from which the following Monumental Inscriptions have been extracted. In this island, as well as in those of St. Christopher and Montserrat, there are many more such records, but in the course of flying visits, the author had not the same opportunities, as in Jamaica, and in Barbados, of making, personally, additions to the present collection.

For an account of the Civil, Military, and Judicial establishments, see "The Colonial List." There is a House of Assembly, of twenty-five members, and a Council, which nominates the Governor, subject to the confirmation of the Crown.

N.B. — The Governor-in-Chief of the Leeward Islands resides at St. John's, Antigua.

CHRONOLOGICAL TABLE.

Date.	Events.	Governor.
1493.	Antigua first discovered by Columbus, who named it after a church in Seville, called Santa Maria, *La Antigua.*	
1623.	First inhabited by a few English, under Col. Thomas Warner, who arrived there from Virginia.	
1625.	Colonel Warner constituted Governor, (Sept. 13).	
1640.	Descent on it by the Caribs. — Great loss of life.	
1651.	Taken by Sir George Ayscue.	
1654.	Descent of the Caribs. — Warner's wife carried off, and after a few days rescued.	
1663.	Charles II. made a formal grant of the island to Lord Willoughby, who sent out a large number of colonists.	
1666.	After an interval of French occupation, it is declared a British possession, by the *Treaty of Breda.*	
1668.	Lord Willoughby of Parham, appointed Governor.	Lord Willoughby.
1681.	Divided into parishes—St. John, St. Peter, St. George, St. Paul, St. Mary, St. Philip.	Rowland Williams.
1693.	Abortive attack on Martinique.	Christopher Codrington.
1702.	Market Place established.	Christopher Codrington.
1703.	Sailing packet for letters established.	Christopher Codrington.
1710.	Revolt and murder of Governor Parke, (Dec. 7).	
1771.	First appearance of sugar ants.	Sir Ralph Payne.
1782.	Great fire at St. John's, the capital.	Sir Thos. Shirley.
1798.	Lord Camelford murders Lieut. Paterson, R.N. [Lord C., afterwards fell in a duel with Capt. Best, a Barbadian.]	John Nugent, (Lt.-Gov.
1798.	Slaves tried by Jury [of whites].	
1825.	Dr. Coleridge, Bishop.	Sir R. Durham.
1834.	Negro Emancipation.	Sir E. M. McGregor.
1835.	Hurricane.	„ „

GOVERNORS, DEPUTY-GOVERNORS, AND LIEUT.-GOVERNORS OF ANTIGUA.

WITH THE YEARS WHEN THEY COMMENCED THEIR ADMINISTRATION.

1625—Colonel (afterwards Sir Thomas) Warner.

Governors.	A.D.	Lt-Gov., Dep.-Govs. and Presidents.	A.D.
Lord Willoughby	1668	(D.G.) Samuel Winthorpe	1668
Philip Warner	1672	(L.G.) William Woodley	1768
Rowland Williams	1675	(L.G.) John Nugent	1788
Sir Wm. Stapleton	1682	(L.G.) William Woodley	1792
Nathaniel Johnson	1682	(L.G.) John Stanley	1793
Christopher Codrington	1689	(P.) John Thomas	1796
Christopher Codrington	1698	(P.) Robt. Thompson	1799
Sir Wm. Matthew	1704	(L.G.) William Woodley	1799
Lord Londonderry	1728	(P.) James Tyson	1809
William Matthew	1730	(P.) John Julius	1810
Sir George Thomas	1752	(P.) John Julius	1813
James Verchild	1766	(P.) Henry Rawlins	1815
Sir Ralph Payne	1771	(L.G.) Henry Light	1836
W. H. Burt	1776	(L.G.) Major Macphail	1840
Sir Thos. Shirley	1781	(L.G.) C. J. Cunningham	1845
Sir Thos. Shirley	1790	(P.) M. H. Daniell	1845
Maj.-Genl. Leigh	1795	(L.G.) Sir Hercules Robinson	1859
Lord Lavington	1801	(P.) B. E. Jarvis	1859
Hugh Elliott	1810	(L.G.) E. J. Eyre	1859
Sir Jas. Leith	1814	(P.) Sir Wm. Byam	1860
Maj.-Genl. Ramsay	1816	(P.) Sir Wm. Byam	1863
G. W. Ramsay	1817	(ADM.) Sir B. C. Pine	1866
Maj.-Genl. Ramsay	1817		
Sir R. Durham	1819		
Sir P. Rose	1826		
Sir E. M. McGregor	1834		
Sir Wm. Colebrooke	1837		
Sir C. A. Fitzroy	1842		

Governors.	A. D.
Sir C. A. Fitzroy	1845
J. M. Higginson	1847
R. J. Mac Intosh	1850
K. B. Hamilton, C.B.	1855
K. B. Hamilton, C.B.	1860
Col. S. J. Hill, C.B.	1863
Col. S. J. Hill, C.B.	1867
Sir B. C. Pine	1869

PARISH OF ST. JOHN.

CHURCH—TOWNSHIP OF OLD ROAD.

1.

AN EPITAPH VPON TH......NOBLE & MVCH LAMENTED GENRL. SIR — THO. WARNER, KT., LIEVETENANT-GENERAL OF YE CARRIBEE IELANDS, & GOVERR. OF YE IELAND OF ST. CHRISTOPHER,—WHO DEPARTED THIS — LIFE THE 10th OF— MARCH, 1648.

> FIRST READ, THEN WEEPE, WHEN THOU ART HEREBY TAUGHT,
> THAT WARNER LYES INTERR'D HERE, ONE WHO BOUGHT,
> WITH LOSS OF NOBLE BLOUD ILLUSTRIOUS NAME
> OF A COMMANDER GREATE IN ACTS OF FAME.
> TRAYN'D FROM HIS YOUTH IN ARMES, HIS COURAGE BOLD
> ATTEMPTED BRAVE EXPLOITES, AND VNCONTROLD
> BY FORTUNES FIERCEST FROWNES, HEE STILL GAVE FORTH
> LARGE NARRATIVES OF MILITARY WORTH :
> ......RITTEN WITH HIS SWORD'S POYNT, BUT WHAT IS MAN
> ......THE MIDST OF HIS GLORY, AND WHO CAN
> ......THIS LIFE A MOMENT, SINCE THAT HEE
> ......AL, MORTAL STROKE AT LENGTH DID YEELD
> ......ACE) TO CONQUERING DEATH THE FIELD,
> > > > FINI CORONAT.

SEE Chronological Table, and Pedigree.

2.

Under the Communion table there is a Latin epitaph—
TO THE MEMORY OF COLONEL WILLIAMS, WHO DIED, AGED EIGHTY YEARS, ON THE 20th ...... 1713.

Slab.

PARISH CHURCH,*

(Founded in 1683-4.—Re-erected 1721—31.)

1.

TO THE MEMORY OF MRS. GILBERT, WIFE OF MR. GILBERT.

Slab.

THE latter introduced Methodism in Antigua, and died in 1747.

---

* This church possesses a curious old silver communion service, inscribed :—1. "Donum Domini Otto Baijer, Ad Templum Divi Johannis in Antigua." 2. "Gulielmus Jones parochialis hujus olim Rector—Donum Dedit." 3. "Donum Petre Lee, Ad Templum Divi Johannis in Antigua."

2.

NEAR TO THIS PLACE IS LAID, WITH THE REMAINS OF HER HONOURED PARENTS, THE BODY OF ELIZABETH......WIFE OF RICHARD OTTLEY; WHO DEPARTED THIS LIFE IN THE ISLAND OF ST. VINCENT, ON THURSDAY, 28th AUGUST, IN THE YEAR OF OUR LORD, ONE THOUSAND SEVEN HUNDRED AND SIXTY-SIX, IN THE THIRTY-SECOND YEAR OF HER AGE.

SHE WAS THE DAUGHTER OF ASHTON WARNER, ESQ., ATTORNEY-GENERAL OF ANTIGUA, BY ELIZABETH HIS WIFE, AND WAS BORN THE 7th JUNE, 1735, O. S.; MARRIED 25th OF OCTOBER, IN THE YEAR 1753, AND LEFT ISSUE SURVIVING HER, ONE SON AND THREE DAUGHTERS — VIZ. — DREWRY, ELIZABETH, MARY TRANT, AND ALICE ....

HER INCONSOLABLE HUSBAND (IN WHOSE ARMS SHE EXPIRED, AFTER BEARING WITH ADMIRABLE FORTITUDE AND RESIGNATION THE EXCRUCIATING PAINS OF A LONG AND DIFFICULT LABOUR) CAUSED THIS MONUMENT TO BE ERECTED TO HER MEMORY.

THE SON WITH WHOM SHE DIED, RECLINES UPON THAT BREAST WHICH WOULD HAVE NOURISHED HIM, HAD THE ALMIGHTY SO PERMITTED.

Mural Monument, W. and B. Marble, with emblematic sculpture.

3.

.... THIS TABLET IS ERECTED BY — ELIZABETH MARY OTTO BAIJER, — TO THE MEMORY OF HER BELOVED FATHER, — THE HONOURABLE SAMUEL OTTO BAIJER,—OF PARES ESTATE IN THIS ISLAND; — WHO DIED AT PHILADELPHIA,— ON THE 20th OF DECEMBER, 1835. — AGED 54 YEARS.—ALSO TO THE MEMORY OF HER MOTHER,— ELIZABETH MARY OTTO BAIJER, — WHO DIED IN 1813, AT DOVE HALL,—IN THE ISLAND OF JAMAICA, — IN THE 27th YEAR OF HER AGE. — ALSO TO THE MEMORY OF HER BROTHER, — ROWLAND ARCHIBALD OTTO BAIJER,— .... WHO DIED AT PARES ESTATE, IN THIS ISLAND, — ON THE 24th OF NOVEMBER, 1827,—AGED 25 YEARS AND 8 MONTHS,—AND WHOSE REMAINS REPOSE NEAR THIS SPOT.

W. M. Gothic Tablet.

4.

SACRED—TO THE MEMORY OF—ELIZABETH JANE HARMAN, — WHO DIED ON THE 16th APRIL, A.D. 1828, — AGED 21 YEARS. — WE HAVE THIS TREASURE IN EARTHEN VESSELS.

Marble Tablet.

5.

...... WILLIAM AND RUTH ATKINSON, ONCE INHABITANTS OF ANTIGUA, AND NOW OF DOMINICA, AS AN INADEQUATE EVIDENCE OF THEIR INTENSE AND AGGRAVATED ANGUISH FOR THE POIGNANT AND CRUSHING TRIAL THEY HAVE UNDERGONE, IN THE LOSS OF BOTH THEIR CHILDREN, PAY THIS MELANCHOLY

TRIBUTE.......... —GEORGE ATKINSON, THEIR FIRST AND LAST SPARED HOPE, HAD NEARLY REACHED HIS TWELFTH YEAR...... QUITTED THIS LIFE WITHOUT A STRUGGLE, ON SUNDAY, 5th DEC., 1779.—WILLIAM ATKINSON, THEIR YOUNGEST, DIED IN INFANCY...... (Verses) .... 1782.

Pyramidal M. Monument. Sculptured with cherubs and scrolls, bearing texts from Scripture.

6.

IN MEMORY OF — AUTHER TEAGLE, — WHO DEPARTED THIS LIFE,—ON THE 20th NOVEMBER, 1839,—AGED 43 YEARS.—THY WILL BE DONE.

W. and B. M. Tablet, surmounted by a laurel chaplet.

7.

TO THE MEMORY OF THE REV. WILLIAM THOMAS BERNARD, A.B. — OF TRINITY COLLEGE, DUBLIN,—LATE CURATE OF THIS PARISH, — WHERE, AFTER A SHORT RESIDENCE OF FOUR MONTHS,—......HE DIED OF FEVER, NOV. 2nd, 1835, IN THE 26th YEAR OF HIS AGE,- .... THIS TRIBUTE OF ESTEEM AND AFFECTION — IS ERECTED, — PARTLY BY HIS MUCH AFFLICTED SISTER,—ELLEN M. BAILY, — AND PARTLY BY THE RIGHT REV. WILLIAM HART COLERIDGE, D.D.—LORD BISHOP OF THIS DIOCESE, — THE CLERGY OF ANTIGUA, — AND OTHER FRIENDS IN THE ISLAND, WHO MOURN HIS EARLY LOSS.

W. M. Monument. Sculptured angel amid clouds.—Bernard Arms, with *Motto*, " Bear and Forbear."

8.

...... TO THE MEMORY OF—THE HONOURABLE WILLIAM WARNER, ESQ.,— WHO WAS A MEMBER OF HIS MAJESTY'S COUNCIL, — AND TREASURER OF THIS ISLAND,—HONOURABLE BY HIS OFFICE OF COUNSELLOR, — BUT—MORE HONOUR- ABLE AS A MAN : — .. .. HE DIED ON FRIDAY, 11 OCTOBER, 1771, IN THE FORTY-THIRD YEAR OF HIS AGE, ... TO COMMEMORATE HER ANGUISH FOR HIS LOSS...... HIS DISCONSOLATE WIDOW HATH—CAUSED THIS MEMORIAL TO BE ERECTED.—GLORIA IN EXCELSIS DEO.

W. M. Monument, with border of variegated brown marble. Female figure leaning on an urn.

9.

TO THE MEMORY OF HER ONLY AND BELOVED DAUGHTER—SARAH KELSICK —WIFE OF MR. JOHN KELSICK, MERCHANT IN ANTIGUA,—WHO DIED ON 20th DAY OF MARCH, 1785,—IN THE 19th YEAR OF HER AGE.—THIS MONUMENT WAS ERECTED BY HER DISCONSOLATE MOTHER—SARAH ECCLESTON,—WIFE OF ISAAC ECCLESTON, ESQ.,—1792.

EULOGISTIC lines follow.

White Pyramidal Monument. Female figure, urn, and flowers.

10.

SACRED—TO THE MEMORY OF—RALPH PAYNE,—LORD LAVINGTON,—OF THE KINGDOM OF IRELAND,—ONE OF HIS MAJESTY'S MOST HONOURABLE PRIVY COUNCIL, —KNIGHT OF THE MOST HONOURABLE ORDER OF THE BATH,—AND CAPTAIN-GENERAL AND COMMANDER-IN-CHIEF OF—THE LEEWARD ISLANDS.

(On the base of the Monument,)

HE WAS BORN IN THE ISLAND OF ST. CHRISTOPHER'S, OF AN ENGLISH FAMILY, DISTINGUISHED FOR ITS LOYALTY AND PUBLIC SPIRIT. HIS EDUCATION HE RECEIVED IN ENGLAND, AND IT PREPARED HIM FOR THE DISTINCTIONS WHICH AWAITED HIS RETURN TO HIS NATIVE ISLE, WHEN HE WAS ELECTED A MEMBER OF THE HOUSE OF ASSEMBLY, AND, ON ITS FIRST MEETING, UNANIMOUSLY CALLED TO THE CHAIR OF THE HOUSE..... ON HIS RETURN TO ENGLAND IN 1762, HE WAS ELECTED A MEMBER OF THE HOUSE OF COMMONS FOR THE BOROUGH OF PLYMPTON, DEVONSHIRE; AND FROM HIS PERFECT KNOWLEDGE OF COLONIAL AFFAIRS, HE WAS APPOINTED IN 1771,—A PERIOD OF NATIONAL INTEREST,—TO BE CAPTAIN-GENERAL AND COMMANDER-IN-CHIEF OF THE LEEWARD ISLANDS, AT WHICH TIME HE WAS INVESTED WITH THE MOST HONOURABLE ORDER OF THE BATH. HE REMAINED IN THE EXERCISE OF HIS GOVERNMENT UNTIL 1774, WHEN HE RETURNED TO ENGLAND, AND WAS APPOINTED A MEMBER OF THE BOARD OF GREEN CLOTH. DURING THE PERIOD OF HIS RESIDENCE IN ENGLAND HE SAT IN FIVE PARLIAMENTS, AND, IN 1795, HIS MAJESTY WAS GRACIOUSLY PLEASED TO RAISE HIM TO THE DIGNITY OF A PEER IN IRELAND, BY THE STYLE AND TITLE OF BARON LAVINGTON OF LAVINGTON. IN 1798, HE WAS SWORN ONE OF HIS MAJESTY'S MOST HONOURABLE PRIVY COUNCIL, AND AGAIN APPOINTED TO THE CHIEF COMMAND OF THE LEEWARD ISLANDS, IN THE WISE AND ABLE ADMINISTRATION OF WHICH HE PASSED HIS LATTER YEARS,—AND CLOSED HIS VENERABLE LIFE. .... THE LEGISLATURE OF ANTIGUA—HAVE ERECTED THIS MONUMENT.—HE DIED AT THE GOVERNMENT HOUSE OF THIS ISLAND, ON THE 3d DAY OF AUG., 1807, AGED 68; AND WAS INTERRED AT HIS OWN ESTATE CALLED "CARLISLES."

Marble Mont. Elaborate sculpture, and statue of the deceased, with his Arms.

11.

"NO WARNING GIVEN! UNCEREMONIOUS FATE!—
A SUDDEN RUSH FROM LIFE'S MERIDIAN JOYS!—
A WRENCH FROM ALL SHE LOVED."*

SACRED TO THE MEMORY—OF—ELIZA MUSGRAVE, WIFE OF WILLIAM MUSGRAVE, ESQ.,—OF THE INNER TEMPLE, BARRISTER-AT-LAW.—SHE DEPARTED THIS LIFE—ON THE MORNING OF THE 12th FEB., 1815,—AGED 24 YEARS.—

EULOGISTIC lines follow.

White M. Mont. Sculpture representing the death of the lady by being thrown out of her carriage.

---

* *See* Young's "Night Thoughts."

CHURCHYARD.

1.

(*Ab.*) .... MEMORY OF .... TROUHTON, ... 1704.

Fragment.

2.

(*Ab.*) COLONEL PHILIP LEE, ... 1704.

HE presented the pair of candlesticks for the communion table. He was an Irishman by birth and education; but after serving in the wars in Flanders, he emigrated to Antigua, and became Speaker of the House of Assembly there, in 1702.

3.

(*Ab.*) CAPTAIN BASTIEN BAIJER, ... 1715 ....

Fragment.

4.

(*Ab.*) THOMAS OASTERMAN, ESQ.,— .... 1724....

Fragment.

5.

(*Ab.*) .... FREDERIC COPE. .... (1739). (An acrostic inscription followed by): HE WAS BORN IN LONDON, OF HONEST PARENTS, ON THE 21st DAY OF MAY, 1710,—AND DIED IN ANTIGUA ON THE 8th ...., 1739.

6.

THE WIFE OF ASHTON WARNER, ESQ., ..., 1748.

7.

(*Ab.*) THE HONORABLE ASHTON WARNER, WHO DIED 11th FEBRUARY, 1762.

Large Marble Tomb.

8.

Inscription obliterated.

Sculptured Monument, flags and anchors, naval trophy.

9.

MAJOR-GENERAL GEORGE W. RAMSEY, GOVERNOR-IN-CHIEF OF ANTIGUA, MONTSERRAT, AND BARBADOS, WHO DEPARTED THIS LIFE, NOVEMBER 1st, 1819, IN THE 58th YEAR OF HIS AGE.

10.

TO THE MEMORY OF PATRICK KIRWAN.

White Marble.

MR. KIRWAN was a planter, and proprietor of estates in Antigua, where he had resided for many years.

He was a native of Galway, and noted for his eccentricities.

53

II.

TO THE MEMORY OF JAMES CULLEN, ... ERECTED BY HIS BROTHER ROBERT CULLEN, THE ARCHITECT OF THE CHURCH.

Mural Mont.

IN A RUIN AT BAY'S LANE.

I.

ANTIGUA.

HERE LIETH THE BODY OF MRS. ELIZABETH WARNER,—LATE WIFE OF EDWARD WARNER, ESQ. .... SHE DEPARTED THIS LIFE THE THIRTEENTH OF AUGUST,— 1723,—IN THE 37th YEAR OF HER AGE.—

2.

HERE LIES THE BODY OF—MR. HENRY WARNER,—WHO DIED ON THE 17th DAY OF SEPT., 1731,—MUCH BELOVED AND LAMENTED BY ALL WHO KNEW HIM, —IN MEMORY OF WHOM HIS—AFFECTIONATE BROTHERS EDWARD AND—ASHTON WARNER—ERECTED THIS MONUMENT.

ST. CHRISTOPHER, NEVIS, AND AUGUILLA.

ST. CHRISTOPHER, NEVIS, AND ANGUILLA.

ST. CHRISTOPHER (Nevis and Anguilla). Until 1866, the Government was administered by a Lieut.-Governor, subordinate to the Governor of Antigua. The first Governor-in-Chief, 1834, was Sir Evan McGregor, Bart., since when it has had (to 1870) thirty-six Governors, Lieut.-Governors, Administrators, and Presidents.

Nevis was discovered in 1498, and settled by the English in 1628. It has had fourteen Lieut.-Governors and Presidents, from 1841 to 1870.

"The latter island," says a correspondent, "I am told, abounds with inscriptions, not only in the churches, but also in private burial grounds about the country." Unfortunately, the author has been unable to obtain but few of these.

LIST OF GOVERNORS &c., OF ST. CHRISTOPHER, NEVIS,
FROM 1834 TO 1870 :—

Sir Evan McGregor, Bart.	1834	E. Kay Drummond Hay, *Lt.-Gov.*	1850
Lt.-Col. I. L. Nixon, *Lt.-Gov.*	"	H. G. R. Robinson, *Lt.-Gov.*	1855
W. G. Crooke, *Pres.*	1835	Ker Baillie Hamilton, C.B., *G.-in-C.*	1856
J. Light, *Adm. Gl.-Gov.*	1837	Thomas Price, *Adm.*	"
Sir H. MacLeod, *Lt.-Gov.*	"	Sir B. C. C. Pine, *Lt.-Gov.*	1860
Sir W. G. Colebrooke, *Gov.-in-Ch.*	1838	T. E. Tudor, *Pres.*	1862
C. T. Cunningham, *Lt.-Gov.*	1839	J. H. King, *Pres.*	"
— Crooke, *Pres.*	1841	Sir B. C. C. Pine, *Lt.-Gov.*	1863
C. T. Cunningham, *Lt.-Gov.*	1842	— Hill, C. B., *Gov.-in-Ch.*	1864
Sir C. A. Fitzroy, *Gov.-in-Ch.*	"	J. R. Holligan, *Pres.*	"
C. T. Cunningham, *Adm.-Gl.-Gov.*	1846	Sir B. C. C. Pine, *Lt.-Gov.*	1865
R. Claxton, *Pres.*	"	Sir B. C. C. Pine, *Adm.-Gl.-Gov.*	1866
C. T. Cunningham, *Lt.-Gov.*	"	J. R. Holligan, *Pres.*	"
R. T. Claxton, *Pres.*	1847	Sir A. Rumbold, Bart., *Adm.*	1867
J. M. Higginson, *Gov.-in-Ch.*	"	Capt. Mackenzie, R.N., *Lt.-Gov.*	"
R. J. Mackintosh, *Gov.-in-Ch.*	"	W. W. Cairns, *Lt.-Gov.*	1868
J. T. Caines, *Pres.*	1850	Sir B. C. C. Pine, *Gov.-in-Ch.*	1869
R. J. Mackintosh, *Gov.-in-Ch.*	"	F. S. Wiglery, *Adm.*	1870

ST. CHRISTOPHER.*

ST. PETER'S CHURCHYARD.

I.

UNDERNEATH LAY THE BODIES OF GILES MARDENBOROUGH, WHO DIED JUNE 25, 1774, AGED 8 MONTHS; OF GEORGE WRIGHT MARDENBOROUGH, WHO DIED JUNE 18, 1775, AGED 2 MONTHS; OF MARGARET WRIGHT MARDENBOROUGH, WHO DIED OCT. 29, 1779, AGED 9 MONTHS; OF GILES MARDENBOROUGH, WHO DIED AUGUST 13, 1785, AGED 2 YEARS AND 4 MONTHS; THE OFFSPRING OF CHRISTOPHER RHODA MARDENBOROUGH. ALSO UNDERNEATH LAYS THE BODY OF RHODA MARDENBOROUGH, WIFE OF CHRISTOPHER MARDENBOROUGH, WHO DIED MARCH 3, 1701, AGED 39 YEARS.

2.

(*Ab.*) CHRISTOPHER MARDENBOROUGH, OF THIS ISLAND, WAS BORN JUNE 1, 1734, AND DIED SEPT. 17, 1806. THIS STONE IS ERECTED TO HIS MEMORY BY HIS GRATEFUL CHILDREN.

3.

HERE LIES CHARLES MARDENBOROUGH, SON OF CHARLES AND MARGARET MARDENBOROUGH, WHO DIED NOV. 3, 1761, AGED 2 YEARS & 9 MONTHS. ALSO, GEORGE MARDENBOROUGH, THEIR SON, WHO DIED NOV. 17, 1767, AGED 7 YEARS. ALSO, ELIZABETH, THEIR DAUGHTER, WHO DIED NOV. 16, 1767, AGED 5 YEARS. ALSO, MARGARET MARDENBOROUGH, WIFE OF CHARLES MARDENBOROUGH, WHO DIED DECR. 2, 1770, AGED 30 YEARS. ALSO, ELIZABETH BROWN, SISTER OF RHODA MARDENBOROUGH, WHO DIED OCT. 18, 1790, AGED 57 YEARS. ALSO, SUSANNA MARDENBOROUGH, DAUGHTER OF CHARLES & RHODA MARDENBOROUGH, WHO DIED MAY 13, 1794, AGED 10 YEARS.

IN ST. PETER'S CHURCH.

I.

HERE LYES THE BODY OF ELIZABETH BRIDGWATER, WIFE TO THOMAS BRIDGWATER, ESQRE., WHO DEPARTED THIS LIFE MAY 16, 1739, AGED 63.

---

* Contributed by the Rev. C. C. Culpeper.

2.

SACRED TO THE MEMORY

OF DANIEL BYAM MATHEW, ESQ., OF CAYON & PENNITENNY, IN THIS ISLAND, WHO DEPARTED THIS LIFE APRIL 26, A.D. 1838, AETATIS SUÆ 82. SON OF DANIEL MATHEW, OF FELIX HALL, IN ESSEX, ESQR., & GRANDSON OF GENERAL WILLIAM MATHEW, GOVERNOR OF THE LEEWARD ISLANDS. HE MARRIED ELIZABETH, DAUGHTER OF SIR EDWARD DERING, OF SURRENDEN-DERING, IN KENT, BART., BY WHOM HE HAD ISSUE, DANIEL DERING, AND MARY ELIZABETH, WHO MARRIED WM. THOS. ROE, ESQR., COMMISSIONER OF THE CUSTOMS, ALSO HIGH STEWARD OF THE SAVOY, &C., &C., &C., WHO DIED APRIL 25, A.D., 1834. THIS TABLET IS ERECTED TO HIS MEMORY BY HIS ONLY DAUGHTER, THE ABOVE MARY ELIZA-BETH ROE, OF WITHDRAN, IN THE COUNTY OF SUSSEX, & HIS SISTER LOUISA, WIDOW OF THE RT. HONBLE. JAMES LORD GAMBIER, OF IVON GROVE, IN THE COUNTY OF BUCKS, ADMIRAL OF THE FLEET, WHO DIED APRIL 19, A.D. 1833.

4.

SACRED TO THE MEMORY

OF MRS. ELIZABETH WILKINSON, NATIVE OF THE COUNTY OF DURHAM, IN ENG-LAND, WHO DEPARTED THIS LIFE MARCH 26, 1805, & WAS BURIED ON THE DAY FOLLOWING, AT THE FOOT OF THIS MARBLE. AS A M. FR. (*i.e.,* mother, friend) & PARENT, SHE WAS HIGHLY RESPECTED.

THIS family is now represented by G. B. Buckley-Mathew, C.B., H.M.'s envoy, Brazil—formerly in the Coldstream Guards—M.P. for Athlone and Shaftesbury, and late Governor of the Bahama Islands.

CHRIST CHURCH, NICOLA TOWN.

1.

IN MEMORIAM CARL : LAVAL : MOLYNEUX INFAN : AETATIS TRI : ANN : HOC SEPULCRUM POSUERE AFFLICTI PARENTES. OBIIT JUNE 30, 1817. EHEW! LECTOR MEMENTO MORI.

THERE was a family of this name, at an early period, in the West Indies, and reputed a branch of that, of the subsequent Earls of Sefton.

2.

SACRED TO THE MEMORY

OF HENRY CHARLES GREENE, ESQUIRE, LATE OF NICHOLA TOWN, WHO DEPARTED THIS LIFE AUGUST 7, 1840, IN THE 19th YEAR OF HIS AGE. HERE LIETH THE BODY OF MARGARET MIDAS, DEPARTED THIS LIFE, AGED 6, ... 1780.

3.

HERE LIETH INTERRED THE BODY OF MRS. MARY CRISP, LATE WIFE OF JOSEPH CRISP, OF THIS ISLAND, ESQR., WHO DEPARTED THIS LIFE JAN. 27, 1730, AGED 38. ALSO, THE BODY OF SAMUEL SHERMAN, ESQR., FATHER OF THE ABOVE SAID MARY, & CORNELIA BROZETT, HER SISTER, WIFE OF MAJOR JAMES BROZETT, WITH HER NIECE ANNE, & HER SISTER-IN-LAW, ELIZABETH BROZETT. NEAR THIS PLACE ALSO LIES THE BODY OF MR. CALEB CRISP AND ANNA HIS WIFE.

BRITISH GUIANA.

BRITISH GUIANA.

THIS territory was first partially settled, by the Dutch West India Company, in 1580. It was from time to time held by Holland, France, and England. It was restored to the Dutch, in 1802; but in the following year, retaken by Great Britain, to whom it was finally ceded, in 1814.*

List of Governors, who have administered the Government since the Union of the three provinces of Demerara, Essequibo, and Berbice, in 1831 :—

1831.—Sir Benjamin D'Urban.
1833.—Lt.-Colonel Courtenay Chambers (*Acting*).
1833.—Sir James Carmichael Smyth (*Lt.-Gov.*)
1835.—Sir Lionel Smith.
1836.—Sir J. Carmichael Smyth.
1838.—Major W. N. Orange (*Acting*).
1838.—Colonel Thomas Bunbury (*Acting*).
1838.—Henry Light.
1848.—W. Walker (*Acting*).
1854.—P. E. Wodehouse.
1857.—W. Walker (*Acting*).
1858.—P. E. Wodehouse.
1861.—W. Walker (*Acting*).
1862.—F. Hincks.
1866.—Major Mundy (*Lt.-Gov.*)
1867.—F. Hincks.
1869.—J. Scott.

---

* "Colonial Office List," 1871.

GEORGE TOWN, DEMERARA.*

CATHEDRAL CHURCH.

1.

SACRED—TO THE MEMORY OF—CAPTAIN WILLIAM PEAKE,—THE BRAVE AND HIGHLY RESPECTED COMMANDER—OF HIS MAJESTY'S BRIG "PEACOCK," — WHOSE DEATH WAS GLORIOUS AS HIS—LIFE WAS HONOURABLE—ENGAGED IN UNEQUAL COMBAT WITH THE AMERICAN SHIP OF WAR, "HORNET," — A CANNON SHOT, IN MERCY TERMINATED HIS EXISTENCE, — ALMOST AT THE SAME MOMENT THAT HIS—GALLANT VESSEL CONSIGNED TO THE DEEP — GAVE A WATERY SEPULCHRE TO THE REMAINS OF—HER LAMENTED CHIEF. — TO COMMEMORATE—THIS GLORIOUS, BUT FATAL ENGAGEMENT, — WHICH TOOK PLACE ON THESE SHORES,—ON THE 24th DAY OF FEBRUARY, 1813, — AND TO PERPETUATE THE MEMORY OF—A DISTINGUISHED OFFICER—HIS EXCELLENCY GENL. CARMICHAEL, ACTING GOVERNOR,—SYMPATHISING WITH THE GENEROUS FEELING OF—THE INHABITANTS OF THIS UNITED COLONY—IN—THE UNIVERSAL EXPRESSION OF SINCERE REGRET,—WAS PLEASED TO GRANT, IN THEIR BEHALF, THIS MEMORIAL TO HIS FAME.

(Verses follow.)

Captain William Peake was the brother of the late Sir Henry Peake, Kt., Surveyor of the Navy, from 1806 to 1822.

The subject of the above inscription is briefly referred to, in the "Naval Biographical Dictionary," as follows :—"Captain William Peake was killed, and his ship, the 'Peacock,' 18 guns and 122 men, was sunk in a desperate action with the American sloop 'Hornet,' 20 guns and 165 men, 24th February, 1813."

It does not appear whether this officer was married and left any descendants. His brother, Sir Henry, however, was the father of two distinguished naval officers, viz., Captain T. L. Peake, who served on the Walcheren Expedition of 1809, and during the memorable action with the French ship "Rivoli," 74 guns, in 1812,—and Commander H. F. Peake. There was also a Lieutenant Charles Peake, (born 1793, died 1847,) who had done good service in his day, but whether he was a member of the above family is not known to the author.

2.

HIS EXCELLENCY MAJOR-GENERAL JOHN MURRAY — AND THE HONOURABLE COURT OF POLICY—IN THE NAME, AND ON THE BEHALF OF THE INHABITANTS —OF THIS UNITED COLONY,—HAVE DEDICATED THIS MONUMENT TO THE MEMORY —OF HUGH LYLE CARMICHAEL, ESQ.,—MAJOR-GENERAL OF HIS MAJESTY'S FORCES,

---

* The Rev. W. G. G. Austin, and the Rev. P. A. Stevenson, have contributed these inscriptions.

—WHO DEPARTED THIS LIFE DURING HIS GOVERNMENT, — ON THE 11th DAY OF MAY, 1813,—AGED 49 YEARS.—AS AN OFFICER HE WAS BRAVE AND LOYAL.—AS A GOVERNOR, ZEALOUS AND INDEFATIGABLE.

3.

SACRED TO THE MEMORY OF — MAJOR-GENERAL — SIR JAMES CARMICHAEL SMYTH, — BARONET, — C.B., K.M.T., K.St.W. — APPOINTED GOVERNOR OF BRITISH GUIANA,—1833,—DIED 4 MARCH, 1838,—AGED 58 YEARS. — ERECTED BY PUBLIC SUBSCRIPTION.

SIR JAMES CARMICHAEL SMYTH, K.C.H., &c., born 22nd Feb., 1780, was created a Baronet 25th August, 1821. He was one of the eight sons of James Carmichael, M.D., F.R.S., Phys. Extraordinary to George III., by his wife, Mary Holyland; and married Harriet, daughter of Genl. Robert Morse.

The family assumed the name of Smyth, in compliance with the testamentary injunction of James Smyth of Atheury, maternal grandfather of James Carmichael, the father of the first Baronet.

4.

SACRED TO THE MEMORY OF—MAJOR-GENERAL—STEPHEN ARTHUR GOOD-MAN, C.B. AND K.H., — BORN 19th JANUARY, 1780, DIED 2d JANUARY, 1841. — HE SERVED THROUGHOUT THE WAR IN THE PENINSULA AND — THE NETHERLANDS —UP TO ITS TERMINATION BY THE GLORIOUS VICTORY OF — WATERLOO. — IN 1821, HE RECEIVED FROM HIS SOVEREIGN, THE OFFICE (PATENT) OF VENDUE MASTER OF DEMERARA AND ESSEQUIBO, — WHICH HE HELD TO HIS DECEASE.— IN 1823—HE WAS APPOINTED TO THE COMMAND OF THE MILITIA,—AND DURING THE MANY YEARS HE HELD IT—RENDERED ESSENTIAL SERVICE TO THE COLONY, —IN THE PRESERVATION OF ITS INTERNAL TRANQUILLITY. — THIS TABLET IS ERECTED LY THE SURVIVING OFFICERS OF THE MILITIA—WHO SERVED UNDER HIM, AND BY FRIENDS — WHO SYMPATHISE WITH HIS SORROWING FAMILY—FOR THE IRREPARABLE LOSS THEY HAVE SUSTAINED.—HE WAS BELOVED IN LIFE AND HIS DEATH—WAS LAMENTED BY THE WHOLE COMMUNITY.—HIS REMAINS WERE IN-TERRED — WITH THE HONOURS DUE TO HIS RANK,—IN THE MILITARY BURIAL GROUND — AT EVE LEARY.*

5.

SACRED TO THE MEMORY OF—ALEXANDER MILNE, ESQ.,—LATE LIEUTENANT-COLONEL 19th REGIMENT,—WHO DEPARTED THIS LIFE ON THE 5th OF NOVEMBER, 1827,—AGED 46 YEARS.—30 OF WHICH HAD BEEN MOST ZEALOUSLY DEVOTED— TO THE SERVICE OF HIS COUNTRY. — THIS TABLET HAS BEEN ERECTED BY THE OFFICERS OF THE 19th REGIMENT, AS A MARK—OF THEIR SINCERE ESTEEM AND RESPECT, TO THE MEMORY—OF THEIR MUCH LAMENTED COMMANDING OFFICER —WHOSE REMAINS, BY HIS OWN PARTICULAR DESIRE,—ARE INTERRED IN THE MILITARY BURIAL GROUND AT EVE LEARY.

---

* Eve Leary is the name of the Cantonment of George Town, Demerara. N.B. The author, while staying there in 1857, witnessed precisely such a phenomenon as that described, in Mr. Waterton's work on South America, as probably due to subterranean volcanic agencies.

THE following are old Dutch Epitaphs, from a Plantation at Coomacha,
150 miles inland.

1.

HIER LEYT BEGRAVEN,
MONSIEUR CORNELIS RASSCHE IN SYN
LEEVEN, RAAT DERER COLONIE,
MR PLANTER OP MARKEY,
GEBOOREN DER 17 NOV. A°. 1689,
IS OVERLEDENDEN 15 MAY, A°. 1726.

Translation.

Here lies buried, Master Cornelis Rassche, during his life Member of Council of
this Colony, Master planter of Markey : born the 17th Nov., in the year 1689 : deceased 15th May, in the year 1726.

HIER BENEDEN LEYT BEGRAVEN SYN
SUSTER JESABETHR (R)ASSCHE GEBORN
DER 19 JUNY, A°. 1694,
EN OVERLEDEN EN YAER DAERNA.

EN SYN BROEDER JOHANNES RASSCHE
GEBOREN DER 18 JANUUWARY, A°. 1692.
EN OVEREEDEN ANNO 1696.

Translation.

Hereunder, lies buried his sister, Elizabeth Rassche, born the 19th June, in the
year 1694, and deceased a year thereafter. And his brother, John Rassche, born the
18th January, in the year 1692, and deceased in the year 1696.

2.

HIER LEYT BEGRAVEN DE HEER
DAVID BALLE, RAATEN
MESTER PLANTER OP DE PLANTAGIE EN
MARKAY. IS GEBOEREN DER
15 NOV., 1692, EN GERLONEE DE
8 NOV., 1734.

Translation.

Here lies buried the Master (Squire ?) David Balle, Member of Council and
Master (chief) planter in the Plantation of Markay,* born on the 15th Nov., 1692, and
died on the 8th Nov., 1734.

---

* Probably named after "the Isle of Marken, a little north-east of Amsterdam."—[R. S. Charnock, in
"Notes and Queries," 5th S., 11, 15.]

WEST INDIA COLONIES

FROM WHICH NO EPITAPHS HAVE BEEN OBTAINED.

N.B.—The Names of the Governors, &c., are given, as many of the latter were descendants of the early Colonists of the islands already noticed.

GRENADA.

GRENADA, discovered in 1498, was at first named Ascension. — Afterwards it was alternately governed by the French and English, until 1783, when it was restored to Great Britain, and Major-General Mathew was appointed Governor.

It is divided into the parishes of Sts. George, John, Patrick, Mark, Andrew, and David.

GOVERNORS, LIEUT.-GOVERNORS, AND PRESIDENTS.

Governors.	A.D.	Lieut.-Governors, and Presidents.	A.D.
Br.-Genl. Robt. Melville	1764	(L.G.) Ulysses Fitzmaurice	1768
Br.-Genl. Melville	1770	Frederick Corsar	1771
Br.-Genl. W. Leybourne	1771	„ „	1775
W. Young	1775	Wm. Lucas	1785
Sir Geo. (afterwards Lord) Macart-		Samuel Williams	1787
ney, K.B............................	1776	James Campbell	1788
Lt.-Genl. Edward Mathew	1784		1789
Colonel Charles Green	1797	Samuel Williams .... {	to
George Vere Hobart	1802		1793
Maj.-Genl. W. D. M. Clephane......	1803	(L.G.) Ninian Home	1793
Br.-Genl. F. Maitland	1805	Kenneth McKenzie	1795
„ „	1810	Samuel Williams	1796
Col. R. Ainslie, Vice-Gov.	1812	(L.G.) Alexr. Houston	1796
Maj.-Genl. Sir C. Shipley	1813	Samuel Mitchell.......................	1798
Maj.-Genl. Phineas Riall............	1816	Rev. Samuel Dent....................	1801
„ „	1821	„ „	1802
Sir James Campbell, K.C.B.	1826	„ „	1803
„ „	1830	A. C. Adye	1804
Sir Lionel Smith, K.C.B.	1833	John Harvey	1807
Sir E. J. M. McGregor, Bt., K.C.B.	1838		1808
Sir Wm. Reid...........................	1847	A. C. Adye............................ {	to
Sir W. M. G. Colebrooke	1849		1811
F. Hincks	1856	John Harvey	1813
James Walker, C.B.	1862	George Paterson	1815
R. W. Rawson, C.B.	1869		1817
		Andw. Houston .... {	to
			1825

LIEUT.-GOVERNORS, AND PRESIDENTS,—*continued.*

	A.D.		A.D.
George Paterson	1821 to 1825	F. Y. Checkley	1855
		„　　„	1856
		(ADM.) James Walker	1856
Andw. Houston	1829	(L.G.) C. H. Kortright	1857
Felix Palmer	1831 to 1832	(ADM.) Lt.-Col. C. Reading	1858
		F. Y. Checkley	1858
(L.G.) Maj.-Genl. G. Middlemore, C.B.	1833	„　　„	1859
		Wm. Stephenson	1860
(L.G.) Maj.-Genl. J. H. Mair	1835	Alexr. Bain	1861
(L.G.) Lt.-Col. C. J. Doyle	1836	„　　„	1863
John Berkeley	1836	(L.G.) C. H. Kortright	1863
Matthew Davis	1840	(L.G.) Major R. M. Mundy	1864
(L.G.) Lt.-Col. C. J. Doyle	1841	„　　„　　„	1865
F. Y. Checkley	1845	(ADM.) E. D. Baynes	1865
(L.G.) Ker B. Hamilton	1846	„　　„	1866
F. Y. Checkley	1850	Andrew Munro	1865
„　　„	1851	„　　„	1866
(L.G.) Ker B. Hamilton	1851	(L.G.) Major R. M. Mundy	1870
(L.G.) R. W. Keate	1853		

———

ST. VINCENT.

St. Vincent.—Discovered in 1498. Granted in 1627 to the Earl of Carlisle. Declared *neutral* in 1660. Granted to Lord Willoughby in 1672. Granted in 1722, by George I., to the Duke of Marlborough. Then followed a settlement by the French. In 1748 declared *neutral.* Captured by General Monckton in 1762, and finally ceded to Great Britain in 1763.

Brigadier-General Robert Melville was (1763) the first Governor, since when it has had fifty-one Governors, Lieut.-Governors, Administrators, and Presidents.

———

MONTSERRAT.

Montserrat.—Discovered in 1493. Colonized by the English in 1632. Taken by the French in 1664. Restored to England, 1668. Taken by the French in 1782. Restored to England, 1784.

ST. LUCIA.

ST. LUCIA.—Discovered in 1502. In 1635 was in possession of the French. Settled by the English in 1639, all of whom were murdered by the Caribs in 1640. In 1642 again in possession of the French. In 1663 Thomas Warner, the natural son of the Governor of St. Christopher, captured the island, which remained in British possession until 1667, when it was restored to France. In 1762 it surrendered to Admiral Rodney and General Monckton; was restored to France the next year. In 1782 Rodney again took it, but it was restored; but again, in 1794, taken by H.R.H. the Duke of Kent.

In 1797 Sir John Moore, the hero of Corunna, was appointed Governor.

In 1802 it was restored to France, but ultimately capitulated to General Grinfield in 1803.

TOBAGO.

TOBAGO.—Discovered 1498. The British flag first planted, 1580. In 1625, an abortive attempt to form a colony. In 1628, granted to the Earl of Pembroke. Settled by the Dutch in 1632. Granted by Charles I., in 1645, to the Duke of Courland. After many changes, it was finally ceded to Great Britain in 1814.

TRINIDAD.

TRINIDAD.—Discovered 1498. First colonized by the Spaniards in 1588. In temporary French possession in 1676. In 1797 it surrendered to Admiral Harvey and Sir Ralph Abercrombie. The latter's A. D. C., Sir Thomas Picton, was left as first Governor. Definitely ceded to Great Britain in 1802. The list of Spanish Governors from 1735 to 1753 includes thirteen names.

Since the British occupation in 1797 there have been of Commissioners, Governors, Lieut.-Governors, and Administrators, fifty-seven.

DOMINICA.

DOMINICA.—Discovered by Columbus, 3rd November, 1493. Granted, by patent, to the Earl of Carlisle, 2nd June, 1627. Under the Treaty of Aix-la-Chapelle, it became a *neutral* island. In 1771 it was formed into a separate government, under Sir William Young. In 1778 it was captured by the French. Restored to England in 1783, Sir John Ord became Governor. In 1805, Sir George Prevost being Governor it gallantly repelled an attack made on it by the French, since when it has remained in the undisturbed possession of the British.

TURKS' AND CAICOS ISLANDS.

TURKS AND CAICOS ISLANDS.—Formerly (until 1848) included in the Bahama group.

THE VIRGIN ISLANDS.

THE VIRGIN ISLANDS.—These islands, discovered in 1493, so far as they are British, became so in 1666, but a regular Government was not established until 1773.

THE BAHAMA ISLANDS.

BAHAMAS.

BAHAMAS.—A group of upwards of nineteen small islands of which St. Salvador is remarkable as having been the first land discovered by Columbus.

New Providence was settled by the English in 1629; was alternately held by them, and the Spaniards, and French, after which it became a rendezvous for pirates until their extirpation in 1718. In 1783 these islands were ultimately annexed to Great Britain.

HONDURAS.

HONDURAS.— On the east coast of Central America. Discovered in 1502. Constituted a Colony in 1861.

GOVERNORS AND ADMINISTRATORS.

	A.D.		A.D.
Col. E. M. Despard	1786	Lt.-Col. Fras. Cockburn	1830
Col. P. Hunter	1790	Lt.-Col. A. McDonald	1837
Col. T. Barrow	1797	Col. C. St. J. Fancourt, K.H.	1843
Genl. Sir R. Basset	1800	Sir P. E. Wodehouse, K.C.B.	1851
Lt.-Col. Gabriel Gordon	1805	Wm. Stevenson	1854
Lt.-Col. A. M. K. Hamilton	1806	Fredk. Seymour	1857
Lt.-Col. J. N. Smyth	1809	T. Price (Acting)	1857
Major George Arthur	1814	J. G. Austin	1864
Maj.-Genl. A. H. Pye	1822	J. R. Longden	1867
Maj.-Genl. E. Codd	1823	W. W. Cairns	1867
Major A. McDonald (Acting)	1829		

INDEX

TO NAMES OF PERSONS OCCURRING IN THE MONUMENTAL INSCRIPTIONS AND
EPITAPHS.

JAMAICA.

BARBADOS, ANTIGUA, AND ST. CHRISTOPHER.

BRITISH GUIANA.

BILLING AND SONS, PRINTERS, GUILDFORD, SURREY.

www.ingramcontent.com/pod-product-compliance
Lightning Source LLC
Chambersburg PA
CBHW081426270326
41932CB00019B/3110